AstroAnalysis

LEO

JULY 21-AUGUST 21

The American AstroAnalysts Institute

GROSSETT & DUNLAP
A FILMWAYS COMPANY
Publishers • New York

**Astrology is astronomy brought to earth
and applied to the affairs of man.**

—Emerson

CONTENTS

The Art of AstroAnalysis

It is not enough to describe you simply as an Aries, Taurus, Gemini or any one of the other nine Sun Sign characters. You are an individual, a unique personality. Quite obviously you can't be lumped in with millions of others born all over the world in the same month and told: "That's you!" Astrology is not that superficial.

In addition to the Sun, several other major planetary influences were acting at the time of your birth. It is these that make all the difference(s) and, together with the Sun Sign, add up to that unique individual, "you."

Astrologers have always recognized this. So, of course, have many of the vast numbers of ordinary people who enjoy reading their character descriptions in books, newspapers and magazines. These descriptions, though basically true and often uncannily accurate, are too wide of the mark to be wholly satisfactory for the serious horoscope reader.

Yet to obtain greater accuracy—that is, a really personal character analysis—you would either have to go to a professional astrologer or wade through a mind-bending mass of figures and technical jargon. Until now. AstroAnalysis has been devised to provide every single reader with his or her own personal astrological particulars and detailed interpretations.

The key to the system is the three sets of colored Planet Tables. They are very easy to follow, and the explanations of what they indicate are written in simple, straightforward language. All you need to know is your birth date or that of the person you wish to AstroAnalyze. Step-by-step instructions accompany each table.

The book is arranged in a natural sequence. It contains much more than the tables and their explanations. It begins with an introduction and history of Astrology from prehistoric to modern times, along with a brief not-too-technical description of how the science works. This will give the newcomer a good idea of what Astrology is all about and should help everyone who reads it make a better job of AstroAnalysis.

Next comes a complete description of your Sun Sign character. Then follows one of the most comprehensive guides ever published on love and romance, describing how you can expect to get along with a man or woman born under any of the Signs, including your own. Next are chapters detailing your health and work prospects, then a guide to all the Signs as business partners, a Compatibility Guide and a section detailing the type of friend, parent and child each Sign makes.

This is followed by an analysis of the zodiacal types as parents and a general description of the traits and needs of children born under the various Signs.

The remainder of the book is given to an AstroAnalysis section from which you can prepare the equivalent of your own "horoscope" or that of anyone else born with the same Sun Sign.

Every AstroAnalysis begins with the Sun Sign, which represents the basic character. Normally it is all that is given. But in order to personalize this, AstroAnalysis uses not one but four standard astrological references.

They are:

1. The Sun Sign, which *determines your basic character.*
2. The position of the planets on the day of birth, which *determines your pattern of behavior.* (Use Pink Tables)
3. The effect of these planets *on each other,* whether for good or bad, which *determines your attitudes and reactions and shows whether you are a strong or weak Aries, Taurus, Gemini, etc.* (Use Yellow Tables)
4. And the Ascendant, which was the Sign rising on the eastern

horizon at the hour of your birth and which *shows how others see you.* (Use Blue Tables)

The art of AstroAnalysis lies in being able to synthesize these results. Put another way, it's obvious that if you know your basic character traits and potentialities (Sun Sign), your likely pattern of behavior and the risks and benefits that may flow therefrom (the planets), combined with the advantage of seeing yourself as you appear to others (Ascendant), you will be in a much better position to assert your talents, correct your shortcomings, exploit your natural possibilities, bring greater harmony into your relationships with others—in short, to live a richer and more meaningful life.

You then don't have to seek for salvation in strange beliefs and doctrines, or to escape in drugs and self-delusion. With this knowledge, you will be "yourself." And to the degree that this self-realization becomes permanent and profound, you will be the master of your fate, a stable personality and an individual well worth having around.

No two people born under the same Sign are identical. Each type is subject to numerous modifications such as nationality, color, environment and heredity. The king's daughter and the underprivileged child born at the same moment in palace and slum will have the same basic thinking and urges, but their vastly different circumstances and conditioning will modify the essential purity of the type.

So, as important as the basic character, the Sun Sign, is, it is only part of the story. The effects of the planets, good and bad, on your Sign, their relationships, friendly and unfriendly, to each other, and the all-important influence of the Ascendant are vital considerations.

With the other books in AstroAnalysis, you can AstroAnalyze your friends (and others who may not be so friendly). All you need to know is the day and year of their birth. It can be fun. It certainly will be revealing.

You will discover who your real friends are, and in business, those who can be depended on and those who cannot. The conspicuous advantage of knowing a rival's innate strengths and weaknesses does not need stressing. You will understand why you feel sympathy for some people and not for others, why some persons of the opposite sex attract you and others leave you cold or even repel you.

Frequently, when making an AstroAnalysis, you will notice that an individual's character clashes with his or her personality. This will help you to understand aggressive and contradictory behavior patterns that otherwise would be baffling. With your new insight, you will be able to ameliorate relationships between husband and wife, partners, co-workers, friends—generally eliminate friction between people who live or work together. Children can be encouraged along positive lines and guided toward a future that provides full scope for their natural abilities and aptitudes.

When you use the colored Planet Tables and references, you will be drawing on the skills of a group of highly experienced international astrologers. It took two years to reduce the complex calculations of all the planet movements over an 80-year period to a simplified table format that uses only words (except for the birth date).

The first tables you'll be referring to are the Pink ones. Here you will find where all ten planets were on your birth date. You will see the Sun (which is called a planet) in your Sun Sign, and the nine others in their particular Signs. In the text, you will read the significance for you of each planet ("The Moon," "Mercury," "Venus," etc.) in its Sign. That's step one.

Remember, the Sun is only *one* influence, though it is by far the most important. Our material existence depends on it absolutely, which is why its position in the Zodiac determines the basic type. But there are nine other planets whose positions in the horoscope modify the basic Sun Sign character. When you turn to read about these, you'll find a short introduction to each planet that shows some surprising correlations between ancient myths and verifiable facts.

It might help the skeptical to know that modern Astrology does not suggest that the planets themselves rule our destinies. The planets are merely dynamic parts of the electromagnetic field in which we exist—a scientific fact. Their constantly altering angular position to the Earth and to each other correlates with distinct changes in human and cosmic affairs.

The Yellow Tables will tell you whether the aspects (or relationships) between your planets are good, adverse or neutral. The descriptions ("Planetary Aspects") will explain what each aspect means. It is here, in evaluating the combined effects of the planets, that you can demonstrate your aptitude for AstroAnalysis. The challenge is to reach a correct conclusion about the person, using judgment, understanding and intuition.

It will help to remember that every good and adverse aspect is helped or made worse by all the other aspects. It is all this pushing and pulling in our natures that make each of us react differently to similar events. The conflicts you will be reading about and assessing are what make us complex, intriguing and interesting personalities—in other words, individuals.

This brings us to the third set of tables, the Blue ones. These give your Ascendant, the Sign that was rising (or ascending) on the eastern horizon at the time of your birth. The Ascendant is a major influence in the formation of your personality and shows how you appear to other people.

To determine your Ascendant, you need to know the hour of your birth. If you don't know the time, try to reach someone, perhaps a relative, who does know. If that fails, there's a good chance you can determine your Ascendant by reading the ascendant-personality descriptions ("Ascendant Signs") following the tables.

Every one of us has negative qualities. No type is all good. The planets' effects sometimes result in pretty rotten behavior. But always we retain our individuality and the capability of ex-

ercising our free will.* It is for you alone to judge which parts of your character revealed in this work need accentuating, changing or correcting. The aim of AstroAnalysis is merely to draw attention to the possibilities and some of the alternatives.

Much unhappiness and frustration result from trying to do the impossible (you can't expect to win the Kentucky Derby with a milking cow), or from striving to succeed in a role for which one is not naturally suited. This book is designed to help you discover your unsuspected aptitudes and the directions in which your goals and happiness are most likely to be found.

Briefly, then—in order to make up your personal character analysis (after reading the Introduction, and "History of Astrology"), follow these steps:

1. Read your Sun Character analysis;
2. Find your birth date in the Planet Tables (Pink) and read the pertinent explanations;
3. Check the Planetary Aspects Tables (Yellow) to see the effects—for good or bad—of the Planets;
4. Study the Ascendant Tables (Blue) to see how you appear to other people.

---

*See "Free Will and Astrology," p. 34.

INTRODUCTION

No Islands in the Universe

It is extraordinary how some of the latest and most dramatic scientific discoveries substantiate the basic premises of Astrology. Skeptics always assumed that the gulf between astrological lore and scientific fact would widen with time, but the opposite is happening. It is not that the two are coming closer together; they will always remain at opposite poles. But the *correspondences* between them, the hitherto invisible lines of longitude like those that connect our earthly north and south poles, are now being revealed. It is a fantastic and exciting story.

The basis of Astrology is that the universe, like the Earth we live on, is a whole and that there is a correlation between what goes on out there and human experience. It maintains that when a massive body, such as a star like our Sun, or the planets or the Moon, changes position, it produces an effect on the rest of the system. This is not disputed by science. The effects are not all observable or measurable, though every schoolchild has heard of some that are. The phases of the Moon, for instance, control the tides in association with the position of the Sun. But some effects are liable to raise scientific eyebrows, and perhaps blood pressures, even though they are undeniable. Correlated with the movements of the Moon, the Sun and the tides are the breeding cycles and habits of fish, which, in turn, are correlated with the economics of the fishing industry and the prosperity of those engaged in it. This is an oversimplification, a generalization; there is no need to belabor it. But it does make a point: the correlations with this one fact are virtually infinite. Correlations can obviously be found for everything. There are no islands in the universe.

The scientific and astrological views of the universe diverge at the point where man enters. Astrology includes the individual in the system. Science, surprisingly, does not—except as a statistic. Astrology says without equivocation that the individual's personality and behavior are influenced by the interaction of the massive solar bodies, particularly at the moment of his or her birth. The conventional scientific mind says: "Definitely not." And then science announces the kind of brilliant discovery—which shall be discussed shortly—that *just about* reaches across the gulf to the outstretched hand of Astrology.

The polarization of the two points of view—that is, their valid existence as an indispensable pair of opposites forming a whole new system of knowledge—seems relatively near. One could go so far as to say it requires only one more scientific breakthrough. But the link can't be forged until scientists are willing to see man's needs in correct perspective to his longings.

We are not here for science, any more than we are here for Astrology. They are only means. Man longs to feel at peace in his psychological self. He does not need many possessions to achieve this. He was happy (and unhappy) in himself long before science heaped its benefits upon him. Astrology recognizes that peace and fulfillment come through understanding, for what a person understands, he can generally control. And it is the scientist's task to enlarge our understanding of the physical universe. But that is the second half of the story. Our immediate problems are not as far away as the Moon, and certainly not as insubstantial as the atom. The individual's universe begins with a reality more immediate and pertinent than the scientist's: an ever-present, interacting world of family, friends, job, self-expression, competition, loneliness, frustration and the rest. And since the scientist is first a human being, he shares in this very personal universe before he turns to his telescope and microscope.

Astrology is a science of people. It is the chronology of observations of individual traits and cosmic correlations since time began. It does not depend on the experiments and observations of less than 300 years, as modern science does; Astrology has been classifying results for about 10,000 years. It has not been restricted by any lack of sophisticated instruments and technical expertise. People are people. And the solar bodies have always been there for the inquiring mind to observe and draw conclusions from. Telescopes and the like have not changed the fundamental principles of Astrology because Astrology is based on observations made from the Earth. And Earth people still live on the Earth and have the same correlations with the cosmos that they did thousands of years ago. The momentous sixteenth-century discovery that the Earth revolved around the Sun did not invalidate Astrology. On the contrary, it has never had so many serious followers, among them a large number of distinguished men and women of science. The famous psychologist C. J. Jung said: "Astrology is assured of recognition from psychology without further restrictions because astrology represents the summation of all the psychological knowledge of antiquity."

Certainly, these Earth people who are the intimate concern of Astrology are stirred and excited almost daily by technological advances—by trips into space they themselves will never make, by the grandeur of the physical universe they can never hope to comprehend—and they share in and benefit from the great discoveries of medicine, physics, chemistry, electronics and the rest. The two standpoints of observation—the scientific and the astrological—represent two distinct realities, neither more important than the other, each essential to human meaning and happiness. Astrology is heart, science is mind. Alone, Astrology degenerates into foolish fancy and superstition; by itself, science dwindles into tedious abstractions and barren statistics. Only together do they make sense. And each has in it a little of the other (Astrology depends on the science of astronomy). Both endeavors are rooted in the individual's compulsive longing to solve the mysteries of life.

The Genetic Code Bombshell

The exciting scientific discovery that makes it possible to speak of an approaching standoff between Astrology and science is DNA—the genetic code. Most people know that the cell is nature's building block for all living things. In the nineteenth century, Gregory Mendel, an Austrian priest and botanist, proposed the first theory of heredity after experiments principally associated with the familiar sweet pea. This led to a new branch of science that established that the medium whereby hereditary features are transmitted from one cell to the next is an element called the gene. At the moment of conception, the genes in the cells of the parents mix in a wild scramble—and suddenly there is a new individual, all packed and ready to go with his or her particular hereditary baggage.

The exact nature of the genes remained pretty much a mystery for some time. But eventually geneticists found that the important material in the genes was an amazing and complex substance called deoxyribonucleic acid, or DNA. On this substance was "stamped" the hereditary data in a code form—something like the perforated cards of a computer program.

And then came the bombshell. Three brilliant biologists, J. D. Watson (U.S.), F. H. C. Crick and M. H. F. Wilkins (Britain), proposed one of the most startling theories of the age:

The fate of every individual is written at birth in the genes. Our predispositions of character, our intelligence, their varying inclinations and strengths throughout youth, maturity and old age, are all stamped there in indelible script. Not only our future physical strengths and weaknesses are written there, but also that moment in the future when our body and its organs will begin to break down and dip toward feebleness and senility.

Astrologers have been saying the same thing, only in a different handwriting, for thousands of years. They call it a horoscope. The three scientists were awarded the Nobel Prize for chemistry.

Researchers have shown that the DNA in the genes is structurally different for every human being. The parallel in Astrology is the "genetic" or natal horoscope, which records the correlated positions of the solar bodies at the moment of birth. The astrologer draws from this information about an individual in much the same way as the geneticists have begun to from the genetic code. Both types of deduction require considerable skill and experience.

The scientific point that our fate is written in our cells has received some verification from research carried out by the late Dr. Franz J. Kallmann of the Psychiatric Institute of New York. In 30 years, he examined 27,000 pairs of identical twins, who must be assumed to possess identical hereditary factors beyond physical characteristics, if the genetic theory is correct. Kallmann quoted a simple example of a case of identical twins who were raised separately by adoptive families from birth in two different countries, and yet who both became professional soldiers and retired with the rank of colonel. He reached the conclusion that inside every being is a clock, set at the moment of birth, that predetermines, among other things, illnesses and accidents.

The case of the colonels could be coincidence. It is not being quoted here to support the case for Astrology (the genetic code it seems to affirm is strictly a scientific triumph). But there are recorded cases of even more astounding similarities that Astrology can explicate and science cannot. To explain these, the conventional scientist must fall back on that old favorite—coincidence. Since the advances in genetics, however, theories that depend on blind chance to explain such similarities don't really stand up.

Take the case of two strangers who met in a hospital in Hackensack, New Jersey. They discovered they had the same first name, Edna, although their surnames, Hanna and Osborne, were different. Then they found out that they had been born in towns not far apart, on the same date of the same year. Pursuing the line of similarity, the astonished women rattled off a string of "coincidences" that has made this a classic example.

Both women had entered the hospital to give birth to a first child. The babies had been born the same hour, had weighed the same and had been given the same name—Patricia Edna.

The women were of identical height and weight and wore the same size dress. Both were brunettes, had blue eyes and had been married on the same date three and a half years earlier. Their husbands were both named Harold, and each was in the same business and owned the same make, model and color of car. The husbands shared the same birth date and year. They also belonged to the same religion; so did the wives (a different religion from that of their husbands). The women had the same number of brothers and sisters. As if all this weren't enough, the women then discovered that both families owned a dog called Spot—and each of the dogs was the same size and breed!

In another well-publicized case, twin brothers, aged 21, from New Rochelle, New York, who had had no recent personal contact, were arraigned on the same day for the deaths of two different men in different places. Both victims were 36 years old.

In Miami, police records show that in 1961 two identical-model poultry trucks that collided were driven by identical twins who had been separated since birth. They were in the same business, had wives with the same first name and had fathered the same number of children who were of identical ages and sexes.

The Planetary Clocks

Despite the genetic breakthrough, there is an outstanding question science has yet to answer: What activates the different stages of the genetic program? Or, who or what pushes the button?

The point of the geneticists' discovery is not that the whole program of our lives is put into motion at the moment of conception or birth; rather it is activated stage by stage. The disorders of age are not selected in the prime of youth; all remain potential in the genetic program. All that is in the program will become reality—but how and when?

Astrology's answer is that the solar system bodies are the eternal clocks that not only order our cycles of days and nights, seasons and tides, but also regulate our own personal behavior cycles—not according to their whims and caprices, but also according to the fate that is inscribed in each of us at the moment of birth.

Science is now well on the way to a similar conclusion. What Astrology might say is written in the stars, science may show is written in the genes.

The genetic code is an extremely recent discovery. Scientists know roughly what is in it, but they can't yet be specific. They have had only a few years to observe the phenomenon, and it may be centuries before its full significance is known. Astrology, on the other hand, has had millennia to observe "genetic" horoscopes. Therefore it offers unparalleled classifications of the basic types of people (12 Sun Signs), as well as variations and refinements of character (Planetary Aspects and Ascendants). "Human personalities," observed Jung, "coincide in the most remarkable way with traditional astrological expectations."

The astrologer, because of his greater experience, is in a much stronger position to predict character and behavior than the scientist. But Astrology is most soundly predictive when it is used by the individual to know himself. If you understand the potentialities and tendencies that were inscribed in you from your beginning, you can use or curb these to advantage and thus have a hand in your own destiny. You are a pawn only as long as you want to be. You have a free will, and you may choose to exercise it.

Earlier, reference was made to the effect that the Moon has on the Earth. Its tidal influence, through gravity acting on the fluid bulk of the oceans, is fairly well understood. But science has recently made remarkable discoveries that back up the astrologer's method of looking at and interpreting this and other influences.

An American biologist, Dr. Frank Brown of Northwestern University, transported some oysters from Long Island Sound in hermetically sealed containers to his laboratory at Evanston, Illinois, 1000 miles inland. He wanted to know how they would behave so far away from their native habitat when feeding time came. As he had suspected, the oysters at first obeyed the East Coast tidal rhythm and opened at the time they had in the Sound. But at the end of 14 days, a remarkable thing happened. Their rhythm shifted progressively until the oysters opened exactly when the tide would have come in had the laboratory been by the water. This was the moment when the Moon reached the meridian overhead. The "lunar clock," correlated to the cell cycle of the oysters, was not confused for very long by the laboratory's experiment.

The same biologist wanted to know if the fiddler crab's change of color was caused only by environmental responses. He put a number of these crabs in a dark room well sheltered from the Moon's light rays and—presto! They changed color according to the Moon's position.

He decided to go further. How would a water creature that had lived all its life in a dark, completely enclosed cave and had never felt the effects of the tide behave? He chose a crayfish and produced evidence that its metabolic processes responded to a rhythm related to the Earth's rotation and the position of the Moon.

Researchers have discovered that mammals—specifically, rats—are also sensitive to the Moon clock's commands. Locked inside a closed room for several months without a clue as to whether it was day or night, the rats showed peaks of activity clearly related to the Moon's positions. They also showed a behavioral rhythm that seemed to depend on the position of the Sun.

After their experiments with animals, researchers now think that conditions they once believed were constant may in reality be continuously influenced by the Sun, the Moon and possibly the other planets—a point Astrology has been making for centuries.

The word "lunatic" was not coined without reason. Modern police departments are well acquainted with the effects of the full Moon on people's behavior. They, like astrologers, know that the waxing Moon is dangerous and that the last phase before the full Moon results in a great increase in crime. The Philadelphia Police Department even made a comprehensive study and in a report entitled, *Effect of Full Moon on Human Behavior* confirmed what thousands of policemen all over the world have learned through experience: man and beast exhibit uncontrollable urges under lunar influences.

"Crimes against the person seem to increase as the night of the full Moon draws near," remarked the inspector of Philadelphia's General Services Division, which was responsibile for the report. "People whose antisocial behavior has psychotic roots—firebugs, kleptomaniacs and homicidal alcoholics—seem to go on a rampage as the Moon rounds. They calm down when the Moon begins to wane."

These findings have been largely confirmed by police in New York, Los Angeles, Detroit, Chicago and San Francisco. Madness, violence and racial rioting usually reach a peak of intensity when the Moon is full. One of the architects of British and American law, Sir William Blackstone (1723–1780), who was the first Solicitor-General of England, remarked: "A lunatic is indeed one that hath lucid intervals . . . frequently depending on the change of the Moon."

Stress Among the Stars

That the planets affect all living things is obvious to astrologers. But despite their own discoveries, this contention is so far unacceptable to scientists. Yet, here too, science is having to consider some extraordinary new evidence.

Most people know that sunspots affect radio reception, but when a technical director of Radio Corporation of America Communications, John H. Nelson, carried out a study over a period of years, he found evidence of an unsuspected factor: the planets. "It is very clear that other forces [than the Sun] are involved," he said. "It is therefore necessary to find a new approach. Study of the planets has revealed encouraging results and a more detailed examination is indicated. A highly developed technique of forecasting radio interference based on the motions of the planets would have the advantage of making possible long-range calculations, since the motions of the planets are well known."

So Nelson made his more detailed study and proved his point: a new approach was necessary. By bringing the planets into his figuring, he was able to predict poor radio reception days with 93 percent accuracy, a result not possible prior to this time.

One of the strange (but to astrologers not so surprising) observations made during the study was that radio interference reached a peak when the planets, in relation to the Sun, were either square to each other (90 degrees), in conjunction (0 degrees) or in opposition (180 degrees). It so happens that in Astrology these same aspects, as they are called, are regarded as causing stress and tension. Conjunctions, however, may be modified in their effect by the nature of the planet concerned—which suggests another field worthy of scientific inquiry.

It has been known for some time that the stars beyond the solar system, and the galaxies even further out in space, are powerful transmitters, many of them more powerful than our Sun. But recently it was discovered that the planets themselves bombard us with electromagnetic waves, especially Jupiter and Venus during the great storms that occur in their atmospheres. What on Earth do these waves affect? What hidden responses do they cause? Are the oysters, crabs, crayfish and rats alone affected?

Certainly not, according to L. F. Tangerman, editor of *Product Engineering*, who saw some significant signs back in 1966. In the July 1966 issue, Tangerman wrote:

I've been told at one time or another that the greatest interference with long-distance radio transmission is not local atmospherics, but electrical effects from planets, notably Saturn. Modern meteorologists have gone so far as to guess that the planets may also affect missile electronic systems and even the human brain, giving some credence to the old astrologers' respect for the heavenly bodies.

The brain is supposedly an electrochemical device. We and the Russians have experimented with tiny radio receivers in damaged brain areas to stimulate nerves from external transmitters so muscles will be activated. Two doctors have just reported that strong but harmless electrical fields are generated when water splashes into a tub or basin; the positive charge goes down the drain but the negative one remains in the atmosphere and may be a greater factor in our postwash feeling of well-being than the water itself. Joseph Molitorisz, ME, also discovered recently that it's an electrical differential that causes sap to flow and makes

trees grow—and a reversal of the polarity will make the trees die.

Now comes a report from Chicago that our fatigue in cars, planes, trucks and office buildings is caused by barring of the Earth's electromagnetic field. It seems that our structures form "Faraday cages" [grounded metal boxes that kill the field]—so we get tired because the human body needs electrical energy.

Who says so? Dr. Cristjo Cristofv, father of the "Cristofv effect." We use the "Cristofv effect" to detect nuclear explosions anywhere in the world, but it was originally applied by the Germans to determine V-1 and V-2 rocket accuracy in World War II. Cristofv got his Ph.D. in Berlin in 1928, was research director of the sound ranging and artillery lab for the Bulgarian Royal Ministry of Defense, as well as an expert on high explosives and teacher of physics. When the Russians entered Bulgaria, Cristofv escaped and came to the U.S. in 1947.

He says the Earth's magnetic field is positively polarized and measures about 200 volts/meter. His antifatigue device" is a metal-enclosed can about the size of an orange in which a solid-state devide is connected to a battery. It is suspended on a slim probe from the ceiling and provides an 800-volt meter field.

Tests of pilots in U-2s, and of truck drivers on the St. Louis—Milwaukee haul, showed greater alertness and less tiredness, according to Cristofv. He reports the 11-hour truck run was cut to 8½, with drivers feeling less tired and able to sleep more restfully afterward. Similar tests in factories and buildings are reported to show similar results.

Metal isn't the only offender, according to Cristofv. Plastics have an inherent high negative charge (as high as 50,000 volts/meter), which degrades performance even more. So plastic seat covers, draperies, bedspreads, and the like can make trouble. He exposed cats to a field of that intensity; in three or four weeks their appetites fell off, [their] sex drive evaporated, and they ran scared from mice.

Ford and Chrysler are reportedly interested. Dr. Cristofv points out that if "efficiency is raised, accidents due to human error can be greatly reduced," so long-distance auto drivers are a particularly good potential for improvement through the findings.

Can it be that the astrologers were right? Are our depressed and non-energetic cycles a result of our efficient structures and the position of the planets or the phase of the Moon? Do we need to recharge our personal batteries? Sounds Moon-mad—but is it?

The Living Sundial

The power of the Sun to affect human behavior is also receiving increasing attention from scientists. One tremendous advance in this study followed an astonishing piece of detective work by a famous Japanese doctor named Maki Takata, a professor at Toho University, Tokyo.

The Takata effect had long been used by gynecologists the world over to indicate the stage of ovarian and menstrual cycles in women patients. The effect was produced by mixing a reactive substance with a blood sample. As male blood did not react, the Takata effect was an excellent aid.

Suddenly, all over the world, blood reactions went wild, canceling out the Takata effect. At the same time, male blood was showing very unstable properties.

Takata and his international colleagues were mystified. He determined to solve the problem. Seventeen years later, he was able to announce that sunspot activity had changed the blood of every person on the planet.

His research showed that the effect on the blood occurred in particular when a group of sunspots moved to the center of the Sun's surface during their 11-year cycle, causing the Sun to shoot a maximum of waves and particles toward the Earth.

"Man is a kind of living sundial," Takata declared. "If the Sun causes irregularities of the blood serum, these must necessarily follow that star's changes of mood."

Takata made another very interesting discovery. Just at the moment when the Sun is about to rise, activity in the blood suddenly shows an enormous increase after having been calm all night. And the odd thing is, he found, the increase begins some minutes *before* sunrise as though the blood anticipated the appearance of the Sun.

This throws some very interesting light on one of the finer aspects of Astrology called the Ascendant. The Ascendant is one determinant of character. It is said to show the purpose of the individual's life and what is possible if he uses his forces rightly. That is its higher octave, what it signifies to him personally. The Ascendant also shows how others are likely to see the individual or how he is apt to act. The Ascendant is the Sign (Aries, Taurus, Gemini, etc.) that is rising or ascending on the eastern horizon at the hour of birth. This will be fully explained later. The point here is that Astrology attaches great importance to the eastern horizon at the time of birth. It says that the finer traits of character are determined for life (as in the genes) at that moment.

One inference of both scientific and astrological research is that waves from the rising Sun carry a personal signal, which is received in the blood.

The Moon's power to interfere with solar radiation next attracted Takata's attention. In tests made during three eclipses, he found that as soon as the Moon began to move across the Sun, the blood activity started to drop, reaching a minimum during full eclipse. The Moon appeared to be intercepting the solar radiation.

The results of the Takata experiments show an extraordinary resemblance to what Astrology has to say about the Sun-Moon relationship. One astrologist theorized that the Moon represents the ability to *absorb the solar currents which pulse through every nerve and tissue of the human and cosmic organism.* In other words, as Takata found, the solar currents throb through human blood and the cosmic plasma.

Russian scientists have been concerned with the effects of sunspot activity on behavior, particularly in regard to wars, revolutions and mass migrations—the last, of course, being quite common among lower animals. One significant point is that intense sunspot reaction occurred in 1938, and the following year the world plunged into the worst war in history. The outbreak of the Korean War was another case in point.

An achievement by the Italian chemist Giorgio Piccardi demonstrates in strictly scientific terms the kind of forces acting on the earth that Astrology has continually tried to draw attention to. Piccardi was asked to explain why activated water descaled boilers and pipes while normal water did not. Also, why activated water only worked sometimes.

After an immense amount of work over a period of years, Piccardi found the answers in the stars, so to speak. He discovered that the inorganic colloids in water were affected by conditions in outer space and varied with the position of the Earth in the galaxy. He found that certain cosmic forces broke down the structure of water. Activated water was structurally suited to dissolve scale, whereas normal water wasn't. But the treatment didn't always work because the *conditions in outer space prevented it. He found success depended on the year, the month, the day and even the hour!*

Since the human body is essentially made up of water and colloids, the Piccardi effect has great ramifications and these are currently the subject of considerable research.

So another striking scientific fact had emerged to confirm astrological method: the time at which experiments were conducted was often of vital importance. Cosmic factors had to be considered as contributory determinants—an obvious parallel to Astrology's concern with the date and moment of birth.

The Cosmogenic Field

Of all the scientific verifications of Astrology, none is quite as astonishing or contains the powerful possibilities as that provided by the new science of cybernetics.

Cybernetics is the youngest of the sciences and in many ways the most important. Although only two decades old, it has already made great steps toward explaining the active principles behind the genetic mystery. Cybernetics is probably the science that is going to provide the link, previously missing, between the microscope and the horoscope.

The story of this new science is fascinating. It begins for our purposes during the International Geophysical Year 1957–1958, when it was discovered that the Earth is surrounded by a great belt of radiation. The original raw data was collected by three satellites—two American (Explorer 1 and Explorer 3) and one Russian (Sputnik 11, which carried the dog Laika). It had the world's scientists puzzled until, after further observations, a U.S. researcher, James A. Van Allen, was able to put the pieces together. There were, he explained, *two* layers of high-intensity radiation surrounding the Earth. One was about 1000 miles out, and the other about 15,000 miles. They were like two cups, one large, one small, inside the other. The larger radiation zone consisted of positively charged hydrogen particles called protons, and the other of negatively charged electrons. A grateful scientific world named these zones the Van Allen Belts.

A remarkable thing about the Van Allen Belts is that their rotation as a unit is symmetrical to the axis of the Earth. This means that they always face the Sun. And the Earth cozily rotates under this vast magnetic umbrella.

After digesting the importance of this discovery, the world's scientists started to put their π-r squares together. They knew, of course, that the Earth had a magnetic field of its own. They quickly established that this had a close relationship to the shape of the Van Allen Belts. They also knew the Earth had a magnetic tail swept out into space by the solar wind (the Sun's radiation streaming toward the Earth) to beyond the Moon's orbit, 238,000 miles distant. But an extraordinary thing that seemed related, but had never been satisfactorily explained, was why the

magnetic poles of the Earth "wandered" many miles every day. This movement altered the magnetic field of the Earth's surface. The "wandering" magnetic poles showed nothing like the stability of the physical north and south poles, which take 26,000 years to revolve once in a conical motion.

After much theorizing, observation and consultation, it was agreed that the Earth's magnetic field and the Van Allen Belts were conjoined in some way to form one giant functional magnetic unit. This was called the magnetosphere.

The presence of such a vast and powerful magnetic force pressed the obvious question: What effect did its interactions with the extraterrestrial radiation have on the biosphere—life on Earth?

It was still a bit early for answers, but the famous Russian physicist Genadin Skuridin, in a work entitled *Cosmic Physics with New Accents*, declared that everyday phenomena now had to be understood in connection with other processes. Life on Earth was affected by electromagnetic interactions—but to what extent? It was left to another Russian scientist, Alexander Pressman, to suggest the startling answer, and in so doing assist at the birth of cybernetics.

There was still a tremendous amount of research to be done before conclusions could be drawn. One group of scientists took the latest measuring equipment to the earthquake areas of the world to study the effects of an earthquake on the local magnetic field. Their discovery was astounding: just before an earthquake, the magnetic field in the area collapses—and this produces panic (some might say a signal) among the animal population, which promptly flees!

The next step was to look beyond the Earth. Did the other planets have magnetospheres? The accepted opinion was that they had either weak magnetic fields or none at all. But Pioneer 10, the U.S. space probe in December 1973, passed 81,000 miles above Jupiter's surface and confirmed that that planet is surrounded by a dense belt of trapped radiation particles from the solar wind. Jupiter is, in fact, a massive cosmic magnet. And in March 1975, against all expectations, it was unequivocally established that Mercury also has a magnetic field.

The cosmic scientists had made the most far-reaching discovery since Galileo raised his home-made telescope in 1610 and detected the moons (satellites) of Jupiter: the cosmos, the world of the Sun and its planets, is one enormous electromagnetic field of force. It is subject to the laws of gravity, and each part acts in a reciprocal manner on the others. The uninterrupted shifting of the celestial bodies creates powerful changes in the field of force, particularly (as far as we are concerned) in the magnetosphere of the Earth. These "shiftings" occur through (1) the daily rotation of the Earth on its axis, (2) its simultaneous orbiting of the Sun, (3) the movements of the Moon and (4) the orbital revolution and rotation of the planets. The whole kaleidoscopic magnetic interaction is continuously vitalized or "refreshed" by the never-waning pressure of the solar wind.

The scientists at last had their answer to the mystery of the wandering magnetic poles. In a relatively few years, they were able to erect a theoretical model of the "cosmogenic" field. Understandably there was very little time for large-scale research to determine the effect of all this on human and animal life, though individual scientists had begun independent investigations and cybernetics was providing the answers.

The Russians, especially Alexander Pressman, say they have been able to recognize "the interrelation between cosmos and bios—the universe and life on Earth"—by utilizing *information*, a concept of cybernetics.

Cybernetics—A New Way of Thinking

It is impossible to explain cybernetics satisfactorily in a few words. It has been defined as the science concerned with the automatic control and communication processes in both animals and machines. With its help, the theoretical laws of the functions of the brain, organisms, machinery and society are investigated. It is the science of the control process in biology, physiology, psychology and sociology. It is the theoretical foundation for the computer industry. Without cybernetic methods, further scientific progress is unthinkable. Or, to put it another way, it embraces "everything."

The Russians, who at first rejected the science, have joined the Americans as leaders in cybernetic studies. They describe cybernetics as the "science of general laws ruling the regulation, control and connection in machines, in organs and the human society." None of these definitions mean a great deal until the underlying idea is grasped, because cybernetics is really a new way of thinking.

Man has always endeavored to discover and understand the laws governing the various forms and expressions of life and society. But until the computer age, there was no chance of developing the concept of cybernetics. It is almost as though the intense concentration on cosmic physics over the last 40 years, when man made tremendous advances in knowledge, has fitted the human mind for the new forms of thinking that cybernetics demands. The "old" scientific mind (of only a generation or so ago) did not have the flexibility—and certainly not the methods—required to approach this scientific analogue to Astrology, for that is what cybernetics is.

The relationship of cybernetics to Astrology becomes much clearer when the electromagnetic fields around the Earth are regarded as information carriers. It became obvious to scientists in the 1960s that these newly discovered fields and belts, together with the immense fields encompassing the Earth and all the other planets, must be felt *here* . . . somewhere, somehow. It had long been known that most of the environmental factors that created and developed life on Earth were electromagnetic in origin. All kinds of radiation played a major role in biology, including gamma rays, infrared and ultraviolet rays, visible light, cosmic radiation and X-rays. All have been independently investigated at various intensities and their effects on various life forms over a long period proved. But it was now realized that energies from the electromagnetic fields around the Earth had accounted for very little of these effects. What, then, was their influence?

It was quite clear that all the known scientific methods of investigation were not going to yield the answer: these had been tried and had revealed nothing. Something was missing. The old methods were based on the two rock-solid fundamental principles of physics that every schoolchild is familiar with: mass and energy. A third principle was now to be introduced: *information*, in the cybernetic form. From now on, there would be three elements in physics—mass, energy and information. The last was to be regarded as the classification of the entirety—the pattern, shape and structure.

So in the laboratories, they again set to work. This time it was decided to simulate Earth conditions by exposing elementary organisms to radiation in an induced electromagnetic field. The results were revolutionary.

The scientists had calculated, based on their previous mass-energy experiments, that to produce certain changes in organisms, a fixed amount of energy would be required. But the actual experiment showed that a thousand times less energy was required, and that it was not the intensity of the radiation that produced the various effects, but *the informational reciprocal between the electromagnetic field and the living organism.*

Thousands of carefully controlled investigations confirmed this (then) astonishing fact. The experiments proved conclusively that various changes in life on Earth were not caused by energy or radiation but by the cosmically induced fluctuations of the magnetosphere.

So the information concept became an integral part of biological science. It is now proved that the Earth's magnetosphere is an information carrier. As the form of the magnetosphere changes, so do the contents of the reciprocal information in living nature. A Russian cybernetics team has revealed that hundreds of observations in very weak electromagnetic fields on specimens from human beings down to one-cell organisms confirmed this. The most frequently observed effects were in the regulations of the vital functions.

Medical research over the last few years has provided additional facts. It has been conclusively proved that during magnetic storms there is a spectacular increase in nervous and mental disorders, heart attacks and defects of the vascular system. A rise in blood pressure is also often reported at these times.

Since 1972 it has also been possible to measure the magnetic fields in the human body caused by the weak electric current that regulates heart activity. The apparatus used for this is a Superconducting Quantum Interferometer Device (SQUID) and the results are called magnetocardiograms. The body's magnetic field is only 100-millionth that of the Earth's. Much research is going into this technique, but at present application is limited because readings can only be taken in temperature conditions approaching absolute zero.

It is also scientific theory that the Earth's geological ages of extreme heat and cold, and the subsequent appearance, evolution and destruction of various prehistoric life forms, as well as the existence of present life forms, are all attributable to electromagnetic variations in the magnetosphere. The extent of these influences on individual human affairs has not yet been defined by science, but from the evidence so far, it seems the final triumph and vindication of Astrology are not too far distant.

While scientists are applying themselves to solving the physical mysteries as they see them, serious astrologers are also hard at work. Astrological research never stops. The modern astrologer does his homework.

The rationales for Astrology are psychological, philosophical and practical. Astrology has always been a study of the frontiers of experience. Therein lies its perennial appeal to the human mind. Wherever the scientist's search leads him, he will find that astrological thought and insight have been there before.

The Ten Life Stages of Man

The correlation of planetary symbolism with the facts of life is quite amazing when considered with an open mind. An interesting example is the astrological scheme of the ten life stages of man. Each stage of seven years is represented by a planet. The sequence follows the actual order of the planets, going away from the Sun. Their "natures," and therefore the particular effect each has on man during the life stage it governs, are the same as has been ascribed to the traditional planets for thousands of years.

The Moon Age (1 to 7 years)

The Moon, the nearest body to the Earth, is treated as a planet. It has always signified the mother, rhythms, water and all other life-giving liquids. It reflects the dual nature of the evolving human spirit, part conscious, part unconscious. It is itself the unconscious side of the personality, bound by instincts, involuntary responses and momentary urges. It is passively receptive to outside influences.

So the child begins its life in a psychologically fluid state, taking its early egotistical shape from the maternal mold. Although an individual with distinct characteristics that will later become conscious, the infant experiences helplessness and vulnerability, and is unable to act for itself except in blind or dim responses. Throughout these first seven years, the child registers the effects of its environment and in so doing displays the acutely impressionable nature of the Moon.

The Mercury Age (7 to 14 years)

Mercury is the intellectual force that governs speech, writing, communication and the mental functions in general. It also rules common sense. It is adaptable, versatile, quick, restless, irresponsible, logical, inquisitive and fast-moving.

The early school years are when the child learns the mechanics of communication, how to write, to speak, to express him- or herself as a mental being and not just as a collection of clamorous desires. He discovers he can contradict the voice of authority sometimes and assert his ideas so that others will listen and pay attention. He makes innumerable connections and contacts, developing a casual attitude toward responsibility and a flexible sense of morality. He moves around incessantly with inquisitive purpose, loses interest as quickly as he gains it and begins to control aspects of his environment through the advancing power of his mental processes.

The Venus Age (14 to 21 years)

Venus is the influence of love, art, culture, sympathy, social relationships, evaluation. All emotions that have a sexual or sensual basis begin here, including the love of beauty. Creative activities—poetry, acting, music, dancing—come under the Venusian force. It aims to unify.

This is the time when the mental enthusiasms of the Mercurial Age turn to love, when intense emotions come and go with brief but remarkable impact. It is the age of fads and crazes that develop in various ways into mature and admirable tastes. The adolescent learns to discriminate, to assess people and situations, to test values, to experiment with the feelings of others, to observe the power of his or her physical presence. The value of cooperation, the social advantages of popularity, the deeper meaning of friendship and the conduct that society demands are also learned. The adolescent prepares for adult life.

The Earth Age (21 to 28 years)

In geocentric (Earth-centered) Astrology, the Earth is not considered a planet, so this period of development is one of self-confrontation. Having come of age, the individual must adjust to material living and all its attendant responsibilities. As the Earth is in the center of the planetary lineup between the extremes of pliability and rigidity, so is the person during the Earth Age. The lessons of the past, ideally, have produced in him or her a sense of balance, proportion and moderation. Other factors not so easy to define may now become influential.

Normally the young adult will endeavor to establish himself in a career or particular occupation—put roots down and set about justifying his existence. The end of the Earth cycle frequently produces a crisis. This is the time when the individual realizes life is not what he thought it was, when he must decide what he is going to make of

it and face the person that he really is. The talents he has uncovered (or covered up) in himself will not easily be denied self-expression. The young man or woman may have to make one or two painful decisions that will mean considerable reorientation. The end of this phase marks the return of the restrictive planet Saturn to the position it occupied in the horoscope at the time of birth, which signifies a new beginning.

The Mars Age (28 to 35 years)

Mars is the planet of energy, activity through enterprise, self-assertion and leadership.

This is a strenuous period when the individual, now stabilized in character, endeavors to make a personal imprint on his or her community. He or she becomes a dynamic influence, responding with vigor to challenges, competing for leadership and acclaim. Ambition is usually the first consideration, money the second. The need to accomplish at almost any cost is paramount. Physical strains are ignored or overcome by aggressive determination to succeed. Those who have laid sound foundations in the previous age now build their edifices with relentless energy. On these, they must now stand or fall.

The Jupiter Age (35 to 42 years)

Jupiter represents expansion—by growth, material acquisition and understanding. It signifies law, banking, philosophy, religion, moderation, reason. It also stands for foreign affairs, including distant journeys.

Now the individual begins to profit from earlier efforts and experience. He or she assumes some authority as a counselor of others, and becomes established in his or her chosen calling. This is the prime of life when the person expands financially, becomes an established citizen, a respectable and reliable member of the community. It is also a time associated with middle-age spread. The growth process reflects itself in a psychological maturity; the person develops an inner sense of law, order and morals. Religious convictions become more certain, and the mature adult reflects the type of person that has been formed through the earlier ages and anticipates future development. Since the direction of life is now probably fairly well fixed, the individual must look for ways of modifying his or her underlying attitudes and illusions in order to experience the deeper fulfillment of self-progression.

The Saturn Age (42 to 49 years)

Saturn is sometimes symbolized as Father Time, the old man with the hourglass and scythe.

It represents the formative principle through restriction, discipline and rigidity. It stands for gravity, profundity, prudence, caution and organization. It is the symbol of the limitation of the physical, through which the human spirit, evolving as mind, must penetrate to go on.

This is the period when the person learns the lessons of self-discipline. The formative years, physically, are over. He or she is now a fixed and determined entity. If mistakes have been made in the creation of the self, this is the age when they are apt to be revealed and demand rectification. Here is where the habitual person finds himself heading for the abyss of decline and depression. But the individual who has fulfilled the earlier stages, it marks the way up, a different kind of path, a compensation for growing old.

This Saturn Age teaches the need for realistic, practical and responsible handling of life's affairs, as distinct from expediency and the habit of self-interest. By the end of the Saturn period, the person has almost concluded his first 50 years. He knows the difference between right and wrong. If he has had to pay, he understands the reasons why. By obeying the community's laws, he upholds these laws and is capable of performing as an authority within the social system. His own endeavors to effect order within himself can now be used to create order in his surroundings. As society once helped to shape him, so now he can help to shape society. And having learned to serve, he may now himself be served. But for the ordinary man or woman, it is difficult to withstand the constrictive and ossifying influence of the Saturn Age. It usually ends in hardening of the arteries, brittleness of the skeleton and a fixation of views that can only be dissolved by the grave.

The Uranus Age (49 to 56 years)

Uranus stands for independence, drastic change, revolt, anarchy, genius, intuition. It also represents Astrology, metaphysics, telepathy and events of a curious or wondrous nature.

This is the age of a second flowering for those who can allow the old self to die. It is the time that the young man or woman at the end of the Earth Age is unconsciously striving toward as the greatest good, but seldom attains. For here is the chance to leap forward, not with enthusiasm, but with wisdom, into a new state of consciousness. This is the age that offers the person the power to break away from the rigidly controlled norm. Here is the realization that uniqueness lies not only in being safe, sober and reliable. Within each individual is the power to be exceptional, if only he can reach it, and this is the stage where he discovers that instead of reaching up, he must reach within to unlock the spontaneous force that will free him from the cyclic rut of accepted limitations. From this renewing impulse springs originality, creative inspiration, scientific thought and inventiveness. Here men and women can produce their most valuable and original work.

The Neptune Age (56 to 63 years)

Neptune symbolizes the evolving human spirit as mind transcending the physical condition. It stands for refinement—through dissolution, subtlety and immateriality. The Neptune function, like the sea with which it is traditionally identified, has no material roots. It is a dissolver of form.

The fully developed person now begins to withdraw from inordinate attachments to the world. His values have a deepening spiritual content that goes beyond the dogma and ceremony of orthodox religions. He meditates without concepts, places less and less dependence on memories of the past and yearns to empty himself of his egotistical cravings.

By rising above the Saturnian need for psychological security and continuity, the ripe man or woman finds both, either in enlightenment or death.

The Pluto Age (63 to 70 years)

Pluto is the last known planet in the solar system. As the Sun represents the beginning of the person, so Pluto symbolizes the cyclic return through experience to that beginning. It is said to be the deliverer. As the Sun is the unexpressed potential at the center, so Pluto, as the final stage of man's progression, represents the seed—a new crystallized beginning.

The fully developed person at this stage knows himself, and in knowing that, comprehends the last mystery.

A HISTORY
OF ASTROLOGY

THE ORIGINS OF ASTROLOGY

11,000 B.C.—Atlantis and the Age of Leo

Recorded history is not sufficient to tell the story of Astrology. Astrology is such an ancient scientific art that it is necessary to go back into tradition to discover its origins, back into the mists of time where nothing is for certain yet the echoes persist in hieroglyphic ruins and stone symbols.

The peoples of all the ancient civilizations—from the first inhabitants of the Tigris-Euphrates valleys (modern Iraq) to the Maya of Mexico, the pre-Incas of South America and the Chinese—practiced Astrology. This is a matter of historical record. But the question that has not been satisfactorily answered is: Where did the concept originate?

It has been speculated that the knowledge, born in Asia Minor, was carried to the Americas by the Asian tribes that trudged across the Bering Strait to Alaska, an event science speculatively places some 17,000 years ago. But perhaps the movement of information was in the opposite direction, from the pre-Incas and Maya to the Asian motherland. No one really knows. What is certain is that by the founding of the Sumerian civilization in ancient Mesopotamia in 4000 B.C., Astrology, the mother of all science, learning and comprehension, was flourishing.

Another theory is that great ideas occur in the collective human psyche and express themselves simultaneously through individuals thousands of miles apart—as happened with the invention of the printing press, the electric light bulb, the discovery of magnetism. The implications of this theory are so profound that, if it is true, there is nothing much more to say.

But the traditional and esoteric answer to the mystery is more conclusive—and fascinating—though perhaps, to some, less convincing. The traditional history of Astrology begins in the legendary story of Atlantis, the Lost Continent. Through the logic of its own method, Astrology traces itself back to this fantastic epoch, which began in 11,000 B.C.

Astrologically, 11,000 B.C. to 8850 B.C. was the Age of Leo, a 2150-year period like the Age of Aquarius, which the world has recently entered. This was the legendary Golden Age when men not only worshiped but also *understood* Sun power, the Solar King, the ruler of the Sign and the Age of Leo, the symbolic royal lion—when, it is said, the self-centered quest for power destroyed a civilization advanced in knowledge beyond the capacity of its people to control it.

The British Pears Encyclopaedia describes Atlantis as: A mythical continent supposed to have lain somewhere between Europe and America and a centre of advanced civilization before it was inundated by some great natural catastrophy in pre-Christian times. There is little, if any, serious historical or archaeological evidence for its existence but the legend of the Golden Land destroyed when the water of the Atlantic closed over it has remarkable staying power. Plato wrote convincingly about the wonders of Atlantis in his dialogues *Timaeus* and *Critias*, while other writers have suggested that the biblical story of the Flood is based on fragmentary accounts of the Atlantean deluge.

Despite the absence of verification, some interesting scientific facts make the story of Atlantis at least plausible. First, science has established that modern man was alive and doing pretty well 30,000 years before the birth of Christ. Anthropologists say he was using small knife blades and engraving tools that were quite an advance on the crude hand axes of his ancestors. That he was painting and sculpturing subjects of a simple astro-religious nature shows he was making observations of the heavens and divinations. The word *divination* is from the Latin, *divus*—a god or constant power. Its original meaning was a casual power whose effect was foreseeable, predictable, as a god or constant force must be when it is correctly understood.

Where a number of gods or constant forces act in the same place at the same time, the result is apparent inconstancy, a medley. There then arises in the human mind a need to propitiate the gods or forces—so it is not surprising that archeologists have found that 30,000 B.C. man made a big thing of magic rites and ceremonies.

So, on the archeological evidence, man was well and truly on his way 20,000 years before the destruction of Atlantis. Considering the astonishing progress he has made in the last 300 years, it is not hard to believe that an amazingly advanced civilization known as Atlantis or Mu could have developed on the Earth by the year 11,000 B.C.

And there are other interesting factors consistent with the final disaster. According to geologists, the last Ice Age reached its peak in 18,000 B.C. Around the same time, human culture underwent important changes, culminating in what is described as the great flowering of Paleolithic art. Then the thaw set in, the Earth's ice jacket began to melt, the seas rose—and if you like to finish the story according to tradition, Atlantis or Mu sank into the sea.

Considering that the last glaciers in Britain didn't disappear until 8000 B.C., Atlantis, which is supposed to have vanished a thousand or so years before, must have been well and truly submerged by then. Just how deeply can be imagined from the fact that it was another 3000 years before the melting ice sheets had raised the sea level enough to cover the land connection with the Continent and make Britain an island.

According to Edgar Cayce, the American trance-clairvoyant, the Atlanteans had perfected the use of solar energy to the point where they were able to regenerate human bodies, as well as use it as a means of propulsion. Their occult and spiritual knowledge was of an astoundingly high order. Not surprisingly, it was founded on an understanding of the Sun's control of life and human affairs through the planetary gyrosystem, which they knew to be a massive electromagnetic field (modern astrologers recognize it is such today).

It is said that although the Atlanteans reached an extremely advanced stage of technical competence and spiritual and artistic response, their society was plagued by bitter power struggles at the executive and priesthood levels. Greed and corruption were prevalent among the general populace.

But the kings or wise men (or both) were of other stuff. They understood the divine astro-science from which flowed their material and spiritual knowledge. This was their religion, and their worship was the living out of that knowledge; life was their only ceremony. To them, the science of energy and the human soul were one. These towering individuals saw human existence as a continuous progression of consciousness through repetition—without a corresponding strength of consciousness, knowledge was devastatingly dangerous. (This seems to parallel twentieth-century fears about proliferation of H-bomb know-how.) Their own "super" society had become precariously imbalanced in this regard.

These wise men of Atlantis, so the story goes, were not like the ambitious and competitive men who governed; they were more like patrons and patriarchs. They had attained a sublime state of quietude, which allowed them to perform naturally without needing to try or to compete to change the order of things. They had replaced the egotistical desire to *find out* with the potent calm of *self-knowing*—in itself an aspect of divination and divinity.

Tradition says it was not just the rising waters that destroyed Atlantis. Possessing the secret of solar fusion—the power source that modern science is now trying to harness—the Atlanteans blew themselves out of existence in a final selfish power clash; or, in astro-religious terms, their consciousness caved in. And the sea did the rest.

Whatever happened, it is said that before the disaster struck, a group of wise men left Atlantis and settled in various places. These became the seven centers of ancient civilization. The Atlanteans took with them the only thing they treasured—their astro-religion. The fragments of this that remain are Astrology.

An interesting end to the traditional story explains the personification of the gods that occurs in the founding mythology of most of the great races. Shortly before the disaster, the spiritual guides who had instructed the colonizing wise men became, in legend, living gods. In the West, they were later known as Zeus, Hermes, Ares, Cronus, Aphrodite and Artemis, and finally as Jupiter, Mercury, Mars, Saturn, Venus and the Moon—the planets.

3000 B.C.—The Babylonians and the Age of Aries

The first "historic" astrologers were the Babylonians or Chaldeans of around 3000 B.C. These were the later occupants of ancient Mesopotamia, the heart of which was the fertile

Tigris and Euphrates river valleys. The period of their ascendancy is known as the Age of Aries, the next precessional fire Sign after Leo. Aries is the Sign of the Ram, of shepherds gazing at the sky, of energetic new beginnings; of great heat and dryness, and of all that is aggressive and pioneering in enterprise.

The Babylonians were the first people to evolve a system of simple mathematics. This they applied to their observations of the movements of the Sun and the planets. In the clear desert skies, they were able to make some remarkably accurate discoveries, considering that there is no record of their having used any method of magnification. They made maps of the heavens and discovered, and named at least two constellations, Pleiades and Orion. It is known that they used towers of some 50 to 70 feet as "observatories," probably to get above the local dust and heat haze. From the calculations of these people developed the basis of astronomy, which for 4500 years was to be the right hand of Astrology.

In the beginning, the observation of planetary movements centered on the Sun and Moon, since they controlled the seasons and growth processes. It was very early established that the success of crop planting depended on the phases of the Moon. And it was not long before the planets—moving against the fixed stars (perceived as pinpoints of light)—were noticed and their regular courses mentally noted. Since the effects of the Sun and Moon on life were evident and predictable, the earliest observers noticed also that various conjunctions of planets in relation to the Moon and Sun corresponded with certain predictable events in the nation's or tribe's affairs. This was not determined in a week or a year. Astrological lore was handed down through the centuries, so that its practitioners were able to draw on a vast accumulation of experience. At some point, the planets were named and assigned appropriate characteristics and the 12 zodiacal Signs were defined and classified.

The mathematical foundations laid by the Babylonians are still in use today. On the basis of their observations, they devised calendars. Throughout the kingdom, a system was set up for the exchange of information among the leading astrologers.

There were no personal horoscopes in those days. Astrology was strictly a state matter; its findings referred to the fate and hopes of the nation. These were personified in the king; what was good for the king was good for the people.

At this stage, prognostications were made from eclipses and major conjunctions of the planets on the basis of what had happened to the nation and its rulers under these conditions in the past.

The Babylonians identified the planets with their gods and invested them with corresponding powers. Some were benign, most were malefic (those weren't easy times). Astrology became the basis of a state religion. The astrologer-priests, who were the king's advisers, kept the whole system shrouded in mystery; it was the preserve of the powerfully privileged. Astrology inevitably became a diabolical political weapon, its predictions and prophecies more expedient than true, especially when an unruly or rebellious populace had to be controlled or placated in times of war or famine.

Meanwhile, in Lower Egypt the first historical dynasty of pharaohs had been established by Menes, and Egyptian culture and learning, revolving around worship of the Sun god Ra, began to develop and flower under the influence of astrological tradition. The earliest extant horoscope was cast by Imhotep, architect of the Step Pyramid at Sakkara, in 2767 B.C. Some authorities say Egyptian Astrology was imported from Babylon, but others contend that Egypt was an "originating" center and that Babylonian Astrology did not reach Egypt until much later—around 400 B.C. They point out that the earliest known Babylonian horoscope—for King Nectanebus—was cast in 358 B.C.

The Old Testament frequently refers to Astrology. It was greatly cultivated by the wisest of the ancient Israelites. Abraham himself, the first of the Hebrew patriarchs, lived with his father's clan in Ur, in the center of Babylonian civilization, before he led his countrymen to Israel in around 2000 B.C. One old Jewish reference work says: "Abraham, the Chaldean, bore upon his breast a large clay astrological tablet on which the fate of every man might be read." It is almost inconceivable that the Hebrews, who wandered between Egypt and Babylonia for 2000 years, did not assimilate astrological knowledge. Also, the Hebrews were the slaves of Egypt for several generations until Moses freed them around 1200 B.C. Moses, before leading the Hebrew revolt, was an Egyptian priest. The evidence that Egyptian Astrology was indigenous and only later incorporated Babylonian techniques is strong.

Under the Egyptians, Astrology was also the jealously guarded power domain of a priesthood that, by using superstition and debasing the art when it suited it, effectively controlled the weaker pharaohs and the people.

The Great Pyramid at Gizeah (2790 B.C.) was built according to measurements said to correspond to astrological relationships and cycles—it is the only pyramid to incorporate these. Erected by King Khufu (or Cheops, as the Greeks called him), the Great Pyramid was originally 481 feet high and 451 feet wide at its base, and it covered 13 acres.

Around 1000 B.C. the Assyrians conquered Babylon. But they preserved the temples and compiled an astrological library of cuneiform clay tablets ranging over nearly 2000 years of Babylonian history. More than 30,000 of these tablets have been found in this century near the site of ancient Babylon.

With the Assyrian conquest, many groups of Babylonians drifted to the northwest and settled in Greece.

600 B.C.—The Greeks and the Age of Pisces

In 600 B.C., the Greek "enlightenment" began. Thales, Anaximander, Anaximenes, Pythagoras, Anagoras, Aristotle, Plato, Hippocrates and others formed a great line of brilliant and creative minds whose scientific inquiry and philosophical speculation graced that remarkable time. Astrology, for a while, seemed to be ignored. But something essential to its continued progress was happening—new astronomical and philosophical concepts were being formulated, preparing the ground for a fresh harvest of astrological inspiration.

The Babylonian settlers taught the Greeks all they knew about astronomy. And the Greeks went on to make a series of astounding discoveries of their own. These included the founding of trigonometry, the basis of all future astronomical calculations.

In 300 B.C., Aristarchus of Samos put forward the theory that the Earth revolved around the Sun in a world almost ferociously committed to the "obvious" truth that the Sun circles the Earth. Seventeen centuries later, Copernicus was to describe the Sun as the center of the universe and become the founder of modern astronomy. But 100 years later, Galileo, after publishing a paper supporting the Copernican theory, encountered the old blind and ignorant forces of priestly superstition and was forced to recant by the Papal Inquisition.

Pythagoras (fifth century B.C.), who studied for a time in Egypt, was supposed to have been the first to contend that the Earth, Moon, planets and fixed stars revolved around the Sun, although he left nothing in writing. Copernicus named him as the originator of the theory he said he was merely reviving.

Around 150 B.C., Hipparchus discovered the precision of the equinoxes, without which accurate astronomical observations were impossible. It is the equinoxes that determine the 2000-year astrological ages. Hipparchus made his discovery after he set out to catalogue all the fixed stars so that he would know if any new ones turned up! When he went back over his lists, he found the stars had "moved," a phenomenon that could only be explained by equinoctial precession. By using Chaldean eclipse data, this gifted Greek was able to work out the mean motion of the Moon.

Gradually, having done all their astronomical homework, the Greeks began to turn their attention to Astrology. Their contribution, as in the other arts and sciences, was massive. After more concentrated study under the tutelage of the Chaldean astrologers, the Greeks quickly developed their own special approach. Instead of accepting Astrology as an exclusive medium for kings and countries, they sought to learn what the stars meant for the individual. And so the personal horoscope was born.

This was not a chance occurrence, according to astrologers, for this period marked the start of the 2000-year Age of Pisces, the emotional, watery Sign that through suffering and compassion dissolves the bonds that bind the individual to temporal authority, whether it be the rock of a church, the sovereignty of a king, the solidarity of a nation or a political ideology. By the twentieth century, the individual should largely have broken away from these constraining traditions and be ready to step into the Age of Aquarius and discover what his new-found freedom means.

In 280 B.C., the Babylonian Berosus set up a school of Astrology on the Greek island of Cos. Over the next two centuries, the Greco-Babylonian Astrology spread as far as Rome and was accompanied by the appearance of various handbooks on the art. One very important change the Greeks made was to substitute the names of their own deities for the "heathen gods" the Babylonians had named the planets for.

In 165 B.C., a Greek stoic philosopher named Posidonius founded a school in Rhodes where the individualized method of casting horoscopes, called Genethliac Astrology, was taught and practiced. Two famous Romans—Pompey and Cicero, orator and statesman—are said to have visited this school. There is also evidence that the classic poem *Astronomica* by Manilius, describing the motions of the heavenly bodies and the properties of the zodiacal Signs, was inspired by the poet's reading of Posidonius' writings.

Under the Greeks, Astrology became an interpretive medium rather than a system predicting the soul-crushing actions of fate. In apprising people of their potentialities—their strengths and weaknesses—it freed them to mold their characters as they saw fit by refusing to bend to their own blind nature and habitual reactions. The Greeks believed that only fools and the weak-willed accepted astrological definitions as statements of fate. More evolved human beings, those who were struggling to develop a truly individual consciousness, would see in the science a pattern of possibilities, warnings, pitfalls, which they could either heed or ignore.

The Greeks also developed Astrology as a system of medical treatment. Later, out of Egypt, came the Hermes cult, which associated various parts of the body with the Signs and the planets, thus erecting what is known as the Zodiacal Man. Although astro-medical science, as it is called, requires a great deal more research, it is considered by most astrologers today to be an extremely valid extension of their art. Research has been neglected because for public acceptance it requires the application of the medical mind, which until very recent times has been too closed and hostile to even consider the possibility. However, the new nucleo-scientific era of bio-cosmology is studying these body-zodiac correspondences.

The scheme of physiological correspondences starts with the first zodiacal Sign, Aries, for the head, and extends through the regions of the body down to the feet, which are connected with the twelfth Sign, Pisces:

Aries—Head
Taurus—Throat, neck
Gemini—Lungs, chest
Cancer—Breasts, stomach
Leo—Heart
Virgo—Intestines, nervous system
Libra—Kidneys, lower back
Scorpio—Genitals, bladder, rectum
Sagittarius—Hips, thighs
Capricorn—Knees
Aquarius—Calves, ankles
Pisces—Feet

Many Piscean types do have trouble with their feet, Libra people with their kidneys and back and so on. But the study is far more profound in its applications than this would suggest. Further correspondences often allow the modern astrologer to make accurate determinations about psychological disturbances that may be causing a particular physical illness, and vice versa. The astrologer may be able to pinpoint a trouble area where medical diagnosis has failed.

The ancient Greeks kept the astro-medical ball rolling with a theory that each horoscope indicated a "climacteric" period in a person's life when he or she should take precautions against certain diseases and sicknesses. They compiled complicated lists of illnesses and treatments that are quite amusing by today's standards. But the important point is that out of this early floundering in ignorance and superstition emerged man's greatest boon—medical science.

Astrology's next phase was accomplished by the Romans. Until the new astro-culture arrived, the Romans had relied for divination on all kinds of symbols, including "readings" from the intestines of animals. The personal horoscope was a lot less mucky. Also, it appealed to the sensitive minds of the more advanced Romans, who were yielding to the refining influence of Greek thought. Once it was accepted that the vista of the heavens held the answers rather than the entrails of some butchered animals, the inner eye turned to more exalted speculation.

In the Roman marketplace, astrologers set up shop in virtually every doorway. Despite some stiff opposition from Cato, Cicero and other heavyweights who warned of the folly of consulting "these mischievous Chaldeans," Astrology flourished and eventually became inseparably bound up with Roman religious life.

Even the lurching expedience of Roman politics failed to suppress Astrology's march into the first millennium A.D. In 33 B.C., Augustus, tussling with Marc Antony for supreme power, banished all astrologers and soothsayers from Rome. Augustus was an ardent believer in the art, but he knew the influence of these people and feared his enemies among them might excite public opinion against him with unfavorable "predictions." After disposing of his rival, Augustus reaffirmed his faith in Astrology by striking a coin showing his Capricorn symbol ruling the world.

Most Roman emperors esteemed their court astrologers. Some of them followed the example of Augustus and minted coinage bearing their Sign symbols or the Sign the Moon occupied on their birthday. In those days, the Moon was considered a most powerful deity. Today, stripped of its religious associations, it is still number three in significance in the horoscope.

Tiberius had a Greek astrologer. Mad Caligula was told the time and conditions under which he would die by the astrologer-mathematician Sylla. Vitellius attempted to banish all astrologers from Rome except his own—but the crafty Chaldeans (as all astrologers were then known) prophesied that the day of their banishment would also be the day the emperor died! Needless to say, the forecast was never put to the test. Claudius, in 52 A.D., also tried to ban Astrology in what was described as a "ruthless but ineffectual" decree. Under Nero, the art once more thrived.

All extant histories of the Roman Empire bear witness to the tremendous influence of Astrology. And these were not times that can be dismissed, as Tacitus and other contemporary historians verify. The end of the old millennium was known as the Golden Age of literature, adorned as it was with the works of Virgil, Horace, Ovid and Livy. These, and other men of equal stature whose ideas have been incorporated into the fabric of Western civilization, were part of this extraordinarily persistent astro-religious persuasion. Under its influence, the masses also raised their sights beyond the obvious. Although their notions may have been ridden with superstition, they saw hope in basing their existence on the depthless sky rather than a grave in the ground. Where they looked with credulous awe, other minds would follow and find the truth.

Roman heroes and ordinary men and women died believing they would be reborn among the stars in the constellations of Hercules, Perseus, Castor and Pollux. There was no one to prove them wrong. And the heavenly mansions referred to around this time by the first Christian also required a faith that, although perhaps more inspirational, was no less vivid in its concepts.

After centuries of isolated development, the Egyptian astrological influence began to assert itself. This was particularly evident following the annexation of Egypt by Rome in 30 B.C.

In the second century A.D., in Alexandria where he resided, the Greek astrologer Claudius Ptolemy made a most remarkable contribution. Ptolemy drew all the threads of astronomical and astrological knowledge together and put them into two books entitled *Almagest* and *Tetrabiblios*. These and his own discoveries have earned him the title "Father of Modern Astrology." His system of astronomy—*Almagest* —lasted for 12 centuries until overthrown by Copernicus. Ptolemy taught correctly that the Earth was round and rotated on its axis. But he made the mistake of believing that the Sun moved around the Earth, as it appears to do. When Copernicus in 1530 proved the opposite, Ptolemy was astronomically eclipsed. But astrologically—through the publication of *Tetrabiblios*—his light has remained undimmed to the present day. And this raises one of the most misunderstood points about Astrology.

Astrological science is based on the *apparent* motions of the heavenly bodies. The rationale for this is simplicity itself: this is how it was when man first observed the sky and this is how it still is when he observes it today. Nothing has changed from an astrological viewpoint. The fact that the Earth revolves around the Sun is an intellectual conception independent of sense perception. It is valid for every science that requires this knowledge, but not for the *abstract* mother of sciences, which was born in man's mind from the genius of his unaided sight. Astrology has no need to put a man on the Moon. It is the science of inner revelation, not overt action. Copernicus' wonderful discovery, which revolutionized astronomy, has made not one iota of difference to the phenomenon of the heavens as viewed by any spectator on Earth. (The locating of the three "new" planets—Uranus, Neptune and Pluto—has extended the system, but not upset it, as will be explained later.) There is a similar discrepancy in the more respected sciences. Newtonian gravitational laws, which work perfectly on Earth, are useless for celestial mechanics, as Einstein proved. But when one is engaged in making jet aircraft, automobiles, washing machines and the like, the Einsteinian theory of relativity is merely an intellectual conception that makes no difference to the product. So, although Ptolemy was wrong, astronomically, this in no way invalidates his astrological information. In fact, he made an enormous contribution by compiling and handing down to us in one encyclopedic volume centuries of knowledge accumulated by the Arabians, Persians, Greeks and Egyptians.

In the *Tetrabiblios*, astrologers found for the first time in one work detailed instructions for interpreting planetary positions in a horoscope based on the then new concept of good and bad aspects. Ptolemy corrected Hipparchus' catalogue of fixed stars and made tables of the motions of the Sun, Moon and planets. He also systemized the combining of Astrology with the doctrine of the four elements—fire, earth, air and water—and the four basic qualities—hot, cold, dry and moist.

By the third century A.D., Plotinus, the Egyptian-born philosopher who settled in Rome and who was regarded as the chief of the Neoplatonists, declared: "It is abundantly evident that the motion of the heavens affects things on Earth."

As Christianity began to spread across Europe, Astrology seemed once again to wane. But this apparent eclipse proved to be only a period of transition. Many centuries had to pass before the Piscean Age would end. Man had to become attached to the authority of the Church before he could chaff under it and be capable of recognizing the powers it stood for in himself as an evolving individual. Much suffering had to be endured in the form of religious wars, poverty and Inquisitional barbarity before this recognition was possible.

The final Roman persecution of the Christians occurred under the emperor Diocletian in 303 A.D. Twenty years later, Rome had its first Christian emperor in Constantine. The old pagan gods were finished and so was Astrology—as a religion. But it was never the ordinary sort of religion, anyway, because essentially it never contended with beliefs. It was a discipline of *revelation*, concerned only with the truth, the understanding of the forces acting on human life whatever they might be called. It had no argument with Christianity or any other faith. It was a principle men could use or leave alone for centuries.

The Christian fathers of the fourth century didn't understand this. Nor did the fanatics of Astrology who tried to fight them. One of Christianity's most fervid spokesmen, St. Augustine, branded Astrology demonic practice, and for 800 years that was that. Once the Church became established with the princes of Europe, Astrology virtually vanished.

But only in that small part of the globe called Europe. In the Arab world, Astrology was lighting the way to new heights of learning. The sheiks of Arabia encouraged education and culture, though their impoverished people must have wondered what for. They spent huge sums setting up libraries, importing books and manuscripts and gathering knowledge through emissaries. They built observatories, developed optics and compiled their own catalogues of the stars. In 777 A.D., a school of astronomy and Astrology was founded in Baghdad. In 815, the Caliph Al-Mamum had Ptolemy's works translated into Arabic. In 850, Albumasar, the most influential of the Arab astrologers, had a thriving school in Baghdad. Albumasar's writings were later translated into Latin by Christian monks. His widely read *Introduction to Astronomy* was one of the first books printed after the invention of the printing press.

It was the Arabic astronomers who first realized that the Greeks were wrong and that the obliquity of the ecliptic (the Sun's apparent path) was not a constant value. They achieved a new degree of accuracy in spherical trigonometry and formulated many of the terms now used in Astrology. The Arabs recognized its importance in physiology and medicine and developed the science of planetary cycles, climacteric periods and critical days. In other words, the Arabs not only kept Astrology alive, they raised it to new heights of competence. And when the Moors conquered Spain, they reintroduced the science into a Europe that was desperately in need of rescue from the ecclesiastical Dark Ages that had strangled culture, progress and free inquiry. It was to be a long haul.

Before proceeding with Western history, it is interesting to glance at what had been happening in Asia and on the subcontinent of India.

THE ASTROLOGY OF ASIA

The Hindus

The Hindus claim they are the oldest surviving civilization in the world and that Astrology is their oldest science. The first point may be disputed by the Chinese and possibly by the Egyptians. But it is unarguable that Astrology is intrinsic to Hindu history, which, like that of all the ancient races, stretches into the antiquity of tradition.

Many authorities are convinced that Hindu Astrology is indigenous—that is, it was "there" in the beginning. It was certainly not imported from Greece or Islamic lands, and its methods bear no resemblance to those of the Chinese. The Hindu system of Astrology was so advanced that its practitioners were casting genethliac, or individual horoscopes, thousands of years before the Greeks and long before the Egyptians.

The Hindus' astrological doctrines were

much more developed than corresponding doctrines in the West, and their understanding of astronomy was extraordinarily advanced. A section of the Vedas—the religio-historical documents of the ancient Aryans of around 1500 B.C. —is devoted to Astrology, the movements of the celestial bodies and their significance.

There is a strong school of thought that the entire structure of Chaldean, Egyptian and Greek learning, especially the more occult sciences, was originally derived from Asia. It is recorded of both the Egyptian Osiris and the Greek Orpheus that they were "dark-skinned men" from the East, who brought the first knowledge of the sacred sciences from a race or order of sages who lived an almost fabled existence in the mountains of northern Hindustan.

It has even been suggested that the Hindus received their spiritual traditions from an older race of Arhats who lived in the "mountain depths remote from men." A similar source of Chinese culture—the "Great Teachers of the Snowy Mountains and the School of the Haimavatas"— is mentioned briefly in the sacred literature of the Tian-T'i sect.

It has been observed that Brahmin priests, who kept their esoteric knowledge secret in the sacred Sanskrit language, were too proud to have borrowed their science from the Greeks, Arabs, Moguls or any nation of Mlechas, as they called those who were ignorant of the Vedas and who had not studied Sanskrit, the "language of the gods."

According to the Hindus, their Astrology was established on the spiritual authority of the gods, who revealed the knowledge to a line of Brahmin sages called *rishis*. *Rishi* means *to shine as a light or a star*. *Maha-rishis* (great lights) were the most illustrious of the sages. They were persons endowed with *Divya Drisati* (superior sight). Among the maharishis who composed the original astrological works was Parasara, the father of Vyasa, who compiled the Vedas as well as the Puranas, another extremely ancient work.

The antiquity of Hindu Astrology can be gauged from the fact that there was time for two ancient subraces to evolve out of one of its premises. As well as possessing the Solar Zodiac, the Hindus founded a parallel system of 27 Lunar Mansions made up of the constellations passed over by the Moon in its daily progress. The symbolism of the Sun and the Moon competing with each other resulted in the emergence of two rival races—the Suryas and the Chandravansas—Children of the Sun and Children of the Moon.

The horoscope of the Hindu god-man Rama, said to be the sixth, seventh or eighth incarnation of Vishnu, the second god of the Hindu Triad, is given in the great epic poem *Ramayana*, which predates Homer's *Iliad* of 900 B.C. Astrologers calculate from the positions of the planets given that the horoscope is of a man born before 3100 B.C. The interesting point is that Rama's horoscope contains the Signs of the Zodiac in which the planets were placed, and these divisions were not made by the Babylonians until around the year 2000 B.C.

In India today, the practice of Astrology is still widespread. As in the West, it is undergoing a gradual scientific realignment, which will allow it to stand on its rightful merits rather than on the shaky emotional ground of popular belief. This, in India more than in most places, has led to ridiculous deceptions and absurdities in the past. In Delhi and several other large cities, courses in Astrology are being conducted in association with local colleges. Hindu Astrology still varies considerably from Western Astrology, and even a cursory study shows it was not derived from any of our sources.

The Chinese

The Chinese are another people who claim to have received their astrological knowledge "direct from the gods." The fact that this vast cultural area was isolated from the rest of the world for thousands of years suggests a source extremely remote in time.

To the ancient Chinese, the outside world did not exist. The national psychology that beyond the gates was abysmal space seems to refute the view that the Chinese derived their Astrology from the Hindus or Arabs. All existing evidence suggests that they discovered and developed their arts and sciences without access to the accumulated knowledge of any of the other historical races.

The ancient Chinese Zodiac is quite independent of that used in the West. Although it was based on the traditional concept, the Chinese related it primarily to a 12-year cycle with different animal symbols for each year. The year 1910, for instance, was the Year of the Dog, 1911, the Year of the Boar, followed by the Rat, Ox, Tiger, Rabbit, Dragon, Snake, Horse, Sheep, Monkey, Cock and back to Dog again in 1922.

People born in a particular year had definite characteristics. These are said to be drawn from the nature to the animals concerned, though they are not obviously appropriate to the animals as we know them today. The descriptions are probably drawn from occult traditions.

For example, people born in 1956 belong to the Year of the Monkey. Monkey people are described as being erratic geniuses. They shine in just about any field. They are original and inventive and very good at making quick decisions. Monkey people have an inborn thirst for knowledge as well as a fine memory. They often become famous. They are clever and possess a great deal of common sense. In love, they are passionate.

As with the Sun in Western Astrology, the year fixes the basic type, which is subject to various modifications that must be considered to arrive at the correct character. This, and the importance that the ancient Chinese sages also ascribed to the Solar Zodiac, is clearly defined in a work called the *Shu King*. It says: "Of the Five Disposers, the first is called the year; the second is called the Moon; the third is named the Sun [Sun Sign]; the fourth is the planetary hour [Ascendant Sign]; and the fifth is known as the astronomical disposition (positions of the planets)."

Historically, Astrology has been firmly established in China since the earliest periods. From the days of the Emperor Fohi, around 2752 B.C. to 200 B.C., astronomy was studied for the sole purpose of astrological prediction. Chinese knowledge of the heavenly motions was extraordinary.

Emperors were chosen on account of their astrological expertise. The Emperor Chueni, in the year 2513 B.C., computed an ephemeris (a book of tables) of the motions of the five planets. There is also evidence suggesting he observed a great conjunction that occurred in 2449 B.C.

Marco Polo, who arrived in China in 1271, wrote: "These astrologers are very skillful in their business and often their words come to pass, so the people have great faith in them."

Chinese legend deifies Fohi as the Divine Emperor. He is referred to as the Dragon Man, the Supreme Sage and the Father of Gods and Men. He is said to have been an avatar (incarnation) of the eternal divinity, Luminous Heaven. Fohi is reputed to have been born of a virgin "without the concurrence of a father."

Fohi was the first educator of the Chinese. He taught them to use written characters and is known as the "literary ancestor of the myriad of ages." He invented diagrams to teach men the formation of the universe from chaos and the succession of the worlds. He instituted marriage and instructed mankind in the useful arts.

Much later the Chinese came under the influence of the Mongolians, starting with the conquest by Genghis Khan in 1213. The Mongolians had also developed a high standard of astrological and astronomical proficiency.

As is usual with legendary historical figures, Genghis Khan's birth is said to have been of divine origin. His mother, a widow, became pregnant, which was against the law, and when arraigned before the chief judge of the tribe, declared that a blinding light had appeared in her room and penetrated her body three times. She said she knew this to mean she would bring three sons into the world, and if this did not happen, she would submit to the cruelest punishment. Three sons were subsequently born and she was regarded as a saint.

When Genghis Khan was born, the astrologers declared that a divine man had come into the world. A modern construction of his horoscope shows a great conjunction of five planets in the Sign of Libra, said to indicate extraordinary genius. The horoscope is for September 1186 A.D. Genghis was trained in Astrology. In an *Outline History of China*, Herbert H. Gowen, F.R.G.S., says that in the midst of his conquests, "the Mogul was impressed with the unfavorable conjunctions of planets as with a presentiment of approaching doom." Deciding to head for home, he died shortly after in northern China. He was 65.

Kublai Khan, the grandson of Genghis who defeated the Sun dynasty of China in 1279 A.D., was a great patron of science, literature and the arts. He encouraged the use of astronomical instruments and some of these were still preserved in the Peking Observatory until the present Communist regime took over.

Kublai Khan encouraged European priests and accepted Tibetan Buddhism as a means of widening the education of his people and hastening the civilization process.

Once he put down a revolt led by dissenting Christians and in a speech to them not only showed his acceptance of Astrology but also revealed his wisdom, maturity and tolerance. With the 15,000 prisoners assembled around him, he addressed them from the back of his elephant, presumably to announce the death sentence:

Though I confess my great victory, this day gotten, was by the power and favor of my gods, the Sun, the Moon and the stars, abiding in the glorious firmament of the heaven; yet because the prisoners, being all or most of them Christians, appear before me not only despoiled of their arms, but mocked and taunted of the Jews, Mohammedans and others, upbraiding them with their god Jesus, who was sometimes fastened unto a cross by the forefathers of these Jews: notwithstanding they have opposed me in battle, and that so many of their ensigns lie here prostrate at my feet; yet that all the nations and languages that live under our principality and dominion, may know, that we in our grace can find as soon will to pardon as power to punish; from this day forward, we forbid, and strictly charge all nations under us, of what quality or religion soever, that they neither deride, injure nor oppress any of these captive Christians, upon penalty to be deprived of their arms, and disgracefully scourged with rods. The main reason inducing us to see this exactly performed, being no other, but that their god Jesus is highly esteemed and honored by us as being one of the greatest among the celestial deities full of all equity and justice.*

MODERN ASTROLOGY IN THE WEST

In the thirteenth century, after the Moorish transfusion, Astrology and intellectual inquiry were again ascendant in Europe. By this time, Astrology had branched into four divisions:

1. *Judicial or Genethliac Astrology*, for interpreting the individual's natal horoscope.
2. *Hororary Astrology*, for answering a question from a horoscope or chart drawn at the moment of asking.
3. *Natural or Mundane Astrology*, for forecasting events of national importance such as wars, weather and financial depressions.
4. *Election Astrology*, for fixing the exact right moment to do something. An example of this was the laying of the foundation stone of Greenwich (England) Observatory at a time astrologically calculated by the first Astronomer Royal, John Flamsteed (1646–1719).

At the new University at Oxford, England, Astrology was part of the study of astronomy. Robert Grosseteste, the first chancellor, regarded Astrology as "the supreme science" and maintained that it gave an insight into all human activities.

Then the Church, through one of its most influential sons, St. Thomas Aquinas, gave Astrology a benign nod. Declaring that God ruled inferior creatures through superior creatures, and

Hierarchy of the Blessed Angels, by Heywood.

so ruled our earthly bodies through the stars, he left room in Astrology for free will, the most contentious point for many people. No ecclesiastic, and few individuals for that matter, could accept a study that suggested all was preordained. The religious poet Dante, who also acknowledged the influence of the stars, repeatedly stressed their partial power. In his *Divine Comedy*, he quotes a tortured spirit as saying: "You lie subject to your freedom to a greater power and to a better nature; and that creates in you, mind, which the heavens have not in their charge. . . ." For Dante, as for Aquinas, the battle was between natural man (controlled by the stars) and aspiring man (subject to God).

By the Renaissance (around the fourteenth century), Astrology was well and truly reestablished in Christian Europe. It enjoyed the support of many of the most prominent thinkers and artists of the time. Over the next four centuries, new foundations were laid that enabled it to survive the skepticism of the eighteenth century.

The scientific discoveries of Newton, Copernicus, Tycho Brahe and Kepler, although they seemed to erode Astrology's position, only served to guarantee it a stronger place in the future. For Astrology had nothing to fear from pure science—but only from uninquiring prejudice. To flourish, all it required was the discernment of minds free from the diehard traditions instilled by church and state and the ingrained habit of worship of authority that freezes men's minds with a fixed and inflexible vision. Astrology needed a chance to look at itself in a pristine state, divested of all but its demonstrable principles correlated with precise astronomical and scientific fact. It needed, in truth, a new breed of astrologers. And this became possible as the vague, emotional and impressionable Piscean Age neared its end.

The transition to the beginning of the scientific age was not easy—for scientists or astrologers. It was difficult to tell who was who.

The Dane, Tycho Brahe (1546–1601), was both. He was recognized as the most distinguished and accurate observer of the heavens since Hipparchus 1700 years before him. He started a scientific ball rolling that culminated in Newton's laws of gravitation published in 1693.

Tycho spent his spare time casting horoscopes. In 1572, he made an extraordinary prediction based on the appearance of a comet. He said that in 1592 a man ordained for a great enterprise in a religious cause would be born in Finland and would die in 1632. The prediction fitted almost exactly the life and career of Gustavus Adolphus of Sweden (of which Finland was a province). Gustavus and his armies won outstanding victories for the Protestant cause during the Thirty-Year War, and he died at the moment of his most glorious victory over the German forces at Lutzen in 1632.

Tycho, under the patronage of King Frederick of Denmark, had all his instruments built of metal instead of wood to ensure greater accuracy. He insisted that theorizing should only begin after the most exacting observations, which he proceeded to make. He prepared and used accurate tables, correcting those of Copernicus.

Among his assistants was a brilliant young German named Johann Kepler (1571–1630). Kepler, using Tycho's records of the motions of the planets, was to revolutionize astronomy with his three great laws of planetary motion, which were only fully explained nearly a century later by Newton's dynamics.

Kepler was also an astrologer. He published annual astrological calendars. For the year 1595, he successfully predicted trouble among the peasants of upper Austria and a Turkish invasion. After casting the horoscope of the famous Austrian General Albrecht von Wallenstein in 1624, Kepler predicted from it that there would be "dreadful disorders over the land" in March 1634. The general was murdered by dissidents on February 25, 1634.

Kepler's laws of motion upset all the previous theories by describing the orbits of the planets as elliptical instead of circular. His astrological ideas also anticipated those of today, which see the Zodiac as a universal genetic pattern correlated with changes in the electromagnetic planetary field of the solar system.

Kepler believed that "the soul bears within itself the idea [Signs?] of the Zodiac" and that the stellar rays act on the soul instinctively, "just as the sense of hearing, endowed with the faculty of discerning chords, lends to music such power that it incites him who hears to dance."

Galileo (1564–1642), a contemporary of Kepler, was the first to use the telescope for astronomical observation. He was also an astrologer. Two of his books contain horoscopes he cast. He died the day Newton was born. It was Newton who explained the real meaning of Kepler's three laws of planetary motion by enunciating the law of universal gravity (which has turned out to be less than universal).

Newton's position regarding Astrology is not too clear, but there is on record the famous retort he made to Halley, the discoverer of the comet that bears his name, when he expressed doubts about Astrology: "Sir, I have studied it, you have not."

One of the most famous astrological predictions about this time was made by the Englishman William Lilly (1602–1681). Lilly was one of the new generation of astrologers who were able to read books translated from Latin and do their own experimenting with horoscopes. In 1651, he predicted both the plague and the Great Fire of London of 1666. A mystified investigating committee summoned him to give evidence but all he could tell them was that both disasters were written in the stars. He records in his autobiography that he was "dismissed by the committee with great civility."

During the eighteenth century, Astrology began to lose ground on the Continent, mainly for want of inspired practitioners. In England, however, the practice flourished and managed even to survive being outlawed by the Witchcraft Act of 1735.

With the rise of literacy in the nineteenth century, people began to read for themselves the rare astrological works and to take a personal interest in what the star they were born under had to say. The professional astrologer, even though intimidated by the threat of prosecution, managed to operate. He was encouraged and sought out by an ever-growing following, who eventually demanded the right to make up their own minds about what was edifying.

Among the ranks of serious astrologers there was an increasing attempt to restate astrological principles in rational scientific terms. By the twentieth century, through the dedicated work of people like William Allan (Alan Leo), Walter Gorn-Old ("Sepharial"), Paul Choisnard, Fomalhaut, Vivian Robson and Max Heindel, the ground had been broken. Today, thanks to scientific astrologers such as Margaret E. Hone, Jeff Mayo, Evangeline Adams, Elbert Benjamine, Marcia Moore and Mark Douglas, the work is ready to be taken up by a new generation that is even more scientific, intuitive, unconventional, original, broadminded and inventive—as befits pioneers of the Aquarian Age.

TODAY'S ASTROLOGY

How the Planets Affect Life

How can the planets possibly influence a person's life? This is a question astrologers have had a hard time answering down through the centuries, and naturally, the credibility of Astrology has suffered because of it. Today, thanks to the advances of late-twentieth-century physics and a greater understanding of the times we live in, the question can finally be answered.

To begin with, if Astrology is to be accepted as a perceptive science, which is what it is, it must be able to justify itself in the light of the latest scientific discoveries in its field—celestial mechanics. Astrology has, in a way, an advantage over science because it claims that although there is still a vast amount to learn and be incorporated into the system, its principle explains the general scheme of life. Science can't do this. It suspects that in time, and in its own way, it will eventually be able to, but its method is to prove each step and to progress gradually from one theory to another toward whatever truth lies at the end. Astrology, in effect, starts with the end.

Obviously, a gap will exist for a very long time between what science discovers and what Astrology claims to know. This limits any explanation and necessitates a certain amount of speculation and theorizing until science catches up. But science and Astrology are on coverging courses and they will meet in the end. There is, even now, enough common ground for a rational explanation, which would have been impossible less than fifty years ago.

Astrology is the science of electromagnetism perceived before its time. Once this basic concept is grasped, the question of how the planets can affect life on Earth is half answered; the other half of the answer depends on the next phase of scientific discovery in the field of cybernetics. The point here is that science has uncovered the underlying verity of Astrology in two specific studies—electromagnetism and cybernetics—and is now in the process of pulling the two strings together. In the bag between we find Astrology.

Since electromagnetism was not even discovered until 1831 by Faraday, what astrologers were up against over the centuries in trying to explain their technical art in rational terms will be appreciated. Like Faraday, they knew through experimentation that their science worked. If it hadn't, it would have died a natural death very early. But how could they express the workings? Faraday couldn't express electromagnetics satisfactorily either. That was to be left to Maxwell, who 40 years later, translated Faraday's discoveries into a single mathematical theory, making possible the development of modern physics and electronics.

How, then, could ancient, medieval and modern astrologers explain the dynamics of their craft if the idea behind it had not even been formulated, the scientific principle not yet conceived? Who could blame the disbelievers and doubters? They just wanted a reasonable answer to a reasonable question: How could Astrology possibly work? It was like asking someone who hadn't heard of electricity to explain how an electric light bulb functioned. The replies down through the ages were stumbling and unconvincing justifications expressed either in occult, metaphysical or magical jargon, the only language available to describe the miracle of electronics. As mathematics is the language of celestial mechanics, so Astrology has its language to express celestial consequences. The symbols used in both languages have the same ancient origins.

The Zodiac

Astrology is based on the Zodiac. The word is from the Greek *zodiakos*, which is from *zoion* (animal) and *kirkos* (circle)—a circle of animals. This alludes to the ancients' naming of the heavenly constellations after various animals. At this point ends all practical correspondence between the fanciful old Zodiac of stars and the modern astrological Zodiac of space.

Astrology is indebted to the ancients, who

saw in the symbolism of the stars the existence of the spatial Zodiac. But there is no connection—except symbolically—between the two. This is rarely made clear and is one of the reasons why Astrology is not understood by more people.

The astrological Zodiac is an abstract division of the sphere of space around us into 12 different segments or Signs. This may sound almost as farfetched as the ancients' idea, but it is not, and the reasons will be clear once the broad picture is described. These 12 Signs inherent in space are patterns of human characteristics, and between them they represent the 12 psychological types of people or the 12 basic ways in which human individuality expresses itself.

The Signs Are:

Aries the Ram	Libra the Scales
Taurus the Bull	Scorpio the Scorpion
Gemini the Twins	Sagittarius the Archer
Cancer the Crab	Capricorn the Goat
Leo the Lion	Aquarius the Water Bearer
Virgo the Virgin	Pisces the Fishes

So the first quality of zodiacal space is it contains 12 distinct divisions of character.

The second quality of space—still represented by the Zodiac—is that it contains 12 basic spheres of human activity. These are called Houses and are numbered from 1 to 12.

The Houses and an abbreviated description of their meanings are:

1. Personality, self-centered interests, outlook on life.
2. Possessions, income, basic security.
3. Communication with the environment; close relatives, neighbors, letters, speech, short trips, intellect.
4. Home, childhood, the unconscious, traditions, the psychological self.
5. Self-projection, pleasure, love affairs, offspring, sensual enjoyment, creativity, ideas, talent.
6. Employment, health, duty, pets, diet, daily tasks, hygiene, basic necessities.
7. The husband or wife, partners, contracts, war, marriage, divorce, legal matters, social awareness.
8. Death, legacies, shared feelings, the sex urge, psychoanalysis, the partner's resources, taxes, the afterlife.
9. Religion, long journeys, philosophical speculation, dreams, foreign countries, publicity, organized sport.
10. Public standing, fame, attainment, career or profession, status, corporations, government.
11. Impersonal relationships, group activities, friends, idealism, humanitarian objectives, unexpected happenings.
12. Sacrificial service, prison, exile, hidden enemies, confinement, seclusion, neuroses, treachery, hospitals, secret motives.

Each House has an affinity with a Sign, beginning with Aries.

The two qualities of space together form the Zodiac—like circles slowly rotating one inside the other. When an energy source (a planet) is in one of the divisions or Signs, it throws that particular character inward into a life situation (House), and the combined image appears on the Earth at the center as the individual and his environment. That's the general idea, absurdly oversimplified.

Since there are ten planets (the Sun and Moon are called planets) always radiating in particular Signs and Houses, the result is fascinating diversity—or human existence as we know it. And it takes quite a bit of skill (astrologer's art) to sort it out into patterns.

It is obvious that the type of energy a planet radiates—and its angular position in relation to the Signs, Houses and other planets—will also have a substantial bearing on the resultant Earth image. Accordingly, the characteristic energies of each of the planets have to be borne in mind. These are:

Sun—Power, self-expression, individuality.
Moon—Response, fluctuation, sensitivity, sympathy.
Mercury—Communication, intelligence, discernment.
Venus—Attraction, unity, beauty, evaluation.
Mars—Activity, energetic expression, self-assertion, heat, enterprise.
Jupiter—Expansion, optimism, foresight.
Saturn—Limitation, restriction, discipline.
Uranus—Drastic change, independence, originality, inventiveness.
Neptune—Transcendence through dissolution, immateriality.
Pluto—Resurrection, elimination, renewal, resolution.

The planets energize the Signs and Houses and the kaleidoscope of life results.

The question remaining is: How is this done—scientifically? The answer, which is not difficult to follow, involves four steps.

The first concerns Einstein's discoveries. In his general theory of relativity, Einstein showed that out among the stars and planets, space is geometrical, possesses peculiarities, assumes "shapes"—is qualifiable. Out there, space is not uniform, as we know it to be on Earth; it has different qualities in different places. It "bends" in a space-time contortion in the presence of massive bodies like the planets and especially the gigantic sun stars and constellations.

Second, sunlight, starlight and radio waves from deep space are electromagnetic in origin. The whole universe is known to be an electromagnetic complex, right down to and including the solar system and our own magnetosphere,* the field surrounding the Earth.

Third, the science of cybernetics †—the new, revolutionary study behind computer development—has introduced into physics an astonishing new concept called information; it recognizes that there is an *informational reciprocal* between any electromagnetic field and the organisms that live in it.

In other words, the "information" that is in an electromagnetic space-field is also inherent in every cell of every organism. This means it is not the power of the Sun's rays or any other form of radiation that produces cellular changes or activity but the informational reciprocal, which is activated in the living thing by fluctuations in the magnetic field responding to that radiation. The planetary radiations, so to speak, trigger a starting bell that sounds in the biocell and starts it on a predetermined program.

Fourth, all the planets cutting through the solar electromagnetic field, while radiating their own energies, create electromagnetic waves, which when in "adverse" aspect to each other and the Earth, cause severe radio disturbance. RCA has developed a prediction system for this along broadly astrological lines.** Those are the scientific considerations.

Now, put astrologically, the Zodiac consists of a circle of 12 different characteristic divisions of outer-space time, which astrologers call the Signs—Aries, Taurus, Gemini, etc. These 12 gigantic divisions taper down to a point that consti-

tutes all Earth space-time. The Signs and their qualities or characteristics, consequently, are universally present in and around every living cell, forming the conditions for electromagnetic activity and expression along precise lines.

It is easier in some respects to understand this cosmic principle than to reason why it has taken science so long to put cybernetics to work in the celestial field. However, through astro-biology—the modern scientific name for Astrology's astro-medicine—this is now being done.

One would have thought that after all the ridicule and derision, science would be moving in a different direction from Astrology. But inexorably it heads toward the Zodiac.

The Horoscope

The horoscope is a reference map. It shows exactly where the planets were in the Zodiac at the time of the person's birth. As with an ordinary map, if the salient features are identified, a fair assessment can be made of the terrain in advance and obvious obstacles can be avoided. The horoscope is a map not only of the character, urges and inclinations working in a person, but also of the forces that actually produced him as a human being. What is in the map will always be his fundamental physical and psychological self. If the time of an event can be fixed, the space characteristic or nature of it may also be determined. The horoscope is Astrology's way of writing science's space-time theory in relation to people and events.

With 10 planets distributed around the 12 Signs of the Zodiac and charted in horoscope form, a starting point has to be found to begin to read from. The most common method, as most people know, is to read the Sign the Sun occupied. The Sun is undoubtedly the most important and powerful body in the solar system, and its energizing force in the zodiacal spectrum is vital and dominant. So the Sign it occupied on the birthday is called the Sun Sign—Aries, Taurus, etc.—and this determines basic character. The Sun character is what you will always feel inside as yourself.

But there is another part of you that in many ways is just as important—that is, how you appear in the world to other people. You don't always reveal your Sun Sign character, although it remains intrinsically you. You often present another character to the outside world, and that is determined by the Ascendant Sign.

The Ascendant is actually the planet Earth.

*See Introduction, p. 15
†See Introduction, p. 16
**See Introduction, p. 12

Generally speaking, the Earth is not considered among the planets because it is the focal point of the horoscope, but it, too, affects our lives through the Zodiac, and the way it does this is by energizing the Ascendant Sign.

The Ascendant is the point at which the Earth meets space at the individual's place of birth—the horizon. Because of the Earth's rotation, a different Sign of the Zodiac rises on the horizon every two hours. To determine your Ascendant, you need to have a fairly accurate idea of your birth time. The Ascendant dictates how you appear to other people. It is your fate, which can't be avoided, your environment (family, home and hereditary circumstances). In most cases, the Ascendant Sign will be different from the Sun Sign. This explains why we often feel totally different from how we act, why we are misunderstood and misunderstand others, and why we have a conscience. The Sun Sign is what we must become—eventually. The Ascendant Sign is what we are now, and what we must use in our struggle to transcend.

The next most important planet in the horoscope is the Moon. This is our emotional self, our deep-rooted past that extends back through childhood, through the maternal influence, beyond memory into the unconscious wisps of other time-space contortions. We respond from the Moon in us with instinct and sensibility.

The positions in the horoscope of all the other planets must then be studied to get a complete picture. All these positions, including the Ascendant, are given in the following pages and their significance is explained.

For the professional astrologer, there are many other considerations in the horoscope that must be taken into account. For instance, each planet "rules" a Sign, sometimes two Signs, and a couple have part ownership. A planet in its own Sign is stronger. But among the planets, there are "enemies" and "friends"—that is, their basic energies are harmonious or disharmonious. Two enemies together will naturally produce tension in the person in regard to matters signified by the Sign and House. There are also Signs in which planets are extrastrong or exalted, as well as those indicating detriment and "fall." Some Houses have special affinity with individual planet qualities.

The Signs themselves have various properties and qualities. Each has an elemental nature, which is either fire, earth, air or water. The fire Signs—Aries, Leo, Sagittarius—are ardent and keen. Earth Signs—Taurus, Virgo, Capricorn—are practical and cautious. Air Signs—Gemini, Libra, Aquarius—are intellectual and communicative. Water Signs—Cancer, Scorpio, Pisces—are emotional, unstable and sensitive.

Each Sign is either positive (Aries, Gemini, Leo, Libra, Sagittarius, Aquarius) or negative (Taurus, Cancer, Virgo, Scorpio, Capricorn, Pisces). The Signs are also divided according to qualities called cardinal, fixed and mutable. The cardinal Signs—Aries, Capricorn, Libra, Cancer—are outgoing; fixed Signs—Taurus, Leo, Scorpio, Aquarius—are resistant to change; mutable Signs—Gemini, Virgo, Sagittarius, Pisces—are adaptable and versatile.

Finally, there are the all-important aspects between the planets. The professional astrologer has to measure the degrees separating the planets in the various Signs from the Houses of the horoscope and decide whether they are in "good" or "bad" angular distance—that is, whether they are producing easy or difficult conditions. In this book, these have been worked out for you, so casting your horoscope is just a simple matter of turning over a few pages and reading. But first you should understand your basic character determined by the Sun.

Free Will and Astrology

Does Astrology preclude free will? This is a question that concerns many people when they begin to understand cosmic significance.

One of the problems is that many of us mistake choice for free will. Astrology shows that there is more than considerable difference between the two.

We all know that at any moment of choice we are free. Otherwise we could not perform as responsible beings. We may have reasons for feeling one thing and choosing to do another—fear, consideration for someone, love—but we are free to choose when the opportunity is presented. Only this is a very limited freedom. A person's choice usually amounts to, will I or won't I stop or go? speak or be silent? say yes or no? Two alternatives obviously do not constitute much of a choice. This limited choosing certainly could not be equated with freedom.

This limited choosing where we feel the burden of our worldly obligations and frequently choose the way of duty rather than what we feel is right for us is presented by the Ascendant Sign. You will remember that this is the second most important factor in the horoscope: the character or personality we show to the world and our environment—rich or poor, orphaned or cherished, healthy or unhealthy—is determined by the Earth's relation to the Zodiac at the moment of birth. Limited choice is limited freedom, the condition of our worldly existence.

Will is quite a different quality. It is represented by the Sun Sign, the character we are becoming by means of our personality and worldly situation. The position of the Sun is the most important point of the horoscope.

Our will, like the Sun, sits behind our choosing personality like an old-fashioned king watching the antics of his prime minister making limited decisions. As was said earlier, the Sun character is what we always feel inside as ourselves. We can fool everyone else, perhaps, but we can't fool it. We get away with our limited choosing, but it won't make us happy or contented for long. We have to choose again, and go on choosing, to enjoy this limited freedom of the Ascendant.

But if through our Ascendant situation we have found a purpose to our lives, we will have the will to do or to be something. Choosing, then, will never really foul us up because we will choose according to our purpose, which is related to our Sun character. An extraordinary thing about purpose is that it has no object. Choice, which is of the Earth-bound Ascendant Sign, always has an object, a goal, an end in mind.

If a person's purpose is to be kind, he will never have to choose what to do—he'll be kind. Unlike the person who chooses an object or a goal, he will never face the question of what to do when enough has been acquired or the goal has been reached. How can he ever be kind enough when every moment of his life is a new opportunity for kindness?

Purpose is timeless and the person seldom has anything in particular to show for it. Purpose is both willing and free—in other words, free will—and it shines like the Sun above the Earth.

Every one of us is a mixture of his or her Sun character and Ascendant Sign. That is why there are so many nice people around.

CUSP CHARTS

IS YOUR LUCKY STAR A DOUBLE-HEADER?

Most people know the 12 Signs of the Zodiac and can tell you at once the name of their stars. Ask people born between February 19 and February 25, for example, and they will say they are Pisces. But are they? Some astrologers say that if you were born when one Sign was giving way to the next, as in the period between February 19 and February 25, then you belong to the *cusp* of Aquarius and Pisces. This means your life is exposed to both sets of stars, because the influence of Aquarius persists for six days (the cusp) from the junction. Consult the following tables and see if you belong to one of these cusps. You may find an aspect of your personality—and a key to your character—that you had never before suspected.

The Cusps Of:

ARIES and TAURUS
April 20—26

TAURUS and GEMINI
May 20—26

GEMINI and CANCER
June 21—27

CANCER and LEO
July 22—28

LEO and VIRGO
August 22—28

VIRGO and LIBRA
September 23—29

LIBRA and SCORPIO
October 23—29

SCORPIO and SAGITTARIUS
November 22—28

SAGITTARIUS and CAPRICORN
December 21—27

CAPRICORN and AQUARIUS
January 20—26

AQUARIUS and PISCES
February 19—25

PISCES and ARIES
March 20—26

YEAR	ARIES MAR.-APR.	TAURUS APR.-MAY	GEMINI MAY-JUNE	CANCER JUNE-JULY	LEO JULY-AUG.	VIRGO AUG.-SEPT.	LIBRA SEPT.-OCT.	SCORPIO OCT.-NOV.	SAGITTARIUS NOV.-DEC.	CAPRICORN DEC.-JAN.	AQUARIUS JAN.-FEB.	PISCES FEB.-MAR.
1910	22-20	21-21	22-21	22-23	24-23	24-23	24-23	24-22	23-22	23-20	21-19	20-21
1911	22-20	21-21	22-22	23-23	24-23	24-23	24-24	25-22	23-22	23-20	21-19	20-21
1912	21-19	20-20	21-21	22-22	23-23	24-22	23-23	24-22	23-21	22-20	21-19	20-20
1913	21-20	21-21	22-21	22-23	24-23	24-23	24-23	24-22	23-21	22-20	21-18	19-20
1914	21-20	21-21	22-21	22-23	24-23	24-23	24-23	24-22	23-22	23-20	21-18	19-20
1915	22-20	21-21	22-22	23-23	24-23	24-23	24-24	25-22	23-22	23-20	21-19	20-21
1916	21-19	20-20	21-21	22-22	23-23	24-22	23-23	24-22	23-21	22-20	21-19	20-20
1917	21-20	21-21	22-21	22-22	23-23	24-23	24-23	24-22	23-21	22-20	21-18	19-20
1918	21-20	21-21	22-21	22-23	24-23	24-23	24-23	24-22	23-22	23-20	21-18	19-20
1919	22-20	21-21	22-21	22-23	24-23	24-23	24-23	24-22	23-22	23-20	21-19	20-21
1920	21-19	20-20	21-21	22-22	23-22	23-22	23-23	24-22	23-21	22-20	21-19	20-20
1921	21-20	21-21	22-21	22-22	23-23	24-23	24-23	24-22	23-21	22-20	21-18	19-20
1922	21-20	21-21	22-21	22-23	24-23	24-23	24-23	24-22	23-22	23-20	21-18	19-20
1923	22-20	21-21	22-21	22-23	24-23	24-23	24-23	24-22	23-22	23-20	21-19	20-21
1924	21-19	20-20	21-21	22-22	23-22	23-22	23-23	24-22	23-21	22-20	21-19	20-20
1925	21-20	21-21	22-21	22-22	23-23	24-23	24-23	24-22	23-21	22-20	21-18	19-20
1926	21-20	21-21	22-21	22-23	24-23	24-23	24-23	24-22	23-22	23-20	21-18	19-20
1927	22-20	21-21	22-21	22-23	24-23	24-23	24-23	24-22	23-22	23-20	21-19	20-21
1928	21-19	20-20	21-21	22-22	23-22	23-22	23-23	24-22	23-21	22-20	21-19	20-20
1929	21-20	21-21	22-21	22-22	23-23	24-23	24-23	24-22	23-21	22-20	21-18	19-20
1930	21-20	21-21	22-21	22-23	24-23	24-23	24-23	24-22	23-22	23-20	21-18	19-20
1931	22-20	21-21	22-21	22-23	24-23	24-23	24-23	24-22	23-22	23-20	21-19	20-21
1932	21-19	20-20	21-21	22-22	23-22	23-22	23-23	24-22	23-21	22-20	21-19	20-20
1933	21-20	21-21	22-21	22-22	23-23	24-23	24-23	24-22	23-21	22-19	20-18	19-20
1934	21-20	21-21	22-21	22-23	24-23	24-23	24-23	24-22	23-22	23-20	21-18	19-20
1935	22-20	21-21	22-21	22-23	24-23	24-23	24-23	24-22	23-22	23-20	21-19	20-21
1936	21-19	20-20	21-21	22-22	23-22	23-22	23-23	24-21	22-21	22-20	21-19	20-20
1937	21-20	21-20	21-21	22-22	23-23	24-22	23-23	24-22	23-21	22-19	20-18	19-20
1938	21-20	21-21	22-21	22-23	24-23	24-23	24-23	24-22	23-22	23-20	21-18	19-20
1939	22-20	21-21	22-21	22-23	24-23	24-23	24-23	24-22	23-22	23-20	21-19	20-21

	ARIES	TAURUS	GEMINI	CANCER	LEO	VIRGO	LIBRA	SCORPIO	SAGITTARIUS	CAPRICORN	AQUARIUS	PISCES
YEAR	MAR.-APR.	APR.-MAY	MAY-JUNE	JUNE-JULY	JULY-AUG.	AUG.-SEPT.	SEPT.-OCT.	OCT.-NOV.	NOV.-DEC.	DEC.-JAN.	JAN.-FEB.	FEB.-MAR.
1940	21-19	20-20	21-21	22-22	23-22	23-22	23-23	24-21	22-21	22-20	21-19	20-20
1941	21-19	20-20	21-21	22-22	23-23	24-22	23-23	24-22	23-21	22-19	20-18	19-20
1942	21-20	21-21	22-21	22-23	24-23	24-23	24-23	24-22	23-21	22-20	21-19	19-20
1943	22-20	21-21	22-21	22-23	24-23	24-23	24-23	24-22	23-22	23-20	21-19	20-21
1944	21-19	20-20	21-21	22-22	23-22	23-22	23-23	24-21	22-21	22-20	21-19	20-20
1945	21-19	20-20	21-21	22-22	23-23	24-22	23-23	24-22	23-21	22-19	20-18	19-20
1946	21-20	21-21	22-21	22-22	23-23	24-23	24-23	24-22	23-21	22-20	21-18	19-20
1947	21-20	21-21	22-21	22-23	24-23	24-23	24-23	24-22	23-22	23-20	21-18	19-20
1948	21-19	20-20	21-21	22-22	23-22	23-22	23-23	24-21	22-21	22-20	21-19	20-20
1949	21-19	20-20	21-21	22-22	23-22	23-22	23-23	24-22	23-21	22-19	20-18	19-20
1950	21-20	21-21	22-21	22-22	23-23	24-23	24-23	24-22	23-21	22-20	21-18	19-20
1951	22-20	21-21	22-22	23-23	24-23	24-23	24-24	25-23	24-22	23-20	21-19	20-21
1952	21-20	21-21	22-21	22-22	23-23	24-23	24-23	24-22	23-21	22-21	22-19	20-20
1953	21-20	21-21	22-21	22-23	24-23	24-23	24-23	24-22	23-22	23-20	21-18	19-20
1954	22-20	21-21	22-21	22-23	24-23	24-23	24-23	24-22	23-22	23-20	21-19	20-21
1955	22-20	21-21	22-22	23-23	24-23	24-23	24-24	25-23	24-22	23-20	21-19	20-21
1956	21-20	21-21	22-21	22-22	23-23	24-23	24-23	24-22	23-21	22-21	22-19	20-20
1957	21-20	21-21	22-21	22-23	24-23	24-23	24-23	24-22	23-22	23-20	21-18	19-20
1958	22-20	21-21	22-21	22-23	24-23	24-23	24-23	24-22	23-22	23-20	21-19	20-21
1959	22-20	21-21	22-22	23-23	24-23	24-23	24-24	25-23	24-22	23-20	21-19	20-21
1960	21-20	21-21	22-21	22-22	23-23	24-23	24-23	24-22	23-21	22-21	22-19	20-20
1961	21-20	21-21	22-21	22-23	24-23	24-23	24-23	24-22	23-22	23-20	21-18	19-20
1962	22-20	21-21	22-21	22-23	24-23	24-23	24-23	24-22	23-22	23-20	21-19	20-21
1963	22-20	21-21	22-22	23-23	24-23	24-23	24-24	25-23	24-22	23-20	21-19	20-21
1964	21-20	21-21	22-21	22-22	23-23	24-23	24-23	24-22	23-21	22-21	22-19	20-20
1965	21-20	21-21	22-21	22-23	24-23	24-23	24-23	24-22	23-22	23-20	21-18	19-20
1966	22-20	21-21	22-21	22-23	24-23	24-23	24-23	24-22	23-22	23-20	21-19	20-21
1967	22-20	21-21	22-22	23-23	24-23	24-23	24-24	25-22	23-22	23-20	21-19	20-21
1968	21-20	21-20	21-21	22-22	23-23	24-22	23-23	24-22	23-21	22-20	21-19	20-20
1969	21-20	21-21	22-21	22-23	24-23	24-23	24-23	24-22	23-22	23-20	21-18	19-20

YEAR	ARIES MAR.-APR.	TAURUS APR.-MAY	GEMINI MAY-JUNE	CANCER JUNE-JULY	LEO JULY-AUG.	VIRGO AUG.-SEPT.	LIBRA SEPT.-OCT.	SCORPIO OCT.-NOV.	SAGITTARIUS NOV.-DEC.	CAPRICORN DEC.-JAN.	AQUARIUS JAN.-FEB.	PISCES FEB.-MAR.
1970	22-20	21-21	22-21	22-23	24-23	24-23	24-23	24-22	23-22	23-20	21-19	20-21
1971	22-20	21-21	22-22	23-23	24-23	24-23	24-24	25-22	23-22	23-20	21-19	20-21
1972	21-19	20-20	21-21	22-22	23-23	24-22	23-23	24-22	23-21	22-20	21-19	20-20
1973	21-20	21-21	22-21	22-22	23-23	24-23	24-23	24-22	23-22	23-20	21-18	19-20
1974	22-20	21-21	22-21	22-23	24-23	24-23	24-23	24-22	23-22	23-20	21-19	20-21
1975	22-20	21-21	22-22	23-23	24-23	24-23	24-24	25-22	23-22	23-20	21-19	20-21
1976	21-19	20-20	21-21	22-22	23-23	24-22	23-23	24-22	23-21	22-20	21-19	20-20
1977	21-20	21-21	22-21	22-22	23-23	24-23	24-23	24-22	23-21	22-20	21-18	19-20
1978	21-20	21-21	22-21	22-23	24-23	24-23	24-23	24-22	23-22	23-20	21-19	20-20
1979	22-20	21-21	22-21	22-23	24-23	24-23	24-24	25-22	23-22	23-20	21-19	20-21
1980	21-19	20-20	21-21	22-22	23-22	23-22	23-23	24-22	23-21	22-20	21-19	20-20
1981	21-20	21-21	22-21	22-22	23-23	24-23	24-23	24-22	23-21	22-20	21-18	19-20
1982	21-20	21-21	22-21	22-23	24-23	24-23	24-23	24-22	23-22	23-20	21-18	19-20
1983	22-20	21-21	22-21	22-23	24-23	24-23	24-23	24-22	23-22	23-20	21-19	20-21
1984	21-19	20-20	21-21	22-22	23-22	23-22	23-23	24-22	23-21	22-20	21-19	20-20
1985	21-20	21-21	22-21	22-22	23-23	24-23	24-23	24-22	23-21	22-20	21-18	19-20
1986	21-20	21-21	22-21	22-23	24-23	24-23	24-23	24-22	23-22	23-20	21-18	19-20
1987	22-20	21-21	22-21	22-23	24-23	24-23	24-23	24-22	23-22	23-20	21-19	20-21
1988	21-19	20-20	21-21	22-22	23-22	23-22	23-23	24-22	23-21	22-20	21-19	20-20
1989	21-20	21-21	22-21	22-22	23-23	24-23	24-23	24-22	23-21	22-20	21-18	19-20
1990	21-20	21-21	22-21	22-23	24-23	24-23	24-23	24-22	23-22	23-20	21-18	19-20

LEO'S CHARACTER

At your best, Leo, you are without doubt the most complete, balanced, commanding and unforgettable personality in the Zodiac. You are Leo the Lion, King of the Jungle, the symbol of royalty, regality and rulership. You were born under the patronage of the Sun itself, the undisputed center of the planetary forces and the source of all life. Like the Sun, you pour out your influence and beneficence without restraint. Unlike the Sun, you are human and your lack of restraint is often your undoing.

A lot of your trouble is that you're too well-meaning. You want everyone to share in what you feel you've got to give. The crunch comes when others resent being told by you what's good for them. They think you're being arrogant, presumptuous and downright interfering.

Still, you're probably one of the easiest people in the world to forgive—especially when you flash that wonderful, ingenuous smile of yours. It's pure sunshine, guaranteed to warm all but the bitterest heart. When a person who matters to you responds, whether it's to excuse your impulsive ways or out of sheer admiration, you're as happy as a lark. When such a person doesn't respond, you are disconsolate, discouraged, shattered.

But only for a brief time. Leo is a champagne Sign; it sparkles with an irrepressible faith in life. As a Leo person, you possess a strong self-sacrificing quality. Your life is virtually a search for a cause to devote your existence to. You have a sense of destiny. Somehow, you're convinced that the world needs you, that your life just won't be allowed to pass unnoticed.

You take command easily in any situation because you are a born leader. Power falls on your shoulders like a royal mantle. And you can be counted on to give a royal performance in any crisis you happen to be coping with. Your self-confidence is immeasurable. So is your self-awareness, or, as some might describe it, your self-centeredness. You seldom do anything without endeavoring to draw attention to yourself.

Have you ever watched a fellow Leo going about an important task? One that he or she is really on top of? Heard the sighing, heaving and snorting? It's all a part of that rather youthful desire to attract notice, in this case to show how hard Leo is working, how deserving he or she is of everyone's recognition and gratitude. An amusing thing to do to friend Leo is to offer to help. Help? Leo? Watch him parry the offer, pooh-pooh the task as a piece of cake *for him*—yet at the same time make a lot of huffing and puffing noises.

The simple fact is that you Leos are usually extraordinarily capable at your job. What you lack in expertise or knowledge you make up for in energy, determination and tenacity—not to mention organizational flair. You have an almost pathological fear of failing to live up to what is expected of you or what you have promised. You will toil day and night to deliver the goods. It is even possible for a Leo to work himself or herself to death, if identification with the task is strong enough.

What else would one expect from a noble and kingly type? Leo's so-called arrogance has deep and worthy origins. Like Caesar, he gets carried away sometimes with his own divinity.

Leo men and women very seldom ask for help. If they do, the request is usually framed in such a way that some sort of exchange is implied. Your unsubtle attempts at subtlety are a rich source of amusement to trained Lion watchers. (If you don't believe this, consult the guy or gal in the next room.)

Proud and self-sufficient Leo is not too convincing, either, when it comes to expressing gratitude. You can be enthusiastic, even fulsome, with your thanks; you can weep if the occasion warrants it. But the astute observer will see that you are merely going through the motions, that you *really* believe when someone does you a good turn, it is only what you deserved. You will repay a favor at the very first opportunity, perhaps in such an extravagant way that it's out of proportion to the original deed and more like a reward. It's the Leo way to be magnanimous, and to make large gestures at unexpected times. You like to receive out of homage, to bestow out of beneficence. You are like a monarch dispensing favors to worthy and devoted subjects.

No matter from which angle they are studied, there is something about Leonine individuals that makes them stand out in a crowd. They have presence, sometimes charisma. What they say or how they say it is usually arresting.

There are, of course, immature Leos whose only claim to recognition is their ability to make a great amount of noise in drawing attention to themselves. These types are boisterous, conceited, critical, boasting, snobbish, swaggering, domineering and—if they get the chance—tyrannical. But because of the Sun's sole rulership of this Sign, even the negative types have a noticeable urge over the years to improve themselves. The spiritual awareness of this Sign, through the Sun's influence, is very strong and in the more evolved types usually takes the form of an intense yearning for self-knowledge. In extreme cases, self-centered awareness can suddenly explode into a self-realization.

Leos generally move quickly and gracefully. They are among the doers of the world. Yet they are sometimes said to have a lazy or indolent streak. This criticism arises from the fact that they don't like wasting their time. They won't build a bridge where there's no river. They've got to be convinced that whatever they put their energies into is worthwhile. Some other Signs, such as Aries or Sagittarius, are so intent on participation and action that they'll go off half-cocked with impatience. Not Leo. What he starts, he finishes. He's inclined to take total responsibility. There'll only be one person to be thanked when the task is finished (the way he looks at it), and he can't afford any white elephants. So when others rush in fired by enthusiasm, Leo often sits back disinterested, languidly sunning himself (and noting every mistake that's being made). He'd love them to ask him to get them out of trouble. Then he'd spring into action. But otherwise—no deal.

Leo is a fixed Sign. This means you're set in your ideas. It doesn't mean you're rigid and inflexible. You will change your opinions. You won't cling to a notion just out of stubborn pride. You'll listen to reason. Perhaps you'll bristle and stamp a bit, but in the face of evidence, you'll concede. First, you may stride off and think about it, but you'll come around.) You are strongly impelled by the desire to be just even when it erodes your own position and standing. It is this quality that wins you the trust and respect of others.

You are acutely observant of all that is happening around you. You hear everything within earshot and are instantly aware of any changes. You have an almost sixth sense about where even the most unimportant objects have been left. Your ideas come mostly from your own experience. You don't rely very much on what others report; you have to find out for yourself. This is the clue to your rather fixed ways. You establish as you go along what works in practice and you remember it. Others are more imaginative, speculative and fanciful, prepared to assume things will be different next time. Not you. You stick to what you know until the facts prove otherwise. Meantime, you tend to disdain or reject the efforts of others. You think you know it all.

Your energy is fantastic. And by a curious quirk of nature, you often seem to be able to transmit it to others, both physically and mentally. Partners born under Pisces and Cancer are apt to draw emotional and vital strength from you. Others are simply inspired by your example or encouragement and go on to realize potentialities that may have lain dormant within them for years. You go out of your way to help others to make the most of their talents. In this regard, you are not the least bit selfish; you don't hold back information others would consider their "trade secrets." It is this helpful tutorial urge that makes you prominent in the teaching professions. Whatever occupation you follow, you will make a point of seeing that others, especially younger people, receive the benefit of your experience and knowledge.

You are very fond of fun and pleasure. All kinds of entertainment appeal to you. You love parties, first nights, all gala occasions where you can dress up and engage in your particular style of theatrics. But however much you clown about in public, you never lose sight of your essential dignity. And woe betide anyone who takes you for the fool you sometimes go to so much trouble to pretend you are. Your gamesmanship has one object only: to draw admiration and applause. You *know* you're the life of any party, but you feel compelled to demonstrate it to others every time. And you are a lot of fun. You've got a sunny, happy personality that inevitably breaks the ice of formality. Your vivacity and magnetism can't help but communicate itself. Quite often you are able to sing, dance or play a musical instrument. This, along with your innate talent for acting and showmanship, makes you a very popular party guest.

There are, of course, quiet Leos, controlled, dignified, very much together. But under that restrained, complaisant exterior beats a boyish or girlish heart waiting for the right circumstances or person to reveal itself. There's no true Leo on earth who won't let his or her hair down . . . sometime. And not one can hide the proud dignity or arrogant vanity that will flare if anyone dares to try to rule him or her.

Astrologically speaking, Leo is the Sign of pleasure and happiness secured through self-expression. So there's little wonder that you're such a natural at entertaining. As a host or hostess, you're fabulous. If you've got the money, you love to live in style. A life of luxury—but not without ambitious effort—is your idea of material paradise. Your home may well reflect your exotic tastes, which can tend toward ostentation if you're not careful. But everything in your home will work, including the color scheme, which is likely to have a strong bias toward gold, scarlet and yellow. You enjoy glamor and like to mix with famous, influential and wealthy people. You're quite prepared to cut down on vacations and other things to ensure that your home is everything that you want it to be.

Both the Leo man and woman are generally fashionable dressers. They're anything but inconspicuous in their choice of clothes, and yet the colors and styles they choose, which might seem outré on others, on them blend into pleasing harmony. The Leo male, unless he's influenced by one of the more subdued ladies of the Zodiac, is likely to be quite a dazzler. He'll splurge on the very latest styles and manage to combine startling reds and golds that no one else could get away with (or want to). Unusual accessories like hats, ties and jewelry give him the chance to express his fondness for sensational contrasts. Being a courtly type of peacock, he can wear frilly cuffs and ruffles without detracting from his vibrant masculinity. Mr. Leo, when he can afford it, loves velvet and rich colors. He's a vest man, more for elegant effect than sobriety. He relaxes at home in satin bathrobes and brocade smoking jackets. In snow country, he looks fantastic in a rugged sheepskin jacket or a sleek fur-collared topcoat—with jaunty fur hat to match, of course.

Ms. Leo is also an expensive dresser when she can afford it. She usually manages to look great in original styles and offbeat color schemes. There's elegance and distinction to her taste, though. As a rule, she loves expensive jewelry and adores furs. Everything about this girl's wardrobe has a touch of class. She'd rather go without than settle for cheap, poor-quality stuff. She spends a fair amount of time in front of the mirror making sure she looks attractive.

Leos are tremendously ambitious. You *have* to get to the top. Although you enjoy the rewards of power and success, it is the position that counts most—the being there. Whatever your scene or group, you have to be top dog, the undisputed focus point of all that is happening. Imperious at work (which is discussed in another chapter), you are just as autocratic where your home and family are concerned. You insist on things being done your way and get irascible when they're not. Your attitude is that if a thing was black yesterday, it's black now. You forget that although the color might not have changed, the people affected by it have. You don't make enough allowance for the preferences and moods of others, which generally waver more than your own. (We'll come to emotions, later.) You know where you are going and what you want. This is the strongest single factor behind the incredible Leo drive. But others don't have the same patient fixity; nor do they always see the necessity for or wisdom of it.

You usually get along well with your family, but not because you're easy to live with. Despite your bold and liberal ideas abroad, you frequently make an issue of trivial matters at home. You can be a Captain Bligh and psychologically keel-haul everyone for hours over an inconsequential point. Once your family has learned how to handle you (they've got to or it will be hell), your quite tractable and domesticated. As long as you feel the whole household revolves around your presence, all is well. Court must be constantly paid you, your efforts on behalf of everyone acknowledged and appreciated. This can become a bore to others—and even if you haven't woken up to it yet, all your loved ones know exactly how to calm you down, how much flattery and praise is required to get you to go along with their plans. It's certainly easier to indulge you than to fight you. You're an absolute terror when opposed. You'll hit the roof with a lightning flash of temper and round on the offending party with cutting acerbity.

Your indignation when you are doubted or disbelieved is monumental. What hurts is the implication that you could possibly hold fallacious opinions or beliefs. Of course, you know you're wrong at times; you are no fool. But a challenge of this kind always seems to catch you off guard, and you instinctively react to defend your infallibility. Fortunately, your anger is short-lived and you are often intelligent and fair enough to realize your own blindness or stupidity. On these occasions, you are apt to apologize and admit your error. This is the humility of the Lion, which because it is so surprising and apparently out of character frequently makes him or her an irresistible partner or buddy.

Sometimes you will take out your worldly frustrations on your family. If you don't build up some sort of empire through work, you may attempt to run your home like a feudal fiefdom, demanding your rights as head of the household while everybody waits on you.

But Leo can't endure an unhappy or discordant situation for long. It is your nature to bring differences and grievances out into the open where you can deal with them. For this reason, you find it difficult to sustain a grudge; you must either forget it or confront the other party and clear the air once and for all. The Lion will choose a fight to the death, any time, rather than have something hanging over his head. It's this attitude that often discourages antagonists and saves you a battle to begin with. But in a cat-and-mouse game, you, the mighty battler, are frequently at a loss.

You like to imagine that you're cunning when it suits you and that you can outsmart the schemers and intriguers of this world on their own ground. You don't stand a chance because you're an open book. All your wily stratagems are usually hopelessly naive. Leo is a noble character and basically uncomplicated. There is no room in your nature for ill-will, for petty squabbles and sinister conspiracies. Only your misplaced pride allows you to think you could outwit those who deal in deception and the double cross. Your duels are fought in the sun. You believe in giving an opponent an even chance. You're fussy about the weapons you use, too. You'd rather perish honorably than prevail dishonorably. Villains who skulk in the shadows taking potshots from behind or who poison with innuendo are out of your league. If a guy won't come out and fight, you'll tear the place down to get to him (perhaps Samson was a Leo).

You're not a very tactful person. You make some horrible gaffes, though never unconsciously; it's your style and you're very much aware of what you're doing. Like all the fire Signs, you're terribly wrapped up in yourself. You have very little time for the frailties of others or the minor subterfuges people use to hide their

uncertainties. You can be blunt to the point of insult. One wonders how you do it; you get away with murder. Sometimes you expose courtesy as a front for cant. You want the truth out. You mean well. But damnit, it does hurt.

It's a pity you're not so adamant in exposing your own hangups, or tolerant of others' criticism of you. Few can dish it out better than Leo, and none is more outraged when he or she is on the receiving end. Fortunately, others appear to sense the absence of malice in your statements. You never seem to see any reason for withholding a frank opinion, whether harsh or favorable. To be fair, though, you are just as likely to hand out an extravagant compliment to an archrival as you are to criticize him.

You have a great deal of heart. In fact, your emotions are both your strongest and your weakest point. You are acutely sympathetic and can't bear to see a person unjustly treated. You have immense respect for the dignity of man and the right of all to find their way (with a little help from you) to a fuller and richer existence. As competent as you are at describing abstractions, you're not sure what they mean; still, you are supremely confident that your advice and wisdom will move others in the right direction. When your compassion or sense of purpose is stirred, you throw yourself into the cause with courage and complete disregard for your own interests. You never give up. You keep pushing and pushing until there's no room left for anyone to maneuver, yourself or the opposition. It's then showdown time, black-and-white time, when you're either victorious or vanquished.

As far as Leo is concerned, the time for compromise is *after* the battle has been won. And remarkably, the loser often receives all or more than he would have had he been victorious. Leo in victory is the spirit of magnanimity. You will never humble a defeated enemy; you will respect a person's pride. The only thing that matters is to prove you were right. As has been said, the only battles you can be bothered waging are those you identify with your own unshakable principles. After victory, you show superb generosity of spirit and mind.

But what an easy person you are to mislead. You're one of the world's worst judges of character. Anyone who makes the effort to praise you can usually win you over. It takes only a few words of flattery to change your countenance and attitude. It doesn't matter what you're doing at the time—you beam. You have a habit of responding to the most outrageously phony compliments. It's not that you're fool enough to believe all of them, but you are unwise enough to feel there is no harm done in benignly excusing an attempt to humor you. After all, it is human nature to try to please the king, isn't it?

When your weakness for flattery is combined with your simple and laudable faith in human nature, there are all the ingredients for a first-class deception. Being a pretty simple and straightforward character yourself, you think others are the same. Perhaps you should read the other books in this series. Until you've learned the errors of Leo's prideful and conceited ways, you're likely to be an easy person for crooks and confidence men to deceive. You may also be a soft touch for the not-so-crook as well, as you've probably discovered by now.

Leo is the Sign of love, romantic love. It represents the passion of the fiery, masterful ideal lover. With this supremely powerful motive force behind you, there's no wonder your emotions are often your Achilles' heel. It seems that as strong, stalwart and steadfast as you are in just about every other department of your life, where love is concerned, you are incredibly vulnerable and quite frequently make an awful mess of things.

Love makes the Lion (both man and woman) throw caution to the wind; his usual discretion seems to desert him (or he it). He is impulsive, erratic, impelled hither and thither by every random wind that promises to head him in the vague direction of his or her beloved.

The Lion doesn't fall this hard every time. But when he or she does, there are no half-measures. In your more temperate romantic affairs, you are still compelled by irresistible ardor. But in the face of unrequited love, you are able to sadly switch your affections elsewhere—happily resuming the chase of another beloved.

Leo is not an easy Sign for women to be born under. The temptation to go wild is very, very great. Perhaps that's what is meant by women's liberation (this is obviously written by a man!). Seriously, though, there is no doubt about the radiant femininity of these Leo girls, their grace, beauty and dignity; no Sign is more female or just plain sexy. But the basic love drive is initiatory, thrusting; the impulses radical rather than conservative. The instinct is that of the huntress—who waits. The mature Leo woman develops a fine balance, giving her a remarkably attractive poise and reserve, despite her vivacious outgoing manner. Ms. Leo can resist any man, except *the* man, if he comes along. The Lioness enjoys her affairs, padding sleekly and untamed among her men. But when she goes overboard, like Mr. Leo, there's no predicting what her emotions will compel her to do.

It seems that both the Lion and the Lioness are fated to learn to control their emotions, eventually. Very few men or women born under this Sign escape at least one torrid love affair that ends disastrously. But Leo's recuperative powers are great. Once restraint in love is learned—and it may take several painful lessons—these people often go on to make happy and enduring marriages. The chances of this happening are discussed in more detail in the "Leo in Love" section.

Leo is also the Sign of children, as well as ideas, which are, of course, the offspring of the mind. Although not fruitful in itself, the Sign inspires productivity and creativity and encourages self-expression in others. Leo people don't possess the same passionate maternal love of children as Cancer-born individuals, for instance. They usually don't have large families. The Leo instinct, rather, is to prepare children—all children—through teaching to carry the flame of creative understanding to the next generation. So you see, Leo's tendency to preach and teach, as maddening as it is, is basically an altruistic urge.

Leo's love is not purely sexual. That's Scorpio's department. It's not discriminating mental love, which is the realm of Libra. Nor is it the love of Taurus, which is feminine, earthy, enveloping. Leo's love is a bit of each—the romantic, unrestrained and compelling starting point of it all.

Your ambitious nature frequently induces you to accept responsibilities beyond your capacity. Out of excessive generosity, you bind yourself to those you love. You're the type to attempt the impossible. Sometimes you go so far out on a limb that you leave yourself without any resources to fall back on. If you don't make it, you don't complain. Often, only your strength of mind and robust constitution get you through. Even so, you are always in danger of undermining your health through taking on too much.

You are fond of sports and the outdoor life. It is imperative that you release your energy in some creative way and not allow it to stagnate or be wasted in gossiping and accumulating useless information. You are more an intellectual being than a physical one, so unless there's a good proportion of creative thinking involved in your activities, you won't feel fulfilled. Your capacity for intense short bursts of concentration should help you to be successful as a professional sportsman or sportswoman.

Artistically, you possess great potential. Your intuition is a rich source of original ideas that can be applied to a wide range of pursuits and interests. Most Leos are naturally skilled at writing and speaking. If they can overcome the tendency to dramatize their statements, they can communicate quickly and expressively. Your love of the dramatic often induces people born under your Sign to join amateur acting groups or to try their hand at other types of entertaining. You have a deep appreciation of nature and a rather poetic turn of mind. Even if you don't write, you use apt, lyrical phrases to describe events. You are quite sentimental and are likely to keep mementos, especially love letters and photographs, long after the people concerned have disappeared from your life.

All typical Leos possess a hidden talent that is not always developed: they can perceive changes that are necessary for society, and sometimes individuals, long before they are generally evident. It is this talent that will cause you to work toward reform often without knowing why. You are frequently at the center or head of a movement. When in charge, you have a knack for distributing jobs to the right people; you can "feel" a person's potential achievements. Unfortunately, your emotional nature often distorts your prophetic gifts. You succeed most when working for others and along idealistic lines. A selfish life makes a Leo-born person shallow and discontented.

You are exceedingly loyal to your buddies and many of your friendships last a lifetime. Although popular, you don't have many really intimate associates. You prefer to keep a degree of aloofness in most relationships.

Probably the most remarkable characteristic of all true Leos is their optimism and almost mystical faith in life. A Leo wrote the following:

My friend Life is death and birth
My friend Life is the whole wide earth
My friend Life is sorrow and a tear
But my friend Life does not know fear.
All the people would drag me down
But not while my friend Life's around
My friend Life is change and pain
But that's all part of my friend's game.
Play the game and it can be fun
Fight to win and the fun's all done
My friend Life is an outstretched hand—
It's your friend, too, if you grab it Man.

LEO

IN LOVE

YOUR LEO MAN

You like him? Love him? What sort of guy is the Leo man?

He wants everything his woman has to give—and more. Sometimes it seems he wants her very soul. And what does he offer in return? The same—all of him. No half-measures are possible on either side.

He puts his woman so high up on a pedestal that sometimes she can't do anything but stand there and be worshipped by him. This can be a bit of a strain on the lady unless she's very, very much in love. In that case, she'll have every single thing her heart desires because Mr. Leo will lay it all at her feet. And while he loves her, she will be the only woman in his life. She will be unable to do any wrong (except one) in his eyes. He will adore her, serve her, idolize her, and with his urgent and passionate lovemaking, make her feel like a goddess.

But if you are disloyal to him, things will never be quite the same. He is big enough not to bear a grudge or want to get even, but his nature is such that he can't ever forgive a woman who destroys his dreams. Disillusionment has an emotional finality for him. If he decides to stay with you (he is feafully noble and proud), he'll continue to demonstrate his affection as though nothing had happened—but the fire will be gone. In these circumstances, unless the woman is able to prove to him that she truly loves him, he will gradually pine away and eat his heart out. A Leo man without love is a dying man.

Of course, in a less than absolute love affair, our Leonine friend won't hang around once a woman's betrayed him. For a time, he'll be dazed because his self-esteem is so towering he just can't believe a woman who said she loved him could possibly change her mind. He'll shake his mane and lick his wounds as he sadly saunters off into the jungle. But don't worry, he'll spot another she-mate shortly (or she him) and it will be the same thing all over again.

Not surprisingly, Mr. Leo is very often unlucky in love. It's one area in which he doesn't seem to have much discretion or judgment.

He's great fun and is usually to be found right in the center of a crowd, roaring about how well he can do something—and then probably doing it even if it kills him. The lengths this guy will go to prove he's the greatest are almost unbelievable. He lives for love and applause. He's a born showman and showoff. If there are any ladies around, he'll be playing up to every one of them, waiting to pounce on the one whose eyes show the greatest admiration and interest.

He's a masterly type who likes to *win* his women. If you fancy him, sit back and be lionized. If you want him to come on a little stronger, just a couple of compliments will do the trick. Even downright flattery is not lost on this guy. He's so sure that every girl he meets is knocked out by him that it never occurs to him to take praise, no matter how extravagant, with a grain of salt.

Despite his domineering and lordly way, he's a bit of a boy at heart, sometimes even naive where love is concerned. It's not difficult for a woman to mislead him. He's terribly trusting in a way, probably because of his simple faith in his own magnetism. There's no doubt he has a compelling presence, and he uses it to great effect in business, where he is generally a top executive or leader.

If you land this man, you may find him difficult to live with at times. He can be exacting and infuriatingly self-centered. He is always looking for approbation and appreciation from his mate and is absurdly wounded if they're not forthcoming. Tickle him under the chin with a little praise, and he'll bounce back to his happy, charming self. Neglect him, and he'll moon around the place as though he's carrying the weight of the world.

When it comes to parties and entertaining, he's a wow. He loves to flirt but will never neglect you. He'll also enjoy showing you off to his buddies. If a Leo male takes to you, it's a safe bet you're an attractive personality with some very special feminine qualities.

YOUR LEO WOMAN

You like her? Love her? What sort of woman is she?

She's a golden girl, a child of the Sun, a real dazzler. A Leo woman can take her place in any company and make her man feel ten feet tall. She's sexy and very attractive to men. You'll have to love her sincerely and give her all the adoring affection she craves to hold her.

Once this woman says she's yours, there'll be no doubt about her loyalty. She'll give you all her attention. She'll wear the type of clothes you admire most and do everything in her power to please you. If you've decided to save up to get married, she'll work just as hard as you and make sure most of her paycheck goes into the joint account. Once she commits herself to a course of action, she seldom swerves.

So what are the disadvantages? Well, you've got to win her first. And with all the competition, that's not going to be easy. Even when you're sure she's yours, your heart will sink with doubts whenever guys crowd around her (which is often). She's terribly confident and sometimes says the most outrageous things that everyone else but you (biting your nails near the door) will think is hilarious. Her quick-thinking mind is a match for just about any male's repartee, and her open sense of humor is infectiously winning.

When you show her off to your buddies, they'll probably all fancy her, much to your chagrin. She's got physical magnetism, charisma, this girl, so she's going to make you jealous even when she's not trying.

She's also likely to infuriate you at times with her bossy manner. Oh sure, she can be one of the most pleasing and agreeable types you've ever met, but when you tread on her ego, or even give it an accidental nudge, watch out! She can turn arrogant and overbearing in a second. Her temper will flare in a thunderous roar of indignation—but as fast as it came, it will be gone, and your Leo girl will be genuinely smiling like the Sun coming out from behind a cloud. She doesn't cherish ill-will. There's no malice in her.

She loves to dress up in the latest fashions and go to parties. She's great at making an impression. Whereas others may be embarrassed at being made a cynosure, she laps up every minute of it. A Leo woman just can't get too much atten-

tion. Perhaps because Leo is a royal Sign, the symbol of kings and queens, she loves to hold court. And as the "royal consort," you'll be pretty important to her. She usually makes a point of only getting involved with men she'll be proud to have by her side.

As a lover, she's fiery and passionate and aggressive in the bedroom. She'll be prepared to leave the lovemaking initiative to you provided you're able to keep her charmed and interested. She doesn't want any caveman haste, though. She wants a *lover* in every sense of the word. Only real men need apply.

Your Leo girl will shower you with presents. She wants to show you in every way she can that she is yours. She is extremely romantic and your flowers, perfume and chocolates will delight her. No one will dare say a detracting word about you in the presence of this proud and dynamic woman. Once she regards you as her man, everything about you will be as dear to her as if it were her own.

Unfortunately, unless her husband is a virile and fairly dominant type of person, this woman will gradually take him over. She won't want to, but her powerful personality and natural talent for making decisions and taking responsibility will make her preeminence almost inevitable.

Always remember that underneath is a kind-hearted, generous and intelligent female. With a strong and masculine husband who loves her, this lady will be content to be his queen and they should live a good and happy life together.

LEO WOMAN—ARIES MAN

He's a feet-first kind of guy. When he falls in love, it's impossible for him to hide his emotions. His passion will overwhelm you. You'll be able to read him like a book, and what you read could put him on your list of bestsellers. He's the sort of man who will fit your ideal pretty well.

He's positive, hard-working and fairly straight in his relationships with the fairer sex. It is not necessarily true that in marriage one person has to lead—doubters will point out that Aries and Leo are born rulers and the fight for power would make this union a nonstarter. This, of course, is rubbish. If two people are in love, a liaison in which all decisions are reached by mutual agreement is the perfect one.

You do both have a very special talent for ruling and it will be in finding out which partner takes the lead and when that will keep your affair alive.

It would be wise to have a fairly long courtship with the Ram. In, the beginning, his passion could sweep you off your feet and make you feel you've met your true love. Do get to know him a little better. He's more fickle than you are and it's not easy for him to settle down to a one-to-one relationship. Certainly, he's the most passionate of all the Signs. His lusty sexual appetite is virtually insatiable.

You may think when you first meet him that because he's so quite, he'll be afraid to make romantic overtures. Don't be fooled. He is ruled by Mars, and you'll find that for him, actions speak louder than words.

There are so many nice things you'll enjoy sharing together. Like you, he will have a fairly acute interest in what's going on in the outside world. You may not have exactly the same attitude to how society's current crop of problems should be solved, but you'll enjoy discussing different approaches.

You are both quite artistic. He will enjoy going to the theater with you and to music concerts as well; one of the special things you have in common is a love of music.

Mr. Aries likes a feminine woman, but he will also admire your guts—your ability to make important decisions and to stand on your own two feet when the going gets rough. He won't mind your having your own career after marriage so long as it doesn't interfere with the smooth running of domestic life. Knowing you, you will be able to cope easily with both.

He is prone to sudden plunges into a new hobby or career, and you'll have to be ready for this. His enthusiasms are boundless but short-lived. He could be absolutely crazy about a pastime for a couple of weeks and then suddenly forget all about it.

Of course, you'll have your arguments, but then, what couple doesn't? You must be sure never to dent his ego. Mr. Aries can't stand being nagged or criticized too harshly. He's really a bit of an overgrown boy in many ways and will need to be constantly reassured of your love.

Don't do too much flirting with other guys when your Aries man's around. He won't be able to take it, even though you think of it as merely harmless fun.

If after you settle down together you have an affair, with another man, it's extremely unlikely that your partnership will ever be the same again. If you love him, your marriage will be far too important to you to play with fire.

You will be a tower of strength to your Aries mate. You are the sort of woman who is clever at

bringing out the very best qualities in this man.

LEO WOMAN—TAURUS MAN

Let's hope you're the sort of woman who likes to take her time over courtship because Mr. Taurus refuses to be rushed into any kind of permanent relationship. He's difficult to pin down because he has a fear of being trapped. He doesn't usually fall for a woman who does the chasing. Where romance is concerned, he likes to feel he's got the initiative. It may take him quite a while to finally decide that you are the woman for him.

It is true that people born under this Sign never reach a decision quickly. Usually they are pretty shrewd businessmen; it is rare for anyone to get away with a sharp practice when dealing with the Bull.

He's a home-loving creature. He likes his comforts and is not too keen on change. He's very true to his friends. If he believes in someone, he'll stick by that person through thick and thin. You may get somewhat bored with his desire to spend so many evenings at home. You're an active kind of person so it will be up to you to put a firecracker under his rocking chair from time to time.

He's very bright and can talk pretty well on any subject. You are both good conversationalists so it's unlikely you'll get bored in each other's company. You could have some fearsome disagreements—but that's another matter.

He has quite a roving eye. You may be surprised to discover how many girls he has lured to the bedroom. It's unlikely, though, that he's found real love with any of them. If he does fall in love with you, his promiscuous ways will soon become a thing of the past.

You both have a penchant for beautiful things and you'll be happy to discover you've met a person who is also a great lover of art. Possessions are important to him. He will want to furnish his home carefully and won't worry how much he spends on decorations and comforts so long as they please him. He's quite handy, too. He can do repair jobs around the house. If you leave him to visit your folks, you'll find he's quite capable of keeping your love nest tidy and of looking after himself.

He's also adept in the kitchen. If you continue your career after marriage—and it's quite likely you'll want to—he will be able to prepare a tasty dinner for you both if he gets home from work before you.

He's a hard worker and will appreciate the drive that keeps you going. You both have inquiring minds and would make a pretty interesting business partnership if you decide to work.

He's a lot of laughs. You'll like his rather aggressive attitude to life. He's a bit of a storyteller. Because he has a vivid imagination, he can't help making out that he's really tougher and shrewder than he is. You will be good for him because you'll help him face up to himself and his failings without being unnecessarily cruel.

This man will be able to offer you security. He's very skillful at looking after the shekels so life will be okay with him from the material point of view. He likes to keep on the right side of the law and will do all he can to stay out of debt.

You will have to be his friend as well as his lover because it's important to him to have a good relationship with his lover outside of bed. He goes in for crazy gadgets and always likes to have the latest in anything.

If you both agree about what you want out of life, there is no reason why you should not be very happy together.

LEO WOMAN—GEMINI MAN

You've heard about the little boy who never grew up? Peter something? Well, it's a dollar to a cent he was a Gemini. A man born under the Sign of the Twins usually maintains his youthfulness throughout his life. What appeals to women most about this character is his naughty schoolboy quality.

The question is, how strong is your maternal instinct? It is extremely unlikely that Mr. Gemini is going to turn out to be the hero type who sweeps you off your feet.

He's very cuddlesome and lovable and you'll always find his company stimulating and entertaining. He has a sharp mind and is quite intuitive about people and situations. His sense of humor will appeal to you, although you may find it a little sick at times because he doesn't know when to stop—which is one of his major problems in life. If he has a drink, he usually has to finish the whole bottle. He finds it almost impossible to cry, "Enough!"

He will admire many of your fine qualities. In fact, you could be the woman of his dreams. He likes a woman with a strong personality. Although he adores freedom and can't beat being dominated, it's important to him to have someone by his side who can pull him up from time to time. But—it's sad to say—that if a woman allows him to, he will trample all over her after a while.

You will certainly have to drive him on at times. He needs plenty of incentive and can easily become bored if he feels tied to his job. He likes change and has the idea that the grass is greener on the other side of the fence. He won't mind your having outside interests so long as they don't interfere with your life together. In fact, he'll encourage you to continue working after marriage because he doesn't want to feel that his partner is going to be a millstone around his neck. He will not expect you to do all the domestic drudgery, either, because he's quite fair and won't demand sacrifices he's not prepared to make himself.

Mr. Gemini loves to move around. Travel excites him. He rates friendship very high and is likely to have numerous close buddies. Let's hope you get on well with them; he'll want to bring them home quite often.

Although he likes a strong lady love, don't ever try to boss him or tell him what to do. He'll run a mile if he feels he's being ordered around. The way to get through to him is by discussion and suggestion.

When it comes to kids, he's great at buying toys and handing out sweets, but not so good at disciplining them. It looks as if that will have to be your department.

He can't help flirting, but then, neither can you. He's not the jealous type unless you go out of your way to tease him.

If you are really hung up on this man, you should be able to cope with him. Remember though, he's not the kind of fellow you should try to change. Don't go into marriage with the idea that he will alter his ways and settle down. He never will.

So long as you can keep up with the all-action life he likes to lead, all will be well. As far as entertaining goes, you'll have a lot in common. When you get into one of your flamboyant moods at a party, he'll sit there genuinely amused. He's quite prepared to let you make a fool of yourself; that's his idea of freedom.

When the children do come along, you must be sure you don't divert your love from him to them. If he feels left out in the cold, it won't be very long before he goes elsewhere in search of love.

LEO WOMAN—CANCER MAN

You'll find it difficult to understand a man born under the Sign of the Crab. When you're first introduced, you'll think he's an easygoing, fun-loving sort of guy without a care in the world. As you get to know him better, you're likely to discover you have gotten involved with a rather complex character. He'll storm into a roomful of strangers and fairly take over. You'll feel you've never come across a man with more confidence. But underneath this bravado, he's basically insecure and is only putting on a big front to cover up his self-doubt.

It may take a long time to discover what he's all about. He won't expose his true feelings until he's sure he can trust you because he is terrified of getting hurt. He will hold out for an inordinate time before he says those three little words.

You'll probably feel that in Mr. Cancer you've met a man who knows exactly what he wants and where he is going. As it turns out, he is very easy to influence and capable of amazingly abrupt changes of mind.

He is quite interested in power and wealth and is usually careful with money.

If you really fall for him, you will have to help him find himself. His tough outer shell hides an exceedingly lovable and gentle soul. Don't think he's a weak man; he's not. He is quite capable of looking after himself and will want to protect you as well.

Both of you will have to be ready to give up rather a lot if you're thinking in terms of marriage. Neither of you really likes to be advised or told what to do. He may talk intimately about his problems to you, but when you give your opinion, he's quite likely to go out and do the reverse. For a straightforward person like you, this can be terribly frustrating.

If he does pop the question, it means he intends to stick by you. Marriage is not something anyone born under the Sign of Cancer enters into lightly. He usually makes a faithful husband. He will want to make your union just what the good book says it should be—for keeps.

He's not mean with money but he can't stand the thought of insecurity. He will make sure you never go without, although he's not one to indulge extravagant tastes. You should not have a problem in this area because you're pretty capable at living within a reasonable budget.

Occasionally, you will have to be his psychiatrist. He needs to talk out his hangups. He knows this will not solve anything, but he can't keep emotions bottled up in an intimate relationship—a thing he feels he has to attempt when dealing with comparative strangers.

You will have to be quite hard on him at times to get him to make the most of his talents. The best way of doing this is to constantly remind him of what he is capable of achieving. Although he's not lazy, this guy's not exactly a self-starter, except when clinching a business deal.

Mr. Cancer will love the way you run the home. He delights in efficiency. His domestic life is very important to him. He likes to know he has a secure refuge to retreat to when outside pressures build up.

In your lovemaking together, there are not likely to be any major problems. He's intuitive about sex and will know what to do to bring you satisfaction.

His family is immensely important to him. His mother will probably be a frequent visitor. You'll just have to make it clear from the start that you rule the roost, not her.

LEO WOMAN—LEO MAN

This might seem an ideal team on the surface: the King and Queen of the Jungle brought together in a right royal linkup. Don't fool yourself—there could be quite a few problems to contend with here.

This is the union of two active and proud personalities. It might be too explosive to be contained under one roof.

You are generous and loyal, and will have to make the most of these qualities if the marriage is to succeed. You both like to lead and this could be a major stumbling block.

You and Mr. Leo will find it easy to become friends because you have a great deal in common. It is essential that you don't mistake friendship for love. Your way of making a marriage partner happy is not likely to be this guy's idea of how his woman should behave.

On first sight, you may feel he matches up to the man of your teenage dreams—strong, courageous, bold and capable of making difficult decisions. Well, he does possess all these qualities, but when your youthful fantasy is offered in the flesh, you may well find out you don't really want what you thought you did. You will find he insists on making certain big decisions on his own, which will not please you because you like to have a say in anything affecting your future well-being and security.

Mr. Leo also craves a great deal of attention. Sometimes you won't be in the mood when he wants petting. Every time he comes into the house, he'll expect you to drop whatever you're doing and give him priority. He can't stand other people finding fault with him, either. You are the sort of woman who says exactly what is on her mind, and this may be a bit too much for him to swallow at times.

He won't be prepared to make many concessions. Once he's laid down the law, he will expect his decisions to be carried out. This all-or-nothing attitude is difficult to live with, especially for a woman as proud as you.

Both of you are capable of extreme jealousy

and possessiveness; this is another area where the relationship could founder. Though both of you like to flirt, neither of you can stand flirtatiousness in your lover. But it's not all bad news. It is possible that you could work out your problems, and this process of accommodation could be rather exciting in itself. In bed, you are both rather aggressive types and neither of you is prepared to play a totally passive role when making love.

He will expect a great deal from you in many other ways—as a housewife and hostess to his business associates, for instance. This could be quite a challenge.

You will need to be many things rolled into one. Sometimes he will treat you like his teenage daughter—yes, he does incline to paternalism—and will like to feel he's looking after you and protecting you from the dangers of the outside world. So long as you can live up to his demands, there will be no problem.

You're the kind of woman who tries very hard to make a go of marriage. You're independent, but you're always on the lookout for Mr. Right should he come along. Like Mr. Leo, you've got fairly high standards, befitting one of the royal Sign. If you can surmount all the difficulties together (which largely means facing up to them to begin with), this could just turn out to be a happy and fruitful union.

LEO WOMAN—VIRGO MAN

Mr. Virgo is too good to be true for a realistic woman like you. He could be just too much of a fussbudget. He's certainly finicky and particular.

Everything has to be spotless, especially his home. You are no slouch when it comes to housework, but there are things you rate as more important in life. He'll notice immediately if the rug hasn't been vacuumed when he comes home from work. He won't overtly criticize you; his method is to get the vacuum cleaner out and go to work himself. He can't help being this way.

He's quite a cool character when it comes to dealing with the fairer sex. His approach is subtle. Though sex is often on his mind, he can do without it for a surprisingly long time.

All this is not to say that your Virgo man does not have a great deal to offer. He does. If you decide to change your name to his, you couldn't ask for a more devoted or loyal husband. He will put you on a pedestal and try to give you everything your heart desires.

The real point is, can you accept someone who is this straightforward and down to earth? He's a man of habit. When his favorite TV program is on, it will be very hard to get him to go out, no matter how exciting the invitation. He's a thinking man who is ruled by logic. If something can't be worked out systematically, he will have little time for it.

If you're going to make a success of life together, it's important that you share many mutual interests. When dating him, note just how much you have in common. It is awfully important to him that his woman have the same taste in music and art and the same opinions on politics and religion. He won't mind converting you, but what a bore that could be if you're already pretty sure of what you enjoy.

You are both fond of going abroad for vacations, and this penchant for travel is one thing you're likely to share together—once Mr. Virgo gets a taste of it, that is.

You could be the right woman to make old stay-at-home Virgo change his ways. You have many qualities he admires, and you'll be able to give him that extra push he so often needs. Although extremely talented, he does not tend to knock himself out getting to the top.

Try to induce him to take more of an interest in sports. Virgo men can often go to seed earlier than they should because they hate physical exercise. You will have to shake him out of his complacency.

He will also have quite a lot to teach and show you. He's pretty sharp about money. He's also exceedingly adept at summing up the strengths and weaknesses of people he meets. He has a computer memory and usually knows a surprising amount about a lot of topics.

You've probably heard wicked rumors that Mr. Virgo is frigid when it comes to lovemaking. He's not. He just has to be turned on, which is the sort of challenge a girl like you might enjoy. You're not forward, but with the right guy, you're not averse to making the overtures. Being a Leo woman, you could find it quite exciting to see what you could do. You'll be able to show him that sex is something to be enjoyed. He sometimes does have a bit of a problem expressing his true feelings.

Mr. Virgo will take his time about proposing. He will want to be really sure before he decides you're the woman for him.

This man usually wants only one or two kids, which will probably suit you. But you can be sure he'll make a fine father.

LEO WOMAN—LIBRA MAN

Your relationship should look pretty good right from the word go. You will admire his mind and speed of thought. The only trouble is the foundations of this affair may not go deep enough to make a permanent liaison possible.

He's super to be with, a charming and amusing companion. He'll know the best places to go and you will soon realize what a compassionate and caring man he is. He feels very deeply for other people and will go out of his way to avoid hurting or upsetting another human being.

Where you may come unstuck is when it comes to setting up home together. There are likely to be a lot of basic differences in your attitude to life and how it should be lived. You look for some sort of consistency and permanence in a man. Mr. Libra will be something of a puzzle to you. In romance, he blows hot and cold. It is extremely difficult for him to settle down with one woman. It isn't that he's madly promiscuous but rather that he's in love with love. He is a great romantic.

Never put pressure on him because he can't stand feeling he has to live by a rule book. Don't tell him dinner will be on the table at a certain hour every night. He's not a person of habit. You will have to be prepared to go along with his moods and lightning changes of mind.

He doesn't like violent confrontations—in fact, he will do everything in his power to avoid them. He doesn't understand why people can't settle their disputes through discussion. He is a real gentleman. He knows how to pay a compliment and will mean what he says. It will not escape his notice when you are wearing a new outfit or have changed your perfume. He's also very tactful; he won't pass comment on matters that aren't his concern.

You, on the other hand, speak your mind. You prefer to bring differences out into the open than to keep your feelings bottled up inside you.

In your courtship with a Libra man, you may wonder if he is really serious in his intentions. He doesn't like to commit himself in a hurry. Like all air Signs, he is terrified of being trapped.

You will enjoy listening to him talk on the subjects in which he specializes. Libra people are often very good teachers because they are capable of making the most dreary and trivial matter sound interesting.

He will love taking you out and showing you the things that really interest him. Art in some form usually strongly appeals to this man. He should be able to open up new worlds for you.

He can be rather cynical at times, and this could get you down. He can also be very tough. If someone tries to double-cross him, he can be absolutely ruthless. Once his mind is made up on a certain course of action, he's very difficult to budge.

Mr. Libra is a survivor because he is able to take the rough with the smooth. He is a good provider, though amassing great wealth and numerous personal possessions is unlikely to appeal to him.

He enjoys traveling. He usually ends up in the sort of job that gives him plenty of scope for being inventive.

Home is important to this man, though he does tend to think of it as a place to recuperate and restore his lost energy. He has lots of acquaintances, but only one or two close friends. He's very tolerant of other people and will always try to see their point of view.

He's a kind father and finds it very difficult to exert discipline with children.

LEO WOMAN—SCORPIO MAN

Oh lady, you'll wonder what you've discovered the first time you get involved with a Scorpio man. He's very passionate and you will have to summon all your strength to keep up with him.

There's no way you can dominate this guy. There isn't a woman going that can lay down the law to him. He likes his women to be feminine and cuddly.

When you have a disagreement, it's unlikely that either of you will be prepared to give ground. If you want a marriage partner who is going to keep you constantly on your toes, then don't look further. You will bring out the man in him and he'll make you realize what being a woman is all about.

When it comes to lovemaking, you should have a ball together. He's lusty and has an insatiable appetite.

You may not hit it off so well when you first meet. This is the kind of union that develops with time. But you won't be able to ignore him when he walks into the room because there's something magnetic about this man.

Mr. Scorpio is not the most romantic man in the world. To him, actions speak louder than words. He won't be standing under your bedroom window trying to woo you with a guitar; he'll be doing his darndest to climb up the ivy and get through the lace curtains. Being a passionate woman, it's unlikely you'll be able to reject his advances for very long.

You will have to curb your flirtatious ways if you do move in with Mr. Scorpio. Of all the Signs, he's the most jealous and possessive. Woe betide you if you're caught having a secret liaison. And woe betide the guy you're caught with. Scorpio's quite capable of resorting to physical violence if aroused.

He probably won't share your tastes in music or art. He likes fairly straightforward reading and theater.

He will regard the house as your domain. He is one of those old-fashioned types who thinks a woman's place is in the home. He will expect your main interest in life to be looking after him. He'll enjoy an odd night out with the boys, and won't mind your having an evening out with your girlfriends, so long as his supper is left ready for him. He can be a bit of a brute. But you may be one of those Leo girls who can take his rough treatment.

This guy is an exceptionally hard worker and, as a rule, pretty astute with money. He is careful about how he invests his cash and his methods are fairly conservative. He will do his best to make sure you have everything you want, but he will frown on unnecessary extravagance. He'll try to get to the top in his career and you'll be very good for him in this respect.

He's not a great night bird. He likes to unwind and relax after a day at the office.

Your Scorpio man keeps his home life and his work in strictly separate compartments. When work is over for the day and he's settled down in his favorite chair, he won't wish to get too involved in discussions with business associates who happen to drop in. If he's got any shop talk to get done—or to listen in on—he prefers to dispose of it over a drink on the way home.

You must try to do what you can to avoid serious confrontations. You are a bright enough girl to know when to draw the line with this man. He needs to be loved and wanted. However, he can be a bit of a loner at times. He requires solitude when he's got problems to work out.

He's extremely fond of children. He will want to rear them in what he considers to be the correct way.

LEO WOMAN—SAGITTARIUS MAN

The Sagittarius man, whose symbol, you'll recall, is a centaur with a bow and arrow, certainly shoots to kill where romance is concerned. Known simply as the Archer, he is often shown galloping along and still trying to speed his effect on the world ahead of his physical presence by means of a well-aimed arrow.

Although he was known to ancient astrologers as the Sign of wisdom and the seeker after truth, we must be a little more critical. His so-called love of adventure is no more than adolescent irresponsibility.

He is a difficult man to trap. He is a bit wary about accepting routine life. You could say he is marriage-shy. He's the kind of guy girls like to have a wild fling with. He's good fun and makes a great companion and escort at parties. You won't forget time spent in his company.

He would not enjoy being trapped in a nine-to-five job. Give him the chance to break through new frontiers, even if it means taking great risks, and he'll jump at the opportunity. He loves the dangerous and unusual and is willing to take a gamble.

He is not exactly what he appears to be on the surface, though. There are hidden depths here. He is basically a sensitive and gentle person. He will always go out of his way to make shy people feel relaxed and at home. Underneath all that bravado and shouting is a man who suffers from an inferiority complex. He has to put on an act for his own sake as much as for the world around him.

He is a faithful person in marriage. Surprisingly enough, there is a strong religious streak in this man. He will take his vows very seriously.

Miss Leo and Mr. Sagittarius should hit it off quite well. You can be a bit wild at times, and you do like a man who speaks his mind and has a touch of the swashbuckler. You are both fire Signs, remember, and you'll discover that you share a great many opinions and beliefs.

You are both fairly sporting types. You could find he is the ideal partner for you at any competitive pastime.

He's something of a Romany, so you might think it's impossible for him to settle down. As a matter of fact, Mr. Sagittarius can quickly adapt to the home life once he has found what he's searching for. He will still like his night out with the boys—some nights he won't be in till the milkman is arriving—but don't get suspicious because it's more than likely that he's been up all night playing poker with his buddies.

This man is generous with money. In fact, he can be rather extravagant. He will spoil you with beautiful clothes and presents. Probably you should have some say in the handling of finances as he doesn't give much thought to tomorrow.

Mr. Sagittarius thinks of money as something to have a good time with. You'll have to remind him from time to time that there are rent bills and income tax payments to be met, and that if you ignore them, landlords and tax agents will get very, very uptight!

He's not the greatest with kids. Oh, he loves them all right, and he's good at telling bedtime stories, but he's not thrilled about changing a diaper or drumming responsibility into a rebellious teenager who got that way from observing his zany example over the years.

Still, if you can accept an occasional screaming match, you could both live happily ever after.

LEO WOMAN—CAPRICORN MAN

He may be shy, but don't be fooled because basically he's as tough as they come. He builds his defenses high around him, so it's not easy to get to know Mr. Capricorn.

He wants a lot of attention and loves to be the center of interest. He may appear self-sufficient but he decidedly is not. Underneath he is an incurable romantic. His trouble is he has great difficulty transforming his dreams into reality. He is a terribly disciplined person and a great conformer. You like helping people and all you expect as a reward is a word of thanks. The trouble with Capricorn is that he finds it very hard to admit he needs help.

If you want to get through to him, you'll have to work your way into his life in exceedingly subtle ways, and subtlety isn't your strongest point.

His humor is of the tongue-in-cheek variety. He can be a bit of a gossip and occasionally he lives his life through other people.

Capricorns like to pretend—especially to themselves—that they can live without compliments, but in fact, they absolutely thrive on them. Just try saying something really nice to a man born under the last earth Sign and watch his face light up.

You adore the good life, he's a bit frugal. He can't bear to waste money. He will travel second class on a train and stand all the way even if he can afford to go luxury.

One wonders if he offers enough to keep you contented for a lifetime. He's not a great mixer, and is likely to have only a handful of close friends. He doesn't feel comfortable at large gatherings. He has a private world that is difficult to break into. It would certainly be easier for you to make him happy than vice versa. The problem is to do this, you would probably have to give up many of your outside interests.

Perhaps the best chance of a successful liaison is with a Capricorn who has weathered the problems of his youth. By the time he hits his late thirties, he's likely to be a far better adjusted person.

If is very difficult to get him enthused about matters outside his sphere of interest. He will find it hard to become involved in something just because it's important to you.

He's unlikely to stray because it's against his nature to have secret love affairs. Of course, you will have to contend with his family. If you marry this man, you'll be taking on another mom and dad and a host of uncles and aunts into the bargain. Be sure you get on well with your mother-in-law because he's likely to have an extremely close relationship with her.

In bed, he'll try to take you by storm. It will be up to you to teach him better and show that you like the slow and gentle approach in lovemaking.

You will have to look after him when he's ill. He likes mollycoddling. He will often retire to his bed at the first sign of a cough or cold.

You'd better give him the idea right from the start that you expect your life with him to have plenty of passion. If not, your relationship will soon develop into something that's mainly platonic with thrill-night coming around every other Saturday.

He will love showing you off to his friends. He will be very proud of the capable way you run the home. He'll always adore you. To him, you'll never look a day older than the day you got married.

LEO WOMAN—AQUARIUS MAN

Mr. Aquarius has certainly struck it rich if he can get hitched to a woman like you. You are exactly the sort of person to bring out the very best in him. This man has many fine qualities; unfortunately, they seldom see the light of day. He needs a woman who can recognize his great potential and coax it out of him.

You will discover he's quite a thinker. If he falls madly in love with you, he will go to the ends of the earth to win you. He's extremely forceful when communicating his own ideas. Don't forget, his is the Sign of friendship, social life, hopes and fears; Aquarius is also known as the house of brotherhood. You will have to bring him down to earth a little bit. If you can stop him from thinking so abstractly all the time, you'll make a more lovable human being of him.

He has many varied interests and it will be better for both of you if you share a few of them. He's very enthusiastic and addicted to causes. Being inquisitive, you'll want to discover what makes him tick. It will be terribly important to him that you care.

The domestic chores will be left to you because he won't even know whether the house is tidy or not. He is out to change the *world* and make it a better place to live in, not the house. What is frustrating to Mr. Aquarius is that he's so often ahead of his time. The innovations he is trying to bring about now could well be generally accepted in fifty years. The Age of Aquarius (we hope) is going to bring us peace and brotherly love—something very dear to this man's heart.

So, how will you fare as a twosome? Well, he doesn't function on quite the same level as you do sexually. With him, love starts in the mind, and from that, all else follows. It is not easy for an Aquarius man to give himself on a casual basis.

He won't share your respect for tradition. As far as he's concerned, the world is in the state it is today because we have hung onto the ways of our ancestors.

Family is important to you; not so with this man. Of course, he loves his parents and his brothers and sisters, but what he believes in usually comes first.

At times you may feel he has lost interest in you completely. This is unlikely to be the case. He just gets so preoccupied with a cause that he becomes vague about everything else.

He will realize what a strong person you are and will expect you to be able to fend for yourself when he's not there.

He's unlikely to be jealous, and this could have its drawbacks. In sheer desperation, you could turn to another man just to see if he cares enough to come and get you back. Unfortunately, you won't get the reaction you hoped for, for he is likely to be philosophical about such matters.

You'll never know what time he's going to arrive home or whom he'll be bringing with him. Often as not, you'll come down in the morning to find some stranger sleeping on your couch; the poor guy probably didn't have anywhere else to go for the night.

Mr. Aquarius is quite likely to change jobs a number of times during the course of his life. Routine doesn't appeal to the Water Bearer.

Don't get too pessimistic, though, because in many ways you will hit it off together. You will learn a lot from each other. Your differences could unite you, if you resist the Leo urge to try to prove you're in the right all the time.

You should be able to show him that what is felt between a man and a woman is just as important as putting the world to rights.

LEO WOMAN—PISCES MAN

Well, one thing is for sure—your life together will be full of surprises. Fortunately, most of them will be pleasant.

When you first meet this man, you may think he's far too dreamy ever to be able to get anything together. True, he is a bit of a dreamer, and he does tend to wander around with his head in the clouds, but when it comes to action, watch him move. He's an expert at clinching business deals in record time. He's also capable of working in sudden spurts that leave even his close friends and family gasping.

Don't forget what his symbol is—two little Fishes swimming in opposite directions. He is a living contradiction. He can be everything you want—and, at times, everything you could well live without. He will keep you guessing.

He is not a weak man but he finds it hard to work up the energy for a project unless he can see a point to it. Work for the sake of work never appeals to him.

Mr. Pisces can be extremely naive. He will take people on face value. When you first go out with him, he'll think you must be the most even-tempered and placid girl he has ever come across. (This is an impression you often give to people.) He'll be very surprised when he finds after a few dates that you're pretty near running the whole damn show.

Let's be honest about Mr. Pisces. If he hasn't got the ball rolling by the time he's 30, he's unlikely to go terribly far in his career. If you don't mind that, all will be well. Being a Leo, though, you'll probably have ambitions for your man.

He can be a loner. This type of man has been known to live without other people for a lifetime. He doesn't hanker after riches or power. Give him enough to fill his belly and a jug of wine and he'll be quite content. If you've got a lot of money, okay. But you must face up to the fact that life with Mr. Pisces is not going to be plain sailing.

That's one Fish. Now, let's have a look at the other Fish, the go-getter. He is a real catch for any girl. His mind will amaze you. He will combine the qualities of many other Signs: the speed of thought of Gemini, the strength of Taurus, the leadership qualities of Leo. He has a live-and-let-live attitude toward life. He won't judge another human by his religion or the color of his skin.

He will do his level best to get on with your family, even if he disagrees with them on many subjects.

Mr. Pisces is not exactly a secretive person but he does believe in letting others know only what is good for them. He may occasionally conceal the truth from you because he doesn't want to hurt your feelings. He's a good talker and is usually capable of holding his own on most subjects. He appreciates a comfortable and settled home life.

He loves company as a rule but the time will come when he wants to be alone with you. You will have many a happy evening together snuggled up in front of the fire. He might take the phone off the hook to make sure you're not disturbed.

If you want to get your own way with him, appeal to his imagination and his feelings. If you try to lay down the law, he will balk.

He's great fun with kids, more like a big brother than a father figure.

LEO MAN—ARIES WOMAN

You'll find her very sexy and a real charmer. She's as bright as a button and her wit is razor sharp. She may be a little too forceful for a man like you, who prefers his relationships with women to be masculine-feminine in the old-fashioned way, because Miss Aries likes to dominate. She won't take orders from anyone. She's positive. And once her mind is made up, she rarely budges.

You do like to be spoiled and made a fuss of and her no-nonsense attitude could be a bit deflating to your male ego.

A woman born under the Sign of the Ram is always on the move. Adventure fascinates her and she is prepared to accept almost anything in the way of a challenge. She knows what she wants, and what is more, she knows how to go about getting it.

Like you, she doesn't play around with passion. If she returns your "I love you," you can bet she means it. You will admire her practicality. But at times you'll wish she relied on you a little more. You can't help wanting to play the protector. Her independent streak may be a little too much for you to take.

Of course, if you both know exactly what you want from life and it happens to be the same thing, then this union could work extremely well.

In a business partnership, you would be unbeatable. A Leo-Aries liaison would be just the right chemistry for getting to the top.

Don't try the masterful approach. She doesn't take kindly to being banged over the head with a club and dragged off to a jungle clearing. She dreams of a more romantic approach, and this should not be difficult for a Leo guy. You know all about soft lights and sweet music.

If this woman is attracted to a man, he soon knows it. It's not uncommon for her to take the lead in a love affair. In fact, she quite likes to do this. Being a bit proper in these things, you may think her rather forward when she asks you out to dinner.

There is no affectation or pretension in this woman's nature. She'll always lay it straight on the line. As a man who likes to know exactly where he stands, you will appreciate her honesty.

It would be wise to keep her guessing. She doesn't really like to get the upper hand in a relationship, although her manner may suggest this is what she's striving to do. Actually, she's only testing you. Play a little hard to get; this sort of behavior always intrigues a Mars-ruled woman.

Miss Aries can be an extremely jealous female. If you start having a bit of fun on the side, be sure she doesn't hear about it because she has a terrible temper and she won't think twice about going to the other woman's place and throwing things at her.

She'll be a great help in your career and will do all in her power to help you get on. A man with an Aries woman behind him will have an advantage over many of his competitors. In marriage, she'll put your interests before her own. She feels you should be the breadwinner.

You'll have no complaint about the way the home is run. She can look after the domestic side of your life together with apparent ease. Her cooking will be different without being exotic. She has the ability to rustle up a tasty snack in five seconds flat. This girl loves licking a house into shape. She's also adept with a pail of paint and a brush.

Basically, she prefers the company of men to women. You must not get jealous if she continues to keep in touch with old boyfriends after marriage. She'll think you're being silly and old-fashioned if you try to lay down the law on this score.

You will admire her fighting qualities, and if you believe in power sharing, all will be well.

LEO MAN—TAURUS WOMAN

This could be an interesting combination. Like you, she's extremely romantic, though people might not guess it on first meeting. Miss Taurus is a bit introverted. She will not easily show what she feels. She's very strong-willed and resilient. She doesn't like to take orders and occasionally seems to be totally without humor. You may find her a little too down to earth. You like a woman to be really feminine. Miss Taurus doesn't always give this impression.

She has great self-control. It is difficult to bait her into losing her temper, but when she does lose it . . . watch out! Try to boss her around, and you'll soon regret it.

This woman doesn't judge other people and expects them to extend her the same courtesy. She has no difficulty mixing with characters from all walks of life. You will find her equally at ease chatting with the postman or the President.

She's not interested in a casual affair. A Taurus woman only subscribes to the real thing. If you are hoping for a weekend with this girl and nothing more, save your breath and imagination. Still, she's very passionate. If you are really gone on each other, there will be no complaints coming from the bedroom. Your type of lovemaking will definitely appeal to her and vice versa.

Miss Taurus is a very reliable person. She would never let a friend down. If you get married, you can be sure your Venus-ruled woman will stand by you come hell or high water.

Her mind may not work as quickly as yours. She reaches the important decisions in life with deliberation. She refuses to be rushed by anybody. She loves feminine things. Angora sweaters and fur coats that she can nestle into will send her into ecstasy. Her sense of touch is highly developed.

She's very good with money and a guy like you may find that with Miss Taurus two can live as cheaply as one. She's quite a saver. She knows a bargain when she sees one and will be able to save dollars on the weekly food bill.

This lady is very set in her opinions, but then, so are you. As long as you are both on the same mental wavelength, all should be well. But it would be a good idea to have a fairly long courtship. Don't trust too much that the first explosion will last a lifetime.

She won't mind you if you wink at a pretty girl or even dance too closely with another woman when you've had a couple too many at a party. Don't go too far, though, because she doesn't miss a trick. She's very jealous so don't take her for a fool and cheat behind her back.

Miss Taurus is quite fashion-conscious. She knows what she looks best in. You will find she's extremely elegant, favoring nicely cut suits.

You are unlikely to be sorry if you do decide to marry a Taurus woman. Once you sort out your differences and come to an understanding, your relationship will be fruitful.

She will be prepared to give up her career if necessary to look after you. She takes great pleasure in doing things for her guy. She's an artist in the kitchen and delights in creating her own dishes to tickle her husband's fancy.

She's great with children in the toddler stage but can be a little too domineering when they hit their teens.

You'll find you haven't married a woman who runs home to mother. And though she won't be after you for your worldly possessions, she will help you to add to them.

LEO MAN—GEMINI WOMAN

A Leo man does like to feel he is following some sort of pattern in his life. You like order and can be quite methodical, so you may run into problems if you get too deeply involved with a girl born under the Sign of the Twins. She can be very confusing. She's apt to change her mind in the blink of an eye. You may feel she's just out to tease you, but this is unlikely.

You see, people born under this Sign have extreme difficulty in working out exactly what they want from life. With patience and understanding, you could help her a great deal. You will soon discover that in linking up with a Gemini, you have taken on more than one woman. After a few dates, you'll be wondering which girl you're going out with next. She just can't hide her moods or her feelings.

Age is quite important. If you meet a Mercury-ruled woman after she's had a chance to mature and experience life, it will be much easier for you to make a go of it. It takes her a long time to grow up and to come to terms with herself. Don't get angry with her or try to lay down the law, as you are in the habit of doing. You won't win her by wielding the big stick. She needs your sympathy and understanding. She'll run a mile if you try to dominate her.

You are a practical man and she certainly needs that. Show her by example and she will learn quickly. She has a sparkling personality and great presence. Just watch the heads turn when you walk into a room together.

Your Gemini woman loves travel and changes of scenery. She can't stand to feel trapped. She always wants to be experiencing something different and new. Jet planes and fast cars are likely to be terribly exciting to her. She's not the type who likes to go to bed early, either. Very often she comes alive at night. She'll get very restless if you expect her to stay home more than a couple of evenings in a row.

It is highly unlikely that this Mercurial woman will allow herself to be cast in the role of the little housewife waiting patiently for the breadwinner to return home demanding dinner. You'll have to allow her to carry on with her own interests or she'll go crazy with boredom. She's not great shakes in the kitchen, as a rule. She doesn't have the patience to prepare lavish banquets.

Miss Gemini needs a lot of loving—but she's capable of giving a lot of love. She can't bear to go on living with someone once the romance has gone out of the relationship, so don't forget to tell her continually how much she means to you. Buy her little presents and remember to take her in your arms occasionally. Even after years of marriage, she'll love it if you flirt with her and hold her hand under the table at a restaurant.

She has a good sense of humor. She'll try to make the best of it if you hit hard times. Miss Gemini can get down in the dumps, but on the whole she's a positive person and a great believer in tomorrow.

Life will never be dull with a Gemini woman. It's unlikely she'll lapse into silence for long. She loves stimulating conversations and discussions.

She makes a great hostess. When you bring your boss home, he's likely to be captivated by her charm and vivacity. She's not too particular about the background of her various friends and may arrive home with some pretty strange characters on occasions. All she requires of people is that they be interesting. When you have a party, leave it to her to do the organizing. She knows how to make an occasion go with a swing.

Her kids may not be the smartest in the playground, but they will be loved and well cared for.

LEO MAN—CANCER WOMAN

Hold on to your hat, Mr. Leo. If you get involved deeply with a Cancer woman, you won't know what's hit you. And the only way you can get involved with this woman is deeply.

You'll find her a constant puzzle. You won't be able to make up your mind whether she's the sweetest, most intelligent woman you've ever met, or if she is totally governed by her ruler, the Moon. Yes, you'll soon discover what an influence the Moon and her element, water, have on her. She turns like the tide itself and is as fathomless as the very deepest portion of any ocean.

Miss Cancer is a rather uncertain lady. She rarely appears to know in what direction she's heading. One minute she'll be vowing undying love, and the next she may be telling you she never really cared for you anyway. The strange thing is she will always appear to be telling the truth—and she probably is. She has great difficulty in recalling what she felt yesterday.

When this girl hits a low, she really gets down. It's almost impossible to shake her out of her mood. Perhaps a powerful personality like you can do it. But you'd better form a good idea of what you're getting involved in.

On first meeting, you'll find she has a way of concerning others in her life and her problems. She likes to be the center of attention and doesn't enjoy competition at all. Her symbol is the Crab, and a pretty apt one it is. When she withdraws into her shell, it will be very difficult to get through to her. Your phone bill could be fairly high because she loves to have long conversations with Mother, which could drive you absolutely insane.

You will have the task of getting her to face up to herself and to accept life for what it really is. She always fears the unknown. Although she is often on the run, she hates to be on her own. She'll worry if she's too fat, likewise if she's too thin. It will be the same with age.

She can be pretty tight with money. Desperate to secure her future, she'll hang on to the last buck. Mind you, she can suddenly go on a spending spree and come home with parcels of expensive new clothes. Her one great weakness is her wardrobe.

If she does fall in love with you, there won't be any doubts about it. She's all woman and will give herself totally. This won't happen, though, until she's absolutely certain of you because she's terrified of being hurt.

You will need to boost her ego constantly. She really does need compliments about her looks and dress. She will never take you for granted and will always be bowled over when you bring her a dozen red roses.

She hangs on to her friends from the past, probably for reasons of security.

Your Cancer wife will make a wonderful home for you. There's nothing she won't do for her man. She'll want you to be a success in your career and will do all she can to help you get to the top. Although she's not a stay-at-home, she does love domestic life because she feels most relaxed in familiar surroundings.

In marriage, she'll become more gentle. Once she feels settled and secure, she will stop hedging and walking sideways. She is devoted to her loved ones. As a mother, no sacrifice is too great for her to make for her children. But you'll have to watch your step when the babies come along. Being a man who needs constant admiration and flattery, you may feel a bit left out when she's fussing over her offspring.

There could also be trouble when the time comes for her kids to find their own way in the world because she does have a tendency to keep them tied to the apron strings.

LEO MAN—LEO WOMAN

This linkup will not be the plain sailing you might imagine. Although on the surface you'll have a great deal in common, there are fundamental differences that will have to be sorted out. When someone is very similar to you in so many ways, there are bound to be aspects of your own personality in them that you find difficult to come to terms with.

Miss Leo is proud, a born leader and unwilling to take orders from anyone. Her freedom is terribly important to her. She hates to feel hemmed in or suffocated. You, on the other hand, like to be cast in the role of protector and provider. It might be hard for you to swallow when this girl proves she is quite capable of taking care of her own affairs.

It will only be because she loves you that she'll allow you to make important decisions. She's not a golddigger. She seeks something higher than money or security in her marriage. She won't be prepared to sit quietly in the background while you hold the floor. She is much admired herself and has plenty to offer other people.

Miss Leo is all woman. Your male friends won't be able to help admiring her, and perhaps even desiring her. She is well aware of the effect she has on men. You will have to hide your jealousy and let her cuddle and hold hands with whom she pleases. You'll soon realize it's all quite harmless and that she'd never dream of doing anything to hurt or upset you. There is definitely something special about a Leo woman. Your friends will be forever reminding you what a lucky guy you are.

Never take her for granted or expect her to sit quietly at home while you live it up. You had better get it straight right from the start that she likes the exciting things in life as much as you do.

She's not the greatest cook or housekeeper.

She'd much prefer to eat out if she's not entertaining. She's capable of rustling up a quick meal or experimenting in the kitchen, but to cook a roast every Sunday is one big yawn for her.

Other women will be pretty jealous of her, or perhaps we should say envious. They'll probably wish they had the strength of character to stand up for their own rights that she has.

Don't expect a lot of flattery, you who like to be tickled under the chin and told how clever you are. Your feline mate will make sure those feet of yours are planted firmly on the ground. You won't be able to pull the wool over her eyes and she certainly won't allow you to fool yourself.

She will be terribly good for you in business. You will never be ashamed to bring home important people. In fact, she could help you to clinch that contract you've been angling for. It won't be what she does or says that tips the scales; it will be her very presence.

She loves to dress up in pretty clothes and you'll enjoy buying them for her. She's very partial to chunky jewelry, expensive perfumes and fur coats she can snuggle into.

Your Leonine partner is a competitive pussycat. She'll give you a run for your money at any card game and will never admit defeat on the tennis court.

Her lovemaking is passionate. She has a vivid imagination and will enjoy experimenting and playing games in the bedroom.

Always remember her birthday. She loves pretty things. Your home is likely to be distinctly feminine. Neither of you is likely to want a large family.

LEO MAN—VIRGO WOMAN

You have a tendency to rush in feet first with your women announcing, "Well, here I am, girl, come and get me." You'd better change your style if you've got your sights set on a Virgo lady. She's quiet, reserved and hates big emotional displays in public. She will never respect you if you embarrass her. If you are interested in more than a casual affair and are prepared to woo her as romantically as only a Leo can when he tries, you'll find her more fascinating every hour you're in her company.

Miss Virgo is not prepared to show her true feelings until she can trust a man. She will expect you to prove yourself before she opens up to you.

Basically, she's shy. People would be amazed if they knew the thoughts that were running through her mind on occasions. It is very often the Mercury-ruled woman who ups and leaves her husband and two kids because she suddenly discovers true love. Her friends will pass such remarks as, ''Well, who would have thought that she. . . .'' Still waters run deep here. Little Miss Virgo cannot be put in a pigeonhole or stamped with a serial number.

She simply cannot or will not admit she's in the wrong, so don't think you can win her by criticizing her. She won't like it at all if you nag and try to change her. The aggravating thing is she's likely to be right most of the time. She's extremely good at summing up people. She may not have joined in the conversation, but when you get home you'll be amazed at how cannily she can pinpoint the strengths and weaknesses of the people you were out with.

If you are at all unsure about which decision to take in connection with your career or an important business deal, you could do a lot worse than discuss the matter with your Virgo woman. Nine times out of ten her advice will be worth following.

Marriage will be about the most important thing in her life so she will certainly try very hard to make a success of it. If, however, something goes wrong, she won't hang on. One thing she won't be able to accept is infidelity. She'll find it extremely hard to trust you again if you betray her.

A Virgo woman will want to share in your life as much as possible. She'll do her best to make your friends her friends.

Keep yourself looking smart. This lady can't bear a man who looks a mess. Keep that beard under control and be sure to splash on plenty of her favorite after-shave lotion.

When it comes to lovemaking, don't rush her. She needs to be treated gently. Whisper sweet nothings in her ear and keep the candles and the incense burning. You have to provide more than physical stimulation to satisfy her. Never say you love her unless you mean it. A woman born under this Sign takes those three little words very seriously. Don't make any promises unless you can deliver the goods.

She's quite capable of keeping on with her career after marriage. She's so well organized that she can run a house and hold down an important job at the same time.

She loves evenings at home but not too many of them. Her happiest times will probably be when you are alone together. Her idea of heaven will be to snuggle up with you in front of a fire on a chill winter's evening. She will keep the home tidy. In fact, you may find it hard to get used to her fetish for cleanliness. Every time you stub out a cigarette, she'll empty the ashtray, and she'll do the washing up while she's still chewing the last mouthful of her dinner.

The Virgo woman makes a good mother but you needn't worry about being displaced by the kids. You'll always come first with her.

LEO MAN—LIBRA WOMAN

You'll hit it off with a Libra woman from the word go. Out of all the Signs of the Zodiac, she is perhaps the most compatible for a man whose symbol is the Lion.

Miss Libra will depend on you without losing her individuality. She will make you feel all man without playing little-girl-lost. You will never feel suffocated or held down by her. Her interests are many and varied. She's an extremely good mixer. She is deeply interested in people and has a very inquiring mind. She is capable of continuing her career and running the home. She's very adaptable, equally poised when having a cheery joke with the mailman and when dazzling your boss with her charm and vivacity.

Harmony and balance are very important to her. She needs more than one interest in life to feel fulfilled. Don't worry, you'll always come first, but you must allow her her independence. Let her carry on with her career after marriage if she wants to.

The Libra woman is usually on the petite side and feminine to their fingertips. Although capable of looking after herself, she will bring out your protective instincts. She will never try to wear the pants. She'll be perfectly happy for you to be head of the house. She likes a man to be a man.

She's very logical and will be able to hold her own in any discussion. There's a mind as sharp as a razor's edge ticking behind that doll-like expression.

Don't forget that Libra is the Sign of partnership and human relationships. You can imagine how important it will be to a woman born under the symbol of the Scales to make a success of her marriage.

You'll have to accept the fact that she likes to flirt. She knows she's attractive to men and can't help playing up to them. You, too, like to play games with the opposite sex, so you will have to be prepared to allow her the same freedom. Don't get hot under the collar. It's unlikely she would ever do anything to put your marriage in jeopardy.

Your Libra woman will be a great ego

booster. She'll put you on a high pedestal. She will tell you you're capable of achieving anything if you really put your mind to it. With this woman behind you, there is no reason why you should not fulfill all your ambitions. For her part, she'll do all she can to get you into the executive seat.

She's just as romantic as you are. She'll adore bouquets of flowers and candlelight dinners. She'll throw her arms around you and shower you with kisses. She does not play games with men so you'll soon know if she is really attracted to you.

This woman needs other people. You aren't likely to find her in a job where she's shut away in some cubbyhole with only a typewriter for company. She'll want to join in as much of your life as she can. In many cases, it will be an advantage to have her along on business dinners.

She will never allow her emotions to get in the way when making an important decision. If she feels a relationship is going wrong, no matter how much it hurts her, she'll break it off. Her analytical powers are quite astonishing.

You'll love the way she organizes things at home. The kitchen is likely to be streamlined. She'll have all the latest gadgets to make life's daily chores easy to handle. The den will be comfortable and in perfect taste.

She's tops with kids—those of others as well as her own. You'll be as proud of her as a mother as you are of her as a wife.

LEO MAN—SCORPIO WOMAN

Brother, if you want to take on a real challenge, if you like to stick your chin out, if you want to dedicate your life to a woman, then pick Miss Scorpio. She'll fit the bill on every count.

She'll be a constant puzzle to you. She's not an easy woman to live with or to understand. Being a very passionate person, her feelings run deep. If she loves you, she'll do anything for you. But if you let her down and make her feel like a fool, watch out.

She's got quite a temper. She will not be dominated unless she wants to be. If you try to lay down the law in your usual way, she'll tell you where to get off in no uncertain manner. Basically, she likes to be in charge. Although she's all woman, she wants to have the upper hand in her close relationships.

Don't try the old-fashioned caveman approach. You won't win her over by dragging her off to the bedroom. She likes to make her own decisions and freedom is very important to her—not just freedom of action but freedom of spirit.

Life with a Scorpio woman will not be smooth sailing because she actually requires a certain amount of conflict in her life in order to function successfully. Her feelings are intense. It is rare for her to be indifferent about anybody. Her opinions are important to her.

She has no use for simpering little girls who play Miss Innocent with men. She's direct to a frightening degree.

She can be pretty ambitious. Scorpio women are usually leaders in their group. She will always retain her individuality and likes to make up her own mind. She is not a camp follower. Her work is pretty important to her and she likes to get to the top in her career. She can't stand to play second fiddle to anybody.

Never make a fool of your Scorpio woman in public. She'll let your remarks pass while others are around, but watch out when you get home. She's extremely truthful. She'll want you to be a success in your job. A hard worker herself, she can't abide laziness in others.

Scorpio people never know when to draw the line. They can go to excess with alcohol and drugs; when their senses are aroused, they lose their self-control.

Sex is one of the dominating factors in their lives. The physical relationship will have to be good for the union to survive. Her appetite in bed is insatiable. Strangely enough, though, she can go for months without sex if she has had a bad experience or doesn't meet the right person. She is quite choosy about whom she gets involved with, and usually goes for a very definite, distinctive type of individual.

You can trust your Scorpio mate to keep a secret. Her friends are terribly important to her. She tries never to let down anybody she respects and loves. She's not as romantic as you are. She'll always put the practicalities of life before her dreams.

Being the type of man you are, you could find life with a Scorpio woman a little draining. It would be advisable to get to know her really well before you marry. Make sure you have a lot more going for you than a purely physical attraction.

You'll find she mixes extremely well with your friends. She'll be just like one of the boys when you go out in a group. Miss Scorpio doesn't mind being the only girl in the party. In fact, she revels in it.

She makes a possessive mother. But then, she is possessive about everything she considers rightfully hers.

LEO MAN—SAGITTARIUS WOMAN

You will have to go easy on a Sagittarius woman. For one thing, she will not tolerate being told what to do. In your Leonine way, you often feel you know what's best for everyone. You appear to be bossy because people sometimes misunderstand your motives. A lady born under the third fire Sign will allow you to make the big decisions as long as you don't try to interfere with what she regards as her domain.

At times she will make you cringe. Sagittarius people have a habit of putting their opinions in a very strong way. She won't mince her words. People will know exactly where they stand with her.

You do like to have your ego boosted regularly. She is not prepared to do this. This woman will bring you to a greater understanding of yourself.

You can't help but appreciate her honesty and good intentions. She will do everything in her power to fulfill her duties as a wife and mother. She will make sure you are always well turned out. It will be important to her to run the home smoothly. She's no slouch when it comes to doing housework and all other duties connected with domestic life.

You'll find her great company. She's very good at parties and is interested in meeting new people. Although a home-loving person, she won't be prepared to stay in the background all the time and play the role of the little woman. You are a bit of a man's man; too many nights out with the boys could land you in hot water with your Sagittarius lady.

She's very ambitious, not only for herself but also for her man. She will stand up for you with other people. You have a bit of a career girl here. Most Sagittarius women go on working after marriage. The home is unlikely to be enough to occupy her mind.

She's quite the outdoors type. Very good at sports, she'll be a willing partner at tennis or squash. She'll enjoy it when you bring your friends home. Even if you give her only a couple hours' notice, she will be able to lay out a nice spread for your poker-playing and beer-drinking pals that will satisfy all.

This woman is exceedingly trusting. Tell her something and she'll believe you. Woe betide the man who lets her down, though, because it is not easy for her to forgive and forget. She'll tolerate the odd flirtation, but if you get involved seriously with another woman, she'll never have quite the same respect for you again.

Miss Sagittarius is a little shy of romance. She's not too keen about displaying her emotions in public. For her, love is something to be shared between two people only.

You haven't got the greatest cook in the world here. Sagittarius women simply don't have the patience to spend hours in the kitchen being creative with a casserole.

A Sagittarius lady will not pry into your business affairs—or into your personal life outside the home, for that matter. She'll feel that as the man of the house, you'll know the best decisions to make as far as your job is concerned.

One motto to remember with your Sagittarius lady is: "If you want a job done, do it yourself." Ask her to mail an important letter and she's quite capable of forgetting to put a stamp on it. Be careful you don't scold her, though. Even if she makes a mess of things on occasions, she'll always do her best to keep you happy.

With kids, she's an absolute wonder, although she does have a tendency to live her life through them as they grow older.

LEO MAN—CAPRICORN WOMAN

All will be well if you are one of those Leo men who are born leaders (that is the category most of you fall into) because Miss Capricorn is an ideal partner for a man who is out to make his mark in the world. Success is very important to her. She will always be there at your side, boosting your confidence and telling you you're the greatest.

Remember, we are dealing with the third of the earth Signs here. This woman is very hung up on possessions and getting to the top. She'll want you to be ambitious and will do all in her power to make you realize your full potential.

A woman born where Saturn rules and Mars is exalted is interested in wealth and security. She wants to feel secure about the future. She's wonderful at getting a home together.

Don't get the wrong idea about her—she doesn't worship money; but she is well aware of its value. She will help you to save and is expert at balancing the family budget. She's also capable of whipping up an interesting and exciting meal for next to nothing.

If you fall for little Miss Capricorn, you will have made a very good choice. If the feeling's mutual, you can count yourself a lucky man for she's a very choosy lady. And you can bet your bottom dollar she's spotted your leadership qualities. It may take some time to get to know her well because she's quite complex. Her head does not always rule her heart. Her emotions are very deeply felt, but she will usually pull back if she thinks she is going to get hurt or is wasting her love on someone who doesn't really deserve it.

Miss Capricorn will take the rough with the smooth and make the necessary sacrifices for the sake of the future. But she is emphatically not the kind of person to put up with second best for the rest of her days.

She has great patience, and if she is really attracted to you, she'll be prepared to play the waiting game. You'll find her wonderful as a partner when it comes to entertaining influential business associates. Miss Capricorn could well help you clinch that all-important deal. She knows how to flirt with men and make them feel very important without allowing the relationship to become heavy.

You won't have any complaints about her lovemaking. Her sexual appetite is pretty near insatiable. She will make you feel all man. As a woman, she likes to be taken. Variety is the spice of life for her. In bed, she has a vivid imagination.

Her family is very important to her, so once you get married, be prepared to see a great deal of her mother.

She will help you build up your bank account. She's shrewd about bargains. You'll never cease to be amazed at how economical she is when shopping for the family groceries. And she's adept, as well as artistic and inventive, at making her own clothes. Occasionally, she might go on a spending spree, but then, can you name a woman who doesn't?

A Capricorn lady can't help being a bit of a flirt. If you catch her fluttering her eyes at another guy, try not to let that jealous streak of yours take over because it's likely to be harmless.

She will make a good mother to your children. As a parent combination, you should agree on how youngsters ought to be brought up. You'll both be firm but just. And she'll give them all the maternal love they need.

LEO MAN—AQUARIUS WOMAN

So you want to marry an Aquarius girl? Well, friend Leo, you'd better decide on a long courtship. Get to know this woman really well before you decide she is the one you want to spend the rest of your natural life with.

There would appear to be quite a lot against this liaison. But then, as they say, love can always find a way. It's possible you two will view life in very opposite ways. She's an extremely difficult girl to pin down. Just when you think you've got her number, she'll do or say something that appears to be totally out of character. You like to know where you stand with a lover, and this is something that's almost impossible to ascertain with Aquarius.

She has a very independent streak and won't allow anyone to lay down the law to her. No sir. She'll always shout "freedom," though when you ask her what exactly that is, she'll find it difficult to articulate.

Plenty of other guys find her desirable so you'll have to contend with a lot of competition if you're out to become the only man in her life.

Aquarius is the Sign of friendship, social life and aspirations—and unexpected happenings. There is not, as a rule, a great deal of interest in domestic matters here (don't forget how much you like your home comforts). An Aquarius woman is likely to be on the go all the time. She's a woman of ideas and can get deeply involved in causes.

As a Leo male, you can be pretty possessive if you feel your woman's life doesn't center around you. A woman born under the Sign of Aquarius could drive you insane. When coming in from a hard day at the office, it's possible you'll find the house empty. You'll have to get used to preparing your own supper quite a lot.

When it comes to getting a home together, this lady has excellent taste. But she's not too good at economizing—in fact, she rather enjoys spending money. Your little chats about how to cut down on unnecessary expenditures will have little effect on her.

This relationship need not be all gloom and despair. She'll ensure that you make the best use of your powers of leadership. She is extremely attracted to people with powerful personalities.

If you can accept change and the fact that Miss Aquarius likes life to be full of surprises, all should be well and good. You do like a certain amount of order, though, and a lifetime of games playing could be a little too much for you.

It could be that a whirlwind romance that ignites great passion for a short period would suit you both best. It is quite likely you'll go on being great chums once your affair is over. She's that sort of woman.

You can't help but admire this girl's pluck. She's always willing to put herself out to help a person in distress.

You'll enjoy taking her out to parties. She doesn't have a jealous nature. If you have an affair with another woman, she'll be very understanding. There is a danger that relationships outside of marriage could become a problem for you both. You will have to work pretty hard at mutual fidelity.

Contrary to expectations, she makes a very responsible mother, who strives to bring up her children in an adult way.

LEO MAN—PISCES WOMAN

The Pisces woman is all woman. She will impress most men with her feminine charms, and you, Mr. Leo, are no exception. She is the zany type who often goes around in circles, occasionally getting confused and frequently changing her mind. She'll have you in a dither, but when you get to know her well, you wouldn't have her any other way.

She's dreamy. Not only is her head in the clouds, but her feet are off the ground. She'll come up with the craziest ideas for travel and for making money—and the surprising thing is that her plans so often pay off.

She likes a man who can take the lead. Masterful Leo is likely to be very much her type. It will be up to you to make the big decisions. She knows who should wear the trousers around the house, and she'll expect a great deal from you. Any lack of confidence you have about your prospects will soon be dispelled by her.

You two make an excellent combination in so many ways because your various strengths and weaknesses balance each other out perfectly.

Don't be taken in by her rather blank and wide-eyed expression. A Pisces woman knows exactly what is going on. There's not a man around who could pull the wool over her eyes for very long. You'll find yourself waiting on her quite often, bringing her a cup of coffee in bed and making sure she's got most of the clothes she desires. But then, what man who loves his woman doesn't enjoy bringing pleasures into her life?

She won't try to match her wits against yours and will enjoy hearing you speak out on your favorite subject.

You are pretty careful with money, although you do enjoy an occasional spending spree. She likes to be extravagant at times, too, but Pisces knows the value of a greenback. You'll have no trouble saving cash for a luxurious vacation or the proverbial rainy day. By the way, Pisces women are reputed to be very astute about property. She knows a bargain in real estate when she sees one.

You will be keen to get home to her most nights after a hard day's work. If occasionally you stop for a couple of beers with the guys, she won't object. Just be sure to let her know if you're going to be late as she may have prepared some special surprise for your supper.

She's an absolute wow at decorating. Her taste is impeccable. One of her pleasures in life is buying new things for the home. One or two of her purchases may turn out to be shrewd investments.

There are, of course, certain drawbacks to this duo. Where you like to be positive and stick to your decisions, this lady born under the last watery Sign of the Zodiac is likely to change her mind as quickly and as many times as the tide ebbs and flows in a day.

The Pisces woman places a lot of importance on anniversaries and birthdays. She'll like you to remember all special occasions. It's one of her ways of reassuring herself of your love. It would be a good idea to keep a record of them.

Physically, you'll discover you are well attuned to each other. She is an uninhibited lover and will like your very masculine attitude. Don't play with her affections. If you let her down, she can be ferocious.

To keep her self-doubts at bay, it will help if you tell her, without being patronizing, whenever she's done a good job. This girl is very artistic and poetic, but in her vain search for perfection, she's likely to destroy her creative efforts in disgust—and the world could miss out on something unusual. She will make an excellent mother for your children—and she'll never relegate you to second place.

LEO'S HEALTH

Since you are one of the hardest workers in the Zodiac, it's not surprising that nature has provided you with an extremely robust constitution. You are probably the healthiest Sign of all. Your nerves, muscles and vital organs are arranged in a fine functional balance, and your fiery, outgoing temperament gives you the will to survive in the most difficult situations.

Leo rules the heart, the central source of the organism's power. Any serious health problems are likely to appear here. Heart disease, epilepsy and rheumatic fever are possible disorders. But generally speaking, the heart is especially strong and healthy in Leo people. They are capable of tremendous exertion (while in good shape) without any ill effects.

You throw off illnesses very rapidly. Your powers of recuperation are quite extraordinary. You can stage a recovery that in other less vibrant types would be impossible. In any kind of sickness, your immense vitality seems to radiate from the heart into every cell, quickly revivifying your entire body.

However, you should never disregard the important effect your emotions can have on your well-being. There may be nothing physically wrong with you, but sorrow, sadness and especially pining disorganize your system. Then you feel unwell and you look unwell. You become lethargic and depressed. You are likely in these circumstances to imagine yourself ill and even talk yourself into going to bed.

Fortunately, the Leo temperament is extraordinarily sanguine. You are usually able to snap out of depression. You can be assisted in this by a person with the right bedside manner, one who admires your strength and capacity to fight back, or by an appeal from a loved one who is dependent on you. The need to take some sort of authoritative action will eventually force a dejected Leo to throw back the sheets and start giving orders.

When you do go succumb to an illness, if it is not heart disease, it is usually connected with the spine, the circulation or the throat. You may suffer from pains in the back, side or shoulders, weakness in the ankles or problems of the reproductive organs. Hoarseness and sore throats are also common. There is also a danger of pleurisy, fevers and convulsions, especially in childhood.

You seldom suffer from chronic or lingering diseases, although periodic eye trouble can be a complaint. When sickness strikes, it is usually sudden. As a patient, you are inclined to require a lot of attention and frequently convince yourself you are in worse shape than you are. You will first think it wonderful to have an opportunity to rest (at last), but soon you will get bored with the inactivity and want to get up.

You are prone to accidents. You are not the most patient driver on the road. Although normally very safety conscious and aware of your responsibilities behind the wheel, you tend to be easily irritated by other motorists and to take silly risks out of churlishness.

A distinct danger period for Leo-born people

occurs in middle age. This is when you are likely to become absorbed in a wide range of mental pursuits and take insufficient exercise. Or, being inclined to extremes and recklessly confident of your own strength, you may suddenly throw yourself into intense physical exertion, which puts a great strain on your heart.

You are usually a great sports lover, the kind who likes to participate. When plunging into superactive games, remember to treat your back with extra consideration.

It is important for Leos as they get older to develop the art of relaxation. You should endeavor to create a philosophical outlook and not react automatically to every emotional situation. In the space of one hour, you can go up and down like a yo-yo, getting all heated up over the most trivial provocations. In middle age, the superb nervous system that served you so well in your youth is easily upset.

Leo's great fondness for pleasure can also be a health hazard. You may burn the candle at both ends just once too often. There is also a danger of drinking and eating to excess because you love good food and are an inveterate party-goer.

Leo individuals are psychologically fearless in the face of danger but not so well equipped to cope with physical pain. You are a sensitive person who can literally fight a duel to the death if necessary to defend a person or a cause, but you may protest at a pinprick and perhaps even faint while giving blood.

LEO

AT WORK

You yearn to be a celebrity. This is a basic Leo urge, so don't be ashamed of it (especially if you're young) and wonder why the limelight seems so much more important to you than to your friends. Leo is the Sign of personal projection. You're going to get to the top in whatever you undertake. If you bury yourself in a dead-end job just because it's safe, you'll always be discontented.

You are a colorful and dominant personality. There's a great deal of the showman in you. You should choose a job or career where you can make the most of these qualities. The entertainment and amusement fields are naturals for you. Many of the most successful actors and actresses were born under your Sign. You possess a wonderful physical magnetism; in the theater or on the screen, this is what is called "star quality." You also possess a fine sense of the dramatic; in fact, you probably have to guard against overdramatizing your actions and words in whatever occupation you follow. The desire to create a sensational effect is not always appreciated by others and may even hinder your advancement.

Leo-born people make fine entrepreneurs, promoters and managers in show biz. They are attuned to public taste and can usually spot talent at a glance. Their promotion methods are usually spectacular. Glamor and gimmickry are props Leo loves to use. Motion picture production, with its almost unlimited opportunities for spectacle, is an excellent medium for your vivid and flamboyant imagination.

But no matter what work you're engaged in, you'll do best when you occupy a position of sole authority because your strongest characteristic is the power to rule. It is as a leader that you make your greatest contribution and impact on the world, and at the same time satisfy your deepest instincts. You'll never be happy in the role of an understudy.

Naturally, everyone has to make a start and learn the business. It is good if you have to knuckle down in your early days and learn to follow orders. There's nothing to stop you from dreaming of the day when you'll be on top while you're working diligently toward it. Fortunately, people born under your Sign have good minds. They can work with great determination and against tremendous odds as long as they know they're progressing. But they need the encouragement of loved ones at home, and appreciation and recognition of their talents by their superiors.

As a Leo, you are well suited for work in one of the professions. Medicine or the law frequently offers the chance of individual expression leading eventually to public acknowledgment. Your vigorous sense of purpose and desire to serve mankind in a dramatic fashion often allow you to change the established order and pioneer new developments and techniques. As an authority, you will have a powerful influence.

Politics is an extremely fertile field for the Leo man or woman. Here you can lead in your inimitable, individualistic style and at the same time satisfy your altruistic urges. Although you may never cease to complain about the weaknesses of the system and the shortsightedness of your colleagues, you have the patience and perseverance to work incessantly toward your goals. Your tactlessness and brash criticism of others is only equaled by your ability to get away with it.

Many Leos end up in executive positions where they can command, organize and distribute duties. Although infuriatingly critical and demanding, they are also extremely fair. They are trusted by their workers.

As a boss, you like to hog all the important jobs for yourself—that is, the ones most likely to impress your clients or the board of directors. But if you get overloaded—which means you can't take a two-hour lunch, meet a client for a game of golf and do the innumerable other things you pack into a single working day—you'll hand the jobs around. Even so, everything has to have your imprimatur on it before it goes out. The fact that someone else worked all night on a job doesn't change this. You'll see that he is rewarded more than amply for his efforts; but when it comes to accolades, you make sure you're the only one in line. Still, your employees usually respect you and will do anything for you, which means working for you can't be all that bad.

In fact, if a worker is having a hard time because of illness or unexpected expenses, you're likely to be on his doorstep as soon as you hear about it with a good-size check in your hand or airline tickets for a holiday in the sun. And no one's ever likely to hear from you what you've done. You might like to blow your trumpet about your achievements, but helping others is one thing you're in no rush to take the credit for. A significant proportion of famous anonymous philanthropists have later been revealed as people born under the Sign of Leo.

As an executive, you expect your staff to be creative and extremely active. You enjoy conferences and think tanks. You like to take the floor and outline your plans with great flourish. You certainly know what you want—and you expect your subordinates to get going on it. You're not a great one for detail yourself (you're strictly an idea person), but you do like everything done precisely, accurately and efficiently. You'll listen to other people's suggestions and encourage them to contribute, but you'll always retain personal control. Everyone must report to you finally. Lone wolves are outlawed in Lion territory.

Although at times you like to appear informal and one of the boys, you want your due respect. Then you are generous in your compliments for a job well done.

You are honest and frank, and therefore sometimes lacerating in your criticism of employees. Insubordination or lack of faith in your pronouncements or leadership is likely to be met with howling rage and derision. There are no palace revolts in Leo's domain. Mutineers get the boot with the first insolent look. The Lion makes terrible enemies while on the warpath putting down a revolt or dealing with a cannonade from the top. He or she shows no mercy and looks for none. You usually win, or die in the attempt. If you do neither, you will simply walk out. Leo, though, only quits as a last resort. You prefer to stand and fight.

As an employee, you've always got your eye on another guy's job—up the ladder. It won't be your boss's job, as a rule, because if he treats you right, you're absolutely loyal. You'll be his num-

ber two in no time, and then you'll move sideways, around him, through some other department, so there'll be no collision of loyalties.

If you've got to wait around to obtain a big promotion you know is coming, you're supremely patient and philosophical. As long as you can see the light at the end of the corridor (burning over that other guy's desk), you can wait in good grace. And in an emergency, you're ever ready to take over, no matter how big the job may be. Can you handle it, Leo? "Yes, just tell me his name and I'll get all I need from him."

You prefer to have a job with a fancy title than an extra few dollars in your paycheck. You'll never really forget a boss who overlooks you. If he does, he's also likely to be a Leo. You're too fond of telling everybody how good you are and too critical of those in command to ever hit it off with a Leo boss, who thinks you're supposed to be telling *him* how great he is. Between the two of you, each jockeying to impress those a little higher up (not to mention all the other employees on the floor), it will be a genuine two-ring circus.

You're a quick thinker, a daring and adventurous operator. Anyone can bounce a decision off you; in a crisis, they come in sure-fire volleys. You'll never pass the buck once you've accepted responsibility. But if anyone's foolish enough to overrule you, you'll let him stew in his own juice and watch the ship go down without batting an eyelid. There's nothing quite so immovable as the imperious disdain of Leo scorned.

You'll be happiest working for an organization where there is contact with the public. You'd prefer a receptionist's job in a high-class or glamorous establishment to working as a secretary-typist. As a personal assistant to a company chief or executive, you are sure to shine, provided you are allowed to achieve the required results your way. You are exceptionally good at implementing orders as long as you are left alone. You also need a job where you can make full use of your vivacious and winning personality.

If you were born between July 21 and July 30, you will do best by pouring your considerable energies into worthwhile projects. There is a danger you'll be distracted by glittering propositions that have no real substance. Glamor and fame may attract you more than solid achievement. You have a talent for writing and for expressing original ideas. You may make a name for yourself in advertising, journalism or public relations. You should be able to rise through the ranks to a high executive post.

The teaching profession, religion and public

welfare work may also serve as an outlet for your talents. You are intense, spontaneous and dynamic. An excessive love of pleasure could affect your health. Emotions may be difficult to control at times, especially where romance is concerned. Work and love affairs may conflict.

If you were born between July 31 and August 10, you will probably do well in some travel-connected occupation. You may write or lecture about your travels. Your judgment in finance and business is first class; your organizational and executive skills excellent. You are quite capable of heading an international operation or company. Artistic decoration and design may offer good commercial prospects. Your personality is forceful, commanding and attractive; you should make friends easily wherever you go. You need to stimulate your thinking by mixing with intellectual types.

You should be able to succeed in a high-level government career where you have responsibility for the interests of large numbers of people. Your vision is broad and independent. Whatever you write or say will have a wider influence than you suspect. In times of stress, you may have to strive to keep your emotions under rational control.

If you were born between August 10 and August 21, you have a good legal mind that is able to perceive the motives of others. Your sharp and alert intellect may be a little daunting and frightening at times. You probably have a strong interest in occult subjects that, given the opportunity, could be turned into a career. Publishing and writing should appeal to you. You may also do particularly well in the entertainment industry or another field that demands close contact with public opinion.

You are likely to gradually build up your estate and by midlife have considerable assets. Much of your success will depend on your ability to control impulsive and speculative actions.

Money

You like to spend money but seldom squander it, except perhaps in your youth. You have expensive tastes but are prepared to work hard and put money aside to buy the best. You are a methodical saver.

People born under your Sign have to learn to make money work for them. Once you mature emotionally, you usually manage to accumulate investment capital. You are a shrewd investor and are often helped by information from people in high places. The real estate and property business can be a bonanza for August-born people.

Your home is often your first worthwhile investment. You enjoy a change and by moving residence can usually manage to improve the value and size of your assets. You should never underestimate your intuition when buying or selling. Leo people often "feel" the right thing to do with money but can be swayed off course by the opinions of loved ones.

You are a good and generous provider. You often find it difficult to say "no" to those who depend on you. You may run yourself into debt for them. Extravagance by family members can cause you considerable anxiety.

There is the danger of loss through gambling. Once started, it's very hard for Leo to stop. Romantic involvements may also be costly.

BUSINESS

PARTNERS

The following guide to business partners for all the Signs is based on the position of the Sun, the most powerful influence in the horoscope. Most people conform to the solar influence. However, variations do take place as a result of the position of the other planets at the time of birth.

For a closer examination of a business partner's character, it is advisable to study his or her personal horoscope, which is available for every Sign in *AstroAnalysis*. All you need to know is the person's date of birth. You can then Astro-Analyze your partner and determine his or her basic characteristics.

Since some Signs are naturally more and less compatible with others, you can obtain a better idea of how you'll hit it off with a partner by referring to the Compatibility Guide on page 91.

YOUR ARIES BUSINESS PARTNER

Teaming up with the Aries person can be a risky business. You will need to understand the type very well to make the partnership work. Much will depend on the restraint you are able to impose without making the Aries feel he or she is being restricted or dictated to.

The Aries partner has much to offer. But there are also quite a few minuses. To begin with, he is a born leader, so he'll want to take charge or feel that he is really the driving force behind the firm. At the outset, he will acknowledge your position as an equal partner and have every intention of keeping to it. But when the action starts, he won't be able to help make decisions on his own. This is one of his greatest faults. He'll assume he knows the best way to deal with a situation, and even if you're in the office across the hall, nine times out of ten, it won't even enter his head to consult with you.

Aries are frightfully impatient. They can't wait to tie things up. To confer with someone else seems to them an unnecessary waste of time. Sometimes their judgment is excellent—they can pull off the most impressive coups, following a decision through with a dash and speed that leave their rivals and competitors hopelessly outdistanced. Other times, using the same technique, Aries make colossal blunders. You will need to get some meaningful assurances from your partner right from the start that he won't act unilaterally in important matters. At the same time, you will have to be careful not to inhibit him too much. His spontaneity is probably his greatest gift, so be cautious how you handle him. He will break up the partnership immediately if he suspects you are trying to give him orders. Despite his faults, the Aries has much inventiveness and resourcefulness to contribute. He just needs that gently restraining hand on his shoulder to prevent him in his eagerness from being rash and impulsive.

Aries is a straight shooter, a person who will never go behind your back. And you won't catch his hand in the cash register, either.

The Aries partner is a person of great energy. He or she is extremely active in all that is going on and is the one to handle the difficult out-front jobs where boldness, courage, fearlessness and originality are required. But your partner is not the best person—in fact, he's probably one of the worst—to cope with a situation requiring tact and diplomacy. Aries are too outspoken and confident of their own simple solutions to the world's problems to reassure a sophisticated and hesitant client.

Aries impress most people with their dynamic energy, quick, intuitive intellect and optimistic and positive approach. But they are a bit reckless, careless, too willing to take a chance, and should not be expected to handle the detail work in a partnership because they very quickly tire of concentrated mental effort. Best at responding to stimulus rather than trying to produce it themselves, Aries have a great deal of initiative yet lack persistence. They are quite good at carrying out instructions but have the infuriating habit of "improving" on them. They like to put their imprimatur on things, as though this alone makes an action worthy of their participation. If in discussions you can give way to your partner on matters that aren't essential to your plans, you will find that he or she works with much greater enthusiasm. And there is no doubt that an Aries person will put immense energy and unlimited time into anything he or she undertakes.

Remember, Aries are very self-willed, quite aggressive and frequently headstrong. Your partner is probably one of the most ambitious types you will ever meet. If you oppose him directly, he will fight you to the last breath (opposition excites him to greater effort). He is fairly fixed in his ideas, but can lose interest in projects very quickly, particularly if they require much hard work apart from the expenditure of energy.

If you run one side of the business and Aries the other, he won't have a great amount of sympathy for your problems. *His* will be the most urgent and important, even though the success of the business is supposed to be a mutual aim. He wants to succeed first in what he is personally doing; the group or partnership objective always remains secondary.

Aries expect to finish a job without much trouble. If complications occur, especially delays and drawn-out discussions about minor points, your partner is likely to walk off in disgust and leave you to sort things out.

It is not in Aries' nature to reflect or do much homework before starting on a project because they prefer to play it by ear. Their great knack is for manufacturing expedients to deal with the exigencies of the moment. As forward-looking planners, they lack depth of vision and are likely to fall into the same old traps—in different trappings—over and over again.

When delicate business negotiations are in progress, you would be wise to try to arrange to do the letter writing yourself. The Aries partner has a habit of being curt and assertive in correspondence. If there are two ways of expressing the same thought, he or she will unwittingly choose the blunter or, in other words, the one more likely to offend.

The Aries is a stickler for conventional behavior where business and partners are concerned, and will expect you to conform. He is rather blind to the fact that his own impatience and impulsiveness often involve him in what amounts to unorthodox methods and actions. He can have quite a volatile temper, which may explode over the simplest issue. But you'll seldom find him holding a grudge. He is inclined to keep to old and proven methods, updating them here and there with a dash of inspiration.

Aries is quite imaginative, though practical, in everyday affairs. Sometimes he gets the facts and his own viewpoint so mixed up he may seem to misrepresent a position.

If you happen to get caught up with the passive or negative type of Aries, you'd better forget a partnership altogether. He's a sad lot. And unless you've seen his birth certificate, you'd never spot him for one of these energetic and very decisive people. This character can't make up his own mind, isn't at all sure of what he's doing, and when he does act, it is usually too late. He spends his time worrying about the outcome when he should be following through.

YOUR TAURUS BUSINESS PARTNER

The Taurus man or woman more often than not makes a fine business partner. If you link up with this person, you will have a lot going for you. But if your aim is to make a quick buck from fly-by-night schemes or any form of risk taking, you'd better look for another buddy.

Taurus is the zodiacal Sign that refers to possessions and money. The Taurus has a natural flair for accumulating both. He or she possesses a very sound business head and is often the solid banker, the clever citizen, extremely good at making money for other people. If you give a Taurus a dollar to invest, in a few years he will hand you back fifty—less expenses, of course. He is not likely to make you any spectacular profits off his own initiative. He is a steady, persevering plodder who makes his fortune by sheer dogged effort, and usually with a bit of luck just when it is needed most.

You'll have to watch that your partnership does not become a rather dull affair. If you leave running the operation to your Taurus associate, you'll discover everything settling deeper and deeper into a pattern. You might have a fine money-making machine, but the boredom will send some of the more adventurous Signs up the wall. Your partner is no experimenter. Taureans loathe taking chances. They play every card by the book, always with an anxious eye to safeguarding their security.

You will have to be the brains of the outfit. You can leave all the tedious organizing and implementing to this tireless and dependable person. If you two hit it off together personally and you are prepared to make a few concessions, you can form an unshakable combination with a Taurus.

The Taurean is intelligent, but not intellectual. He or she is a very conservative, down-to-earth person. You will find you are able to discuss your ideas and problems in an adult way, and your partner's great good common sense and very practical approach will help keep your more imaginative schemes on the rails. When it comes to making expansive moves or undertaking any project that requires a bit of a risk, you will have to handle this person with kid gloves—and be ready to answer some very searching questions. Taureans hate change. But even more, they resist disturbing their resources. They don't care how much time and effort they put in, but when it comes to spending their own money or mortgaging their hard-earned assets, they will dig in their toes. And what big toes the zodiacal Bull has! It will take a sound case, as well as some very persuasive talk, to enlist your partner's cooperation.

The obstinacy of these people can be truly incredible. They are rather slow to grasp an idea. You may think at times you are talking to a brick wall for all the comprehension they show. But when they do catch on, and a proposition appeals to them, they really go for it. They put the objective up there on their mental horizon and head toward it with astounding dedication and one-eyed purposefulness. Once they've decided on a course, nothing will make them deviate from it. Virtually every consideration thereafter is referred to that particular aim. Their amazing stubbornness works the same way. If they decide they don't like your idea, that's the end of it. They won't come around. You'll have to find a way to deal with this extraordinary trait, which can often blind a Taurus person to his own obvious good. And, of course, in a partnership, it can spell stormy weather.

Similarly, you'll find your partner very fixed in his ways and not too keen to learn new ones. The mental effort seems to tire him. Perhaps it bores him. He likes to be physically and psychologically comfortable, undisturbed, at rest. By sticking to routine and going about their job in a methodical and habitual way, Taureans achieve a soothing peace and contentment. They are always in great danger of going into a waking sleep, of wrapping themselves in a cocoon of comfort and regulated doings and virtually dis-

appearing from the creative scene when needed.

You'll find it necessary to give your partner a shake now and again. How to do this without undermining the association will depend a lot on your personal relationship. But there is a way of reaching Taureans and getting them to sit up and take notice, and this is through their feelings. Their sensibilities are far more acutely developed than their intellectual processes. They feel things continuously that never reach the level of their conscious mind. It's a sort of inner self-sufficiency. If their feelings are not penetrated so that they feel emotionally involved with what's going on, Taureans remain unmoved and uncommitted. This is why others often regard them as mentally sluggish. It is also why Taurus children are slow to learn from an intellectually top-heavy education system. Your business partner is no exception.

Taureans are emotionally attached to everything they own, and this includes their loved ones. Any proposition they feel endangers these they will probably turn down. They are moved by art and beauty and are quick to respond to nature. A day out in the country can resensitize them emotionally, especially if they have sunk into the habit of town or city life, which actually doesn't suit them. Too much movement around them is upsetting and makes them heap more protective layers around themselves. Taurus is an earth Sign and these people are inclined to bury themselves digging for material treasures.

Your Taurus partner is honest and loyal. He won't touch you personally for a penny and will be most scrupulous in keeping accounts correct and up to date. But since he does enjoy the good life, his expenses may be very high for entertainment, clothes and especially food. He is very good at making influential friends and usually moves freely with a natural self-assurance among the affluent.

These men and women are kind and gentle. Just as they're not easy to get started on a project, they're not easy to provoke to anger. They are certainly one of the least temperamental Signs of the Zodiac. They exude patience and self-control. But there is a limit to their restraint. Under sufficient goading, they are capable of breaking out into an irrational fury that can be physically dangerous to the person it's directed at.

The negative type of Taurus is not as bad for business as some of the other unevolved characters—at least he'll grab every penny he can and stash it away with the ardor of the traditional miser. But you will probably find this partner's grasping and heavy materialistic ways just too much. This weaker type may be so downright lazy, stodgy, self-indulgent and stubborn about even the simplest matters that you'll willingly leave him down in the basement counting out his gold.

YOUR GEMINI BUSINESS PARTNER

At first meeting, the Gemini man or woman may seem the ideal person to co-opt as a business partner. But be careful, for all is not as it seems.

These people can adapt to just about any situation. They have the happy knack of being able to provide any conversationalist with just the audience he wants. If you're talking business, Gemini will show intense interest and an amazing grasp of what you're saying. His replies will be everything you want to hear. And when it comes to discussing a partnership, you couldn't wish for a more understanding mind, one that seems to see things exactly as you do. Well . . . that's now. In five minutes, it may all be different. Gemini will have changed his tune and be agreeing with a contrary point of view or indulging in the sort of tantrum that would appall any partner.

A partnership with this elusive, Mercurial Sign can work, but it is a iffy proposition. Much will depend on you. If you can handle this bright and clever chameleon character, you could have yourself a winner. *If!*

Geminis are changeable and unpredictable. They find it difficult to keep at one thing for long. But while they are engaged in something that appeals to them, they are exceedingly deft, competent and quite often just plain brilliant.

Your Gemini partner will be unbeatable when you are meeting or entertaining clients. Amiable, often suave, intensely communicative and possessing a sophisticated sense of humor, he or she can discuss practically any topic. Instinctively these people know just where to put the emphasis if the task is to convince a difficult client. They have a flair for making strangers feel like old friends and putting clients at their ease. Even the standoffish types soon wilt before the charm, wit and affability of these extremely pleasant and outgoing people.

Since Gemini is a mental creature—intellectual, logical, reasonable—you can count on this partner to come up with a constant succession of bright ideas. All you have to do is point him or her at a problem and, quick as a flash, you'll have an answer and (probably a good solution). A challenge that tests their ingenuity and mental powers is what these people enjoy most. So, if you are an individual who likes to deal with the bread-and-butter side of the business, there is no better type to leave the ideas and public relations to than Mr. or Ms. Gemini.

They are very perceptive and discerning people. If anyone is going to put anything over on anyone in a business deal, it will be your Gemini partner and not the other way around. Not that he'll double-cross you; he knows where his bread is buttered. If you're a good bet, he'll be keen and honest. But in the whiz-biz he's handy to have around because he can detect a lie or a fishy story with the first "ahem." Gemini is the zodiacal Sign of mental activity, the raw nerve ends that are pulsing with information waiting to be communicated. The brain processes are so highly strung here that the mind and body are extremely restless. Gemini people operate on a nervous energy that needs positive direction or it is likely to go haywire. They require a steadying hand, but certainly not a constraining one. You'll have to handle your Gemini partner literally without touching him. Since he understands completely an appeal to reason and logic, he'll be the first to appreciate your argument or to catch on to what you're driving at. He'll cooperate all the way and work very hard to please you. But you mustn't try to hem him in. He's the type who wants to come and go as he pleases. You'll never find him sitting beside you from nine till five pouring over accounts or writing tedious reports. He'll do those things—and about 50 others as well during a normal day. He's extremely good with figures and writing. But he's not going to take over one aspect of the partnership and make it his routine. He'll pull his weight, but the load must be in numerous small parcels.

You can call your Gemini partner up at any time of the night to solve a problem. Chances are, if he's had a hard day, he'll have been out "relaxing" with lots of friends or amid the bright lights. He has amazing energy and the more active he keeps, the less rest he seems to need. He recharges his batteries through continual human contact.

If there's any heavy manual work to do, you'd better not count on Gemini. These people's bodies are built for speed, not labor. Physical toil soon depletes their vitality and makes them unnaturally depressed and morose. They're very capable with their hands, though, and even if they haven't learned to type, they can knock out a presentable letter on the office machine in very short order.

Your partner will be a great asset as a go-between or middleman. He'll rap with the bank manager, tick a slow payer off (preferably over the telephone) with stinging expertise while giving you a puckish wink, make the most plausible excuses for late deliveries and do his darndest (with a great amount of success) to keep everyone happy from the biggest client down to the messenger boy.

Gemini men and women are not really combative. They prefer to circumvent trouble and tend to compromise or reason their way out of things without looking for the source of the trouble. Although able administrators, they are likely to upset their employees by treating them as numbers and being generally unsympathetic. Geminis can become irritable when things aren't going well and fuss around the office in an ineffectual way.

If your Gemini partner hasn't got much of a head for business, it's not filled with criticism or malice either. If you have an argument, he won't be the one to hold a grudge. Neither will he nag you or try to shout you down. He believes passionately in freedom of speech—so if you have the occasion to tell him a few home truths, he'll respect your right to do so.

By taking on a Gemini partner, you'll be doing him or her a good turn because these people need the stability that a sober and understanding partner can provide. Their numerous outstanding talents will be fair exchange.

Gemini's creative mind sometimes makes it difficult for him to stick to a decision once he's made one. No sooner does he make up his mind than he discerns other possibilities. He lives in his head and is constantly outdistancing himself. With an intellect that works like lightning and seldom stops, he is continually revising and dissecting his own thoughts. He's really in business more for the mental stimulus than for the profit.

The negative Gemini type should be written off as a partner because he's likely to be devious and a bit of a con man, living for the moment on what he can get away with rather than what he can earn. This person doesn't know his own mind from one minute to the next—is unreliable, lacks continuity and quite often is heartless.

YOUR CANCER BUSINESS PARTNER

The developed Cancer person has a natural flair for business. He or she understands finance, has a superb sense of timing and seems to find a constructive release for gnawing ambitions in the business world. But as a partner whom you must be able to work and cooperate with personally, Cancer is not ideal.

These men and women are rather moody. You may feel you don't know where you stand with your partner from one day to the next. Cancerians can be effusive and communicative, and then turn sullen or introverted. They can disturb the atmosphere of the office. If they have been offended at home or crossed in a love affair, they won't shake off their despondency quickly. Like the Crab, which is their zodiacal symbol, they are all soft and fleshy inside, nothing like what their crusty exterior suggests. They hurt easily and retreat very quickly into their shells.

Your Cancer partner will soon display his business acumen. He may not have a lot to say on occasions, but you would be well advised to be guided by him when he recommends a course. Cancerians do not, as a rule, make idle proposals or suggest moves they have not thought or "felt" through thoroughly. These people are highly intuitive and rely more on the communications of their inner feelings than on their intellectual processes. They often "know" things, though if you question them logically, their conclusions may seem unreasonably based.

You will discover that your business partner is extremely persistent. He does not expect to attain his objectives with the same speed that others do, but has an extraordinary tenacity that allows him to hang on even when everything seems to be crashing down around him. As long as he maintains faith in what he is doing, he will not give up. The Cancer business person is a master of the war of attrition. He prefers to concoct a good corrosive plan and to wear the opposition away with it, often without their even knowing a battle is on. He is a silent worker, a takeover specialist who bides his time, *quietly* buys up company stock until suddenly he's got control. He is not deterred by setbacks or rebuffs. Even when all his work has been negated, he carries on, building up again as though nothing had happened.

It is your Cancer partner's nature to remain in the background as much as he can. He doesn't like participating in overt action or making a scene about things. For you two to get along, you'll have to tolerate his rather old-fashioned methods, for he won't change. You might say: If he gets results, why should he? A good point. He's pretty fixed in his habits. And he has a great respect for precedent. He sincerely believes the "good old days" were preferable. If you're a modern whiz kid embued with novel ideas, don't expect him to share your enthusiasm. Even modern furniture goes against the Cancer grain. And as for discotheque decor—if this is your choice—you'll definitely need separate offices. His office will be relaxingly redolent of some past period, comfortable, homely and liberally sprinkled with relics, souvenirs and the like.

Despite their natural reserve, Cancer people are surprisingly ambitious. They need to succeed and enjoy being looked up to. Cancer will cooperate with you as a business partner as long as he feels you can help him get where he wants to go. Otherwise, he'll judge you as a person, and you'll soon know from his moods and responses whether he likes you or not.

The danger with a Cancer partner is that he is too quickly contented with his lot. If everything is going along okay, why rock the boat? Well, without some new activity, the boat may very well start rocking on its own. It will be in your interest to take the initiative, to see that business keeps moving. Cancer often needs a kick in the backside—if you can get him off it long enough to do it!

To mention a few other debits, the Cancer business partner can be indecisive. He's not the sort to take along to a client meeting where everyone is expecting mind-blowing ideas because he can be terribly ponderous and give the impression of missing the message when he's under fire. What he's actually doing is feeling his way, taking everything in and preparing to digest it afterward in the snug isolation of his office or home. He'll give you an answer tomorrow or the day after (and it will probably be a good one), but just now, he'd like to be the hell out of here! Cancers hate being pressured, can't stand the big heat or the spotlight. They are feeling creatures, remember, and feeling surfaces more slowly than bright ideas or palliatives. When your partner does make a suggestion, it won't be superficial. The trouble is that by the time he comes up with it, the client may have gone elsewhere.

Having a Cancer partner around makes some people feel a bit dusty because these people are usually preoccupied with the past. They clutter the office with bric-a-brac and pieces of junk. They never seem to throw anything away. They are romantic, idealistic, sentimental and easily hurt. They have exalted ideas about themselves and may lead you to believe their function in life is far more profound than the prosaic business role. If you offend your Crablike partner, he'll

scurry into his familiar crevice and may become morbid. When he doesn't get the attention he feels is due him, he will be restless, touchy and probably irritable.

Cancer is economical and cautious. He won't want to spend the partnership's money except perhaps on a library of good old books and a few tasteful antiques. You'll get along much better with him if you share his views on the essential aspects of life and are able to dish out some approval and praise from time to time. If he thinks you think well of him, he'll try much harder. Although he may say he wants to be let alone, he tends to flounder when left to his own devices. You should tactfully keep him on course.

Cancer is quite hospitable, especially when entertaining at home. He or she can often cook a meal that will impress the most fastidious client. These people have an excellent memory and a good sense of the dramatic, which help to make them quiet but pleasing hosts. They like to chat with amiable company and will move around to find it. Quite often they are very well informed. They would rather entertain clients at home than take them out.

Cancer tends to imagine slights where none exist or were intended. These people are thin-skinned characters. Once they've been affronted, like the elephant, they never forget. They're not malicious or vengeful, but they'll never let the offender get close to them again.

The negative Cancer person might be all right as a silent partner, but in an active capacity, his moods, indecisiveness, complaints and unprogressive attitude make him a crustacean delicacy you can well do without.

YOUR LEO BUSINESS PARTNER

You'd better face it from the word go: your Leo partner is not going to take a secondary role. He'll work alongside you, give your partnership all he's got, but at the first sign of any high-handedness on your part, there will be a showdown. He's a good partner, but if anyone is going to take over, it will be him. That's his attitude, anyway.

In Leo, you have the most complete and balanced representative of all the Signs. These men and women are big-hearted, strong willed and reliable. They possess tremendous energy for work—when they really get involved in a project, there is a danger that they will literally work themselves to death. They don't seem to realize their own limitations, physical or mental (perhaps they just refuse to acknowledge them). But if you can learn to handle Leo, you can point your partner in just about any direction and he or she will return you more than your money's worth.

The first move to guarantee a successful partnership is to concede Leo sufficient control from the start. You won't regret this, for while you're engaged in your side of the business, you can be sure his side is being handled capably and conscientiously. But see that he *stays* on his side of the fence. In Lionlike fashion, he's apt to leap across and start lording it over your territory. Leo is trustworthy and more inclined to choose the noble way than the surreptitious. As a rule, he is too proud and cognizant of his own dignity to stoop to mean and dishonest actions. But if he believes he is right and acting according to his rather idealistic principles, he will stick to his guns come what may and regardless of what others think of him.

Your partner is a good contact man and you would be wise to use him in this capacity. His personality is usually impressive, his disposition positive and optimistic. People tend to respect him. Personally, he's a bristly character and not so easy to get along with. But when he's turning on the charm—say, as the public relations part of the outfit—he's a likable and popular figure. Toward you, his partner, he will develop an infuriating I-told-you-so habit. Leo men and women imagine themselves to be oracles, and when things turn out the way they thought they would, they'll draw your attention to it every time. They are know-it-alls in many ways, who love to be right and want everyone to be aware of it. What you would let slide, they tend to make big news of. It's the petty side of their nature.

Leo is basically a showman. He is addicted to the big flourish, the exaggerated gesture. Nothing delights him more than the roar of admiration from an audience. To make this Lion purr and literally eat out of your hand, all you have to do is show him you appreciate his efforts and keep the compliments coming. He's a bit of a fool where flattery is concerned. But you should have no reason to be insincere in acknowledging his willingness and conscientiousness.

Your Leo partner is not so well suited to routine, detailed work. Being born leaders, Leo people need to feel they are directing matters. They can be very happy and productive in creative work that allows a broad scope. They are solid idea types who are often drawn to literary work or the entertainment industry. Their sense of the dramatic is highly developed. If allowed to go too far, though, they can be embarrassing show-offs and nauseating boasters.

In dealing with clients, you will find your Leo partner quickly wins their trust and confidence. Although his manner is dominant and forceful, his sincerity is seldom questioned. He hardly ever attempts a venture unless his heart is in it because it is essential for him to believe in what he is doing. He doesn't like selling spurious goods or ideas. Sometimes he identifies so completely with what he's doing that to criticize it is to criticize him. And Leos do not enjoy criticism. In fact, they can't believe it! They are so self-assured that when they hear a complaint about themselves, they dismiss it as a misunderstanding on the other party's part.

You'll find your partner excitable and quite irritable at times. He will flare up without warning and say exactly what he thinks. He will then go on as though nothing had happened. If you take umbrage, he is likely to be hurt, although, there is little risk he will hold a grudge. Leos consider malice and revenge beneath them, but they are capable of maintaining a clear-meaning aloof distance which is difficult to penetrate.

Leos are first-class organizers and enjoy taking a chance or two, though usually they will be pretty sure of their ground before risking money or reputation. Capable enough with finances, they may seem extravagant on occasions, especially when it comes to entertainment or amusement. Usually, though, they have a little put away for emergencies or know exactly how far their resources can be stretched. Worrying about the morning coffee money is not these people's style; they like to think and talk in big round figures.

Your Leo partner will want to expand the business as quickly as possible. He's not in it so much for the money as for the opportunities to direct and control. He may show some impatience, which can develop into recklessness if not wisely monitored. Being generous and fond of display and keeping up a good front, he may also overspend on unnecessary items at a time when budgetary restraint is necessary.

Leo's head for business in the art of wheeling and dealing is not so good. These men and women are not as shrewd in this department as they think—in fact, they are rather easy to see through. Their capacity is very much dependent on their interest. Only when their imagination is vividly excited do they go on to succeed. Half-measures and incomplete commitments leave them languid and yawning.

You'll discover your Leo partner is able to sum up or generalize a situation with a few bold verbal brushmarks. He or she can discard details that, although essential, may obscure the human interest and even the beauty of some arrangement. Leo can present a picture that is not only informative but also satisfying. Being somewhat mystically inclined because of the Sun's lordship of this Sign, Leo often catches sight of the wood and not the trees.

If your partner gets bossy or domineering, you'll just have to have it out. Generally speaking, the advanced Leo type is easy to reason with and will see the error of his or her ways. Don't try to lecture a Leo; handle him. If he disagrees with your observations, you can bet your life it is because he has examined them against his own experience. But if pride prevents him from acknowledging that you were correct, once he sees your point, he will endeavor to change.

In adversity, your Leo partner tends to become downcast. He can fight the drawn-out battle only so long. Here, a sympathetic and understanding partner with a few right words of encouragement can restore his heart. Otherwise, alone, he will use his last energy to force a fight to the death.

The undeveloped Leo is too loud-mouthed, brash, reckless, dogmatic and overweaning for any business partner to tolerate for long.

YOUR VIRGO BUSINESS PARTNER

Here is a steady, reliable partner who will work hard with great patience. You won't have to worry about this man or woman trying to steal the limelight or attempting to take over. Virgos are rather shy and retiring and would prefer that you take the public bows while they concentrate on getting the books and the business generally in better running order.

This doesn't mean your Virgo partner is antisocial. Far from it. These individuals like being with people they know, and enjoy meeting others in familiar circumstances. They are intensely chatty. It's only the unfamiliar face or situation that puts them off. They enjoy moving around and visiting old friends and clients. They are intelligent and good conversationalists.

You'll find your Virgo buddy extremely cooperative. He will make helpful suggestions and do much to improve the business in practical ways. But he will never try to force issues or impose his will. He does *not* want to lead. He is best suited for a secondary role, for implementing orders, for serving others. Don't worry about offending him when a menial job comes up and everyone else happens to have suddenly vanished; this is what he enjoys. You couldn't find a more willing or dependable person to look after the detail and routine side of the partnership. He'll absorb himself in this with obvious, though restrained, delight. He is painstaking and meticulous and will work all day—without looking over his shoulder to discover what, if anything, you are doing.

Virgo is a progressive thinker, but strictly in the practical sense. His ideas seldom rise to greatness. But once you get going together, you may wonder how you ever managed to cope before without his novel ideas. He has a knack for evolving specialized ways of handling work. If you've got a logjam in the office or *on* the factory floor, your Virgo partner is the one to solve it. He's what you might call a budding expert at all sorts of production-line work. What others may regard as tiresome detail or statistical euthanasia, he revels in, and will arrange facts with exacting discrimination into an acceptable and proper order. He strives for efficiency in himself and everything around him, and he is not afraid to get down on his hands and knees and scrub the floor, if that's the job that has to be done. Virgos are modest and unassuming, frequently humble. Their egos are not affronted by tasks others may regard as below their station.

This does not mean you can bully or ride roughshod over your Virgo partner. You wouldn't want to do this anyway to anyone so obliging and lacking in airs and graces. But if you try it, you will soon realize your partner is very sensitive about the dignity he or she retains, little though it may be.

Your partner's main fault is that he is extremely critical, quite unnecessarily so at times. His mind is always discriminating, observing things and actions that to him are out of order. If your behavior doesn't come up to scratch, he'll tell you so with outrageous frankness and frequently unerring accuracy. This is not a malicious or destructive trait in Virgo. It is an attempt to be helpful, to allow you (or anyone in his company) to distinguish in yourself what needs to be rectified. But it's a very vexing habit all the same. The gems that dart from the mouths of these people—especially when you are entertaining important clients—are likely to bring on an attack of apoplexy. But still, Virgo's criticisms do not offend as easily or as deeply as those that come from more egotistical types.

Your Virgo associate is very good with money. He or she is quite capable of taking over the financial side of the business and keeping accurate accounts, though you must prevent this partner from putting too much emphasis on economizing and constricting all ambitious projects. Virgo can drive a hard bargain and is just the person to handle final negotiations. He enjoys taking the mickey out of smart-alecky or more lofty minds in these deals. Being a rather cold and unsympathetic person, he can show great control and dispassion at these times and hold out to the last minute. But in normal business affairs, your Virgo partner is hampered by a lack of understanding of how irrational human beings can be. His approach is purely intellectual, so he is apt to miss the vital subtleties of response that distinguish normal business relations from horse trading.

Virgos are a bit straitlaced and narrow-minded, or appear to be. They *know* what is right and wrong, rather than feel it. It was all implanted in their heads in their early years, and their moral code is like a reference book that rarely undergoes any change. Actually, they are less concerned with morals than with propriety. Being unemotional themselves and often lacking the fire of enthusiasm, they don't have much experience of the passionate side of life.

They are perfectionists whose striving for this impossible ideal is reflected in every aspect of their nature. That's why Virgos are prepared to labor at just about any job. Someone's got to do it, to make a perfect world. It's an unconscious motivation, of course. And some less earthy and practical Signs may argue that these people should seek the perfection more in themselves. But thank goodness, Virgo is Virgo. He wants everything to be working in its right place, and he's prepared to do more than talk about it.

Your partner may be a terrible fusspot around the office: putting things back after they've been deliberately moved, tidying up his desk a dozen times a day, restacking the phone books almost before you've finished looking at them. He is never satisfied, complains ceaselessly and lives on a nervous energy that requires his constant application to some task or duty.

Despite his small number of faults, you'll find your Virgo partner a very easy person to get along with, personally. He doesn't pretend to be what he isn't and doesn't expect a great amount out of life in the way of material rewards. He is almost embarrassingly obliging at times and is prepared to try out just about any idea that is new and novel. You can't ask for much more than that! But if you are a Sagittarius, Pisces or Gemini, you may find him a bit too detailed, and almost facelessly dull.

The negative type of Virgo will seldom want to become a partner but will prefer to work as an employee, either among numerous other employees or in an inferior position where he can follow instructions precisely and be as persnickety and fault-finding as he wishes, knowing that he will not be endangering his job.

YOUR LIBRA BUSINESS PARTNER

In the Libra person, you have the ideal partner. Libra is the Sign of partnership, symbolized by the balanced Scales of justice. So you can't go far wrong taking Libra as an associate because his or her whole makeup is adapted to cooperation. Libras are the most composed, rational and temperate people of all the Signs.

Librans love to be successful. They will do all in their power to achieve the objectives mutually agreed upon. They enjoy the good things of life that usually accompany success and are very aware of the power of money to make the going easy. Your Libra associate will make all the sacrifices necessary in the early stages while the firm is being established. But when the money is there, you can expect your partner to spend his or her share of it—and perhaps a bit more. Librans enjoy luxury and would rather have a gracious home, an elegantly furnished office and a first-rate wardrobe than money in the bank.

Your business finances will be in competent hands as a rule if that side is left to your partner. Librans are extremely good with figures, and when responsible for budgeting, their judgment is usually remarkably accurate. But if the character is not developed, the individual's mathematical ability and love of what money can buy may lead to juggling the books. But one thing is certain: any embezzlement will be done well—and very neatly.

Librans are rather conservative and definitely not revolutionaries. Rarely enterprising themselves, they will support advanced and unusual schemes with shrewdness and ingenuity. You will find a Libra partner a great asset to a business connected with one of the learned professions, the arts or a beautifying pursuit. Objects these people handle or produce must be finely worked or contain materials of pleasing grain or texture. To give their best, they require clean, harmonious and, if possible, beautiful surroundings. This may sound a bit much, but in vulgar or squalid conditions, Libra quickly wilts and becomes unhappy and nervous. He is then likely to retreat inside himself and become moody and unproductive. It is not unusual for a Libra person forced to work in ugly or uncongenial surroundings to become physically ill. Even if your partner is not consciously aware of this propensity, it will be in the business's interest to see that he or she is not forced to perform in these conditions by you or by the needs of a client.

Libra is a charming person to be associated with. He will never intrude or try to dominate you. He will certainly influence you in the direction he feels you should take—at this he is really brilliant—but it will not be by pushing or arguing. Libra uses gentle and subtle persuasion. His tactic is to sow the seed of an idea in your mind and then quietly nurture it with suggestion. By the time you implement it, you will believe it was your own creation. Libra will just smile knowling to himself and never mention it again.

Librans are difficult people to fight or to pin down. They are suave, immensely tactful and equipped with every attribute to please. They will not dispute with you on your own ground. They tend to regard their partners as a means of gaining their own ends. They genuinely want their partners to be content, for to wish otherwise would be to go against themselves. They know their destiny lies in partnership, that this is their psychological niche. And they won't leave you—unless they find a better partner.

Libra men and women believe passionately in freedom and equality. They demand these qualities for themselves and insist on them for others. This is one area where you may find your partner surprisingly singly aggressive and ready for open conflict, if necessary. He is a champion of the underdog and may put up a vehement defense for any employee he feels is being unfairly treated by the firm or his co-workers.

But as a rule, your Libra partner will do his best to avoid an argument or any unpleasantness. He is an excellent person to entertain clients, the essence of diplomacy and genteel hosting. He speaks and writes in a pleasing way and is one of the most plausible types you will ever meet. Underneath his poise and composure is a very active mind. He is highly intellectual and analytical and is gifted at understanding a problem very quickly. Since Librans are not emotional, they seldom allow their feelings to influence their judgments. Therefore, in business, they have the advantage of being able to take a dispassionate view of a situation. You will find your associate's advice extremely helpful and objective, especially when passions are aroused.

Your Libra partner will never upstage you. He will always see that you receive your rightful recognition and respect, even when you are absent. Because he does not want to be associated with anyone about whom others might harbor a bad opinion, while he remains your associate, he will never try to undercut your confidence or dispute your competence. He will aim to create an aura of agreement and harmony around the partnership. If he sees faults—which he will—and is unable to rectify them, he will ignore them and proceed as though they didn't exist.

One of the problems with Librans is that they are often indecisive. They are at their best when responding rather than initiating. In the course of trying to reach a decision, they are inclined to see so many alternatives that the moment for action passes. This can be exasperating to you as a partner. Another thing you have to be alert for is the tendency of the Libran to drift. He loses direction quickly by relating to other events going on around him and needs to be gently pulled back on course. Librans are fairly curious-minded; they are very content to be eternal sightseers quietly absorbing the changing scene without paying much attention to where they are going. Being smooth talkers, the weaker types are likely to camouflage their innate lack of purpose with a convincing spiel that contains nothing more than diplomatic platitudes, admirable intentions and questionable "facts."

Librans also tend to sit on the fence in discussions, bending this way and that according to the direction in which the wind of opinion seems to be blowing. They will support contending views in the space of a few minutes, as though the object is to restore harmony rather than to batter out a workable solution. Their basic urge is to please everyone at the same time!

Their unwillingness to say "no" often gives the impression that they are easily led. They *can* be manipulated by difficult employees, who may take advantage of the Libran preference for using persuasion rather than disciplinary action. In a partnership, however, this agreeable and amiable characteristic has obvious advantages.

A negative type of Libra partner is still likely to be a better bet than some other Signs, even though he or she will be indecisive, changeable, frivolous and lazy. If you can balance these shortcomings, much may come of the association.

YOUR SCORPIO BUSINESS PARTNER

Forget Scorpio as a business partner. Well . . . almost. These people do have some tremendous qualities such as unlimited patience, superhuman endurance and a passionate drive to get at the truth. But the scalding nature of their temperament makes them almost unthinkable candidates for partnership. Fortunately, the Scorpio character is rarely met in its pure state; the type is normally modified by the positions of the other planets in the horoscope. It's fair to say that *any* modification of this extreme Sign has to be an improvement. Perhaps the partner you have in mind is a suitably toned-down version. (You can ascertain this from the Yellow Tables found in the Scorpio book of *AstroAnalysis*.)

The first thing that strikes you about Scorpio men and women is their penetrative intelligence. They go straight to the heart of the matter with an economy of words and astonishing accuracy. You won't even get around to a discussion with your prospective Scorpio partner if he doesn't think you're very bright. Unless, of course, he has an ulterior motive. In which case, he will mentally note all your weak spots with terrifying insight, butter you up and prepare to dispose of you to his advantage.

But let us say he sees the partnership as desirable and you as a reasonably acceptable representative of the human race. He will want to get down to business immediately and be told exactly what preparations have been made, the objectives and the market potential. Here is where you'll need to have done your homework, for Scorpio has an uncanny gift of assessing the chances of success and failure for an enterprise. He can look years ahead and see future developments, anticipate trends. And he'll analyze your scheme on the spot with computerlike precision—and with about the same type of emotional involvement. If the plan is any good, he'll probably appreciate the possibilities better than you—at least the long-term ones. This, you must admit, makes Scorpio an exceptionally handy business partner.

Next, you'll be impressed by Scorpio's thoroughness. This guy or lady never goes off half-cocked. Everything is worked out, analyzed, schemed beforehand—particularly the strengths and weaknesses of the personalities involved. The shrewdness of the Scorpio mind is almost inconceivable. It quite easily degenerates into the Machiavellian doctrine that any means, however unscrupulous, may be justifiably employed to achieve a desired end. This tendency can be carried to diabolical lengths. But let's assume your partner is a modified type. To outwit your rivals, you couldn't have the assistance of a more fertiley cunning and relentless mind.

Your Scorpio partner's incredible power of persistence may even weary you. He never, ever gives up. Whereas the Taurus partner will perservere with great plodding determination, your Scorpio buddy will keep up such a high-pitched scream of pressure that the opposition will usually give up, give in, compromise or surrender in some way just to escape the perpetual nerve-pinching pain. Scorpio himself is quite unaffected by the exertion and tension involved in maintaining such pressure. He can keep it up for years. And he hasn't got a weak stomach, either, if you're in the rackets and it comes to a bit of physical torture. He has such a massive and enduring constitutional strength that to win he will literally press on to the point of his own destruction—which is normally far beyond any other individual's. Out of *all* this emerges Scorpio's reputation for dependability. He doesn't accept challenges lightly; he dismisses fools; he manipulates and struggles to the death. Such a temperament, if nothing else, has to be dependable.

Well, that's about it for the pluses.

On the debit side, Scorpios are exceedingly obstinate. Their amazing willpower makes them unbending psychological beings. They keep their attitudes intact in separate watertight compartments so there is no overlapping. Scorpio people know exactly what is in each department of their mind, but have little idea of what they add up to as a whole. If they did, they would be more tolerant, more forgiving, more failing, more human. As it is, they respond from fixed opinions. One opinion may oppose another, but since the mind can have only one conscious thought at a time, no serious conflict arises. Scorpios will defend their conflicting views with implacable severity, which is aimed at destroying an antagonist rather than considering the logic of the argument. If you, as Scorpio's partner, dare to point out his inconsistency, he will erupt into a vituperative rage—and perhaps create another secret, seething department in his mind with your name written on it!

Scorpios can be cruel and vengeful enemeis. And yet, by the strange quirks of opposites that distinguish this Sign, they are capable of devoting themselves with the same tireless, repressed passion to a loved one, work or a cause. You take a lottery ticket when you select Scorpio—the odds are against you, but someone wins somewhere every draw.

Scorpio will expect you to work as hard as he does. If you—or members of your staff—try to keep pace with him or emulate him, you will probably endanger your health.

He is no diplomat. He believes in going directly to the point. He'll tell you, or perhaps even your top client, a raw-boned home truth without the slightest regard for personal feelings. He is contemptuous of displays of emotion and expects everyone to be as dispassionate as he is on the surface. Inside he twists and creaks with personal dissatisfaction and repressed desire. He wants desperately to rise above himself, but is not sure how to do this except by suppressing one or more of his emotions.

Scorpio finds it difficult to adapt to new conditions. Once you've fixed your mutual aims, he'll want to go on, come what may. He's the old-fashioned type who'd rather let his business disintegrate under him than change his methods. You may wish to take advantage of a profitable year and enjoy an extra holiday—but not Scorpio. His mind will be fixed on the agreed future objective; there must be not letup until it is achieved. If he feels his position may be weakened by his absence, he won't take a holiday, for years if necessary. And if he's dying, he'll still come to the office and put in a full day's work.

Your partner loves power. It is this desire that drives him. His thirst for it is unquenchable. He is a budding tyrant with a stormtrooper's baton in his kit bag. His moral consciousness has no outside reference. His own opinion is what is right. Sometimes the Sign produces the ennobled human being; in that case, this doctrine works wonderfully. But in the lesser Scorpio mortal, it is his own selfish purposes that count. Financially, this may lead to fiddling and recklessness on a ruinous scale. Although your partner possesses great personal magnetism, he is unlikely to be a favorite among your clientele. He is a type who attracts or repels people violently—a dubious credential for any business partner.

YOUR SAGITTARIUS BUSINESS PARTNER

Sagittarius has much to offer as a business partner. If you manage to link up with one of the highly developed types, you've really got it made. These people have incredible breadth of vision, which they can apply in practical ways. They are highly intelligent, extremely active and temperamentally equipped to handle the largest business enterprises. The bigger the scheme, the better Sagittarius performs.

Needless to say, your Sagittarius partner is not going to take to a partnership that involves him in a lot of petty detail or small transactions and fiddling correspondence. He doesn't get the decimal point easily. He's definitely no clerk.

Sagittarians are marvelously adaptable. They can succeed solo or in double harness. They like people and people take to them, though they do not form deep attachments. To a Sagittarius, buddies are to talk to and share adventures with, not feelings. You, as his partner, will enjoy his cheery, outgoing sociability, though you may never feel really close to him. He's just not built that way. He literally loves the whole wide world and longs to serve it in his way. He doesn't find the individual such a reliable proposition. Your Sagittarius partner will always be looking ahead, beyond the current scene that occupies and captivates most people.

He is an inordinately lucky person—which is lucky for you. You will be surprised at how often he lands on his feet when the mat is pulled from under him. This probably accounts for his unbounded optimism. Even when he loses out, he immediately looks to the future with the same, almost naive expectation of success as before. As a consequence, he is inclined to take too many chances—and for stakes that are far too big for comfort. He needs a wise, restraining hand. Wise, because he won't tolerate being ordered about. But he will submit to tactful treatment and listen to advice. However, when the temptation to take a chance is high, you won't want to leave him to his own devices for too long.

In normal financial business matters, the Sagittarian judgment is most reliable. You will find your partner's approach impersonal and balanced because he is swift to discern the advantages and disadvantages of a situation. It is when he gets the feel of personal adventure—often the opportunity to be a rover or to experience new situations—that he seems to become emotionally involved and lose his perspective. As a result, your Sagittarius partner is likely to enjoy a plunge on the horses or a session at the gambling tables. Once the gambling bug bites him, he is very difficult to reason with—until either he loses disastrously or has lived it up with his winnings. He'll squander all his ready cash on a night out because money doesn't mean that much to him. Sagittarius, in fact, is the original big spender. Easy come, easy go is his attitude. The ruler of his Sign is Jupiter, the jovial and luckiest planet of them all. So your partner's faith and confidence in his continuing good fortune are not hard to understand.

Novel and way-out business ventures have an odd attraction for him. Although definitely no fool, he frequently gets mixed up with people whose ideas normally would not be considered a safe business bet. For instance, he might decide with great enthusiasm to back an invention that no one really wants. It is the *idea* that impresses him rather its practical uses. He's often a sucker for fly-by-night projects and may be left holding the baby (with you as assistant nursemaid). But if the preliminaries drag on, he'll lose interest very quickly and turn his attention to another new gimmick. These distractions are usually secondary to the mainstream of business activity, so it's not all that bad.

Naturally, some of the people Sagittarius attracts are not sterling characters. Since he is not a suspicious or critical person, he is likely to be deceived. Reputations can be damaged through such associations and it could be in your interests to keep an eye on this aspect of the partnership.

Sagittarius is extremely energetic. He works hard, plays hard and lives hard. You will need tons of vitality to keep up with him. He can scatter his energies, running from project to project and not getting a great amount done in any particular area. But he is a colorful and likable character and his sense of the dramatic gives him style. He usually possesses a tremendous sense of fun and humor, and in any social situation, you'll find him surrounded by an appreciative audience. You can leave the entertaining to him any time and be sure he'll keep your guests happy and amused. He is an expansive, generous and innovative host.

Your partner will be a valuable asset at business conferences. He is skilled at getting a point across, enjoys a verbal dual and has a flair of repartee. He is also clever at cross-examination. With a few words he can expose the merits or demerits of a proposition. His intuition is quite extraordinary at times. He senses weak spots in his antagonists immediately. In an undeveloped Sagittarius, this ability expresses itself as a bluntness that can be offensive. The natural frankness of the type is refreshing, but it does require a modifying emotional concern for other people's feelings.

In business transactions, impatience is likely to force your Sagittarius partner to jump the gun. He often finds it difficult to wait while necessary preliminaries are concluded and his hastiness may ruin delicate negotiations. His confidence in his own ability to be tactful—which is generally warranted—can convince him he is persuading others when he is not. A negative response the next day is apt to prove the point occasionally.

Promises, promises . . . this is another Sagittarian fault that may reveal itself quite early in your association. Your partner, in his enthusiasm, often promises results that are far beyond his capabilities or the potential of the venture. Explaining to disappointed clients or trying to match promises with performance can be a frustrating and annoying business.

Despite his shortcomings, which are not all that important to a successful partnership, Sagittarius will not try to throw his share of the responsibilities back onto you. He will handle his side of the business energetically and efficiently. He is not a fusser. He is an understanding person and will amaze you on occasions with the soundness and sagacity of his counsel.

From a health point of view, you should know it is of the utmost importance for your partner to get enough exercise. Although he is constantly on the move, he usually requires a sport or regular exercise to keep his body toned up and his liver in good order.

The undeveloped Sagittarius will be restless, talkative and highly imaginative. The freedom he insists on may be to do as he wishes. He is likely to be boisterous and an out-and-out gambler.

YOUR CAPRICORN BUSINESS PARTNER

There are two distinct types of Capricorn people, whose zodiacal symbol is the Goat. One type is contented to be tethered to a stick in the ground, provide domestic milk with machinelike regularity and wander around in circles thinking he's going places. The other is a self-centered and deliberate mountain Goat who might not stray too far from his favorite peak, but at least is always climbing toward the summit.

A business partner with the imagination and aspirations of the Capricorn milk machine is guaranteed to sour the association in no time, but the active mountain Goat variety is a different proposition.

The mature Capricorn person is a mighty solid type. He's honest, practical, persevering, cautious and probably has a better grasp of business and the commercial setup in general than any other Sign in the Zodiac. Sagittarius might be exceptional in breadth of vision, but Capricorn has the capacity to administer and understand a worldwide conglomerate while knowing essentially what is going on in any department!

His ability to grasp the practical intricacies of a mammoth business operation is incomparable. Now, coming down from those giddy heights to your partnership, there are bound to be some problems. For a start, your Capricorn associate will want to have the last word. A departmentalized mind capable of exercising centralized control on a huge scale is going to insist on a good deal of authority for itself. And chances are, a severe or rigid discipline will be required to maintain it.

Capricorn is extremely conservative and patient. Although one of the most ambitious types of the Zodiac, he or she doesn't believe in new-fangled methods of getting to the top. Capricorn's faith is in what has been tried and proven in the past. Why experiment? The old way is safe and sure. And if you're prepared to work hard enough and long enough, you'll make it, says Capricorn.

Well, he'll certainly work hard with unremitting dedication—and he'll expect you to do the same, the old slave driver. If you're looking for plaudits because you've put in 12 hours straight, forget it. That sort of exertion is routine to Mr. or Ms. Capricorn. These people might not believe in shortcut tactics, but they do think time is precious, and once they have begun a task, they won't allow one minute to be wasted. Yet to get Capricorn started can be a job in itself. He's inclined to circle and hover, sizing up the situation carefully to protect himself from surprises.

Capricorn prefers steady advancement to spectacular gains. He's suspicious of anything that doesn't follow a pattern. Actually, he is uneasy until he settles into a routine, so the first thing you'll find him doing is reducing the work to familiar forms, methods, procedures and routines—an obsession of his you might be tempted to describe as organized drudgery or mind-pinching tedium. Still, someone's got to attend to details and ensure accuracy, so you could be onto a good thing with a Capricorn partner.

You'll need to be the public relations part of the outfit, though. This guy or lady takes life too seriously to put much store in the sociable side of business. Pleasure, as most other people know it, is not that important to the Goat perched on a rugged outcrop—work is the thing. With Capricorn's single-track nature, there's not much chance of producing stereo sounds out of this partnership unless you can provide the stylus. You'll probably need to get out and about regularly, anyway, as relief from this stern and uncompromising influence.

Whether or not a partnership with Capricorn works out depends on your personal attitude. Your associate is really not built for double harness, as you've no doubt gathered. He's got enormous business sense, but his disposition is austere and intense, and all the business capability in the world doesn't add up to much if two people can't hit it off together as partners.

Capricorn people won't waste pennies. But they might be a bit foolish with the dollars. They know exactly how much is left in the morning coffee tin. If your partner is in charge of accounts, there'll be no errors. These men and women are meticulous in everything they do. They would rather stick to the letter of the law than take a chance on the spirit. They accept the limitations of their environment—their task, as they see it, is to do the best they can with what's at their disposal. Besides, it's less trouble that way . . . and a darn sight less risky. Capricorns like to be looked up to, regarded as dependable, steady and persevering. Others may want to be remembered for more human qualities, but not these people. Needless to say, they take to responsibility like a duck to water. Extra business burdens or problems never daunt them. They just knuckle down, and with amazing methodical grace, proceed step by step toward the conclusion they know lies at the end of all relentless effort. They don't conceptualize the end; they concentrate on the means.

Old Capricorn's only fear is loss of security, psychological or material. He finds comforting reassurance in the respect that others show him. He will never commit an act that might bring him into public disrepute if it can be helped. Not being a particularly warm person himself, he tends to underestimate the potency of feelings in others and their effect on hitherto fixed situations. He is thrown off balance by sudden changes, becomes unsure of himself, edgy, until he can settle down again into routine. He works and saves for the future. The strain of modern living never gets him down, no matter how hard it presses him. He doesn't develop "nerves." He often displays a surprising sense of humor that allows him to laugh at himself, even in company. You mustn't, but he can! It's a fair enough concession for an otherwise painfully self-conscious type of person.

Your partner is rarely generous. Fair, but not spontaneous. In dealing with employees, he will pay them exactly what has been agreed to—and they can forget about bonuses. But he will sometimes take up a fight on behalf of someone he feels has a rightful grievance. Time and effort he will give unsparingly, but money and resources he likes to keep for himself and his dependants.

With a Capricorn partner, most of the good ideas and original thinking will have to come from you because he is too conventional and careful to be inventive or creative. But he is highly resourceful and adroit when it comes to materialistic dealings. Although he may be unable to visualize an end in itself because he is basically a self-centered individual, he knows every moment precisely where he is and the direction in which he is heading. That direction is *always* toward his own best interests. As long as your own interests lie in the same quarter, you should prosper as a partnership. But remember, like the mountain Goat, he really prefers to climb alone—the pickings might be too sparse for two.

With only a little bit more hardening, a Capricorn partner can be dogmatic, tyrannical, mean, hard—and just about impossible for a normal human being to stay teamed up with.

YOUR AQUARIUS BUSINESS PARTNER

Aquarius people make good partners. Their calm and moderate ways help balance out just about any other zodiacal type. This partnership should be able to build a reputation for solid and sensible performance. But mind you, Aquarius is no ball of fire. He's not very good in a fight or in trying to cope with emergencies. He comes into his own *after* the battle, healing the rifts and handling everyday affairs with extraordinarily good common sense and practical wisdom. If you can handle the crises—and for a business to succeed there can't be too many of these—your Aquarius partner will look after the rest, admirably.

Aquarians are not troublemakers. Dissension of any kind disturbs them. They won't quarrel and they have a natural discretion that steers them around awkward situations. Good-natured, friendly types, they would rather talk things over in a calm and civilized way than pommel you with their point of view.

It is a fact that the Water-Bearer doesn't usually possess any special flair for business. (Perhaps that's oil in his jug and he's too busy pouring it over troubled waters.) But each of his characteristics can be useful to a partnership in one way or another, more so than most of the other Signs. The Aquarian is a sort of composite man or woman, containing a little bit of good from all the other types. Here, you'll have to consider the Compatibility Guide (page 91) because some Signs find Aquarius just a little too much of a good thing to be in harness with.

His or her mind is not that quick in action. But it is very broad in its attitudes, tolerant and receptive. And the Aquarian power to receive flashes of inspiration about new trends and desirable improvements is quite remarkable. Aquarius has a lot of the gentleness of Libra and the vision of Sagittarius, and is progressive in a very special way. This man or woman will never try to upset the established order to introduce new ideas. Aquarius would rather put them before you—or society—and allow you to judge their merits for yourself. This is an evolutionary rather than a revolutionary character. Generally, the Water-Bearer's insights are so obviously beneficial that they are quickly adopted into the system, and this is a quality you will find particularly helpful in your Aquarius partner. If you pay attention to his or her suggestions, your business should prosper along modern and efficient lines.

With money, your buddy is completely trustworthy. In a personal sense, Aquarius can be extravagant, but you won't find him spending beyond his means and dipping into the till for the deficit. He's not so interested in accumulating money, although he will work diligently enough to earn it. He won't appreciate penny-pinching methods where the business is concerned; he'll want it to advance, and he's realistic enough to know that you must keep up a presentable image and spend money to make money. If he doesn't approve of some expenditure, you can bet your life he's had a brainstorm about where the money can be used to greater advantage. It will pay you to listen to him.

Don't be put off by a certain coldness in your partner's makeup. Aquarians are not excitable or emotive, but they are tremendously optimistic—to the extent that they will let things slide. On occasions, Aquarians will be greatly enthused and determined to show what they can do. But if you're looking for dash and bubbling fervor, you're not going to get it here. There are few or no extremes in the Water-Bearer's nature. Basically, he or she is built for bigger things than our usual daily aspirations allow. (This is something we will all come to appreciate now that the world has entered the 2000-year Aquarian Age.) Aquarians are intellectual beings, equipped to deal with the problems of humanity rather than with those of the individual. Although they have intense inner feelings, they rarely show them in individual cases. These people are not sentimentalists, though they are very kind and sincere. Just don't expect emotionalism.

Your Aquarius partner won't make any special demands on you. He will respect your independence as a person and expect you to return the consideration. One thing you will find pleasing is his habit of anticipating the likes and dislikes of people he comes into contact with. This is a great asset in a partnership when it comes to close dealings with clients.

There are many people who admire the Aquarius trait of maintaining an impassive front in all situations. This apparent unflappability often masks tumultuous feelings. Aquarius is the Sign of friends, so your partner's congenial and amiable nature will attract a wide variety of acquaintances. His conversation is usually on a fairly high plane. He won't gossip about you or your friends or break any confidences. But don't expect him to show any fanatical zeal either when the partnership agrees to implement one of your really bright ideas. If he goes along with it, you can be certain it makes good sense. That may have to be enough.

You'll find your Aquarius buddy is quite conventional in moral outlook. His ideas of freedom and progress seldom include any watering down of the golden rules. He enjoys traveling and working and living in new surroundings, but he is upset and confused by sudden changes, which seem to be forced on him more often than on most other Signs.

To get the best out of your partner, you must understand he is an idealist. Any suggestion of crooked dealings or exploitation of others will meet with his instant disapproval. He won't compromise with his conscience. In fact, the more your business leans toward some form of acceptable public service or worthwhile objectives in humanitarian terms, the more you will appreciate the talents he has to offer.

Aquarians are splendid mediators and can be counted on to mend differences and alleviate friction. They have a sensible word for everyone. Of course, we don't always want the proper advice but rather some form of partisanship—and Aquarius is a bit too advanced intellectually to play that emotional game. So, nice placid person that your partner is, you might find him at times too adaptable and lacking in definite response.

He may also seem a bit hesitant or uncertain if you are pushing him for a decision. He's got a mind that understands a situation from all angles, and that sort of comprehension often cancels out the desire to act.

You may never be able to get a decision out of the backward-type Aquarius. His or her life is lived on the premise that if you don't do anything, you can't possibly make a mistake—which is probably the biggest mistake of all!

YOUR PISCES BUSINESS PARTNER

Pisces people can make excellent partners, but only if you are lucky—or astute—enough to select one of the developed types. Any lesser Fish will slip through your fingers every time you try to catch him or pin him down. No Sign is more talented, pleasing and sympathetic. And none is more infuriatingly indecisive, vague and impressionable.

Assuming your partner is at the right end of the yardstick, you have here a person with extraordinary insight and intuition. He or she has an incredible knack for making the right decision at exactly the right time. But you're not going to get the answers when *you* want them because the Pisces doesn't work that way. In fact, when pressured, he tends to go to pieces. His method is to wait, his patience when working "his way" is unequaled. To his business associates, what he is doing may seem like ineffectual muddling,

It has been said that the Pisces makes a better sleeping partner than an active one. This is largely because in the hustle and bustle of the commercial system, the Pisces' insouciance seems out of place. In business, when we're worried or intense, we usually expect our associates to show similar concern. Pisces won't. Although no mean actor when he wants to be, he is incapable of this basic betrayal of his own inner workings. His attitude has been called "escapism," among other uncomplimentary things, but it's really a matter of faith in himself and proper timing. If you understand and appreciate this trait in your partner, you will be able to make a success of your association.

Not that Pisces is not a worrier. He very definitely is whenever things are not going the way *he* thinks they should. This may not coincide with your view of things, so you will need to remember that though Pisces works at a different level, he is just as intent as you are on advancing your mutual interests. Once you fully understand this, you'll be able to appreciate this extremely sensitive, perceptive and creative character.

The partnership finances, though, would be better left in other hands. Pisces is a bit of a contradiction when it comes to handling money. He is generous but careless, saving but extravagant. He spends without getting a great deal of value for the money. He is also a sucker for a hard-luck story. His sympathetic nature makes him dig into his pocket to help—without considering the sacrifices it might mean for others, such as his dependants or partners. It's just too risky to allow Pisces to handle partnership funds, though he wouldn't deliberately rob you of a single cent and is extremely good at managing when funds are short because he can make the pennies go a long way. But anything he manages to save is likely to be dissipated in one impulsive action. In good times, he is a profuse and indiscriminate spender.

Your Pisces partner is a very kind and trusting person. At the same time, he doesn't miss much. So, he is a superb judge of character, yet extremely tolerant and forgiving of the failings of human nature. He will know all your shortcomings, and yet won't nag you about them or even bother to mention inconsistencies others would make an issue of. He won't try to overshadow or dominate you. He is retiring, often shy, and prefers to work in the background. He has a way of literally dreaming up schemes and manipulating people and events to make his dreams come true! Linked with a harmoniously balanced and active partner, he can be an acceptable power behind the throne.

If he accepts you as his business partner, he will never blame you for what goes wrong and will stand by you through thick and thin. Neither will he allow others to run you down in his presence. If you are active and dynamic honestly, he will help make your work easier and more effective, even though it inconveniences him.

The Fish is essentially lazy and doesn't relate easily to the world of physical action. It would rather drift with the tide and gets its kicks from an emotional dream world of its own making. But once it senses a really stimulating enterprise—say, your exciting new partnership—it will swim against the current toward the objectives with great resourcefulness and determination. The secret, of course, is that Pisces has to be excited by a project to be induced to start swimming; only then can he show his special skills and talents. He tends to favor artistic pursuits and the professions, especially writing and publishing.

Your partner will be popular with the business's employees. He may be too indulgent of them at times, for he has a deep feeling for people in an inferior position, even though they may not be deprived or exploited in any way. He will often give in to them when a sterner course is indicated. However, through his caring, he attracts a loyalty that often produces better work results and less labor dissension.

Pisces enjoys the good life and sometimes gets carried away with the glamour of a situation, losing sight of the realties. His judgment may be more unreliable when he is confronted with an opportunity for self-indulgence. Pisces feels that if he must live in this world, then he ought to have the best of it—physical comfort, respect, admiration and harmonious surroundings.

Although naturally reserved, Pisces are social creatures who enjoy the passing parade rather than lead it. In the company of familiar people whom they like, they often discard their inhibitions temporarily to reveal the fun-loving and extroverted person underneath. When your partner attends a business conference or lunch, you'd better check that he doesn't leave his briefcase or papers behind; since he's usually thinking (you might say benignly scheming) and is a bit absentminded. His impressionable nature is very easily disturbed by the presence of rigid and uncompromising personalities. He can't stand the exacting, standover type, who, in turn, is irritated by his vagueness and tries to pin him down. He can be surprisingly obstinate, and if forced to work in uncongenial surroundings or with incompatible people, will become moody and manage to make everyone aware of his unhappiness.

The Fish is capable of reaching unfathomable depths of creative understanding, but is rather badly equipped to withstand pressure. A partnership that corrects this serious imbalance can be a winner!

COMPATIBILITY

GUIDE

ARIES	*RAM*	**March 21 – April 20**
TAURUS	*BULL*	**April 21 – May 20**
GEMINI	*TWINS*	**May 21 – June 20**
CANCER	*CRAB*	**June 21 – July 20**
LEO	*LION*	**July 21 – August 21**
VIRGO	*VIRGIN*	**August 22 — September 22**
LIBRA	*SCALES*	**September 23 – October 22**
SCORPIO	*SCORPION*	**October 23 – November 22**
SAGITTARIUS	*ARCHER*	**November 23 – December 20**
CAPRICORN	*GOAT*	**December 21 – January 19**
AQUARIUS	*WATER-BEARER*	**January 20 – February 18**
PISCES	*FISHES*	**February 19 – March 20**

ARIES

Most Compatible Signs: *Leo* and *Sagittarius*.
Next Best: *Taurus, Gemini, Pisces* and *Aquarius*.
Doubtful: *Cancer*—too moody and easily hurt.
Libra—too indecisive and cautious.
Capricorn—unimaginative and too conservative.
Neutral: *Virgo* and *Scorpio*.

TAURUS

Most Compatible Signs: *Virgo* and *Capricorn*.
Next Best: *Gemini, Cancer, Pisces* and *Aries*.
Doubtful: *Aquarius*—too fond of change.
Leo—too dominating, conceited.
Scorpio—too scheming, subtle.
Neutral: *Libra* and *Sagittarius*.

GEMINI

Most Compatible Signs: *Libra* and *Aquarius*.
Next Best: *Cancer, Leo, Aries* and *Taurus*.
Doubtful: *Virgo*—fusspot, too exacting.
             Sagittarius—too restless, like yourself.
             Pisces—too doomy, introspective.
Neutral: *Scorpio* and *Capricorn*.

CANCER

Most Compatible Signs: *Scorpio* and *Pisces*.
Next Best: *Leo, Virgo, Taurus* and *Gemini*.
Doubtful: *Aries*—blunt, bruising.
             Libra—frivolous.
             Capricorn—too earthy.
Neutral: *Sagittarius* and *Aquarius*.

LEO

Most Compatible Signs: *Sagittarius* and *Aries*.
Next Best: *Virgo, Libra, Gemini* and *Cancer*.
Doubtful: *Scorpio*—too calculating.
             Aquarius—airy-fairy, unresponsive.
             Taurus—obstinate, sluggish.
Neutral: *Pisces* and *Capricorn*.

VIRGO

Most Compatible Signs: *Capricorn* and *Taurus*.
Next Best: *Libra, Scorpio, Leo* and *Cancer*.
Doubtful: *Sagittarius*—irresponsible.
             Pisces—unreachable, moody.
             Gemini—unreliable, unsettling.
Neutral: *Aquarius* and *Aries*.

LIBRA

Most Compatible Signs: *Aquarius* and *Gemini*.
Next Best: *Scorpio, Sagittarius, Leo* and *Virgo*.
Doubtful: *Aries*—aggressive, brusque.
             Capricorn—pedestrian, dull.
             Cancer—smothering.
Neutral: *Pisces* and *Taurus*.

Compatible

Gemini - May 22 - June 21

Capricorn - Dec. 23 - Jan. 20

Capricorn - Some
       Sept. 24 - Oct 23

Libra - early to middle. last Sept, early Oct.
       Nov. 23. Dec. 22

Sag. - honest, generous, funny loving

Scorpio - Some Oct 24 - Nov 22

✓ Sun in Sagittarius (mom)

✓ Moon in Capricorn

✓ Ascending Sign Cancer

  Pluto in Leo

  Neptune in Libra ⎤ in 2nd house

  Mercury in Virgo

✓ Venus in Virgo   Sq. Saturn?

  Mars in Taurus

  Jupiter in Libra?

✓ Saturn in Gemini

✓ Uranus in Gemini

  Neptune in

Venus ⎤
Mars ⎦→ Tri
Moon

SCORPIO

Most Compatible Signs: *Pisces* and *Cancer*.
Next Best: *Sagittarius, Capricorn, Virgo* and *Libra*.
Doubtful: *Aquarius*—irritatingly detached, impersonal.
Taurus—clash of wills.
Leo—showy, arrogant.
Neutral: *Aries* and *Gemini*.

SAGITTARIUS

Most Compatible Signs: *Aries* and *Leo*.
Next Best: *Capricorn, Aquarius, Libra* and *Scorpio*.
Doubtful: *Pisces*—too introverted.
Gemini—superficial, flighty.
Virgo—narrow-minded, fussy.
Neutral: *Taurus* and *Cancer*.

CAPRICORN

Most Compatible Signs: *Taurus* and *Virgo*.
Next Best: *Aquarius, Pisces, Scorpio* and *Sagittarius*.
Doubtful: *Aries*—impulsive, erratic.
Cancer—depressing.
Libra—insincere, affected.
Neutral: *Gemini* and *Leo*.

AQUARIUS

Most Compatible Signs: *Gemini* and *Libra*.
Next Best: *Sagittarius, Capricorn, Pisces* and *Aries*.
Doubtful: *Taurus*—too staid.
Leo—too demanding.
Scorpio—too possessive.
Neutral: *Cancer* and *Virgo*.

PISCES

Most Compatible Signs: *Cancer* and *Scorpio*.
Next Best: *Capricorn, Aquarius, Aries* and *Taurus*.
Doubtful: *Gemini*—disturbingly restless.
Virgo—dull.
Sagittarius—too offhand.
Neutral: *Leo* and *Libra*.

Should any of your relationships not conform to this guide, it means other powerful influences are at work in the person's horoscope. These can be ascertained in detail from *AstroAnalysis* for that Sign.

FRIENDS

The following descriptions of the various Signs as friends are based on the position of the Sun, the most powerful influence in the horoscope. Most people conform to the solar influence. However, variations do take place because of the position of the other planets at the time of birth.

For a closer examination of a friend's character, it is advisable to study the individual's personal horoscope, which is available for every Sign in *AstroAnalysis*. All you need to know is the person's date of birth.

Since some Signs are naturally more and less compatible with others, you can obtain a further idea of how you'll hit it off with a friend by referring to the Compatibility Guide, page 91.

ARIES AS A FRIEND

The Aries person enjoys friendship, but it has to be largely on his or her terms. Aries people are too self-willed and organizing to fit everybody's notion of the ideal buddy. Yet their closest companions think they're really great—they love the male and female Ram's way of getting things moving and stirring up the entertainment. After all, it does suit some people to have a personal master of ceremonies around—and anyone with an Aries pal will agree that that just about sums up the favorite role of these very active and decisive individuals.

Aries are always eager to meet new faces. They need them. It's suicide for Aries people to try to cut themselves off from the mainstream of life that is people. They temper their mental and emotional mettle on relationships and require contact with the widest range of personalities to bring out the best in themselves. Mixing with others also instills in them the need for restraint and consideration, not their strongest points.

Aries quickly become part of a group. But no matter how enthusiastic and communicative they may appear, they hold a little bit of themselves back. They don't give that part away on casual acquaintance. True friendship means a great deal to them, and they are selective and discriminating in this regard. Which is one reason why they usually don't have many close friends. Another is that they have some very fixed opinions, which they propound and defend passionately. Close relationships can't always stand the strain of their fierce, combative verbal outbursts. They're too quick on the jaw. After a smashing start, people go cold on them. Aries individuals, as a rule, don't hold grudges, and they don't try to get even (there's no malice in them). When a relationship doesn't work out, they just wheel away, Ramlike, and charge off in another direction.

In company, people born under this Sign are very entertaining. They've got that audacious boyish or girlish impulsiveness, which sometimes comes very close to naiveté. They're a little bit unbelievable, amusingly impertinent, refreshing. What they'll say or do next is anybody's guess. This, of course, makes them exciting characters to be with—for some people. When they want to, they can mix easily with the most sophisticated company. But only for a time. The two types pretty quickly tire of each other.

Aries people are constantly on the alert in social circles for an appreciative ear, someone who laughs or applauds one of their clever, humorous or insightful remarks. They are then spurred on to outdo themselves, and before they know it they have corralled a mate (audience) for the evening.

They are staunchly loyal to close friends and generous to a fault. If a buddy is in trouble, they won't waste time spouting sympathetic platitudes. They'll bound into instant action, set on doing something practical to help. Without a single reservation, these spontaneous people will dig into their pocket or purse or run around organizing whatever they think is necessary to relieve a situation.

Being extremely idealistic, they have a habit of seeing others as they are not. Given the right emotional stimulus, they project their deeper longings onto individuals and pursue friendship with a vigor that frequently ends in disillusionment—and shock—when the truth is finally revealed to them.

As much as Aries enjoy and need numbers of people at times, they prefer mainly the company of a few close and trusted comrades who understand them and appreciate the sincerity that underlies their self-assertive nature.

They also require brief periods of seclusion.

TAURUS AS A FRIEND

No one makes a more faithful friend than dear, loyal Taurus. It's true Taureans do not excite great inspiration—what they offer is solid, sympathetic, warmhearted companionship. They satisfy where the need is greatest. And what is more desirable in a friend?

Taurus can also be a hatful of fun. But usually these men and women are quiet and reserved to begin with. They truly value friendship and don't offer theirs haphazardly.

Taurus individuals frequently have friends in the higher echelons of society where money and position count. They may not be wealthy or powerful themselves, but they are accepted by the affluent and influential and take their place among them naturally without awkwardness.

One side of the Taurean character that appeals to others is an innate appreciation of the artistic side of life. Your Taurus friend may not be a Michelangelo or Hemingway or possess any special knowledge, but his or her affinity with most that is creative, harmonious and beautiful seldom fails to come through.

Even though they may work hard all day in an office, Taureans are almost sure to have a creative outlet that they share with special friends at night or on weekends. This may be anything ranging from handicrafts to entertaining (Taurus usually love giving dinner parties). Most of them are quite capable of preparing a small banquet with Cordon Bleu expertise and flourish. And what is more, they—especially Ms. Taurus—will manage to emerge from the kitchen unruffled, impeccably dressed and at ease.

Friends enjoy visiting a Taurus home because these people are wonderful hosts and hostesses. They can also be counted on to have very pleasant accommodations, if they can manage it, with a garden or in a rural setting. But very definitely their home will be nicely furnished and comfortable, with as many touches of luxury as they can afford.

They are a little hesitant and unsure when it comes to making friends. They don't think of themselves as great conversationalists and they're never quite sure how to break the ice. They are inclined to hold off making contact and to wait for events to dictate the action. Taureans prefer not to take the initiative. None of that bumptious bouncing up to strangers for these people. Their fraternizing methods are subdued and dignified.

It is not unusual for Taurus to become close personal friends with the boss and other superiors and their families. They may visit each other's homes and carry on a friendship for years without ever disturbing the workday relations. These people have intuitive tact; they never give those in important positions the impression that they will take advantage of the friendship. They themselves are easily put off by presumptuous behavior, and when they make up their minds to end a relationship, there are no two ways about it. When Taureans lose faith in a person, they obliterate that person from their thinking.

Taurus' closest friends are those who share their love of beautiful things. This includes a distinct penchant for rambling in the great outdoors.

They are inclined, however, to settle too comfortably into a niche among special buddies and to gradually lose their spontaneity. They get caught up in the same old conversations and habitual recreations. They don't like changing friends and sometimes fail to keep their relationships alive and vital. It pays Taurus to circulate and bring new companions into the fold every now and again.

And the friends of Taurus should be careful that they, too, don't get into a rut.

GEMINI AS A FRIEND

Gemini people love having loads of friends—but as few deep attachments as possible. To them, friendship is for fun, kicks and mental stimulation, but no obligations, please. They don't want to be pinned down to what they said last week. Geminis are likely to say anything in the excitement of a racy moment, and they expect their friends to understand this. Not that they're illogical, not by any means. They can make logic out of just about any nonsense, so quick and shrewd are their reasoning powers. But, try to tie a Gemini down to something he or she said yesterday? You have to be joking.

The strange thing is that the real friends of these Peter Pan characters *do* understand them. And they don't find them unreliable because they accept them for what they are—very likable, entertaining, optimistic, helpful, intelligent bundles of (mostly) good-humored energy.

Gemini probably has more telephone numbers of pals in his or her head than most other people keep in their address books. These men and women have a memory for facts and figures that is as remarkable as their ability to strike up casual acquaintanceships. Their friends are usually spread over a vast area. When Geminis visit a town where they're not known, you can bet that by the time they leave, they'll have a dozen new addresses memorized. These Mercurial individuals make enough friends for two people—which is probably why Gemini's symbol is the Twins.

The Geminian doesn't stick to one type of friend like some other Signs. He or she chooses buddies from all walks of life. They're just as likely to include a couple of tramps as the governor himself. Gemini must have various personalities to bounce off his ideas. And the more types he can gather together at one time, the happier he is. He or she can handle two or three conversations simultaneously—and do two jobs or have two or three love affairs going at the same time.

Geminis love novelty. Their minds are intensely keen and curious. They get bored very quickly, especially with ponderous types who take themselves and life too seriously. They can enjoy a good laugh with or at these people, but only so long as they're entertained or collecting interesting information. Otherwise, these children of Mercury are off to the next unexpected meeting. For anyone who tries to tag along, it can be a very tiring threesome.

They love to argue but not at the emotional level. Sometimes they rub people the wrong way at first meetings because they are quite capable of taking an opposite point of view just for the sake of exercising their formidable intellect at another's expense.

These Mercurial characters may seem inconsistent, flighty and frivolous, and some may regard them as insincere, but none of their friends will ever call them dull. They are the nerve end of any party or gathering.

In social circles, they sail along famously. They can adapt to just about any situation and keep up a patter of well-informed or inconsequential talk, depending on what's required. They sprinkle their conversation with amusing anecdotes. At repartee, they are down-right brilliant. They have a wonderful knack of changing their personality to fit the mood of the room.

Geminis' closest buddies are intellectual types who can discuss the more abstract subjects that interest them—and who don't object to being called up at the oddest hours simply for a chat!

CANCER AS A FRIEND

Cancer people enjoy having a few loyal intimates. They like to feel they are of service to these pals, and that they enjoy their respect and esteem in return. They choose their friends more by feeling than by intellectual discrimination. If the person "feels" right to a Cancer, it is almost certain he or she will enjoy the same interests or hold similar views. The point is that these June—July-born men and women are almost inspirational in their sensitivity to other people's vibes.

They have such a fine rapport with their closest buddies that it is often not necessary for them to speak at all for hours at a time. They literally absorb the presence of their friends in a way that transcends the normal idea of communication. But they do enjoy chatting with different acquaintances and can be surprisingly loquacious as well as interesting.

Cancers are moody characters, and can be very irritating to people who don't know them very well. They are seldom the same person from one day to the next. Their temperament fluctuates according to where they are and whom they're with, and sometimes even with the weather! However, the male and female Crab are far deeper individuals than they appear to be, and their real friends appreciate this and love them for what they are.

The intensity of a close Cancer friendship can be a bit claustrophobic. Although wonderfully sympathetic and helpful, the Cancer individual tends to be overprotective, too solicitous of his or her friend's welfare. The object of this solicitude sometimes feels he is being taken over, that his individual expression is being stifled. When Cancers are trying most to give, they are likely to be excessively demanding. These very sensitive people have a great need for affection. They often end up being hurt when their friends decide it's time to disentangle themselves and take a break.

Although Cancers are not vain or egotistical, they do possess considerable personal pride, which means they have to be appreciated and constantly assured of their worth and value.

This is not difficult because they are rather lovable characters. Still, they're touchy and easily offended and will sometimes sulk or sink into sullen silence when they aren't getting enough attention. It is excruciating to them to sense that their friends are underrating them. They know, in a humble kind of way, exactly what they are worth.

Friends and acquaintances have a habit of confiding in Cancer. The Crab often shares more secrets than all of his or her companions put together, but would never think of divulging another's private affairs even in the most intimate exchange of confidences. It is this kind of loyalty and understanding, together with an aura of high-minded seriousness, that make even casual acquaintances tell Cancer intimate details and seek advice. The Crab has a great deal of patience and good old common sense.

Cancers intensely dislike arguments and discord. They'd much rather give in to a friend or walk quietly away than engage in a stand-up, knock-down fight. Mixing with aggressive and rowdy people literally upsets their stomachs and can make them ill.

Many people don't realize just how sensitive these gentle Moon children are because they manage to conceal their emotions under a calm and confident exterior.

LEO AS A FRIEND

The problem with Leo friends is they're likely to be *too* generous and giving. They often deny their buddies the satisfaction of feeling friendship is a two-way affair. This is not so much related to the things money can buy. Leo's friendship is not as smothering as Cancer's can be. It's just apt to be overwhelming!

Of course, we're talking about the developed Leonine character. The immature type is too bossy and brash to hold friends for long. But even the openhanded and magnanimous Leo often has to realize it's possible to kill or at least mar a friendship with overdoses of well-intended goodwill. This is likely to include handing out good advice. Neither the Lion nor the Lioness can resist giving his or her opinion whether it has been asked for or not.

Make no mistake, though, Leos are true and tried friends. And they usually manage to attract companions who are also generous and kind. This is indeed fortunate because these are the only people with whom they can have any reasonably good kind of relationship.

These proud and usually commanding characters demand a great deal of respect, applause and loyalty from their pals. Worldly gifts are nothing to them in comparison. Anyone who's not something of an admirer won't be calling a Leo "friend" for long.

Leos really believe all that talk about being King of the Jungle. They tend to gather around them friends who are their intellectual equals but emotionally dependent on them. They enjoy holding court, giving good advice here, solving someone's problems there. When they can smile on their friends and feel like big mommy or daddy, they are happy. In adversity, although they are unlikely to admit it, they need their buddies desperately.

If you're a friend of a Leo, you probably enjoy showing off a bit too. You have probably noticed that this intensely competitive character will stay in his or her seat as long as you are not getting all the attention. If that happens, you can bet the Lion will think up something to steal the spotlight.

Leo people are rather fixed and one-pointed in their ideas and aspirations. They therefore find restless types with many interests fascinating but vaguely unsettling. These comrades disturb Leo's enormous self-assurance that he's on the right track, and force him to examine his goals and wishes more closely. He usually recovers his equilibrium (which means his self-confidence) fairly quickly, but for a time he may be confused. Friends like this actually do Leo a service by breaking down some of his rigid ideas and shaking his complacency. He needs to learn he can't be right *all* the time.

Leo people can get mixed up in dubious company and often their friends have to extricate them. They are not great judges of character at first meeting. They may fall for flattery and insincere gestures, particularly if these have a touch of glamour. In this way, so-called friends and casual acquaintances manage to penetrate their guard and make chumps of them. Oddly, they are seldom offended by people who try to get favors out of them by phony compliments.

Both the Leo man and woman have strong personal magnetism and make loads of friends. Many of their buddies are apt to be prominent in government and community circles. Some of their friendships last a lifetime. They like to entertain their pals at home as well as at popular night spots.

Leo usually establishes one or two lasting

friendships with people from abroad.

Come what may, neither the Lion nor the Lioness will ever let a friend down.

VIRGO AS A FRIEND

Virgos are not the easiest people to get close to. They may say they have many friends, but others are more likely to call these acquaintances. It's not so simple for people born under the Sign of the Virgin to understand the profundity of real friendship, the emotional and sympathetic link that can't be put into words. Virgos make friends largely at the intellectual level; the relationship has to make sense to them. Their personal alliances generally lack resilience.

This is not to say that these practical people don't have numerous friends they can phone, visit and call upon for help at any time—and vice versa. But they are very choosy and don't encourage friends who want to share intimate details because they resent all kinds of intrusion. They don't intrude on others and they expect the same consideration. Virgo people enjoy good healthy relationships where there is open discussion of mutual interests. Their private affairs they consider sacrosanct. Only to an unusually compatible person of tried and trusted integrity will they confide. Here again, they don't go looking for this type of person with whom to share their most intimate secrets.

You are most likely to find a Virgo friend among a group of people who share one of the many interests of these intelligent and discerning individuals. They are reserved and a little apprehensive at first meeting. They prefer to stay in the background until they get their bearings—which usually means a pretty acute summing up of everyone present.

Although quiet personalities, Virgos are certainly not dummies. In discussions, their shrewd and scholastic mind allows them to see the practicalities of a proposition in a flash. They speak up and people listen, for it is obvious they are being constructive even though critical.

People with similar interests usually take a liking to Virgos. They might be a bit severe in their outspokenness, but they are refreshingly honest. In fact, honesty is one of their most impressive characteristics. People always know where they stand with them. They are both conscientious and idealistic.

Frequently, however, Virgo individuals break with their friends over differences of opinion. Whereas other types may be able to ignore a divergence of fundamental views with a fast friend, Virgo men and women can't—as a rule. For as long as possible, they will tolerate such a situation, but eventually their own nature compels them to force a showdown. They must get to the bottom of things. Their minds insist on a logical analysis. It's the principle that counts. And so friendship, that indefinable thing, too often flies out the window.

Some of Virgo's closest friends are met through sporting and outdoor activities. They are not the rough-and-tumble type, but are keenly aware of the need to keep fit through exercise and plenty of fresh air. Most of their buddies share their absorbing interest in diet and food.

When Virgos do choose a pal, they are scrupulously honest in the relationship. They won't tolerate another person talking behind their friend's back. They will always come out into the open and confront you if they have any grievances. They are honorable people and can be depended on to do the correct thing.

LIBRA AS A FRIEND

Librans need to belong. Friendship is as essential to them as breathing. But their alliances often seem much more intimate than is actually the case. Librans don't, as a rule, form deep, soul-stirring friendships. The agony and the ecstacy are usually missing. Friendship to them is a dignified and entertaining way of ensuring they are seldom alone or isolated.

Libra is the Sign of partnership. And as far as Librans are concerned, there's no essential difference between a marriage and a fraternal partnership. The reason for this is they are idealists, not sensualists. To them, a lover is first a friend.

Librans seldom give themselves entirely in any liaison. Always they hold a vital bit in reserve which gives them an appearance of slight formality, the discretion that says: "Not too close, please." This discretion, with their other positive attributes, makes them interesting and desirable companions; nothing is quite so irresistible as that which entices but gently demurs.

Librans are charming, easygoing, polite and terribly diplomatic. They want everyone they meet to love them, to want them as a friend—everyone, that is, except bullying, aggressive, course types, who literally make them ill if they are forced to remain in their company for any length of time.

Libra, as most people know, is ruled by Venus, the planet of love, beauty and harmony, and these are the essential qualities that Librans look for in all their relationships. Wherever they work, live or play, they gravitate toward that which is artistic, elegant and pleasing. Their favorite companions are those who are skilled in the creative or fine arts or who have an appreciation or specialized knowledge of them. Libran people themselves are often talented in these ways and may go into partnerships with friends as color consultants, interior decorators, designers, hair stylists and other occupations connected with beauty and beautifying.

They love entertaining, dressing up and visiting friends in their homes. Their manner as guest or host is gracious and amusing. Often their friends are among the most influential and socially prominent people in town.

Libra friends will do all they can to bring new and interesting people into their circle. Often they are responsible for making romantic matches for others. They delight in seeing people enjoying themselves.

These mentally active and self-expressive individuals are a bit moody and unpredictable. Sometimes when their guard is down, they become critical, sharp and quick to anger. However, they recover their balance quickly. After all, their symbol is the Scales.

They have a fiery sense of dignity and justice. Any companion who unfairly attacks an underdog in their presence can expect a stinging rebuke. Libra men and women believe wholeheartedly in the brotherhood of man. But when it comes to actually doing something about it, they're frequently missing, because, as a rule, they are too fond of comfort and ease to embrace unnecessary effort.

These individuals are delightful companions, but they do have a way of using their friends to get what they want out of life.

SCORPIO AS A FRIEND

Scorpio people can be the most demanding friends of all. They are basically loners, they won't share their feelings and they want everything their way. They expect their friends to be as intense about their interests as they are. If not, they're out. A Scorpio doesn't have a friend around unless he or she has something to give.

As harsh as this sounds, it's the key to the extraordinary personality of the pure Scorpio type. Fortunately, the pure type is always modified by other factors in the horoscope, although the essential framework remains.

It is not easy for Scorpio to attract true friends because he and she doesn't have a great need for them. And what is not needed, normally becomes expendable under stress.

But Scorpio generally does have a compulsive desire to satisfy the sex drive, which is intensely strong in him or her. This drive in this remarkable Sign may go to the opposite extreme and propel Scorpio, still alone, to the self-denying heights of mystical experience. But usually the Scorpio man or woman directs libidinal energies in one way or another into love. So he or she *needs* a lover, and will serve or treat that person according to that need.

So what is it that Scorpio needs in a friend? An echo of his or her own idea, a sounding board, a captive audience? The problem is, Scorpio's friends usually need Scorpio, and this places them in a most unenviable position.

The Scorpio personality is intensely magnetic to some people; to others, it is exceptionally repulsive. Those who are attracted frequently have great feelings of love and devotion, which the Scorpio person probably does not require. To remain in his company, they must indulge this generally selfish, tyrannical, vindictive, suspicious, scheming, stubborn and quite often cruel and violent personality.

But, of course, there are always exceptions, produced by positive and favorable influences elsewhere in the chart. These more developed Scorpio types—when not emotionally aroused—are staunch and sympathetic friends. They will work and fight courageously on behalf of a comrade. Weaker companions often draw inspiration and strength from their dauntless determination and patience.

However, when a Scorpio person encourages a friendship, it usually means he has an ulterior motive. For instance, he is likely to be a personal friend of his boss. He has an astonishing gift for weighing situations and seeing who will come out on top—and therefore is the best person to cultivate—in a future power struggle. His ability for intrigue is unmatched by any other zodiacal type, for there is no limit to his perfidy and wily patience when self-interest is involved.

The Scorpio person can passionately and devotedly serve a cause or a person he or she loves—and be just as violent in his or her hatred or loathing of either.

Scorpio seldom gives an opinion unless it's asked for, and doesn't accept the views of others without investigation.

If friendship is understood to be based on trust and sharing, Scorpio friendships do not have a lot going for them.

Ask Scorpio, for he or she has that chilling, detached honesty that would probably agree.

SAGITTARIUS AS A FRIEND

Sagittarius people are wonderful companions. Lighthearted, witty and extremely intelligent, they make and attract friends from all levels of society. They have a passion for experimenting with life, for traveling as widely and as often as possible—and people enjoy the adventure of tagging along with them for a time. There's seldom a dull moment when these good-humored individuals are around. They adore novelty and jump from experience to experience with a lust for living that may leave less strenuous types bewildered and breathless.

Yet they can be intensely serious. Their love of fun, uncomplicated manner and tendency to clown constitute only one-half of their nature. This half has undeniable appeal and makes Sagittarius one of the most popular of the zodiacal types. But these people are deeply interested in the problems of their fellow man and will support all kinds of projects aimed at making his life easier and freer.

The Sagittarian's closest companions are usually like him- or herself. They never tie each other down—the link is pure comradeship. Sagittarians manage to divide their time without conflict between the serious and lighter sides of existence. Their energy and enthusiasm are exuberantly boundless.

The above characteristics describe the positive and mature type of person born under this Sign. The negative type manages to distort the higher qualities into odd but still recognizable shapes. For a start, he or she is a boisterous kind of individual who lives mainly for a good time and attracts shallow, showy friends of similar temperament. Negative Sagittarians also eat and drink excessively, make promises they have no intention of honoring, can't resist gambling and usually are chronically in debt. Because of their innate magnetism, these people can be a bad influence on others. Their levity and contempt for responsibility may appear glamorous; the young, especially, may admire and imitate their swashbuckling freedom.

Even the higher types of this Sign need occasionally to restrain their exuberance and impulsiveness where pleasure is concerned. The party life and all forms of revelry can be irresistible. Even the serious, high-minded and respected Sagittarius, a pillar of his community or the business world, can suddenly break out and land himself and his friends in embarrassing and ridiculous situations that are impossible to explain in the light of day.

Although the Sagittarian's breezy manner may suggest unconcern for what others think of him, his conscience pricks him painfully and he will always try to make amends in some way.

These people are generous and sincere friends. Their intimates respect their outspoken honesty and high ideals regarding the treatment of others. They love their freedom and independence and will never, even in a position of judicial power, deprive another of his liberty without deep soul-searching.

Sagittarians try to give their friends the benefit of their experience by taking a personal interest in their problems and endeavoring to offer solutions. Their hospitality, kindness and openhandedness with money is usually legendary among their intimates.

CAPRICORN AS A FRIEND

People born under Capricorn do not have many intimate friends. Their main interest is their work. When that's done for the day, they do enjoy relaxing with someone who understands that any discussion of personal affairs must be initiated by Capricorn. Their friends are mostly casual types who don't expect any exchange of intimacies.

Capricorns are capable of making fast friendships, and in those rare instances, they are as staunch and loyal as any one type in the Zodiac. But the individual Goat's fraternity club has a very restricted membership, and members don't meet that often. It's enough for these characters to know there's someone in this world they can discuss their troubles with—if the necessity ever arises. This gives them the feeling of security that is so essential to their happiness and well-being. It isn't the actual exercising of this option that matters, for deep, confiding friendship is something Capricorn holds in reserve—or in his mind—and probably never needs to make use of.

So it's on with the surface show. These people are easily entertained: a quiet chat, a few drinks, listening to music, watching TV or discussing business and current affairs will often satisfy them. They are not romantic types with social aspirations and they're not addicted to pleasure. All they really want is a temporary break from their main concern, which, as they mature, is to get as far ahead as they can in their job or career, and if possible to make a name for themselves.

Their closest friends and all those who love them realize they are supersensitive. They may appear solid, stable and practical, but, deep inside, they are aquiver with diffidence, uncertainty and vague, indefinable fears.

On first meeting, Capricorns appear to many to be standoffish and cold. This is frequently a pose they affect to compensate for their uneasiness. They are so determined that no one shall hurt their feelings that they won't give others the chance to rebuff or slight them by making overt moves of friendship. Their emotions are generally tucked safely away where nobody can get at them.

The real friends of Capricorn men and women are those who care enough to patiently and affectionately penetrate to the real person. There is no doubt that this protective veneer begins growing on Capricorn people early in life. Their childhood is frequently sad or disorganized, which teaches them to be wary of so-called close relationships.

They sometimes appear distrustful and suspicious when others extend a friendly hand. It's not that they don't want to grasp it; but they worry about the price that must be paid in pain if one fails the other. They are deep and serious people, these Capricorns.

A Capricorn person who allows his or her fears to dominate becomes withdrawn and uncommunicative. The process can start very early, sometimes in the middle of the happy and fun-loving teens. This person is often critical and builds up a repressed passion, which expresses itself in instant and violent dislikes.

All in all, the odds are against Capricorn being a very satisfactory friend for most people.

AQUARIUS AS A FRIEND

Aquarius friendship is of the highest order. It gives what might be called soul satisfaction, and for those who get close to these likable individuals, it is often a source of inspiration. This is not surprising because Aquarius is the Sign that rules friendship, associations and commitments to groups. In other words, Aquarius can make the ideal buddy.

These people are neither jealous nor possessive. In fact, the clinging-vine type of person who looks for some form of exclusiveness in a friendship will be bitterly disappointed here. Aquarians are attached to the ideal of comradeship, its intrinsic freedom and lack of demand, and not so much to the individual. They make more successful friends than lovers or marriage partners, as a rule. Marriage tends to confine and restrict when their whole nature craves variety of intellectual experience through different companions.

None of this means they are supertypes who don't need warmth and affection. In fact, they are idealists, and their aloneness is often the result of having standards of thought and behavior that don't conform to those of the crowd. Yet they seem to possess a built-in loadstone that attracts others to them, even if only for a short time.

These people are genuinely interested in human relationships. Although not so intense and possessive as most others, they are tremendously aware of the deeper aspect of friendship. They know it's not just a convenient way to fill up a few pleasant hours. There's a dignity to their friendship, which they always manage to preserve and endow with meaningful significance. Both sides retain their individuality in an Aquarius friendship.

The friends of Aquarius are usually intellectually serious types who agree with their somewhat advanced ideas about social reform and making life easier for the masses. Those who advance the course of progress are seldom social butterflies. Their views usually separate them and their closest pals from the ordinary run-of-the-mill people.

In some cases, these people even earn a reputation as radicals and revolutionaries. Occasionally, little bands of Aquarians and their friends strike out and refuse to join the Establishment. They may live a bohemian-type existence to underline their refusal to conform to comfortable, accepted standards, which they regard as outdated and socially inhibiting. They may dress differently. In some cases, their overzealous identification with a cause may lead to serious clashes with authority.

But generally, Aquarians are reasonable individuals who are extremely just and generous to their friends. They have a fine sense of give and take. And their inventiveness and brilliant intellects often elevate the minds of their companions and bring out the best in those people.

The true Aquarius—because of his or her intelligence—is very selective in the choice of intimates but is never a snob.

PISCES AS A FRIEND

Pisces people are always looking for the perfect friend; naturally, they are frequently disillusioned. Their problem is they have an ideal of friendship that often is beyond the capacity of any human being to fulfill. They expect too much. When they don't get the impossible, they tend to lose active interest in that particular person. Not that they would ever "disown" someone they have called a friend. They are aware of their irrational expectations, and in any case, possess a superb sense of loyalty. They simply push those who "fail" them gently to the back of their mind and keep on searching for the impossible.

Love and friendship are not easy for the Pisces person to maintain in separate compartments. It's too often both together or nothing.

They loathe being alone—and yet, they must have periods of seclusion. This is one of the qualities of their nature that new acquaintances are apt to find confusing.

They enjoy stimulating company and can work themselves into a near-frenzy of excitement. Yet, the next day, they may be withdrawn, almost self-reproachful, unable to face those with whom they have shared such fun and comradeship. This disturbing emotional turbulence is a subjective experience only the Piscean is really

familiar with. So when the phone or doorbell rings, they answer and are able to respond naturally and charmingly—though quietly—to their friend. There is much of the instant actor or actress in these strange and gentle people.

Pisceans sometimes choose their friends unwisely. They get carried away with their enthusiasm for contact and sharing. They start sympathizing and confiding before they know where they are, or more importantly, before they've bothered to assess the caliber of their companions. In personal relationships, they tend to think things will improve, even when experience has taught them just the opposite.

A Pisces' friends are almost certain to be artistically inclined. They just can't tolerate heavy or coarse company. They themselves are highly and prolifically artistic. Although they may not be accomplished in any of the arts as such, they have a way of inspiring those who are.

There are not many Pisceans who have not poured their sensitive feelings into writing poems at some time or other. But it will be a very dear friend indeed, as a rule, who has the privilege of reading them because poems will be quickly destroyed by these oddly self-critical people.

Pisces individuals have a great gift for making those around them happy—except when they are trying to turn a friendship into a romance in their own imagination. Then they may be cloying and just too, too obliging and loving.

These people are wonderful at entertaining and making their friends feel deliciously at home. Pleasing others pleases Pisces most.

The following descriptions of the various Signs as parents are based on the position of the Sun, the most powerful influence in the horoscope. Most people conform to the solar influence. However, variations do occur because of the placement of the other planets at the time of birth. And, of course, the birth Sign of the child will also be an important consideration.

For a closer examination of these factors, it is advisable to study the individual parent's and child's horoscopes, which are available for every Sign in *AstroAnalysis*. All you need to know is the person's date of birth.

Since some Signs are naturally more and less compatible with others, you can obtain a further idea of how parents and children will hit it off by referring to the Compatibility Guide on page 91.

THE ARIES PARENT

The Aries parent is kind, generous and fairly strict. The Aries woman often makes a better parent than the Aries man. Neither is particularly sympathetic or understanding; Aries people have difficulty seeing things through a child's eyes, possibly because they want too much to be proud of their offspring.

But the Aries woman takes parenting very much to heart. She's determined to bring up her children the way she thinks is right, even if it kills her—or drives her neighbors crazy, which is more likely.

Aries mothers have some very advanced ideas about child rearing. Their methods are often unconventional. They believe in teaching their youngsters initiative from the outset. And that may include permitting the three-year-old pride of the household to toddle over and pour himself a cup of coffee from Aunt Nellie's best bonechina set. Or to get busy with a pair of scissors or a crayon, perhaps on the wallpaper, while mother's attention is elsewhere. Not that Mrs. Aries is irresponsible. Far from it. But one freedom is likely to lead to another in the child's eyes, and she is impelled to go along with it. Still, it's the child that counts with her, and you've got to

admire the way she tries to prepare him to cope with the practical side of life without putting a stranglehold on his self-expression.

The Aries dad is somewhat different. He's also progressive, extremely proud of his offspring and wants the very best for them. But he won't allow kids to take over his whole life the way some fathers do. They occupy a very special place in his affections and he'll see they never want for any material things. But he's a busy man, and although he'll do his best to satisfy their emotional needs, he's not particularly good at it—consciously anyway. But children usually love him and they do delight in the way he'll do things they enjoy on the spur of the moment.

The Aries father tends to become impatient and irritable under the constant demands of his children. Both parents believe that experience is a great teacher. If the child has to burn himself to learn not to touch the hot stove, then the attitude is, okay, let's let him get on with it. Mother is the softer and more efficient parent of the two. But they're both wonderful examples to the growing child of initiative and independence.

The birth Sign of the child, of course, will have a large bearing on the success of the individual Aries parent.

THE TAURUS PARENT

Taurus men and women adore their children and make them the center of family life. But these loving and affectionate people are far too wise in normal circumstances to put the children before their mate. In fact, this question just doesn't arise with them. They manage in a wonderfully sensible way to make the family a unit. And the youngsters usually grow up with a keen respect for the virtues of family life based on their Taurus parent's example. These children often go on to make happy marriages themselves.

It's not surprising, therefore, that Taurus is frequently considered to be the ideal mom or dad. These people are kind-hearted and sympathetic personalities with a deep, intuitive understanding of those they love. As homemakers, they are generally considered to be without peer as a rule.

Because of their sensitive nature, they are conscious at all times of the emotional impact that unpleasant scenes and quarreling have on children. They have their marital disagreements, of course, but would rather lose an argument—or eat humble pie for a while—than disturb the tranquillity of the home.

Their views on child rearing are rather conventional. They believe generally in the old-fashioned way—teaching children good manners, good behavior and good morals right from the start. Freedom and independence, they feel, are qualities of character natural to children who feel loved and secure. If they are given correct values—and who, asks the Taurus parent, would argue against goodness and kindness as the golden rule?—then youngsters will have a firm foundation on which to build for themselves.

One of the secrets of the Taurean's success as a parent is that he or she loves home life; the domestic routine is never a bore, as it is to several other zodiacal types. Home, to these people, is not just a place to sleep and eat—it's a place to live in with as much comfort, elegance and harmony as is humanly possible.

Taurus parents are acutely aware of surroundings and the importance of environment on a child's development. They prefer to make their home in a suburb well away from the city, or ideally in the country.

Taureans have a strong protective instinct. They are among the last people to seek a divorce because they fear it would unsettle the children. They will endure considerable personal hardship for the sake of a growing family.

The birth Sign of the child, of course, will have a large bearing on the success of the individual Taurus parent.

THE GEMINI PARENT

Parenthood is not an easy role for a typical Gemini man or woman. Their temperament and outlook are generally too youthful and adaptable to impart the solid direction and psychological security so necessary for a developing personality. Children who compare Gemini's example of restless activity and nervous excitement with conventional ideas of steady citizenship may become confused and uncertain of themselves.

The Gemini mother is likely to make a better fist of it than the Gemini dad. These versatile women are inclined to carry on with an outside activity after marriage, but when the children come along, they will probably realize they can't manage both. Or can they? There's no telling with ingenious, energetic Gemini. These women, although appearing domestically slack at times, loathe untidiness and are very fussy about how their home is run. What they would prefer is to have someone else do the housekeeping while they get out and on with their other interests.

Both parents love their children, but they're not prepared to make them their whole life. To do so, they feel, would be to give the youngsters a wrong impression of what living is all about. They are deeply interested in their children's intellectual development. They don't believe they should have second-hand ideas and values stuffed into them. They believe in free speech, free thought and independence—and this is what they try to teach their offspring. After all, that's what democracy is about, isn't it?

Geminis put a lot more thought than emotion into their relationships with Children. Critics may say they show a deficiency of heart. They tend to reason with them rather than try to "feel" with them. Emotionally, the Twins and their children may be miles apart.

The Gemini father is very quickly bored by the routine of family life. He's inclined to go out as often as possible, and may even seek an occupation that requires him to spend odd days away from home. However, he has a great deal of affection for his children as well as his home base. He is apt to rush in after a short absence in a flurry of expectation and excitement, stimulating everyone (especially the youngsters) to fever pitch.

The Gemini father may at times be unduly strict. He is likely to put on a display of irate authority to cover up his own feelings of uncertainty and insecurity.

Both Gemini parents find, as a rule, that they are able to guide their children more effectively by creating a restful atmosphere in the home.

The birth Sign of the child, of course, will have a large bearing on the success of the individual Gemini parent.

THE CANCER PARENT

A person born under Cancer often feels he or she is the best mom or dad in the world. Cancers do have some remarkably fine parental qualities (some even say that Cancer is the personification of motherhood), yet they are at the opposite extreme to Gemini: Cancer is all heart or feeling and not enough reason.

Both Cancer parents love their children in a

most possessive, effusive and sentimental way. They are determined to nourish and protect them—and often succeed in almost suffocating them with affection in the process.

The Cancer parent is completely devoted to home and family. Every other activity is incidental to this one great absorbing idea. While the children are growing up, they receive every consideration. Nothing is too much trouble; no desired object is denied them while there is any money available.

The Cancer mom and dad are of much the same temperament. But since this is a mothering Sign, the characteristcs generally fit the woman better than the man. He's moody, changeable, sentimental and and often oblivious to the exacting demands he makes on his family in exchange for his devotion to them. If you call him selfish, he will be flabbergasted, then highly indignant—and reel off incontrovertible evidence of all the sacrifices he's made for his family over the years. Yet his family might feel that despite his loving kindness, he has cheated them emotionally—that the price he has extorted in sympathy, approval and recognition of his virtues down the years was just not worth it. His fussiness around the home, insistence on accepted forms of behavior and corrective criticism may make the children nervous and self-conscious paragons. He can't seem to see beyond his own feelings of devotion and worthiness.

The Cancer mother will indulge and coddle her children with doting kindness, and then punish them with undue severity when they are naughty. Her moods change abruptly with irritation. Then this woman, who normally serves her children day in and day out and regards it as a privilege, will flare into a near-hysterical outburst. The children are often left bewildered and puzzled by this adult inconsistency.

Cancer parents need to exercise more reasoning and control over their fluctuating emotions if they are to balance their love with wisdom.

The birth Sign of the child, of course, will have a large bearing on the success of the individual Cancer parent.

THE LEO PARENT

Leo, as most people know, is the Sign of children, so it is to be expected that both the man and woman make fairly good parents.

They are exceedingly ambitious for their offspring. They want them to succeed in everything they attempt and are prepared to ensure that they enjoy every possible advantage. They won't take the initiative from their youngsters, but they will let them know they expect big things from them.

The success of these tactics depends to a great degree on the character of the child. If some of the zodiacal types are driven too hard or too much is expected of them, their development will probably be impaired or they will become resentful of the parent in later years.

Fortunately, Leo is also the Sign of deep love. The parent's ambitions for the children are usually tempered with profound affection and understanding. A typical Leo won't push a child beyond safe limits. Leo's style is more showmanship than shovemanship.

Children, whatever their Sign, can't help but be aware of the strength and loving concern of these parents. They will frequently indulge their offspring with extravagance, yet usually manage to attach some sort of condition that encourages a responsible attitude toward life. Despite their strong desire to be able to show off their youngsters to others, when it comes down to fundamentals, they want what is best for each child.

Leo parents (particularly dad) are likely to run the home as though it were their own private kingdom. Unless they receive homage and attention from their family, they are apt to become silent and sulky or stride off in a huff. This is more a device for drawing attention to the ingratitude of loved ones (who really should know better!) than moodiness or brooding. Once the acknowledgments are forthcoming, the whole household smiles again.

When Leo parents feel a visitor or friend is receiving more attention and admiration than they are from their offspring, they'll sometimes do ridiculous things to go one better. Junior may enjoy this, but the effects of such egocentric contests on his outlook are hard to gauge.

Leo parents have a habit of going from one extreme to another with their children; they either lavish too much attention on them or demand too much.

The birth Sign of the child, of course, will have a large bearing on the success of the individual Leo parent.

THE VIRGO PARENT

Virgo men and women make first-class parents, although their mates may have to see to the emotional development of the children because this side of child rearing is not one of Virgo's strong points.

These parents are practical, neat and orderly. They teach their children admirably how to cope with the problems of everyday life. They are especially mindful of diet and careful to instill in youngsters the necessity for cleanliness and good hygiene.

The Virgo mother instructs her youngsters from an early age in the virtues of good manners, tidy appearance and moral behavior. She doesn't believe in waste and makes sure that the children, both boys and girls, do their share of the chores around the house and learn to be methodical.

Sometimes she's a bit tight with the purse-strings where small personal luxuries are concerned. Occasionally, though, she is unexpectedly indulgent, particularly when she feels the child has earned a treat. Her youngsters never want for necessities, and they always have good, nutritious food to eat.

Both Mr. and Mrs. Virgo encourage their children right from the start to save for a rainy day. They are not social climbers nor particularly ambitious for themselves, but they do with all their heart want to see their children get a good start in life. They are very much aware of the benefits of a good education and will themselves help with lessons at home. They can grasp a subject very quickly from a textbook and have a knack for explaining things in clear, concise, and logical concepts.

Both Virgo parents want their children to stand on their own two feet, and will do everything possible to encourage this. However, they are apt to overlook a child's emotional needs because they feel the practical side is more important in the youngster's development. It is not easy for them to demonstrate love and affection. Although highly sensitive within themselves, they find it very difficult to show their real feelings. Although they love and care deeply for their offspring, a child may miss the warmth of cuddling and close physical contact.

The Virgo mom and dad both have a strong tendency to nag children. They may also be very possessive and fail to extend the freedom of choice in play that other children normally enjoy.

The birth Sign of the child, of course, will have a large bearing on the success of the individual Virgo parent.

THE LIBRA PARENT

Librans make excellent parents, probably the best of all the zodiacal types. They have an affinity with children that shines through their relationships in many delightful ways. They love to play with them. As the youngsters grow up, they genuinely enjoy having them and their young friends around. They help with the entertainment and can join in games and conversation without appearing to be intruding.

Basically, Libran men and women treat children with the same consideration and regard for dignity that they extend to their own many friends. They are gentle and patient; persuasive rather than pushy. They know instinctively what is right for a child, but would rather guide him to choose for himself than put an object into his hands with a ready-made explanation.

Because Librans are very fair, they won't allow themselves to inflict their own hangups and prejudices on a developing mind; nor do they permit others to intrude in this way. They can be surprisingly adamant and forceful if an adult—whatever his position—attempts to bully or tyrannize a child. Although they are the last people to go looking for a fight, they are the first to resist injustice in any form.

The Libra parent loves beauty and harmony and will do all in his or her power to awaken similar feelings in the children. Librans endeavor to interest their children early in one of the arts—say music or painting—believing that this will aid their higher development and enable them to mix with creative and socially refined people. They are not snobs by any means, but they do appreciate sophistication and culture, so they can't help but endeavor to educate their children along many of these same lines.

Librans have a way of making instruction interesting for children. And children do their best to please them. These individuals make loving and affectionate parents, but not stupid ones. They don't spoil their young ones by overindulging them in material possessions or waiting on them hand and foot. They believe in moderation in all things. Gushing sentiment and insincere platitudes cut no ice with them.

Having an independent and spontaneous nature themselves, they endeavor to see that these qualities are not inhibited in the young personality. They will never attempt to hold back or delay progress out of jealousy.

The birth Sign of the child, of course, will have a large bearing on the success of the individual Libra parent.

THE SCORPIO PARENT

The Scorpio parent usually runs a tight family ship. Oh, these moms and dads are generous enough, keenly solicitous of the physical and moral welfare of their children and intent on providing a good home for them with every modern convenience. No one could say they aren't deeply devoted, but they are rarely capable of appreciating the child's point of view. Everything must be as they divine it. The result is often a rigid and unyielding discipline that cramps the child's style.

Scorpio is one of the clearest-thinking, no-nonsense Signs of the Zodiac. It seems a pity these men and women can't always humanize their gift for dealing with realities when it comes to child rearing.

Their function as parents is to help form an integrated personality through which the reality of the youngster's character can unfold. But too often the Scorpio parent's stern methods of discipline disintegrate the child's personality. The child's main concern, then, is to obey—it is, after all, his or her best means of defense. The personality such a child presents to the family may have no relationship at all to his or her inner state. Some children of Scorpio parents wait only for the day when they can quit the rigorous regimen of their home. Others may be so intimidated that they grow up repressed and cowardly.

The Scorpio dad is often the worse offender of the two parents. He frequently runs his home like an old feudal baron, insisting that his wife as well as his children follow his instructions to the letter. The overbearing and tyrannical methods that he often employs to become a successful businessman are imposed on his household.

The Scorpio mother is a great homemaker and she idolizes her children. As long as she is in love with her husband, all is relatively well. But if the marriage breaks up or if she falls in love with another man, she will usually follow the dictates of her passionate nature. Although the children's material needs will be looked after in every respect, their psychological development may be seriously impaired.

Both parents are likely to suffer from inordinate and irrational jealousy, which may intensify their urge to restrict their child's personal freedom.

The birth Sign of the child, of course, will have a great bearing on the success of the individual Scorpio parent.

THE SAGITTARIUS PARENT

The Sagittarius man is usually too in love with his own freedom to make a really good father. He's a great sport, a fine companion and a real man's man. But when it comes to supervising children, he's usually a dead loss. He gets impatient with his own family. He wants to be out and about, roaming and sharing his ideas and comradeship with the rest of humanity.

The Sagittarius mother is a much more stable and settled character as far as the home and parenthood are concerned. She has a deep inner wisdom and a lot of common sense, which allow her to bring up her children in a balanced way. She also believes in freedom, but is more inclined to regard it as a state of mind than as the absence of any physical restriction; she teaches her children accordingly.

Both parents are intellectual types, have a broad outlook and are usually well informed on world affairs. They are also likely to approach religion from a philosophic rather than dogmatic angle, and to encourage their children to be tolerant of the opinions of others but to make decisions for themselves.

Both mother and father are splendid influences from a moral point of view. Although sometimes bluntly outspoken, their frankness and honesty are among their finest attributes. They are also good-hearted, kind and generous, but not foolishly so (except dad sometimes when he's out with the boys).

The children of Sagittarius parents will probably be more at ease confiding their personal problems to their mother. Dad, although just as capable of giving sound and helpful advice, may become a little uneasy when intimate matters are discussed. He prefers to stay clear—if possible—of emotional problems concerning his family. He feels more comfortable if his wife deals with them and lets him know the happy result when it's all over! Both parents will see that their youngsters take an early interest in sports and get plenty of exercise and fresh air. With a Sagittarius parent, a child is almost sure to develop great affection for animals of all kinds.

The birth Sign of the youngster, of course, will have a great bearing on the success of the individual Sagittarius parent.

THE CAPRICORN PARENT

The personality of the Capricorn parent ranges between two extremes. On the one hand, these people may be too indulgent with their children. On the other, they may be unduly stern, demanding and forbidding.

The Capricorn woman, especially, finds motherhood an outlet for her often cruelly repressed emotions. Capricorn is nowhere near as self-sufficient as the individuals born under this Sign usually manage to convey.

Generally speaking, Capricorn parents do have a deep love for their children and regard them as necessary to complete a marriage. The parents' own childhood is often memorable for its unstable conditions, particularly in the relationship between their mother and father. They tend to retain vivid emotional impressions of any unhappiness suffered in those days and endeavor to protect their own children from such similar and painful experiences.

However, the less mature Capricorn parent, especially dad, may have been so bitterly affected by his past that he is unsympathetic and intolerant of his own children. He is likely to impose rules that restrict normal pleasures and emphasize responsibility and duty. He may justify his harshness by saying it is for the children's own good. This parent may feel he enjoys the respect of his children, when in fact they fear him and in later years may detest him.

The Capricorn mother is frequently very ambitious for her offspring. She will see that they are always well dressed when going out, but may not worry so much when they're around the house. She will tend to nag continually, trying to improve their speech, their manners and their behavior. Her object is to make them more socially acceptable and popular. She will take a close interest in their education and insist on homework (as well as chores about the house) being done.

Both parents may be possessive or jealous. Those who spoil and indulge their own youngsters may find that they are irritated by other people's children.

Capricorn mothers and fathers will instruct their children to be careful with money, although they themselves may be quite unwise in their spending habits.

The birth Sign of the child, of course, will have a large bearing on the success of the individual Capricorn parent.

THE AQUARIUS PARENT

Aquarius men and women make wise and mature parents. They are intent on allowing the child to develop as himself or herself and not as a carbon copy of either mom or dad.

Aquarius is the Sign that rules brotherhood and understanding, and Aquarius parents base their relationships with their children on these qualities. Although intensely devoted to them, they keep their emotional distance. The child is never stifled or confused by displays of jealousy or the inconsistencies of sickly sentimentality.

The Aquarius mother and father both encourage their youngsters to be intellectually fearless, to question rather than blindly accept the opinions of others. The children are taught to be keen and considerate rather than purely competitive. These people desire their children to succeed as much as any parent, but they put less emphasis on materialistic values and egocentric pride. The Aquarius parent likes first to think of his or her child as a successful human being.

Aquarians are gentle and reasonable with children. They endeavor at all times to awaken the youngster's interest so that he feels he is making his own way under their sympathetic and helpful supervision.

Both are exceedingly independent, with strong ideals and humanitarian feelings. Their views on child rearing are often well ahead of the times, and may be criticized by conventional members of the family. But they are firm in their beliefs and will not allow in-laws or other relatives to interfere.

When it comes to discipline, both parents are likely to have an enlightened and original approach. They are usually most reluctant to resort to corporal punishment. They find it difficult to rebuke children who are too young to heed an appeal to reason. They are sometimes accused of being permissive by stalwarts of the old school.

The Aquarius mother will usually manage to dress her children in a distinctive way. She will encourage them to be honest and not to compromise with their conscience. The child with an Aquarian parent will be brought up with a high regard for loyalty to family and friends.

The birth Sign of the youngster, of course, will have a large bearing on the success of the individual Aquarian parent.

THE PISCES PARENT

Pisces mothers and fathers are both gentle and loving—but it's debatable whether they are really up to coping with the practical demands of their parenthood.

No one derives more pleasure from their children than these parents. They wait on their charges hand and foot, listen sympathetically to their small talk and problems, welcome their friends and spoil them in every way.

The problem is they are reluctant to face up to the often unpleasant and disagreeable side of parenthood—training and discipline. The child is frequently so indulged that unless the other parent is strong and determined, the child will grow up thoroughly spoiled and unreasonably demanding in his or her personal relationships.

However, there is a saving grace. These people do all in their power to encourage their children to be socially acceptable. It is extremely important to Pisces' own happiness and contentment that their offspring be liked by others.

So although they may adroitly sidestep the nasty and serious business of disciplining youngsters, they will use their splendid gifts of persuasion to inculcate the social graces—correcting speech, manners, deportment and so forth at every opportunity.

Both the Pisces mother and father are inclined to crack emotionally under pressure in the home or in disharmonious surroundings. Trying to cope with intractable young children or willful teenagers is apt to send them screaming for the door—or the bar.

Pisces parents usually imagine they are good parents—and they are more than half right. But for the sake of their mate, as well as for their children, it will pay them to learn to be a little less softhearted and permissive.

There is no doubt that the children of Pisces have a rare opportunity to be associated with spiritually uplifting influences. Also, their parents' fondness for all that is artistic and aesthetically pleasing can have a most beneficial effect on children's developing personalities.

If tangible direction is lacking, there is certainly no absence of love, affection and a subtle appreciation of beauty and graciousness in the home of a Pisces parent.

The birth Sign of the child, of course, will have a great bearing on the success of the individual Pisces parent.

CHILDREN

The following descriptions of children born under the various Signs are based on the position of the Sun, the most powerful influence in the horoscope. Most individuals conform to the solar influence. However, variations do occur because of the placement of the other planets at the time of birth. And, of course, the birth Signs of the parents will also be reflected in the child's conditioning.

For a closer examination of these factors, it is advisable to study the individual child's and the parents' horoscopes, which are available for every Sign in *AstroAnalysis*. All you need to know is the person's date of birth.

Since some Signs are naturally more and less compatible with others, you can obtain a further idea of how children and parents will hit it off by referring to the Compatibility Guide on page 91.

THE ARIES CHILD

The Aries child is extremely bright (sometimes brilliant) and usually very advanced for his or her age.

Too much applause and reference to the child's precocity by admiring adults is likely to make him strive to outdo himself and overexcite his nervous system. This could result in sleeplessness, supersensitivity and an overcritical approach to his playmates and later all his associates. The Aries child is high-strung and needs to be intelligently quieted. His mind is so alert to the possibilities for action in his environment that he finds it difficult to concentrate on one thing for very long. He begins new interests with great enthusiasm, but usually veers off well before they are finished. Sometimes it is because he has discovered the challenge is within his capabilities and so loses interest in it. But if a toy or game is beyond him, he will petulantly turn his back on it—or perhaps break it or throw it away. He should be taught to apply himself to finish what he starts. The chances of success will be greater in an atmosphere where he feels there is due recognition of the importance of what he is doing.

From the start, these youngsters should be taught the advantages of slowing down without inhibiting their spontaneity. Their excited, sudden movements are apt to lead to more than their share of accidents. They will usually be recovering from a bruise, scald or cut somewhere on their body. It is terribly important for Aries boys and girls to be physically active; it helps to work off the excess nervous energy that subtracts from their powers of concentration. But they need to learn the value of deliberate, measured movement as against unrestrained hustle and bustle; their parents should inculcate in them a sense of grace of rhythm, which their impulsive actions seldom allow.

Sports are good for the Aries child and he or she is usually proficient at them. It is wise to have children coached from an early age so that they express themselves with style and expertise. Abounding energy and desire to succeed will prevent them from becoming performing cogs in a wheel. Either they'll get to the top of the team or they'll quit and try another activity until they make their mark.

In none of his activities should the Aries child be encouraged to show off. If restraint or discipline is required, it should be exercised tactfully so it won't injure the youngster's pride. Aries is a fiercely proud Sign, and this is the key to the nobility that can readily be developed in this character.

It is important that this type of child be allowed to discover things for himself and not constantly be told what to do. He likes to experiment. Too much supervision and interference make him resentful. He learns from making mistakes. He might make the same mistake more than once (which can be rather exasperating for a parent), but this is his style. He packs a lot of experience into his life. He is attracted by the challenge rather than by the end result.

The Aries child often reveals creative talents quite early. These should be nurtured and developed as soon as they appear, without stressing the competitive angle.

One of the main problems is an overactive imagination. Young Aries should be taught not to exaggerate and to learn to describe objects and events as they really are, not as he or she fancies them to be.

THE TAURUS CHILD

Taurus is usually a lovely child, both to look at and in disposition. But he has some very definite characteristics that are not immediately discernible. These need to be understood, especially by his teachers, for him to develop in a normal, balanced way.

Above everything else, young Taureans need love and affection. They are deeply sensitive and unsure of themselves inside. They often give the appearance of being wonderfully self-assured, but this is to compensate for their uncertainty, which can amount almost to an inferiority complex at times.

Taureans are not intellectual beings, essentially. They live on their feelings, which need to be constantly stimulated by the demonstration and knowledge that they are loved and appreciated. You can't just tell a Taurus child that you love him or her. You have to show it in physical terms by cuddling and petting—or with caring actions. If you don't do this, the child will become more and more indifferent, and as he gets older, will turn to sensual self-indulgence as a substitute for the loving stimulation he missed as a child. Failing this, Taurus may become increasingly stolid, and, in maturity, a rather dull and uninteresting person.

Young Taurus has exceptional willpower, which may, at times, reveal itself as a fearful obstinacy. If he digs in his toes, no argument or threat will shake him. He can be absolutely unreasonable. Again, only an appeal to his emotional self is apt to make him relent. Should he ever lose his temper, it could be a devastatingly memorable occasion.

He is an extremely modest child and tends to underrate his own abilities. He should not be criticized to make him "do better" because criticism will only make him feel more inferior and then, perhaps, defiantly overconfident and prone to making silly mistakes. He responds much better to praise and encouragement.

Taurus children are not studious types. Normal education methods don't work so well with them. To learn, it is vital that they have their feelings aroused so they can take a genuine interest in the subject. These boys and girls need to relate to topics through their senses; if they're to learn about nature, they must examine the specimen, touch it, smell it. With arithmetic and other abstract subjects, the teacher must find a way of exciting them into participation with demonstrations, models. The failure to realize this often leads to branding the Taurus child a slow learner, when he is, in fact, nothing of the sort.

Friendship and playmates are very important to Taurean youngsters. If they can't mix with children they like, they will slow down physically and mentally, and may easily become lazy and indifferent. Having a great love of pleasure (because it helps them learn to be intellectual creatures), they might choose companions who teach them bad habits.

Properly handled and encouraged, the Taurus child quickly puts aside his timidity and becomes a friendly and congenial little person. He is likely to be artistic with his hands and any sign of this should be cultivated.

THE GEMINI CHILD

Gemini children are usually filled with restless, nervous energy. It comes from their minds, which are like delicately tuned electronic instruments. They simply can't keep still, mentally or physically. They must be constantly engaged in something that interests them. Parents and teachers may find this an exhausting business, mainly because these lovable little imps lose interest more quickly than most children. And when that happens, and no one's around, their capacity for mischief is almost unbelievable!

Young Gemini is an exceedingly bright child. He or she learns instantaneously and has an alert, inquiring mind that demands to know the reason behind everything that catches his or her attention.

As often as practical, Gemini children should be answered factually and not put off because the question happens to be irrelevant. This is the way they absorb, and every fact goes into their formidable memory, where it will be recalled as soon as it's required. In a very short time, you can teach a Gemini child practically anything.

He may not be physically strong in his early years because his whole system is under the continual tension of febrile nervous activity. As his body adapts to this, he will get stronger, until finally, in maturity, his health will be dictated largely by his state of mind. Just as Gemini can stage remarkable recoveries when new and novel interests appear, so he can become listless when assailed by boredom and depression.

The pure Gemini child needs plenty of exercise, but usually not in the form of rough and strenuous sports. His lithe, agile body and quick actions enable him to excel in games requiring thought and technique rather than brute strength and endurance.

It is especially necessary for these boys and girls to get as much sleep and rest as possible. But this is usually easier said than arranged. At bedtime, the aim should be to avoid excitement that stimulates the imagination. Stories and television shows should be carefully selected. Horror movies and the like are almost certain to cause nightmares and extreme anxiety. The child may be afraid of the dark well into his or her teens.

Gemini youngsters frequently exaggerate and tell outrageous lies—with remarkable plausibility. Their imagination is so active and vivid that they live out adventures and dramas in their heads and can't (or would rather not) separate fiction from reality.

They make excellent actors, able to mimic sounds and reproduce the characteristics of people they observe. Sometimes these children suffer from a slight speech impediment—the brain is too fast for the vocal equipment. But with patience and understanding, this can be overcome. Otherwise, the Gemini child is usually well advanced in his speech and comprehension. He may be a terrible chatterbox, though.

A child of this Sign is more intellectual than sentimental and may sometimes be slow at showing love and affection.

THE CANCER CHILD

The Cancer child looks for love and a placid existence. These boys and girls are extremely sensitive and timid. Even though they crave to make friends, their retiring nature renders it difficult to make the first move. They do not enjoy being alone; they need to feel they belong. A Cancer child will cling tenaciously to anyone who loves him. The most difficult parental task is to push this sensitive little creature gently forward into the world.

Although the Cancer child is not necessarily the smartest or brightest of children, he possesses innate talents that a sensible upbringing will help make manifest. The tendency for late development makes the formative years extremely important for them.

Young Cancer responds remarkably to adults who show they have faith in him. For those who love him, he will do almost anything. A responsive and understanding parent or teacher will try to arouse his interest in games and activities that he can confidently share with other children. He should not be left to feel lonely. The object is to coax the child out, to make him more independent and outspoken. It is best to encourage him to do as much as possible for himself and let him feel he is actually achieving results. These should be praised and appreciated.

Cancer children are splendidly conscientious when they have been entrusted with a task. Psychologically, the reason for this is they are in constant need of approbation and learn quickly that one way of guaranteeing this is to do a job assiduously.

These children are not studious and intellectual, although they may become so in adulthood. They learn through their feelings. Unless they are very clearly associated with sensation, concepts and ideas confuse them. They need to smell a flower, to sing a song, to taste a piece of fruit if they are going to be taught about these things. You can't assume that a Cancer child has got the idea of a subject from a verbal description—which would suffice for most other children. Cancer is the Sign of the senses and intuition, so the child's intellectual development depends on *emotional* understanding. Once a parent or teacher manages to arouse an absorbing interest in him, the Cancer child may apply himself to this subject for the rest of his life. Great artistic and creative careers may be begun with the right treatment of these finely balanced little people.

Otherwise, the younger person of this Sign is tempted to become introverted and live off his own emotions—moody, changeable and lethargic.

Being exceedingly sensitive, the Cancer child is easily discouraged and takes criticism much to heart. Worry may upset his stomach. He is also apt to suffer from colds and chills. His health in his earlier years may be indifferent. He may pick at his food and cry more than most youngsters.

Cancer children are usually competent at making handicrafts. In later years, they often show an extraordinary flair for business coupled with an intensely ambitious spirit.

THE LEO CHILD

The Leo child has a vast amount of vital and mental energy at his or her disposal. It is important for parents and teachers to see that this is directed along positive lines. This youngster, because of his forceful determination, is apt to find that success comes fairly readily. He may get so carried away with applause and admiration that he overlooks the value of accomplishment itself.

Young Leo has a natural gift for leadership and will assert this as his or her right in the presence of other youngsters. The problem is a tendency to become domineering, to throw his weight around unnecessarily, show off and generally bore everyone within earshot with his boasting. In some cases, little Leo becomes "little Caesar" and exhibits a distinct love of power, which may be harmless in a child but is an objectionable quality in an adult.

The Leo child is an active and lovable little person. Quite apart from the early "ego flexing," there is a dignity and nobility to his nature. His unquestionable courage becomes obvious early. Although as disobedient as any child, he will seldom resort to mean and spiteful actions. He or she will probably only have to be told once that it is dishonest to tell tales. This child's sense of loyalty is ingrained and at times may be carried to absurd lengths.

Leos are deeply affectionate children, and despite their love of display and applause, are keenly sensitive. Their intuition is often remarkable. They have a great sense of pride and yet are quick to forget and forgive. Once they make up their minds to do something, they are unswervingly determined.

A Leo child often acts impulsively, especially where pleasure is concerned, finding it very difficult to turn down an opportunity to enjoy himself. When playing, he is likely to lose all sense of time and arrive home at nine o'clock at night for his evening meal. He has a love of the great outdoors and is likely to acquit himself well at all kinds of sports.

Young Leo, although enjoying his periods of seclusion, will usually be found among groups and clubs where he can demonstrate his organizing ability and powers of leadership.

Parents of the Leo teenager should endeavor to have him trained in any profession or line of work he shows an interest in. He has a great capacity for learning, not by gathering and memorizing information but by inquiring and understanding its significance. He is never really satisfied unless he comprehends the reason for an action or instruction. A natural commander of men and women in the making, Leo will never be a shallow echo of another person's caprices.

The Leo youngster has a deep-seated ambition to get to the top even though he or she may not understand this inner drive. This child's considerable energies and diverse talents work better harnessed in a definite direction, whether in the arts, literature, politics, journalism, science or executive management.

Young Leo also benefits from a good example. Conversely, he or she should not be allowed to fall into bad company.

THE VIRGO CHILD

Virgo children are worriers. They take the smallest disappointments very seriously. They want to be liked, and yet have an unfortunate way of upsetting others by being unduly critical and faultfinding. A Virgo child is often exasperated and discouraged by other people's negative reactions to his or her good intentions, and by his or her own frustrated desire to please.

Young Virgo needs to be taught to accent the positive side of his or her nature. Although reserved and modest, these children are naturally optimistic and progressive. They are also keenly intelligent. But the slightest antagonism and adversity tend to deflate them. They live on their nerves to a great extent. They are continually analyzing other people's motives and endeavoring to find a rationale for everything. The sheer impossibility of satisfying this desire explains their basic problem.

The Virgo child loves order and method. Once these are established at home or in school, he or she will settle down emotionally and seldom be any trouble. But in a disorganized system where people are uncertain, Virgo becomes disoriented. That's why it's often a traumatic experience for a Virgo child—or a Virgo adult for that matter—to move to a new home, school or job. One astrologer has even claimed you can cause great agitation in a Virgo cat by relocating its saucer!

Schoolwork itself, however, is seldom much of a problem for the Virgo youngster. Along with Gemini, he is one of the easiest types in the Zodiac to teach. He has an inquiring and logical mind, which is always trying to make practical sense out of the information received. Naturally, school lessons make sense to these boys and girls. They often take a special interest in science and mathematics. They are also quite inventive and enjoy devising new methods of doing things.

Young Virgo makes friends cautiously. He's not a sentimental or emotional character and prefers to judge people on their actions and achievements rather than their words. He is an idealist and at heart a perfectionist who wants to see everything in its proper place and logical order. When he discerns that a person is not being honest with himself or true to his type (his intellectual acuity is first rate), he will say so, not with the desire to hurt, but to help. This trait is naturally often misinterpreted, and his playmates may resent his remarks and attitude and ostracize him for them.

The Virgo child needs a good education so that he doesn't feel inferior to others. He doesn't, as a rule, enjoy close physical contact—in fact, he may feel that cuddling and caressing are unnecessary and embarrassing. His finer feelings have to be handled delicately and with understanding to prevent fussiness and queasiness from becoming fixed in his character.

Virgo children are apt to be faddish about certain foods and instantly dislike some kinds. They may refuse to eat in a place they feel is dirty, although they are unable to give a conscious reason for this attitude.

These children are very quick to learn about cleanliness and hygiene, but the subjects should not be overemphasized.

THE LIBRA CHILD

The Libra child is a delicate flower because he or she is a meeting point of intellect and emotion and these two don't integrate easily. The child is usually very intelligent and bright but unsure of how to handle his or her feelings.

Libras crave love yet are reserved and shy about reaching out for it. Consequently, they may cling and yet be unable to give in return. They are constantly weighing up what to do in their relationships, which way to go, what is best. The result is they don't appear to have much initiative, and unless guided and directed by an understanding parent or teacher, may grow up unable to make positive use of their many potential talents.

Young Libras don't seem to have much willpower, mainly for the reasons given above. They become excited by an idea, plunge into action with enthusiasm—and then lose interest and look around for something new. If they can't find something special, they may lapse into apathy. These children have very little urge to develop their capabilities; ambition is something they have to learn. They prefer to depend on others without exerting themselves. They need to develop the habit of working along methodical

lines—games and hobbies can be used for this. If their interest is not maintained—by the parent acting as a sort of partner—they will quickly get into mischief.

The wise parent of a Libra youngster will realize right from the start that his or her child is artistically inclined and that a harsh, uncongenial, severe or ugly environment will inhibit natural expression. In such an environment, the child is likely to become highly nervous and a constant problem for the parent. But once the innate Libran love of beauty and harmony is acknowledged and cultivated, the prospects of steady development and accomplishment are much improved. For these reasons, it is advisable for the parent to observe the child's proclivities in the formative years and coax him along in the right direction.

A Libra child is much more likely to become a successful dancer, actor, singer, writer, painter, interior decorator, architect or beauty specialist than shine in a cutthroat commercial occupation.

Moodiness and jealousy are often a problem. These children want desperately to be liked, but their attitude often suggests indifference to their playmates. They may be happy and gay one moment, and inexplicably depressed and silent the next. The more they are left alone, the more temperamental and introspective they become. If this is allowed to continue, the child may grow up with few friends and unreasonable possessiveness may cause great unhappiness in his or her future love life.

Libran children are usually well formed and attractive. They have a magnetic appeal that makes other childrren want to be with them, but they seem unable to maintain the initial attraction. This confuses them. The parents' task is to teach the Libra child, with love and understanding, to integrate his or her emotional and mental activities and express them in unselfish ways such as in art and social endeavors.

THE SCORPIO CHILD

The Scorpio child is a tight concentration of intense energy and the direction of his or her development will depend largely on the influence parents or guardians bring to bear.

Young Scorpio is particularly strong-willed. He or she also possesses abundant capabilities that bode success in future life as a surgeon, dentist, psychiatrist, scientist, occult investigator, researcher, lawyer, detective or military person.

If you can interest this youngster in constructive and productive activities, there is not much he or she is incapable of achieving. Once this child fixes a goal, he will pursue it relentlessly. And his capacity for hard work and endurance is unequaled by any of the other Sign of the Zodiac.

The problem is that Scorpio can go from one extreme to the other; that is, he or she can be very good and very bad. If early training is neglected or haphazard, or if the child happens to fall into bad company, he may grow up to be a selfish and tyrannical adult.

Young Scorpio has a keen and penetrating mind and cannot long be entertained by frivolous and pointless games and pastimes. At every stage, Scorpios enjoy grappling with sturdy problems that are not so easy for others of their age or experience to solve. Everything they attempt, they do with zest and relish—provided they are genuinely interested.

Schoolwork comes easy to Scorpio children. Trouble occurs when they can't find sufficiently satisfying outlets for their tremendous vitality.

It is wise for the parents of a Scorpio child to be honest and straightforward with him or her from the beginning because these children possess an almost mystical ability to detect lies and attempts to deceive them. Also, the negative side of a Scorpio nature is less likely to assert itself in an atmosphere of frank and open commitment. The habitual faults of the Scorpio character include brooding resentment, secretiveness and jealousy. These have less opportunity to fester in a young personality used to candid and truthful parents.

Young Scorpio is fiercely independent but surprisingly tractable if handled with subtlety and sensitivity. He or she resents being ordered about, and may react violently and willfully to this sort of treatment. Parents who reason with their Scorpio children and deal with them in an adult fashion will get the best results.

The shrewdness and comprehension of these youngsters may develop into an infuriating air of superiority when they are with less mentally acute adults. Their self-confidence is enormous. Their vanty is a weak spot.

The Scorpio child is sometimes so bent on getting his own way that when opposed by young playmates, he may resort to underhanded methods. He can be vindictive, and in extreme cases, exact cruel reprisals. If the negative qualities are strong in these boys and girls, they may plot revenge while pretending to be sorry.

THE SAGITTARIUS CHILD

The Sagittarius child is not a fast developer. He or she is cheerful, trusting, optimistic and a very congenial little person to have around, if you can tolerate some changeable and unpredictable ways. Sagittarius sometimes retains these childlike qualities well into adulthood, and in some cases, for his entrie life. His trust and faith in humanity is one of his most admirable traits. Yet, as many parents are pained to find out, this faith is often violated and imposed upon.

Still, not to worry—little Sagittarius certainly doesn't. He loves to play, to roam far afield, to visit people, to go on "adventures." These boys and girls are too interested in being on the move and experiencing life as it actually is to have much time for reading and study. However, they are mentally eager, bright and quick to learn, though lacking in concentration.

Sagittarius is passionately fond of animals. If he can get hold of a horse and ride it on his explorations and adventures, he is in his element. The parents of a Sagittarius child can expect to have around the house a menagerie of pets on which their youngster will lavish considerable affection. He may sometimes in his haste forget to feed the animals and afterward cry inconsolably with remorse. He is so genuine in his affection and sincere in his intentions that it is not wise to make a fuss over this kind of neglect.

Young Sagittarius tends to think everyone is good. He himself is truthful, spontaneous and honest. He doesn't have a selfish or vindictive bone in his body. He has to be taught, though, that there is such a thing as deceit and that he must practice putting his inherently good judgment to full use.

The Sagittarius child is not possessive. Emotionally, he or she loves to have a home, family (and pets) to return to. But these children can't stand the thought of being tied down to a confined or regimented existence. Their sense of freedom is essential to their continued and broadening development.

Here, a parent must exercise great care, striking a balance between the child's need to be restrained and taught responsibility and his or her fundamental urge to learn. The most effective way of securing this child's cooperation and interest, as well as this objective, is to treat him or her like a buddy and not try to dictate. Sagittarius is built for companionship and affection rather than for possessive love. He makes one of the finest friends of all.

Young Sagittarius *has* to be guided toward a more responsible attitude to life. He thinks he can look after himself, but rarely can unless his parents have managed to cultivate in him the judgment that curbs impatience, restlessness, recklessness, extravagance and all that goes with a personality trying to throw off authority and its controls.

When it comes to a career, the Sagittarius youth is ambitious and resourceful. But he is inclined to jump from one job to another because he just can't stand the tedium of waiting for normal advancement.

THE CAPRICORN CHILD

The Capricorn child is often far too serious for his or her own good. And frequently, it is the fault of one of the parents. This child needs mature but cheerful and happy handling that makes a point of *not* overstressing duty, responsibility and restriction. There are enough of these sobering elements in the Capricorn temperament already. Exaggeration will only create further problems for the youngster as he or she grows up.

Young Capricorn needs a great deal of praise and affection. These boys and girls often feel afraid and deeply dissatisfied with themselves. Criticism wounds them deeply, not because they resent it, but because they unwittingly believe it to be true. Obviously, these little people require a very special parental technique to help them develop a balanced and buoyant personality.

Never nag this child. Criticism should be leveled so that the positive alternative appears as the ideal solution. Every effort to instruct should be made optimistically and encouragingly.

With this Sign, the positions of the other planets in the child's horoscope are extremely important. If there are sunnier and more easygoing influences such as Jupiter in Leo, Sagittarius or Aries, the youngster's disposition will be correspondingly less grave. These other planetary configurations can be checked out in the Capricorn book of *AstroAnalysis*.

The true Capricorn child is very self-conscious. He wants to make friends, but is uneasy in the presence of others, especially strangers. Being withdrawn and a rather solitary figure, he doesn't attract the usual number of playmates. Without friends to help draw him out, he is inclined to become distrustful and wary of personal relationships, thus isolating himself even more.

Young Capricorn is very good at schoolwork and a willing little helper around the house. He enjoys running errands and completing small tasks for elders who display trust in him. He is extremely conscientious and wants to please. He usually enjoys study and reading and has a great capacity for sorting out detail and cataloging data. He is well suited for all kinds of hobbies connected with sciences such as chemistry, biology, astronomy, and the like where he can apply his considerable reasoning abilities.

The longer his education can be continued, the better, especially from the social angle. He needs to be in the company of people his own age to help overcome his shyness.

As Capricorn has a distinct talent for practical pursuits, he or she will generally feel more confident with an education along these lines rather than one that is strictly academic.

People of this Sign are born leaders and vauntingly ambitious. When young Capricorn does get around to organizing young friends, he or she is enterprising and frequently bossy.

THE AQUARIUS CHILD

The Aquarian child is often precocious in a shy and rather retiring way. Juvenile pastimes and games don't hold his or her interest for as long in the formative years as they do other children's. Aquarians "grow up" mentally very quickly and often prefer the company of elders "when they should be out playing." Sometimes they are called "old-fashioned" because of their adult ways, but these are only a reflection of the advanced understanding of life which is peculiar to Aquarius.

The Aquarius child is naturally affectionate and very obedient if parents or teachers are reasonable. He or she enjoys a position of trust and is particular about honoring obligations. The cooperation of these children can't be secured by threat or force. They are highly intellectual and demand to know from a very early age why they should or should not do certain things.

The most effective parental policy is to treat an Aquarian youngster as a mental equal, to confide in him or her and encourage confidences in return—in other words, to regard the child as an intelligent companion.

Although young Aquarius is a loving child with a sweet and kind disposition, he is noticeably impersonal in the way he shows affection. He doesn't cling to people in sentimental ways and is more likely to be adult and friendly.

These boys and girls are not great students and need to be encouraged and helped with their schoolwork. They find routine book learning and formal concentration arduous. Their independent minds tend to reject attempts to condition their thinking. However, if they can be convinced that education is a means to a personally desirable end, they will apply themselves and work conscientiously. They need to know there is progressive development for them in whatever they tackle. To accumulate indiscriminate knowledge is just not their style.

The Aquarian child is uniquely lacking in self-centered drive. Basically, he or she wants to be of use to the community. Material possessions are not all that important, and over the years this indifference becomes more and more evident. A strong humanitarian tendency is apt to appear. Finally, Aquarians will probably choose a career in science or medicine, one connected with large welfare projects or social reform where they can satisfy their urge to serve on a wide scale. They are not so concerned with the individual as they are with the masses, which accounts for their sometimes detached attitude.

Young Aquarius often has a great love of animals. Here, he or she begins to demonstrate a deep protective instinct.

This child sometimes has the potential of brilliance—even genius—but not necessarily in conventional forms. His or her inclinations need to be closely observed so that any unusual aptitude can be cultivated and guided.

THE PISCES CHILD

The true Pisces child is very intelligent but emotionally unstable. He or she is born believing that everything and everyone are good. Thus Pisces' life seems to be a progression of disillusionment.

Faced with an unacceptable reality, Pisces children retreat into a dream world where all is as perfect as they originally thought. The problem for the parent is to coax these little people back without smashing their dreams, to teach them it's not so bad after all and that every human being has within them the power to cope.

These children are essentially artistic and often show a talent for dancing, painting, music and writing—especially poetry. They are terribly self-conscious and need to be encouraged at every step with love, praise and admiration.

They are very critical of their own efforts and never seem to reach the standard of perfection their nature calls for. In despair, they will tear up what they've written or drawn, even though by normal standards it might be excellent. Or, more likely as they grow up, they will decide not to try at all anymore, that indolence is better than the pain of failure.

Young Pisces have no confidence in their own ability. They are great actors and can put on a show of indifference and self-assurance, for a short time. But then they are likely to go away on their own and cry until they sink into the delicious world of their own vivid imaginings. These boys and girls are generally timid, shy, secretive and very loving. But they also possess a strong spiritual quality.

A Pisces child has to be taught that harsh self-judgment is damaging to his or her attempts to be productive and expressive. These boys and girls must be led to understand that they are highly artistic, and that even their compassion for others (stronger in them than in any other Sign) is an act of love and creation—sublime artistry—that most others are not capable of. On the practical side, they must learn to allow those who are competent to judge their efforts to do so, since no one will be as cruelly critical of their work as they are themselves.

These boys and girls must be given a sense of proportion so that they understand every success means "failure" for someone. The important thing is to instill in the child a desire to perform, and especially to complete, for the sake of the work itself, without encouraging a competitive spirit or even acknowledging that it is necessary.

Your AstroProfile

The following section contains Planet Tables showing their positions on your birth date (Pink Tables). The check lists provided here can be used in conjunction with the Tables to serve both as a permanent reference and as a basis for establishing your own horoscope (see chart page 120).

At the time of my birth the Moon was in:

- Aries ☐
- Taurus ☐
- Gemini ☐
- Cancer ☐
- Leo ☐
- Virgo ☐
- Libra ☐
- Scorpio ☐
- Sagittarius ☐
- Capricorn ☐
- Aquarius ☐
- Pisces ☐

At the time of my birth the Mercury was in:

- Aries ☐
- Taurus ☐
- Gemini ☐
- Cancer ☐
- Leo ☐
- Virgo ☐
- Libra ☐
- Scorpio ☐
- Sagittarius ☐
- Capricorn ☐
- Aquarius ☐
- Pisces ☐

At the time of my birth Venus was in:

- Aries ☐
- Taurus ☐
- Gemini ☐
- Cancer ☐
- Leo ☐
- Virgo ☐
- Libra ☐
- Scorpio ☐
- Sagittarius ☐
- Capricorn ☐
- Aquarius ☐
- Pisces ☐

At the time of my birth Mars was in:

- Aries ☐
- Taurus ☐
- Gemini ☐
- Cancer ☐
- Leo ☐
- Virgo ☐
- Libra ☐
- Scorpio ☐
- Sagittarius ☐
- Capricorn ☐
- Aquarius ☐
- Pisces ☐

At the time of my birth Jupiter was in:

- Aries ☐
- Taurus ☐
- Gemini ☐
- Cancer ☐
- Leo ☐
- Virgo ☐
- Libra ☐
- Scorpio ☐
- Sagittarius ☐
- Capricorn ☐
- Aquarius ☐
- Pisces ☐

At the time of my birth Saturn was in:

- Aries ☐
- Taurus ☐
- Gemini ☐
- Cancer ☐
- Leo ☐
- Virgo ☐
- Libra ☐
- Scorpio ☐
- Sagittarius ☐
- Capricorn ☐
- Aquarius ☐
- Pisces ☐

At the time of my birth Uranus was in:

- Aries ☐
- Taurus ☐
- Gemini ☐
- Cancer ☐
- Leo ☐
- Virgo ☐
- Libra ☐
- Scorpio ☐
- Sagittarius ☐
- Capricorn ☐
- Aquarius ☐
- Pisces ☐

At the time of my birth Neptune was in:

- Aries ☐
- Taurus ☐
- Gemini ☐
- Cancer ☐
- Leo ☐
- Virgo ☐
- Libra ☐
- Scorpio ☐
- Sagittarius ☐
- Capricorn ☐
- Aquarius ☐
- Pisces ☐

At the time of my birth Pluto was in:

- Aries ☐
- Taurus ☐
- Gemini ☐
- Cancer ☐
- Leo ☐
- Virgo ☐
- Libra ☐
- Scorpio ☐
- Sagittarius ☐
- Capricorn ☐
- Aquarius ☐
- Pisces ☐

YOUR HOROSCOPE CHART

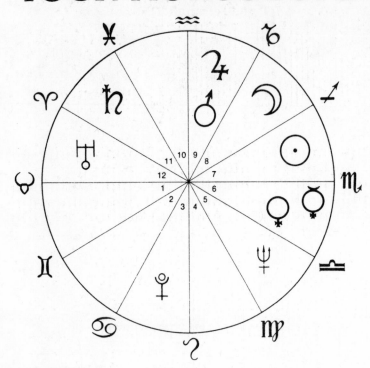

This person was born at 5:15 p.m. October 31 in New York City. The Sun is in Scorpio and is found in the 7th house. The Rising Sign, or the Sign governing house number 1, is Taurus, so this person is a blend of Scorpio and Taurus.

HOW TO CONSTRUCT YOUR OWN HOROSCOPE CHART:

1. Label house number 1: 4 a.m.—6 a.m.
2. In a counterclockwise direction, label the rest of the houses: 2 a.m.—4 a.m., Midnight—2 a.m., 10 p.m.—Midnight, 8 p.m.—10 p.m., 6 p.m.,—8 p.m., 4 p.m.—6 p.m., 2 p.m.—4 p.m., Noon—2 p.m., 10 a.m.—Noon, 8 a.m.—10 a.m., and 6 a.m.—8 a.m.
3. Now find out what time you were born and place the Sun in the appropriate house.
4. Label the edge of that house with your Sun Sign. You now have a description of your basic character and your fundamental drives. You can also see in what areas of life on Earth you will be most likely to focus your constant energy and center your activity.
5. Label the rest of the houses with the Signs, starting with your Sun Sign, in order, still in a *counterclockwise direction*. When you get to Pisces, start over with Aries and keep going until you reach the house behind the Sun.
6. Now refer to your Astro Check List and fill in the rest of your Chart.

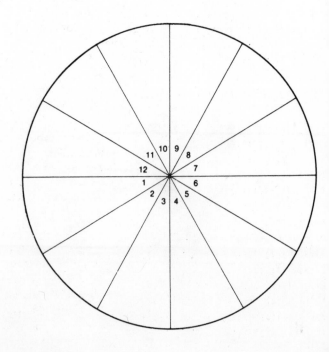

YOUR PLANETS

AND WHAT THEY SIGNIFY

LEO

The Pink Tables contain all the information you need to construct your own AstroAnalysis in a short time—or that of anyone born between July 21st and August 21st, when the Sun was in Leo.

As you know, the Leo Character Analysis (pages 41—46) is the same for every person born between July 21st and August 21st. No doubt you recognized your basic self in those descriptions. There were probably areas where your character did not conform. Naturally. You are a Leo, but you are also an individual. You share many common traits with your Leo cousins, but in behavior there are distinct, special, unique traits that make you what you are.

How does Astrology account for all this? By "reading" the position of planets other than the Sun on the day of your birth. The Sun is only *one* influence, although it is by far the most important. Our existence depends on it absolutely which is why its position in the Zodiac determines our basic type. But there are nine other planets whose positions in the horoscope affect and modify the basic Sun Sign character.

For instance, where were Jupiter and Saturn, the largest of the planets, on the day you were born? These two planets exert tremendous influence on both the actual solar system and on the individual's character and life. Suppose Jupiter and Saturn were together in Aquarius, the Sign exactly opposite the Sun in Leo. Science has established that this powerful lineup causes severe radio disturbance on the Earth. What effect does it have on you—on your electromagnetic receiver, your conscious and your subconscious mind? So here goes:

Turn to the Pink Tables and read along the columns to the right beside your birth date. This will tell you the exact location of every planet on every day. Begin with the Moon and see what Sign it was visiting. Then turn to the Moon chapter and read the appropriate descriptions. Do the same for all the other planets. If you wish, this information can then be transferred to the check list provided in the preceding Astro Profile. Remember that in Astrology the Sun and the Moon are considered to be planets and that it is not unusual for a Sign to contain more than one planet.

Following this introduction are brief descriptions of the influences exerted on your life by the ten planets. Next you will find a Time Zone Map to help you establish the position of the Moon at the exact time of your birth. The Time Zone Map is explained on the overleaf and is followed by the Pink Tables. These Tables are simplicity itself, since all the complex mathematical calculations involved in the science of Astrology have been done for you. They show the positions of all the planets for every day in your Sign between 1910 and 1990. Refer to these tables and then to the descriptions which follow the tables and which are applicable to you (Moon in Virgo, Neptune in Cancer, etc.). As you progress, you will be amazed at how many facets of your own personality reveal themselves to you. You may discover hidden strengths and weaknesses—you may have suspected their existence before but never quite put them into words. You will be astounded as your AstroAnalysis helps you on your voyage of self-discovery and, as the mystery unfolds, you'll be startled to see just how Astrology is zeroing in on your character.

PLANETARY INFLUENCES

While the Sun, undeniably, is the center of our existence, the planets modify its influence according to their own special natures, strengths and positions. Because the planets revolve around the Sun, their positions must be calculated for each day, each year, in order to determine their function and expression in your horoscope—hence the Pink Tables. The significance of these planets is described briefly on these pages, but to understand fully the extent to which your own life has been—and continues to be—affected by these planets, you must use the Tables to find their location on your birthdate.

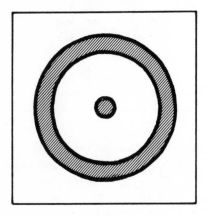

SUN—the constant, ever-shining source of life in the daytime. It symbolizes strength, vigor, ardor, generosity and the ability to function as a mature individual and a creative force; it also indicates the complete potential of every human being.

MOON—rules our feelings, customs, habits and moods, and its position is an indicator of rapidly changing phases of behavior and personality. The Moon rules the female element in both women and men, the women in a man's life, fertility, food, health in general and the masses.

MERCURY—is the planet of the mind and the power of communication. It rules speaking, language, mathematics, drafting and design, students, messengers and, indeed, any profession in which the mind of man has wings!

VENUS—symbolizes that rare and elusive harmony and radiance which is true beauty. Its ideal is the flame of spiritual love, Aphrodite, goddess of love. It indicates grace, delicacy, sensitivity and charm; and it rules the love of nature and pleasure, luck and wealth.

MARS—is energy and drive, courage and daring; but it can be thoughtless and cruel, wild and angry. It rules soldiers, butchers, surgeons and salesmen—any calling that requires daring, bold skill, refined techniques and self-promotion.

JUPITER—rules good luck and good cheer, health, wealth, optimism, happiness, success and joy. It is the symbol of opportunity; it rules actors, statesmen, professional people, publishing and religion.

SATURN—creates limitations and boundaries and shows the consequences of being human. It rules time, old age and sobriety. It symbolizes selfishness, reticence and diplomacy; and can bring depression, jealousy and greed.

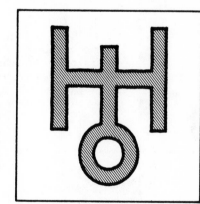

URANUS—rules upheaval and revolution and sudden changes for good or evil. It governs intellectual genius, inventiveness, technology and electronic advancement and influences mankind's great forward leaps. Uranus, Neptune and Pluto are known as the outer planets.

NEPTUNE—is the planet of illusion. At its best, it is the planet of emotional genius, poetry, music and inspiration and has dominance over many of the arts. It is a cheap intoxicant, and its worst aspects include drugs and fraud. It is associated with all forms of escapism and mass delusion.

PLUTO—symbolizes the capacity to change totally and forever a person's lifestyle, thought and behavior. Pluto rules all the powerful forces of creation and destruction; it can bring a lust for power with strong obsessions. It creates, destroys and re-creates.

WORLD TIME

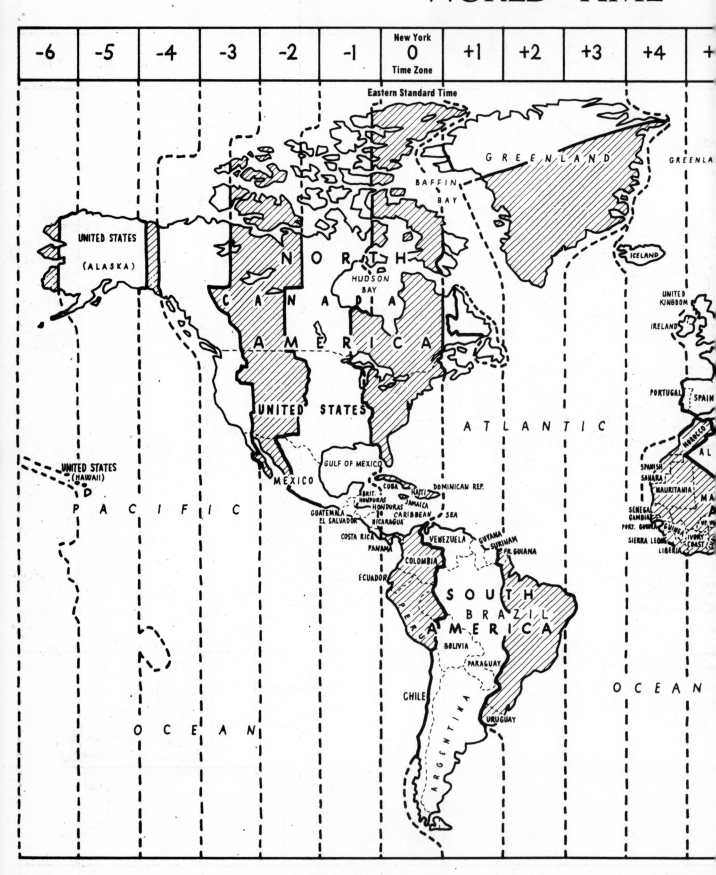

| -6 | -5 | -4 | -3 | -2 | -1 | New York 0 Time Zone | +1 | +2 | +3 | +4 | + |

ZONE MAP

+7	+8	+9	+10	+11	+12	+13	+14	+15	+16	+17

FINLAND

UNION OF SOVIET SOCIALIST REPUBLICS

BERING SEA

E U R O P E

A S I A

FINLAND

HUNG.

YUGO.

BULG.

ALB.

BLACK SEA

GREECE

TURKEY

MONGOLIA

N. KOREA

CYP. LEB. SYRIA

ISRAEL

IRAQ

JORD.

KUWAIT

IRAN

AFGHANISTAN

S. KOREA

CHINA

PACIFIC

MEAN SEA

LYBA

U.A.R. (EGYPT)

SAUDI

ARABIA

PAKISTAN

NEPAL

BANGLADESH

BURMA

HONG KONG

TAIWAN

OCEAN

CHAD

SUDAN

YEMEN

SOUTH YEMEN

MUSCAT & OMAN

ARABIAN

SEA

INDIA

LAOS

THAI.

VIETNAM

CAMB.

REP. OF THE PHILIPPINES

ICA

I C A

ETHIOPIA

SOMALIA

I N D I A N

CENT. AFR. REP.

REP. OF THE CONGO

DEM. REP. OF THE CONGO

UGANDA

RWANDA

BURUNDI

KENYA

TANZANIA

MALAYSIA

SINGAPORE

I N D O N E S I A

NEW GUINEA

NGOLA

ZAMBIA

MALAWI

MALAGASY REP.

O C E A N

CORAL SEA

WEST

RHOD.

MOZAMBIQUE

BOTSWANA

MAURITIUS

ICA

SWAZILAND

A U S T R A L I A

SOUTH AFRICA

LESOTHO

TASMAN SEA

NEW ZEALAND

For explanation of Time Zone Map, see page 126.

The exact time of your birth is important in determining an exact horoscope. This is particularly important when considering the position of the Moon, since you will notice in the Pink Planet Tables that the Moon moves from Sign to Sign through the whole Zodiac. Since it makes the trip through all twelve Signs in a month, the Moon stays in each Sign only about two and a half days.

In addition to helping you find what particular Sign the Moon is "visiting" each day, the Pink Planet Tables will tell you at what *time* the Moon will enter a new Sign.

For example:

March	MOON	
22	7:56 P.M.	VIRGO
23		
24		
25	6:45 A.M.	LIBRA

This means that at 7:56 in New York, on the evening of the 22nd, the Moon entered the Sign of Virgo and remained in that Sign until 6:45 in the morning of March 25th, when it entered the Sign of Libra.

You will notice that the map on the preceding two pages is divided into zones. Locate the place of your birth on the map. If you were born in the zone marked "0," no calculation is needed. However, if you were born outside this zone, the number at the top of the zone in which you were born represents the number of hours you must add to or subtract from the time of your birth in order to use the times given in the Tables. (These times are based on Eastern Standard Time.)

For example:

You were born in San Francisco on March 25 at 6:30 A.M. Since the time on the Tables is applicable only to those people born in the zone marked "0", look at the number at the top of the zone in which California is found. The number is -3. Therefore, to convert to New York "0" time, going eastward, you must *add* 3 hours to the time of your birth. The result is 9:30 A.M., indicating that the Moon was in Libra at the time of your birth.

March	MOON	
22	7:56 P.M.	VIRGO
23		
24		
25	6:45 A.M.	LIBRA
26		
27	7:06 P.M.	SCORPIO

On the other hand, if you were born on March 25 in London at 9:30 A.M., the number at the top of the zone is +5. *Subtracting* 5 hours, going westward to New York "0" time, the result is 4:30 A.M. This indicates that the Moon was in Virgo at the time of your birth.

1910   LEO

	MOON FROM IN	MERCURY	VENUS	MARS	JUPITER	SATURN	URANUS	NEPTUNE	PLUTO
JULY									
24	11:56 AM PISCES	LEO	GEMINI	LEO	LIBRA	TAURUS	CAPRICORN	CANCER	GEMINI
25		LEO	CANCER	LEO	LIBRA	TAURUS	CAPRICORN	CANCER	GEMINI
26	4:07 PM ARIES	LEO	CANCER	LEO	LIBRA	TAURUS	CAPRICORN	CANCER	GEMINI
27		LEO	CANCER	LEO	LIBRA	TAURUS	CAPRICORN	CANCER	GEMINI
28	7:26 PM TAURUS	LEO	CANCER	LEO	LIBRA	TAURUS	CAPRICORN	CANCER	GEMINI
29		LEO	CANCER	LEO	LIBRA	TAURUS	CAPRICORN	CANCER	GEMINI
30	10:19 PM GEMINI	LEO	CANCER	LEO	LIBRA	TAURUS	CAPRICORN	CANCER	GEMINI
31		LEO	CANCER	LEO	LIBRA	TAURUS	CAPRICORN	CANCER	GEMINI
AUGUST									
1		LEO	CANCER	LEO	LIBRA	TAURUS	CAPRICORN	CANCER	GEMINI
2	0:53 AM CANCER	LEO	CANCER	LEO	LIBRA	TAURUS	CAPRICORN	CANCER	GEMINI
3		LEO	CANCER	LEO	LIBRA	TAURUS	CAPRICORN	CANCER	GEMINI
4	4:39 AM LEO	LEO	CANCER	LEO	LIBRA	TAURUS	CAPRICORN	CANCER	GEMINI
5		LEO	CANCER	LEO	LIBRA	TAURUS	CAPRICORN	CANCER	GEMINI
6	9:57 AM VIRGO	LEO	CANCER	LEO	LIBRA	TAURUS	CAPRICORN	CANCER	GEMINI
7		VIRGO	CANCER	VIRGO	LIBRA	TAURUS	CAPRICORN	CANCER	GEMINI
8	6:12 PM LIBRA	VIRGO	CANCER	VIRGO	LIBRA	TAURUS	CAPRICORN	CANCER	GEMINI
9		VIRGO	CANCER	VIRGO	LIBRA	TAURUS	CAPRICORN	CANCER	GEMINI
10		VIRGO	CANCER	VIRGO	LIBRA	TAURUS	CAPRICORN	CANCER	GEMINI
11	5:33 AM SCORPIO	VIRGO	CANCER	VIRGO	LIBRA	TAURUS	CAPRICORN	CANCER	GEMINI
12		VIRGO	CANCER	VIRGO	LIBRA	TAURUS	CAPRICORN	CANCER	GEMINI
13	6:26 PM SAGITTARIUS	VIRGO	CANCER	VIRGO	LIBRA	TAURUS	CAPRICORN	CANCER	GEMINI
14		VIRGO	CANCER	VIRGO	LIBRA	TAURUS	CAPRICORN	CANCER	GEMINI
15		VIRGO	CANCER	VIRGO	LIBRA	TAURUS	CAPRICORN	CANCER	GEMINI
16	6:04 AM CAPRICORN	VIRGO	CANCER	VIRGO	LIBRA	TAURUS	CAPRICORN	CANCER	GEMINI
17		VIRGO	CANCER	VIRGO	LIBRA	TAURUS	CAPRICORN	CANCER	GEMINI
18	2:29 PM AQUARIUS	VIRGO	CANCER	VIRGO	LIBRA	TAURUS	CAPRICORN	CANCER	GEMINI
19		VIRGO	LEO	VIRGO	LIBRA	TAURUS	CAPRICORN	CANCER	GEMINI
20	7:39 PM PISCES	VIRGO	LEO	VIRGO	LIBRA	TAURUS	CAPRICORN	CANCER	GEMINI
21		VIRGO	LEO	VIRGO	LIBRA	TAURUS	CAPRICORN	CANCER	GEMINI
22	10:41 PM ARIES	VIRGO	LEO	VIRGO	LIBRA	TAURUS	CAPRICORN	CANCER	GEMINI
23		VIRGO	LEO	VIRGO	LIBRA	TAURUS	CAPRICORN	CANCER	GEMINI

1911   MOON

	FROM IN	MERCURY	VENUS	MARS	JUPITER	SATURN	URANUS	NEPTUNE	PLUTO
JULY									
24		LEO	VIRGO	TAURUS	SCORPIO	TAURUS	CAPRICORN	CANCER	GEMINI
25	12:24 PM LEO	LEO	VIRGO	TAURUS	SCORPIO	TAURUS	CAPRICORN	CANCER	GEMINI
26		LEO	VIRGO	TAURUS	SCORPIO	TAURUS	CAPRICORN	CANCER	GEMINI
27	1:26 PM VIRGO	LEO	VIRGO	TAURUS	SCORPIO	TAURUS	CAPRICORN	CANCER	GEMINI
28		LEO	VIRGO	TAURUS	SCORPIO	TAURUS	CAPRICORN	CANCER	GEMINI
29	5:32 PM LIBRA	LEO	VIRGO	TAURUS	SCORPIO	TAURUS	CAPRICORN	CANCER	GEMINI
30		LEO	VIRGO	TAURUS	SCORPIO	TAURUS	CAPRICORN	CANCER	GEMINI
31		VIRGO	VIRGO	TAURUS	SCORPIO	TAURUS	CAPRICORN	CANCER	GEMINI
AUGUST									
1	1:45 AM SCORPIO	VIRGO	VIRGO	TAURUS	SCORPIO	TAURUS	CAPRICORN	CANCER	GEMINI
2		VIRGO	VIRGO	TAURUS	SCORPIO	TAURUS	CAPRICORN	CANCER	GEMINI
3	1:23 PM SAGITTARIUS	VIRGO	VIRGO	TAURUS	SCORPIO	TAURUS	CAPRICORN	CANCER	GEMINI
4		VIRGO	VIRGO	TAURUS	SCORPIO	TAURUS	CAPRICORN	CANCER	GEMINI
5		VIRGO	VIRGO	TAURUS	SCORPIO	TAURUS	CAPRICORN	CANCER	GEMINI
6	2:08 AM CAPRICORN	VIRGO	VIRGO	TAURUS	SCORPIO	TAURUS	CAPRICORN	CANCER	GEMINI
7		VIRGO	VIRGO	TAURUS	SCORPIO	TAURUS	CAPRICORN	CANCER	GEMINI
8	2:01 PM AQUARIUS	VIRGO	VIRGO	TAURUS	SCORPIO	TAURUS	CAPRICORN	CANCER	GEMINI
9		VIRGO	VIRGO	TAURUS	SCORPIO	TAURUS	CAPRICORN	CANCER	GEMINI
10	11:59 PM PISCES	VIRGO	VIRGO	TAURUS	SCORPIO	TAURUS	CAPRICORN	CANCER	GEMINI
11		VIRGO	VIRGO	TAURUS	SCORPIO	TAURUS	CAPRICORN	CANCER	GEMINI
12		VIRGO	VIRGO	TAURUS	SCORPIO	TAURUS	CAPRICORN	CANCER	GEMINI
13	8:01 AM ARIES	VIRGO	VIRGO	TAURUS	SCORPIO	TAURUS	CAPRICORN	CANCER	GEMINI
14		VIRGO	VIRGO	TAURUS	SCORPIO	TAURUS	CAPRICORN	CANCER	GEMINI
15	2:10 PM TAURUS	VIRGO	VIRGO	TAURUS	SCORPIO	TAURUS	CAPRICORN	CANCER	GEMINI
16		VIRGO	VIRGO	TAURUS	SCORPIO	TAURUS	CAPRICORN	CANCER	GEMINI
17	6:22 PM GEMINI	VIRGO	VIRGO	TAURUS	SCORPIO	TAURUS	CAPRICORN	CANCER	GEMINI
18		VIRGO	VIRGO	TAURUS	SCORPIO	TAURUS	CAPRICORN	CANCER	GEMINI
19	8:41 PM CANCER	VIRGO	VIRGO	TAURUS	SCORPIO	TAURUS	CAPRICORN	CANCER	GEMINI
20		VIRGO	VIRGO	TAURUS	SCORPIO	TAURUS	CAPRICORN	CANCER	GEMINI
21	9:53 PM LEO	VIRGO	VIRGO	TAURUS	SCORPIO	TAURUS	CAPRICORN	CANCER	GEMINI
22		VIRGO	VIRGO	TAURUS	SCORPIO	TAURUS	CAPRICORN	CANCER	GEMINI
23	11:26 PM VIRGO	VIRGO	VIRGO	TAURUS	SCORPIO	TAURUS	CAPRICORN	CANCER	GEMINI

1912

	MOON FROM IN	MERCURY	VENUS	MARS	JUPITER	SATURN	URANUS	NEPTUNE	PLUTO
JULY									
23	10:21 AM SAGITTARIUS	LEO	LEO	VIRGO	SAGITTARIUS	GEMINI	AQUARIUS	CANCER	GEMINI
24		LEO	LEO	VIRGO	SAGITTARIUS	GEMINI	AQUARIUS	CANCER	GEMINI
25	11:41 PM CAPRICORN	LEO	LEO	VIRGO	SAGITTARIUS	GEMINI	AQUARIUS	CANCER	GEMINI
26		VIRGO	LEO	VIRGO	SAGITTARIUS	GEMINI	AQUARIUS	CANCER	GEMINI
27		VIRGO	LEO	VIRGO	SAGITTARIUS	GEMINI	AQUARIUS	CANCER	GEMINI
28	11:59 AM AQUARIUS	VIRGO	LEO	VIRGO	SAGITTARIUS	GEMINI	AQUARIUS	CANCER	GEMINI
29		VIRGO	LEO	VIRGO	SAGITTARIUS	GEMINI	AQUARIUS	CANCER	GEMINI
30		VIRGO	LEO	VIRGO	SAGITTARIUS	GEMINI	AQUARIUS	CANCER	GEMINI
31	0:39 AM PISCES	VIRGO	LEO	VIRGO	SAGITTARIUS	GEMINI	AQUARIUS	CANCER	GEMINI
AUGUST									
1		VIRGO	LEO	VIRGO	SAGITTARIUS	GEMINI	AQUARIUS	CANCER	GEMINI
2	12:38 PM ARIES	VIRGO	LEO	VIRGO	SAGITTARIUS	GEMINI	AQUARIUS	CANCER	GEMINI
3		VIRGO	LEO	VIRGO	SAGITTARIUS	GEMINI	AQUARIUS	CANCER	GEMINI
4	10:35 PM TAURUS	VIRGO	LEO	VIRGO	SAGITTARIUS	GEMINI	AQUARIUS	CANCER	GEMINI
5		VIRGO	LEO	VIRGO	SAGITTARIUS	GEMINI	AQUARIUS	CANCER	GEMINI
6		VIRGO	LEO	VIRGO	SAGITTARIUS	GEMINI	AQUARIUS	CANCER	GEMINI
7	5:08 AM GEMINI	VIRGO	LEO	VIRGO	SAGITTARIUS	GEMINI	AQUARIUS	CANCER	GEMINI
8		VIRGO	LEO	VIRGO	SAGITTARIUS	GEMINI	AQUARIUS	CANCER	GEMINI
9	7:56 AM CANCER	VIRGO	LEO	VIRGO	SAGITTARIUS	GEMINI	AQUARIUS	CANCER	GEMINI
10		VIRGO	LEO	VIRGO	SAGITTARIUS	GEMINI	AQUARIUS	CANCER	GEMINI
11	7:59 AM LEO	VIRGO	LEO	VIRGO	SAGITTARIUS	GEMINI	AQUARIUS	CANCER	GEMINI
12		VIRGO	LEO	VIRGO	SAGITTARIUS	GEMINI	AQUARIUS	CANCER	GEMINI
13	7:13 AM VIRGO	VIRGO	VIRGO	VIRGO	SAGITTARIUS	GEMINI	AQUARIUS	CANCER	GEMINI
14		VIRGO	VIRGO	VIRGO	SAGITTARIUS	GEMINI	AQUARIUS	CANCER	GEMINI
15	7:48 AM LIBRA	VIRGO	VIRGO	VIRGO	SAGITTARIUS	GEMINI	AQUARIUS	CANCER	GEMINI
16		VIRGO	VIRGO	VIRGO	SAGITTARIUS	GEMINI	AQUARIUS	CANCER	GEMINI
17	11:28 AM SCORPIO	VIRGO	VIRGO	VIRGO	SAGITTARIUS	GEMINI	AQUARIUS	CANCER	GEMINI
18		VIRGO	VIRGO	VIRGO	SAGITTARIUS	GEMINI	AQUARIUS	CANCER	GEMINI
19	6:58 PM SAGITTARIUS	VIRGO	VIRGO	VIRGO	SAGITTARIUS	GEMINI	AQUARIUS	CANCER	GEMINI
20		VIRGO	VIRGO	VIRGO	SAGITTARIUS	GEMINI	AQUARIUS	CANCER	GEMINI
21		LEO	VIRGO	VIRGO	SAGITTARIUS	GEMINI	AQUARIUS	CANCER	GEMINI
22	5:42 AM CAPRICORN	LEO	VIRGO	VIRGO	SAGITTARIUS	GEMINI	AQUARIUS	CANCER	GEMINI
23		LEO	VIRGO	VIRGO	SAGITTARIUS	GEMINI	AQUARIUS	CANCER	GEMINI

1913

	MOON FROM IN	MERCURY	VENUS	MARS	JUPITER	SATURN	URANUS	NEPTUNE	PLUTO
JULY									
24		LEO	GEMINI	TAURUS	CAPRICORN	GEMINI	AQUARIUS	CANCER	CANCER
25	11:28 PM TAURUS	LEO	GEMINI	TAURUS	CAPRICORN	GEMINI	AQUARIUS	CANCER	CANCER
26		LEO	GEMINI	TAURUS	CAPRICORN	GEMINI	AQUARIUS	CANCER	CANCER
27		LEO	GEMINI	TAURUS	CAPRICORN	GEMINI	AQUARIUS	CANCER	CANCER
28	8:56 AM GEMINI	LEO	GEMINI	TAURUS	CAPRICORN	GEMINI	AQUARIUS	CANCER	CANCER
29		LEO	GEMINI	GEMINI	CAPRICORN	GEMINI	AQUARIUS	CANCER	CANCER
30	2:21 PM CANCER	LEO	GEMINI	GEMINI	CAPRICORN	GEMINI	AQUARIUS	CANCER	CANCER
31		LEO	GEMINI	GEMINI	CAPRICORN	GEMINI	AQUARIUS	CANCER	CANCER
AUGUST									
1	4:23 PM LEO	LEO	GEMINI	GEMINI	CAPRICORN	GEMINI	AQUARIUS	CANCER	CANCER
2		LEO	GEMINI	GEMINI	CAPRICORN	GEMINI	AQUARIUS	CANCER	CANCER
3	4:43 PM VIRGO	LEO	GEMINI	GEMINI	CAPRICORN	GEMINI	AQUARIUS	CANCER	CANCER
4		LEO	GEMINI	GEMINI	CAPRICORN	GEMINI	AQUARIUS	CANCER	CANCER
5	5:12 PM LIBRA	LEO	GEMINI	GEMINI	CAPRICORN	GEMINI	AQUARIUS	CANCER	CANCER
6		LEO	CANCER	GEMINI	CAPRICORN	GEMINI	AQUARIUS	CANCER	CANCER
7	7:21 PM SCORPIO	LEO	CANCER	GEMINI	CAPRICORN	GEMINI	AQUARIUS	CANCER	CANCER
8		LEO	CANCER	GEMINI	CAPRICORN	GEMINI	AQUARIUS	CANCER	CANCER
9		LEO	CANCER	GEMINI	CAPRICORN	GEMINI	AQUARIUS	CANCER	CANCER
10	0:03 AM SAGITTARIUS	LEO	CANCER	GEMINI	CAPRICORN	GEMINI	AQUARIUS	CANCER	CANCER
11		LEO	CANCER	GEMINI	CAPRICORN	GEMINI	AQUARIUS	CANCER	CANCER
12	7:24 AM CAPRICORN	LEO	CANCER	GEMINI	CAPRICORN	GEMINI	AQUARIUS	CANCER	CANCER
13		LEO	CANCER	GEMINI	CAPRICORN	GEMINI	AQUARIUS	CANCER	CANCER
14	5:09 PM AQUARIUS	LEO	CANCER	GEMINI	CAPRICORN	GEMINI	AQUARIUS	CANCER	CANCER
15		LEO	CANCER	GEMINI	CAPRICORN	GEMINI	AQUARIUS	CANCER	CANCER
16		LEO	CANCER	GEMINI	CAPRICORN	GEMINI	AQUARIUS	CANCER	CANCER
17	4:51 AM PISCES	LEO	CANCER	GEMINI	CAPRICORN	GEMINI	AQUARIUS	CANCER	CANCER
18		LEO	CANCER	GEMINI	CAPRICORN	GEMINI	AQUARIUS	CANCER	CANCER
19	5:47 PM ARIES	LEO	CANCER	GEMINI	CAPRICORN	GEMINI	AQUARIUS	CANCER	CANCER
20		LEO	CANCER	GEMINI	CAPRICORN	GEMINI	AQUARIUS	CANCER	CANCER
21		LEO	CANCER	GEMINI	CAPRICORN	GEMINI	AQUARIUS	CANCER	CANCER
22	6:29 AM TAURUS	LEO	CANCER	GEMINI	CAPRICORN	GEMINI	AQUARIUS	CANCER	CANCER
23		LEO	CANCER	GEMINI	CAPRICORN	GEMINI	AQUARIUS	CANCER	CANCER

1914   LEO

	MOON FROM / IN	MERCURY	VENUS	MARS	JUPITER	SATURN	URANUS	NEPTUNE	PLUTO
JULY									
24		CANCER	VIRGO	VIRGO	AQUARIUS	GEMINI	AQUARIUS	CANCER	CANCER
25	2:59 AM VIRGO	CANCER	VIRGO	VIRGO	AQUARIUS	GEMINI	AQUARIUS	CANCER	CANCER
26		CANCER	VIRGO	VIRGO	AQUARIUS	GEMINI	AQUARIUS	CANCER	CANCER
27	6:04 AM LIBRA	CANCER	VIRGO	VIRGO	AQUARIUS	GEMINI	AQUARIUS	CANCER	CANCER
28		CANCER	VIRGO	VIRGO	AQUARIUS	GEMINI	AQUARIUS	CANCER	CANCER
29	8:44 AM SCORPIO	CANCER	VIRGO	VIRGO	AQUARIUS	GEMINI	AQUARIUS	CANCER	CANCER
30		CANCER	VIRGO	VIRGO	AQUARIUS	GEMINI	AQUARIUS	CANCER	CANCER
31	11:35 AM SAGITTARIUS	CANCER	VIRGO	VIRGO	AQUARIUS	GEMINI	AQUARIUS	CANCER	CANCER
AUGUST									
1		CANCER	VIRGO	VIRGO	AQUARIUS	GEMINI	AQUARIUS	CANCER	CANCER
2	3:14 PM CAPRICORN	CANCER	VIRGO	VIRGO	AQUARIUS	GEMINI	AQUARIUS	CANCER	CANCER
3		CANCER	VIRGO	VIRGO	AQUARIUS	GEMINI	AQUARIUS	CANCER	CANCER
4	8:26 PM AQUARIUS	CANCER	VIRGO	VIRGO	AQUARIUS	GEMINI	AQUARIUS	CANCER	CANCER
5		CANCER	VIRGO	VIRGO	AQUARIUS	GEMINI	AQUARIUS	CANCER	CANCER
6		CANCER	VIRGO	VIRGO	AQUARIUS	GEMINI	AQUARIUS	CANCER	CANCER
7	4:03 AM PISCES	CANCER	VIRGO	VIRGO	AQUARIUS	GEMINI	AQUARIUS	CANCER	CANCER
8		CANCER	VIRGO	VIRGO	AQUARIUS	GEMINI	AQUARIUS	CANCER	CANCER
9	2:25 PM ARIES	CANCER	VIRGO	VIRGO	AQUARIUS	GEMINI	AQUARIUS	CANCER	CANCER
10		CANCER	VIRGO	VIRGO	AQUARIUS	GEMINI	AQUARIUS	CANCER	CANCER
11		LEO	LIBRA	VIRGO	AQUARIUS	GEMINI	AQUARIUS	CANCER	CANCER
12	2:45 AM TAURUS	LEO	LIBRA	VIRGO	AQUARIUS	GEMINI	AQUARIUS	CANCER	CANCER
13		LEO	LIBRA	VIRGO	AQUARIUS	GEMINI	AQUARIUS	CANCER	CANCER
14	3:05 PM GEMINI	LEO	LIBRA	VIRGO	AQUARIUS	GEMINI	AQUARIUS	CANCER	CANCER
15		LEO	LIBRA	LIBRA	AQUARIUS	GEMINI	AQUARIUS	CANCER	CANCER
16		LEO	LIBRA	LIBRA	AQUARIUS	GEMINI	AQUARIUS	CANCER	CANCER
17	1:09 AM CANCER	LEO	LIBRA	LIBRA	AQUARIUS	GEMINI	AQUARIUS	CANCER	CANCER
18		LEO	LIBRA	LIBRA	AQUARIUS	GEMINI	AQUARIUS	CANCER	CANCER
19	7:51 AM LEO	LEO	LIBRA	LIBRA	AQUARIUS	GEMINI	AQUARIUS	CANCER	CANCER
20		LEO	LIBRA	LIBRA	AQUARIUS	GEMINI	AQUARIUS	CANCER	CANCER
21	11:29 AM VIRGO	LEO	LIBRA	LIBRA	AQUARIUS	GEMINI	AQUARIUS	CANCER	CANCER
22		LEO	LIBRA	LIBRA	AQUARIUS	GEMINI	AQUARIUS	CANCER	CANCER
23	1:17 PM LIBRA	LEO	LIBRA	LIBRA	AQUARIUS	GEMINI	AQUARIUS	CANCER	CANCER

1915

	MOON FROM / IN	MERCURY	VENUS	MARS	JUPITER	SATURN	URANUS	NEPTUNE	PLUTO
JULY									
24	2:04 AM CAPRICORN	CANCER	CANCER	GEMINI	PISCES	CANCER	AQUARIUS	LEO	CANCER
25		CANCER	CANCER	GEMINI	PISCES	CANCER	AQUARIUS	LEO	CANCER
26	3:11 AM AQUARIUS	CANCER	CANCER	GEMINI	PISCES	CANCER	AQUARIUS	LEO	CANCER
27		CANCER	CANCER	GEMINI	PISCES	CANCER	AQUARIUS	LEO	CANCER
28	6:05 AM PISCES	CANCER	CANCER	GEMINI	PISCES	CANCER	AQUARIUS	LEO	CANCER
29		CANCER	CANCER	GEMINI	PISCES	CANCER	AQUARIUS	LEO	CANCER
30	12:08 PM ARIES	CANCER	CANCER	GEMINI	PISCES	CANCER	AQUARIUS	LEO	CANCER
31		CANCER	CANCER	GEMINI	PISCES	CANCER	AQUARIUS	LEO	CANCER
AUGUST									
1	9:40 PM TAURUS	CANCER	CANCER	GEMINI	PISCES	CANCER	AQUARIUS	LEO	CANCER
2		CANCER	CANCER	GEMINI	PISCES	CANCER	AQUARIUS	LEO	CANCER
3		CANCER	CANCER	GEMINI	PISCES	CANCER	AQUARIUS	LEO	CANCER
4	9:43 AM GEMINI	LEO	LEO	GEMINI	PISCES	CANCER	AQUARIUS	LEO	CANCER
5		LEO	LEO	GEMINI	PISCES	CANCER	AQUARIUS	LEO	CANCER
6	10:11 PM CANCER	LEO	LEO	GEMINI	PISCES	CANCER	AQUARIUS	LEO	CANCER
7		LEO	LEO	GEMINI	PISCES	CANCER	AQUARIUS	LEO	CANCER
8		LEO	LEO	GEMINI	PISCES	CANCER	AQUARIUS	LEO	CANCER
9	9:08 AM LEO	LEO	LEO	GEMINI	PISCES	CANCER	AQUARIUS	LEO	CANCER
10		LEO	LEO	GEMINI	PISCES	CANCER	AQUARIUS	LEO	CANCER
11	5:42 PM VIRGO	LEO	LEO	GEMINI	PISCES	CANCER	AQUARIUS	LEO	CANCER
12		LEO	LEO	GEMINI	PISCES	CANCER	AQUARIUS	LEO	CANCER
13	11:55 PM LIBRA	LEO	LEO	GEMINI	PISCES	CANCER	AQUARIUS	LEO	CANCER
14		LEO	LEO	GEMINI	PISCES	CANCER	AQUARIUS	LEO	CANCER
15		LEO	LEO	GEMINI	PISCES	CANCER	AQUARIUS	LEO	CANCER
16	4:16 AM SCORPIO	LEO	LEO	GEMINI	PISCES	CANCER	AQUARIUS	LEO	CANCER
17		LEO	LEO	GEMINI	PISCES	CANCER	AQUARIUS	LEO	CANCER
18	7:19 AM SAGITTARIUS	LEO	LEO	GEMINI	PISCES	CANCER	AQUARIUS	LEO	CANCER
19		VIRGO	LEO	CANCER	PISCES	CANCER	AQUARIUS	LEO	CANCER
20	9:38 AM CAPRICORN	VIRGO	LEO	CANCER	PISCES	CANCER	AQUARIUS	LEO	CANCER
21		VIRGO	LEO	CANCER	PISCES	CANCER	AQUARIUS	LEO	CANCER
22	12:04 PM AQUARIUS	VIRGO	LEO	CANCER	PISCES	CANCER	AQUARIUS	LEO	CANCER
23		VIRGO	LEO	CANCER	PISCES	CANCER	AQUARIUS	LEO	CANCER

1916

JULY	MOON FROM IN	MERCURY	VENUS	MARS	JUPITER	SATURN	URANUS	NEPTUNE	PLUTO
23		CANCER	CANCER	LIBRA	TAURUS	CANCER	AQUARIUS	LEO	CANCER
24	5:36 AM GEMINI	CANCER	CANCER	LIBRA	TAURUS	CANCER	AQUARIUS	LEO	CANCER
25		CANCER	CANCER	LIBRA	TAURUS	CANCER	AQUARIUS	LEO	CANCER
26	6:53 PM CANCER	LEO	CANCER	LIBRA	TAURUS	CANCER	AQUARIUS	LEO	CANCER
27		LEO	CANCER	LIBRA	TAURUS	CANCER	AQUARIUS	LEO	CANCER
28		LEO	CANCER	LIBRA	TAURUS	CANCER	AQUARIUS	LEO	CANCER
29	7:56 AM LEO	LEO	CANCER	LIBRA	TAURUS	CANCER	AQUARIUS	LEO	CANCER
30		LEO	CANCER	LIBRA	TAURUS	CANCER	AQUARIUS	LEO	CANCER
31	8:18 PM VIRGO	LEO	CANCER	LIBRA	TAURUS	CANCER	AQUARIUS	LEO	CANCER
AUGUST									
1		LEO	CANCER	LIBRA	TAURUS	CANCER	AQUARIUS	LEO	CANCER
2		LEO	CANCER	LIBRA	TAURUS	CANCER	AQUARIUS	LEO	CANCER
3	6:54 AM LIBRA	LEO	CANCER	LIBRA	TAURUS	CANCER	AQUARIUS	LEO	CANCER
4		LEO	CANCER	LIBRA	TAURUS	CANCER	AQUARIUS	LEO	CANCER
5	2:55 PM SCORPIO	LEO	CANCER	LIBRA	TAURUS	CANCER	AQUARIUS	LEO	CANCER
6		LEO	CANCER	LIBRA	TAURUS	CANCER	AQUARIUS	LEO	CANCER
7	7:57 PM SAGITTARIUS	LEO	CANCER	LIBRA	TAURUS	CANCER	AQUARIUS	LEO	CANCER
8		LEO	CANCER	LIBRA	TAURUS	CANCER	AQUARIUS	LEO	CANCER
9	10:08 PM CAPRICORN	LEO	CANCER	LIBRA	TAURUS	CANCER	AQUARIUS	LEO	CANCER
10		VIRGO	CANCER	LIBRA	TAURUS	CANCER	AQUARIUS	LEO	CANCER
11	10:28 PM AQUARIUS	VIRGO	CANCER	LIBRA	TAURUS	CANCER	AQUARIUS	LEO	CANCER
12		VIRGO	CANCER	LIBRA	TAURUS	CANCER	AQUARIUS	LEO	CANCER
13	10:30 PM PISCES	VIRGO	CANCER	LIBRA	TAURUS	CANCER	AQUARIUS	LEO	CANCER
14		VIRGO	CANCER	LIBRA	TAURUS	CANCER	AQUARIUS	LEO	CANCER
15		VIRGO	CANCER	LIBRA	TAURUS	CANCER	AQUARIUS	LEO	CANCER
16	0:03 AM ARIES	VIRGO	CANCER	LIBRA	TAURUS	CANCER	AQUARIUS	LEO	CANCER
17		VIRGO	CANCER	LIBRA	TAURUS	CANCER	AQUARIUS	LEO	CANCER
18	4:46 AM TAURUS	VIRGO	CANCER	LIBRA	TAURUS	CANCER	AQUARIUS	LEO	CANCER
19		VIRGO	CANCER	LIBRA	TAURUS	CANCER	AQUARIUS	LEO	CANCER
20	1:28 PM GEMINI	VIRGO	CANCER	LIBRA	TAURUS	CANCER	AQUARIUS	LEO	CANCER
21		VIRGO	CANCER	LIBRA	TAURUS	CANCER	AQUARIUS	LEO	CANCER
22		VIRGO	CANCER	LIBRA	TAURUS	CANCER	AQUARIUS	LEO	CANCER
23	1:22 AM CANCER	VIRGO	CANCER	LIBRA	TAURUS	CANCER	AQUARIUS	LEO	CANCER

1917

JULY	MOON FROM IN	MERCURY	VENUS	MARS	JUPITER	SATURN	URANUS	NEPTUNE	PLUTO
23		LEO	LEO	GEMINI	GEMINI	LEO	AQUARIUS	LEO	CANCER
24	7:33 AM LIBRA	LEO	LEO	GEMINI	GEMINI	LEO	AQUARIUS	LEO	CANCER
25		LEO	LEO	GEMINI	GEMINI	LEO	AQUARIUS	LEO	CANCER
26	6:41 PM SCORPIO	LEO	LEO	GEMINI	GEMINI	LEO	AQUARIUS	LEO	CANCER
27		LEO	LEO	GEMINI	GEMINI	LEO	AQUARIUS	LEO	CANCER
28		LEO	LEO	CANCER	GEMINI	LEO	AQUARIUS	LEO	CANCER
29	2:37 AM SAGITTARIUS	LEO	VIRGO	CANCER	GEMINI	LEO	AQUARIUS	LEO	CANCER
30		LEO	VIRGO	CANCER	GEMINI	LEO	AQUARIUS	LEO	CANCER
31	6:48 AM CAPRICORN	LEO	VIRGO	CANCER	GEMINI	LEO	AQUARIUS	LEO	CANCER
AUGUST									
1		LEO	VIRGO	CANCER	GEMINI	LEO	AQUARIUS	LEO	CANCER
2	7:50 AM AQUARIUS	LEO	VIRGO	CANCER	GEMINI	LEO	AQUARIUS	LEO	CANCER
3		VIRGO	VIRGO	CANCER	GEMINI	LEO	AQUARIUS	LEO	CANCER
4	7:20 AM PISCES	VIRGO	VIRGO	CANCER	GEMINI	LEO	AQUARIUS	LEO	CANCER
5		VIRGO	VIRGO	CANCER	GEMINI	LEO	AQUARIUS	LEO	CANCER
6	7:19 AM ARIES	VIRGO	VIRGO	CANCER	GEMINI	LEO	AQUARIUS	LEO	CANCER
7		VIRGO	VIRGO	CANCER	GEMINI	LEO	AQUARIUS	LEO	CANCER
8	9:38 AM TAURUS	VIRGO	VIRGO	CANCER	GEMINI	LEO	AQUARIUS	LEO	CANCER
9		VIRGO	VIRGO	CANCER	GEMINI	LEO	AQUARIUS	LEO	CANCER
10	3:25 PM GEMINI	VIRGO	VIRGO	CANCER	GEMINI	LEO	AQUARIUS	LEO	CANCER
11		VIRGO	VIRGO	CANCER	GEMINI	LEO	AQUARIUS	LEO	CANCER
12		VIRGO	VIRGO	CANCER	GEMINI	LEO	AQUARIUS	LEO	CANCER
13	0:40 AM CANCER	VIRGO	VIRGO	CANCER	GEMINI	LEO	AQUARIUS	LEO	CANCER
14		VIRGO	VIRGO	CANCER	GEMINI	LEO	AQUARIUS	LEO	CANCER
15	12:20 PM LEO	VIRGO	VIRGO	CANCER	GEMINI	LEO	AQUARIUS	LEO	CANCER
16		VIRGO	VIRGO	CANCER	GEMINI	LEO	AQUARIUS	LEO	CANCER
17		VIRGO	VIRGO	CANCER	GEMINI	LEO	AQUARIUS	LEO	CANCER
18	1:02 AM VIRGO	VIRGO	VIRGO	CANCER	GEMINI	LEO	AQUARIUS	LEO	CANCER
19		VIRGO	VIRGO	CANCER	GEMINI	LEO	AQUARIUS	LEO	CANCER
20	1:42 PM LIBRA	VIRGO	VIRGO	CANCER	GEMINI	LEO	AQUARIUS	LEO	CANCER
21		VIRGO	VIRGO	CANCER	GEMINI	LEO	AQUARIUS	LEO	CANCER
22		VIRGO	LIBRA	CANCER	GEMINI	LEO	AQUARIUS	LEO	CANCER
23	1:15 AM SCORPIO	VIRGO	LIBRA	CANCER	GEMINI	LEO	AQUARIUS	LEO	CANCER

1918   LEO

	MOON FROM IN	MERCURY	VENUS	MARS	JUPITER	SATURN	URANUS	NEPTUNE	PLUTO
JULY									
24		LEO	GEMINI	LIBRA	CANCER	LEO	AQUARIUS	LEO	CANCER
25	5:32 PM PISCES	LEO	CANCER	LIBRA	CANCER	LEO	AQUARIUS	LEO	CANCER
26		LEO	CANCER	LIBRA	CANCER	LEO	AQUARIUS	LEO	CANCER
27	6:59 PM ARIES	LEO	CANCER	LIBRA	CANCER	LEO	AQUARIUS	LEO	CANCER
28		VIRGO	CANCER	LIBRA	CANCER	LEO	AQUARIUS	LEO	CANCER
29	9:07 PM TAURUS	VIRGO	CANCER	LIBRA	CANCER	LEO	AQUARIUS	LEO	CANCER
30		VIRGO	CANCER	LIBRA	CANCER	LEO	AQUARIUS	LEO	CANCER
31		VIRGO	CANCER	LIBRA	CANCER	LEO	AQUARIUS	LEO	CANCER
AUGUST									
1	0:49 AM GEMINI	VIRGO	CANCER	LIBRA	CANCER	LEO	AQUARIUS	LEO	CANCER
2		VIRGO	CANCER	LIBRA	CANCER	LEO	AQUARIUS	LEO	CANCER
3	6:22 AM CANCER	VIRGO	CANCER	LIBRA	CANCER	LEO	AQUARIUS	LEO	CANCER
4		VIRGO	CANCER	LIBRA	CANCER	LEO	AQUARIUS	LEO	CANCER
5	1:50 PM LEO	VIRGO	CANCER	LIBRA	CANCER	LEO	AQUARIUS	LEO	CANCER
6		VIRGO	CANCER	LIBRA	CANCER	LEO	AQUARIUS	LEO	CANCER
7	11:18 PM VIRGO	VIRGO	CANCER	LIBRA	CANCER	LEO	AQUARIUS	LEO	CANCER
8		VIRGO	CANCER	LIBRA	CANCER	LEO	AQUARIUS	LEO	CANCER
9		VIRGO	CANCER	LIBRA	CANCER	LEO	AQUARIUS	LEO	CANCER
10	10:46 AM LIBRA	VIRGO	CANCER	LIBRA	CANCER	LEO	AQUARIUS	LEO	CANCER
11		VIRGO	CANCER	LIBRA	CANCER	LEO	AQUARIUS	LEO	CANCER
12	11:27 PM SCORPIO	VIRGO	CANCER	LIBRA	CANCER	LEO	AQUARIUS	LEO	CANCER
13		VIRGO	CANCER	LIBRA	CANCER	LEO	AQUARIUS	LEO	CANCER
14		VIRGO	CANCER	LIBRA	CANCER	LEO	AQUARIUS	LEO	CANCER
15	11:22 AM SAGITTARIUS	VIRGO	CANCER	LIBRA	CANCER	LEO	AQUARIUS	LEO	CANCER
16		VIRGO	CANCER	LIBRA	CANCER	LEO	AQUARIUS	LEO	CANCER
17	8:17 PM CAPRICORN	VIRGO	CANCER	SCORPIO	CANCER	LEO	AQUARIUS	LEO	CANCER
18		VIRGO	CANCER	SCORPIO	CANCER	LEO	AQUARIUS	LEO	CANCER
19		VIRGO	LEO	SCORPIO	CANCER	LEO	AQUARIUS	LEO	CANCER
20	1:10 AM AQUARIUS	VIRGO	LEO	SCORPIO	CANCER	LEO	AQUARIUS	LEO	CANCER
21		VIRGO	LEO	SCORPIO	CANCER	LEO	AQUARIUS	LEO	CANCER
22	2:48 AM PISCES	VIRGO	LEO	SCORPIO	CANCER	LEO	AQUARIUS	LEO	CANCER
23		VIRGO	LEO	SCORPIO	CANCER	LEO	AQUARIUS	LEO	CANCER

1919

	MOON FROM IN	MERCURY	VENUS	MARS	JUPITER	SATURN	URANUS	NEPTUNE	PLUTO
JULY									
24	4:25 PM CANCER	LEO	VIRGO	CANCER	CANCER	LEO	PISCES	LEO	CANCER
25		LEO	VIRGO	CANCER	CANCER	LEO	PISCES	LEO	CANCER
26	7:04 PM LEO	LEO	VIRGO	CANCER	CANCER	LEO	PISCES	LEO	CANCER
27		LEO	VIRGO	CANCER	CANCER	LEO	PISCES	LEO	CANCER
28	11:29 PM VIRGO	LEO	VIRGO	CANCER	CANCER	LEO	PISCES	LEO	CANCER
29		LEO	VIRGO	CANCER	CANCER	LEO	PISCES	LEO	CANCER
30		LEO	VIRGO	CANCER	CANCER	LEO	PISCES	LEO	CANCER
31	7:07 AM LIBRA	LEO	VIRGO	CANCER	CANCER	LEO	PISCES	LEO	CANCER
AUGUST									
1		LEO	VIRGO	CANCER	CANCER	LEO	PISCES	LEO	CANCER
2	6:08 PM SCORPIO	LEO	VIRGO	CANCER	LEO	LEO	PISCES	LEO	CANCER
3		LEO	VIRGO	CANCER	LEO	LEO	PISCES	LEO	CANCER
4		LEO	VIRGO	CANCER	LEO	LEO	PISCES	LEO	CANCER
5	6:58 AM SAGITTARIUS	LEO	VIRGO	CANCER	LEO	LEO	PISCES	LEO	CANCER
6		LEO	VIRGO	CANCER	LEO	LEO	PISCES	LEO	CANCER
7	6:52 PM CAPRICORN	LEO	VIRGO	CANCER	LEO	LEO	PISCES	LEO	CANCER
8		LEO	VIRGO	CANCER	LEO	LEO	PISCES	LEO	CANCER
9		LEO	VIRGO	CANCER	LEO	LEO	PISCES	LEO	CANCER
10	3:56 AM AQUARIUS	LEO	VIRGO	CANCER	LEO	LEO	PISCES	LEO	CANCER
11		LEO	VIRGO	CANCER	LEO	LEO	PISCES	LEO	CANCER
12	9:59 AM PISCES	LEO	VIRGO	CANCER	LEO	VIRGO	PISCES	LEO	CANCER
13		LEO	VIRGO	CANCER	LEO	VIRGO	PISCES	LEO	CANCER
14	1:59 PM ARIES	LEO	VIRGO	CANCER	LEO	VIRGO	PISCES	LEO	CANCER
15		LEO	VIRGO	CANCER	LEO	VIRGO	PISCES	LEO	CANCER
16	5:05 PM TAURUS	LEO	VIRGO	CANCER	LEO	VIRGO	PISCES	LEO	CANCER
17		LEO	VIRGO	CANCER	LEO	VIRGO	AQUARIUS	LEO	CANCER
18	8:03 PM GEMINI	LEO	VIRGO	CANCER	LEO	VIRGO	AQUARIUS	LEO	CANCER
19		LEO	VIRGO	CANCER	LEO	VIRGO	AQUARIUS	LEO	CANCER
20	11:14 PM CANCER	LEO	VIRGO	CANCER	LEO	VIRGO	AQUARIUS	LEO	CANCER
21		LEO	VIRGO	CANCER	LEO	VIRGO	AQUARIUS	LEO	CANCER
22		LEO	VIRGO	CANCER	LEO	VIRGO	AQUARIUS	LEO	CANCER
23	3:00 AM LEO	LEO	VIRGO	LEO	LEO	VIRGO	AQUARIUS	LEO	CANCER

	MOON FROM IN	MERCURY	VENUS	MARS	JUPITER	SATURN	URANUS	NEPTUNE	PLUTO
JULY									
23		LEO	LEO	SCORPIO	LEO	VIRGO	PISCES	LEO	CANCER
24		LEO	LEO	SCORPIO	LEO	VIRGO	PISCES	LEO	CANCER
25	2:32 AM SAGITTARIUS	LEO	LEO	SCORPIO	LEO	VIRGO	PISCES	LEO	CANCER
26		LEO	LEO	SCORPIO	LEO	VIRGO	PISCES	LEO	CANCER
27	3:22 PM CAPRICORN	LEO	LEO	SCORPIO	LEO	VIRGO	PISCES	LEO	CANCER
28		LEO	LEO	SCORPIO	LEO	VIRGO	PISCES	LEO	CANCER
29		LEO	LEO	SCORPIO	LEO	VIRGO	PISCES	LEO	CANCER
30	3:36 AM AQUARIUS	LEO	LEO	SCORPIO	LEO	VIRGO	PISCES	LEO	CANCER
31		LEO	LEO	SCORPIO	LEO	VIRGO	PISCES	LEO	CANCER
AUGUST									
1	2:18 PM PISCES	LEO	LEO	SCORPIO	LEO	VIRGO	PISCES	LEO	CANCER
2		LEO	LEO	SCORPIO	LEO	VIRGO	PISCES	LEO	CANCER
3	11:09 PM ARIES	CANCER	LEO	SCORPIO	LEO	VIRGO	PISCES	LEO	CANCER
4		CANCER	LEO	SCORPIO	LEO	VIRGO	PISCES	LEO	CANCER
5		CANCER	LEO	SCORPIO	LEO	VIRGO	PISCES	LEO	CANCER
6	5:56 AM TAURUS	CANCER	LEO	SCORPIO	LEO	VIRGO	PISCES	LEO	CANCER
7		CANCER	LEO	SCORPIO	LEO	VIRGO	PISCES	LEO	CANCER
8	10:14 AM GEMINI	CANCER	LEO	SCORPIO	LEO	VIRGO	PISCES	LEO	CANCER
9		CANCER	LEO	SCORPIO	LEO	VIRGO	PISCES	LEO	CANCER
10	12:11 PM CANCER	LEO	LEO	SCORPIO	LEO	VIRGO	PISCES	LEO	CANCER
11		LEO	LEO	SCORPIO	LEO	VIRGO	PISCES	LEO	CANCER
12	12:42 PM LEO	LEO	VIRGO	SCORPIO	LEO	VIRGO	PISCES	LEO	CANCER
13		LEO	VIRGO	SCORPIO	LEO	VIRGO	PISCES	LEO	CANCER
14	1:28 PM VIRGO	LEO	VIRGO	SCORPIO	LEO	VIRGO	PISCES	LEO	CANCER
15		LEO	VIRGO	SCORPIO	LEO	VIRGO	PISCES	LEO	CANCER
16	4:29 PM LIBRA	LEO	VIRGO	SCORPIO	LEO	VIRGO	PISCES	LEO	CANCER
17		LEO	VIRGO	SCORPIO	LEO	VIRGO	PISCES	LEO	CANCER
18	11:14 PM SCORPIO	LEO	VIRGO	SCORPIO	LEO	VIRGO	PISCES	LEO	CANCER
19		LEO	VIRGO	SCORPIO	LEO	VIRGO	PISCES	LEO	CANCER
20		LEO	VIRGO	SCORPIO	LEO	VIRGO	PISCES	LEO	CANCER
21	9:46 AM SAGITTARIUS	LEO	VIRGO	SCORPIO	LEO	VIRGO	PISCES	LEO	CANCER
22		LEO	VIRGO	SCORPIO	LEO	VIRGO	PISCES	LEO	CANCER

1921

	MOON FROM IN	MERCURY	VENUS	MARS	JUPITER	SATURN	URANUS	NEPTUNE	PLUTO
JULY									
23		CANCER	GEMINI	CANCER	VIRGO	VIRGO	PISCES	LEO	CANCER
24		CANCER	GEMINI	CANCER	VIRGO	VIRGO	PISCES	LEO	CANCER
25	2:41 AM ARIES	CANCER	GEMINI	CANCER	VIRGO	VIRGO	PISCES	LEO	CANCER
26		CANCER	GEMINI	CANCER	VIRGO	VIRGO	PISCES	LEO	CANCER
27	12:57 PM TAURUS	CANCER	GEMINI	CANCER	VIRGO	VIRGO	PISCES	LEO	CANCER
28		CANCER	GEMINI	CANCER	VIRGO	VIRGO	PISCES	LEO	CANCER
29	7:37 PM GEMINI	CANCER	GEMINI	CANCER	VIRGO	VIRGO	PISCES	LEO	CANCER
30		CANCER	GEMINI	CANCER	VIRGO	VIRGO	PISCES	LEO	CANCER
31	10:17 PM CANCER	CANCER	GEMINI	CANCER	VIRGO	VIRGO	PISCES	LEO	CANCER
AUGUST									
1		CANCER	GEMINI	CANCER	VIRGO	VIRGO	PISCES	LEO	CANCER
2	10:11 PM LEO	CANCER	GEMINI	CANCER	VIRGO	VIRGO	PISCES	LEO	CANCER
3		CANCER	GEMINI	LEO	VIRGO	VIRGO	PISCES	LEO	CANCER
4	9:19 PM VIRGO	CANCER	GEMINI	LEO	VIRGO	VIRGO	PISCES	LEO	CANCER
5		CANCER	GEMINI	LEO	VIRGO	VIRGO	PISCES	LEO	CANCER
6	9:53 PM LIBRA	CANCER	CANCER	LEO	VIRGO	VIRGO	PISCES	LEO	CANCER
7		CANCER	CANCER	LEO	VIRGO	VIRGO	PISCES	LEO	CANCER
8		LEO	CANCER	LEO	VIRGO	VIRGO	PISCES	LEO	CANCER·
9	1:35 AM SCORPIO	LEO	CANCER	LEO	VIRGO	VIRGO	PISCES	LEO	CANCER
10		LEO	CANCER	LEO	VIRGO	VIRGO	PISCES	LEO	CANCER
11	9:00 AM SAGITTARIUS	LEO	CANCER	LEO	VIRGO	VIRGO	PISCES	LEO	CANCER
12		LEO	CANCER	LEO	VIRGO	VIRGO	PISCES	LEO	CANCER
13	7:30 PM CAPRICORN	LEO	CANCER	LEO	VIRGO	VIRGO	PISCES	LEO	CANCER
14		LEO	CANCER	LEO	VIRGO	VIRGO	PISCES	LEO	CANCER
15		LEO	CANCER	LEO	VIRGO	VIRGO	PISCES	LEO	CANCER
16	7:42 AM AQUARIUS	LEO	CANCER	LEO	VIRGO	VIRGO	PISCES	LEO	CANCER
17		LEO	CANCER	LEO	VIRGO	VIRGO	PISCES	LEO	CANCER
18	8:20 PM PISCES	LEO	CANCER	LEO	VIRGO	VIRGO	PISCES	LEO	CANCER
19		LEO	CANCER	LEO	VIRGO	VIRGO	PISCES	LEO	CANCER
20		LEO	CANCER	LEO	VIRGO	VIRGO	PISCES	LEO	CANCER
21	8:30 AM ARIES	LEO	CANCER	LEO	VIRGO	VIRGO	PISCES	LEO	CANCER
22		LEO	CANCER	LEO	VIRGO	VIRGO	PISCES	LEO	CANCER
23	7:07 PM TAURUS	LEO	CANCER	LEO	VIRGO	VIRGO	PISCES	LEO	CANCER

1922

MOON		MERCURY	VENUS	MARS	JUPITER	SATURN	URANUS	NEPTUNE	PLUTO
FROM	IN								
JULY									
24	6:27 AM LEO	CANCER	VIRGO	SAGITTARIUS	LIBRA	LIBRA	PISCES	LEO	CANCER
25		CANCER	VIRGO	SAGITTARIUS	LIBRA	LIBRA	PISCES	LEO	CANCER
26	7:22 AM VIRGO	CANCER	VIRGO	SAGITTARIUS	LIBRA	LIBRA	PISCES	LEO	CANCER
27		CANCER	VIRGO	SAGITTARIUS	LIBRA	LIBRA	PISCES	LEO	CANCER
28	7:09 AM LIBRA	CANCER	VIRGO	SAGITTARIUS	LIBRA	LIBRA	PISCES	LEO	CANCER
29		CANCER	VIRGO	SAGITTARIUS	LIBRA	LIBRA	PISCES	LEO	CANCER
30	11:00 AM SCORPIO	CANCER	VIRGO	SAGITTARIUS	LIBRA	LIBRA	PISCES	LEO	CANCER
31		CANCER	VIRGO	SAGITTARIUS	LIBRA	LIBRA	PISCES	LEO	CANCER
AUGUST									
1	3:36 PM SAGITTARIUS	LEO	VIRGO	SAGITTARIUS	LIBRA	LIBRA	PISCES	LEO	CANCER
2		LEO	VIRGO	SAGITTARIUS	LIBRA	LIBRA	PISCES	LEO	CANCER
3	10:23 PM CAPRICORN	LEO	VIRGO	SAGITTARIUS	LIBRA	LIBRA	PISCES	LEO	CANCER
4		LEO	VIRGO	SAGITTARIUS	LIBRA	LIBRA	PISCES	LEO	CANCER
5		LEO	VIRGO	SAGITTARIUS	LIBRA	LIBRA	PISCES	LEO	CANCER
6	7:19 AM AQUARIUS	LEO	VIRGO	SAGITTARIUS	LIBRA	LIBRA	PISCES	LEO	CANCER
8	6:23 PM PISCES	LEO	VIRGO	SAGITTARIUS	LIBRA	LIBRA	PISCES	LEO	CANCER
9		LEO	VIRGO	SAGITTARIUS	LIBRA	LIBRA	PISCES	LEO	CANCER
10		LEO	LIBRA	SAGITTARIUS	LIBRA	LIBRA	PISCES	LEO	CANCER
11	7:06 AM ARIES	LEO	LIBRA	SAGITTARIUS	LIBRA	LIBRA	PISCES	LEO	CANCER
12		LEO	LIBRA	SAGITTARIUS	LIBRA	LIBRA	PISCES	LEO	CANCER
13	7:57 PM TAURUS	LEO	LIBRA	SAGITTARIUS	LIBRA	LIBRA	PISCES	LEO	CANCER
14		LEO	LIBRA	SAGITTARIUS	LIBRA	LIBRA	PISCES	LEO	CANCER
15		VIRGO	LIBRA	SAGITTARIUS	LIBRA	LIBRA	PISCES	LEO	CANCER
16	6:43 AM GEMINI	VIRGO	LIBRA	SAGITTARIUS	LIBRA	LIBRA	PISCES	LEO	CANCER
17		VIRGO	LIBRA	SAGITTARIUS	LIBRA	LIBRA	PISCES	LEO	CANCER
18	1:39 PM CANCER	VIRGO	LIBRA	SAGITTARIUS	LIBRA	LIBRA	PISCES	LEO	CANCER
19		VIRGO	LIBRA	SAGITTARIUS	LIBRA	LIBRA	PISCES	LEO	CANCER
20	4:45 PM LEO	VIRGO	LIBRA	SAGITTARIUS	LIBRA	LIBRA	PISCES	LEO	CANCER
21		VIRGO	LIBRA	SAGITTARIUS	LIBRA	LIBRA	PISCES	LEO	CANCER
22	5:16 PM VIRGO	VIRGO	LIBRA	SAGITTARIUS	LIBRA	LIBRA	PISCES	LEO	CANCER
23		VIRGO	LIBRA	SAGITTARIUS	LIBRA	LIBRA	PISCES	LEO	CANCER

1923

MOON		MERCURY	VENUS	MARS	JUPITER	SATURN	URANUS	NEPTUNE	PLUTO
FROM	IN								
JULY									
24		LEO	CANCER	LEO	SCORPIO	LIBRA	PISCES	LEO	CANCER
25	6:33 AM CAPRICORN	LEO	CANCER	LEO	SCORPIO	LIBRA	PISCES	LEO	CANCER
26		LEO	CANCER	LEO	SCORPIO	LIBRA	PISCES	LEO	CANCER
27	10:43 AM AQUARIUS	LEO	CANCER	LEO	SCORPIO	LIBRA	PISCES	LEO	CANCER
28		LEO	CANCER	LEO	SCORPIO	LIBRA	PISCES	LEO	CANCER
29	5:24 PM PISCES	LEO	CANCER	LEO	SCORPIO	LIBRA	PISCES	LEO	CANCER
30		LEO	CANCER	LEO	SCORPIO	LIBRA	PISCES	LEO	CANCER
31		LEO	CANCER	LEO	SCORPIO	LIBRA	PISCES	LEO	CANCER
AUGUST									
1	3:12 AM ARIES	LEO	CANCER	LEO	SCORPIO	LIBRA	PISCES	LEO	CANCER
2		LEO	CANCER	LEO	SCORPIO	LIBRA	PISCES	LEO	CANCER
3	3:22 PM TAURUS	LEO	CANCER	LEO	SCORPIO	LIBRA	PISCES	LEO	CANCER
4		LEO	LEO	LEO	SCORPIO	LIBRA	PISCES	LEO	CANCER
5		LEO	LEO	LEO	SCORPIO	LIBRA	PISCES	LEO	CANCER
6	3:47 AM GEMINI	LEO	LEO	LEO	SCORPIO	LIBRA	PISCES	LEO	CANCER
7		LEO	LEO	LEO	SCORPIO	LIBRA	PISCES	LEO	CANCER
8	2:07 PM CANCER	VIRGO	LEO	LEO	SCORPIO	LIBRA	PISCES	LEO	CANCER
9		VIRGO	LEO	LEO	SCORPIO	LIBRA	PISCES	LEO	CANCER
10	9:19 PM LEO	VIRGO	LEO	LEO	SCORPIO	LIBRA	PISCES	LEO	CANCER
11		VIRGO	LEO	LEO	SCORPIO	LIBRA	PISCES	LEO	CANCER
12		VIRGO	LEO	LEO	SCORPIO	LIBRA	PISCES	LEO	CANCER
13	1:43 AM VIRGO	VIRGO	LEO	LEO	SCORPIO	LIBRA	PISCES	LEO	CANCER
14		VIRGO	LEO	LEO	SCORPIO	LIBRA	PISCES	LEO	CANCER
15	4:27 AM LIBRA	VIRGO	LEO	LEO	SCORPIO	LIBRA	PISCES	LEO	CANCER
16		VIRGO	LEO	LEO	SCORPIO	LIBRA	PISCES	LEO	CANCER
17	6:38 AM SCORPIO	VIRGO	LEO	LEO	SCORPIO	LIBRA	PISCES	LEO	CANCER
18		VIRGO	LEO	LEO	SCORPIO	LIBRA	PISCES	LEO	CANCER
19	9:12 AM SAGITTARIUS	VIRGO	LEO	LEO	SCORPIO	LIBRA	PISCES	LEO	CANCER
20		VIRGO	LEO	LEO	SCORPIO	LIBRA	PISCES	LEO	CANCER
21	12:50 PM CAPRICORN	VIRGO	LEO	LEO	SCORPIO	LIBRA	PISCES	LEO	CANCER
22		VIRGO	LEO	LEO	SCORPIO	LIBRA	PISCES	LEO	CANCER
23	6:03 PM AQUARIUS	VIRGO	LEO	LEO	SCORPIO	LIBRA	PISCES	LEO	CANCER

	MOON FROM IN	MERCURY	VENUS	MARS	JUPITER	SATURN	URANUS	NEPTUNE	PLUTO
JULY									
23	10:37 AM TAURUS	LEO	CANCER	PISCES	SAGITTARIUS	LIBRA	PISCES	LEO	CANCER
24		LEO	CANCER	PISCES	SAGITTARIUS	LIBRA	PISCES	LEO	CANCER
25	10:37 PM GEMINI	LEO	CANCER	PISCES	SAGITTARIUS	LIBRA	PISCES	LEO	CANCER
26		LEO	CANCER	PISCES	SAGITTARIUS	LIBRA	PISCES	LEO	CANCER
27		LEO	CANCER	PISCES	SAGITTARIUS	LIBRA	PISCES	LEO	CANCER
28	11:11 AM CANCER	LEO	CANCER	PISCES	SAGITTARIUS	LIBRA	PISCES	LEO	CANCER
29		LEO	CANCER	PISCES	SAGITTARIUS	LIBRA	PISCES	LEO	CANCER
30	10:38 PM LEO	LEO	CANCER	PISCES	SAGITTARIUS	LIBRA	PISCES	LEO	CANCER
31		VIRGO	CANCER	PISCES	SAGITTARIUS	LIBRA	PISCES	LEO	CANCER
AUGUST									
1		VIRGO	CANCER	PISCES	SAGITTARIUS	LIBRA	PISCES	LEO	CANCER
2	8:05 AM VIRGO	VIRGO	CANCER	PISCES	SAGITTAIUS	LIBRA	PISCES	LEO	CANCER
3		VIRGO	CANCER	PISCES	SAGITTARIUS	LIBRA	PISCES	LEO	CANCER
4	3:19 PM LIBRA	VIRGO	CANCER	PISCES	SAGITTARIUS	LIBRA	PISCES	LEO	CANCER
5		VIRGO	CANCER	PISCES	SAGITTARIUS	LIBRA	PISCES	LEO	CANCER
6	8:24 PM SCORPIO	VIRGO	CANCER	PISCES	SAGITTARIUS	LIBRA	PISCES	LEO	CANCER
7		VIRGO	CANCER	PISCES	SAGITTARIUS	LIBRA	PISCES	LEO	CANCER
8	11:31 PM SAGITTARIUS	VIRGO	CANCER	PISCES	SAGITTARIUS	LIBRA	PISCES	LEO	CANCER
9		VIRGO	CANCER	PISCES	SAGITTARIUS	LIBRA	PISCES	LEO	CANCER
10		VIRGO	CANCER	PISCES	SAGITTARIUS	LIBRA	PISCES	LEO	CANCER
11	1:20 AM CAPRICORN	VIRGO	CANCER	PISCES	SAGITTARIUS	LIBRA	PISCES	LEO	CANCER
12		VIRGO	CANCER	PISCES	SAGITTARIUS	LIBRA	PISCES	LEO	CANCER
13	2:52 AM AQUARIUS	VIRGO	CANCER	PISCES	SAGITTARIUS	LIBRA	PISCES	LEO	CANCER
14		VIRGO	CANCER	PISCES	SAGITTARIUS	LIBRA	PISCES	LEO	CANCER
15	5:29 AM PISCES	VIRGO	CANCER	PISCES	SAGITTARIUS	LIBRA	PISCES	LEO	CANCER
16		VIRGO	CANCER	PISCES	SAGITTARIUS	LIBRA	PISCES	LEO	CANCER
17	10:33 AM ARIES	VIRGO	CANCER	PISCES	SAGITTARIUS	LIBRA	PISCES	LEO	CANCER
18		VIRGO	CANCER	PISCES	SAGITTARIUS	LIBRA	PISCES	LEO	CANCER
19	6:54 PM TAURUS	VIRGO	CANCER	PISCES	SAGITTARIUS	LIBRA	PISCES	LEO	CANCER
20		VIRGO	CANCER	PISCES	SAGITTARIUS	LIBRA	PISCES	LEO	CANCER
21		VIRGO	CANCER	PISCES	SAGITTARIUS	LIBRA	PISCES	LEO	CANCER
22	6:15 AM GEMINI	VIRGO	CANCER	PISCES	SAGITTARIUS	LIBRA	PISCES	LEO	CANCER

1925

	MOON FROM IN	MERCURY	VENUS	MARS	JUPITER	SATURN	URANUS	NEPTUNE	PLUTO
JULY									
23	10:17 AM VIRGO	LEO	LEO	LEO	CAPRICORN	SCORPIO	PISCES	LEO	CANCER
24		LEO	LEO	LEO	CAPRICORN	SCORPIO	PISCES	LEO	CANCER
25	9:29 PM LIBRA	LEO	LEO	LEO	CAPRICORN	SCORPIO	PISCES	LEO	CANCER
26		VIRGO	LEO	LEO	CAPRICORN	SCORPIO	PISCES	LEO	CANCER
27		VIRGO	LEO	LEO	CAPRICORN	SCORPIO	PISCES	LEO	CANCER
28	5:56 AM SCORPIO	VIRGO	VIRGO	LEO	CAPRICORN	SCORPIO	PISCES	LEO	CANCER
29		VIRGO	VIRGO	LEO	CAPRICORN	SCORPIO	PISCES	LEO	CANCER
30	10:55 AM SAGITTARIUS	VIRGO	VIRGO	LEO	CAPRICORN	SCORPIO	PISCES	LEO	CANCER
31		VIRGO	VIRGO	LEO	CAPRICORN	SCORPIO	PISCES	LEO	CANCER
AUGUST									
1	12:46 PM CAPRICORN	VIRGO	VIRGO	LEO	CAPRICORN	SCORPIO	PISCES	LEO	CANCER
2		VIRGO	VIRGO	LEO	CAPRICORN	SCORPIO	PISCES	LEO	CANCER
3	12:41 PM AQUARIUS	VIRGO	VIRGO	LEO	CAPRICORN	SCORPIO	PISCES	LEO	CANCER
4		VIRGO	VIRGO	LEO	CAPRICORN	SCORPIO	PISCES	LEO	CANCER
5	12:24 PM PISCES	VIRGO	VIRGO	LEO	CAPRICORN	SCORPIO	PISCES	LEO	CANCER
6		VIRGO	VIRGO	LEO	CAPRICORN	SCORPIO	PISCES	LEO	CANCER
7	1:48 PM ARIES	VIRGO	VIRGO	LEO	CAPRICORN	SCORPIO	PISCES	LEO	CANCER
8		VIRGO	VIRGO	LEO	CAPRICORN	SCORPIO	PISCES	LEO	CANCER
9	6:25 PM TAURUS	VIRGO	VIRGO	LEO	CAPRICORN	SCORPIO	PISCES	LEO	CANCER
10		VIRGO	VIRGO	LEO	CAPRICORN	SCORPIO	PISCES	LEO	CANCER
11		VIRGO	VIRGO	LEO	CAPRICORN	SCORPIO	PISCES	LEO	CANCER
12	2:58 AM GEMINI	VIRGO	VIRGO	LEO	CAPRICORN	SCORPIO	PISCES	LEO	CANCER
13		VIRGO	VIRGO	VIRGO	CAPRICORN	SCORPIO	PISCES	LEO	CANCER
14	2:39 PM CANCER	VIRGO	VIRGO	VIRGO	CAPRICORN	SCORPIO	PISCES	LEO	CANCER
15		VIRGO	VIRGO	VIRGO	CAPRICORN	SCORPIO	PISCES	LEO	CANCER
16		VIRGO	VIRGO	VIRGO	CAPRICORN	SCORPIO	PISCES	LEO	CANCER
17	3:41 AM LEO	VIRGO	VIRGO	VIRGO	CAPRICORN	SCORPIO	PISCES	LEO	CANCER
18		VIRGO	VIRGO	VIRGO	CAPRICORN	SCORPIO	PISCES	LEO	CANCER
19	4:12 PM VIRGO	VIRGO	VIRGO	VIRGO	CAPRICORN	SCORPIO	PISCES	LEO	CANCER
20		VIRGO	VIRGO	VIRGO	CAPRICORN	SCORPIO	PISCES	LEO	CANCER
21		VIRGO	VIRGO	VIRGO	CAPRICORN	SCORPIO	PISCES	LEO	CANCER
22	3:05 AM LIBRA	VIRGO	LIBRA	VIRGO	CAPRICORN	SCORPIO	PISCES	LEO	CANCER
23		VIRGO	LIBRA	VIRGO	CAPRICORN	SCORPIO	PISCES	LEO	CANCER

1926

	MOON										
	FROM	IN	MERCURY	VENUS	MARS	JUPITER	SATURN	URANUS	NEPTUNE	PLUTO
JULY										
24	9:48 PM	AQUARIUS	LEO	CANCER	ARIES	AQUARIUS	SCORPIO	PISCES	LEO	CANCER
25			LEO	CANCER	ARIES	AQUARIUS	SCORPIO	PISCES	LEO	CANCER
26	9:46 PM	PISCES	LEO	CANCER	ARIES	AQUARIUS	SCORPIO	PISCES	LEO	CANCER
27			LEO	CANCER	ARIES	AQUARIUS	SCORPIO	PISCES	LEO	CANCER
28	10:14 PM	ARIES	LEO	CANCER	ARIES	AQUARIUS	SCORPIO	PISCES	LEO	CANCER
29			LEO	CANCER	ARIES	AQUARIUS	SCORPIO	PISCES	LEO	CANCER
30			LEO	CANCER	ARIES	AQUARIUS	SCORPIO	PISCES	LEO	CANCER
31	0:48 AM	TAURUS	LEO	CANCER	ARIES	AQUARIUS	SCORPIO	PISCES	LEO	CANCER
AUGUST										
1			LEO	CANCER	TAURUS	AQUARIUS	SCORPIO	PISCES	LEO	CANCER
2	6:25 AM	GEMINI	LEO	CANCER	TAURUS	AQUARIUS	SCORPIO	PISCES	LEO	CANCER
3			LEO	CANCER	TAURUS	AQUARIUS	SCORPIO	PISCES	LEO	CANCER
4	3:09 PM	CANCER	LEO	CANCER	TAURUS	AQUARIUS	SCORPIO	PISCES	LEO	CANCER
5			LEO	CANCER	TAURUS	AQUARIUS	SCORPIO	PISCES	LEO	CANCER
6			LEO	CANCER	TAURUS	AQUARIUS	SCORPIO	PISCES	LEO	CANCER
7	2:13 AM	LEO	LEO	CANCER	TAURUS	AQUARIUS	SCORPIO	PISCES	LEO	CANCER
8			LEO	CANCER	TAURUS	AQUARIUS	SCORPIO	PISCES	LEO	CANCER
9	2:39 PM	VIRGO	LEO	CANCER	TAURUS	AQUARIUS	SCORPIO	PISCES	LEO	CANCER
10			LEO	CANCER	TAURUS	AQUARIUS	SCORPIO	PISCES	LEO	CANCER
11			LEO	CANCER	TAURUS	AQUARIUS	SCORPIO	PISCES	LEO	CANCER
12	3:26 AM	LIBRA	LEO	CANCER	TAURUS	AQUARIUS	SCORPIO	PISCES	LEO	CANCER
13			LEO	CANCER	TAURUS	AQUARIUS	SCORPIO	PISCES	LEO	CANCER
14	3:17 PM	SCORPIO	LEO	CANCER	TAURUS	AQUARIUS	SCORPIO	PISCES	LEO	CANCER
15			LEO	CANCER	TAURUS	AQUARIUS	SCORPIO	PISCES	LEO	CANCER
16			LEO	CANCER	TAURUS	AQUARIUS	SCORPIO	PISCES	LEO	CANCER
17	0:38 AM	SAGITTARIUS	LEO	CANCER	TAURUS	AQUARIUS	SCORPIO	PISCES	LEO	CANCER
18			LEO	LEO	TAURUS	AQUARIUS	SCORPIO	PISCES	LEO	CANCER
19	6:23 AM	CAPRICORN	LEO	LEO	TAURUS	AQUARIUS	SCORPIO	PISCES	LEO	CANCER
20			LEO	LEO	TAURUS	AQUARIUS	SCORPIO	PISCES	LEO	CANCER
21	8:30 AM	AQUARIUS	LEO	LEO	TAURUS	AQUARIUS	SCORPIO	PISCES	LEO	CANCER
22			LEO	LEO	TAURUS	AQUARIUS	SCORPIO	PISCES	LEO	CANCER
23	8:14 AM	PISCES	LEO	LEO	TAURUS	AQUARIUS	SCORPIO	PISCES	LEO	CANCER

1927

	MOON										
	FROM	IN	MERCURY	VENUS	MARS	JUPITER	SATURN	URANUS	NEPTUNE	PLUTO
JULY										
24			CANCER	VIRGO	LEO	ARIES	SAGITTARIUS	ARIES	LEO	CANCER
25	9:31 PM	CANCER	CANCER	VIRGO	VIRGO	ARIES	SAGITTARIUS	ARIES	LEO	CANCER
26			CANCER	VIRGO	VIRGO	ARIES	SAGITTARIUS	ARIES	LEO	CANCER
27			CANCER	VIRGO	VIRGO	ARIES	SAGITTARIUS	ARIES	LEO	CANCER
28	4:01 AM	LEO	CANCER	VIRGO	VIRGO	ARIES	SAGITTARIUS	ARIES	LEO	CANCER
29			CANCER	VIRGO	VIRGO	ARIES	SAGITTARIUS	ARIES	LEO	CANCER
30	12:43 PM	VIRGO	CANCER	VIRGO	VIRGO	ARIES	SAGITTARIUS	ARIES	LEO	CANCER
31			CANCER	VIRGO	VIRGO	ARIES	SAGITTARIUS	ARIES	LEO	CANCER
AUGUST										
1	11:44 PM	LIBRA	CANCER	VIRGO	VIRGO	ARIES	SAGITTARIUS	ARIES	LEO	CANCER
2			CANCER	VIRGO	VIRGO	ARIES	SAGITTARIUS	ARIES	LEO	CANCER
3			CANCER	VIRGO	VIRGO	ARIES	SAGITTARIUS	ARIES	LEO	CANCER
4	12:16 PM	SCORPIO	CANCER	VIRGO	VIRGO	ARIES	SAGITTARIUS	ARIES	LEO	CANCER
5			CANCER	VIRGO	VIRGO	ARIES	SAGITTARIUS	ARIES	LEO	CANCER
6			CANCER	VIRGO	VIRGO	ARIES	SAGITTARIUS	ARIES	LEO	CANCER
7	0:13 AM	SAGITTARIUS	CANCER	VIRGO	VIRGO	ARIES	SAGITTARIUS	ARIES	LEO	CANCER
8			CANCER	VIRGO	VIRGO	ARIES	SAGITTARIUS	ARIES	LEO	CANCER
9	9:22 AM	CAPRICORN	CANCER	VIRGO	VIRGO	ARIES	SAGITTARIUS	ARIES	LEO	CANCER
10			CANCER	VIRGO	VIRGO	ARIES	SAGITTARIUS	ARIES	LEO	CANCER
11	2:45 PM	AQUARIUS	CANCER	VIRGO	VIRGO	ARIES	SAGITTARIUS	ARIES	LEO	CANCER
12			LEO	VIRGO	VIRGO	ARIES	SAGITTARIUS	ARIES	LEO	CANCER
13	5:05 PM	PISCES	LEO	VIRGO	VIRGO	ARIES	SAGITTARIUS	ARIES	LEO	CANCER
14			LEO	VIRGO	VIRGO	ARIES	SAGITTARIUS	ARIES	LEO	CANCER
15	5:57 PM	ARIES	LEO	VIRGO	VIRGO	ARIES	SAGITTARIUS	ARIES	LEO	CANCER
16			LEO	VIRGO	VIRGO	ARIES	SAGITTARIUS	ARIES	LEO	CANCER
17	7:12 PM	TAURUS	LEO	VIRGO	VIRGO	ARIES	SAGITTARIUS	ARIES	LEO	CANCER
18			LEO	VIRGO	VIRGO	ARIES	SAGITTARIUS	ARIES	LEO	CANCER
19	10:09 PM	GEMINI	LEO	VIRGO	VIRGO	ARIES	SAGITTARIUS	ARIES	LEO	CANCER
20			LEO	VIRGO	VIRGO	ARIES	SAGITTARIUS	ARIES	LEO	CANCER
21			LEO	VIRGO	VIRGO	ARIES	SAGITTARIUS	ARIES	LEO	CANCER
22	3:20 AM	CANCER	LEO	VIRGO	VIRGO	ARIES	SAGITTARIUS	ARIES	LEO	CANCER
23			LEO	VIRGO	VIRGO	ARIES	SAGITTARIUS	ARIES	LEO	CANCER

MOON FROM	IN	MERCURY	VENUS	MARS	JUPITER	SATURN	URANUS	NEPTUNE	PLUTO
JULY									
23		CANCER	LEO	TAURUS	TAURUS	SAGITTARIUS	ARIES	LEO	CANCER
24	6:48 AM SCORPIO	CANCER	LEO	TAURUS	TAURUS	SAGITTARIUS	ARIES	LEO	CANCER
25		CANCER	LEO	TAURUS	TAURUS	SAGITTARIUS	ARIES	LEO	CANCER
26	7:34 PM SAGITTARIUS	CANCER	LEO	TAURUS	TAURUS	SAGITTARIUS	ARIES	LEO	CANCER
27		CANCER	LEO	TAURUS	TAURUS	SAGITTARIUS	ARIES	LEO	CANCER
28		CANCER	LEO	TAURUS	TAURUS	SAGITTARIUS	ARIES	LEO	CANCER
29	7:47 AM CAPRICORN	CANCER	LEO	TAURUS	TAURUS	SAGITTARIUS	ARIES	LEO	CANCER
30		CANCER	LEO	TAURUS	TAURUS	SAGITTARIUS	ARIES	LEO	CANCER
31	5:33 PM AQUARIUS	CANCER	LEO	TAURUS	TAURUS	SAGITTARIUS	ARIES	LEO	CANCER
AUGUST									
1		CANCER	LEO	TAURUS	TAURUS	SAGITTARIUS	ARIES	LEO	CANCER
2		CANCER	LEO	TAURUS	TAURUS	SAGITTARIUS	ARIES	LEO	CANCER
3	0:34 AM PISCES	CANCER	LEO	TAURUS	TAURUS	SAGITTARIUS	ARIES	LEO	CANCER
4		CANCER	LEO	TAURUS	TAURUS	SAGITTARIUS	ARIES	LEO	CANCER
5	5:33 AM ARIES	LEO	LEO	TAURUS	TAURUS	SAGITTARIUS	ARIES	LEO	CANCER
6		LEO	LEO	TAURUS	TAURUS	SAGITTARIUS	ARIES	LEO	CANCER
7	9:18 AM TAURUS	LEO	LEO	TAURUS	TAURUS	SAGITTARIUS	ARIES	LEO	CANCER
8		LEO	LEO	TAURUS	TAURUS	SAGITTARIUS	ARIES	LEO	CANCER
9	12:22 PM GEMINI	LEO	LEO	GEMINI	TAURUS	SAGITTARIUS	ARIES	LEO	CANCER
10		LEO	LEO	GEMINI	TAURUS	SAGITTARIUS	ARIES	LEO	CANCER
11	3:03 PM CANCER	LEO	LEO	GEMINI	TAURUS	SAGITTARIUS	ARIES	LEO	CANCER
12		LEO	VIRGO	GEMINI	TAURUS	SAGITTARIUS	ARIES	LEO	CANCER
13	5:57 PM LEO	LEO	VIRGO	GEMINI	TAURUS	SAGITTARIUS	ARIES	LEO	CANCER
14		LEO	VIRGO	GEMINI	TAURUS	SAGITTARIUS	ARIES	LEO	CANCER
15	10:08 PM VIRGO	LEO	VIRGO	GEMINI	TAURUS	SAGITTARIUS	ARIES	LEO	CANCER
16		LEO	VIRGO	GEMINI	TAURUS	SAGITTARIUS	ARIES	LEO	CANCER
17		LEO	VIRGO	GEMINI	TAURUS	SAGITTARIUS	ARIES	LEO	CANCER
18	4:54 AM LIBRA	LEO	VIRGO	GEMINI	TAURUS	SAGITTARIUS	ARIES	LEO	CANCER
19		LEO	VIRGO	GEMINI	TAURUS	SAGITTARIUS	ARIES	LEO	CANCER
20	2:58 PM SCORPIO	VIRGO	VIRGO	GEMINI	TAURUS	SAGITTARIUS	ARIES	LEO	CANCER
21		VIRGO	VIRGO	GEMINI	TAURUS	SAGITTARIUS	ARIES	LEO	CANCER
22		VIRGO	VIRGO	GEMINI	TAURUS	SAGITTARIUS	ARIES	LEO	CANCER

1929

MOON FROM	IN	MERCURY	VENUS	MARS	JUPITER	SATURN	URANUS	NEPTUNE	PLUTO
JULY									
23		CANCER	GEMINI	VIRGO	GEMINI	SAGITTARIUS	ARIES	LEO	CANCER
24	4:39 AM PISCES	CANCER	GEMINI	VIRGO	GEMINI	SAGITTARIUS	ARIES	VIRGO	CANCER
25		CANCER	GEMINI	VIRGO	GEMINI	SAGITTARIUS	ARIES	VIRGO	CANCER
26	2:13 PM ARIES	CANCER	GEMINI	VIRGO	GEMINI	SAGITTARIUS	ARIES	VIRGO	CANCER
27		CANCER	GEMINI	VIRGO	GEMINI	SAGITTARIUS	ARIES	VIRGO	CANCER
28	9:25 PM TAURUS	LEO	GEMINI	VIRGO	GEMINI	SAGITTARIUS	ARIES	VIRGO	CANCER
29		LEO	GEMINI	VIRGO	GEMINI	SAGITTARIUS	ARIES	VIRGO	CANCER
30		LEO	GEMINI	VIRGO	GEMINI	SAGITTARIUS	ARIES	VIRGO	CANCER
31	1:43 AM GEMINI	LEO	GEMINI	VIRGO	GEMINI	SAGITTARIUS	ARIES	VIRGO	CANCER
AUGUST									
1		LEO	GEMINI	VIRGO	GEMINI	SAGITTARIUS	ARIES	VIRGO	CANCER
2	3:15 AM CANCER	LEO	GEMINI	VIRGO	GEMINI	SAGITTARIUS	ARIES	VIRGO	CANCER
3		LEO	GEMINI	VIRGO	GEMINI	SAGITTARIUS	ARIES	VIRGO	CANCER
4	3:11 AM LEO	LEO	GEMINI	VIRGO	GEMINI	SAGITTARIUS	ARIES	VIRGO	CANCER
5		LEO	CANCER	VIRGO	GEMINI	SAGITTARIUS	ARIES	VIRGO	CANCER
6	3:23 AM VIRGO	LEO	CANCER	VIRGO	GEMINI	SAGITTARIUS	ARIES	VIRGO	CANCER
7		LEO	CANCER	VIRGO	GEMINI	SAGITTARIUS	ARIES	VIRGO	CANCER
8	5:56 AM LIBRA	LEO	CANCER	VIRGO	GEMINI	SAGITTARIUS	ARIES	VIRGO	CANCER
9		LEO	CANCER	VIRGO	GEMINI	SAGITTARIUS	ARIES	VIRGO	CANCER
10	12:22 PM SCORPIO	LEO	CANCER	VIRGO	GEMINI	SAGITTARIUS	ARIES	VIRGO	CANCER
11		LEO	CANCER	VIRGO	GEMINI	SAGITTARIUS	ARIES	VIRGO	CANCER
12	10:45 PM SAGITTARIUS	VIRGO	CANCER	VIRGO	GEMINI	SAGITTARIUS	ARIES	VIRGO	CANCER
13		VIRGO	CANCER	VIRGO	GEMINI	SAGITTARIUS	ARIES	VIRGO	CANCER
14		VIRGO	CANCER	VIRGO	GEMINI	SAGITTARIUS	ARIES	VIRGO	CANCER
15	11:21 AM CAPRICORN	VIRGO	CANCER	VIRGO	GEMINI	SAGITTARIUS	ARIES	VIRGO	CANCER
16		VIRGO	CANCER	VIRGO	GEMINI	SAGITTARIUS	ARIES	VIRGO	CANCER
17	11:50 PM AQUARIUS	VIRGO	CANCER	VIRGO	GEMINI	SAGITTARIUS	ARIES	VIRGO	CANCER
18		VIRGO	CANCER	VIRGO	GEMINI	SAGITTARIUS	ARIES	VIRGO	CANCER
19		VIRGO	CANCER	VIRGO	GEMINI	SAGITTARIUS	ARIES	VIRGO	CANCER
20	10:46 AM PISCES	VIRGO	CANCER	VIRGO	GEMINI	SAGITTARIUS	ARIES	VIRGO	CANCER
21		VIRGO	CANCER	VIRGO	GEMINI	SAGITTARIUS	ARIES	VIRGO	CANCER
22	7:47 PM ARIES	VIRGO	CANCER	LIBRA	GEMINI	SAGITTARIUS	ARIES	VIRGO	CANCER
23		VIRGO	CANCER	LIBRA	GEMINI	SAGITTARIUS	ARIES	VIRGO	CANCER

1930   LEO

	MOON FROM	IN	MERCURY	VENUS	MARS	JUPITER	SATURN	URANUS	NEPTUNE	PLUTO
JULY										
24			LEO	VIRGO	GEMINI	CANCER	CAPRICORN	ARIES	VIRGO	CANCER
25	12:19 PM	LEO	LEO	VIRGO	GEMINI	CANCER	CAPRICORN	ARIES	VIRGO	CANCER
26			LEO	VIRGO	GEMINI	CANCER	CAPRICORN	ARIES	VIRGO	CANCER
27	11:35 AM	VIRGO	LEO	VIRGO	GEMINI	CANCER	CAPRICORN	ARIES	VIRGO	CANCER
28			LEO	VIRGO	GEMINI	CANCER	CAPRICORN	ARIES	VIRGO	CANCER
29	12:19 PM	LIBRA	LEO	VIRGO	GEMINI	CANCER	CAPRICORN	ARIES	VIRGO	CANCER
30			LEO	VIRGO	GEMINI	CANCER	CAPRICORN	AIRES	VIRGO	CANCER
31	4:08 PM	SCORPIO	LEO	VIRGO	GEMINI	CANCER	CAPRICORN	AIRES	VIRGO	CANCER
AUGUST										
1			LEO	VIRGO	GEMINI	CANCER	CAPRICORN	ARIES	VIRGO	CANCER
2	11:25 PM	SAGITTARIUS	LEO	VIRGO	GEMINI	CANCER	CAPRICORN	ARIES	VIRGO	CANCER
3			LEO	VIRGO	GEMINI	CANCER	CAPRICORN	ARIES	VIRGO	CANCER
4			VIRGO	VIRGO	GEMINI	CANCER	CAPRICORN	ARIES	VIRGO	CANCER
5	9:35 AM	CAPRICORN	VIRGO	VIRGO	GEMINI	CANCER	CAPRICORN	ARIES	VIRGO	CANCER
6			VIRGO	VIRGO	GEMINI	CANCER	CAPRICORN	ARIES	VIRGO	CANCER
7	9:27 PM	AQUARIUS	VIRGO	VIRGO	GEMINI	CANCER	CAPRICORN	ARIES	VIRGO	CANCER
8			VIRGO	VIRGO	GEMINI	CANCER	CAPRICORN	ARIES	VIRGO	CANCER
9			VIRGO	VIRGO	GEMINI	CANCER	CAPRICORN	ARIES	VIRGO	CANCER
10	10:03 AM	PISCES	VIRGO	LIBRA	GEMINI	CANCER	CAPRICORN	ARIES	VIRGO	CANCER
11			VIRGO	LIBRA	GEMINI	CANCER	CAPRICORN	ARIES	VIRGO	CANCER
12	10:32 PM	ARIES	VIRGO	LIBRA	GEMINI	CANCER	CAPRICORN	ARIES	VIRGO	CANCER
13			VIRGO	LIBRA	GEMINI	CANCER	CAPRICORN	ARIES	VIRGO	CANCER
14			VIRGO	LIBRA	GEMINI	CANCER	CAPRICORN	ARIES	VIRGO	CANCER
15	9:37 AM	TAURUS	VIRGO	LIBRA	GEMINI	CANCER	CAPRICORN	ARIES	VIRGO	CANCER
16			VIRGO	LIBRA	GEMINI	CANCER	CAPRICORN	ARIES	VIRGO	CANCER
17	5:46 PM	GEMINI	VIRGO	LIBRA	GEMINI	CANCER	CAPRICORN	ARIES	VIRGO	CANCER
18			VIRGO	LIBRA	GEMINI	CANCER	CAPRICORN	ARIES	VIRGO	CANCER
19	10:01 PM	CANCER	VIRGO	LIBRA	GEMINI	CANCER	CAPRICORN	ARIES	VIRGO	CANCER
20			VIRGO	LIBRA	GEMINI	CANCER	CAPRICORN	ARIES	VIRGO	CANCER
21	10:57 PM	LEO	VIRGO	LIBRA	GEMINI	CANCER	CAPRICORN	ARIES	VIRGO	CANCER
22			VIRGO	LIBRA	GEMINI	CANCER	CAPRICORN	ARIES	VIRGO	CANCER
23	10:14 PM	VIRGO	VIRGO	LIBRA	GEMINI	CANCER	CAPRICORN	ARIES	VIRGO	CANCER

1931

	MOON FROM	IN	MERCURY	VENUS	MARS	JUPITER	SATURN	URANUS	NEPTUNE	PLUTO
JULY										
24	7:19 AM	SAGITTARIUS	LEO	CANCER	VIRGO	LEO	CAPRICORN	ARIES	VIRGO	CANCER
25			LEO	CANCER	VIRGO	LEO	CAPRICORN	ARIES	VIRGO	CANCER
26	1:23 PM	CAPRICORN	LEO	CANCER	VIRGO	LEO	CAPRICORN	ARIES	VIRGO	CANCER
27			LEO	CANCER	VIRGO	LEO	CAPRICORN	ARIES	VIRGO	CANCER
28	9:25 PM	AQUARIUS	LEO	CANCER	VIRGO	LEO	CAPRICORN	ARIES	VIRGO	CANCER
29			VIRGO	CANCER	VIRGO	LEO	CAPRICORN	ARIES	VIRGO	CANCER
30			VIRGO	CANCER	VIRGO	LEO	CAPRICORN	ARIES	VIRGO	CANCER
31	7:46 AM	PISCES	VIRGO	CANCER	VIRGO	LEO	CAPRICORN	ARIES	VIRGO	CANCER
AUGUST										
1			VIRGO	CANCER	VIRGO	LEO	CAPRICORN	ARIES	VIRGO	CANCER
2	8:10 PM	ARIES	VIRGO	CANCER	LIBRA	LEO	CAPRICORN	ARIES	VIRGO	CANCER
3			VIRGO	LEO	LIBRA	LEO	CAPRICORN	ARIES	VIRGO	CANCER
4			VIRGO	LEO	LIBRA	LEO	CAPRICORN	ARIES	VIRGO	CANCER
5	9:05 AM	TAURUS	VIRGO	LEO	LIBRA	LEO	CAPRICORN	ARIES	VIRGO	CANCER
6			VIRGO	LEO	LIBRA	LEO	CAPRICORN	ARIES	VIRGO	CANCER
7	8:01 PM	GEMINI	VIRGO	LEO	LIBRA	LEO	CAPRICORN	ARIES	VIRGO	CANCER
8			VIRGO	LEO	LIBRA	LEO	CAPRICORN	ARIES	VIRGO	CANCER
9			VIRGO	LEO	LIBRA	LEO	CAPRICORN	ARIES	VIRGO	CANCER
10	3:09 AM	CANCER	VIRGO	LEO	LIBRA	LEO	CAPRICORN	ARIES	VIRGO	CANCER
11			VIRGO	LEO	LIBRA	LEO	CAPRICORN	ARIES	VIRGO	CANCER
12	6:31 AM	LEO	VIRGO	LEO	LIBRA	LEO	CAPRICORN	ARIES	VIRGO	CANCER
13			VIRGO	LEO	LIBRA	LEO	CAPRICORN	ARIES	VIRGO	CANCER
14	7:25 AM	VIRGO	VIRGO	LEO	LIBRA	LEO	CAPRICORN	ARIES	VIRGO	CANCER
15			VIRGO	LEO	LIBRA	LEO	CAPRICORN	ARIES	VIRGO	CANCER
16	7:45 AM	LIBRA	VIRGO	LEO	LIBRA	LEO	CAPRICORN	ARIES	VIRGO	CANCER
17			VIRGO	LEO	LIBRA	LEO	CAPRICORN	ARIES	VIRGO	CANCER
18	9:11 AM	SCORPIO	VIRGO	LEO	LIBRA	LEO	CAPRICORN	ARIES	VIRGO	CANCER
19			VIRGO	LEO	LIBRA	LEO	CAPRICORN	ARIES	VIRGO	CANCER
20	12:48 PM	SAGITTARIUS	VIRGO	LEO	LIBRA	LEO	CAPRICORN	ARIES	VIRGO	CANCER
21			VIRGO	LEO	LIBRA	LEO	CAPRICORN	ARIES	VIRGO	CANCER
22	6:58 PM	CAPRICORN	VIRGO	LEO	LIBRA	LEO	CAPRICORN	ARIES	VIRGO	CANCER
23			VIRGO	LEO	LIBRA	LEO	CAPRICORN	ARIES	VIRGO	CANCER

LEO

MOON FROM IN	MERCURY	VENUS	MARS	JUPITER	SATURN	URANUS	NEPTUNE	PLUTO
JULY								
23	LEO	GEMINI	GEMINI	LEO	AQUARIUS	ARIES	VIRGO	CANCER
24	LEO	GEMINI	GEMINI	LEO	AQUARIUS	ARIES	VIRGO	CANCER
25 3:54 AM TAURUS	LEO	GEMINI	GEMINI	LEO	AQUARIUS	ARIES	VIRGO	CANCER
26	LEO	GEMINI	GEMINI	LEO	AQUARIUS	ARIES	VIRGO	CANCER
27 4:26 PM GEMINI	LEO	GEMINI	GEMINI	LEO	AQUARIUS	ARIES	VIRGO	CANCER
28	VIRGO	CANCER	GEMINI	LEO	AQUARIUS	ARIES	VIRGO	CANCER
29	VIRGO	CANCER	GEMINI	LEO	AQUARIUS	ARIES	VIRGO	CANCER
30 3:07 AM CANCER	VIRGO	CANCER	GEMINI	LEO	AQUARIUS	ARIES	VIRGO	CANCER
31	VIRGO	CANCER	GEMINI	LEO	AQUARIUS	ARIES	VIRGO	CANCER
AUGUST								
1 10:57 AM LEO	VIRGO	CANCER	GEMINI	LEO	AQUARIUS	ARIES	VIRGO	CANCER
2	VIRGO	CANCER	GEMINI	LEO	AQUARIUS	ARIES	VIRGO	CANCER
3 4:15 PM VIRGO	VIRGO	CANCER	GEMINI	LEO	AQUARIUS	ARIES	VIRGO	CANCER
4	VIRGO	CANCER	GEMINI	LEO	AQUARIUS	ARIES	VIRGO	CANCER
5 7:56 PM LIBRA	VIRGO	CANCER	CANCER	LEO	AQUARIUS	ARIES	VIRGO	CANCER
6	VIRGO	CANCER	CANCER	LEO	AQUARIUS	ARIES	VIRGO	CANCER
7 10:49 PM SCORPIO	VIRGO	CANCER	CANCER	LEO	AQUARIUS	ARIES	VIRGO	CANCER
8	VIRGO	CANCER	CANCER	LEO	AQUARIUS	ARIES	VIRGO	CANCER
9	VIRGO	CANCER	CANCER	LEO	AQUARIUS	AIRES	VIRGO	CANCER
10 1:32 AM SAGITTARIUS	LEO	CANCER	CANCER	LEO	AQUARIUS	ARIES	VIRGO	CANCER
11	LEO	CANCER	CANCER	VIRGO	AQUARIUS	ARIES	VIRGO	CANCER
12 4:38 AM CAPRICORN	LEO	CANCER	CANCER	VIRGO	AQUARIUS	ARIES	VIRGO	CANCER
13	LEO	CANCER	CANCER	VIRGO	AQUARIUS	ARIES	VIRGO	CANCER
14 8:54 AM AQUARIUS	LEO	CANCER	CANCER	VIRGO	AQUARIUS	ARIES	VIRGO	CANCER
15	LEO	CANCER	CANCER	VIRGO	AQUARIUS	ARIES	VIRGO	CANCER
16 3:14 PM PISCES	LEO	CANCER	CANCER	VIRGO	AQUARIUS	ARIES	VIRGO	CANCER
17	LEO	CANCER	CANCER	VIRGO	AQUARIUS	ARIES	VIRGO	CANCER
18	LEO	CANCER	CANCER	VIRGO	AQUARIUS	ARIES	VIRGO	CANCER
19 0:18 AM ARIES	LEO	CANCER	CANCER	VIRGO	AQUARIUS	ARIES	VIRGO	CANCER
20	LEO	CANCER	CANCER	VIRGO	AQUARIUS	ARIES	VIRGO	CANCER
21 11:56 AM TAURUS	LEO	CANCER	CANCER	VIRGO	AQUARIUS	ARIES	VIRGO	CANCER
22	LEO	CANCER	CANCER	VIRGO	AQUARIUS	ARIES	VIRGO	CANCER

1933

MOON FROM IN	MERCURY	VENUS	MARS	JUPITER	SATURN	URANUS	NEPTUNE	PLUTO
JULY								
23	LEO	LEO	LIBRA	VIRGO	AQUARIUS	ARIES	VIRGO	CANCER
24 10:35 PM VIRGO	LEO	LEO	LIBRA	VIRGO	AQUARIUS	ARIES	VIRGO	CANCER
25	LEO	LEO	LIBRA	VIRGO	AQUARIUS	ARIES	VIRGO	CANCER
26	LEO	LEO	LIBRA	VIRGO	AQUARIUS	ARIES	VIRGO	CANCER
27 6:44 AM LIBRA	LEO	LEO	LIBRA	VIRGO	AQUARIUS	ARIES	VIRGO	CANCER
28	LEO	VIRGO	LIBRA	VIRGO	AQUARIUS	ARIES	VIRGO	CANCER
29 12:20 PM SCORPIO	LEO	VIRGO	LIBRA	VIRGO	AQUARIUS	ARIES	VIRGO	CANCER
30	LEO	VIRGO	LIBRA	VIRGO	AQUARIUS	ARIES	VIRGO	CANCER
31 3:26 PM SAGITTARIUS	LEO	VIRGO	LIBRA	VIRGO	AQUARIUS	ARIES	VIRGO	CANCER
AUGUST								
1	LEO	VIRGO	LIBRA	VIRGO	AQUARIUS	ARIES	VIRGO	CANCER
2 4:40 PM CAPRICORN	LEO	VIRGO	LIBRA	VIRGO	AQUARIUS	ARIES	VIRGO	CANCER
3	LEO	VIRGO	LIBRA	VIRGO	AQUARIUS	ARIES	VIRGO	CANCER
4 5:22 PM AQUARIUS	LEO	VIRGO	LIBRA	VIRGO	AQUARIUS	ARIES	VIRGO	CANCER
5	LEO	VIRGO	LIBRA	VIRGO	AQUARIUS	ARIES	VIRGO	CANCER
6 7:11 PM PISCES	LEO	VIRGO	LIBRA	VIRGO	AQUARIUS	ARIES	VIRGO	CANCER
7	LEO	VIRGO	LIBRA	VIRGO	AQUARIUS	ARIES	VIRGO	CANCER
8 11:42 PM ARIES	LEO	VIRGO	LIBRA	VIRGO	AQUARIUS	ARIES	VIRGO	CANCER
9	LEO	VIRGO	LIBRA	VIRGO	AQUARIUS	ARIES	VIRGO	CANCER
10	LEO	VIRGO	LIBRA	VIRGO	AQUARIUS	ARIES	VIRGO	CANCER
11 7:45 AM TAURUS	LEO	VIRGO	LIBRA	VIRGO	AQUARIUS	ARIES	VIRGO	CANCER
12	LEO	VIRGO	LIBRA	VIRGO	AQUARIUS	ARIES	VIRGO	CANCER
13 6:57 PM GEMINI	LEO	VIRGO	LIBRA	VIRGO	AQUARIUS	ARIES	VIRGO	CANCER
14	LEO	VIRGO	LIBRA	VIRGO	AQUARIUS	ARIES	VIRGO	CANCER
15	LEO	VIRGO	LIBRA	VIRGO	AQUARIUS	ARIES	VIRGO	CANCER
16 7:32 AM CANCER	LEO	VIRGO	LIBRA	VIRGO	AQUARIUS	ARIES	VIRGO	CANCER
17	LEO	VIRGO	LIBRA	VIRGO	AQUARIUS	ARIES	VIRGO	CANCER
18 7:23 PM LEO	LEO	VIRGO	LIBRA	VIRGO	AQUARIUS	ARIES	VIRGO	CANCER
19	LEO	VIRGO	LIBRA	VIRGO	AQUARIUS	ARIES	VIRGO	CANCER
20	LEO	VIRGO	LIBRA	VIRGO	AQUARIUS	ARIES	VIRGO	CANCER
21 5:07 AM VIRGO	LEO	VIRGO	LIBRA	VIRGO	AQUARIUS	ARIES	VIRGO	CANCER
22	LEO	LIBRA	LIBRA	VIRGO	AQUARIUS	ARIES	VIRGO	CANCER
23 12:29 PM LIBRA	LEO	LIBRA	LIBRA	VIRGO	AQUARIUS	ARIES	VIRGO	CANCER

1934

LEO

	MOON FROM IN	MERCURY	VENUS	MARS	JUPITER	SATURN	URANUS	NEPTUNE	PLUTO
JULY									
24	3:04 AM CAPRICORN	CANCER	CANCER	CANCER	LIBRA	AQUARIUS	TAURUS	VIRGO	CANCER
25		CANCER	CANCER	CANCER	LIBRA	AQUARIUS	TAURUS	VIRGO	CANCER
26	2:43 AM AQUARIUS	CANCER	CANCER	CANCER	LIBRA	AQUARIUS	TAURUS	VIRGO	CANCER
27		CANCER	CANCER	CANCER	LIBRA	AQUARIUS	TAURUS	VIRGO	CANCER
28	2:20 AM PISCES	CANCER	CANCER	CANCER	LIBRA	AQUARIUS	TAURUS	VIRGO	CANCER
29		CANCER	CANCER	CANCER	LIBRA	AQUARIUS	TAURUS	VIRGO	CANCER
30	3:46 AM ARIES	CANCER	CANCER	CANCER	LIBRA	AQUARIUS	TAURUS	VIRGO	CANCER
31		CANCER	CANCER	CANCER	LIBRA	AQUARIUS	TAURUS	VIRGO	CANCER
AUGUST									
1	8:25 AM TAURUS	CANCER	CANCER	CANCER	LIBRA	AQUARIUS	TAURUS	VIRGO	CANCER
2		CANCER	CANCER	CANCER	LIBRA	AQUARIUS	TAURUS	VIRGO	CANCER
3	4:49 PM GEMINI	CANCER	CANCER	CANCER	LIBRA	AAUARIUS	TAURUS	VIRGO	CANCER
4		CANCER	CANCER	CANCER	LIBRA	AQUARIUS	TAURUS	VIRGO	CANCER
5		CANCER	CANCER	CANCER	LIBRA	AQUARIUS	TAURUS	VIRGO	CANCER
6	4:13 AM CANCER	CANCER	CANCER	CANCER	LIBRA	AQUARIUS	TAURUS	VIRGO	CANCER
7		CANCER	CANCER	CANCER	LIBRA	AQUARIUS	TAURUS	VIRGO	CANCER
8	5:08 PM LEO	CANCER	CANCER	CANCER	LIBRA	AQUARIUS	TAURUS	VIRGO	CANCER
9		CANCER	CANCER	CANCER	LIBRA	AQUARIUS	TAURUS	VIRGO	CANCER
10		LEO	CANCER	CANCER	LIBRA	AQUARIUS	TAURUS	VIRGO	CANCER
11	5:59 AM VIRGO	LEO	CANCER	CANCER	LIBRA	AQUARIUS	TAURUS	VIRGO	CANCER
12		LEO	CANCER	CANCER	LIBRA	AQUARIUS	TAURUS	VIRGO	CANCER
13	5:32 PM LIBRA	LEO	CANCER	CANCER	LIBRA	AQUARIUS	TAURUS	VIRGO	CANCER
14		LEO	CANCER	CANCER	LIBRA	AQUARIUS	TAURUS	VIRGO	CANCER
15		LEO	CANCER	CANCER	LIBRA	AQUARIUS	TAURUS	VIRGO	CANCER
16	2:51 AM SCORPIO	LEO	CANCER	CANCER	LIBRA	AQUARIUS	TAURUS	VIRGO	CANCER
17		LEO	CANCER	CANCER	LIBRA	AQUARIUS	TAURUS	VIRGO	CANCER
18	9:11 AM SAGITTARIUS	LEO	LEO	CANCER	LIBRA	AQUARIUS	TAURUS	VIRGO	CANCER
19		LEO	LEO	CANCER	LIBRA	AQUARIUS	TAURUS	VIRGO	CANCER
20	12:27 PM CAPRICORN	LEO	LEO	CANCER	LIBRA	AQUARIUS	TAURUS	VIRGO	CANCER
21		LEO	LEO	CANCER	LIBRA	AQUARIUS	TAURUS	VIRGO	CANCER
22	1:18 PM AQUARIUS	LEO	LEO	CANCER	LIBRA	AQUARIUS	TAURUS	VIRGO	CANCER
23		LEO	LEO	CANCER	LIBRA	AQUARIUS	TAURUS	VIRGO	CANCER

1935

	MOON FROM IN	MERCURY	VENUS	MARS	JUPITER	SATURN	URANUS	NEPTUNE	PLUTO
JULY									
24	9:42 PM GEMINI	CANCER	VIRGO	LIBRA	SCORPIO	PISCES	TAURUS	VIRGO	CANCER
25		CANCER	VIRGO	LIBRA	SCORPIO	PISCES	TAURUS	VIRGO	CANCER
26		CANCER	VIRGO	LIBRA	SCORPIO	PISCES	TAURUS	VIRGO	CANCER
27	5:43 AM CANCER	CANCER	VIRGO	LIBRA	SCORPIO	PISCES	TAURUS	VIRGO	CANCER
28		CANCER	VIRGO	LIBRA	SCORPIO	PISCES	TAURUS	VIRGO	CANCER
29	4:04 PM LEO	CANCER	VIRGO	LIBRA	SCORPIO	PISCES	TAURUS	VIRGO	CANCER
30		CANCER	VIRGO	SCORPIO	SCORPIO	PISCES	TAURUS	VIRGO	CANCER
31		CANCER	VIRGO	SCORPIO	SCORPIO	PISCES	TAURUS	VIRGO	CANCER
AUGUST									
1	4:06 AM VIRGO	CANCER	VIRGO	SCORPIO	SCORPIO	PISCES	TAURUS	VIRGO	CANCER
2		LEO	VIRGO	SCORPIO	SCORPIO	PISCES	TAURUS	VIRGO	CANCER
3	4:54 PM LIBRA	LEO	VIRGO	SCORPIO	SCORPIO	PISCES	TAURUS	VIRGO	CANCER
4		LEO	VIRGO	SCORPIO	SCORPIO	PISCES	TAURUS	VIRGO	CANCER
5		LEO	VIRGO	SCORPIO	SCORPIO	PISCES	TAURUS	VIRGO	CANCER
6	4:57 AM SCORPIO	LEO	VIRGO	SCORPIO	SCORPIO	PISCES	TAURUS	VIRGO	CANCER
7		LEO	VIRGO	SCORPIO	SCORPIO	PISCES	TAURUS	VIRGO	CANCER
8	2:24 PM SAGITTARIUS	LEO	VIRGO	SCORPIO	SCORPIO	PISCES	TAURUS	VIRGO	CANCER
9		LEO	VIRGO	SCORPIO	SCORPIO	PISCES	TAURUS	VIRGO	CANCER
10	8:10 PM CAPRICORN	LEO	VIRGO	SCORPIO	SCORPIO	PISCES	TAURUS	VIRGO	CANCER
11		LEO	VIRGO	SCORPIO	SCORPIO	PISCES	TAURUS	VIRGO	CANCER
12	10:21 PM AQUARIUS	LEO	VIRGO	SCORPIO	SCORPIO	PISCES	TAURUS	VIRGO	CANCER
13		LEO	VIRGO	SCORPIO	SCORPIO	PISCES	TAURUS	VIRGO	CANCER
14	10:18 PM PISCES	LEO	VIRGO	SCORPIO	SCORPIO	PISCES	TAURUS	VIRGO	CANCER
15		LEO	VIRGO	SCORPIO	SCORPIO	PISCES	TAURUS	VIRGO	CANCER
16	9:55 PM ARIES	LEO	VIRGO	SCORPIO	SCORPIO	PISCES	TAURUS	VIRGO	CANCER
17		VIRGO	VIRGO	SCORPIO	SCORPIO	PISCES	TAURUS	VIRGO	CANCER
18	11:08 PM TAURUS	VIRGO	VIRGO	SCORPIO	SCORPIO	PISCES	TAURUS	VIRGO	CANCER
19		VIRGO	VIRGO	SCORPIO	SCORPIO	PISCES	TAURUS	VIRGO	CANCER
20		VIRGO	VIRGO	SCORPIO	SCORPIO	PISCES	TAURUS	VIRGO	CANCER
21	3:25 AM GEMINI	VIRGO	VIRGO	SCORPIO	SCORPIO	PISCES	TAURUS	VIRGO	CANCER
22		VIRGO	VIRGO	SCORPIO	SCORPIO	PISCES	TAURUS	VIRGO	CANCER
23	11:17 AM CANCER	VIRGO	VIRGO	SCORPIO	SCORPIO	PISCES	TAURUS	VIRGO	CANCER

	MOON										
	FROM IN	MERCURY	VENUS	MARS	JUPITER	SATURN	URANUS	NEPTUNE	PLUTO
JULY									
23	12:31 PM LIBRA	CANCER	LEO	CANCER	SAGITTARIUS	PISCES	TAURUS	VIRGO	CANCER
24		LEO	LEO	CANCER	SAGITTARIUS	PISCES	TAURUS	VIRGO	CANCER
25		LEO	LEO	CANCER	SAGITTARIUS	PISCES	TAURUS	VIRGO	CANCER
26	0:54 AM SCORPIO	LEO	LEO	CANCER	SAGITTARIUS	PISCES	TAURUS	VIRGO	CANCER
27		LEO	LEO	CANCER	SAGITTARIUS	PISCES	TAURUS	VIRGO	CANCER
28	12:36 PM SAGITTARIUS	LEO	LEO	CANCER	SAGITTARIUS	PISCES	TAURUS	VIRGO	CANCER
29		LEO	LEO	CANCER	SAGITTARIUS	PISCES	TAURUS	VIRGO	CANCER
30	10:23 PM CAPRICORN	LEO	LEO	CANCER	SAGITTARIUS	PISCES	TAURUS	VIRGO	CANCER
31		LEO	LEO	CANCER	SAGITTARIUS	PISCES	TAURUS	VIRGO	CANCER
AUGUST									
1		LEO	LEO	CANCER	SAGITTARIUS	PISCES	TAURUS	VIRGO	CANCER
2	4:25 AM AQUARIUS	LEO	LEO	CANCER	SAGITTARIUS	PISCES	TAURUS	VIRGO	CANCER
3		LEO	LEO	CANCER	SAGITTARIUS	PISCES	TAURUS	VIRGO	CANCER
4	7:36 AM PISCES	LEO	LEO	CANCER	SAGITTARIUS	PISCES	TAURUS	VIRGO	CANCER
5		LEO	LEO	CANCER	SAGITTARIUS	PISCES	TAURUS	VIRGO	CANCER
6	9:21 AM ARIES	LEO	LEO	CANCER	SAGITTARIUS	PISCES	TAURUS	VIRGO	CANCER
7		LEO	LEO	CANCER	SAGITTARIUS	PISCES	TAURUS	VIRGO	CANCER
8	11:12 AM TAURUS	VIRGO	LEO	CANCER	SAGITTARIUS	PISCES	TAURUS	VIRGO	CANCER
9		VIRGO	LEO	LEO	SAGITTARIUS	PISCES	TAURUS	VIRGO	CANCER
10	2:12 PM GEMINI	VIRGO	LEO	LEO	SAGITTARIUS	PISCES	TAURUS	VIRGO	CANCER
11		VIRGO	VIRGO	LEO	SAGITTARIUS	PISCES	TAURUS	VIRGO	CANCER
12	6:52 PM CANCER	VIRGO	VIRGO	LEO	SAGITTARIUS	PISCES	TAURUS	VIRGO	CANCER
13		VIRGO	VIRGO	LEO	SAGITTARIUS	PISCES	TAURUS	VIRGO	CANCER
14		VIRGO	VIRGO	LEO	SAGITTARIUS	PISCES	TAURUS	VIRGO	CANCER
15	1:20 AM LEO	VIRGO	VIRGO	LEO	SAGITTARIUS	PISCES	TAURUS	VIRGO	CANCER
16		VIRGO	VIRGO	LEO	SAGITTARIUS	PISCES	TAURUS	VIRGO	CANCER
17	9:45 AM VIRGO	VIRGO	VIRGO	LEO	SAGITTARIUS	PISCES	TAURUS	VIRGO	CANCER
18		VIRGO	VIRGO	LEO	SAGITTARIUS	PISCES	TAURUS	VIRGO	CANCER
19	8:17 PM LIBRA	VIRGO	VIRGO	LEO	SAGITTARIUS	PISCES	TAURUS	VIRGO	CANCER
20		VIRGO	VIRGO	LEO	SAGITTARIUS	PISCES	TAURUS	VIRGO	CANCER
21		VIRGO	VIRGO	LEO	SAGITTARIUS	PISCES	TAURUS	VIRGO	CANCER
22	8:36 AM SCORPIO	VIRGO	VIRGO	LEO	SAGITTARIUS	PISCES	TAURUS	VIRGO	CANCER

1937

	MOON										
	FROM IN	MERCURY	VENUS	MARS	JUPITER	SATURN	URANUS	NEPTUNE	PLUTO
JULY									
23	7:19 AM AQUARIUS	LEO	GEMINI	SCORPIO	CAPRICORN	ARIES	TAURUS	VIRGO	CANCER
24		LEO	GEMINI	SCORPIO	CAPRICORN	ARIES	TAURUS	VIRGO	CANCER
25	3:18 PM PISCES	LEO	GEMINI	SCORPIO	CAPRICORN	ARIES	TAURUS	VIRGO	CANCER
26		LEO	GEMINI	SCORPIO	CAPRICORN	ARIES	TAURUS	VIRGO	CANCER
27	9:13 PM ARIES	LEO	GEMINI	SCORPIO	CAPRICORN	ARIES	TAURUS	VIRGO	CANCER
28		LEO	GEMINI	SCORPIO	CAPRICORN	ARIES	TAURUS	VIRGO	CANCER
29		LEO	GEMINI	SCORPIO	CAPRICORN	ARIES	TAURUS	VIRGO	CANCER
30	1:29 AM TAURUS	LEO	GEMINI	SCORPIO	CAPRICORN	ARIES	TAURUS	VIRGO	CANCER
31		LEO	GEMINI	SCORPIO	CAPRICORN	ARIES	TAURUS	VIRGO	CANCER
AUGUST									
1	4:28 AM GEMINI	VIRGO	GEMINI	SCORPIO	CAPRICORN	ARIES	TAURUS	VIRGO	CANCER
2		VIRGO	GEMINI	SCORPIO	CAPRICORN	ARIES	TAURUS	VIRGO	CANCER
3	6:33 AM CANCER	VIRGO	GEMINI	SCORPIO	CAPRICORN	ARIES	TAURUS	VIRGO	CANCER
4		VIRGO	GEMINI	SCORPIO	CAPRICORN	ARIES	TAURUS	VIRGO	CANCER
5	8:36 AM LEO	VIRGO	CANCER	SCORPIO	CAPRICORN	ARIES	TAURUS	VIRGO	CANCER
6		VIRGO	CANCER	SCORPIO	CAPRICORN	ARIES	TAURUS	VIRGO	CANCER
7	11:56 AM VIRGO	VIRGO	CANCER	SCORPIO	CAPRICORN	ARIES	TAURUS	VIRGO	CANCER
8		VIRGO	CANCER	SCORPIO	CAPRICORN	ARIES	TAURUS	VIRGO	CANCER
9	6:03 PM LIBRA	VIRGO	CANCER	SAGITTARIUS	CAPRICORN	ARIES	TAURUS	VIRGO	CANCER
10		VIRGO	CANCER	SAGITTARIUS	CAPRICORN	ARIES	TAURUS	VIRGO	CANCER
11		VIRGO	CANCER	SAGITTARIUS	CAPRICORN	ARIES	TAURUS	VIRGO	CANCER
12	3:38 AM SCORPIO	VIRGO	CANCER	SAGITTARIUS	CAPRICORN	ARIES	TAURUS	VIRGO	CANCER
13		VIRGO	CANCER	SAGITTARIUS	CAPRICORN	ARIES	TAURUS	VIRGO	CANCER
14	3:59 PM SAGITTARIUS	VIRGO	CANCER	SAGITTARIUS	CAPRICORN	ARIES	TAURUS	VIRGO	CANCER
15		VIRGO	CANCER	SAGITTARIUS	CAPRICORN	ARIES	TAURUS	VIRGO	CANCER
16		VIRGO	CANCER	SAGITTARIUS	CAPRICORN	ARIES	TAURUS	VIRGO	CANCER
17	4:36 AM CAPRICORN	VIRGO	CANCER	SAGITTARIUS	CAPRICORN	ARIES	TAURUS	VIRGO	CANCER
18		VIRGO	CANCER	SAGITTARIUS	CAPRICORN	ARIES	TAURUS	VIRGO	CANCER
19	3:02 PM AQUARIUS	VIRGO	CANCER	SAGITTARIUS	CAPRICORN	ARIES	TAURUS	VIRGO	CANCER
20		VIRGO	CANCER	SAGITTARIUS	CAPRICORN	ARIES	TAURUS	VIRGO	CANCER
21	10:25 PM PISCES	VIRGO	CANCER	SAGITTARIUS	CAPRICORN	ARIES	TAURUS	VIRGO	CANCER
22		VIRGO	CANCER	SAGITTARIUS	CAPRICORN	ARIES	TAURUS	VIRGO	CANCER
23		VIRGO	CANCER	SAGITTARIUS	CAPRICORN	ARIES	TAURUS	VIRGO	CANCER

1938   LEO

	MOON FROM	IN	MERCURY	VENUS	MARS	JUPITER	SATURN	URANUS	NEPTUNE	PLUTO
JULY										
24	5:54 AM	CANCER	LEO	VIRGO	LEO	PISCES	ARIES	TAURUS	VIRGO	CANCER
25			LEO	VIRGO	LEO	PISCES	ARIES	TAURUS	VIRGO	CANCER
26	5:25 PM	LEO	LEO	VIRGO	LEO	PISCES	ARIES	TAURUS	VIRGO	CANCER
27			VIRGO	VIRGO	LEO	PISCES	ARIES	TAURUS	VIRGO	CANCER
28	5:18 PM	VIRGO	VIRGO	VIRGO	LEO	PISCES	ARIES	TAURUS	VIRGO	CANCER
29			VIRGO	VIRGO	LEO	PISCES	ARIES	TAURUS	VIRGO	CANCER
30	7:42 PM	LIBRA	VIRGO	VIRGO	LEO	AQUARIUS	ARIES	TAURUS	VIRGO	CANCER
31			VIRGO	VIRGO	LEO	AQUARIUS	ARIES	TAURUS	VIRGO	CANCER
AUGUST										
1			VIRGO	VIRGO	LEO	AQUARIUS	ARIES	TAURUS	VIRGO	CANCER
2	1:53 AM	SCORPIO	VIRGO	VIRGO	LEO	AQUARIUS	ARIES	TAURUS	VIRGO	LEO
3			VIRGO	VIRGO	LEO	AQUARIUS	ARIES	TAURUS	VIRGO	LEO
4	12:04 PM	SAGITTARIUS	VIRGO	VIRGO	LEO	AQUARIUS	ARIES	TAURUS	VIRGO	LEO
5			VIRGO	VIRGO	LEO	AQUARIUS	ARIES	TAURUS	VIRGO	LEO
6			VIRGO	VIRGO	LEO	AQUARIUS	ARIES	TAURUS	VIRGO	LEO
7	0:34 AM	CAPRICORN	VIRGO	VIRGO	LEO	AQUARIUS	ARIES	TAURUS	VIRGO	LEO
8			VIRGO	VIRGO	LEO	AQUARIUS	ARIES	TAURUS	VIRGO	LEO
9	1:15 PM	AQUARIUS	VIRGO	VIRGO	LEO	AQUARIUS	ARIES	TAURUS	VIRGO	LEO
10			VIRGO	LIBRA	LEO	AQUARIUS	ARIES	TAURUS	VIRGO	LEO
11			VIRGO	LIBRA	LEO	AQUARIUS	ARIES	TAURUS	VIRGO	LEO
12	0:43 AM	PISCES	VIRGO	LIBRA	LEO	AQUARIUS	ARIES	TAURUS	VIRGO	LEO
13			VIRGO	LIBRA	LEO	AQUARIUS	ARIES	TAURUS	VIRGO	LEO
14	10:33 AM	ARIES	VIRGO	LIBRA	LEO	AQUARIUS	ARIES	TAURUS	VIRGO	LEO
15			VIRGO	LIBRA	LEO	AQUARIUS	ARIES	TAURUS	VIRGO	LEO
16	6:22 PM	TAURUS	VIRGO	LIBRA	LEO	AQUARIUS	ARIES	TAURUS	VIRGO	LEO
17			VIRGO	LIBRA	LEO	AQUARIUS	ARIES	TAURUS	VIRGO	LEO
18	11:47 PM	GEMINI	VIRGO	LIBRA	LEO	AQUARIUS	ARIES	TAURUS	VIRGO	LEO
19			VIRGO	LIBRA	LEO	AQUARIUS	ARIES	TAURUS	VIRGO	LEO
20			VIRGO	LIBRA	LEO	AQUARIUS	ARIES	TAURUS	VIRGO	LEO
21	2:37 AM	CANCER	VIRGO	LIBRA	LEO	AQUARIUS	ARIES	TAURUS	VIRGO	LEO
22			VIRGO	LIBRA	LEO	AQUARIUS	ARIES	TAURUS	VIRGO	LEO
23	3:26 AM	LEO	VIRGO	LIBRA	LEO	AQUARIUS	ARIES	TAURUS	VIRGO	LEO

1939

	MOON FROM	IN	MERCURY	VENUS	MARS	JUPITER	SATURN	URANUS	NEPTUNE	PLUTO
JULY										
24			LEO	CANCER	CAPRICORN	ARIES	TAURUS	TAURUS	VIRGO	LEO
25	2:13 PM	SAGITTARIUS	LEO	CANCER	CAPRICORN	ARIES	TAURUS	TAURUS	VIRGO	LEO
26			LEO	CANCER	CAPRICORN	ARIES	TAURUS	TAURUS	VIRGO	LEO
27	11:53 PM	CAPRICORN	LEO	CANCER	CAPRICORN	ARIES	TAURUS	TAURUS	VIRGO	LEO
28			LEO	CANCER	CAPRICORN	ARIES	TAURUS	TAURUS	VIRGO	LEO
29			LEO	CANCER	CAPRICORN	ARIES	TAURUS	TAURUS	VIRGO	LEO
30	11:15 AM	AQUARIUS	LEO	CANCER	CAPRICORN	ARIES	TAURUS	TAURUS	VIRGO	LEO
31			LEO	CANCER	CAPRICORN	ARIES	TAURUS	TAURUS	VIRGO	LEO
AUGUST										
1	11:41 PM	PISCES	LEO	CANCER	CAPRICORN	ARIES	TAURUS	TAURUS	VIRGO	LEO
2			LEO	CANCER	CAPRICORN	ARIES	TAURUS	TAURUS	VIRGO	LEO
3			LEO	LEO	CAPRICORN	ARIES	TAURUS	TAURUS	VIRGO	LEO
4	12:21 PM	ARIES	LEO	LEO	CAPRICORN	ARIES	TAURUS	TAURUS	VIRGO	LEO
5			LEO	LEO	CAPRICORN	ARIES	TAURUS	TAURUS	VIRGO	LEO
6			LEO	LEO	CAPRICORN	ARIES	TAURUS	TAURUS	VIRGO	LEO
7	4:04 AM	TAURUS	LEO	LEO	CAPRICORN	ARIES	TAURUS	TAURUS	VIRGO	LEO
8			LEO	LEO	CAPRICORN	ARIES	TAURUS	TAURUS	VIRGO	LEO
9	8:04 AM	GEMINI	LEO	LEO	CAPRICORN	ARIES	TAURUS	TAURUS	VIRGO	LEO
10			LEO	LEO	CAPRICORN	ARIES	TAURUS	TAURUS	VIRGO	LEO
11	12:18 PM	CANCER	LEO	LEO	CAPRICORN	ARIES	TAURUS	TAURUS	VIRGO	LEO
12			LEO	LEO	CAPRICORN	ARIES	TAURUS	TAURUS	VIRGO	LEO
13	1:07 PM	LEO	LEO	LEO	CAPRICORN	ARIES	TAURUS	TAURUS	VIRGO	LEO
14			LEO	LEO	CAPRICORN	ARIES	TAURUS	TAURUS	VIRGO	LEO
15	12:20 PM	VIRGO	LEO	LEO	CAPRICORN	ARIES	TAURUS	TAURUS	VIRGO	LEO
16			LEO	LEO	CAPRICORN	ARIES	TAURUS	TAURUS	VIRGO	LEO
17	12:05 PM	LIBRA	LEO	LEO	CAPRICORN	ARIES	TAURUS	TAURUS	VIRGO	LEO
18			LEO	LEO	CAPRICORN	ARIES	TAURUS	TAURUS	VIRGO	LEO
19	2:25 PM	SCORPIO	LEO	LEO	CAPRICORN	ARIES	TAURUS	TAURUS	VIRGO	LEO
20			LEO	LEO	CAPRICORN	ARIES	TAURUS	TAURUS	VIRGO	LEO
21	8:18 PM	SAGITTARIUS	LEO	LEO	CAPRICORN	ARIES	TAURUS	TAURUS	VIRGO	LEO
22			LEO	LEO	CAPRICORN	ARIES	TAURUS	TAURUS	VIRGO	LEO
23			LEO	LEO	CAPRICORN	ARIES	TAURUS	TAURUS	VIRGO	LEO

LEO

	MOON FROM	IN	MERCURY	VENUS	MARS	JUPITER	SATURN	URANUS	NEPTUNE	PLUTO
JULY										
23			CANCER	GEMINI	LEO	TAURUS	TAURUS	TAURUS	VIRGO	LEO
24	9:02 AM	ARIES	CANCER	GEMINI	LEO	TAURUS	TAURUS	TAURUS	VIRGO	LEO
25			CANCER	GEMINI	LEO	TAURUS	TAURUS	TAURUS	VIRGO	LEO
26	9:53 PM	TAURUS	CANCER	GEMINI	LEO	TAURUS	TAURUS	TAURUS	VIRGO	LEO
27			CANCER	GEMINI	LEO	TAURUS	TAURUS	TAURUS	VIRGO	LEO
28			CANCER	GEMINI	LEO	TAURUS	TAURUS	TAURUS	VIRGO	LEO
29	9:03 AM	GEMINI	CANCER	GEMINI	LEO	TAURUS	TAURUS	TAURUS	VIRGO	LEO
30			CANCER	GEMINI	LEO	TAURUS	TAURUS	TAURUS	VIRGO	LEO
31	4:27 PM	CANCER	CANCER	GEMINI	LEO	TAURUS	TAURUS	TAURUS	VIRGO	LEO
AUGUST										
1			CANCER	CANCER	LEO	TAURUS	TAURUS	TAURUS	VIRGO	LEO
2	8:16 PM	LEO	CANCER	CANCER	LEO	TAURUS	TAURUS	TAURUS	VIRGO	LEO
3			CANCER	CANCER	LEO	TAURUS	TAURUS	TAURUS	VIRGO	LEO
4	9:49 PM	VIRGO	CANCER	CANCER	LEO	TAURUS	TAURUS	TAURUS	VIRGO	LEO
5			CANCER	CANCER	LEO	TAURUS	TAURUS	TAURUS	VIRGO	LEO
6	10:51 PM	LIBRA	CANCER	CANCER	LEO	TAURUS	TAURUS	TAURUS	VIRGO	LEO
7			CANCER	CANCER	LEO	TAURUS	TAURUS	TAURUS	VIRGO	LEO
8			CANCER	CANCER	LEO	TAURUS	TAURUS	TAURUS	VIRGO	LEO
9	0:48 AM	SCORPIO	CANCER	CANCER	LEO	TAURUS	TAURUS	TAURUS	VIRGO	LEO
10			CANCER	CANCER	LEO	TAURUS	TAURUS	TAURUS	VIRGO	LEO
11	4:30 AM	SAGITTARIUS	LEO	CANCER	LEO	TAURUS	TAURUS	TAURUS	VIRGO	LEO
12			LEO	CANCER	LEO	TAURUS	TAURUS	TAURUS	VIRGO	LEO
13	10:17 AM	CAPRICORN	LEO	CANCER	LEO	TAURUS	TAURUS	TAURUS	VIRGO	LEO
14			LEO	CANCER	LEO	TAURUS	TAURUS	TAURUS	VIRGO	LEO
15	6:11 PM	AQUARIUS	LEO	CANCER	LEO	TAURUS	TAURUS	TAURUS	VIRGO	LEO
16			LEO	CANCER	LEO	TAURUS	TAURUS	TAURUS	VIRGO	LEO
17			LEO	CANCER	LEO	TAURUS	TAURUS	TAURUS	VIRGO	LEO
18	4:11 AM	PISCES	LEO	CANCER	LEO	TAURUS	TAURUS	TAURUS	VIRGO	LEO
19			LEO	CANCER	VIRGO	TAURUS	TAURUS	TAURUS	VIRGO	LEO
20	4:16 PM	ARIES	LEO	CANCER	VIRGO	TAURUS	TAURUS	TAURUS	VIRGO	LEO
21			LEO	CANCER	VIRGO	TAURUS	TAURUS	TAURUS	VIRGO	LEO
22			LEO	CANCER	VIRGO	TAURUS	TAURUS	TAURUS	VIRGO	LEO

	MOON FROM	IN	MERCURY	VENUS	MARS	JUPITER	SATURN	URANUS	NEPTUNE	PLUTO
JULY										
23			CANCER	LEO	ARIES	GEMINI	TAURUS	TAURUS	VIRGO	LEO
24	0:46 AM	LEO	CANCER	LEO	ARIES	GEMINI	TAURUS	TAURUS	VIRGO	LEO
25			CANCER	LEO	ARIES	GEMINI	TAURUS	TAURUS	VIRGO	LEO
26	7:04 AM	VIRGO	CANCER	LEO	ARIES	GEMINI	TAURUS	TAURUS	VIRGO	LEO
27			CANCER	VIRGO	ARIES	GEMINI	TAURUS	TAURUS	VIRGO	LEO
28	11:40 AM	LIBRA	CANCER	VIRGO	ARIES	GEMINI	TAURUS	TAURUS	VIRGO	LEO
29			CANCER	VIRGO	ARIES	GEMINI	TAURUS	TAURUS	VIRGO	LEO
30	3:07 PM	SCORPIO	CANCER	VIRGO	ARIES	GEMINI	TAURUS	TAURUS	VIRGO	LEO
31			CANCER	VIRGO	ARIES	GEMINI	TAURUS	TAURUS	VIRGO	LEO
AUGUST										
1	5:49 PM	SAGITTARIUS	CANCER	VIRGO	ARIES	GEMINI	TAURUS	TAURUS	VIRGO	LEO
2			CANCER	VIRGO	ARIES	GEMINI	TAURUS	TAURUS	VIRGO	LEO
3	9:27 PM	CAPRICORN	CANCER	VIRGO	ARIES	GEMINI	TAURUS	TAURUS	VIRGO	LEO
4			CANCER	VIRGO	ARIES	GEMINI	TAURUS	TAURUS	VIRGO	LEO
5	11:35 PM	AQUARIUS	CANCER	VIRGO	ARIES	GEMINI	TAURUS	TAURUS	VIRGO	LEO
6			LEO	VIRGO	ARIES	GEMINI	TAURUS	TAURUS	VIRGO	LEO
7			LEO	VIRGO	ARIES	GEMINI	TAURUS	GEMINI	VIRGO	LEO
8	4:52 AM	PISCES	LEO	VIRGO	ARIES	GEMINI	TAURUS	GEMINI	VIRGO	LEO
9			LEO	VIRGO	ARIES	GEMINI	TAURUS	GEMINI	VIRGO	LEO
10	1:15 PM	ARIES	LEO	VIRGO	ARIES	GEMINI	TAURUS	GEMINI	VIRGO	LEO
11			LEO	VIRGO	ARIES	GEMINI	TAURUS	GEMINI	VIRGO	LEO
12			LEO	VIRGO	ARIES	GEMINI	TAURUS	GEMINI	VIRGO	LEO
13	0:33 AM	TAURUS	LEO	VIRGO	ARIES	GEMINI	TAURUS	GEMINI	VIRGO	LEO
14			LEO	VIRGO	ARIES	GEMINI	TAURUS	GEMINI	VIRGO	LEO
15	1:08 PM	GEMINI	LEO	VIRGO	ARIES	GEMINI	TAURUS	GEMINI	VIRGO	LEO
16			LEO	VIRGO	ARIES	GEMINI	TAURUS	GEMINI	VIRGO	LEO
17			LEO	VIRGO	ARIES	GEMINI	TAURUS	GEMINI	VIRGO	LEO
18	0:34 AM	CANCER	LEO	VIRGO	ARIES	GEMINI	TAURUS	GEMINI	VIRGO	LEO
19			LEO	VIRGO	ARIES	GEMINI	TAURUS	GEMINI	VIRGO	LEO
20	9:14 AM	LEO	LEO	VIRGO	ARIES	GEMINI	TAURUS	GEMINI	VIRGO	LEO
21			VIRGO	LIBRA	ARIES	GEMINI	TAURUS	GEMINI	VIRGO	LEO
22	2:50 PM	VIRGO	VIRGO	LIBRA	ARIES	GEMINI	TAURUS	GEMINI	VIRGO	LEO
23			VIRGO	LIBRA	ARIES	GEMINI	TAURUS	GEMINI	VIRGO	LEO

1942 LEO

Date	MOON FROM IN	MERCURY	VENUS	MARS	JUPITER	SATURN	URANUS	NEPTUNE	PLUTO
JULY									
24		CANCER	CANCER	LEO	CANCER	GEMINI	GEMINI	VIRGO	LEO
25	7:38 AM CAPRICORN	CANCER	CANCER	LEO	CANCER	GEMINI	GEMINI	VIRGO	LEO
26		CANCER	CANCER	LEO	CANCER	GEMINI	GEMINI	VIRGO	LEO
27	7:37 AM AQUARIUS	CANCER	CANCER	LEO	CANCER	GEMINI	GEMINI	VIRGO	LEO
28		CANCER	CANCER	LEO	CANCER	GEMINI	GEMINI	VIRGO	LEO
29	8:51 AM PISCES	LEO	CANCER	LEO	CANCER	GEMINI	GEMINI	VIRGO	LEO
30		LEO	CANCER	LEO	CANCER	GEMINI	GEMINI	VIRGO	LEO
31	12:59 PM ARIES	LEO	CANCER	LEO	CANCER	GEMINI	GEMINI	VIRGO	LEO
AUGUST									
1		LEO	CANCER	VIRGO	CANCER	GEMINI	GEMINI	VIRGO	LEO
2		LEO	CANCER	VIRGO	CANCER	GEMINI	GEMINI	VIRGO	LEO
3	0:26 AM TAURUS	LEO	CANCER	VIRGO	CANCER	GEMINI	GEMINI	VIRGO	LEO
4		LEO	CANCER	VIRGO	CANCER	GEMINI	GEMINI	VIRGO	LEO
5	7:55 AM GEMINI	LEO	CANCER	VIRGO	CANCER	GEMINI	GEMINI	VIRGO	LEO
6		LEO	CANCER	VIRGO	CANCER	GEMINI	GEMINI	VIRGO	LEO
7	8:29 PM CANCER	LEO	CANCER	VIRGO	CANCER	GEMINI	GEMINI	VIRGO	LEO
8		LEO	CANCER	VIRGO	CANCER	GEMINI	GEMINI	VIRGO	LEO
9		LEO	CANCER	VIRGO	CANCER	GEMINI	GEMINI	VIRGO	LEO
10	8:39 AM LEO	LEO	CANCER	VIRGO	CANCER	GEMINI	GEMINI	VIRGO	LEO
11		LEO	CANCER	VIRGO	CANCER	GEMINI	GEMINI	VIRGO	LEO
12	7:06 PM VIRGO	LEO	CANCER	VIRGO	CANCER	GEMINI	GEMINI	VIRGO	LEO
13		VIRGO	CANCER	VIRGO	CANCER	GEMINI	GEMINI	VIRGO	LEO
14		VIRGO	CANCER	VIRGO	CANCER	GEMINI	GEMINI	VIRGO	LEO
15	3:29 AM LIBRA	VIRGO	CANCER	VIRGO	CANCER	GEMINI	GEMINI	VIRGO	LEO
16		VIRGO	CANCER	VIRGO	CANCER	GEMINI	GEMINI	VIRGO	LEO
17	9:36 AM SCORPIO	VIRGO	LEO	VIRGO	CANCER	GEMINI	GEMINI	VIRGO	LEO
18		VIRGO	LEO	VIRGO	CANCER	GEMINI	GEMINI	VIRGO	LEO
19	1:33 PM SAGITTARIUS	VIRGO	LEO	VIRGO	CANCER	GEMINI	GEMINI	VIRGO	LEO
20		VIRGO	LEO	VIRGO	CANCER	GEMINI	GEMINI	VIRGO	LEO
21	3:45 PM CAPRICORN	VIRGO	LEO	VIRGO	CANCER	GEMINI	GEMINI	VIRGO	LEO
22		VIRGO	LEO	VIRGO	CANCER	GEMINI	GEMINI	VIRGO	LEO
23	5:07 PM AQUARIUS	VIRGO	LEO	VIRGO	CANCER	GEMINI	GEMINI	VIRGO	LEO

1943

Date	MOON FROM IN	MERCURY	VENUS	MARS	JUPITER	SATURN	URANUS	NEPTUNE	PLUTO
JULY									
24		LEO	VIRGO	TAURUS	LEO	GEMINI	GEMINI	VIRGO	LEO
25		LEO	VIRGO	TAURUS	LEO	GEMINI	GEMINI	VIRGO	LEO
26	7:04 AM GEMINI	LEO	VIRGO	TAURUS	LEO	GEMINI	GEMINI	VIRGO	LEO
27		LEO	VIRGO	TAURUS	LEO	GEMINI	GEMINI	VIRGO	LEO
28	6:05 PM CANCER	LEO	VIRGO	TAURUS	LEO	GEMINI	GEMINI	VIRGO	LEO
29		LEO	VIRGO	TAURUS	LEO	GEMINI	GEMINI	VIRGO	LEO
30		LEO	VIRGO	TAURUS	LEO	GEMINI	GEMINI	VIRGO	LEO
31	6:43 AM LEO	LEO	VIRGO	TAURUS	LEO	GEMINI	GEMINI	VIRGO	LEO
AUGUST									
1		LEO	VIRGO	TAURUS	LEO	GEMINI	GEMINI	VIRGO	LEO
2	7:44 PM VIRGO	LEO	VIRGO	TAURUS	LEO	GEMINI	GEMINI	LIBRA	LEO
3		LEO	VIRGO	TAURUS	LEO	GEMINI	GEMINI	LIBRA	LEO
4		LEO	VIRGO	TAURUS	LEO	GEMINI	GEMINI	LIBRA	LEO
5	7:51 AM LIBRA	VIRGO	VIRGO	TAURUS	LEO	GEMINI	GEMINI	LIBRA	LEO
6		VIRGO	VIRGO	TAURUS	LEO	GEMINI	GEMINI	LIBRA	LEO
7	5:35 PM SCORPIO	VIRGO	VIRGO	TAURUS	LEO	GEMINI	GEMINI	LIBRA	LEO
8		VIRGO	VIRGO	TAURUS	LEO	GEMINI	GEMINI	LIBRA	LEO
9		VIRGO	VIRGO	TAURUS	LEO	GEMINI	GEMINI	LIBRA	LEO
10	0:03 AM SAGITTARIUS	VIRGO	VIRGO	TAURUS	LEO	GEMINI	GEMINI	LIBRA	LEO
11		VIRGO	VIRGO	TAURUS	LEO	GEMINI	GEMINI	LIBRA	LEO
12	3:06 AM CAPRICORN	VIRGO	VIRGO	TAURUS	LEO	GEMINI	GEMINI	LIBRA	LEO
13		VIRGO	VIRGO	TAURUS	LEO	GEMINI	GEMINI	LIBRA	LEO
14	3:36 AM AQUARIUS	VIRGO	VIRGO	TAURUS	LEO	GEMINI	GEMINI	LIBRA	LEO
15		VIRGO	VIRGO	TAURUS	LEO	GEMINI	GEMINI	LIBRA	LEO
16	3:07 AM PISCES	VIRGO	VIRGO	TAURUS	LEO	GEMINI	GEMINI	LIBRA	LEO
17		VIRGO	VIRGO	TAURUS	LEO	GEMINI	GEMINI	LIBRA	LEO
18	3:34 AM ARIES	VIRGO	VIRGO	TAURUS	LEO	GEMINI	GEMINI	LIBRA	LEO
19		VIRGO	VIRGO	TAURUS	LEO	GEMINI	GEMINI	LIBRA	LEO
20	6:39 AM TAURUS	VIRGO	VIRGO	TAURUS	LEO	GEMINI	GEMINI	LIBRA	LEO
21		VIRGO	VIRGO	TAURUS	LEO	GEMINI	GEMINI	LIBRA	LEO
22	1:39 PM GEMINI	VIRGO	VIRGO	TAURUS	LEO	GEMINI	GEMINI	LIBRA	LEO
23		VIRGO	VIRGO	TAURUS	LEO	GEMINI	GEMINI	LIBRA	LEO

	MOON		MERCURY	VENUS	MARS	JUPITER	SATURN	URANUS	NEPTUNE	PLUTO
	FROM	IN								
JULY										
23			LEO	LEO	VIRGO	LEO	CANCER	GEMINI	LIBRA	LEO
24			LEO	LEO	VIRGO	LEO	CANCER	GEMINI	LIBRA	LEO
25	6:07 AM	LIBRA	LEO	LEO	VIRGO	LEO	CANCER	GEMINI	LIBRA	LEO
26			LEO	LEO	VIRGO	VIRGO	CANCER	GEMINI	LIBRA	LEO
27	6:14 PM	SCORPIO	LEO	LEO	VIRGO	VIRGO	CANCER	GEMINI	LIBRA	LEO
28			LEO	LEO	VIRGO	VIRGO	CANCER	GEMINI	LIBRA	LEO
29			VIRGO	LEO	VIRGO	VIRGO	CANCER	GEMINI	LIBRA	LEO
30	3:48 AM	SAGITTARIUS	VIRGO	LEO	VIRGO	VIRGO	CANCER	GEMINI	LIBRA	LEO
31			VIRGO	LEO	VIRGO	VIRGO	CANCER	GEMINI	LIBRA	LEO
AUGUST										
1	9:39 AM	CAPRICORN	VIRGO	LEO	VIRGO	VIRGO	CANCER	GEMINI	LIBRA	LEO
2			VIRGO	LEO	VIRGO	VIRGO	CANCER	GEMINI	LIBRA	LEO
3	12:09 PM	AQUARIUS	VIRGO	LEO	VIRGO	VIRGO	CANCER	GEMINI	LIBRA	LEO
4			VIRGO	LEO	VIRGO	VIRGO	CANCER	GEMINI	LIBRA	LEO
5	10:02 AM	PISCES	VIRGO	LEO	VIRGO	VIRGO	CANCER	GEMINI	LIBRA	LEO
6			VIRGO	LEO	VIRGO	VIRGO	CANCER	GEMINI	LIBRA	LEO
7	12:45 PM	ARIES	VIRGO	LEO	VIRGO	VIRGO	CANCER	GEMINI	LIBRA	LEO
8			VIRGO	LEO	VIRGO	VIRGO	CANCER	GEMINI	LIBRA	LEO
9	2:23 PM	TAURUS	VIRGO	LEO	VIRGO	VIRGO	CANCER	GEMINI	LIBRA	LEO
10			VIRGO	LEO	VIRGO	VIRGO	CANCER	GEMINI	LIBRA	LEO
11	6:43 PM	GEMINI	VIRGO	VIRGO	VIRGO	VIRGO	CANCER	GEMINI	LIBRA	LEO
12			VIRGO	VIRGO	VIRGO	VIRGO	CANCER	GEMINI	LIBRA	LEO
13			VIRGO	VIRGO	VIRGO	VIRGO	CANCER	GEMINI	LIBRA	LEO
14	2:06 AM	CANCER	VIRGO	VIRGO	VIRGO	VIRGO	CANCER	GEMINI	LIBRA	LEO
15			VIRGO	VIRGO	VIRGO	VIRGO	CANCER	GEMINI	LIBRA	LEO
16	12:09 PM	LEO	VIRGO	VIRGO	VIRGO	VIRGO	CANCER	GEMINI	LIBRA	LEO
17			VIRGO	VIRGO	VIRGO	VIRGO	CANCER	GEMINI	LIBRA	LEO
18			VIRGO	VIRGO	VIRGO	VIRGO	CANCER	GEMINI	LIBRA	LEO
19	0:01 AM	VIRGO	VIRGO	VIRGO	VIRGO	VIRGO	CANCER	GEMINI	LIBRA	LEO
20			VIRGO	VIRGO	VIRGO	VIRGO	CANCER	GEMINI	LIBRA	LEO
21	12:44 PM	LIBRA	VIRGO	VIRGO	VIRGO	VIRGO	CANCER	GEMINI	LIBRA	LEO
22			VIRGO	VIRGO	VIRGO	VIRGO	CANCER	GEMINI	LIBRA	LEO

1945

	MOON		MERCURY	VENUS	MARS	JUPITER	SATURN	URANUS	NEPTUNE	PLUTO
	FROM	IN								
JULY										
23			LEO	GEMINI	GEMINI	VIRGO	CANCER	GEMINI	LIBRA	LEO
24	6:12 PM	AQUARIUS	LEO	GEMINI	GEMINI	VIRGO	CANCER	GEMINI	LIBRA	LEO
25			LEO	GEMINI	GEMINI	VIRGO	CANCER	GEMINI	LIBRA	LEO
26	10:25 PM	PISCES	LEO	GEMINI	GEMINI	VIRGO	CANCER	GEMINI	LIBRA	LEO
27			VIRGO	GEMINI	GEMINI	VIRGO	CANCER	GEMINI	LIBRA	LEO
28			VIRGO	GEMINI	GEMINI	VIRGO	CANCER	GEMINI	LIBRA	LEO
29	1:07 AM	ARIES	VIRGO	GEMINI	GEMINI	VIRGO	CANCER	GEMINI	LIBRA	LEO
30			VIRGO	GEMINI	GEMINI	VIRGO	CANCER	GEMINI	LIBRA	LEO
31	3:30 AM	TAURUS	VIRGO	GEMINI	GEMINI	VIRGO	CANCER	GEMINI	LIBRA	LEO
AUGUST										
1			VIRGO	GEMINI	GEMINI	VIRGO	CANCER	GEMINI	LIBRA	LEO
2	6:22 AM	GEMINI	VIRGO	GEMINI	GEMINI	VIRGO	CANCER	GEMINI	LIBRA	LEO
3			VIRGO	GEMINI	GEMINI	VIRGO	CANCER	GEMINI	LIBRA	LEO
4	10:23 AM	CANCER	VIRGO	CANCER	GEMINI	VIRGO	CANCER	GEMINI	LIBRA	LEO
5			VIRGO	CANCER	GEMINI	VIRGO	CANCER	GEMINI	LIBRA	LEO
6	3:54 PM	LEO	VIRGO	CANCER	GEMINI	VIRGO	CANCER	GEMINI	LIBRA	LEO
7			VIRGO	CANCER	GEMINI	VIRGO	CANCER	GEMINI	LIBRA	LEO
8	11:26 PM	VIRGO	VIRGO	CANCER	GEMINI	VIRGO	CANCER	GEMINI	LIBRA	LEO
9			VIRGO	CANCER	GEMINI	VIRGO	CANCER	GEMINI	LIBRA	LEO
10			VIRGO	CANCER	GEMINI	VIRGO	CANCER	GEMINI	LIBRA	LEO
11	9:23 AM	LIBRA	VIRGO	CANCER	GEMINI	VIRGO	CANCER	GEMINI	LIBRA	LEO
12			VIRGO	CANCER	GEMINI	VIRGO	CANCER	GEMINI	LIBRA	LEO
13	9:26 PM	SCORPIO	VIRGO	CANCER	GEMINI	VIRGO	CANCER	GEMINI	LIBRA	LEO
14			VIRGO	CANCER	GEMINI	VIRGO	CANCER	GEMINI	LIBRA	LEO
15			VIRGO	CANCER	GEMINI	VIRGO	CANCER	GEMINI	LIBRA	LEO
16	9:55 AM	SAGITTARIUS	VIRGO	CANCER	GEMINI	VIRGO	CANCER	GEMINI	LIBRA	LEO
17			LEO	CANCER	GEMINI	VIRGO	CANCER	GEMINI	LIBRA	LEO
18	8:25 PM	CAPRICORN	LEO	CANCER	GEMINI	VIRGO	CANCER	GEMINI	LIBRA	LEO
19			LEO	CANCER	GEMINI	VIRGO	CANCER	GEMINI	LIBRA	LEO
20			LEO	CANCER	GEMINI	VIRGO	CANCER	GEMINI	LIBRA	LEO
21	3:29 AM	AQUARIUS	LEO	CANCER	GEMINI	VIRGO	CANCER	GEMINI	LIBRA	LEO
22			LEO	CANCER	GEMINI	VIRGO	CANCER	GEMINI	LIBRA	LEO
23	7:05 AM	PISCES	LEO	CANCER	GEMINI	VIRGO	CANCER	GEMINI	LIBRA	LEO

	MOON FROM	IN	MERCURY	VENUS	MARS	JUPITER	SATURN	URANUS	NEPTUNE	PLUTO
JULY										
23	8:15 PM	GEMINI	LEO	VIRGO	VIRGO	LIBRA	CANCER	GEMINI	LIBRA	LEO
24			LEO	VIRGO	VIRGO	LIBRA	CANCER	GEMINI	LIBRA	LEO
25	9:43 PM	CANCER	LEO	VIRGO	VIRGO	LIBRA	CANCER	GEMINI	LIBRA	LEO
26			LEO	VIRGO	VIRGO	LIBRA	CANCER	GEMINI	LIBRA	LEO
27	11:01 PM	LEO	LEO	VIRGO	VIRGO	LIBRA	CANCER	GEMINI	LIBRA	LEO
28			LEO	VIRGO	VIRGO	LIBRA	CANCER	GEMINI	LIBRA	LEO
29			LEO	VIRGO	VIRGO	LIBRA	CANCER	GEMINI	LIBRA	LEO
30	1:41 AM	VIRGO	LEO	VIRGO	VIRGO	LIBRA	CANCER	GEMINI	LIBRA	LEO
31			LEO	VIRGO	VIRGO	LIBRA	CANCER	GEMINI	LIBRA	LEO
AUGUST										
1	7:09 AM	LIBRA	LEO	VIRGO	VIRGO	LIBRA	CANCER	GEMINI	LIBRA	LEO
2			LEO	VIRGO	VIRGO	LIBRA	LEO	GEMINI	LIBRA	LEO
3	4:30 PM	SCORPIO	LEO	VIRGO	VIRGO	LIBRA	LEO	GEMINI	LIBRA	LEO
4			LEO	VIRGO	VIRGO	LIBRA	LEO	GEMINI	LIBRA	LEO
5			LEO	VIRGO	VIRGO	LIBRA	LEO	GEMINI	LIBRA	LEO
6	4:38 AM	SAGITTARIUS	LEO	VIRGO	VIRGO	LIBRA	LEO	GEMINI	LIBRA	LEO
7			LEO	VIRGO	VIRGO	LIBRA	LEO	GEMINI	LIBRA	LEO
8	5:19 PM	CAPRICORN	LEO	VIRGO	VIRGO	LIBRA	LEO	GEMINI	LIBRA	LEO
9			LEO	LIBRA	VIRGO	LIBRA	LEO	GEMINI	LIBRA	LEO
10			LEO	LIBRA	LIBRA	LIBRA	LEO	GEMINI	LIBRA	LEO
11	4:19 AM	AQUARIUS	LEO	LIBRA	LIBRA	LIBRA	LEO	GEMINI	LIBRA	LEO
12			LEO	LIBRA	LIBRA	LIBRA	LEO	GEMINI	LIBRA	LEO
13	12:36 PM	PISCES	LEO	LIBRA	LIBRA	LIBRA	LEO	GEMINI	LIBRA	LEO
14			LEO	LIBRA	LIBRA	LIBRA	LEO	GEMINI	LIBRA	LEO
15	6:33 PM	ARIES	LEO	LIBRA	LIBRA	LIBRA	LEO	GEMINI	LIBRA	LEO
16			LEO	LIBRA	LIBRA	LIBRA	LEO	GEMINI	LIBRA	LEO
17	10:56 PM	TAURUS	LEO	LIBRA	LIBRA	LIBRA	LEO	GEMINI	LIBRA	LEO
18			LEO	LIBRA	LIBRA	LIBRA	LEO	GEMINI	LIBRA	LEO
19			LEO	LIBRA	LIBRA	LIBRA	LEO	GEMINI	LIBRA	LEO
20	2:20 AM	GEMINI	LEO	LIBRA	LIBRA	LIBRA	LEO	GEM NI	LIBRA	LEO
21			LEO	LIBRA	LIBRA	LIBRA	LEO	GEMINI	LIBRA	LEO
22	5:07 AM	CANCER	LEO	LIBRA	LIBRA	LIBRA	LEO	GEMINI	LIBRA	LEO
23			LEO	LIBRA	LIBRA	LIBRA	LEO	GEMINI	LIBRA	LEO

1947

	MOON FROM	IN	MERCURY	VENUS	MARS	JUPITER	SATURN	URANUS	NEPTUNE	PLUTO
JULY										
24	3:46 PM	SCORPIO	CANCER	CANCER	GEMINI	SCORPIO	LEO	GEMINI	LIBRA	LEO
25			CANCER	CANCER	GEMINI	SCORPIO	LEO	GEMINI	LIBRA	LEO
26			CANCER	CANCER	GEMINI	SCORPIO	LEO	GEMINI	LIBRA	LEO
27	1:44 AM	SAGITTARIUS	CANCER	CANCER	GEMINI	SCORPIO	LEO	GEMINI	LIBRA	LEO
28			CANCER	CANCER	GEMINI	SCORPIO	LEO	GEMINI	LIBRA	LEO
29	2:02 PM	CAPRICORN	CANCER	CANCER	GEMINI	SCORPIO	LEO	GEMINI	LIBRA	LEO
30			CANCER	CANCER	GEMINI	SCORPIO	LEO	GEMINI	LIBRA	LEO
31			CANCER	CANCER	GEMINI	SCORPIO	LEO	GEMINI	LIBRA	LEO
AUGUST										
1	2:50 AM	AQUARIUS	CANCER	CANCER	GEMINI	SCORPIO	LEO	GEMINI	LIBRA	LEO
2			CANCER	LEO	GEMINI	SCORPIO	LEO	GEMINI	LIBRA	LEO
3	2:48 PM	PISCES	CANCER	LEO	GEMINI	SCORPIO	LEO	GEMINI	LIBRA	LEO
4			CANCER	LEO	GEMINI	SCORPIO	LEO	GEMINI	LIBRA	LEO
5			CANCER	LEO	GEMINI	SCORPIO	LEO	GEMINI	LIBRA	LFO
6	1:19 AM	ARIES	CANCER	LEO	GEMINI	SCORPIO	LEO	GEMINI	LIBRA	LEO
7			CANCER	LEO	GEMINI	SCORPIO	LEO	GEMINI	LIBRA	LEO
8	10:37 AM	TAURUS	CANCER	LEO	GEMINI	SCORPIO	LEO	GEMINI	LIBRA	LEO
9			CANCER	LEO	GEMINI	SCORPIO	LEO	GEMINI	LIBRA	LEO
10	3:14 PM	GEMINI	CANCER	LEO	GEMINI	SCORPIO	LEO	GEMINI	LIBRA	LEO
11			LEO	LEO	GEMINI	SCORPIO	LEO	GEMINI	LIBRA	LEO
12	5:45 PM	CANCER	LEO	LEO	GEMINI	SCORPIO	LEO	GEMINI	LIBRA	LEO
13			LEO	LEO	GEMINI	SCORPIO	LEO	GEMINI	LIBRA	LEO
14	6:06 PM	LEO	LEO	LEO	CANCER	SCORPIO	LEO	GEMINI	LIBRA	LEO
15			LEO	LEO	CANCER	SCORPIO	LEO	GEMINI	LIBRA	LEO
16	5:53 PM	VIRGO	LEO	LEO	CANCER	SCORPIO	LEO	GEMINI	LIBRA	LEO
17			LEO	LEO	CANCER	SCORPIO	LEO	GEMINI	LIBRA	LEO
18	7:10 PM	LIBRA	LEO	LEO	CANCER	SCORPIO	LEO	GEMINI	LIBRA	LEO
19			LEO	LEO	CANCER	SCORPIO	LEO	GEMINI	LIBRA	LEO
20	11:40 PM	SCORPIO	LEO	LEO	CANCER	SCORPIO	LEO	GEMINI	LIBRA	LEO
21			LEO	LEO	CANCER	SCORPIO	LEO	GEMINI	LIBRA	LEO
22			LEO	LEO	CANCER	SCORPIO	LEO	GEMINI	LIBRA	LEO
23	8:36 AM	SAGITTARIUS	LEO	LEO	CANCER	SCORPIO	LEO	GEMINI	LIBRA	LEO

	MOON FROM	MOON IN	MERCURY	VENUS	MARS	JUPITER	SATURN	URANUS	NEPTUNE	PLUTO
JULY										
23	1:14 PM	PISCES	CANCER	GEMINI	LIBRA	SAGITTARIUS	LEO	GEMINI	LIBRA	LEO
24			CANCER	GEMINI	LIBRA	SAGITTARIUS	LEO	GEMINI	LIBRA	LEO
25			CANCER	GEMINI	LIBRA	SAGITTARIUS	LEO	GEMINI	LIBRA	LEO
26	1:57 AM	ARIES	CANCER	GEMINI	LIBRA	SAGITTARIUS	LEO	GEMINI	LIBRA	LEO
27			CANCER	GEMINI	LIBRA	SAGITTARIUS	LEO	GEMINI	LIBRA	LEO
28	1:30 PM	TAURUS	CANCER	GEMINI	LIBRA	SAGITTARIUS	LEO	GEMINI	LIBRA	LEO
29			CANCER	GEMINI	LIBRA	SAGITTARIUS	LEO	GEMINI	LIBRA	LEO
30	9:56 PM	GEMINI	CANCER	GEMINI	LIBRA	SAGITTARIUS	LEO	GEMINI	LIBRA	LEO
31			CANCER	GEMINI	LIBRA	SAGITTARIUS	LEO	GEMINI	LIBRA	LEO
AUGUST										
1			CANCER	GEMINI	LIBRA	SAGITTARIUS	LEO	GEMINI	LIBRA	LEO
2	2:17 AM	CANCER	CANCER	GEMINI	LIBRA	SAGITTARIUS	LEO	GEMINI	LIBRA	LEO
3			LEO	CANCER	LIBRA	SAGITTARIUS	LEO	GEMINI	LIBRA	LEO
4	3:11 AM	LEO	LEO	CANCER	LIBRA	SAGITTARIUS	LEO	GEMINI	LIBRA	LEO
5			LEO	CANCER	LIBRA	SAGITTARIUS	LEO	GEMINI	LIBRA	LEO
6	2:26 AM	VIRGO	LEO	CANCER	LIBRA	SAGITTARIUS	LEO	GEMINI	LIBRA	LEO
7			LEO	CANCER	LIBRA	SAGITTARIUS	LEO	GEMINI	LIBRA	LEO
8	2:33 AM	LIBRA	LEO	CANCER	LIBRA	SAGITTARIUS	LEO	GEMINI	LIBRA	LEO
9			LEO	CANCER	LIBRA	SAGITTARIUS	LEO	GEMINI	LIBRA	LEO
10	4:58 AM	SCORPIO	LEO	CANCER	LIBRA	SAGITTARIUS	LEO	GEMINI	LIBRA	LEO
11			LEO	CANCER	LIBRA	SAGITTARIUS	LEO	GEMINI	LIBRA	LEO
12	10:52 AM	SAGITTARIUS	LEO	CANCER	LIBRA	SAGITTARIUS	LEO	GEMINI	LIBRA	LEO
13			LEO	CANCER	LIBRA	SAGITTARIUS	LEO	GEMINI	LIBRA	LEO
14	7:54 PM	CAPRICORN	LEO	CANCER	LIBRA	SAGITTARIUS	LEO	GEMINI	LIBRA	LEO
15			LEO	CANCER	LIBRA	SAGITTARIUS	LEO	GEMINI	LIBRA	LEO
16			LEO	CANCER	LIBRA	SAGITTARIUS	LEO	GEMINI	LIBRA	LEO
17	7:02 AM	AQUARIUS	VIRGO	CANCER	LIBRA	SAGITTARIUS	LEO	GEMINI	LIBRA	LEO
18			VIRGO	CANCER	LIBRA	SAGITTARIUS	LEO	GEMINI	LIBRA	LEO
19	7:23 PM	PISCES	VIRGO	CANCER	LIBRA	SAGITTARIUS	LEO	GEMINI	LIBRA	LEO
20			VIRGO	CANCER	LIBRA	SAGITTARIUS	LEO	GEMINI	LIBRA	LEO
21			VIRGO	CANCER	LIBRA	SAGITTARIUS	LEO	GEMINI	LIBRA	LEO
22	8:04 AM	ARIES	VIRGO	CANCER	LIBRA	SAGITTARIUS	LEO	GEMINI	LIBRA	LEO

1949

	MOON FROM	MOON IN	MERCURY	VENUS	MARS	JUPITER	SATURN	URANUS	NEPTUNE	PLUTO
JULY										
23	5:51 AM	CANCER	CANCER	LEO	CANCER	CAPRICORN	VIRGO	CANCER	LIBRA	LEO
24			CANCER	LEO	CANCER	CAPRICORN	VIRGO	CANCER	LIBRA	LEO
25	10:18 AM	LEO	LEO	LEO	CANCER	CAPRICORN	VIRGO	CANCER	LIBRA	LEO
26			LEO	LEO	CANCER	CAPRICORN	VIRGO	CANCER	LIBRA	LEO
27	12:35 PM	VIRGO	LEO	VIRGO	CANCER	CAPRICORN	VIRGO	CANCER	LIBRA	LEO
28			LEO	VIRGO	CANCER	CAPRICORN	VIRGO	CANCER	LIBRA	LEO
29	2:21 PM	LIBRA	LEO	VIRGO	CANCER	CAPRICORN	VIRGO	CANCER	LIBRA	LEO
30			LEO	VIRGO	CANCER	CAPRICORN	VIRGO	CANCER	LIBRA	LEO
31	4:46 PM	SCORPIO	LEO	VIRGO	CANCER	CAPRICORN	VIRGO	CANCER	LIBRA	LEO
AUGUST										
1			LEO	VIRGO	CANCER	CAPRICORN	VIRGO	CANCER	LIBRA	LEO
2	8:26 PM	SAGITTARIUS	LEO	VIRGO	CANCER	CAPRICORN	VIRGO	CANCER	LIBRA	LEO
3			LEO	VIRGO	CANCER	CAPRICORN	VIRGO	CANCER	LIBRA	LEO
4			LEO	VIRGO	CANCER	CAPRICORN	VIRGO	CANCER	LIBRA	LEO
5	1:37 AM	CAPRICORN	LEO	VIRGO	CANCER	CAPRICORN	VIRGO	CANCER	LIBRA	LEO
6			LEO	VIRGO	CANCER	CAPRICORN	VIRGO	CANCER	LIBRA	LEO
7	8:34 AM	AQUARIUS	LEO	VIRGO	CANCER	CAPRICORN	VIRGO	CANCER	LIBRA	LEO
8			LEO	VIRGO	CANCER	CAPRICORN	VIRGO	CANCER	LIBRA	LEO
9	5:49 PM	PISCES	VIRGO	VIRGO	CANCER	CAPRICORN	VIRGO	CANCER	LIBRA	LEO
10			VIRGO	VIRGO	CANCER	CAPRICORN	VIRGO	CANCER	LIBRA	LEO
11			VIRGO	VIRGO	CANCER	CAPRICORN	VIRGO	CANCER	LIBRA	LEO
12	5:20 AM	ARIES	VIRGO	VIRGO	CANCER	CAPRICORN	VIRGO	CANCER	LIBRA	LEO
13			VIRGO	VIRGO	CANCER	CAPRICORN	VIRGO	CANCER	LIBRA	LEO
14	6:18 PM	TAURUS	VIRGO	VIRGO	CANCER	CAPRICORN	VIRGO	CANCER	LIBRA	LEO
15			VIRGO	VIRGO	CANCER	CAPRICORN	VIRGO	CANCER	LIBRA	LEO
16			VIRGO	VIRGO	CANCER	CAPRICORN	VIRGO	CANCER	LIBRA	LEO
17	6:22 AM	GEMINI	VIRGO	VIRGO	CANCER	CAPRICORN	VIRGO	CANCER	LIBRA	LEO
18			VIRGO	VIRGO	CANCER	CAPRICORN	VIRGO	CANCER	LIBRA	LEO
19	3:09 PM	CANCER	VIRGO	VIRGO	CANCER	CAPRICORN	VIRGO	CANCER	LIBRA	LEO
20			VIRGO	VIRGO	CANCER	CAPRICORN	VIRGO	CANCER	LIBRA	LEO
21	8:02 PM	LEO	VIRGO	LIBRA	CANCER	CAPRICORN	VIRGO	CANCER	LIBRA	LEO
22			VIRGO	LIBRA	CANCER	CAPRICORN	VIRGO	CANCER	LIBRA	LEO

1950

MOON		MERCURY	VENUS	MARS	JUPITER	SATURN	URANUS	NEPTUNE	PLUTO
FROM	IN								
JULY									
23		LEO	CANCER	LIBRA	PISCES	VIRGO	CANCER	LIBRA	LEO
24	9:54 AM SAGITTARIUS	LEO	CANCER	LIBRA	PISCES	VIRGO	CANCER	LIBRA	LEO
25		LEO	CANCER	LIBRA	PISCES	VIRGO	CANCER	LIBRA	LEO
26	11:39 AM CAPRICORN	LEO	CANCER	LIBRA	PISCES	VIRGO	CANCER	LIBRA	LEO
27		LEO	CANCER	LIBRA	PISCES	VIRGO	CANCER	LIBRA	LEO
28	1:58 PM AQUARIUS	LEO	CANCER	LIBRA	PISCES	VIRGO	CANCER	LIBRA	LEO
29		LEO	CANCER	LIBRA	PISCES	VIRGO	CANCER	LIBRA	LEO
30	6:24 PM PISCES	LEO	CANCER	LIBRA	PISCES	VIRGO	CANCER	LIBRA	LEO
31		LEO	CANCER	LIBRA	PISCES	VIRGO	CANCER	LIBRA	LEO
AUGUST									
1		LEO	CANCER	LIBRA	PISCES	VIRGO	CANCER	LIBRA	LEO
2	2:05 AM ARIES	VIRGO	CANCER	LIBRA	PISCES	VIRGO	CANCER	LIBRA	LEO
3		VIRGO	CANCER	LIBRA	PISCES	VIRGO	CANCER	LIBRA	LEO
4	1:07 PM TAURUS	VIRGO	CANCER	LIBRA	PISCES	VIRGO	CANCER	LIBRA	LEO
5		VIRGO	CANCER	LIBRA	PISCES	VIRGO	CANCER	LIBRA	LEO
6		VIRGO	CANCER	LIBRA	PISCES	VIRGO	CANCER	LIBRA	LEO
7	1:43 AM GEMINI	VIRGO	CANCER	LIBRA	PISCES	VIRGO	CANCER	LIBRA	LEO
8		VIRGO	CANCER	LIBRA	PISCES	VIRGO	CANCER	LIBRA	LEO
9	11:28 AM CANCER	VIRGO	CANCER	LIBRA	PISCES	VIRGO	CANCER	LIBRA	LEO
10		VIRGO	CANCER	LIBRA	PISCES	VIRGO	CANCER	LIBRA	LEO
11	10:33 PM LEO	VIRGO	CANCER	SCORPIO	PISCES	VIRGO	CANCER	LIBRA	LEO
12		VIRGO	CANCER	SCORPIO	PISCES	VIRGO	CANCER	LIBRA	LEO
13		VIRGO	CANCER	SCORPIO	PISCES	VIRGO	CANCER	LIBRA	LEO
14	5:02 AM VIRGO	VIRGO	CANCER	SCORPIO	PISCES	VIRGO	CANCER	LIBRA	LEO
15		VIRGO	CANCER	SCORPIO	PISCES	VIRGO	CANCER	LIBRA	LEO
16	9:30 AM LIBRA	VIRGO	CANCER	SCORPIO	PISCES	VIRGO	CANCER	LIBRA	LEO
17		VIRGO	LEO	SCORPIO	PISCES	VIRGO	CANCER	LIBRA	LEO
18	12:48 PM SCORPIO	VIRGO	LEO	SCORPIO	PISCES	VIRGO	CANCER	LIBRA	LEO
19		VIRGO	LEO	SCORPIO	PISCES	VIRGO	CANCER	LIBRA	LEO
20	3:35 PM SAGITTARIUS	VIRGO	LEO	SCORPIO	PISCES	VIRGO	CANCER	LIBRA	LEO
21		VIRGO	LEO	SCORPIO	PISCES	VIRGO	CANCER	LIBRA	LEO
22	6:23 PM CAPRICORN	VIRGO	LEO	SCORPIO	PISCES	VIRGO	CANCER	LIBRA	LEO
23		VIRGO	LEO	SCORPIO	PISCES	VIRGO	CANCER	LIBRA	LEO

1951

MOON		MERCURY	VENUS	MARS	JUPITER	SATURN	URANUS	NEPTUNE	PLUTO
FROM	IN								
JULY									
24		LEO	VIRGO	CANCER	ARIES	VIRGO	CANCER	LIBRA	LEO
25	10:08 AM TAURUS	LEO	VIRGO	CANCER	ARIES	VIRGO	CANCER	LIBRA	LEO
26		LEO	VIRGO	CANCER	ARIES	VIRGO	CANCER	LIBRA	LEO
27	9:09 PM GEMINI	LEO	VIRGO	CANCER	ARIES	VIRGO	CANCER	LIBRA	LEO
28		VIRGO	VIRGO	CANCER	ARIES	VIRGO	CANCER	LIBRA	LEO
29		VIRGO	VIRGO	CANCER	ARIES	VIRGO	CANCER	LIBRA	LEO
30	9:42 AM CANCER	VIRGO	VIRGO	CANCER	ARIES	VIRGO	CANCER	LIBRA	LEO
31		VIRGO	VIRGO	CANCER	ARIES	VIRGO	CANCER	LIBRA	LEO
AUGUST									
1	10:06 PM LEO	VIRGO	VIRGO	CANCER	ARIES	VIRGO	CANCER	LIBRA	LEO
2		VIRGO	VIRGO	CANCER	ARIES	VIRGO	CANCER	LIBRA	LEO
3		VIRGO	VIRGO	CANCER	ARIES	VIRGO	CANCER	LIBRA	LEO
4	9:17 AM VIRGO	VIRGO	VIRGO	CANCER	ARIES	VIRGO	CANCER	LIBRA	LEO
5		VIRGO	VIRGO	CANCER	ARIES	VIRGO	CANCER	LIBRA	LEO
6	6:30 PM LIBRA	VIRGO	VIRGO	CANCER	ARIES	VIRGO	CANCER	LIBRA	LEO
7		VIRGO	VIRGO	CANCER	ARIES	VIRGO	CANCER	LIBRA	LEO
8		VIRGO	VIRGO	CANCER	ARIES	VIRGO	CANCER	LIBRA	LEO
9	1:21 AM SCORPIO	VIRGO	VIRGO	CANCER	ARIES	VIRGO	CANCER	LIBRA	LEO
10		VIRGO	VIRGO	CANCER	ARIES	VIRGO	CANCER	LIBRA	LEO
11	5:29 AM SAGITTARIUS	VIRGO	VIRGO	CANCER	ARIES	VIRGO	CANCER	LIBRA	LEO
12		VIRGO	VIRGO	CANCER	ARIES	VIRGO	CANCER	LIBRA	LEO
13	7:18 AM CAPRICORN	VIRGO	VIRGO	CANCER	ARIES	VIRGO	CANCER	LIBRA	LEO
14		VIRGO	VIRGO	CANCER	ARIES	LIBRA	CANCER	LIBRA	LEO
15	7:54 AM AQUARIUS	VIRGO	VIRGO	CANCER	ARIES	LIBRA	CANCER	LIBRA	LEO
16		VIRGO	VIRGO	CANCER	ARIES	LIBRA	CANCER	LIBRA	LEO
17	9:20 PM PISCES	VIRGO	VIRGO	CANCER	ARIES	LIBRA	CANCER	LIBRA	LEO
18		VIRGO	VIRGO	CANCER	ARIES	LIBRA	CANCER	LIBRA	LEO
19	12:01 PM ARIES	VIRGO	VIRGO	LEO	ARIES	LIBRA	CANCER	LIBRA	LEO
20		VIRGO	VIRGO	LEO	ARIES	LIBRA	CANCER	LIBRA	LEO
21	6:31 PM TAURUS	VIRGO	VIRGO	LEO	ARIES	LIBRA	CANCER	LIBRA	LEO
22		VIRGO	VIRGO	LEO	ARIES	LIBRA	CANCER	LIBRA	LEO
23		VIRGO	VIRGO	LEO	ARIES	LIBRA	CANCER	LIBRA	LEO

1952   LEO

	MOON		MERCURY	VENUS	MARS	JUPITER	SATURN	URANUS	NEPTUNE	PLUTO
	FROM	IN								
JULY											
23			LEO	LEO	SCORPIO	TAURUS	LIBRA	CANCER	LIBRA	LEO
24	9:26 AM	VIRGO	LEO	LEO	SCORPIO	TAURUS	LIBRA	CANCER	LIBRA	LEO
25			LEO	LEO	SCORPIO	TAURUS	LIBRA	CANCER	LIBRA	LEO
26	9:36 PM	LIBRA	LEO	LEO	SCORPIO	TAURUS	LIBRA	CANCER	LIBRA	LEO
27			LEO	LEO	SCORPIO	TAURUS	LIBRA	CANCER	LIBRA	LEO
28			LEO	LEO	SCORPIO	TAURUS	LIBRA	CANCER	LIBRA	LEO
29	8:08 AM	SCORPIO	LEO	LEO	SCORPIO	TAURUS	LIBRA	CANCER	LIBRA	LEO
30			LEO	LEO	SCORPIO	TAURUS	LIBRA	CANCER	LIBRA	LEO
31	2:57 PM	SAGITTARIUS	LEO	LEO	SCORPIO	TAURUS	LIBRA	CANCER	LIBRA	LEO
AUGUST											
1			LEO	LEO	SCORPIO	TAURUS	LIBRA	CANCER	LIBRA	LEO
2	5:52 PM	CAPRICORN	LEO	LEO	SCORPIO	TAURUS	LIBRA	CANCER	LIBRA	LEO
3			LEO	LEO	SCORPIO	TAURUS	LIBRA	CANCER	LIBRA	LEO
4	6:26 PM	AQUARIUS	LEO	LEO	SCORPIO	TAURUS	LIBRA	CANCER	LIBRA	LEO
5			LEO	LEO	SCORPIO	TAURUS	LIBRA	CANCER	LIBRA	LEO
6	5:42 PM	PISCES	LEO	LEO	SCORPIO	TAURUS	LIBRA	CANCER	LIBRA	LEO
7			LEO	LEO	SCORPIO	TAURUS	LIBRA	CANCER	LIBRA	LEO
8	6:08 PM	ARIES	LEO	LEO	SCORPIO	TAURUS	LIBRA	CANCER	LIBRA	LEO
9			LEO	LEO	SCORPIO	TAURUS	LIBRA	CANCER	LIBRA	LEO
10	9:01 PM	TAURUS	LEO	VIRGO	SCORPIO	TAURUS	LIBRA	CANCER	LIBRA	LEO
11			LEO	VIRGO	SCORPIO	TAURUS	LIBRA	CANCER	LIBRA	LEO
12			LEO	VIRGO	SCORPIO	TAURUS	LIBRA	CANCER	LIBRA	LEO
13	3:36 AM	GEMINI	LEO	VIRGO	SCORPIO	TAURUS	LIBRA	CANCER	LIBRA	LEO
14			LEO	VIRGO	SCORPIO	TAURUS	LIBRA	CANCER	LIBRA	LEO
15	2:24 PM	CANCER	LEO	VIRGO	SCORPIO	TAURUS	LIBRA	CANCER	LIBRA	LEO
16			LEO	VIRGO	SCORPIO	TAURUS	LIBRA	CANCER	LIBRA	LEO
17			LEO	VIRGO	SCORPIO	TAURUS	LIBRA	CANCER	LIBRA	LEO
18	2:23 AM	LEO	LEO	VIRGO	SCORPIO	TAURUS	LIBRA	CANCER	LIBRA	LEO
19			LEO	VIRGO	SCORPIO	TAURUS	LIBRA	CANCER	LIBRA	LEO
20	3:04 PM	VIRGO	LEO	VIRGO	SCORPIO	TAURUS	LIBRA	CANCER	LIBRA	LEO
21			LEO	VIRGO	SCORPIO	TAURUS	LIBRA	CANCER	LIBRA	LEO
22			LEO	VIRGO	SCORPIO	TAURUS	LIBRA	CANCER	LIBRA	LEO
23	3:01 AM	LIBRA	LEO	VIRGO	SCORPIO	TAURUS	LIBRA	CANCER	LIBRA	LEO

1953   MOON

	MOON		MERCURY	VENUS	MARS	JUPITER	SATURN	URANUS	NEPTUNE	PLUTO
	FROM	IN								
JULY											
24			LEO	GEMINI	CANCER	GEMINI	LIBRA	CANCER	LIBRA	LEO
25			LEO	GEMINI	CANCER	GEMINI	LIBRA	CANCER	LIBRA	LEO
26	2:13 AM	AQUARIUS	LEO	GEMINI	CANCER	GEMINI	LIBRA	CANCER	LIBRA	LEO
27			LEO	GEMINI	CANCER	GEMINI	LIBRA	CANCER	LIBRA	LEO
28	3:15 AM	PISCES	LEO	GEMINI	CANCER	GEMINI	LIBRA	CANCER	LIBRA	LEO
29			CANCER	GEMINI	CANCER	GEMINI	LIBRA	CANCER	LIBRA	LEO
30	4:07 AM	ARIES	CANCER	GEMINI	LEO	GEMINI	LIBRA	CANCER	LIBRA	LEO
31			CANCER	GEMINI	LEO	GEMINI	LIBRA	CANCER	LIBRA	LEO
AUGUST											
1	5:50 AM	TAURUS	CANCER	GEMINI	LEO	GEMINI	LIBRA	CANCER	LIBRA	LEO
2			CANCER	GEMINI	LEO	GEMINI	LIBRA	CANCER	LIBRA	LEO
3	10:26 AM	GEMINI	CANCER	GEMINI	LEO	GEMINI	LIBRA	CANCER	LIBRA	LEO
4			CANCER	GEMINI	LEO	GEMINI	LIBRA	CANCER	LIBRA	LEO
5	5:14 PM	CANCER	CANCER	CANCER	LEO	GEMINI	LIBRA	CANCER	LIBRA	LEO
6			CANCER	CANCER	LEO	GEMINI	LIBRA	CANCER	LIBRA	LEO
7			CANCER	CANCER	LEO	GEMINI	LIBRA	CANCER	LIBRA	LEO
8	2:23 AM	LEO	CANCER	CANCER	LEO	GEMINI	LIBRA	CANCER	LIBRA	LEO
9			CANCER	CANCER	LEO	GEMINI	LIBRA	CANCER	LIBRA	LEO
10	1:19 PM	VIRGO	CANCER	CANCER	LEO	GEMINI	LIBRA	CANCER	LIBRA	LEO
11			CANCER	CANCER	LEO	GEMINI	LIBRA	CANCER	LIBRA	LEO
12			LEO	CANCER	LEO	GEMINI	LIBRA	CANCER	LIBRA	LEO
13	1:45 AM	LIBRA	LEO	CANCER	LEO	GEMINI	LIBRA	CANCER	LIBRA	LEO
14			LEO	CANCER	LEO	GEMINI	LIBRA	CANCER	LIBRA	LEO
15	2:33 PM	SCORPIO	LEO	CANCER	LEO	GEMINI	LIBRA	CANCER	LIBRA	LEO
16			IIO	CANCER	LEO	GEMINI	LIBRA	CANCER	LIBRA	LEO
17			LEO	CANCER	LEO	GEMINI	LIBRA	CANCER	LIBRA	LEO
18	1:38 AM	SAGITTARIUS	LEO	CANCER	LEO	GEMINI	LIBRA	CANCER	LIBRA	LEO
19			LEO	CANCER	LEO	GEMINI	LIBRA	CANCER	LIBRA	LEO
20	9:16 AM	CAPRICORN	LEO	CANCER	LEO	GEMINI	LIBRA	CANCER	LIBRA	LEO
21			LEO	CANCER	LEO	GEMINI	LIBRA	CANCER	LIBRA	LEO
22	12:21 PM	AQUARIUS	LEO	CANCER	LEO	GEMINI	LIBRA	CANCER	LIBRA	LEO
23			LEO	CANCER	LEO	GEMINI	LIBRA	CANCER	LIBRA	LEO

1954

DATE	MOON FROM/IN	MERCURY	VENUS	MARS	JUPITER	SATURN	URANUS	NEPTUNE	PLUTO
JULY									
24		CANCER	VIRGO	SAGITTARIUS	CANCER	SCORPIO	CANCER	LIBRA	LEO
25	2:36 AM GEMINI	CANCER	VIRGO	SAGITTARIUS	CANCER	SCORPIO	CANCER	LIBRA	LEO
26		CANCER	VIRGO	SAGITTARIUS	CANCER	SCORPIO	CANCER	LIBRA	LEO
27	5:48 AM CANCER	CANCER	VIRGO	SAGITTARIUS	CANCER	SCORPIO	CANCER	LIBRA	LEO
28		CANCER	VIRGO	SAGITTARIUS	CANCER	SCORPIO	CANCER	LIBRA	LEO
29	10:10 AM LEO	CANCER	VIRGO	SAGITTARIUS	CANCER	SCORPIO	CANCER	LIBRA	LEO
30		CANCER	VIRGO	SAGITTARIUS	CANCER	SCORPIO	CANCER	LIBRA	LEO
31	3:09 PM VIRGO	CANCER	VIRGO	SAGITTARIUS	CANCER	SCORPIO	CANCER	LIBRA	LEO
AUGUST									
1		CANCER	VIRGO	SAGITTARIUS	CANCER	SCORPIO	CANCER	LIBRA	LEO
2	9:57 PM LIBRA	CANCER	VIRGO	SAGITTARIUS	CANCER	SCORPIO	CANCER	LIBRA	LEO
3		CANCER	VIRGO	SAGITTARIUS	CANCER	SCORPIO	CANCER	LIBRA	LEO
4		CANCER	VIRGO	SAGITTARIUS	CANCER	SCORPIO	CANCER	LIBRA	LEO
5	10:01 AM SCORPIO	CANCER	VIRGO	SAGITTARIUS	CANCER	SCORPIO	CANCER	LIBRA	LEO
6		CANCER	VIRGO	SAGITTARIUS	CANCER	SCORPIO	CANCER	LIBRA	LEO
7	10:52 PM SAGITTARIUS	CANCER	VIRGO	SAGITTARIUS	CANCER	SCORPIO	CANCER	LIBRA	LEO
8		LEO	VIRGO	SAGITTARIUS	CANCER	SCORPIO	CANCER	LIBRA	LEO
9		LEO	VIRGO	SAGITTARIUS	CANCER	SCORPIO	CANCER	LIBRA	LEO
10	9:27 AM CAPRICORN	LEO	LIBRA	SAGITTARIUS	CANCER	SCORPIO	CANCER	LIBRA	LEO
11		LEO	LIBRA	SAGITTARIUS	CANCER	SCORPIO	CANCER	LIBRA	LEO
12	4:44 PM AQUARIUS	LEO	LIBRA	SAGITTARIUS	CANCER	SCORPIO	CANCER	LIBRA	LEO
13		LEO	LIBRA	SAGITTARIUS	CANCER	SCORPIO	CANCER	LIBRA	LEO
14	9:10 PM PISCES	LEO	LIBRA	SAGITTARIUS	CANCER	SCORPIO	CANCER	LIBRA	LEO
15		LEO	LIBRA	SAGITTARIUS	CANCER	SCORPIO	CANCER	LIBRA	LEO
16	11:34 PM ARIES	LEO	LIBRA	SAGITTARIUS	CANCER	SCORPIO	CANCER	LIBRA	LEO
17		LEO	LIBRA	SAGITTARIUS	CANCER	SCORPIO	CANCER	LIBRA	LEO
18		LEO	LIBRA	SAGITTARIUS	CANCER	SCORPIO	CANCER	LIBRA	LEO
19	1:33 AM TAURUS	LEO	LIBRA	SAGITTARIUS	CANCER	SCORPIO	CANCER	LIBRA	LEO
20		LEO	LIBRA	SAGITTARIUS	CANCER	SCORPIO	CANCER	LIBRA	LEO
21	4:13 AM GEMINI	LEO	LIBRA	SAGITTARIUS	CANCER	SCORPIO	CANCER	LIBRA	LEO
22		LEO	LIBRA	SAGITTARIUS	CANCER	SCORPIO	CANCER	LIBRA	LEO
23	8:04 AM CANCER	LEO	LIBRA	SAGITTARIUS	CANCER	SCORPIO	CANCER	LIBRA	LEO

1955

DATE	MOON FROM/IN	MERCURY	VENUS	MARS	JUPITER	SATURN	URANUS	NEPTUNE	PLUTO
JULY									
24		CANCER	CANCER	LEO	LEO	SCORPIO	CANCER	LIBRA	LEO
25		CANCER	CANCER	LEO	LEO	SCORPIO	CANCER	LIBRA	LEO
26	5:28 AM SCORPIO	CANCER	CANCER	LEO	LEO	SCORPIO	CANCER	LIBRA	LEO
27		CANCER	CANCER	LEO	LEO	SCORPIO	CANCER	LIBRA	LEO
28	5:41 PM SAGITTARIUS	CANCER	CANCER	LEO	LEO	SCORPIO	CANCER	LIBRA	LEO
29		CANCER	CANCER	LEO	LEO	SCORPIO	CANCER	LIBRA	LEO
30		CANCER	CANCER	LEO	LEO	SCORPIO	CANCER	LIBRA	LEO
31	6:36 AM CAPRICORN	LEO	CANCER	LEO	LEO	SCROPIO	CANCER	LIBRA	LEO
AUGUST									
1		LEO	CANCER	LEO	LEO	SCORPIO	CANCER	LIBRA	LEO
2	5:19 PM AQUARIUS	LEO	LEO	LEO	LEO	SCORPIO	CANCER	LIBRA	LEO
3		LEO	LEO	LEO	LEO	SCORPIO	CANCER	LIBRA	LEO
4		LEO	LEO	LEO	LEO	SCORPÍO	CANCER	LIBRA	LEO
5	2:33 AM PISCES	LEO	LEO	LEO	LEO	SCORPIO	CANCER	LIBRA	LEO
6		LEO	LEO	LEO	LEO	SCORPIO	CANCER	LIBRA	LEO
7	10:03 AM ARIES	LEO	LEO	LEO	LEO	SCORPIO	CANCER	LIBRA	LEO
8		LEO	LEO	LEO	LEO	SCORPIO	CANCER	LIBRA	LEO
9	3:04 PM TAURUS	LEO	LEO	LEO	LEO	SCORPIO	CANCER	LIBRA	LEO
10		LEO	LEO	LEO	LEO	SCORPIO	CANCER	LIBRA	LEO
11	6:51 PM GEMINI	LEO	LEO	LEO	LEO	SCORPIO	CANCER	LIBRA	LEO
12		LEO	LEO	LEO	LEO	SCORPIO	CANCER	LIBRA	LEO
13	8:50 PM CANCER	LEO	LEO	LEO	LEO	SCORPIO	CANCER	LIBRA	LEO
14		LEO	LEO	LEO	LEO	SCORPIO	CANCER	LIBRA	LEO
15	10:44 PM LEO	VIRGO	LEO	LEO	LEO	SCORPIO	CANCER	LIBRA	LEO
16		VIRGO	LEO	LEO	LEO	SCORPIO	CANCER	LIBRA	LEO
17		VIRGO	LEO	LEO	LEO	SCORPIO	CANCER	LIBRA	LEO
18	1:11 AM VIRGO	VIRGO	LEO	LEO	LEO	SCORPIO	CANCER	LIBRA	LEO
19		VIRGO	LEO	LEO	LEO	SCORPIO	CANCER	LIBRA	LEO
20	5:32 AM LIBRA	VIRGO	LEO	LEO	LEO	SCORPIO	CANCER	LIBRA	LEO
21		VIRGO	LEO	LEO	LEO	SCORPIO	CANCER	LIBRA	LEO
22	1:38 PM SCORPIO	VIRGO	LEO	LEO	LEO	SCORPIO	CANCER	LIBRA	LEO
23		VIRGO	LEO	LEO	LEO	SCORPIO	CANCER	LIBRA	LEO

MOON FROM IN	MERCURY	VENUS	MARS	JUPITER	SATURN	URANUS	NEPTUNE	PLUTO
JULY								
23	LEO	GEMINI	PISCES	VIRGO	SCORPIO	LEO	LIBRA	LEO
24	LEO	GEMINI	PISCES	VIRGO	SCORPIO	LEO	LIBRA	LEO
25 4:49 AM PISCES	LEO	GEMINI	PISCES	VIRGO	SCORPIO	LEO	LIBRA	LEO
26	LEO	GEMINI	PISCES	VIRGO	SCORPIO	LEO	LIBRA	LEO
27 4:12 PM ARIES	LEO	GEMINI	PISCES	VIRGO	SCORPIO	LEO	LIBRA	LEO
28	LEO	GEMINI	PISCES	VIRGO	SCORPIO	LEO	LIBRA	LEO
29	LEO	GEMINI	PISCES	VIRGO	SCORPIO	LEO	LIBRA	LEO
30 1:09 AM TAURUS	LEO	GEMINI	PISCES	VIRGO	SCORPIO	LEO	LIBRA	LEO
31	LEO	GEMINI	PISCES	VIRGO	SCORPIO	LEO	LIBRA	LEO
AUGUST								
1 6:29 AM GEMINI	LEO	GEMINI	PISCES	VIRGO	SCORPIO	LEO	LIBRA	LEO
2	LEO	GEMINI	PISCES	VIRGO	SCORPIO	LEO	LIBRA	LEO
3 8:27 AM CANCER	LEO	GEMINI	PISCES	VIRGO	SCORPIO	LEO	LIBRA	LEO
4	LEO	GEMINI	PISCES	VIRGO	SCORPIO	LEO	LIBRA	LEO
5 8:25 AM LEO	LEO	CANCER	PISCES	VIRGO	SCORPIO	LEO	LIBRA	LEO
6	VIRGO	CANCER	PISCES	VIRGO	SCORPIO	LEO	LIBRA	LEO
7 8:08 AM VIRGO	VIRGO	CANCER	PISCES	VIRGO	SCORPIO	LEO	LIBRA	LEO
8	VIRGO	CANCER	PISCES	VIRGO	SCORPIO	LEO	LIBRA	LEO
9 9:13 AM LIBRA	VIRGO	CANCER	PISCES	VIRGO	SCORPIO	LEO	LIBRA	LEO
10	VIRGO	CANCER	PISCES	VIRGO	SCORPIO	LEO	LIBRA	LEO
11 1:45 PM SCORPIO	VIRGO	CANCER	PISCES	VIRGO	SCORPIO	LEO	LIBRA	LEO
12	VIRGO	CANCER	PISCES	VIRGO	SCORPIO	LEO	LIBRA	LEO
13 9:54 PM SAGITTARIUS	VIRGO	CANCER	PISCES	VIRGO	SCORPIO	LEO	LIBRA	LEO
14	VIRGO	CANCER	PISCES	VIRGO	SCORPIO	LEO	LIBRA	LEO
15	VIRGO	CANCER	PISCES	VIRGO	SCORPIO	LEO	LIBRA	LEO
16 9:51 AM CAPRICORN	VIRGO	CANCER	PISCES	VIRGO	SCORPIO	LEO	LIBRA	LEO
17	VIRGO	CANCER	PISCES	VIRGO	SCORPIO	LEO	LIBRA	LEO
18 10:44 PM AQUARIUS	VIRGO	CANCER	PISCES	VIRGO	SCORPIO	LEO	LIBRA	LEO
19	VIRGO	CANCER	PISCES	VIRGO	SCORPIO	LEO	LIBRA	LEO
20	VIRGO	CANCER	PISCES	VIRGO	SCORPIO	LEO	LIBRA	LEO
21 10:55 AM PISCES	VIRGO	CANCER	PISCES	VIRGO	SCORPIO	LEO	LIBRA	LEO
22	VIRGO	CANCER	PISCES	VIRGO	SCORPIO	LEO	LIBRA	LEO
23 9:38 PM ARIES	VIRGO	CANCER	PISCES	VIRGO	SCORPIO	LEO	LIBRA	LEO

1957

MOON FROM IN	MERCURY	VENUS	MARS	JUPITER	SATURN	URANUS	NEPTUNE	PLUTO
JULY								
24 3:58 PM CANCER	LEO	LEO	LEO	VIRGO	SAGITTARIUS	LEO	LIBRA	LEO
25	LEO	LEO	LEO	VIRGO	SAGITTARIUS	LEO	LIBRA	LEO
26 5:24 PM LEO	LEO	LEO	LEO	VIRGO	SAGITTARIUS	LEO	LIBRA	LEO
27	LEO	VIRGO	LEO	VIRGO	SAGITTARIUS	LEO	LIBRA	LEO
28 5:24 PM VIRGO	LEO	VIRGO	LEO	VIRGO	SAGITTARIUS	LEO	LIBRA	LEO
29	LEO	VIRGO	LEO	VIRGO	SAGITTARIUS	LEO	LIBRA	LEO
30 5:54 PM LIBRA	LEO	VIRGO	LEO	VIRGO	SAGITTARIUS	LEO	LIBRA	LEO
31	VIRGO	VIRGO	LEO	VIRGO	SAGITTARIUS	LEO	LIBRA	LEO
AUGUST								
1 8:02 PM SCORPIO	VIRGO	VIRGO	LEO	VIRGO	SAGITTARIUS	LEO	LIBRA	LEO
2	VIRGO	VIRGO	LEO	VIRGO	SAGITTARIUS	LEO	LIBRA	LEO
3	VIRGO	VIRGO	LEO	VIRGO	SAGITTARIUS	LEO	LIBRA	LEO
4 1:44 AM SAGITTARIUS	VIRGO	VIRGO	LEO	VIRGO	SAGITTARIUS	LEO	LIBRA	LEO
5	VIRGO	VIRGO	LEO	VIRGO	SAGITTARIUS	LEO	LIBRA	LEO
6 10:08 AM CAPRICORN	VIRGO	VIRGO	LEO	VIRGO	SAGITTARIUS	LEO	LIBRA	LEO
7	VIRGO	VIRGO	LEO	VIRGO	SAGITTARIUS	LEO	SCORPIO	LEO
8 9:10 PM AQUARIUS	VIRGO	VIRGO	LEO	LIBRA	SAGITTARIUS	LEO	SCORPIO	LEO
9	VIRGO	VIRGO	VIRGO	LIBRA	SAGITTARIUS	LEO	SCORPIO	LEO
10	VIRGO	VIRGO	VIRGO	LIBRA	SAGITTARIUS	LEO	SCORPIO	LEO
11 9:02 AM PISCES	VIRGO	VIRGO	VIRGO	LIBRA	SAGITTARIUS	LEO	SCORPIO	LEO
12	VIRGO	VIRGO	VIRGO	LIBRA	SAGITTARIUS	LEO	SCORPIO	LEO
13 9:46 PM ARIES	VIRGO	VIRGO	VIRGO	LIBRA	SAGITTARIUS	LEO	SCORPIO	LEO
14	VIRGO	VIRGO	VIRGO	LIBRA	SAGITTARIUS	LEO	SCORPIO	LEO
15	VIRGO	VIRGO	VIRGO	LIBRA	SAGITTARIUS	LEO	SCORPIO	LEO
16 10:08 AM TAURUS	VIRGO	VIRGO	VIRGO	LIBRA	SAGITTARIUS	LEO	SCORPIO	LEO
17	VIRGO	VIRGO	VIRGO	LIBRA	SAGITTARIUS	LEO	SCORPIO	LEO
18 7:50 PM GEMINI	VIRGO	VIRGO	VIRGO	LIBRA	SAGITTARIUS	LEO	SCORPIO	LEO
19	VIRGO	VIRGO	VIRGO	LIBRA	SAGITTARIUS	LEO	SCORPIO	LEO
20	VIRGO	VIRGO	VIRGO	LIBRA	SAGITTARIUS	LEO	SCORPIO	VIRGO
21 1:45 AM CANCER	VIRGO	LIBRA	VIRGO	LIBRA	SAGITTARIUS	LEO	SCORPIO	VIRGO
22	VIRGO	LIBRA	VIRGO	LIBRA	SAGITTARIUS	LEO	SCORPIO	VIRGO
23 3:52 AM LEO	VIRGO	LIBRA	VIRGO	LIBRA	SAGITTARIUS	LEO	SCORPIO	VIRGO

1958 LEO

	MOON		MERCURY	VENUS	MARS	JUPITER	SATURN	URANUS	NEPTUNE	PLUTO
	FROM	IN								
JULY										
24			LEO	CANCER	TAURUS	LIBRA	SAGITTARIUS	LEO	SCORPIO	VIRGO
25	12:22 PM	SAGITTARIUS	LEO	CANCER	TAURUS	LIBRA	SAGITTARIUS	LEO	SCORPIO	VIRGO
26			LEO	CANCER	TAURUS	LIBRA	SAGITTARIUS	LEO	SCORPIO	VIRGO
27	5;02 PM	CAPRICORN	VIRGO	CANCER	TAURUS	LIBRA	SAGITTARIUS	LEO	SCORPIO	VIRGO
28			VIRGO	CANCER	TAURUS	LIBRA	SAGITTARIUS	LEO	SCORPIO	VIRGO
29	11:15 PM	AQUARIUS	VIRGO	CANCER	TAURUS	LIBRA	SAGITTARIUS	LEO	SCORPIO	VIRGO
30			VIRGO	CANCER	TAURUS	LIBRA	SAGITTARIUS	LEO	SCORPIO	VIRGO
31			VIRGO	CANCER	TAURUS	LIBRA	SAGITTARIUS	LEO	SCORPIO	VIRGO
AUGUST										
1	7;24 AM	PISCES	VIRGO	CANCER	TAURUS	LIBRA	SAGITTARIUS	LEO	SCORPIO	VIRGO
2			VIRGO	CANCER	TAURUS	LIBRA	SAGITTARIUS	LEO	SCORPIO	VIRGO
3	6:24 PM	ARIES	VIRGO	CANCER	TAURUS	LIBRA	SAGITTARIUS	LEO	SCORPIO	VIRGO
4			VIRGO	CANCER	TAURUS	LIBRA	SAGITTARIUS	LEO	SCORPIO	VIRGO
5			VIRGO	CANCER	TAURUS	LIBRA	SAGITTARIUS	LEO	SCORPIO	VIRGO
6	6:48 AM	TAURUS	VIRGO	CANCER	TAURUS	LIBRA	SAGITTARIUS	LEO	SCORPIO	VIRGO
7			VIRGO	CANCER	TAURUS	LIBRA	SAGITTARIUS	LEO	SCORPIO	VIRGO
8	7:47 PM	GEMINI	VIRGO	CANCER	TAURUS	LIBRA	SAGITTARIUS	LEO	SCORPIO	VIRGO
9			VIRGO	CANCER	TAURUS	LIBRA	SAGITTARIUS	LEO	SCORPIO	VIRGO
10			VIRGO	CANCER	TAURUS	LIBRA	SAGITTARIUS	LEO	SCORPIO	VIRGO
11	4:45 AM	CANCER	VIRGO	CANCER	TAURUS	LIBRA	SAGITTARIUS	LEO	SCORPIO	VIRGO
12			VIRGO	CANCER	TAURUS	LIBRA	SAGITTARIUS	LEO	SCORPIO	VIRGO
13	9:45 AM	LEO	VIRGO	CANCER	TAURUS	LIBRA	SAGITTARIUS	LEO	SCORPIO	VIRGO
14			VIRGO	CANCER	TAURUS	LIBRA	SAGITTARIUS	LEO	SCORPIO	VIRGO
15	12:27 PM	VIRGO	VIRGO	CANCER	TAURUS	LIBRA	SAGITTARIUS	LEO	SCORPIO	VIRGO
16			VIRGO	CANCER	TAURUS	LIBRA	SAGITTARIUS	LEO	SCORPIO	VIRGO
17	1:41 PM	LIBRA	VIRGO	LEO	TAURUS	LIBRA	SAGITTARIUS	LEO	SCORPIO	VIRGO
18			VIRGO	LEO	TAURUS	LIBRA	SAGITTARIUS	LEO	SCORPIO	VIRGO
19	2:44 PM	SCORPIO	VIRGO	LEO	TAURUS	LIBRA	SAGITTARIUS	LEO	SCORPIO	VIRGO
20			VIRGO	LEO	TAURUS	LIBRA	SAGITTARIUS	LEO	SCORPIO	VIRGO
21	5:34 PM	SAGITTARIUS	VIRGO	LEO	TAURUS	LIBRA	SAGITTARIUS	LEO	SCORPIO	VIRGO
22			VIRGO	LEO	TAURUS	LIBRA	SAGITTARIUS	LEO	SCORPIO	VIRGO
23	10:30 PM	CAPRICORN	VIRGO	LEO	TAURUS	LIBRA	SAGITTARIUS	LEO	SCORPIO	VIRGO

1959

	MOON		MERCURY	VENUS	MARS	JUPITER	SATURN	URANUS	NEPTUNE	PLUTO
	FROM	IN								
JULY										
24	3:12 PM	ARIES	LEO	VIRGO	VIRGO	SCORPIO	CAPRICORN	LEO	SCORPIO	VIRGO
25			LEO	VIRGO	VIRGO	SCORPIO	CAPRICORN	LEO	SCORPIO	VIRGO
26			LEO	VIRGO	VIRGO	SCORPIO	CAPRICORN	LEO	SCORPIO	VIRGO
27	1:51 PM	TAURUS	LEO	VIRGO	VIRGO	SCORPIO	CAPRICORN	LEO	SCORPIO	VIRGO
28			LEO	VIRGO	VIRGO	SCORPIO	CAPRICORN	LEO	SCORPIO	VIRGO
29	2:37 PM	GEMINI	LEO	VIRGO	VIRGO	SCORPIO	CAPRICORN	LEO	SCORPIO	VIRGO
30			LEO	VIRGO	VIRGO	SCORPIO	CAPRICORN	LEO	SCORPIO	VIRGO
31			LEO	VIRGO	VIRGO	SCORPIO	CAPRICORN	LEO	SCORPIO	VIRGO
AUGUST										
1	2:31 AM	CANCER	LEO	VIRGO	VIRGO	SCORPIO	CAPRICORN	LEO	SCORPIO	VIRGO
2			LEO	VIRGO	VIRGO	SCORPIO	CAPRICORN	LEO	SCORPIO	VIRGO
3	12:21 PM	LEO	LEO	VIRGO	VIRGO	SCORPIO	CAPRICORN	LEO	SCORPIO	VIRGO
4			LEO	VIRGO	VIRGO	SCORPIO	CAPRICORN	LEO	SCORPIO	VIRGO
5	7:26 PM	VIRGO	LEO	VIRGO	VIRGO	SCORPIO	CAPRICORN	LEO	SCORPIO	VIRGO
6			LEO	VIRGO	VIRGO	SCORPIO	CAPRICORN	LEO	SCORPIO	VIRGO
7			LEO	VIRGO	VIRGO	SCORPIO	CAPRICORN	LEO	SCORPIO	VIRGO
8	0:53 AM	LIBRA	LEO	VIRGO	VIRGO	SCORPIO	CAPRICORN	LEO	SCORPIO	VIRGO
9			LEO	VIRGO	VIRGO	SCORPIO	CAPRICORN	LEO	SCORPIO	VIRGO
10	4:35 AM	SCORPIO	LEO	VIRGO	VIRGO	SCORPIO	CAPRICORN	LEO	SCORPIO	VIRGO
11			LEO	VIRGO	VIRGO	SCORPIO	CAPRICORN	LEO	SCORPIO	VIRGO
12	7:41 AM	SAGITTARIUS	LEO	VIRGO	VIRGO	SCORPIO	CAPRICORN	LEO	SCORPIO	VIRGO
13			LEO	VIRGO	VIRGO	SCORPIO	CAPRICORN	LEO	SCORPIO	VIRGO
14	10:14 AM	CAPRICORN	LEO	VIRGO	VIRGO	SCORPIO	CAPRICORN	LEO	SCORPIO	VIRGO
15			LEO	VIRGO	VIRGO	SCORPIO	CAPRICORN	LEO	SCORPIO	VIRGO
16	1:13 PM	AQUARIUS	LEO	VIRGO	VIRGO	SCORPIO	CAPRICORN	LEO	SCORPIO	VIRGO
17			LEO	VIRGO	VIRGO	SCORPIO	CAPRICORN	LEO	SCORPIO	VIRGO
18	5:19 PM	PISCES	LEO	VIRGO	VIRGO	SCORPIO	CAPRICORN	LEO	SCORPIO	VIRGO
19			LEO	VIRGO	VIRGO	SCORPIO	CAPRICORN	LEO	SCORPIO	VIRGO
20			LEO	VIRGO	VIRGO	SCORPIO	CAPRICORN	LEO	SCORPIO	VIRGO
21	0:09 AM	ARIES	LEO	VIRGO	VIRGO	SCORPIO	CAPRICORN	LEO	SCORPIO	VIRGO
22			LEO	VIRGO	VIRGO	SCORPIO	CAPRICORN	LEO	SCORPIO	VIRGO
23	9:38 AM	TAURUS	LEO	VIRGO	VIRGO	SCORPIO	CAPRICORN	LEO	SCORPIO	VIRGO

	MOON FROM	IN	MERCURY	VENUS	MARS	JUPITER	SATURN	URANUS	NEPTUNE	PLUTO
JULY										
23	12:03 PM	LEO	CANCER	LEO	TAURUS	SAGITTARIUS	CAPRICORN	LEO	SCORPIO	VIRGO
24			CANCER	LEO	TAURUS	SAGITTARIUS	CAPRICORN	LEO	SCORPIO	VIRGO
25	11:44 PM	VIRGO	CANCER	LEO	TAURUS	SAGITTARIUS	CAPRICORN	LEO	SCORPIO	VIRGO
26			CANCER	LEO	TAURUS	SAGITTARIUS	CAPRICORN	LEO	SCORPIO	VIRGO
27			CANCER	LEO	TAURUS	SAGITTARIUS	CAPRICORN	LEO	SCORPIO	VIRGO
28	9:38 AM	LIBRA	CANCER	LEO	TAURUS	SAGITTARIUS	CAPRICORN	LEO	SCORPIO	VIRGO
29			CANCER	LEO	TAURUS	SAGITTARIUS	CAPRICORN	LEO	SCORPIO	VIRGO
30	5:02 PM	SCORPIO	CANCER	LEO	TAURUS	SAGITTARIUS	CAPRICORN	LEO	SCORPIO	VIRGO
31			CANCER	LEO	TAURUS	SAGITTARIUS	CAPRICORN	LEO	SCORPIO	VIRGO
AUGUST										
1	8:52 PM	SAGITTARIUS	CANCER	LEO	TAURUS	SAGITTARIUS	CAPRICORN	LEO	SCORPIO	VIRGO
2			CANCER	LEO	TAURUS	SAGITTARIUS	CAPRICORN	LEO	SCORPIO	VIRGO
3	10:51 PM	CAPRICORN	CANCER	LEO	GEMINI	SAGITTARIUS	CAPRICORN	LEO	SCORPIO	VIRGO
4			CANCER	LEO	GEMINI	SAGITTARIUS	CAPRICORN	LEO	SCORPIO	VIRGO
5	10:42 PM	AQUARIUS	CANCER	LEO	GEMINI	SAGITTARIUS	CAPRICORN	LEO	SCORPIO	VIRGO
6			CANCER	LEO	GEMINI	SAGITTARIUS	CAPRICORN	LEO	SCORPIO	VIRGO
7	11:20 PM	PISCES	CANCER	LEO	GEMINI	SAGITTARIUS	CAPRICORN	LEO	SCORPIO	VIRGO
8			CANCER	LEO	GEMINI	SAGITTARIUS	CAPRICORN	LEO	SCORPIO	VIRGO
9			CANCER	LEO	GEMINI	SAGITTARIUS	CAPRICORN	LEO	SCORPIO	VIRGO
10	1:30 AM	ARIES	CANCER	VIRGO	GEMINI	SAGITTARIUS	CAPRICORN	LEO	SCORPIO	VIRGO
11			LEO	VIRGO	GEMINI	SAGITTARIUS	CAPRICORN	LEO	SCORPIO	VIRGO
12	7:45 AM	TAURUS	LEO	VIRGO	GEMINI	SAGITTARIUS	CAPRICORN	LEO	SCORPIO	VIRGO
13			LEO	VIRGO	GEMINI	SAGITTARIUS	CAPRICORN	LEO	SCORPIO	VIRGO
14	5:41 PM	GEMINI	LEO	VIRGO	GEMINI	SAGITTARIUS	CAPRICORN	LEO	SCORPIO	VIRGO
15			LEO	VIRGO	GEMINI	SAGITTARIUS	CAPRICORN	LEO	SCORPIO	VIRGO
16			LEO	VIRGO	GEMINI	SAGITTARIUS	CAPRICORN	LEO	SCORPIO	VIRGO
17	6:23 AM	CANCER	LEO	VIRGO	GEMINI	SAGITTARIUS	CAPRICORN	LEO	SCORPIO	VIRGO
18			LEO	VIRGO	GEMINI	SAGITTARIUS	CAPRICORN	LEO	SCORPIO	VIRGO
19	6:42 PM	LEO	LEO	VIRGO	GEMINI	SAGITTARIUS	CAPRICORN	LEO	SCORPIO	VIRGO
20			LEO	VIRGO	GEMINI	SAGITTARIUS	CAPRICORN	LEO	SCORPIO	VIRGO
21			LEO	VIRGO	GEMINI	SAGITTARIUS	CAPRICORN	LEO	SCORPIO	VIRGO
22	5:50 AM	VIRGO	LEO	VIRGO	GEMINI	SAGITTARIUS	CAPRICORN	LEO	SCORPIO	VIRGO
23			LEO	VIRGO	GEMINI	SAGITTARIUS	CAPRICORN	LEO	SCORPIO	VIRGO

1961

	MOON FROM	IN	MERCURY	VENUS	MARS	JUPITER	SATURN	URANUS	NEPTUNE	PLUTO
JULY										
24			CANCER	GEMINI	VIRGO	AQUARIUS	CAPRICORN	LEO	SCORPIO	VIRGO
25	7:49 AM	CAPRICORN	CANCER	GEMINI	VIRGO	AQUARIUS	CAPRICORN	LEO	SCORPIO	VIRGO
26			CANCER	GEMINI	VIRGO	AQUARIUS	CAPRICORN	LEO	SCORPIO	VIRGO
27	8:17 AM	AQUARIUS	CANCER	GEMINI	VIRGO	AQUARIUS	CAPRICORN	LEO	SCORPIO	VIRGO
28			CANCER	GEMINI	VIRGO	AQUARIUS	CAPRICORN	LEO	SCORPIO	VIRGO
29	7:38 AM	PISCES	CANCER	GEMINI	VIRGO	AQUARIUS	CAPRICORN	LEO	SCORPIO	VIRGO
30			CANCER	GEMINI	VIRGO	AQUARIUS	CAPRICORN	LEO	SCORPIO	VIRGO
31	8:10 AM	ARIES	CANCER	GEMINI	VIRGO	AQUARIUS	CAPRICORN	LEO	SCORPIO	VIRGO
AUGUST										
1			CANCER	GEMINI	VIRGO	AQUARIUS	CAPRICORN	LEO	SCORPIO	VIRGO
2	11:08 AM	TAURUS	CANCER	GEMINI	VIRGO	AQUARIUS	CAPRICORN	LEO	SCORPIO	VIRGO
3			CANCER	GEMINI	VIRGO	AQUARIUS	CAPRICORN	LEO	SCORPIO	VIRGO
4	5:53 PM	GEMINI	CANCER	CANCER	VIRGO	AQUARIUS	CAPRICORN	LEO	SCORPIO	VIRGO
5			LEO	CANCER	VIRGO	AQUARIUS	CAPRICORN	LEO	SCORPIO	VIRGO
6			LEO	CANCER	VIRGO	AQUARIUS	CAPRICORN	LEO	SCORPIO	VIRGO
7	4:02 AM	CANCER	LEO	CANCER	VIRGO	AQUARIUS	CAPRICORN	LEO	SCORPIO	VIRGO
8			LEO	CANCER	VIRGO	AQUARIUS	CAPRICORN	LEO	SCORPIO	VIRGO
9	4:17 PM	LEO	LEO	CANCER	VIRGO	AQUARIUS	CAPRICORN	LEO	SCORPIO	VIRGO
10			LEO	CANCER	VIRGO	AQUARIUS	CAPRICORN	LEO	SCORPIO	VIRGO
11			LEO	CANCER	VIRGO	AQUARIUS	CAPRICORN	LEO	SCORPIO	VIRGO
12	4:48 AM	VIRGO	LEO	CANCER	VIRGO	AQUARIUS	CAPRICORN	LEO	SCORPIO	VIRGO
13			LEO	CANCER	VIRGO	CAPRICORN	CAPRICORN	LEO	SCORPIO	VIRGO
14	5:05 PM	LIBRA	LEO	CANCER	VIRGO	CAPRICORN	CAPRICORN	LEO	SCORPIO	VIRGO
15			LEO	CANCER	VIRGO	CAPRICORN	CAPRICORN	LEO	SCORPIO	VIRGO
16			LEO	CANCER	VIRGO	CAPRICORN	CAPRICORN	LEO	SCORPIO	VIRGO
17	4:30 AM	SCORPIO	LEO	CANCER	VIRGO	CAPRICORN	CAPRICORN	LEO	SCORPIO	VIRGO
18			LEO	CANCER	LIBRA	CAPRICORN	CAPRICORN	LEO	SCORPIO	VIRGO
19	12:47 PM	SAGITTARIUS	VIRGO	CANCER	LIBRA	CAPRICORN	CAPRICORN	LEO	SCORPIO	VIRGO
20			VIRGO	CANCER	LIBRA	CAPRICORN	CAPRICORN	LEO	SCORPIO	VIRGO
21	5:28 PM	CAPRICORN	VIRGO	CANCER	LIBRA	CAPRICORN	CAPRICORN	LEO	SCORPIO	VIRGO
22			VIRGO	CANCER	LIBRA	CAPRICORN	CAPRICORN	LEO	SCORPIO	VIRGO
23	6:37 PM	AQUARIUS	VIRGO	CANCER	LIBRA	CAPRICORN	CAPRICORN	LEO	SCORPIO	VIRGO

1962 LEO

DAY	MOON FROM	MOON IN	MERCURY	VENUS	MARS	JUPITER	SATURN	URANUS	NEPTUNE	PLUTO
JULY										
24			CANCER	VIRGO	GEMINI	PISCES	AQUARIUS	LEO	SCORPIO	VIRGO
25			CANCER	VIRGO	GEMINI	PISCES	AQUARIUS	LEO	SCORPIO	VIRGO
26	2:24 AM	GEMINI	CANCER	VIRGO	GEMINI	PISCES	AQUARIUS	LEO	SCORPIO	VIRGO
27			LEO	VIRGO	GEMINI	PISCES	AQUARIUS	LEO	SCORPIO	VIRGO
28	8:40 AM	CANCER	LEO	VIRGO	GEMINI	PISCES	AQUARIUS	LEO	SCORPIO	VIRGO
29			LEO	VIRGO	GEMINI	PISCES	AQUARIUS	LEO	SCORPIO	VIRGO
30	4:43 PM	LEO	LEO	VIRGO	GEMINI	PISCES	AQUARIUS	LEO	SCORPIO	VIRGO
31			LEO	VIRGO	GEMINI	PISCES	AQUARIUS	LEO	SCORPIO	VIRGO
AUGUST										
1			LEO	VIRGO	GEMINI	PISCES	AQUARIUS	LEO	SCORPIO	VIRGO
2	2:43 AM	VIRGO	LEO	VIRGO	GEMINI	PISCES	AQUARIUS	LEO	SCORPIO	VIRGO
3			LEO	VIRGO	GEMINI	PISCES	AQUARIUS	LEO	SCORPIO	VIRGO
4	2:52 PM	LIBRA	LEO	VIRGO	GEMINI	PISCES	AQUARIUS	LEO	SCORPIO	VIRGO
5			LEO	VIRGO	GEMINI	PISCES	AQUARIUS	LEO	SCORPIO	VIRGO
6			LEO	VIRGO	GEMINI	PISCES	AQUARIUS	LEO	SCORPIO	VIRGO
7	3:33 AM	SCORPIO	LEO	VIRGO	GEMINI	PISCES	AQUARIUS	LEO	SCORPIO	VIRGO
8			LEO	VIRGO	GEMINI	PISCES	AQUARIUS	LEO	SCORPIO	VIRGO
9	2:50 PM	SAGITTARIUS	LEO	LIBRA	GEMINI	PISCES	AQUARIUS	LEO	SCORPIO	VIRGO
10			LEO	LIBRA	GEMINI	PISCES	AQUARIUS	VIRGO	SCORPIO	VIRGO
11	10:24 PM	CAPRICORN	VIRGO	LIBRA	GEMINI	PISCES	AQUARIUS	VIRGO	SCORPIO	VIRGO
12			VIRGO	LIBRA	GEMINI	PISCES	AQUARIUS	VIRGO	SCORPIO	VIRGO
13			VIRGO	LIBRA	GEMINI	PISCES	AQUARIUS	VIRGO	SCORPIO	VIRGO
14	1:59 AM	AQUARIUS	VIRGO	LIBRA	GEMINI	PISCES	AQUARIUS	VIRGO	SCORPIO	VIRGO
15			VIRGO	LIBRA	GEMINI	PISCES	AQUARIUS	VIRGO	SCORPIO	VIRGO
16	3:16 AM	PISCES	VIRGO	LIBRA	GEMINI	PISCES	AQUARIUS	VIRGO	SCORPIO	VIRGO
17			VIRGO	LIBRA	GEMINI	PISCES	AQUARIUS	VIRGO	SCORPIO	VIRGO
18	3:16 AM	ARIES	VIRGO	LIBRA	GEMINI	PISCES	AQUARIUS	VIRGO	SCORPIO	VIRGO
19			VIRGO	LIBRA	GEMINI	PISCES	AQUARIUS	VIRGO	SCORPIO	VIRGO
20	4:43 AM	TAURUS	VIRGO	LIBRA	GEMINI	PISCES	AQUARIUS	VIRGO	SCORPIO	VIRGO
21			VIRGO	LIBRA	GEMINI	PISCES	AQUARIUS	VIRGO	SCORPIO	VIRGO
22	7:43 AM	GEMINI	VIRGO	LIBRA	GEMINI	PISCES	AQUARIUS	VIRGO	SCORPIO	VIRGO
23			VIRGO	LIBRA	GEMINI	PISCES	AQUARIUS	VIRGO	SCORPIO	VIRGO

1963

DAY	MOON FROM	MOON IN	MERCURY	VENUS	MARS	JUPITER	SATURN	URANUS	NEPTUNE	PLUTO
JULY										
24			LEO	CANCER	VIRGO	ARIES	AQUARIUS	VIRGO	SCORPIO	VIRGO
25	10:56 AM	LIBRA	LEO	CANCER	VIRGO	ARIES	AQUARIUS	VIRGO	SCORPIO	VIRGO
26			LEO	CANCER	VIRGO	ARIES	AQUARIUS	VIRGO	SCORPIO	VIRGO
27	10:44 PM	SCORPIO	LEO	CANCER	VIRGO	ARIES	AQUARIUS	VIRGO	SCORPIO	VIRGO
28			LEO	CANCER	LIBRA	ARIES	AQUARIUS	VIRGO	SCORPIO	VIRGO
29			LEO	CANCER	LIBRA	ARIES	AQUARIUS	VIRGO	SCORPIO	VIRGO
30	11:39 AM	SAGITTARIUS	LEO	CANCER	LIBRA	ARIES	AQUARIUS	VIRGO	SCORPIO	VIRGO
31			LEO	CANCER	LIBRA	ARIES	AQUARIUS	VIRGO	SCORPIO	VIRGO
AUGUST										
1	10:25 PM	CAPRICORN	LEO	LEO	LIBRA	ARIES	AQUARIUS	VIRGO	SCORPIO	VIRGO
2			LEO	LEO	LIBRA	ARIES	AQUARIUS	VIRGO	SCORPIO	VIRGO
3			LEO	LEO	LIBRA	ARIES	AQUARIUS	VIRGO	SCORPIO	VIRGO
4	6:18 AM	AQUARIUS	VIRGO	LEO	LIBRA	ARIES	AQUARIUS	VIRGO	SCORPIO	VIRGO
5			VIRGO	LEO	LIBRA	ARIES	AQUARIUS	VIRGO	SCORPIO	VIRGO
6	11:23 AM	PISCES	VIRGO	LEO	LIBRA	ARIES	AQUARIUS	VIRGO	SCORPIO	VIRGO
7			VIRGO	LEO	LIBRA	ARIES	AQUARIUS	VIRGO	SCORPIO	VIRGO
8	3:04 PM	ARIES	VIRGO	LEO	LIBRA	ARIES	AQUARIUS	VIRGO	SCORPIO	VIRGO
9			VIRGO	LEO	LIBRA	ARIES	AQUARIUS	VIRGO	SCORPIO	VIRGO
10	5:41 PM	TAURUS	VIRGO	LEO	LIBRA	ARIES	AQUARIUS	VIRGO	SCORPIO	VIRGO
11			VIRGO	LEO	LIBRA	ARIES	AQUARIUS	VIRGO	SCORPIO	VIRGO
12	8:31 PM	GEMINI	VIRGO	LEO	LIBRA	ARIES	AQUARIUS	VIRGO	SCORPIO	VIRGO
13			VIRGO	LEO	LIBRA	ARIES	AQUARIUS	VIRGO	SCORPIO	VIRGO
14	11:56 PM	CANCER	VIRGO	LEO	LIBRA	ARIES	AQUARIUS	VIRGO	SCORPIO	VIRGO
15			VIRGO	LEO	LIBRA	ARIES	AQUARIUS	VIRGO	SCORPIO	VIRGO
16			VIRGO	LEO	LIBRA	ARIES	AQUARIUS	VIRGO	SCORPIO	VIRGO
17	4:21 AM	LEO	VIRGO	LEO	LIBRA	ARIES	AQUARIUS	VIRGO	SCORPIO	VIRGO
18			VIRGO	LEO	LIBRA	ARIES	AQUARIUS	VIRGO	SCORPIO	VIRGO
19	10:44 AM	VIRGO	VIRGO	LEO	LIBRA	ARIES	AQUARIUS	VIRGO	SCORPIO	VIRGO
20			VIRGO	LEO	LIBRA	ARIES	AQUARIUS	VIRGO	SCORPIO	VIRGO
21	7:18 PM	LIBRA	VIRGO	LEO	LIBRA	ARIES	AQUARIUS	VIRGO	SCORPIO	VIRGO
22			VIRGO	LEO	LIBRA	ARIES	AQUARIUS	VIRGO	SCORPIO	VIRGO
23			VIRGO	LEO	LIBRA	ARIES	AQUARIUS	VIRGO	SCORPIO	VIRGO

	MOON		MERCURY	VENUS	MARS	JUPITER	SATURN	URANUS	NEPTUNE	PLUTO
	FROM	IN								
JULY										
23			LEO	GEMINI	GEMINI	TAURUS	PISCES	VIRGO	SCORPIO	VIRGO
24	7:24 AM	AQUARIUS	LEO	GEMINI	GEMINI	TAURUS	PISCES	VIRGO	SCORPIO	VIRGO
25			LEO	GEMINI	GEMINI	TAURUS	PISCES	VIRGO	SCORPIO	VIRGO
26	5:18 PM	PISCES	LEO	GEMINI	GEMINI	TAURUS	PISCES	VIRGO	SCORPIO	VIRGO
27			LEO	GEMINI	GEMINI	TAURUS	PISCES	VIRGO	SCORPIO	VIRGO
28			VIRGO	GEMINI	GEMINI	TAURUS	PISCES	VIRGO	SCORPIO	VIRGO
29	1:31 AM	ARIES	VIRGO	GEMINI	GEMINI	TAURUS	PISCES	VIRGO	SCORPIO	VIRGO
30			VIRGO	GEMINI	GEMINI	TAURUS	PISCES	VIRGO	SCORPIO	VIRGO
31	7:31 AM	TAURUS	VIRGO	GEMINI	CANCER	TAURUS	PISCES	VIRGO	SCORPIO	VIRGO
AUGUST										
1			VIRGO	GEMINI	CANCER	TAURUS	PISCES	VIRGO	SCORPIO	VIRGO
2	10:42 AM	GEMINI	VIRGO	GEMINI	CANCER	TAURUS	PISCES	VIRGO	SCORPIO	VIRGO
3			VIRGO	GEMINI	CANCER	TAURUS	PISCES	VIRGO	SCORPIO	VIRGO
4	12:14 PM	CANCER	VIRGO	GEMINI	CANCER	TAURUS	PISCES	VIRGO	SCORPIO	VIRGO
5			VIRGO	GEMINI	CANCER	TAURUS	PISCES	VIRGO	SCORPIO	VIRGO
6	1:06 PM	LEO	VIRGO	CANCER	CANCER	TAURUS	PISCES	VIRGO	SCORPIO	VIRGO
7			VIRGO	CANCER	CANCER	TAURUS	PISCES	VIRGO	SCORPIO	VIRGO
8	2:51 PM	VIRGO	VIRGO	CANCER	CANCER	TAURUS	PISCES	VIRGO	SCORPIO	VIRGO
9			VIRGO	CANCER	CANCER	TAURUS	PISCES	VIRGO	SCORPIO	VIRGO
10	6:50 PM	LIBRA	VIRGO	CANCER	CANCER	TAURUS	PISCES	VIRGO	SCORPIO	VIRGO
11			VIRGO	CANCER	CANCER	TAURUS	PISCES	VIRGO	SCORPIO	VIRGO
12			VIRGO	CANCER	CANCER	TAURUS	PISCES	VIRGO	SCORPIO	VIRGO
13	2:24 AM	SCORPIO	VIRGO	CANCER	CANCER	TAURUS	PISCES	VIRGO	SCORPIO	VIRGO
14			VIRGO	CANCER	CANCER	TAURUS	PISCES	VIRGO	SCORPIO	VIRGO
15	1:52 PM	SAGITTARIUS	VIRGO	CANCER	CANCER	TAURUS	PISCES	VIRGO	SCORPIO	VIRGO
16			VIRGO	CANCER	CANCER	TAURUS	PISCES	VIRGO	SCORPIO	VIRGO
17			VIRGO	CANCER	CANCER	TAURUS	PISCES	VIRGO	SCORPIO	VIRGO
18	2:46 AM	CAPRICORN	VIRGO	CANCER	CANCER	TAURUS	PISCES	VIRGO	SCORPIO	VIRGO
19			VIRGO	CANCER	CANCER	TAURUS	PISCES	VIRGO	SCORPIO	VIRGO
20	2:32 PM	AQUARIUS	VIRGO	CANCER	CANCER	TAURUS	PISCES	VIRGO	SCORPIO	VIRGO
21			VIRGO	CANCER	CANCER	TAURUS	PISCES	VIRGO	SCORPIO	VIRGO
22	11:53 PM	PISCES	VIRGO	CANCER	CANCER	TAURUS	PISCES	VIRGO	SCORPIO	VIRGO
23			VIRGO	CANCER	CANCER	TAURUS	PISCES	VIRGO	SCORPIO	VIRGO

1965   MOON

	MOON		MERCURY	VENUS	MARS	JUPITER	SATURN	URANUS	NEPTUNE	PLUTO
	FROM	IN								
JULY										
24			LEO	LEO	LIBRA	GEMINI	PISCES	VIRGO	SCORPIO	VIRGO
25	10:58 PM	CANCER	LEO	LEO	LIBRA	GEMINI	PISCES	VIRGO	SCORPIO	VIRGO
26			LEO	VIRGO	LIBRA	GEMINI	PISCES	VIRGO	SCORPIO	VIRGO
27	10:55 PM	LEO	LEO	LEO	LIBRA	GEMINI	PISCES	VIRGO	SCORPIO	VIRGO
28			LEO	VIRGO	LIBRA	GEMINI	PISCES	VIRGO	SCORPIO	VIRGO
29	10:16 PM	VIRGO	LEO	VIRGO	LIBRA	GEMINI	PISCES	VIRGO	SCORPIO	VIRGO
30			LEO	VIRGO	LIBRA	GEMINI	PISCES	VIRGO	SCORPIO	VIRGO
31	11:14 PM	LIBRA	LEO	VIRGO	LIBRA	GEMINI	PISCES	VIRGO	SCORPIO	VIRGO
AUGUST										
1			VIRGO	VIRGO	LIBRA	GEMINI	PISCES	VIRGO	SCORPIO	VIRGO
2			VIRGO	VIRGO	LIBRA	GEMINI	PISCES	VIRGO	SCORPIO	VIRGO
3	3:35 AM	SCORPIO	VIRGO	VIRGO	LIBRA	GEMINI	PISCES	VIRGO	SCORPIO	VIRGO
4			LEO	VIRGO	LIBRA	GEMINI	PISCES	VIRGO	SCORPIO	VIRGO
5	11:44 AM	SAGITTARIUS	LEO	VIRGO	LIBRA	GEMINI	PISCES	VIRGO	SCORPIO	VIRGO
6			LEO	VIRGO	LIBRA	GEMINI	PISCES	VIRGO	SCORPIO	VIRGO
7	11:24 PM	CAPRICORN	LEO	VIRGO	LIBRA	GEMINI	PISCES	VIRGO	SCORPIO	VIRGO
8			LEO	VIRGO	LIBRA	GEMINI	PISCES	VIRGO	SCORPIO	VIRGO
9			LEO	VIRGO	LIBRA	GEMINI	PISCES	VIRGO	SCORPIO	VIRGO
10	12:06 PM	AQUARIUS	LEO	VIRGO	LIBRA	GEMINI	PISCES	VIRGO	SCORPIO	VIRGO
11			LEO	VIRGO	LIBRA	GEMINI	PISCES	VIRGO	SCORPIO	VIRGO
12			LEO	VIRGO	LIBRA	GEMINI	PISCES	VIRGO	SCORPIO	VIRGO
13	0:33 AM	PISCES	LEO	VIRGO	LIBRA	GEMINI	PISCES	VIRGO	SCORPIO	VIRGO
14			LEO	VIRGO	LIBRA	GEMINI	PISCES	VIRGO	SCORPIO	VIRGO
15	12:04 PM	ARIES	LEO	VIRGO	LIBRA	GEMINI	PISCES	VIRGO	SCORPIO	VIRGO
16			LEO	VIRGO	LIBRA	GEMINI	PISCES	VIRGO	SCORPIO	VIRGO
17	9:44 PM	TAURUS	LEO	VIRGO	LIBRA	GEMINI	PISCES	VIRGO	SCORPIO	VIRGO
18			LEO	VIRGO	LIBRA	GEMINI	PISCES	VIRGO	SCORPIO	VIRGO
19			LEO	VIRGO	LIBRA	GEMINI	PISCES	VIRGO	SCORPIO	VIRGO
20	4:39 AM	GEMINI	LEO	LIBRA	LIBRA	GEMINI	PISCES	VIRGO	SCORPIO	VIRGO
21			LEO	LIBRA	SCORPIO	GEMINI	PISCES	VIRGO	SCORPIO	VIRGO
22	8:10 AM	CANCER	LEO	LIBRA	SCORPIO	GEMINI	PISCES	VIRGO	SCORPIO	VIRGO
23			LEO	LIBRA	SCORPIO	GEMINI	PISCES	VIRGO	SCORPIO	VIRGO

1966   LEO

	MOON FROM IN	MERCURY	VENUS	MARS	JUPITER	SATURN	URANUS	NEPTUNE	PLUTO
JULY									
24	11:44 AM SCORPIO	LEO	CANCER	CANCER	CANCER	PISCES	VIRGO	SCORPIO	VIRGO
25		LEO	CANCER	CANCER	CANCER	PISCES	VIRGO	SCORPIO	VIRGO
26	5:18 PM SAGITTARIUS	LEO	CANCER	CANCER	CANCER	PISCES	VIRGO	SCORPIO	VIRGO
27		LEO	CANCER	CANCER	CANCER	PISCES	VIRGO	SCORPIO	VIRGO
28		LEO	CANCER	CANCER	CANCER	PISCES	VIRGO	SCORPIO	VIRGO
29	1:08 AM CAPRICORN	LEO	CANCER	CANCER	CANCER	PISCES	VIRGO	SCORPIO	VIRGO
30		LEO	CANCER	CANCER	CANCER	PISCES	VIRGO	SCORPIO	VIRGO
31	11:05 AM AQUARIUS	LEO	CANCER	CANCER	CANCER	PISCES	VIRGO	SCORPIO	VIRGO
AUGUST									
1		LEO	CANCER	CANCER	CANCER	PISCES	VIRGO	SCORPIO	VIRGO
2	10:40 PM PISCES	LEO	CANCER	CANCER	CANCER	PISCES	VIRGO	SCORPIO	VIRGO
3		LEO	CANCER	CANCER	CANCER	PISCES	VIRGO	SCORPIO	VIRGO
4		LEO	CANCER	CANCER	CANCER	PISCES	VIRGO	SCORPIO	VIRGO
5	11:17 AM ARIES	LEO	CANCER	CANCER	CANCER	PISCES	VIRGO	SCORPIO	VIRGO
6		LEO	CANCER	CANCER	CANCER	PISCES	VIRGO	SCORPIO	VIRGO
7	11:50 PM TAURUS	LEO	CANCER	CANCER	CANCER	PISCES	VIRGO	SCORPIO	VIRGO
8		LEO	CANCER	CANCER	CANCER	PISCES	VIRGO	SCORPIO	VIRGO
9		LEO	CANCER	CANCER	CANCER	PISCES	VIRGO	SCORPIO	VRIGO
10	9:37 AM GEMINI	LEO	CANCER	CANCER	CANCER	PISCES	VIRGO	SCORPIO	VIRGO
11		LEO	CANCER	CANCER	CANCER	PISCES	VIRGO	SCORPIO	VIRGO
12	3:38 PM CANCER	LEO	CANCER	CANCER	CANCER	PISCES	VIRGO	SCORPIO	VIRGO
13		LEO	CANCER	CANCER	CANCER	PISCES	VIRGO	SCORPIO	VIRGO
14	5:51 PM LEO	LEO	CANCER	CANCER	CANCER	PISCES	VIRGO	SCORPIO	VIRGO
15		LEO	CANCER	CANCER	CANCER	PISCES	VIRGO	SCORPIO	VRIGO
16	6:02 PM VIRGO	LEO	LEO	CANCER	CANCER	PISCES	VIRGO	SCORPIO	VIRGO
17		LEO	LEO	CANCER	CANCER	PISCES	VIRGO	SCORPIO	VIRGO
18	5:36 PM LIBRA	LEO	LEO	CANCER	CANCER	PISCES	VIRGO	SCORPIO	VIRGO
19		LEO	LEO	CANCER	CANCER	PISCES	VIRGO	SCORPIO	VIRGO
20	6:51 PM SCORPIO	LEO	LEO	CANCER	CANCER	PISCES	VIRGO	SCORPIO	VIRGO
21		LEO	LEO	CANCER	CANCER	PISCES	VIRGO	SCORPIO	VIRGO
22	10:54 PM SAGITTARIUS	LEO	LEO	CANCER	CANCER	PISCES	VIRGO	SCORPIO	VIRGO
23		LEO	LEO	CANCER	CANCER	PISCES	VIRGO	SCORPIO	VIRGO

1967   MOON

	MOON FROM IN	MERCURY	VENUS	MARS	JUPITER	SATURN	URANUS	NEPTUNE	PLUTO
JULY									
24		CANCER	VIRGO	SCORPIO	LEO	ARIES	VIRGO	SCORPIO	VIRGO
25		CANCER	VIRGO	SCORPIO	LEO	ARIES	VIRGO	SCORPIO	VIRGO
26	7:12 AM ARIES	CANCER	VIRGO	SCORPIO	LEO	ARIES	VIRGO	SCORPIO	VIRGO
27		CANCER	VIRGO	SCORPIO	LEO	ARIES	VIRGO	SCORPIO	VIRGO
28	7:55 PM TAURUS	CANCER	VIRGO	SCORPIO	LEO	ARIES	VIRGO	SCORPIO	VIRGO
29		CANCER	VIRGO	SCORPIO	LEO	ARIES	VIRGO	SCORPIO	VIRGO
30		CANCER	VIRGO	SCORPIO	LEO	ARIES	VIRGO	SCORPIO	VIRGO
31	8:11 AM GEMINI	CANCER	VIRGO	SCORPIO	LEO	ARIES	VIRGO	SCORPIO	VIRGO
AUGUST									
1		CANCER	VIRGO	SCORPIO	LEO	ARIES	VIRGO	SCORPIO	VIRGO
2	5:24 PM CANCER	CANCER	VIRGO	SCORPIO	LEO	ARIES	VIRGO	SCORPIO	VIRGO
3		CANCER	VIRGO	SCORPIO	LEO	ARIES	VIRGO	SCORPIO	VIRGO
4	11:21 PM LEO	CANCER	VIRGO	SCORPIO	LEO	ARIES	VIRGO	SCORPIO	VIRGO
5		CANCER	VIRGO	SCORPIO	LEO	ARIES	VIRGO	SCORPIO	VIRGO
6		CANCER	VIRGO	SCORPIO	LEO	ARIES	VIRGO	SCORPIO	VIRGO
7	2:52 AM VIRGO	CANCER	VIRGO	SCORPIO	LEO	ARIES	VIRGO	SCORPIO	VIRGO
8		CANCER	VIRGO	SCORPIO	LEO	ARIES	VIRGO	SCORPIO	VIRGO
9	4:43 AM LIBRA	LEO	VIRGO	SCORPIO	LEO	ARIES	VIRGO	SCORPIO	VIRGO
10		LEO	VIRGO	SCORPIO	LEO	ARIES	VIRGO	SCORPIO	VIRGO
11	6:41 AM SCORPIO	LEO	VIRGO	SCORPIO	LEO	ARIES	VIRGO	SCORPIO	VIRGO
12		LEO	VIRGO	SCORPIO	LEO	ARIES	VIRGO	SCORPIO	VIRGO
13	9:45 AM SAGITTARIUS	LEO	VIRGO	SCORPIO	LEO	ARIES	VIRGO	SCORPIO	VIRGO
14		LEO	VIRGO	SCORPIO	LEO	ARIES	VIRGO	SCORPIO	VIRGO
15	2:17 PM CAPRICORN	LEO	VIRGO	SCORPIO	LEO	ARIES	VIRGO	SCORPIO	VIRGO
16		LEO	VIRGO	SCORPIO	LEO	ARIES	VIRGO	SCORPIO	VIRGO
17	8:29 PM AQUARIUS	LEO	VIRGO	SCORPIO	LEO	ARIES	VIRGO	SCORPIO	VIRGO
18		LEO	VIRGO	SCORPIO	LEO	ARIES	VIRGO	SCORPIO	VIRGO
19		LEO	VIRGO	SCORPIO	LEO	ARIES	VIRGO	SCORPIO	VIRGO
20	4:33 AM PISCES	LEO	VIRGO	SCORPIO	LEO	ARIES	VIRGO	SCORPIO	VIRGO
21		LEO	VIRGO	SCORPIO	LEO	ARIES	VIRGO	SCORPIO	VIRGO
22	2:56 PM ARIES	LEO	VIRGO	SCORPIO	LEO	ARIES	VIRGO	SCORPIO	VIRGO
23		LEO	VIRGO	SCORPIO	LEO	ARIES	VIRGO	SCORPIO	VIRGO

1968

	MOON FROM IN	MERCURY	VENUS	MARS	JUPITER	SATURN	URANUS	NEPTUNE	PLUTO
JULY									
23		CANCER	LEO	CANCER	VIRGO	ARIES	VIRGO	SCORPIO	VIRGO
24		CANCER	LEO	CANCER	VIRGO	ARIES	VIRGO	SCORPIO	VIRGO
25	2:11 AM LEO	CANCER	LEO	CANCER	VIRGO	ARIES	VIRGO	SCORPIO	VIRGO
26		CANCER	LEO	CANCER	VIRGO	ARIES	VIRGO	SCORPIO	VIRGO
27	10:20 AM VIRGO	CANCER	LEO	CANCER	VIRGO	ARIES	VIRGO	SCORPIO	VIRGO
28		CANCER	LEO	CANCER	VIRGO	ARIES	VIRGO	SCORPIO	VIRGO
29	4:34 PM LIBRA	CANCER	LEO	CANCER	VIRGO	ARIES	VIRGO	SCORPIO	VIRGO
30		CANCER	LEO	CANCER	VIRGO	ARIES	VIRGO	SCORPIO	VIRGO
31	8:53 PM SCORPIO	CANCER	LEO	CANCER	VIRGO	ARIES	VIRGO	SCORPIO	VIRGO
AUGUST									
1		LEO	LEO	CANCER	VIRGO	ARIES	VIRGO	SCORPIO	VIRGO
2	11:52 PM SAGITTARIUS	LEO	LEO	CANCER	VIRGO	ARIES	VIRGO	SCORPIO	VIRGO
3		LEO	LEO	CANCER	VIRGO	ARIES	VIRGO	SCORPIO	VIRGO
4		LEO	LEO	CANCER	VIRGO	ARIES	VIRGO	SCORPIO	VIRGO
5	2:02 AM CAPRICORN	LEO	LEO	CANCER	VIRGO	ARIES	VIRGO	SCORPIO	VIRGO
6		LEO	LEO	LEO	VIRGO	ARIES	VIRGO	SCORPIO	VIRGO
7	3:53 AM AQUARIUS	LEO	LEO	LEO	VIRGO	ARIES	VIRGO	SCORPIO	VIRGO
8		LEO	LEO	LEO	VIRGO	ARIES	VIRGO	SCORPIO	VIRGO
9	7:21 AM PISCES	LEO	VIRGO	LEO	VIRGO	ARIES	VIRGO	SCORPIO	VIRGO
10		LEO	VIRGO	LEO	VIRGO	ARIES	VIRGO	SCORPIO	VIRGO
11	1:07 PM ARIES	LEO	VIRGO	LEO	VIRGO	ARIES	VIRGO	SCORPIO	VIRGO
12		LEO	VIRGO	LEO	VIRGO	ARIES	VIRGO	SCORPIO	VIRGO
13	10:25 PM TAURUS	LEO	VIRGO	LEO	VIRGO	ARIES	VIRGO	SCORPIO	VIRGO
14		LEO	VIRGO	LEO	VIRGO	ARIES	VIRGO	SCORPIO	VIRGO
15		LEO	VIRGO	LEO	VIRGO	ARIES	VIRGO	SCORPIO	VIRGO
16	10:52 AM GEMINI	VIRGO	VIRGO	LEO	VIRGO	ARIES	VIRGO	SCORPIO	VIRGO
17		VIRGO	VIRGO	LEO	VIRGO	ARIES	VIRGO	SCORPIO	VIRGO
18	11:24 PM CANCER	VIRGO	VIRGO	LEO	VIRGO	ARIES	VIRGO	SCORPIO	VIRGO
19		VIRGO	VIRGO	LEO	VIRGO	ARIES	VIRGO	SCORPIO	VIRGO
20		VIRGO	VIRGO	LEO	VIRGO	ARIES	VIRGO	SCORPIO	VIRGO
21	10:02 AM LEO	VIRGO	VIRGO	LEO	VIRGO	ARIES	VIRGO	SCORPIO	VIRGO
22		VIRGO	VIRGO	LEO	VIRGO	ARIES	VIRGO	SCORPIO	VIRGO
23	7:19 PM VIRGO	VIRGO	VIRGO	LEO	VIRGO	ARIES	VIRGO	SCORPIO	VIRGO

1969

	MOON FROM IN	MERCURY	VENUS	MARS	JUPITER	SATURN	URANUS	NEPTUNE	PLUTO
JULY									
24	12:12 PM SAGITTARIUS	LEO	GEMINI	SAGITTARIUS	LIBRA	TAURUS	LIBRA	SCORPIO	VIRGO
25		LEO	GEMINI	SAGITTARIUS	LIBRA	TAURUS	LIBRA	SCORPIO	VIRGO
26	1:22 PM CAPRICORN	LEO	GEMINI	SAGITTARIUS	LIBRA	TAURUS	LIBRA	SCORPIO	VIRGO
27		LEO	GEMINI	SAGITTARIUS	LIBRA	TAURUS	LIBRA	SCORPIO	VIRGO
28	1:05 PM AQUARIUS	LEO	GEMINI	SAGITTARIUS	LIBRA	TAURUS	LIBRA	SCORPIO	VIRGO
29		LEO	GEMINI	SAGITTARIUS	LIBRA	TAURUS	LIBRA	SCORPIO	VIRGO
30	1:03 PM PISCES	LEO	GEMINI	SAGITTARIUS	LIBRA	TAURUS	LIBRA	SCORPIO	VIRGO
31		LEO	GEMINI	SAGITTARIUS	LIBRA	TAURUS	LIBRA	SCORPIO	VIRGO
AUGUST									
1	3:01 PM ARIES	LEO	GEMINI	SAGITTARIUS	LIBRA	TAURUS	LIBRA	SCORPIO	VIRGO
2		LEO	GEMINI	SAGITTARIUS	LIBRA	TAURUS	LIBRA	SCORPIO	VIRGO
3	8:57 PM TAURUS	LEO	GEMINI	SAGITTARIUS	LIBRA	TAURUS	LIBRA	SCORPIO	VIRGO
4		LEO	CANCER	SAGITTARIUS	LIBRA	TAURUS	LIBRA	SCORPIO	VIRGO
5		LEO	CANCER	SAGITTARIUS	LIBRA	TAURUS	LIBRA	SCORPIO	VIRGO
6	6:37 AM GEMINI	LEO	CANCER	SAGITTARIUS	LIBRA	TAURUS	LIBRA	SCORPIO	VIRGO
7		LEO	CANCER	SAGITTARIUS	LIBRA	TAURUS	LIBRA	SCORPIO	VIRGO
8	7:19 PM CANCER	VIRGO	CANCER	SAGITTARIUS	LIBRA	TAURUS	LIBRA	SCORPIO	VIRGO
9		VIRGO	CANCER	SAGITTARIUS	LIBRA	TAURUS	LIBRA	SCORPIO	VIRGO
10		VIRGO	CANCER	SAGITTARIUS	LIBRA	TAURUS	LIBRA	SCORPIO	VIRGO
11	8:00 AM LEO	VIRGO	CANCER	SAGITTARIUS	LIBRA	TAURUS	LIBRA	SCORPIO	VIRGO
12		VIRGO	CANCER	SAGITTARIUS	LIBRA	TAURUS	LIBRA	SCORPIO	VIRGO
13	7:24 PM VIRGO	VIRGO	CANCER	SAGITTARIUS	LIBRA	TAURUS	LIBRA	SCORPIO	VIRGO
14		VIRGO	CANCER	SAGITTARIUS	LIBRA	TAURUS	LIBRA	SCORPIO	VIRGO
15		VIRGO	CANCER	SAGITTARIUS	LIBRA	TAURUS	LIBRA	SCORPIO	VIRGO
16	5:39 AM LIBRA	VIRGO	CANCER	SAGITTARIUS	LIBRA	TAURUS	LIBRA	SCORPIO	VIRGO
17		VIRGO	CANCER	SAGITTARIUS	LIBRA	TAURUS	LIBRA	SCORPIO	VIRGO
18	1:14 PM SCORPIO	VIRGO	CANCER	SAGITTARIUS	LIBRA	TAURUS	LIBRA	SCORPIO	VIRGO
19		VIRGO	CANCER	SAGITTARIUS	LIBRA	TAURUS	LIBRA	SCORPIO	VIRGO
20	6:59 PM SAGITTARIUS	VIRGO	CANCER	SAGITTARIUS	LIBRA	TAURUS	LIBRA	SCORPIO	VIRGO
21		VIRGO	CANCER	SAGITTARIUS	LIBRA	TAURUS	LIBRA	SCORPIO	VIRGO
22	7:54 PM CAPRICORN	VIRGO	CANCER	SAGITTARIUS	LIBRA	TAURUS	LIBRA	SCORPIO	VIRGO
23		VIRGO	CANCER	SAGITTARIUS	LIBRA	TAURUS	LIBRA	SCORPIO	VIRGO

1970

	MOON FROM IN	MERCURY	VENUS	MARS	JUPITER	SATURN	URANUS	NEPTUNE	PLUTO
JULY									
24		LEO	VIRGO	LEO	LIBRA	TAURUS	LIBRA	SCORPIO	VIRGO
25	2:36 AM TAURUS	LEO	VIRGO	LEO	LIBRA	TAURUS	LIBRA	SCORPIO	VIRGO
26		LEO	VIRGO	LEO	LIBRA	TAURUS	LIBRA	SCORPIO	VIRGO
27	9:17 AM GEMINI	LEO	VIRGO	LEO	LIBRA	TAURUS	LIBRA	SCORPIO	VIRGO
28		LEO	VIRGO	LEO	LIBRA	TAURUS	LIBRA	SCORPIO	VIRGO
29	6:53 PM CANCER	LEO	VIRGO	LEO	LIBRA	TAURUS	LIBRA	SCORPIO	VIRGO
30		LEO	VIRGO	LEO	LIBRA	TAURUS	LIBRA	SCORPIO	VIRGO
31		LEO	VIRGO	LEO	LIBRA	TAURUS	LIBRA	SCORPIO	VIRGO
AUGUST									
1	6:02 AM LEO	VIRGO	VIRGO	LEO	LIBRA	TAURUS	LIBRA	SCORPIO	VIRGO
2		VIRGO	VIRGO	LEO	LIBRA	TAURUS	LIBRA	SCORPIO	VIRGO
3	6:30 PM VIRGO	VIRGO	VIRGO	LEO	LIBRA	TAURUS	LIBRA	SCORPIO	VIRGO
4		VIRGO	VIRGO	LEO	LIBRA	TAURUS	LIBRA	SCORPIO	VIRGO
5		VIRGO	VIRGO	LEO	LIBRA	TAURUS	LIBRA	SCORPIO	VIRGO
6	7:12 AM LIBRA	VIRGO	VIRGO	LEO	LIBRA	TAURUS	LIBRA	SCORPIO	VIRGO
7		VIRGO	VIRGO	LEO	LIBRA	TAURUS	LIBRA	SCORPIO	VIRGO
8	6:43 PM SCORPIO	VIRGO	VIRGO	LEO	LIBRA	TAURUS	LIBRA	SCORPIO	VIRGO
9		VIRGO	LIBRA	LEO	LIBRA	TAURUS	LIBRA	SCORPIO	VIRGO
10		VIRGO	LIBRA	LEO	LIBRA	TAURUS	LIBRA	SCORPIO	VIRGO
11	3:28 AM SAGITTARIUS	VIRGO	LIBRA	LEO	LIBRA	TAURUS	LIBRA	SCORPIO	VIRGO
12		VIRGO	LIBRA	LEO	LIBRA	TAURUS	LIBRA	SCORPIO	VIRGO
13	7:41 AM CAPRICORN	VIRGO	LIBRA	LEO	LIBRA	TAURUS	LIBRA	SCORPIO	VIRGO
14		VIRGO	LIBRA	LEO	LIBRA	TAURUS	LIBRA	SCORPIO	VIRGO
15	8:55 AM AQUARIUS	VIRGO	LIBRA	LEO	LIBRA	TAURUS	LIBRA	SCORPIO	VIRGO
16		VIRGO	LIBRA	LEO	SCORPIO	TAURUS	LIBRA	SCORPIO	VIRGO
17	8:25 AM PISCES	VIRGO	LIBRA	LEO	SCORPIO	TAURUS	LIBRA	SCORPIO	VIRGO
18		VIRGO	LIBRA	LEO	SCORPIO	TAURUS	LIBRA	SCORPIO	VIRGO
19	8:09 AM ARIES	VIRGO	LIBRA	LEO	SCORPIO	TAURUS	LIBRA	SCORPIO	VIRGO
20		VIRGO	LIBRA	LEO	SCORPIO	TAURUS	LIBRA	SCORPIO	VIRGO
21	10:04 AM TAURUS	VIRGO	LIBRA	LEO	SCORPIO	TAURUS	LIBRA	SCORPIO	VIRGO
22		VIRGO	LIBRA	LEO	SCORPIO	TAURUS	LIBRA	SCORPIO	VIRGO
23	3:08 PM GEMINI	VIRGO	LIBRA	LEO	SCORPIO	TAURUS	LIBRA	SCORPIO	VIRGO

1971

	MOON FROM IN	MERCURY	VENUS	MARS	JUPITER	SATURN	URANUS	NEPTUNE	PLUTO
JULY									
24	4:15 PM VIRGO	LEO	CANCER	AQUARIUS	SCORPIO	GEMINI	LIBRA	SAGITTARIUS	VIRGO
25		LEO	CANCER	AQUARIUS	SCORPIO	GEMINI	LIBRA	SAGITTARIUS	VIRGO
26		LEO	CANCER	AQUARIUS	SCORPIO	GEMINI	LIBRA	SAGITTARIUS	VIRGO
27	4:00 AM LIBRA	VIRGO	CANCER	AQUARIUS	SCORPIO	GEMINI	LIBRA	SAGITTARIUS	VIRGO
28		VIRGO	CANCER	AQUARIUS	SCORPIO	GEMINI	LIBRA	SAGITTARIUS	VIRGO
29	4:53 PM SCORPIO	VIRGO	CANCER	AQUARIUS	SCORPIO	GEMINI	LIBRA	SAGITTARIUS	VIRGO
31		VIRGO	CANCER	AQUARIUS	SCORPIO	GEMINI	LIBRA	SAGITTARIUS	VIRGO
AUGUST									
1	4:06 AM SAGITTARIUS	VIRGO	LEO	AQUARIUS	SCORPIO	GEMINI	LIBRA	SAGITTARIUS	VIRGO
2		VIRGO	LEO	AQUARIUS	SCORPIO	GEMINI	LIBRA	SAGITTARIUS	VIRGO
3	11:50 AM CAPRICORN	VIRGO	LEO	AQUARIUS	SCORPIO	GEMINI	LIBRA	SAGITTARIUS	VIRGO
4		VIRGO	LEO	AQUARIUS	SCORPIO	GEMINI	LIBRA	SAGITTARIUS	VIRGO
5	3:53 PM AQUARIUS	VIRGO	LEO	AQUARIUS	SCORPIO	GEMINI	LIBRA	SAGITTARIUS	VIRGO
6		VIRGO	LEO	AQUARIUS	SCORPIO	GEMINI	LIBRA	SAGITTARIUS	VIRGO
7	5:40 PM PISCES	VIRGO	LEO	AQUARIUS	SCORPIO	GEMINI	LIBRA	SAGITTARIUS	VIRGO
8		VIRGO	LEO	AQUARIUS	SCORPIO	GEMINI	LIBRA	SAGITTARIUS	VIRGO
9	6:26 PM ARIES	VIRGO	LEO	AQUARIUS	SCORPIO	GEMINI	LIBRA	SAGITTARIUS	VIRGO
10		VIRGO	LEO	AQUARIUS	SCORPIO	GEMINI	LIBRA	SAGITTARIUS	VIRGO
11	8:00 PM TAURUS	VIRGO	LEO	AQUARIUS	SCORPIO	GEMINI	LIBRA	SAGITTARIUS	VIRGO
12		VIRGO	LEO	AQUARIUS	SCORPIO	GEMINI	LIBRA	SAGITTARIUS	VIRGO
13	11:14 PM GEMINI	VIRGO	LEO	AQUARIUS	SCORPIO	GEMINI	LIBRA	SAGITTARIUS	VIRGO
14		VIRGO	LEO	AQUARIUS	SCORPIO	GEMINI	LIBRA	SAGITTARIUS	VIRGO
15		VIRGO	LEO	AQUARIUS	SCORPIO	GEMINI	LIBRA	SAGITTARIUS	VIRGO
16	5:13 AM CANCER	VIRGO	LEO	AQUARIUS	SCORPIO	GEMINI	LIBRA	SAGITTARIUS	VIRGO
17		VIRGO	LEO	AQUARIUS	SCORPIO	GEMINI	LIBRA	SAGITTARIUS	VIRGO
18	1:25 PM LEO	VIRGO	LEO	AQUARIUS	SCORPIO	GEMINI	LIBRA	SAGITTARIUS	VIRGO
19		VIRGO	LEO	AQUARIUS	SCORPIO	GEMINI	LIBRA	SAGITTARIUS	VIRGO
20	11:31 PM VIRGO	VIRGO	LEO	AQUARIUS	SCORPIO	GEMINI	LIBRA	SAGITTARIUS	VIRGO
21		VIRGO	LEO	AQUARIUS	SCORPIO	GEMINI	LIBRA	SAGITTARIUS	VIRGO
22		VIRGO	LEO	AQUARIUS	SCORPIO	GEMINI	LIBRA	SAGITTARIUS	VIRGO
23	11:04 AM LIBRA	VIRGO	LEO	AQUARIUS	SCORPIO	GEMINI	LIBRA	SAGITTARIUS	VIRGO

	MOON		MERCURY	VENUS	MARS	JUPITER	SATURN	URANUS	NEPTUNE	PLUTO
	FROM	IN								
JULY										
23	11:26 AM	CAPRICORN	LEO	GEMINI	LEO	CAPRICORN	GEMINI	LIBRA	SAGITTARIUS	VIRGO
24			LEO	GEMINI	LEO	CAPRICORN	GEMINI	LIBRA	SAGITTARIUS	VIRGO
25	8:12 PM	AQUARIUS	LEO	GEMINI	LEO	SAGITTARIUS	GEMINI	LIBRA	SAGITTARIUS	VIRGO
26			LEO	GEMINI	LEO	SAGITTARIUS	GEMINI	LIBRA	SAGITTARIUS	VIRGO
27			LEO	GEMINI	LEO	SAGITTARIUS	GEMINI	LIBRA	SAGITTARIUS	VIRGO
28	2:30 AM	PISCES	LEO	GEMINI	LEO	SAGITTARIUS	GEMINI	LIBRA	SAGITTARIUS	VIRGO
29			LEO	GEMINI	LEO	SAGITTARIUS	GEMINI	LIBRA	SAGITTARIUS	VIRGO
30	7:00 AM	ARIES	LEO	GEMINI	LEO	SAGITTARIUS	GEMINI	LIBRA	SAGITTARIUS	VIRGO
31			LEO	GEMINI	LEO	SAGITTARIUS	GEMINI	LIBRA	SAGITTARIUS	LIBRA
AUGUST										
1	10:02 AM	TAURUS	LEO	GEMINI	LEO	SAGITTARIUS	GEMINI	LIBRA	SAGITTARIUS	LIBRA
2			LEO	GEMINI	LEO	SAGITTARIUS	GEMINI	LIBRA	SAGITTARIUS	LIBRA
3	12:45 PM	GEMINI	LEO	GEMINI	LEO	SAGITTARIUS	GEMINI	LIBRA	SAGITTARIUS	LIBRA
4			LEO	GEMINI	LEO	SAGITTARIUS	GEMINI	LIBRA	SAGITTARIUS	LIBRA
5	3:31 PM	CANCER	LEO	GEMINI	LEO	SAGITTARIUS	GEMINI	LIBRA	SAGITTARIUS	LIBRA
6			LEO	GEMINI	LEO	SAGITTARIUS	GEMINI	LIBRA	SAGITTARIUS	LIBRA
7	7:08 PM	LEO	LEO	CANCER	LEO	SAGITTARIUS	GEMINI	LIBRA	SAGITTARIUS	LIBRA
8			LEO	CANCER	LEO	SAGITTARIUS	GEMINI	LIBRA	SAGITTARIUS	LIBRA
9			LEO	CANCER	LEO	SAGITTARIUS	GEMINI	LIBRA	SAGITTARIUS	LIBRA
10	0:19 AM	VIRGO	LEO	CANCER	LEO	SAGITTARIUS	GEMINI	LIBRA	SAGITTARIUS	LIBRA
11			LEO	CANCER	LEO	SAGITTARIUS	GEMINI	LIBRA	SAGITTARIUS	LIBRA
12	8:10 AM	LIBRA	LEO	CANCER	LEO	SAGITTARIUS	GEMINI	LIBRA	SAGITTARIUS	LIBRA
13			LEO	CANCER	LEO	SAGITTARIUS	GEMINI	LIBRA	SAGITTARIUS	LIBRA
14	7:06 PM	SCORPIO	LEO	CANCER	LEO	SAGITTARIUS	GEMINI	LIBRA	SAGITTARIUS	LIBRA
15			LEO	CANCER	LEO	SAGITTARIUS	GEMINI	LIBRA	SAGITTARIUS	LIBRA
16			LEO	CANCER	VIRGO	SAGITTARIUS	GEMINI	LIBRA	SAGITTARIUS	LIBRA
17	7:49 AM	SAGITTARIUS	LEO	CANCER	VIRGO	SAGITTARIUS	GEMINI	LIBRA	SAGITTARIUS	LIBRA
18			LEO	CANCER	VIRGO	SAGITTARIUS	GEMINI	LIBRA	SAGITTARIUS	LIBRA
19	7:53 PM	CAPRICORN	LEO	CANCER	VIRGO	SAGITTARIUS	GEMINI	LIBRA	SAGITTARIUS	LIBRA
20			LEO	CANCER	VIRGO	SAGITTARIUS	GEMINI	LIBRA	SAGITTARIUS	LIBRA
21			LEO	CANCER	VIRGO	SAGITTARIUS	GEMINI	LIBRA	SAGITTARIUS	LIBRA
22	4:49 AM	AQUARIUS	LEO	CANCER	VIRGO	SAGITTARIUS	GEMINI	LIBRA	SAGITTARIUS	LIBRA
23			LEO	CANCER	VIRGO	SAGITTARIUS	GEMINI	LIBRA	SAGITTARIUS	LIBRA

1973

	MOON		MERCURY	VENUS	MARS	JUPITER	SATURN	URANUS	NEPTUNE	PLUTO
JULY	FROM	IN								
23			CANCER	LEO	ARIES	AQUARIUS	GEMINI	LIBRA	SAGITTARIUS	LIBRA
24			CANCER	LEO	ARIES	AQUARIUS	GEMINI	LIBRA	SAGITTARIUS	LIBRA
25	2:27 AM	GEMINI	CANCER	LEO	ARIES	AQUARIUS	GEMINI	LIBRA	SAGITTARIUS	LIBRA
26			CANCER	VIRGO	ARIES	AQUARIUS	GEMINI	LIBRA	SAGITTARIUS	LIBRA
27	3:24 AM	CANCER	CANCER	VIRGO	ARIES	AQUARIUS	GEMINI	LIBRA	SAGITTARIUS	LIBRA
28			CANCER	VIRGO	ARIES	AQUARIUS	GEMINI	LIBRA	SAGITTARIUS	LIBRA
29	3:51 AM	LEO	CANCER	VIRGO	ARIES	AQUARIUS	GEMINI	LIBRA	SAGITTARIUS	LIBRA
30			CANCER	VIRGO	ARIES	AQUARIUS	GEMINI	LIBRA	SAGITTARIUS	LIBRA
31	4:52 AM	VIRGO	CANCER	VIRGO	ARIES	AQAARIUS	GEMINI	LIBRA	SAGITTARIUS	LIBRA
AUGUST										
1			CANCER	VIRGO	ARIES	AQUARIUS	GEMINI	LIBRA	SAGITTARIUS	LIBRA
2	7:55 AM	LIBRA	CANCER	VIRGO	ARIES	AQUARIUS	CANCER	LIBRA	SAGITTARIUS	LIBRA
3			CANCER	VIRGO	ARIES	AQUARIUS	CANCER	LIBRA	SAGITTARIUS	LIBRA
4	3:33 PM	SCORPIO	CANCER	VIRGO	ARIES	AQUARIUS	CANCER	LIBRA	SAGITTARIUS	LIBRA
5			CANCER	VIRGO	ARIES	AQUARIUS	CANCER	LIBRA	SAGITTARIUS	LIBRA
6			CANCER	VIRGO	ARIES	AQUARIUS	CANCER	LIBRA	SAGITTARIUS	LIBRA
7	2:39 AM	SAGITTARIUS	CANCER	VIRGO	ARIES	AQUARIUS	CANCER	LIBRA	SAGITTARIUS	LIBRA
8			CANCER	VIRGO	ARIES	AQUARIUS	CANCER	LIBRA	SAGITTARIUS	LIBRA
9	3:39 PM	CAPRICORN	CANCER	VIRGO	ARIES	AQUARIUS	CANCER	LIBRA	SAGITTARIUS	LIBRA
10			CANCER	VIRGO	ARIES	AQUARIUS	CANCER	LIBRA	SAGITTARIUS	LIBRA
11			CANCER	VIRGO	ARIES	AQUARIUS	CANCER	LIBRA	SAGITTARIUS	LIBRA
12	3:40 AM	AQUARIUS	LEO	VIRGO	ARIES	AQUARIUS	CANCER	LIBRA	SAGITTARIUS	LIBRA
13			LEO	VIRGO	TAURUS	AQUARIUS	CANCER	LIBRA	SAGITTARIUS	LIBRA
14	1:53 PM	PISCES	LEO	VIRGO	TAURUS	AQUARIUS	CANCER	LIBRA	SAGITTARIUS	LIBRA
15			LEO	VIRGO	TAURUS	AQUARIUS	CANCER	LIBRA	SAGITTARIUS	LIBRA
16	10:16 PM	ARIES	LEO	VIRGO	TAURUS	AQUARIUS	CANCER	LIBRA	SAGITTARIUS	LIBRA
17			LEO	VIRGO	TAURUS	AQUARIUS	CANCER	LIBRA	SAGITTARIUS	LIBRA
18			LEO	VIRGO	TAURUS	AQUARIUS	CANCER	LIBRA	SAGITTARIUS	LIBRA
19	4:10 AM	TAURUS	LEO	VIRGO	TAURUS	AQUARIUS	CANCER	LIBRA	SAGITTARIUS	LIBRA
20			LEO	LIBRA	TAURUS	AQUARIUS	CANCER	LIBRA	SAGITTARIUS	LIBRA
21	8:41 AM	GEMINI	LEO	LIBRA	TAURUS	AQUARIUS	CANCER	LIBRA	SAGITTARIUS	LIBRA
22			LEO	LIBRA	TAURUS	AQUARIUS	CANCER	LIBRA	SAGITTARIUS	LIBRA
23	11:20 AM	CANCER	LEO	LIBRA	TAURUS	AQUARIUS	CANCER	LIBRA	SAGITTARIUS	LIBRA

1974   LEO

	MOON FROM	IN	MERCURY	VENUS	MARS	JUPITER	SATURN	URANUS	NEPTUNE	PLUTO
JULY										
24			CANCER	CANCER	LEO	PISCES	CANCER	LIBRA	SAGITTARIUS	LIBRA
25	6:01 PM	SCORPIO	CANCER	CANCER	LEO	PISCES	CANCER	LIBRA	SAGITTARIUS	LIBRA
26			CANCER	CANCER	LEO	PISCES	CANCER	LIBRA	SAGITTARIUS	LIBRA
27			CANCER	CANCER	LEO	PISCES	CANCER	LIBRA	SAGITTARIUS	LIBRA
28	2:02 AM	SAGITTARIUS	CANCER	CANCER	VIRGO	PISCES	CANCER	LIBRA	SAGITTARIUS	LIBRA
29			CANCER	CANCER	VIRGO	PISCES	CANCER	LIBRA	SAGITTARIUS	LIBRA
30	1:25 PM	CAPRICORN	CANCER	CANCER	VIRGO	PISCES	CANCER	LIBRA	SAGITTARIUS	LIBRA
31			CANCER	CANCER	VIRGO	PISCES	CANCER	LIBRA	SAGITTARIUS	LIBRA
AUGUST										
1			CANCER	CANCER	VIRGO	PISCES	CANCER	LIBRA	SAGITTARIUS	LIBRA
2	1:33 AM	AQUARIUS	CANCER	CANCER	VIRGO	PISCES	CANCER	LIBRA	SAGITTARIUS	LIBRA
3			CANCER	CANCER	VIRGO	PISCES	CANCER	LIBRA	SAGITTARIUS	LIBRA
4	2:04 PM	PISCES	CANCER	CANCER	VIRGO	PISCES	CANCER	LIBRA	SAGITTARIUS	LIBRA
5			CANCER	CANCER	VIRGO	PISCES	CANCER	LIBRA	SAGITTARIUS	LIBRA
6			LEO	CANCER	VIRGO	PISCES	CANCER	LIBRA	SAGITTARIUS	LIBRA
7	2:11 AM	ARIES	LEO	CANCER	VIRGO	PISCES	CANCER	LIBRA	SAGITTARIUS	LIBRA
8			LEO	CANCER	VIRGO	PISCES	CANCER	LIBRA	SAGITTARIUS	LIBRA
9	12:27 PM	TAURUS	LEO	CANCER	VIRGO	PISCES	CANCER	LIBRA	SAGITTARIUS	LIBRA
10			LEO	CANCER	VIRGO	PISCES	CANCER	LIBRA	SAGITTARIUS	LIBRA
11	7:14 PM	GEMINI	LEO	CANCER	VIRGO	PISCES	CANCER	LIBRA	SAGITTARIUS	LIBRA
12			LEO	CANCER	VIRGO	PISCES	CANCER	LIBRA	SAGITTARIUS	LIBRA
13	10:37 PM	CANCER	LEO	CANCER	VIRGO	PISCES	CANCER	LIBRA	SAGITTARIUS	LIBRA
14			LEO	CANCER	VIRGO	PISCES	CANCER	LIBRA	SAGITTARIUS	LIBRA
15	11:20 PM	LEO	LEO	LEO	VIRGO	PISCES	CANCER	LIBRA	SAGITTARIUS	LIBRA
16			LEO	LEO	VIRGO	PISCES	CANCER	LIBRA	SAGITTARIUS	LIBRA
17	10:46 PM	VIRGO	LEO	LEO	VIRGO	PISCES	CANCER	LIBRA	SAGITTARIUS	LIBRA
18			LEO	LEO	VIRGO	PISCES	CANCER	LIBRA	SAGITTARIUS	LIBRA
19	11:07 PM	LIBRA	LEO	LEO	VIRGO	PISCES	CANCER	LIBRA	SAGITTARIUS	LIBRA
20			LEO	LEO	VIRGO	PISCES	CANCER	LIBRA	SAGITTARIUS	LIBRA
21			VIRGO	LEO	VIRGO	PISCES	CANCER	LIBRA	SAGITTARIUS	LIBRA
22	1:51 AM	SCORPIO	VIRGO	LEO	VIRGO	PISCES	CANCER	LIBRA	SAGITTARIUS	LIBRA
23			VIRGO	LEO	VIRGO	PISCES	CANCER	LIBRA	SAGITTARIUS	LIBRA

1975

	MOON FROM	IN	MERCURY	VENUS	MARS	JUPITER	SATURN	URANUS	NEPTUNE	PLUTO
JULY										
24			CANCER	VIRGO	TAURUS	ARIES	CANCER	LIBRA	SAGITTARIUS	LIBRA
25	12:12 PM	PISCES	CANCER	VIRGO	TAURUS	ARIES	CANCER	LIBRA	SAGITTARIUS	LIBRA
26			CANCER	VIRGO	TAURUS	ARIES	CANCER	LIBRA	SAGITTARIUS	LIBRA
27			CANCER	VIRGO	TAURUS	ARIES	CANCER	LIBRA	SAGITTARIUS	LIBRA
28	0:51 AM	ARIES	CANCER	VIRGO	TAURUS	ARIES	CANCER	LIBRA	SAGITTARIUS	LIBRA
29			LEO	VIRGO	TAURUS	ARIES	CANCER	LIBRA	SAGITTARIUS	LIBRA
30	1:19 PM	TAURUS	LEO	VIRGO	TAURUS	ARIES	CANCER	LIBRA	SAGITTARIUS	LIBRA
31			LEO	VIRGO	TAURUS	ARIES	CANCER	LIBRA	SAGITTARIUS	LIBRA
AUGUST										
1	11:00 PM	GEMINI	LEO	VIRGO	TAURUS	ARIES	CANCER	LIBRA	SAGITTARIUS	LIBRA
2			LEO	VIRGO	TAURUS	ARIES	CANCER	LIBRA	SAGITTARIUS	LIBRA
3			LEO	VIRGO	TAURUS	ARIES	CANCER	LIBRA	SAGITTARIUS	LIBRA
4	5:15 AM	CANCER	LEO	VIRGO	TAURUS	ARIES	CANCER	LIBRA	SAGITTARIUS	LIBRA
5			LEO	VIRGO	TAURUS	ARIES	CANCER	LIBRA	SAGITTARIUS	LIBRA
6	7:40 AM	LEO	LEO	VIRGO	TAURUS	ARIES	CANCER	LIBRA	SAGITTARIUS	LIBRA
7			LEO	VIRGO	TAURUS	ARIES	CANCER	LIBRA	SAGITTARIUS	LIBRA
8	8:07 AM	VIRGO	LEO	VIRGO	TAURUS	ARIES	CANCER	LIBRA	SAGITTARIUS	LIBRA
9			LEO	VIRGO	TAURUS	ARIES	CANCER	LIBRA	SAGITTARIUS	LIBRA
10	8:10 AM	LIBRA	LEO	VIRGO	TAURUS	ARIES	CANCER	LIBRA	SAGITTARIUS	LIBRA
11			LEO	VIRGO	TAURUS	ARIES	CANCER	LIBRA	SAGITTARIUS	LIBRA
12	8:17 AM	SCORPIO	LEO	VIRGO	TAURUS	ARIES	CANCER	LIBRA	SAGITTARIUS	LIBRA
13			VIRGO	VIRGO	TAURUS	ARIES	CANCER	LIBRA	SAGITTARIUS	LIBRA
14	2:04 PM	SAGITTARIUS	VIRGO	VIRGO	TAURUS	ARIES	CANCER	LIBRA	SAGITTARIUS	LIBRA
15			VIRGO	VIRGO	GEMINI	ARIES	CANCER	LIBRA	SAGITTARIUS	LIBRA
16	9:29 PM	CAPRICORN	VIRGO	VIRGO	GEMINI	ARIES	CANCER	LIBRA	SAGITTARIUS	LIBRA
17			VIRGO	VIRGO	GEMINI	ARIES	CANCER	LIBRA	SAGITTARIUS	LIBRA
18			VIRGO	VIRGO	GEMINI	ARIES	CANCER	LIBRA	SAGITTARIUS	LIBRA
19	7:12 AM	AQUARIUS	VIRGO	VIRGO	GEMINI	ARIES	CANCER	LIBRA	SAGITTARIUS	LIBRA
20			VIRGO	VIRGO	GEMINI	ARIES	CANCER	LIBRA	SAGITTARIUS	LIBRA
21	6:30 PM	PISCES	VIRGO	VIRGO	GEMINI	ARIES	CANCER	LIBRA	SAGITTARIUS	LIBRA
22			VIRGO	VIRGO	GEMINI	ARIES	CANCER	LIBRA	SAGITTARIUS	LIBRA
23			VIRGO	VIRGO	GEMINI	ARIES	CANCER	LIBRA	SAGITTARIUS	LIBRA

	MOON FROM	IN	MERCURY	VENUS	MARS	JUPITER	SATURN	URANUS	NEPTUNE	PLUTO
JULY											
23			LEO	LEO	VIRGO	TAURUS	LEO	SCORPIO	SAGITTARIUS	LIBRA
24	6:49 AM	CANCER	LEO	LEO	VIRGO	TAURUS	LEO	SCORPIO	SAGITTARIUS	LIBRA
25			LEO	LEO	VIRGO	TAURUS	LEO	SCORPIO	SAGITTARIUS	LIBRA
26	1:23 PM	LEO	LEO	LEO	VIRGO	TAURUS	LEO	SCORPIO	SAGITTARIUS	LIBRA
27			LEO	LEO	VIRGO	TAURUS	LEO	SCORPIO	SAGITTARIUS	LIBRA
28	5:38 PM	VIRGO	LEO	LEO	VIRGO	TAURUS	LEO	SCORPIO	SAGITTARIUS	LIBRA
29			LEO	LEO	VIRGO	TAURUS	LEO	SCORPIO	SAGITTARIUS	LIBRA
30	8:36 PM	LIBRA	LEO	LEO	VIRGO	TAURUS	LEO	SCORPIO	SAGITTARIUS	LIBRA
31			LEO	LEO	VIRGO	TAURUS	LEO	SCORPIO	SAGITTARIUS	LIBRA
AUGUST											
1	10:57 PM	SCORPIO	LEO	LEO	VIRGO	TAURUS	LEO	SCORPIO	SAGITTARIUS	LIBRA
2			LEO	LEO	VIRGO	TAURUS	LEO	SCORPIO	SAGITTARIUS	LIBRA
3			LEO	LEO	VIRGO	TAURUS	LEO	SCORPIO	SAGITTARIUS	LIBRA
4	1:54 AM	SAGITTARIUS	VIRGO	LEO	VIRGO	TAURUS	LEO	SCORPIO	SAGITTARIUS	LIBRA
5			VIRGO	LEO	VIRGO	TAURUS	LEO	SCORPIO	SAGITTARIUS	LIBRA
6	5:38 AM	CAPRICORN	VIRGO	LEO	VIRGO	TAURUS	LEO	SCORPIO	SAGITTARIUS	LIBRA
7			VIRGO	LEO	VIRGO	TAURUS	LEO	SCORPIO	SAGITTARIUS	LIBRA
8	11:00 AM	AQUARIUS	VIRGO	LEO	VIRGO	TAURUS	LEO	SCORPIO	SAGITTARIUS	LIBRA
9			VIRGO	VIRGO	VIRGO	TAURUS	LEO	SCORPIO	SAGITTARIUS	LIBRA
10	6:19 PM	PISCES	VIRGO	VIRGO	VIRGO	TAURUS	LEO	SCORPIO	SAGITTARIUS	LIBRA
11			VIRGO	VIRGO	VIRGO	TAURUS	LEO	SCORPIO	SAGITTARIUS	LIBRA
12			VIRGO	VIRGO	VIRGO	TAURUS	LEO	SCORPIO	SAGITTARIUS	LIBRA
13	4:02 AM	ARIES	VIRGO	VIRGO	VIRGO	TAURUS	LEO	SCORPIO	SAGITTARIUS	LIBRA
14			VIRGO	VIRGO	VIRGO	TAURUS	LEO	SCORPIO	SAGITTARIUS	LIBRA
15	4:10 PM	TAURUS	VIRGO	VIRGO	VIRGO	TAURUS	LEO	SCORPIO	SAGITTARIUS	LIBRA
16			VIRGO	VIRGO	VIRGO	TAURUS	LEO	SCORPIO	SAGITTARIUS	LIBRA
17			VIRGO	VIRGO	VIRGO	TAURUS	LEO	SCORPIO	SAGITTARIUS	LIBRA
18	4:49 AM	GEMINI	VIRGO	VIRGO	VIRGO	TAURUS	LEO	SCORPIO	SAGITTARIUS	LIBRA
19			VIRGO	VIRGO	VIRGO	TAURUS	LEO	SCORPIO	SAGITTARIUS	LIBRA
20	3:46 PM	CANCER	VIRGO	VIRGO	VIRGO	TAURUS	LEO	SCORPIO	SAGITTARIUS	LIBRA
21			VIRGO	VIRGO	VIRGO	TAURUS	LEO	SCORPIO	SAGITTARIUS	LIBRA
22	10:39 PM	LEO	VIRGO	VIRGO	VIRGO	TAURUS	LEO	SCORPIO	SAGITTARIUS	LIBRA
23			VIRGO	VIRGO	VIRGO	TAURUS	LEO	SCORPIO	SAGITTARIUS	LIBRA

1977

	MOON FROM	IN	MERCURY	VENUS	MARS	JUPITER	SATURN	URANUS	NEPTUNE	PLUTO
JULY											
23	1:18 PM	SCORPIO	LEO	GEMINI	GEMINI	GEMINI	LEO	SCORPIO	SAGITTARIUS	LIBRA
24			LEO	GEMINI	GEMINI	GEMINI	LEO	SCORPIO	SAGITTARIUS	LIBRA
25	4:07 PM	SAGITTARIUS	LEO	GEMINI	GEMINI	GEMINI	LEO	SCORPIO	SAGITTARIUS	LIBRA
26			LEO	GEMINI	GEMINI	GEMINI	LEO	SCORPIO	SAGITTARIUS	LIBRA
27	5:17 PM	CAPRICORN	LEO	GEMINI	GEMINI	GEMINI	LEO	SCORPIO	SAGITTARIUS	LIBRA
28			LEO	GEMINI	GEMINI	GEMINI	LEO	SCORPIO	SAGITTARIUS	LIBRA
29	6:36 PM	AQUARIUS	VIRGO	GEMINI	GEMINI	GEMINI	LEO	SCORPIO	SAGITTARIUS	LIBRA
30			VIRGO	GEMINI	GEMINI	GEMINI	LEO	SCORPIO	SAGITTARIUS	LIBRA
31	8:53 PM	PISCES	VIRGO	GEMINI	GEMINI	GEMINI	LEO	SCORPIO	SAGITTARIUS	LIBRA
AUGUST											
1			VIRGO	GEMINI	GEMINI	GEMINI	LEO	SCORPIO	SAGITTARIUS	LIBRA
2			VIRGO	GEMINI	GEMINI	GEMINI	LEO	SCORPIO	SAGITTARIUS	LIBRA
3	2:04 AM	ARIES	VIRGO	CANCER	GEMINI	GEMINI	LEO	SCORPIO	SAGITTARIUS	LIBRA
4			VIRGO	CANCER	GEMINI	GEMINI	LEO	SCORPIO	SAGITTARIUS	LIBRA
5	11:21 AM	TAURUS	VIRGO	CANCER	GEMINI	GEMINI	LEO	SCORPIO	SAGITTARIUS	LIBRA
6			VIRGO	CANCER	GEMINI	GEMINI	LEO	SCORPIO	SAGITTARIUS	LIBRA
7	11:32 PM	GEMINI	VIRGO	CANCER	GEMINI	GEMINI	LEO	SCORPIO	SAGITTARIUS	LIBRA
8			VIRGO	CANCER	GEMINI	GEMINI	LEO	SCORPIO	SAGITTARIUS	LIBRA
9			VIRGO	CANCER	GEMINI	GEMINI	LEO	SCORPIO	SAGITTARIUS	LIBRA
10	12:15 PM	CANCER	VIRGO	CANCER	GEMINI	GEMINI	LEO	SCORPIO	SAGITTARIUS	LIBRA
11			VIRGO	CANCER	GEMINI	GEMINI	LEO	SCORPIO	SAGITTARIUS	LIBRA
12	11:15 PM	LEO	VIRGO	CANCER	GEMINI	GEMINI	LEO	SCORPIO	SAGITTARIUS	LIBRA
13			VIRGO	CANCER	GEMINI	GEMINI	LEO	SCORPIO	SAGITTARIUS	LIBRA
14			VIRGO	CANCER	GEMINI	GEMINI	LEO	SCORPIO	SAGITTARIUS	LIBRA
15	7:44 AM	VIRGO	VIRGO	CANCER	GEMINI	GEMINI	LEO	SCORPIO	SAGITTARIUS	LIBRA
16			VIRGO	CANCER	GEMINI	GEMINI	LEO	SCORPIO	SAGITTARIUS	LIBRA
17	1:38 PM	LIBRA	VIRGO	CANCER	GEMINI	GEMINI	LEO	SCORPIO	SAGITTARIUS	LIBRA
18			VIRGO	CANCER	GEMINI	GEMINI	LEO	SCORPIO	SAGITTARIUS	LIBRA
19	6:25 PM	SCORPIO	VIRGO	CANCER	GEMINI	GEMINI	LEO	SCORPIO	SAGITTARIUS	LIBRA
20			VIRGO	CANCER	GEMINI	GEMINI	LEO	SCORPIO	SAGITTARIUS	LIBRA
21	9:46 PM	SAGITTARIUS	VIRGO	CANCER	GEMINI	CANCER	LEO	SCORPIO	SAGITTARIUS	LIBRA
22			VIRGO	CANCER	GEMINI	CANCER	LEO	SCORPIO	SAGITTARIUS	LIBRA
23			VIRGO	CANCER	GEMINI	CANCER	LEO	SCORPIO	SAGITTARIUS	LIBRA

	MOON FROM IN	MERCURY	VENUS	MARS	JUPITER	SATURN	URANUS	NEPTUNE	PLUTO
JULY									
24	5:14 AM ARIES	LEO	VIRGO	VIRGO	CANCER	LEO	SCORPIO	SAGITTARIUS	LIBRA
25		LEO	VIRGO	VIRGO	CANCER	LEO	SCORPIO	SAGITTARIUS	LIBRA
26	10:48 AM TAURUS	LEO	VIRGO	VIRGO	CANCER	LEO	SCORPIO	SAGITTARIUS	LIBRA
27		LEO	VIRGO	VIRGO	CANCER	VIRGO	SCORPIO	SAGITTARIUS	LIBRA
28	8:42 PM GEMINI	VIRGO	VIRGO	VIRGO	CANCER	VIRGO	SCORPIO	SAGITTARIUS	LIBRA
29		VIRGO	VIRGO	VIRGO	CANCER	VIRGO	SCORPIO	SAGITTARIUS	LIBRA
30		VIRGO	VIRGO	VIRGO	CANCER	VIRGO	SCORPIO	SAGITTARIUS	LIBRA
31	8:49 AM CANCER	VIRGO	VIRGO	VIRGO	CANCER	VIRGO	SCORPIO	SAGITTARIUS	LIBRA
AUGUST									
1		VIRGO	VIRGO	VIRGO	CANCER	VIRGO	SCORPIO	SAGITTARIUS	LIBRA
2	9:21 PM LEO	VIRGO	VIRGO	VIRGO	CANCER	VIRGO	SCORPIO	SAGITTARIUS	LIBRA
3		VIRGO	VIRGO	VIRGO	CANCER	VIRGO	SCORPIO	SAGITTARIUS	LIBRA
4		VIRGO	VIRGO	VIRGO	CANCER	VIRGO	SCORPIO	SAGITTARIUS	LIBRA
5	9:13 AM VIRGO	VIRGO	VIRGO	LIBRA	CANCER	VIRGO	SCORPIO	SAGITTARIUS	LIBRA
6		VIRGO	VIRGO	LIBRA	CANCER	VIRGO	SCORPIO	SAGITTARIUS	LIBRA
7	8:15 PM LIBRA	VIRGO	VIRGO	LIBRA	CANCER	VIRGO	SCORPIO	SAGITTARIUS	LIBRA
8		VIRGO	VIRGO	LIBRA	CANCER	VIRGO	SCORPIO	SAGITTARIUS	LIBRA
9		VIRGO	LIBRA	LIBRA	CANCER	VIRGO	SCORPIO	SAGITTARIUS	LIBRA
10	4:57 AM SCORPIO	VIRGO	LIBRA	LIBRA	CANCER	VIRGO	SCORPIO	SAGITTARIUS	LIBRA
11		VIRGO	LIBRA	LIBRA	CANCER	VIRGO	SCORPIO	SAGITTARIUS	LIBRA
12	10:37 AM SAGITTARIUS	VIRGO	LIBRA	LIBRA	CANCER	VIRGO	SCORPIO	SAGITTARIUS	LIBRA
13		VIRGO	LIBRA	LIBRA	CANCER	VIRGO	SCORPIO	SAGITTARIUS	LIBRA
14	1:08 PM CAPRICORN	LEO	LIBRA	LIBRA	CANCER	VIRGO	SCORPIO	SAGITTARIUS	LIBRA
15		LEO	LIBRA	LIBRA	CANCER	VIRGO	SCORPIO	SAGITTARIUS	LIBRA
16	1:32 PM AQUARIUS	LEO	LIBRA	LIBRA	CANCER	VIRGO	SCORPIO	SAGITTARIUS	LIBRA
17		LEO	LIBRA	LIBRA	CANCER	VIRGO	SCORPIO	SAGITTARIUS	LIBRA
18	1:37 PM PISCES	LEO	LIBRA	LIBRA	CANCER	VIRGO	SCORPIO	SAGITTARIUS	LIBRA
19		LEO	LIBRA	LIBRA	CANCER	VIRGO	SCORPIO	SAGITTARIUS	LIBRA
20	2:54 PM ARIES	LEO	LIBRA	LIBRA	CANCER	VIRGO	SCORPIO	SAGITTARIUS	LIBRA
21		LEO	LIBRA	LIBRA	CANCER	VIRGO	SCORPIO	SAGITTARIUS	LIBRA
22	7:11 PM TAURUS	LEO	LIBRA	LIBRA	CANCER	VIRGO	SCORPIO	SAGITTARIUS	LIBRA
23		LEO	LIBRA	LIBRA	CANCER	VIRGO	SCORPIO	SAGITTARIUS	LIBRA

1979

	MOON FROM IN	MERCURY	VENUS	MARS	JUPITER	SATURN	URANUS	NEPTUNE	PLUTO
JULY									
24		LEO	CANCER	GEMINI	LEO	VIRGO	SCORPIO	SAGITTARIUS	LIBRA
25		LEO	CANCER	GEMINI	LEO	VIRGO	SCORPIO	SAGITTARIUS	LIBRA
26	8:01 AM VIRGO	LEO	CANCER	GEMINI	LEO	VIRGO	SCORPIO	SAGITTARIUS	LIBRA
27		LEO	CANCER	GEMINI	LEO	VIRGO	SCORPIO	SAGITTARIUS	LIBRA
28	8:56 PM LIBRA	LEO	CANCER	GEMINI	LEO	VIRGO	SCORPIO	SAGITTARIUS	LIBRA
29		LEO	CANCER	GEMINI	LEO	VIRGO	SCORPIO	SAGITTARIUS	LIBRA
30		LEO	CANCER	GEMINI	LEO	VIRGO	SCORPIO	SAGITTARIUS	LIBRA
31	8:44 AM SCORPIO	LEO	LEO	GEMINI	LEO	VIRGO	SCORPIO	SAGITTARIUS	LIBRA
AUGUST									
1		LEO	LEO	GEMINI	LEO	VIRGO	SCORPIO	SAGITTARIUS	LIBRA
2	5:01 PM SAGITTARIUS	LEO	LEO	GEMINI	LEO	VIRGO	SCORPIO	SAGITTARIUS	LIBRA
3		LEO	LEO	GEMINI	LEO	VIRGO	SCORPIO	SAGITTARIUS	LIBRA
4	9:16 PM CAPRICORN	LEO	LEO	GEMINI	LEO	VIRGO	SCORPIO	SAGITTARIUS	LIBRA
5		LEO	LEO	GEMINI	LEO	VIRGO	SCORPIO	SAGITTARIUS	LIBRA
6	10:38 PM AQUARIUS	LEO	LEO	GEMINI	LEO	VIRGO	SCORPIO	SAGITTARIUS	LIBRA
7		LEO	LEO	GEMINI	LEO	VIRGO	SCORPIO	SAGITTARIUS	LIBRA
8	10:17 PM PISCES	LEO	LEO	GEMINI	LEO	VIRGO	SCORPIO	SAGITTARIUS	LIBRA
9		LEO	LEO	CANCER	LEO	VIRGO	SCORPIO	SAGITTARIUS	LIBRA
10	10:21 PM ARIES	LEO	LEO	CANCER	LEO	VIRGO	SCORPIO	SAGITTARIUS	LIBRA
11		LEO	LEO	CANCER	LEO	VIRGO	SCORPIO	SAGITTARIUS	LIBRA
12		LEO	LEO	CANCER	LEO	VIRGO	SCORPIO	SAGITTARIUS	LIBRA
13	0:16 AM TAURUS	LEO	LEO	CANCER	LEO	VIRGO	SCORPIO	SAGITTARIUS	LIBRA
14		LEO	LEO	CANCER	LEO	VIRGO	SCORPIO	SAGITTARIUS	LIBRA
15	5:33 AM GEMINI	LEO	LEO	CANCER	LEO	VIRGO	SCORPIO	SAGITTARIUS	LIBRA
16		LEO	LEO	CANCER	LEO	VIRGO	SCORPIO	SAGITTARIUS	LIBRA
17	2:28 PM CANCER	LEO	LEO	CANCER	LEO	VIRGO	SCORPIO	SAGITTARIUS	LIBRA
18		LEO	LEO	CANCER	LEO	VIRGO	SCORPIO	SAGITTARIUS	LIBRA
19		LEO	LEO	CANCER	LEO	VIRGO	SCORPIO	SAGITTARIUS	LIBRA
20	1:51 AM LEO	LEO	LEO	CANCER	LEO	VIRGO	SCORPIO	SAGITTARIUS	LIBRA
21		LEO	LEO	CANCER	LEO	VIRGO	SCORPIO	SAGITTARIUS	LIBRA
22	2:13 PM VIRGO	LEO	LEO	CANCER	LEO	VIRGO	SCORPIO	SAGITTARIUS	LIBRA
23		LEO	LEO	CANCER	LEO	VIRGO	SCORPIO	SAGITTARIUS	LIBRA

	MOON FROM	IN	MERCURY	VENUS	MARS	JUPITER	SATURN	URANUS	NEPTUNE	PLUTO
JULY										
23			CANCER	GEMINI	LIBRA	VIRGO	VIRGO	SCORPIO	SAGITTARIUS	LIBRA
24			CANCER	GEMINI	LIBRA	VIRGO	VIRGO	SCORPIO	SAGITTARIUS	LIBRA
25	1:12 AM	CAPRICORN	CANCER	GEMINI	LIBRA	VIRGO	VIRGO	SCORPIO	SAGITTARIUS	LIBRA
26			CANCER	GEMINI	LIBRA	VIRGO	VIRGO	SCORPIO	SAGITTARIUS	LIBRA
27	5:38 AM	AQUARIUS	CANCER	GEMINI	LIBRA	VIRGO	VIRGO	SCORPIO	SAGITTARIUS	LIBRA
28			CANCER	GEMINI	LIBRA	VIRGO	VIRGO	SCORPIO	SAGITTARIUS	LIBRA
29	8:29 AM	PISCES	CANCER	GEMINI	LIBRA	VIRGO	VIRGO	SCORPIO	SAGITTARIUS	LIBRA
30			CANCER	GEMINI	LIBRA	VIRGO	VIRGO	SCORPIO	SAGITTARIUS	LIBRA
31	9:49 AM	ARIES	CANCER	GEMINI	LIBRA	VIRGO	VIRGO	SCORPIO	SAGITTARIUS	LIBRA
AUGUST										
1			CANCER	GEMINI	LIBRA	VIRGO	VIRGO	SCORPIO	SAGITTARIUS	LIBRA
2	11:53 AM	TAURUS	CANCER	GEMINI	LIBRA	VIRGO	VIRGO	SCORPIO	SAGITTARIUS	LIBRA
3			CANCER	GEMINI	LIBRA	VIRGO	VIRGO	SCORPIO	SAGITTARIUS	LIBRA
4	3:21 PM	GEMINI	CANCER	GEMINI	LIBRA	VIRGO	VIRGO	SCORPIO	SAGITTARIUS	LIBRA
5			CANCER	GEMINI	LIBRA	VIRGO	VIRGO	SCORPIO	SAGITTARIUS	LIBRA
6	8:32 PM	CANCER	CANCER	GEMINI	LIBRA	VIRGO	VIRGO	SCORPIO	SAGITTARIUS	LIBRA
7			CANCER	CANCER	LIBRA	VIRGO	VIRGO	SCORPIO	SAGITTARIUS	LIBRA
8			CANCER	CANCER	LIBRA	VIRGO	VIRGO	SCORPIO	SAGITTARIUS	LIBRA
9	3:51 AM	LEO	CANCER	CANCER	LIBRA	VIRGO	VIRGO	SCORPIO	SAGITTARIUS	LIBRA
10			LEO	CANCER	LIBRA	VIRGO	VIRGO	SCORPIO	SAGITTARIUS	LIBRA
11	1:07 PM	VIRGO	LEO	CANCER	LIBRA	VIRGO	VIRGO	SCORPIO	SAGITTARIUS	LIBRA
12			LEO	CANCER	LIBRA	VIRGO	VIRGO	SCORPIO	SAGITTARIUS	LIBRA
13			LEO	CANCER	LIBRA	VIRGO	VIRGO	SCORPIO	SAGITTARIUS	LIBRA
14	0:12 AM	LIBRA	LEO	CANCER	LIBRA	VIRGO	VIRGO	SCORPIO	SAGITTARIUS	LIBRA
15			LEO	CANCER	LIBRA	VIRGO	VIRGO	SCORPIO	SAGITTARIUS	LIBRA
16	1:04 PM	SCORPIO	LEO	CANCER	LIBRA	VIRGO	VIRGO	SCORPIO	SAGITTARIUS	LIBRA
17			LEO	CANCER	LIBRA	VIRGO	VIRGO	SCORPIO	SAGITTARIUS	LIBRA
18			LEO	CANCER	LIBRA	VIRGO	VIRGO	SCORPIO	SAGITTARIUS	LIBRA
19	1:26 AM	SAGITTARIUS	LEO	CANCER	LIBRA	VIRGO	VIRGO	SCORPIO	SAGITTARIUS	LIBRA
20			LEO	CANCER	LIBRA	VIRGO	VIRGO	SCORPIO	SAGITTARIUS	LIBRA
21	10:40 AM	CAPRICORN	LEO	CANCER	LIBRA	VIRGO	VIRGO	SCORPIO	SAGITTARIUS	LIBRA
22			LEO	CANCER	LIBRA	VIRGO	VIRGO	SCORPIO	SAGITTARIUS	LIBRA
23	3:38 PM	AQUARIUS	LEO	CANCER	LIBRA	VIRGO	VIRGO	SCORPIO	SAGITTARIUS	LIBRA

1981

	MOON FROM	IN	MERCURY	VENUS	MARS	JUPITER	SATURN	URANUS	NEPTUNE	PLUTO
JULY										
23			CANCER	LEO	CANCER	LIBRA	LIBRA	SCORPIO	SAGITTARIUS	LIBRA
24	2:41 AM	TAURUS	CANCER	LEO	CANCER	LIBRA	LIBRA	SCORPIO	SAGITTARIUS	LIBRA
25			CANCER	VIRGO	CANCER	LIBRA	LIBRA	SCORPIO	SAGITTARIUS	LIBRA
26	5:19 AM	GEMINI	CANCER	VIRGO	CANCER	LIBRA	LIBRA	SCORPIO	SAGITTARIUS	LIBRA
27			CANCER	VIRGO	CANCER	LIBRA	LIBRA	SCORPIO	SAGITTARIUS	LIBRA
28	7:30 AM	CANCER	CANCER	VIRGO	CANCER	LIBRA	LIBRA	SCORPIO	SAGITTARIUS	LIBRA
29			CANCER	VIRGO	CANCER	LIBRA	LIBRA	SCORPIO	SAGITTARIUS	LIBRA
30	9:54 AM	LEO	CANCER	VIRGO	CANCER	LIBRA	LIBRA	SCORPIO	SAGITTARIUS	LIBRA
31			CANCER	VIRGO	CANCER	LIBRA	LIBRA	SCORPIO	SAGITTARIUS	LIBRA
AUGUST										
1	1:55 PM	VIRGO	CANCER	VIRGO	CANCER	LIBRA	LIBRA	SCORPIO	SAGITTARIUS	LIBRA
2			LEO	VIRGO	CANCER	LIBRA	LIBRA	SCORPIO	SAGITTARIUS	LIBRA
3	8:59 PM	LIBRA	LEO	VIRGO	CANCER	LIBRA	LIBRA	SCORPIO	SAGITTARIUS	LIBRA
4			LEO	VIRGO	CANCER	LIBRA	LIBRA	SCORPIO	SAGITTARIUS	LIBRA
5			LEO	VIRGO	CANCER	LIBRA	LIBRA	SCORPIO	SAGITTARIUS	LIBRA
6	7:37 AM	SCORPIO	LEO	VIRGO	CANCER	LIBRA	LIBRA	SCORPIO	SAGITTARIUS	LIBRA
7			LEO	VIRGO	CANCER	LIBRA	LIBRA	SCORPIO	SAGITTARIUS	LIBRA
8	8:38 PM	SAGITTARIUS	LEO	VIRGO	CANCER	LIBRA	LIBRA	SCORPIO	SAGITTARIUS	LIBRA
9			LEO	VIRGO	CANCER	LIBRA	LIBRA	SCORPIO	SAGITTARIUS	LIBRA
10			LEO	VIRGO	CANCER	LIBRA	LIBRA	SCORPIO	SAGITTARIUS	LIBRA
11	8:34 AM	CAPRICORN	LEO	VIRGO	CANCER	LIBRA	LIBRA	SCORPIO	SAGITTARIUS	LIBRA
12			LEO	VIRGO	CANCER	LIBRA	LIBRA	SCORPIO	SAGITTARIUS	LIBRA
13	5:48 PM	AQUARIUS	LEO	VIRGO	CANCER	LIBRA	LIBRA	SCORPIO	SAGITTARIUS	LIBRA
14			LEO	VIRGO	CANCER	LIBRA	LIBRA	SCORPIO	SAGITTARIUS	LIBRA
15			LEO	VIRGO	CANCER	LIBRA	LIBRA	SCORPIO	SAGITTARIUS	LIBRA
16	0:28 AM	PISCES	LEO	VIRGO	CANCER	LIBRA	LIBRA	SCORPIO	SAGITTARIUS	LIBRA
17			VIRGO	VIRGO	CANCER	LIBRA	LIBRA	SCORPIO	SAGITTARIUS	LIBRA
18	4:31 AM	ARIES	VIRGO	VIRGO	CANCER	LIBRA	LIBRA	SCORPIO	SAGITTARIUS	LIBRA
19			VIRGO	LIBRA	CANCER	LIBRA	LIBRA	SCORPIO	SAGITTARIUS	LIBRA
20	7:51 AM	TAURUS	VIRGO	LIBRA	CANCER	LIBRA	LIBRA	SCORPIO	SAGITTARIUS	LIBRA
21			VIRGO	LIBRA	CANCER	LIBRA	LIBRA	SCORPIO	SAGITTARIUS	LIBRA
22	10:35 PM	GEMINI	VIRGO	LIBRA	CANCER	LIBRA	LIBRA	SCORPIO	SAGITTARIUS	LIBRA
23			VIRGO	LIBRA	CANCER	LIBRA	LIBRA	SCORPIO	SAGITTARIUS	LIBRA

1982   LEO

	MOON FROM IN	MERCURY	VENUS	MARS	JUPITER	SATURN	URANUS	NEPTUNE	PLUTO
JULY									
24	9:53 PM LIBRA	CANCER	CANCER	LIBRA	SCORPIO	LIBRA	SAGITTARIUS	SAGITTARIUS	LIBRA
25		LEO	CANCER	LIBRA	SCORPIO	LIBRA	SAGITTARIUS	SAGITTARIUS	LIBRA
26		LEO	CANCER	LIBRA	SCORPIO	LIBRA	SAGITTARIUS	SAGITTARIUS	LIBRA
27	4:57 AM SCORPIO	LEO	CANCER	LIBRA	SCORPIO	LIBRA	SAGITTARIUS	SAGITTARIUS	LIBRA
28		LEO	CANCER	LIBRA	SCORPIO	LIBRA	SAGITTARIUS	SAGITTARIUS	LIBRA
29	4:13 PM SAGITTARIUS	LEO	CANCER	LIBRA	SCORPIO	LIBRA	SAGITTARIUS	SAGITTARIUS	LIBRA
30		LEO	CANCER	LIBRA	SCORPIO	LIBRA	SAGITTARIUS	SAGITTARIUS	LIBRA
31		LEO	CANCER	LIBRA	SCORPIO	LIBRA	SAGITTARIUS	SAGITTARIUS	LIBRA
AUGUST									
1	4:49 PM CAPRICORN	LEO	CANCER	LIBRA	SCORPIO	LIBRA	SAGITTARIUS	SAGITTARIUS	LIBRA
2		LEO	CANCER	LIBRA	SCORPIO	LIBRA	SAGITTARIUS	SAGITTARIUS	LIBRA
3	5:15 PM AQUARIUS	LEO	CANCER	LIBRA	SCORPIO	LIBRA	SAGITTARIUS	SAGITTARIUS	LIBRA
4		LEO	CANCER	SCORPIO	SCORPIO	LIBRA	SAGITTARIUS	SAGITTARIUS	LIBRA
5		LEO	CANCER	SCORPIO	SCORPIO	LIBRA	SAGITTARIUS	SAGITTARIUS	LIBRA
6	3:53 AM PISCES	LEO	CANCER	SCORPIO	SCORPIO	LIBRA	SAGITTARIUS	SAGITTARIUS	LIBRA
7		LEO	CANCER	SCORPIO	SCORPIO	LIBRA	SAGITTARIUS	SAGITTARIUS	LIBRA
8	1:12 PM ARIES	LEO	CANCER	SCORPIO	SCORPIO	LIBRA	SAGITTARIUS	SAGITTARIUS	LIBRA
9		VIRGO	CANCER	SCORPIO	SCORPIO	LIBRA	SAGITTARIUS	SAGITTARIUS	LIBRA
10	8:06 PM TAURUS	VIRGO	CANCER	SCORPIO	SCORPIO	LIBRA	SAGITTARIUS	SAGITTARIUS	LIBRA
11		VIRGO	CANCER	SCORPIO	SCORPIO	LIBRA	SAGITTARIUS	SAGITTARIUS	LIBRA
12		VIRGO	CANCER	SCORPIO	SCORPIO	LIBRA	SAGITTARIUS	SAGITTARIUS	LIBRA
13	0:39 AM GEMINI	VIRGO	CANCER	SCORPIO	SCORPIO	LIBRA	SAGITTARIUS	SAGITTARIUS	LIBRA
14		VIRGO	CANCER	SCORPIO	SCORPIO	LIBRA	SAGITTARIUS	SAGITTARIUS	LIBRA
15	3:02 AM CANCER	VIRGO	LEO	SCORPIO	SCORPIO	LIBRA	SAGITTARIUS	SAGITTARIUS	LIBRA
16		VIRGO	LEO	SCORPIO	SCORPIO	LIBRA	SAGITTARIUS	SAGITTARIUS	LIBRA
17	3:58 AM LEO	VIRGO	LEO	SCORPIO	SCORPIO	LIBRA	SAGITTARIUS	SAGITTARIUS	LIBRA
18		VIRGO	LEO	SCORPIO	SCORPIO	LIBRA	SAGITTARIUS	SAGITTARIUS	LIBRA
19	4:34 AM VIRGO	VIRGO	LEO	SCORPIO	SCORPIO	LIBRA	SAGITTARIUS	SAGITTARIUS	LIBRA
20		VIRGO	LEO	SCORPIO	SCORPIO	LIBRA	SAGITTARIUS	SAGITTARIUS	LIBRA
21	7:21 AM LIBRA	VIRGO	LEO	SCORPIO	SCORPIO	LIBRA	SAGITTARIUS	SAGITTARIUS	LIBRA
22		VIRGO	LEO	SCORPIO	SCORPIO	LIBRA	SAGITTARIUS	SAGITTARIUS	LIBRA
23	1:25 PM SCORPIO	VIRGO	LEO	SCORPIO	SCORPIO	LIBRA	SAGITTARIUS	SAGITTARIUS	LIBRA

1983

	MOON FROM IN	MERCURY	VENUS	MARS	JUPITER	SATURN	URANUS	NEPTUNE	PLUTO
JULY									
24	3:37 PM AQUARIUS	LEO	VIRGO	CANCER	SAGITTARIUS	LIBRA	SAGITTARIUS	SAGITTARIUS	LIBRA
25		LEO	VIRGO	CANCER	SAGITTARIUS	LIBRA	SAGITTARIUS	SAGITTARIUS	LIBRA
26		LEO	VIRGO	CANCER	SAGITTARIUS	LIBRA	SAGITTARIUS	SAGITTARIUS	LIBRA
27	4:34 AM PISCES	LEO	VIRGO	CANCER	SAGITTARIUS	LIBRA	SAGITTARIUS	SAGITTARIUS	LIBRA
28		LEO	VIRGO	CANCER	SAGITTARIUS	LIBRA	SAGITTARIUS	SAGITTARIUS	LIBRA
29	4:46 PM ARIES	LEO	VIRGO	CANCER	SAGITTARIUS	LIBRA	SAGITTARIUS	SAGITTARIUS	LIBRA
30		LEO	VIRGO	CANCER	SAGITTARIUS	LIBRA	SAGITTARIUS	SAGITTARIUS	LIBRA
31		LEO	VIRGO	CANCER	SAGITTARIUS	LIBRA	SAGITTARIUS	SAGITTARIUS	LIBRA
AUGUST									
1	2:41 AM TAURUS	LEO	VIRGO	CANCER	SAGITTARIUS	LIBRA	SAGITTARIUS	SAGITTARIUS	LIBRA
2		VIRGO	VIRGO	CANCER	SAGITTARIUS	LIBRA	SAGITTARIUS	SAGITTARIUS	LIBRA
3	9:56 AM GEMINI	VIRGO	VIRGO	CANCER	SAGITTARIUS	LIBRA	SAGITTARIUS	SAGITTARIUS	LIBRA
4		VIRGO	VIRGO	CANCER	SAGITTARIUS	LIBRA	SAGITTARIUS	SAGITTARIUS	LIBRA
5	1:03 PM CANCER	VIRGO	VIRGO	CANCER	SAGITTARIUS	LIBRA	SAGITTARIUS	SAGITTARIUS	LIBRA
6		VIRGO	VIRGO	CANCER	SAGITTARIUS	LIBRA	SAGITTARIUS	SAGITTARIUS	LIBRA
7	1:29 PM LEO	VIRGO	VIRGO	CANCER	SAGITTARIUS	LIBRA	SAGITTARIUS	SAGITTARIUS	LIBRA
8		VIRGO	VIRGO	CANCER	SAGITTARIUS	LIBRA	SAGITTARIUS	SAGITTARIUS	LIBRA
9	12:45 PM VIRGO	VIRGO	VIRGO	CANCER	SAGITTARIUS	LIBRA	SAGITTARIUS	SAGITTARIUS	LIBRA
10		VIRGO	VIRGO	CANCER	SAGITTARIUS	LIBRA	SAGITTARIUS	SAGITTARIUS	LIBRA
11	1:08 PM LIBRA	VIRGO	VIRGO	CANCER	SAGITTARIUS	LIBRA	SAGITTARIUS	SAGITTARIUS	LIBRA
12		VIRGO	VIRGO	CANCER	SAGITTARIUS	LIBRA	SAGITTARIUS	SAGITTARIUS	LIBRA
13	3:56 PM SCORPIO	VIRGO	VIRGO	CANCER	SAGITTARIUS	LIBRA	SAGITTARIUS	SAGITTARIUS	LIBRA
14		VIRGO	VIRGO	LEO	SAGITTARIUS	LIBRA	SAGITTARIUS	SAGITTARIUS	LIBRA
15	10:49 PM SAGITTARIUS	VIRGO	VIRGO	LEO	SAGITTARIUS	LIBRA	SAGITTARIUS	SAGITTARIUS	LIBRA
16		VIRGO	VIRGO	LEO	SAGITTARIUS	LIBRA	SAGITTARIUS	SAGITTARIUS	LIBRA
17		VIRGO	VIRGO	LEO	SAGITTARIUS	LIBRA	SAGITTARIUS	SAGITTARIUS	LIBRA
18	9:00 AM CAPRICORN	VIRGO	VIRGO	LEO	SAGITTARIUS	LIBRA	SAGITTARIUS	SAGITTARIUS	LIBRA
19		VIRGO	VIRGO	LEO	SAGITTARIUS	LIBRA	SAGITTARIUS	SAGITTARIUS	LIBRA
20	9:21 PM AQUARIUS	VIRGO	VIRGO	LEO	SAGITTARIUS	LIBRA	SAGITTARIUS	SAGITTARIUS	LIBRA
21		VIRGO	VIRGO	LEO	SAGITTARIUS	LIBRA	SAGITTARIUS	SAGITTARIUS	LIBRA
22		VIRGO	VIRGO	LEO	SAGITTARIUS	**LIBRA**	SAGITTARIUS	SAGITTARIUS	LIBRA
23	4:51 AM PISCES	VIRGO	VIRGO	LEO	SAGITTARIUS	**LIBRA**	SAGITTARIUS	SAGITTARIUS	LIBRA

	MOON FROM	IN	MERCURY	VENUS	MARS	JUPITER	SATURN	URANUS	NEPTUNE	PLUTO
JULY										
23	12:27 PM	GEMINI	LEO	LEO	SCORPIO	CAPRICORN	SCORPIO	SAGITTARIUS	SAGITTARIUS	LIBRA
24			LEO	LEO	SCORPIO	CAPRICORN	SCORPIO	SAGITTARIUS	SAGITTARIUS	LIBRA
25	6:49 PM	CANCER	LEO	LEO	SCORPIO	CAPRICORN	SCORPIO	SAGITTARIUS	SAGITTARIUS	LIBRA
26			LEO	LEO	SCORPIO	CAPRICORN	SCORPIO	SAGITTARIUS	SAGITTARIUS	LIBRA
27	9:46 PM	LEO	VIRGO	LEO	SCORPIO	CAPRICORN	SCORPIO	SAGITTARIUS	SAGITTARIUS	LIBRA
28			VIRGO	LEO	SCORPIO	CAPRICORN	SCORPIO	SAGITTARIUS	SAGITTARIUS	LIBRA
29	10:44 PM	VIRGO	VIRGO	LEO	SCORPIO	CAPRICORN	SCORPIO	SAGITTARIUS	SAGITTARIUS	LIBRA
30			VIRGO	LEO	SCORPIO	CAPRICORN	SCORPIO	SAGITTARIUS	SAGITTARIUS	LIBRA
31	11:23 PM	LIBRA	VIRGO	LEO	SCORPIO	CAPRICORN	SCORPIO	SAGITTARIUS	SAGITTARIUS	LIBRA
AUGUST										
1			VIRGO	LEO	SCORPIO	CAPRICORN	SCORPIO	SAGITTARIUS	SAGITTARIUS	LIBRA
2			VIRGO	LEO	SCORPIO	CAPRICORN	SCORPIO	SAGITTARIUS	SAGITTARIUS	LIBRA
3	1:13 AM	SCORPIO	VIRGO	LEO	SCORPIO	CAPRICORN	SCORPIO	SAGITTARIUS	SAGITTARIUS	LIBRA
4			VIRGO	LEO	SCORPIO	CAPRICORN	SCORPIO	SAGITTARIUS	SAGITTARIUS	LIBRA
5	5:37 AM	SAGITTARIUS	VIRGO	LEO	SCORPIO	CAPRICORN	SCORPIO	SAGITTARIUS	SAGITTARIUS	LIBRA
6			VIRGO	LEO	SCORPIO	CAPRICORN	SCORPIO	SAGITTARIUS	SAGITTARIUS	LIBRA
7	12:27 PM	CAPRICORN	VIRGO	LEO	SCORPIO	CAPRICORN	SCORPIO	SAGITTARIUS	SAGITTARIUS	LIBRA
8			VIRGO	VIRGO	SCORPIO	CAPRICORN	SCORPIO	SAGITTARIUS	SAGITTARIUS	LIBRA
9	9:18 PM	AQUARIUS	VIRGO	VIRGO	SCORPIO	CAPRICORN	SCORPIO	SAGITTARIUS	SAGITTARIUS	LIBRA
10			VIRGO	VIRGO	SCORPIO	CAPRICORN	SCORPIO	SAGITTARIUS	SAGITTARIUS	LIBRA
11			VIRGO	VIRGO	SCORPIO	CAPRICORN	SCORPIO	SAGITTARIUS	SAGITTARIUS	LIBRA
12	8:12 AM	PISCES	VIRGO	VIRGO	SCORPIO	CAPRICORN	SCORPIO	SAGITTARIUS	SAGITTARIUS	LIBRA
13			VIRGO	VIRGO	SCORPIO	CAPRICORN	SCORPIO	SAGITTARIUS	SAGITTARIUS	LIBRA
14	8:38 PM	ARIES	VIRGO	VIRGO	SCORPIO	CAPRICORN	SCORPIO	SAGITTARIUS	SAGITTARIUS	LIBRA
15			VIRGO	VIRGO	SCORPIO	CAPRICORN	SCORPIO	SAGITTARIUS	SAGITTARIUS	LIBRA
16			VIRGO	VIRGO	SCORPIO	CAPRICORN	SCORPIO	SAGITTARIUS	SAGITTARIUS	LIBRA
17	9:15 AM	TAURUS	VIRGO	VIRGO	SCORPIO	CAPRICORN	SCORPIO	SAGITTARIUS	SAGITTARIUS	LIBRA
18			VIRGO	VIRGO	SAGITTARIUS	CAPRICORN	SCORPIO	SAGITTARIUS	SAGITTARIUS	LIBRA
19	8:37 PM	GEMINI	VIRGO	VIRGO	SAGITTARIUS	CAPRICORN	SCORPIO	SAGITTARIUS	SAGITTARIUS	LIBRA
20			VIRGO	VIRGO	SAGITTARIUS	CAPRICORN	SCORPIO	SAGITTARIUS	SAGITTARIUS	LIBRA
21			VIRGO	VIRGO	SAGITTARIUS	CAPRICORN	SCORPIO	SAGITTARIUS	SAGITTARIUS	LIBRA
22	4:30 AM	CANCER	VIRGO	VIRGO	SAGITTARIUS	CAPRICORN	SCORPIO	SAGITTARIUS	SAGITTARIUS	LIBRA

1985 MOON

	FROM	IN	MERCURY	VENUS	MARS	JUPITER	SATURN	URANUS	NEPTUNE	PLUTO
JULY										
23			LEO	GEMINI	CANCER	AQUARIUS	SCORPIO	SAGITTARIUS	CAPRICORN	SCORPIO
24	3:41 PM	SCORPIO	LEO	GEMINI	CANCER	AQUARIUS	SCORPIO	SAGITTARIUS	CAPRICORN	SCORPIO
25			LEO	GEMINI	CANCER	AQUARIUS	SCORPIO	SAGITTARIUS	CAPRICORN	SCORPIO
26	6:10 PM	SAGITTARIUS	LEO	GEMINI	LEO	AQUARIUS	SCORPIO	SAGITTARIUS	CAPRICORN	SCORPIO
27			LEO	GEMINI	LEO	AQUARIUS	SCORPIO	SAGITTARIUS	CAPRICORN	SCORPIO
28	9:37 PM	CAPRICORN	LEO	GEMINI	LEO	AQUARIUS	SCORPIO	SAGITTARIUS	CAPRICORN	SCORPIO
29			LEO	GEMINI	LEO	AQUARIUS	SCORPIO	SAGITTARIUS	CAPRICORN	SCORPIO
30			LEO	GEMINI	LEO	AQUARIUS	SCORPIO	SAGITTARIUS	CAPRICORN	SCORPIO
31	1:38 AM	AQUARIUS	LEO	GEMINI	LEO	AQUARIUS	SCORPIO	SAGITTARIUS	CAPRICORN	SCORPIO
AUGUST										
1			LEO	GEMINI	LEO	AQUARIUS	SCORPIO	SAGITTARIUS	CAPRICORN	SCORPIO
2	7:33 AM	PISCES	LEO	GEMINI	LEO	AQUARIUS	SCORPIO	SAGITTARIUS	CAPRICORN	SCORPIO
3			LEO	CANCER	LEO	AQUARIUS	SCORPIO	SAGITTARIUS	CAPRICORN	SCORPIO
4	4:57 PM	ARIES	LEO	CANCER	LEO	AQUARIUS	SCORPIO	SAGITTARIUS	CAPRICORN	SCORPIO
5			LEO	CANCER	LEO	AQUARIUS	SCORPIO	SAGITTARIUS	CAPRICORN	SCORPIO
6			LEO	CANCER	LEO	AQUARIUS	SCORPIO	SAGITTARIUS	CAPRICORN	SCORPIO
7	4:57 AM	TAURUS	LEO	CANCER	LEO	AQUARIUS	SCORPIO	SAGITTARIUS	CAPRICORN	SCORPIO
8			LEO	CANCER	LEO	AQUARIUS	SCORPIO	SAGITTARIUS	CAPRICORN	SCORPIO
9	5:30 PM	GEMINI	LEO	CANCER	LEO	AQUARIUS	SCORPIO	SAGITTARIUS	CAPRICORN	SCORPIO
10			LEO	CANCER	LEO	AQUARIUS	SCORPIO	SAGITTARIUS	CAPRICORN	SCORPIO
11			LEO	CANCER	LEO	AQUARIUS	SCORPIO	SAGITTARIUS	CAPRICORN	SCORPIO
12	4:33 AM	CANCER	LEO	CANCER	LEO	AQUARIUS	SCORPIO	SEGITTARIUS	CAPRICORN	SCORPIO
13			LEO	CANCER	LEO	AQUARIUS	SCORPIO	SAGITTARIUS	CAPRICORN	SCORPIO
14	11:59 AM	LEO	LEO	CANCER	LEO	AQUARIUS	SCORPIO	SAGITTARIUS	CAPRICORN	SCORPIO
15			LEO	CANCER	LEO	AQUARIUS	SCORPIO	SAGITTARIUS	CAPRICORN	SCORPIO
16	4:28 PM	VIRGO	LEO	CANCER	LEO	AQUARIUS	SCORPIO	SAGITTARIUS	CAPRICORN	SCORPIO
17			LEO	CANCER	LEO	AQUARIUS	SCORPIO	SAGITTARIUS	CAPRICORN	SCORPIO
18	6:56 PM	LIBRA	LEO	CANCER	LEO	AQUARIUS	SCORPIO	SAGITTARIUS	CAPRICORN	SCORPIO
19			LEO	CANCER	LEO	AQUARIUS	SCORPIO	SAGITTARIUS	CAPRICORN	SCORPIO
20	9:04 PM	SCORPIO	LEO	CANCER	LEO	AQUARIUS	SCORPIO	SAGITTARIUS	CAPRICORN	SCORPIO
21			LEO	CANCER	LEO	AQUARIUS	SCORPIO	SAGITTARIUS	CAPRICORN	SCORPIO
22	11:24 PM	SAGITTARIUS	LEO	CANCER	LEO	AQUARIUS	SCORPIO	SAGITTARIUS	CAPRICORN	SCORPIO
23			LEO	CANCER	LEO	AQUARIUS	SCORPIO	SAGITTARIUS	CAPRICORN	SCORPIO

1986

	MOON		MERCURY	VENUS	MARS	JUPITER	SATURN	URANUS	NEPTUNE	PLUTO
	FROM	IN								
JULY										
24			CANCER	VIRGO	CAPRICORN	PISCES	SAGITTARIUS	SAGITTARIUS	CAPRICORN	SCORPIO
25	3:26 PM	ARIES	CANCER	VIRGO	CAPRICORN	PISCES	SAGITTARIUS	SAGITTARIUS	CAPRICORN	SCORPIO
26			CANCER	VIRGO	CAPRICORN	PISCES	SAGITTARIUS	SAGITTARIUS	CAPRICORN	SCORPIO
27			CANCER	VIRGO	CAPRICORN	PISCES	SAGITTARIUS	SAGITTARIUS	CAPRICORN	SCORPIO
28	0:30 AM	TAURUS	CANCER	VIRGO	CAPRICORN	PISCES	SAGITTARIUS	SAGITTARIUS	CAPRICORN	SCORPIO
29			CANCER	VIRGO	CAPRICORN	PISCES	SAGITTARIUS	SAGITTARIUS	CAPRICORN	SCORPIO
30	12:27 PM	GEMINI	CANCER	VIRGO	CAPRICORN	PISCES	SAGITTARIUS	SAGITTARIUS	CAPRICORN	SCORPIO
31			CANCER	VIRGO	CAPRICORN	PISCES	SAGITTARIUS	SAGITTARIUS	CAPRICORN	SCORPIO
AUGUST										
1			CANCER	VIRGO	CAPRICORN	PISCES	SAGITTARIUS	SAGITTARIUS	CAPRICORN	SCORPIO
2	1:09 AM	CANCER	CANCER	VIRGO	CAPRICORN	PISCES	SAGITTARIUS	SAGITTARIUS	CAPRICORN	SCORPIO
3			CANCER	VIRGO	CAPRICORN	PISCES	SAGITTARIUS	SAGITTARIUS	CAPRICORN	SCORPIO
4	12:19 PM	LEO	CANCER	VIRGO	CAPRICORN	PISCES	SAGITTARIUS	SAGITTARIUS	CAPRICORN	SCORPIO
5			CANCER	VIRGO	CAPRICORN	PISCES	SAGITTARIUS	SAGITTARIUS	CAPRICORN	SCORPIO
6	9:44 PM	VIRGO	CANCER	VIRGO	CAPRICORN	PISCES	SAGITTARIUS	SAGITTARIUS	CAPRICORN	SCORPIO
7			CANCER	VIRGO	CAPRICORN	PISCES	SAGITTARIUS	SAGITTARIUS	CAPRICORN	SCORPIO
8			CANCER	LIBRA	CAPRICORN	PISCES	SAGITTARIUS	SAGITTARIUS	CAPRICORN	SCORPIO
9	5:12 AM	LIBRA	CANCER	LIBRA	CAPRICORN	PISCES	SAGITTARIUS	SAGITTARIUS	CAPRICORN	SCORPIO
10			CANCER	LIBRA	CAPRICORN	PISCES	SAGITTARIUS	SAGITTARIUS	CAPRICORN	SCORPIO
11	10:20 AM	SCORPIO	CANCER	LIBRA	CAPRICORN	PISCES	SAGITTARIUS	SAGITTARIUS	CAPRICORN	SCORPIO
12			LEO	LIBRA	CAPRICORN	PISCES	SAGITTARIUS	SAGITTARIUS	CAPRICORN	SCORPIO
13	1:53 PM	SAGITTARIUS	LEO	LIBRA	CAPRICORN	PISCES	SAGITTARIUS	SAGITTARIUS	CAPRICORN	SCORPIO
14			LEO	LIBRA	CAPRICORN	PISCES	SAGITTARIUS	SAGITTARIUS	CAPRICORN	SCORPIO
5	4:21 PM	CAPRICORN	LEO	LIBRA	CAPRICORN	PISCES	SAGITTARIUS	SAGITTARIUS	CAPRICORN	SCORPIO
16			LEO	LIBRA	CAPRICORN	PISCES	SAGITTARIUS	SAGITTARIUS	CAPRICORN	SCORPIO
17	5:50 PM	AQUARIUS	LEO	LIBRA	CAPRICORN	PISCES	SAGITTARIUS	SAGITTARIUS	CAPRICORN	SCORPIO
18			LEO	LIBRA	CAPRICORN	PISCES	SAGITTARIUS	SAGITTARIUS	CAPRICORN	SCORPIO
19	8:38 PM	PISCES	LEO	LIBRA	CAPRICORN	PISCES	SAGITTARIUS	SAGITTARIUS	CAPRICORN	SCORPIO
20			LEO	LIBRA	CAPRICORN	PISCES	SAGITTARIUS	SAGITTARIUS	CAPRICORN	SCORPIO
21			LEO	LIBRA	CAPRICORN	PISCES	SAGITTARIUS	SAGITTARIUS	CAPRICORN	SCORPIO
22	0:47 AM	ARIES	LEO	LIBRA	CAPRICORN	PISCES	SAGITTARIUS	SAGITTARIUS	CAPRICORN	SCORPIO
23			LEO	LIBRA	CAPRICORN	PISCES	SAGITTARIUS	SAGITTARIUS	CAPRICORN	SCORPIO

1987

	MOON		MERCURY	VENUS	MARS	JUPITER	SATURN	URANUS	NEPTUNE	PLUTO
	FROM	IN								
JULY										
24			CANCER	CANCER	LEO	ARIES	SAGITTARIUS	SAGITTARIUS	CAPRICORN	SCORPIO
25	11:13 AM	LEO	CANCER	CANCER	LEO	ARIES	SAGITTARIUS	SAGITTARIUS	CAPRICORN	SCORPIO
26			CANCER	CANCER	LEO	ARIES	SAGITTARIUS	SAGITTARIUS	CAPRICORN	SCORPIO
27	11:32 PM	VIRGO	CANCER	CANCER	LEO	ARIES	SAGITTARIUS	SAGITTARIUS	CAPRICORN	SCORPIO
28			CANCER	CANCER	LEO	ARIES	SAGITTARIUS	SAGITTARIUS	CAPRICORN	SCORPIO
29			CANCER	CANCER	LEO	ARIES	SAGITTARIUS	SAGITTARIUS	CAPRICORN	SCORPIO
30	10:55 AM	LIBRA	CANCER	CANCER	LEO	ARIES	SAGITTARIUS	SAGITTARIUS	CAPRICORN	SCORPIO
31			CANCER	LEO	LEO	ARIES	SAGITTARIUS	SAGITTARIUS	CAPRICORN	SCORPIO
AUGUST										
1	7:49 PM	SCORPIO	CANCER	LEO	LEO	ARIES	SAGITTARIUS	SAGITTARIUS	CAPRICORN	SCORPIO
2			CANCER	LEO	LEO	ARIES	SAGITTARIUS	SAGITTARIUS	CAPRICORN	SCORPIO
3			CANCER	LEO	LEO	ARIES	SAGITTARIUS	SAGITTARIUS	CAPRICORN	SCORPIO
4	1:35 AM	SAGITTARIUS	CANCER	LEO	LEO	ARIES	SAGITTARIUS	SAGITTARIUS	CAPRICORN	SCORPIO
5			CANCER	LEO	LEO	ARIES	SAGITTARIUS	SAGITTARIUS	CAPRICORN	SCORPIO
6	3:41 AM	CAPRICORN	CANCER	LEO	LEO	ARIES	SAGITTARIUS	SAGITTARIUS	CAPRICORN	SCORPIO
7			LEO	LEO	LEO	ARIES	SAGITTARIUS	SAGITTARIUS	CAPRICORN	SCORPIO
8	3:53 AM	AQUARIUS	LEO	LEO	LEO	ARIES	SAGITTARIUS	SAGITTARIUS	CAPRICORN	SCORPIO
9			LEO	LEO	LEO	ARIES	SAGITTARIUS	SAGITTARIUS	CAPRICORN	SCORPIO
10	3:32 AM	PISCES	LEO	LEO	LEO	ARIES	SAGITTARIUS	SAGITTARIUS	CAPRICORN	SCORPIO
11			LEO	LEO	LEO	ARIES	SAGITTARIUS	SAGITTARIUS	CAPRICORN	SCORPIO
12	4:34 AM	ARIES	LEO	LEO	LEO	ARIES	SAGITTARIUS	SAGITTARIUS	CAPRICORN	SCORPIO
13			LEO	LEO	LEO	ARIES	SAGITTARIUS	SAGITTARIUS	CAPRICORN	SCORPIO
14	8:39 AM	TAURUS	LEO	LEO	LEO	ARIES	SAGITTARIUS	SAGITTARIUS	CAPRICORN	SCORPIO
15			LEO	LEO	LEO	ARIES	SAGITTARIUS	SAGITTARIUS	CAPRICORN	SCORPIO
16	4:52 PM	GEMINI	LEO	LEO	LEO	ARIES	SAGITTARIUS	SAGITTARIUS	CAPRICORN	SCORPIO
17			LEO	LEO	LEO	ARIES	SAGITTARIUS	SAGITTARIUS	CAPRICORN	SCORPIO
18			LEO	LEO	LEO	ARIES	SAGITTARIUS	SAGITTARIUS	CAPRICORN	SCORPIO
19	4:25 AM	CANCER	LEO	LEO	LEO	ARIES	SAGITTARIUS	SAGITTARIUS	CAPRICORN	SCORPIO
20			LEO	LEO	LEO	ARIES	SAGITTARIUS	SAGITTARIUS	CAPRICORN	SCORPIO
21	5:24 PM	LEO	LEO	LEO	LEO	ARIES	SAGITTARIUS	SAGITTARIUS	CAPRICORN	SCORPIO
22			VIRGO	LEO	LEO	ARIES	SAGITTARIUS	SAGITTARIUS	CAPRICORN	SCORPIO
23			VIRGO	LEO	VIRGO	ARIES	SAGITTARIUS	SAGITTARIUS	CAPRICORN	SCORPIO

	MOON FROM IN	MERCURY	VENUS	MARS	JUPITER	SATURN	URANUS	NEPTUNE	PLUTO
JULY									
23		CANCER	GEMINI	ARIES	GEMINI	SAGITTARIUS	SAGITTARIUS	CAPRICORN	SCORPIO
24	7:00 AM SAGITTARIUS	CANCER	GEMINI	ARIES	GEMINI	SAGITTARIUS	SAGITTARIUS	CAPRICORN	SCORPIO
25		CANCER	GEMINI	ARIES	GEMINI	SAGITTARIUS	SAGITTARIUS	CAPRICORN	SCORPIO
26	11:15 AM CAPRICORN	CANCER	GEMINI	ARIES	GEMINI	SAGITTARIUS	SAGITTARIUS	CAPRICORN	SCORPIO
27		CANCER	GEMINI	ARIES	GEMINI	SAGITTARIUS	SAGITTARIUS	CAPRICORN	SCORPIO
28	12:58 PM AQUARIUS	CANCER	GEMINI	ARIES	GEMINI	SAGITTARIUS	SAGITTARIUS	CAPRICORN	SCORPIO
29		LEO	GEMINI	ARIES	GEMINI	SAGITTARIUS	SAGITTARIUS	CAPRICORN	SCORPIO
30	12:45 PM PISCES	LEO	GEMINI	ARIES	GEMINI	SAGITTARIUS	SAGITTARIUS	CAPRICORN	SCORPIO
31		LEO	GEMINI	ARIES	GEMINI	SAGITTARIUS	SAGITTARIUS	CAPRICORN	SCORPIO
AUGUST									
1	12:48 PM ARIES	LEO	GEMINI	ARIES	GEMINI	SAGITTARIUS	SAGITTARIUS	CAPRICORN	SCORPIO
2		LEO	GEMINI	ARIES	GEMINI	SAGITTARIUS	SAGITTARIUS	CAPRICORN	SCORPIO
3	3:12PM TAURUS	LEO	GEMINI	ARIES	GEMINI	SAGITTARIUS	SAGITTARIUS	CAPRICORN	SCORPIO
4		LEO	GEMINI	ARIES	GEMINI	SAGITTARIUS	SAGITTARIUS	CAPRICORN	SCORPIO
5	8:34 PM GEMINI	LEO	GEMINI	ARIES	GEMINI	SAGITTARIUS	SAGITTARIUS	CAPRICORN	SCORPIO
6		LEO	GEMINI	ARIES	GEMINI	SAGITTARIUS	SAGITTARIUS	CAPRICORN	SCORPIO
7		LEO	CANCER	ARIES	GEMINI	SAGITTARIUS	SAGITTARIUS	CAPRICORN	SCORPIO
8	5:07 AM CANCER	LEO	CANCER	ARIES	GEMINI	SAGITTARIUS	SAGITTARIUS	CAPRICORN	SCORPIO
9		LEO	CANCER	ARIES	GEMINI	SAGITTARIUS	SAGITTARIUS	CAPRICORN	SCORPIO
10	3:57 PM LEO	LEO	CANCER	ARIES	GEMINI	SAGITTARIUS	SAGITTARIUS	CAPRICORN	SCORPIO
11		LEO	CANCER	ARIES	GEMINI	SAGITTARIUS	SAGITTARIUS	CAPRICORN	SCORPIO
12		LEO	CANCER	ARIES	GEMINI	SAGITTARIUS	SAGITTARIUS	CAPRICORN	SCORPIO
13	3:37 AM VIRGO	VIRGO	CANCER	ARIES	GEMINI	SAGITTARIUS	SAGITTARIUS	CAPRICORN	SCORPIO
14		VIRGO	CANCER	ARIES	GEMINI	SAGITTARIUS	SAGITTARIUS	CAPRICORN	SCORPIO
15	4:26 PM LIBRA	VIRGO	CANCER	ARIES	GEMINI	SAGITTARIUS	SAGITTARIUS	CAPRICORN	SCORPIO
16		VIRGO	CANCER	ARIES	GEMINI	SAGITTARIUS	SAGITTARIUS	CAPRICORN	SCORPIO
17		VIRGO	CANCER	ARIES	GEMINI	SAGITTARIUS	SAGITTARIUS	CAPRICORN	SCORPIO
18	4:37 AM SCORPIO	VIRGO	CANCER	ARIES	GEMINI	SAGITTARIUS	SAGITTARIUS	CAPRICORN	SCORPIO
19		VIRGO	CANCER	ARIES	GEMINI	SAGITTARIUS	SAGITTARIUS	CAPRICORN	SCORPIO
20	2:49 PM SAGITTARIUS	VIRGO	CANCER	ARIES	GEMINI	SAGITTARIUS	SAGITTARIUS	CAPRICORN	SCORPIO
21		VIRGO	CANCER	ARIES	GEMINI	SAGITTARIUS	SAGITTARIUS	CAPRICORN	SCORPIO
22	8:45 PM CAPRICORN	VIRGO	CANCER	ARIES	GEMINI	SAGITTARIUS	SAGITTARIUS	CAPRICORN	SCORPIO

	MOON FROM IN	MERCURY	VENUS	MARS	JUPITER	SATURN	URANUS	NEPTUNE	PLUTO
JULY									
23	1:30 AM ARIES	LEO	LEO	LEO	GEMINI	CAPRICORN	CAPRICORN	CAPRICORN	SCORPIO
24		LEO	LEO	LEO	GEMINI	CAPRICORN	CAPRICORN	CAPRICORN	SCORPIO
25	4:07 AM TAURUS	LEO	VIRGO	LEO	GEMINI	CAPRICORN	CAPRICORN	CAPRICORN	SCORPIO
26		LEO	VIRGO	LEO	GEMINI	CAPRICORN	CAPRICORN	CAPRICORN	SCORPIO
27	7:21 AM GEMINI	LEO	VIRGO	LEO	GEMINI	CAPRICORN	CAPRICORN	CAPRICORN	SCORPIO
28		LEO	VIRGO	LEO	GEMINI	CAPRICORN	CAPRICORN	CAPRICORN	SCORPIO
29	12:08 PM CANCER	LEO	VIRGO	LEO	GEMINI	CAPRICORN	CAPRICORN	CAPRICORN	SCORPIO
30		LEO	VIRGO	LEO	GEMINI	CAPRICORN	CAPRICORN	CAPRICORN	SCORPIO
31	6:04 PM LEO	LEO	VIRGO	LEO	CANCER	CAPRICORN	CAPRICORN	CAPRICORN	SCORPIO
AUGUST									
1		LEO	VIRGO	LEO	CANCER	CAPRICORN	CAPRICORN	CAPRICORN	SCORPIO
2		LEO	VIRGO	LEO	CANCER	CAPRICORN	CAPRICORN	CAPRICORN	SCORPIO
3	2:22 AM VIRGO	LEO	VIRGO	LEO	CANCER	CAPRICORN	CAPRICORN	CAPRICORN	SCORPIO
4		LEO	VIRGO	VIRGO	CANCER	CAPRICORN	CAPRICORN	CAPRICORN	SCORPIO
5	1:00 PM LIBRA	LEO	VIRGO	VIRGO	CANCER	CAPRICORN	CAPRICORN	CAPRICORN	SCORPIO
6		VIRGO	VIRGO	VIRGO	CANCER	CAPRICORN	CAPRICORN	CAPRICORN	SCORPIO
7		VIRGO	VIRGO	VIRGO	CANCER	CAPRICORN	CAPRICORN	CAPRICORN	SCORPIO
8	1:50 AM SCORPIO	VIRGO	VIRGO	VIRGO	CANCER	CAPRICORN	CAPRICORN	CAPRICORN	SCORPIO
9		VIRGO	VIRGO	VIRGO	CANCER	CAPRICORN	CAPRICORN	CAPRICORN	SCORPIO
10	12:50 PM SAGITTARIUS	VIRGO	VIRGO	VIRGO	CANCER	CAPRICORN	CAPRICORN	CAPRICORN	SCORPIO
11		VIRGO	VIRGO	VIRGO	CANCER	CAPRICORN	CAPRICORN	CAPRICORN	SCORPIO
12	11:26 PM CAPRICORN	VIRGO	VIRGO	VIRGO	CANCER	CAPRICORN	CAPRICORN	CAPRICORN	SCORPIO
13		VIRGO	VIRGO	VIRGO	CANCER	CAPRICORN	CAPRICORN	CAPRICORN	SCORPIO
14		VIRGO	VIRGO	VIRGO	CANCER	CAPRICORN	CAPRICORN	CAPRICORN	SCORPIO
15	5:05 AM AQUARIUS	VIRGO	VIRGO	VIRGO	CANCER	CAPRICORN	CAPRICORN	CAPRICORN	SCORPIO
16		VIRGO	VIRGO	VIRGO	CANCER	CAPRICORN	CAPRICORN	CAPRICORN	SCORPIO
17	7:40 AM PISCES	VIRGO	VIRGO	VIRGO	CANCER	CAPRICORN	CAPRICORN	CAPRICORN	SCORPIO
18		VIRGO	VIRGO	VIRGO	CANCER	CAPRICORN	CAPRICORN	CAPRICORN	SCORPIO
19	8:50 AM ARIES	VIRGO	LIBRA	VIRGO	CANCER	CAPRICORN	CAPRICORN	CAPRICORN	SCORPIO
20		VIRGO	LIBRA	VIRGO	CANCER	CAPRICORN	CAPRICORN	CAPRICORN	SCORPIO
21	10:00 AM TAURUS	VIRGO	LIBRA	VIRGO	CANCER	CAPRICORN	CAPRICORN	CAPRICORN	SCORPIO
22		VIRGO	LIBRA	VIRGO	CANCER	CAPRICORN	CAPRICORN	CAPRICORN	SCORPIO
23	12:46 PM GEMINI	VIRGO	LIBRA	VIRGO	CANCER	CAPRICORN	CAPRICORN	CAPRICORN	SCORPIO

LEO

	MOON FROM IN	MERCURY	VENUS	MARS	JUPITER	SATURN	URANUS	NEPTUNE	PLUTO
JULY									
24	3:22 AM VIRGO	LEO	CANCER	TAURUS	CANCER	CAPRICORN	CAPRICORN	CAPRICORN	SCORPIO
25		LEO	CANCER	TAURUS	CANCER	CAPRICORN	CAPRICORN	CAPRICORN	SCORPIO
26	9:54 AM LIBRA	LEO	CANCER	TAURUS	CANCER	CAPRICORN	CAPRICORN	CAPRICORN	SCORPIO
27		LEO	CANCER	TAURUS	CANCER	CAPRICORN	CAPRICORN	CAPRICORN	SCORPIO
28	8:42 PM SCORPIO	LEO	CANCER	TAURUS	CANCER	CAPRICORN	CAPRICORN	CAPRICORN	SCORPIO
29		LEO	CANCER	TAURUS	CANCER	CAPRICORN	CAPRICORN	CAPRICORN	SCORPIO
30		VIRGO	CANCER	TAURUS	CANCER	CAPRICORN	CAPRICORN	CAPRICORN	SCORPIO
31	9:13 AM SAGITTARIUS	VIRGO	CANCER	TAURUS	CANCER	CAPRICORN	CAPRICORN	CAPRICORN	SCORPIO
AUGUST									
1		VIRGO	CANCER	TAURUS	CANCER	CAPRICORN	CAPRICORN	CAPRICORN	SCORPIO
2	9:17 PM CAPRICORN	VIRGO	CANCER	TAURUS	CANCER	CAPRICORN	CAPRICORN	CAPRICORN	SCORPIO
3		VIRGO	CANCER	TAURUS	CANCER	CAPRICORN	CAPRICORN	CAPRICORN	SCORPIO
4		VIRGO	CANCER	TAURUS	CANCER	CAPRICORN	CAPRICORN	CAPRICORN	SCORPIO
5	7:11 AM AQUARIUS	VIRGO	CANCER	TAURUS	CANCER	CAPRICORN	CAPRICORN	CAPRICORN	SCORPIO
6		VIRGO	CANCER	TAURUS	CANCER	CAPRICORN	CAPRICORN	CAPRICORN	SCORPIO
7	2:35 PM PISCES	VIRGO	CANCER	TAURUS	CANCER	CAPRICORN	CAPRICORN	CAPRICORN	SCORPIO
8		VIRGO	CANCER	TAURUS	CANCER	CAPRICORN	CAPRICORN	CAPRICORN	SCORPIO
9	7:47 PM ARIES	VIRGO	CANCER	TAURUS	CANCER	CAPRICORN	CAPRICORN	CAPRICORN	SCORPIO
10		VIRGO	CANCER	TAURUS	CANCER	CAPRICORN	CAPRICORN	CAPRICORN	SCORPIO
11	11:52 PM TAURUS	VIRGO	CANCER	TAURUS	CANCER	CAPRICORN	CAPRICORN	CAPRICORN	SCORPIO
12		VIRGO	CANCER	TAURUS	CANCER	CAPRICORN	CAPRICORN	CAPRICORN	SCORPIO
13		VIRGO	CANCER	TAURUS	CANCER	CAPRICORN	CAPRICORN	CAPRICORN	SCORPIO
14	2:50 AM GEMINI	VIRGO	LEO	TAURUS	CANCER	CAPRICORN	CAPRICORN	CAPRICORN	SCORPIO
15		VIRGO	LEO	TAURUS	CANCER	CAPRICORN	CAPRICORN	CAPRICORN	SCORPIO
16	5:29 AM CANCER	VIRGO	LEO	TAURUS	CANCER	CAPRICORN	CAPRICORN	CAPRICORN	SCORPIO
17		VIRGO	LEO	TAURUS	CANCER	CAPRICORN	CAPRICORN	CAPRICORN	SCORPIO
18	8:14 AM LEO	VIRGO	LEO	TAURUS	CANCER	CAPRICORN	CAPRICORN	CAPRICORN	SCORPIO
19		VIRGO	LEO	TAURUS	LEO	CAPRICORN	CAPRICORN	CAPRICORN	SCORPIO
20	12:23 PM VIRGO	VIRGO	LEO	TAURUS	LEO	CAPRICORN	CAPRICORN	CAPRICORN	SCORPIO
21		VIRGO	LEO	TAURUS	LEO	CAPRICORN	CAPRICORN	CAPRICORN	SCORPIO
22	7:00 PM LIBRA	VIRGO	LEO	TAURUS	LEO	CAPRICORN	CAPRICORN	CAPRICORN	SCORPIO
23		VIRGO	LEO	TAURUS	LEO	CAPRICORN	CAPRICORN	CAPRICORN	SCORPIO

YOUR ASTRO CHECK LIST

Following you will find a list of words usually linked to Leo. On the left-hand side of the page are those qualities generally considered negative. On the right side you'll find the positive traits of the Leo nature. Being as honest as you can, put a check mark beside each trait that best describes you.

Then add up the number of check marks on the left and on the right. If the number on the left exceeds the number on the right by ten, then you are truly way out of whack, and must hasten to restore balance to your life. If, on the other hand, you have checked ten more traits on the right-hand side than on the left, you are an excellent example of a well-balanced Leo. Congratulations!

If every year you can erase one check mark on the left-hand column and add one to the right, you are proceeding well along the road to happiness and fulfillment.

LEO

Negative	Positive
_____bossy, demanding	_____honorable, noble
_____arrogant	_____warm, loving
_____intolerant	_____generous
_____stubborn, unyielding	_____positive, healthy
_____lacking in integrity	_____creative, inspiring
_____over conscious of image	_____courageous, daring
_____childishly, insecure	_____stalwart, loyal
_____credit-grabbing	_____ardent, passionate
_____vain, selfish	_____stylish, filled with flair
_____boastful	_____regal, proud
_____devious, untruthful	_____strong of purpose
_____loud but, ineffective	_____constant, stable
_____cruel, destructive	_____flowing with life, vitality
_____controlling, despotic	_____graceful, elegant
_____unspontaneous, self-conscious	_____commanding, decisive
_____obsessed with getting attention	_____entertaining
_____suffering from ego-neglect	_____organized, capable
_____vulnerable to flattery	_____thoughtful, gracious
_____cowardly, falsely heroic	_____cheerful, game
_____ostentatious, over-dramatic	_____masterful, dynamic
_____Total	_____Total

THE MOON

The Planet

The Moon is the Earth's satellite. It is 238,000 miles away and is the only planet in the solar system that revolves around the Earth. The Moon is about a quarter of the size of the Earth, having a diameter of just over 2000 miles. It orbits the Earth in 27 days, 7 hours and 43 minutes. This is also the time it takes to rotate on its axis, so the same face is always kept toward us.

The Moon has no protective atmosphere. For eons of time, it has been exposed to every kind of cosmic influence, including solar radiation. Its surface is pockmarked from innumerable collisions with solid particles of all sizes.

All moonlight is a reflection of sunlight. But the Moon is a poor reflector and gives back only 7 percent of the light it receives.

On the Earth we see the Moon change from crescent shape to full and back again in 29½ days. From out in space, we would see that about half the moon is always lit up by the Sun and half is always in darkness, except during an eclipse. When the Moon is in a direct line between us and the Sun, we see only the dark side. When the Moon is on the other side of its orbit so that the Earth is in line between it and the Sun, we see the Moon's fully illuminated side and can watch it as a full Moon from sunset to the next sunrise. All the other stages (called phases of the Moon) are in between. When the Moon is a quarter of the way around its orbit, we still see half of its surface, but half of this half is dark and half is illuminated, giving us a quarter Moon.

Although the Moon is Earth's satellite, the Sun's pull on it is far greater; the Sun is the common center of gravity for both bodies. The Earth-Moon system is, in effect, a double planet.

The influence of the Moon (with the Sun) causes the tides. As the Earth rotates and the Moon revolves, most places receive alternating high and low tides. When the Sun and Moon both pull in line at new and full Moon, the tides are higher. When they pull at right angles and partly counteract one another, the tides are lower. Tide timetables can be prepared years ahead on the basis of the Moon's predicted movements. The tidal range is 3 to 10 feet, but in narrow bays, tides may rise to 50 feet.

Symbolism

In mythology, the Moon is personified as the goddess Luna, Selene, Artemis or Diana. She is the queen of the night, the twin sister of Apollo, the Sun. She is a huntress, the mistress of animals and goddess of the chase. She governs chastity as well as fertility.

As sister of Apollo, she shares many of his characteristics. She carries a bow and arrows and has the power to send plague and sudden death. She is also the protectress of children and young animals. Like Apollo, she is unmarried, a maiden goddess who severely punishes sexual lapses. As Artemis, she changed Acteon to a stag so that he was torn to pieces by his own hounds because he had seen her bathing. She was said to have killed the handsome Orion because of his unchastity. The hounds of Artemis also hunted down the nymph Callisto after she had been seduced by Zeus.

The poets and lyricists throughout the ages have sung praises to her beauty. She has been worshipped by the priests of all races. She waxes childlike, innocent, passive and receptive. She shines at her fullest as the glorious virgin wisdom of the Sun, inspiring us with fantastic dreams of attaining the unattainable. She wanes with a wan, sad smile that luringly invites us to try again.

The ancient association of the Moon phases with fertility, growth and decay has been confirmed by science. It is now common knowledge that plant growth is influenced by the Moon, that the tidal rhythms depend upon her movements, that the female menstrual cycle corresponds to the sidereal lunar month.

Astrology

Astrologically, the Moon's influence is cold, moist, fruitful and feminine. Because its visual image alters daily, it characterizes changeability. Consequntly, its influence is often unsettling. People born with the Moon prominent in their horoscopes (Cancer Sun Sign or Ascendant, or Moon in Cancer) will be emotionally unsettled.

The Moon signifies the past. It rules all life-giving and life-sustaining liquids. In the fluids of brain and body, it accumulates and carries forward man's personal evolutionary history. Through the psychological and physical digestive actions, it transmutes experiences into the instinctive functions. It brings the past into the present, pleasing and paining man with his memories and subjective feelings. It cautions him to protect himself psychologically by forming habitual patterns that become predictable behavioral reactions and responses.

The Moon is the rhythm between now and then. It rules the ebb and flow of sensation and emotion, from the present to the past and from the past back to the present—that inner correspondence that allows man to revitalize his mind and thinking, to know inwardly where he stands today against yesterday, to separate both periods as concepts of time. As his being is revitalized in sleep by sinking into the deep pool of unconsciousness, so his waking imagination is revivified by the ebbing and flowing of his feelings between the past and the present.

The Sun is the conscious side and the Moon the unconscious side of the personality. The Sun indicates what a person is trying to become, whereas the Moon effects what he or she is trying to overcome. All that is instinctive and unconscious is in the Moon.

The Moon represents the mother and any strong matriarchal or family influence that has left a deep impression on the psyche. It often reveals itself in patriotism and a vivid awareness of traditional values and ancestral worth.

The Moon governs conception, pregnancy, birth and animal instinct. It rules the infant, most impressionable stage of a person.

Representing the weight of the past, the Moon acts like a brake on the progressive Sun and regulates our evolution toward cosmic consciousness. This, the Sun, in its unrestrained beneficence, would bestow prematurely with a mind-disintegrating flash.

The Moon is the regulator on the pendulum of time. It preserves—not the balance between past and present—but the essential *interaction* between the two, which is man's continual and gradual development. In so doing, it protects, nourishes and lovingly nurtures the spark of life wherever it appears.

The Moon's feeling nature is dual, but not erratic—it is changeable in that it swings from one side to the other, but it is constant in that the rhythm is measured and predictable (like the tidal phases). So the individual will fluctuate between painful and pleasurable emotions according to the pressure of time and circumstance.

The Moon rules the movement and volume of the sea but not the sea's nature. The Moon provides the raw and simple forms of life for consciousness to make the most of. It governs the public, the faceless masses and their combined emotional response, as distinct from the individual and the social order.

Physiologically, the Moon rules the digestive juices, the glandular secretions of the lymphatic system, the stomach, breasts, ovaries and the sympathetic nervous system. The last is intimately associated with the emotions, affections and desires. Hence the origin of the term *lunacy* to describe severe emotional disturbances.

MOON IN ARIES

Wham! Here is a head-on collision between the immovable cold of the Moon and the irresistible heat of Aries. Neither mixes with the other, and the result is a frenetic inner tension; either you handle it and accomplish much, or it handles you and converts your life into a constant nervous conflict.

You act instinctively. You have great faith in your senses. You don't wait to think, to weigh things, but accept them as you see them. Your assessments are instantaneous and often brilliant. You are at your best when working in an action atmosphere that requires moment-to-moment adjustments. You don't need to know where you are heading; you just follow the trail with greased-lightning speed and in so doing find an essential balance. When you stop, you lose your equilibrium and become restless, high-strung, edgy. You are easily provoked and upset. You flare up quickly, hit out blindly and say things you may later regret.

You are intensely emotional, always plugged in to what is happening around you. Success makes you even more excitable, sharper and prone to push yourself harder. You are extremely enthusiastic and ready to jump on any new bandwagon that may come along. On the surface, you may appear conventional, but you are always looking for a chance to take the initiative, to lead others, to strike out on your own. In no time at all, you'll be up there with the bandmaster's baton—playing your own tune. You are supremely sure of yourself and would rather depend on your own impressions than listen to the advice of others. This can be dangerous; you make mistakes in this way. You don't take kindly to people who try to tell you how to do things. You have a very independent mind. You are usually interested in occult studies. Your sense of sight is the most developed.

The dual nature of the Moon makes you inclined to fuss over trifles, but in major issues, you are swift and decisive. You seem to wear yourself out on lesser things and stumble around them with the persnicketiness of a mothering hen. Your talents are best suited for professions where success depends on quick decisions. The higher the stakes, the greater your satisfaction and competence. If you have a choice of jobs, you will often deliberately take the one that offers a risk, a gamble. You live to feel and to act without the necessity for pause. You are impulsive and quite often rash. But your enterprise and inventiveness make others, especially employers, tolerant of these lapses. You usually succeed by ending up in a position of authority.

You are fond of travel and are often employed in work connected with the public. You have a strongly persuasive manner; you can rally numbers to follow you and support your causes. You are acutely idealistic and apt to advocate changing conditions on a wide scale, but you may lack the perseverance and concentration to bring your crusading efforts to any notable success.

A man with Moon in Aries may have difficulty with the women in his life. He is apt to be inconstant, striding from one affair to another, never really ready to settle down. He is not a cozy domestic type. He will attract women who are passionate, headstrong and impractical. They may be highly intelligent but difficult. They certainly won't live under his thumb. Marriage for the Moon-Aries man may be a tempestuous and short-lived experience. But if the Moon is well aspected by other planets, women can be a great help to him in his career and professional life.

You may love your parents and family but there will always be tensions and conflict. It has been said that the Moon in Aries is like a rose in a fire. Usually you will prefer to communicate with older loved ones from a distance than to risk misunderstandings and arguments.

You may have strong memories of your mother's earlier ambitions for you and harbor some subconscious resentment about this.

Mothers with this Moon-Aries combination may try to run their children's lives even into adulthood. These same mothers may also lack the ability to cope with the practical side of life.

The Other Side of the Story

You may pour out vast amounts of energy in great spurts of enthusiasm and achieve nothing. You may be all show, all puff and wind. Your ideas are likely to be magnificently unworkable. You may start a project and drop it because you have lost interest, without a thought for any others involved. Your idealism may reach fanatical levels. You are likely to make indiscreet public statements and ruin your reputation through rash actions. Your temper may be uncontrollable and destructive. Your lack of inner stability may lead to a breakdown. You are likely to be a troublesome rebel without a cause. Your marital infidelities may cause unhappiness. You may be a thoughtless and dictatorial parent.

MOON IN TAURUS

This is an excellent position for the Moon, and it usually brings a fair amount of life's comforts and possessions. Here the Moon is exalted; here its emotional sensors find a compatible and fertile place in the Earth to put down deep and fruitful roots. The Moon in Taurus can be productive, not of change, but of constructive material activities.

You are a reliable person. You don't change your ideas easily or capriciously, and you don't intend to lose what you own in any silly sort of experimentation. You are a builder who likes to erect your estate on solid foundations.

You are intuitive and very impressionable. Your powers of concentration are good. You are attentive and know how to listen when you want to. You absorb the feeling of things to begin with rather than the idea of them. No instant decisions and reactions for you—you like to quietly and leisurely digest all your impressions before reaching a conclusion. But when you make up your mind, it's for keeps. You stick to your principles, come what may. And you proceed to implement them, working relentlessly toward your predetermined goals.

You love your family. There is something about the past, your childhood, that nothing that has happened since can displace. You are deeply nostalgic and these yearnings are satisfied by the constant stirrings of your memory. You often think about your home, your grandparents, ancestors and links with the past. You are ruminative and find delight in the fond recollection of bygone days. Your memory is tenacious.

You have a good feel for business and are not short of influential or affluent friends, even though you may not be wealthy yourself. You have a knack for making money and investing it wisely. Your funds usually grow, not overnight, but with an inexorable certainty that makes you a safe bet for being comfortable or well off one day. You have a developed sense of timing where public opinion and tastes are concerned. You can make money out of raw materials, and especially out of farm products; a sixth sense tells you the right time to buy and sell. Cooperative societies, wholesale associations and syndicates where you can pool your interests with others are usually fortunate. Restaurants, health food shops and other places that cater to the public taste are also likely to provide a lucrative living. Housing and land offer special opportunities, particularly large estates that attract small communities. Bricks and mortar are lucky for you.

You are courteous, affable and sympathetic. But you are not an adventurous type. Revolutionary fashions and fads are not for you. You enjoy the best of all that is established—the classical and the traditional. You don't mind at all having the old dressed up as the new as long as it is stylish and attractive. You have a strong attachment to the good things of life. You may overindulge your appetite for comfort, food and sex. Your senses of taste and touch are highly developed. You may be secretive about some of your activities. You gather friends easily and are a responsive host or hostess. You are romantic, and although innately cautious, attracted by the opposite sex. You are ambitious and eager to excel in whatever you undertake.

You are conservative and conventional, although your emotional life may at times seem to contradict this. You are not a great propounder of new ideas; more a renovator than an innovator, you are inclined to remold old ideas into attractive new shapes.

The women in a Moon-Taurus man's life are practical, affectionate and domestically inclined. He can count on their loyalty and unwavering support in difficult times and situations. But they may be emotional clinging vines, difficult to break away from once the decision to part is made. If you are a woman, you will observe these characteristics in your own makeup as well as in your female companions.

People with Moon in Taurus often have fine singing and speaking voices. They may choose occupations connected with broadcasting, public speaking or recording.

The Other Side of the Story

You may be boringly conservative and totally lack originality. You are likely to be gluttonous and undermine your health through obesity. Your fondness for liquor may be a problem, especially for your family. You may mix with shady company or choose companions with dubious reputations and secretive or sly habits. You may be overly possessive toward your loved ones; your children may be driven to seek sympathy and understanding from others. You may marry too young and suffer for it. You are likely to stand by and watch others be unfairly treated rather than risk your own discomfort. You may pay lip service to your ideals but be too lazy or inept to take action.

MOON IN GEMINI

This is a restless combination. It imbues you with great intellectual ability, but indicates a tendency to skate on the surface of subjects, intent on covering a lot of ground rather than making any great or lasting impression. You have the ability but not much inclination to tackle fundamentals. You are very active both physically and mentally. You like to read, to study various topics at once and to visit other people, especially in their homes. You enjoy short trips, brisk walks, much chat. You often have a flair for math or science, and your literary ability can be quite impressive. Your sense perception is extraordinary. You pick up impressions with tremendous speed and are able to verbalize them with fascinating fluency or write them down in the form of poetry or prose. You then throw them away and forget them, just as though they had never existed in the first place.

You find most of your enjoyments in the mind, not in actual sensation. But you are sympathetic and humane. To you, the emotions are most valuable for the ideas they provoke, the opportunities they present for action and distraction, the contact and movement that flow from them. You have little time for sentiment; you will never wallow in your feelings. But you are very aware of what is happening in the family circle; you are acutely interested in what loved ones are doing and like to keep tabs on them through letters, phone calls and visits. You enjoy talking about the past but not with the nostalgic desire to repeat it. Your most serious moments relate to domestic and personal affairs.

You are instantly excitable and quickly propelled into new activities with a great display of enthusiasm. You are eager and quick to learn and a natural mimic. You can file information away with the speed of a computer and retail it exactly wherever there is an attentive ear. But you seldom add anything of yourself to what you repeat; you are too busy communicating to reach down into your deeper feelings and come up with a seasoned package. With you, a half-baked loaf is better than no bread at all, it seems.

You have a keen sense of smell and an ear for music. Without continual mental stimulation and variety, your health is likely to suffer because you become nervous and irritable. You need to keep your imagination functioning vividly in full color. You are one of the few people who can half-read a book or story without any desire to finish it; it is not the satisfaction of endings or conclusions that you are after, but the opportunity to be able to start something fresh. You love to travel. You adore novelty.

You have a feel for language and languages. You prefer to tell people what they want to hear rather than be bothered trying to put your own point of view across. Or you may tell a lie because it will be better received than the truth. To you, the intellect is something of a toy with which you never tire of playing with. It is this attitude that makes the Gemini temperament so suited to "conning" people. The compulsive need is to match wits, to change poses convincingly without losing a step, to trip unsuspected through the credulous minds of others. Material gains are only a bonus to you. It's the game that counts, not the petty satisfaction of winning some egotistical point.

You are not a malicious person, nor are you deliberately cruel, but sometimes you have to manufacture (or you might say, stir) your own intellectual sparring partners to keep your mind razor sharp.

You are capricious and likely to sweep your problems under the rug rather than face them. You detest disputes and quarreling—in fact, you'll run a mile (and enjoy the run) to avoid a scene. But you usually manage through indiscretion or lack of caution to land yourself in difficult and embarrassing situations.

You are inclined to change houses and jobs regularly. If you can settle down, you would make a good reporter, salesperson, writer, teacher or agent. A job that means contact with the masses is often lucrative for you.

For career women, this is a favorable position for the Moon. It creates no particular liking for domestic duties and no great emphasis on ro-

mance and love affairs. But the Moon does provide the necessary feminine vitality for these women to apply themselves to accomplishment with considerable fixity of purpose. Without a strong intellectual drive, the female mind in this position can be especially frivolous.

The women in the life of a man with the Moon in Gemini must have more brains than beauty to keep his interest and attention alive. They are seldom enthusiastic homemakers and may be fickle in love and avid seekers after novelty and excitement.

The Other Side of the Story

You may be a cheat and a plausible liar, incapable of concentrating for long on anything besides your own selfish interests. You may talk to hear the sound of your own voice and take pleasure in causing dissension among others. You think nothing of being inconsiderate, unsympathetic and shallowly calculating in order to bring about your own designs. Your mother and family may dislike you. You are apt to be unreliable, inconsistent and childish. What is expedient may be more important to you than what is fair or right. Your carefree and cheerful manner may be a subterfuge to hide a person who is undisciplined, immature and unwilling to face life on any terms.

MOON IN CANCER

You are a true child of nature. You love beauty and your senses are keenly attuned to your surroundings and the people you mix with. You fit snugly into your environment and are prepared to go along with whatever is happening, provided there is sufficient harmony and a little tenderness exhibited.

Cancer is the Moon's own Sign and here the Moon is truly at home. Its positive qualities are emphasized and its negative aspects watered down. But there is the possibility that you are too comfortably inclined (mildness and placidity can be carried too far). With this combination, you may find it easy to sink into a state of drifting and effortless inertia.

You are less changeable and your temperament is a little warmer than those who have the Moon in other positions. You are extremely solicitous of the welfare of your family and offspring. You are vividly attached to the memories of your childhood, especially to your mother. The sorrows and joys of those early days occupy much of your thoughts. You love to think and reminisce about the past and sometimes brood over old disappointments and injustices. It is not unusual with this combination to have a mother complex. You may be unconsciously drawn to people you feel are protective and dependable. You also exhibit a strong nurturing instinct yourself and are inclined to fuss over your loved ones.

You make a loving parent and marriage partner. You lavish affection on your mate and all those who are emotionally dependent on you. You would prefer to work at or out of your home, and will actually accept a smaller income to do this if the opportunity comes along. You do all in your power to make your living quarters comfortable and homey. You like to have a few relics and antiques around. Your library usually includes quite a bit of historical matter.

You are extremely impressionable. Your mind is receptive rather than active—that is, you are more contemplative than cogitative. Thought to you is more a feeling than a mental image. Being hypersensitive to atmospheres, you absorb them instantaneously. But, your reactions are slow and uncertain and you take your time rendering a verdict. You don't like unsettled conditions or being disturbed yourself. You prefer to be left alone to ruminate and assimilate your impressions until you decide it's time to venture out into the world again and give it the benefit of your conclusions. By that time, though, it's often too late, the opportunity has slipped by. You will get nothing much done unless you push yourself to the limit or there are other energizing factors in your horoscope.

You may be too thorough in your reflections to be outstandingly creative. You have the raw material for brilliance but seldom the spontaneity. Languorous contentment and mental torpor are the obstacles.

You love ease and comfort and are at your best at home with congenial people. You also enjoy visiting and conversation. Since you have a penchant for good food and drink, weight can be a problem, especially if you get insufficient exercise. You are very adaptable to harmonious company and sensitive to the deeper feelings of others, so much so that you are easily swept out of your depth emotionally. Your enthusiasms come and go. Though you can fight with all your might for a worthy cause, a sudden change of mood will leave you high and dry without the will to go on.

Paradoxically, you have a way of projecting yourself into the public eye. Although you are reserved and your whole temperament recoils from this kind of thing, you get drawn into controversies and disputes that attract wide attention. Your own behavior is conspicuously erratic at times; you can blithely swing between two contradictory stands with the polished unconcern of a trapeze artist. Your extreme sensitivity often produces an awareness of psychic activity that is hidden to others. You "know" things without being told.

You are sentimental, sympathetic and humane. Although acutely aware of your senses, you don't allow them to plunge you into a great amount of physical activity. You infinitely prefer sensuous pleasures.

You make a good actor and mimic. You can call up emotion the way others call upon their memory. You are usually fond of poetry, music, and the theater.

This placing of the Moon is not so favorable for women because it inclines them to be too much at the mercy of the men in their lives. Being passive and impressionable, they are easily influenced and often subjected to domineering and oppressive treatment. Almost all Moon-in-Cancer people run the risk of being imposed upon.

For men, this position usually means the women in their lives are the mothering type. Deeply affectionate and romantic, these females are apt to stick with the tenacity of limpets. Once committed, their loyalty is unquestionable.

The Other Side of the Story

You may be physically lazy and mentally inert. You are likely to be impressionable to the point of foolishness and have no mind of your own. An inordinate love of your mother or her memory may make you a difficult person to live with or be married to. You may be moody and morose—up one minute, down the next. Your changeability is apt to make others wary of your promises. You may blame "fate" for your weaknesses and failures and fail to develop a workable sense of responsibility. You are likely to be spoiled and feel you have a right to be looked after by society without exerting yourself. You may be excessively voluptuous and preoccupied with the search for sensuous gratification.

MOON IN LEO

You are very sure of yourself and a great one for dramatizing situations. Although your mind is alert and quick, you are largely controlled by your emotions. Love and affection come first with you and unless you have them you become downhearted and retreat into yourself. You need desperately to be needed, appreciated, applauded. Fortunately, you have a warm and likable personality that attracts others, so you are rarely short of admirers, collaborators and pleasant companions whose presence shields you from the uncertainties that hover in the deeper recesses of your psyche.

You are intensely ambitious, have good business sense and are not afraid of responsibility. You intend to impress the world in some way or another. Sometimes this urge gets out of control, degenerating into flamboyance, ostentation and posturing conceit. You are a born actor whose wonderful emotional range of expression requires mature curbing.

Usually you are very popular with the opposite sex. In fact, your capacity to love might be called "all-consuming." No matter how often you fall in love, you love each time with your entire being—which is flattering, comforting and reassuring to the other party. But after a while—if you still happen to be around—your affection may be regarded as somewhat smothering, and definitely overly protective.

You are self-sacrificing. If you give your word or your heart, you will see the obligation through. Though you may fret under the pressure of adversity, you will seldom go back on a promise. The exception is if the person concerned takes your loyalty and effort for granted. Then you break all ties in a sensational show of independence and indignation.

You are positive and decisive, optimistic and hopeful. The power to lead and to be followed inheres in you. Your initiative prevents you from acknowledging limitations; where there's a will there's definitely a way for those born with the Moon in Leo. But it takes something special to arouse your participation; you're not the type of person who goes looking for any old cause or crusade to invest your energies in. You are fairly fixed in your beliefs and emotions. Unless you are interested in a project or a subject there's no hope of its attracting your attention. You're not as curious as others, at least not intellectually. You require emotional stimulus to set you off. You're at peace lying in the Sun with Leonine ease. At least, until someone treads on your tail! Given the interest, you learn very quickly.

You are proud, honorable and generous, fond of your home and ambitious for your offspring. If a man, the women in your life might be a bit bossy and inclined to try to organize your activities "for your own good." However, they will exert a strongly beneficial influence, especially in the mental and spiritual realms. Women with the Moon in Leo usually have more balanced personalities than the men. The men are that much more egotistical and tend to crunch ahead, ignoring people's feelings and contemptuously dismissing outside influences.

You are a neat type of person and take care with your appearance. You're almost certain to gravitate toward a position of prominence in your community. In many cases, people with this combination become public figures, especially in the entertainment world. You can usually count on the support of those in high places.

You are self-indulgent and very fond of pleasure. But somehow you choose your times for relaxation, entertainment and excess fairly judiciously and manage to prevent them from interfering with your work or reputation, both of which are of the utmost importance to you. You are seldom lucky in your love life; impulsive affairs with willing and coaxing playmates are extremely hard for you to resist.

Luxuries, including jewelry, furs, expensive suits and flashy cars may be a weakness. You enjoy music, art, literature and often are creative in these fields, and earn your living from them. Organized sport may appeal, either as a pastime or a business.

The Other Side of the Story

You may reduce yourself to a self-indulgent wreck. Your conceited and overbearing attitude may make you unpopular and propel you to constantly look out for new people to impress. Self-importance is probably a fetish with you. Although physically developed, you are apt to be mentally and emotionally immature. Your idea of love and affection may not go much further than permissiveness and voluptuousness. What you regard as sensitivity in yourself, others might see as self-pity and a complaining nature. Your striving for the limelight is apt to rebound—notoriety is more likely than fame. Scandal is a danger until you learn the necessary lesson of self-restraint.

MOON IN VIRGO

You are intelligent and practical—and probably the most efficient and uncomplaining worker in the zodiacal lineup. You can slice through a sea of detail like the prow of a cutter.

You possess a special flair for devising more efficient ways of handling the work load, and you don't look for any special privileges or kudos. In many ways, you are the ideal employee—trustworthy, diligent, meticulous, practical and amazingly unassuming.

You are rather reserved and much less sure of yourself than you make out. This lack of confidence can often be traced to the influence of your mother or some maternal figure who had the habit of nagging you. Sympathetic warmth may have been lacking in your early family life. It is also possible that as a child you assumed emotional responsibility for another hard-pressed member of the family. Prejudices you picked up from the dominating figures of those days are probably still with you. An inability to come to terms with your own feelings makes it difficult for you to understand the emotions of others. You have your feelings very much under control, or so it seems. The danger is that you never really understand them.

You are basically an intellectual person, but you don't acquire knowledge just to be well informed, as your Mercurial Gemini counterpart does. Everything you learn or absorb you try to put to practical use. You're a very steady, reliable, down-to-earth character.

You are fastidious about health and diet and a terror when it comes to hygiene. You know disease and illness are spread by bacteria and you jolly well don't intend to be immobilized in that way, if you can help it. You keep your body clean and your house spotless. You can't stand being sick—in fact, nothing is more nerve-racking to you than being laid up in bed.

You're a food faddist, usually enjoy the health-food kick and can't resist trying out exciting new recipes featuring plenty of fresh produce, fruit juices and possibly meat substitutes. Unless you take care with your diet, you are inclined to suffer from stomach disorders.

Left to your own devices, you're pretty easygoing. You're quietly ambitious and will do well working for a large organization.

Your memory is excellent and you learn easily. You have many talents, some of which your associates may not be aware of, because you are anything but egotistical. You put your views forward with clarity and candor but do not strive to impress people. Inadvertently you do, especially with your novel ideas and fresh approach to problems. You are unpretentious, disarmingly modest to the point of consistently underselling yourself. You like to know you're appreciated. You won't get uptight if someone makes a fortune out of one of your good ideas as long as he gives you a wave of recognition.

You're not greedy or avaricious with money. You don't expect any more than what's fair for your labor. You can be careful with the pennies and you're a very astute financial manager.

Women with the Moon in Virgo run the home like a well-oiled machine—everything in its place, working efficiently and contributing to comfort and serviceability—but their hearth is a bit cold. Perhaps this excessive efficiency implies an intolerance of human failings and disorder. It is in the area of personal relations that the Moon-in-Virgo person usually suffers most, basically because of an inability to identify with the feelings of others. Passion and romance are more mental concepts to these people than painful longings and ecstatic feelings. These women become intellectually rather than emotionally involved with their men. They have to be deeply soul-stirred, to begin to love in ordinary terms. Usually they learn in a negative fashion from an unhappy marriage or love affair, suffering secretly and silently.

You have an irritating way of instantly analyzing people and trying to correct their faults. Though you are basically well intentioned, too often the urge becomes compulsive and inevitably degenerates into carping criticism or wounding outspokenness.

You enjoy scientific studies and have more than a passing interest in the occult. Your own intuition often borders on clairvoyance.

The Other Side of the Story

You are acrimonious, bitterly critical and always complaining. You don't have a kind word for many people. In your family life, you use your clever mind to skim across the surface of problems and offer panaceas but seldom any real solutions. Your ceaseless peppering turns children and those you live with against you. You seem incapable of keeping your nose out of other people's affairs. You are boringly repetitive, superficial and fussy. You are quite likely a hypochondriac. Cleanliness and dietary fears may eventually be phobic.

MOON IN LIBRA

You love companionship and are indeed a fine partner. Everything about you seems to fit into a pattern designed for attracting and pleasing others. You have a charisma that, even if you are not particularly striking to look at, makes even a brief encounter with you memorable. And on closer acquaintance you become even more interesting—as a possible lover, friend or trusted business partner.

Libra is the Sign of partnership and the Moon is the power of the senses. Together, as you may imagine, they add up to some heady connections with the opposite sex.

Emotionally, you are very easygoing. You accept others as you find them and are one of the most understanding types in the Zodiac. You don't want to reform others, educate them or correct them; you just want to enjoy their company. Not surprisingly, you are very popular. You are an excellent listener and can be depended on to make all the right noises at precisely the right time. When people tell you their troubles you are sympathetic, encouraging and terribly concerned. But though you express the most comforting sentiments, the chances of your doing anything practical about the problem are nil!

Not that you're two-faced or spurious. You just don't have much capacity for initiating action. You're not essentially a physical being. You're sensuous more than sensual. Your trouble is you are incredibly adaptable emotionally and respond idealistically to every feeling that others chuck at you. You give people exactly what they need to restore their emotional equilibrium. It might be concluded, then, that you have no genuine feelings of your own, but that's not true. Your fundamental desire is to restore emotional harmony wherever it is lacking.

Therefore, it's easy to understand why you are so courteous and diplomatic—and why you are so sociable, visiting people in their homes, entertaining them at your place and generally being wherever groups are gathered together. It's your zodiacal function to bring people together in harmony, to build all the bridges you can over personally troubled waters.

But there is a kind of disharmony you'll run a mile from. That's any form of argument, coarseness or discord. You can't stand quarrels and fights. When you see one looming, you're off! In conversation, you'll adroitly skirt around controversial points. If anyone accuses you of dodging issues or vacillating you'll deny it with self-convincing fervor and disarming charm. Your wizardry at subtly producing red herrings is such that people will be put off the scent, giving you a chance to change the subject! Okay, this

might be done unconsciously, but still, you are deluding yourself and eventually may be thought deceptive or devious by others.

Dirty, unpleasant and disharmonious surroundings upset you awfully. You become moody and unhappy in these conditions and can't perform.

Your finely developed senses heighten your natural proclivity to all that is aesthetically pleasing. Your appreciation of music, painting and the other fine arts often indicates a creative aptitude that could provide a satisfying and lucrative career, if exploited.

You are fond of smart and fashionable clothes. Your taste in most things is expensive. You have more chance of making a success of your life through partnerships than by trying to go it alone. You will probably marry young.

The women in the life of men born with the Moon in Libra are likely to be accomplished, detached, gentle, refined and undemandingly passionate. They may insist on living their own lives, even after marriage, which is also a characteristic of women born with this combination. The need to be accepted by others is crucial to happiness and makes you highly susceptible to flattery. What people say or think is probably more important to you than the truth. Attachment to social affairs and amusements tends to produce a frivolous personality.

The Other Side of the Story
You are likely to be a scatterbrained goodtime gal or guy. You're very difficult to take seriously because you don't seem to have any permanent values. You are easily influenced and sometimes can't say "no" even for your own good. You are lazy, inclined to overeat and have no aim in life apart from being accepted by those with more money and superior status. Peace at any price may be a fixed attitude that costs you plenty—especially in self-respect.

MOON IN SCORPIO
There is something of the extremist, even the fanatic, in your nature. If you ever discover a cause to serve, you will never give it up, irrespective of the forces that oppose you. But if you never find a way to absorb this demolishing energy of yours, you'll have problems. For a start, there is likely to be a strong sensual bias in your makeup. The search for sexual gratification could lead you into tortuous and sometimes emotionally self-torturing paths. Erotic dreams and

thoughts are likely to absorb you and stimulate your imagination to intense levels. There is much that is both creative and destructive in this sort of combination.

You are vigorously active, strong-willed and passionate. You don't confide your inner feelings or secret thoughts to anyone. When others are revealing their secrets in an affable exchange of confidences, you stay mum. Openness is not your style. You tend to tell people only what you want them to know. Although in many ways you are impulsive, you seldom allow a spontaneous disclosure of your inner feelings. Such self-repression leads to a tremendous buildup of energy that must have a constructive outlet.

The unevolved type of person with this combination is an out-and-out hedonist. The senses are used almost exclusively as mediums of pleasures; knowledge is regarded as an incidental by-product whose main function is to produce more opportunities for sensational excitation. These people can sink to terrible depths of perversion and often end up destroying themselves in one way or another. Drugs and drinking are likely to contribute to their misery. Having no real values to speak of, they are treacherous, vindictive and cruel. Revengeful hate is their automatic reaction to anyone who crosses them.

You are a loner with a great faith in your own abilities. When there's is job to be done, you rarely find it necessary to seek assistance. You much prefer to work in isolation, locked up in your office, away from co-workers' camaraderie. You are highly efficient, quick to eliminate unnecessary detail and capable of working incredibly long hours without tiring or losing your concentration. You will never be imposed upon. You are easily irritated but will remember a kindness with unsuspected tenderness. Your manner is abrupt and often blunt. You like to come straight to the point. You don't talk much unless discussing a pet subject. Then you can display voluble enthusiasm, discoursing in quick-fire sentences and leaving no doubt as to your mastery of the subject and perceptive insights. You have a special talent for grasping basic facts instantly.

You usually take an interest in scientific studies and are especially competent at extracting ideas and organizing them into an applicable pattern. The acuteness of your senses frequently gives you extraordinary powers of observation.

The women in your life are likely to be very determined and a little unscrupulous. They will know exactly what they want and be prepared to use deviously subtle means to get it. Time means nothing in the gaining of their ends. These women are intelligent, ambitious and courageous.

You don't like change and are fairly fixed in your opinions. When you do switch views or decide to support a particular line of action, you are capable of producing revolutionary changes. These may be quite unsettling and uncomfortable for others at the time, but in the end, they will probably be recognized as timely reforms or essential bits of surgery.

Mothers with the Moon in Scorpio should take care that their ambitions for their children do not stifle the youngsters' natural talents and creative urges. The willpower of people with this combination is so immense that even with the best of intentions they can overwhelm and misshape a developing personality.

The Other Side of the Story

You may be hopelessly corrupt, devoid of moral scruples and sexually degenerate. Addiction to drugs and alcohol may render you impossible to live with. You could betray your best friend to achieve your ends. You are likely to be utterly ruined by a woman or, going to the other extreme, be denied women's company for most of your life. Jealousy may destroy any chance of a happy marriage. Various perversions may be your idea of recreation. Your domineering and heartlessly ambitious plans for your children may produce carbon copies of yourself.

MOON IN SAGITTARIUS

You are an idealist and find it hard to obtain what you are looking for, which you probably can't even define. But you don't need an explicit end to push ahead; you often change your place of residence, more often your job, and are always on the move in one way or another toward a new horizon.

The important consideration at all times is for you to feel free. You don't object to discipline but you'll never cease testing its validity. You don't want to be tied down to other people's views or be limited by their beliefs. If there is any truth in this world—and you are certain there is—you are going to find it for yourself. You're a pretty volatile, free-wheeling package of good-humored energy.

You are extremely sociable and enjoy mixed company. You're passionate enough when it comes to sex but enjoy good companionship even more. You like listening to others' views about life and you filter these finely through your own experience. You are something of a wandering philosopher; keen to absorb the meaning of things and not averse to holding forth in company with your own notions of what life is all about. You are as tolerant of others' viewpoints as you expect them to be of yours. Probably you had an early introduction to one-eyed beliefs by clashing with family members in your youth. You'll listen to anyone and form your own conclusions, but you won't stand for being told what to believe in.

You are seldom at rest either in mind or body. Usually you're considering some far-ranging scheme, which your incurable impatience insists on starting before the necessary preliminaries are completed. This is why you often make mistakes—you're inclined to overlook essential details. Optimism is almost an illness with you. You'll plunge into a venture with the confidence of a nine-year-old and then wonder what went wrong when you find yourself in over your head. You don't learn quickly from your rash errors. Even though you are usually cutting your losses in one way or another, you're still a sucker for a long shot.

Lady Luck smiles on you more than on most. Perhaps your generous, kind-hearted and benevolent ways bring the same sort of treatment back to you. You get along very well with people in authority; they are more often likely to show favors than to refuse them. You also have a knack of exploiting your personal popularity so that, given the goods to sell or the creative talent to display, you can attract the attention of the crowd and go on to become famous. There is a danger that you will play on the public's emotions and tell them what they want to hear rather than the truth. Once you have success, you have a tendency to moral posturing and expedience.

Your easygoing attitude makes you a pleasant friend and associate but not such a good marital partner. You are not built for domestic happiness because you are too impersonal and unpossessive to make a go of it with other zodiacal people who need to be wanted. You're inclined to live and let live, and in love that means you go your own way when you feel like it. Any display of jealousy will usually send women with this influence racing off—probably straight into the arms of some temporarily interesting and very (temporarily) understanding gentleman.

You love the outdoor life and the feeling of freedom and independence it gives you. At times,

you are quick-tempered, especially if someone—your lover, for instance—tries to order you about. You have the discomforting ability to see deep inside people and announce aloud piercing truths about their motives and attitudes. For this reason, you are often regarded as a terror, though more often than not the words come out of you with no deliberation and you just take the blame or the bows. Your disposition is open and frank.

You are genuinely solicitous of others' welfare and have an understanding relationship with all animals.

The Other Side of the Story

You are apt to be a swaggering braggart, wasting money in stupid and careless ways. You are usually prepared to back your inflated opinion of yourself with impossible promises. Your profligate and irresponsible habits may keep you constantly in debt, so that though you are recklessly open-handed with boon companions, you are unable to maintain a consistent standard of living for your dependents. You may live off your wits. A good time probably tops your list of priorities. You may be a narrow-minded bigot and bore behind a facade of righteousness.

MOON IN CAPRICORN

This is not such a good position, especially for women. It tends to make both sexes cold, unresponsive and authoritarian, even though they may not wish to be this way. Circumstances, particularly in childhood, probably exposed you to the harsher side of life. Most people with this combination have unconsciously steeled themselves against being hurt again. Women have to make a special effort to keep their feminine charm. Both men and women feel, with some justification, that their lives will be austere and difficult.

Remember, though, other influences in the chart can mitigate these effects. The tendency toward discipline and restraint, with help elsewhere, can be turned to good account. Moon in Capricorn can be the makings of a most successful business tycoon. But you must expect some grinding hard work and isolating dedication to achieve this kind of success.

Moon in Capricorn dulls the responsiveness to human sentiment. The senses do not flow over into an impressionable plasmic sympathy; they are mainly carriers of information, which is used with astute efficiency in the individual's struggle for achievement and power. Ambition is the driving force. The capacity to persevere under oppressively daunting conditions is truly amazing. The sheer force of sustained exertion usually results in success, and quite commonly in fame or public renown.

There is also a chance of things going wrong—notoriety may be the reward of all this struggle. With such emphasis on ambition, a calculating mind and not a great deal of regard for other people's feelings, Moon-in-Capricorn people usually make enemies and generate ill-will over a long period. When success does come, a secret or open foe often endeavors to destroy the person's reputation or influence.

You are extremely well suited to be a top administrator in situations where generalship and stern authority count. You are quite capable of inspiring confidence. Your ability to organize and to interest others in helping you to attain your particular objectives has to be respected. That you are aloof and somewhat standoffish helps to enhance your air of authority. Inside, you may be shy and uncertain, even fearful.

It is not unusual for a Moon-in-Capricorn child to be forced to take on responsibilities far beyond his or her years and to absorb the hardest lesson of all—that rewards come only to those who earn them. This isn't true, of course, but to a developing mind starved for love and sympathy, the lesson seems clear and final: when you excel, you are admired. So the will to succeed in concrete and unarguable terms consumes energies that might otherwise be more happily expended in tenderness and understanding.

If you are a man, the women in your life are apt to be upright, dependable, exacting and somewhat off-putting in their lack of warmth. If you are a woman, the men in your life will not be jealous of you, but very down-to-earth and practical. Incidentally, there will be no misunderstandings about your relationship, from which they are more likely to gain than you.

Men with Moon in Capricorn often marry older women or wed late in life. Their wives or lovers seldom bring them happiness and sometimes contribute to their downfall. Bachelorhood is not a difficult or unusual role for these males.

Mothers with this combination should go out of their way to give their children love and sympathy. They don't need to worry about being efficient in the home and providing practical instruction; these are disciplines they have naturally. Above any other duty to their offspring they should choose to show loving kindness and

understanding. What will make a man or woman of their child in their eyes probably won't; it will merely make a crippled and thwarted adult.

The Other Side of the Story

You are ambitious but vague and uncertain about the direction in which you are heading. You never cease to worry. Given any form of authority, you are petty, critical, carping, whining and callous. You resent others who are popular or more productive and gifted than you. You are a snide character assassin, unable to give praise where it's due and never capable of a complimentary word for anyone. You lack creative ability. Desperate to attract attention, you are apt to toady to your bosses and tell tales. Frustration at being unable to materialize your desires often renders you a chronic depressive.

MOON IN AQUARIUS

You are an interesting and nicely balanced person. As a pleasant companion, you're probably unbeatable, but as a serious romantic prospect, you're not such a good bet. You're too independent and unconventional to settle down for long with one partner. You're very loyal, mind you, and mean to keep your word, but you're really built for brotherhood and wider alliances. And when the call comes to circulate or serve some unusual cause, well, you gotta go when you've gotta go. You're not necessarily unfaithful to your mate during your peregrinations, but these sudden freedom jaunts can be very hard on the nerves and emotions of anyone who's attached to you.

Freedom is probably the key to your nature. And it's not just a physical impulse. You are mainly a mental creature, a creative idealist. You like to speak out. You not only believe passionately in freedom of thought, you practice it in constructive ways. You refuse to be inhibited by acceptable forms of thinking and custom. Your ideas are truly original, inventive, inspired. You have a rare gift for visualization and sometimes a touch of genius. The power of ideas to change and update society is frequently demonstrated through the Lunar Aquarian.

Being out front like this incurs some risks. For one thing, you might be thought eccentric. This won't worry you unduly because you are aware you see things differently. You also possess an admirable tolerance for all points of view. In fact, your sympathies are as wide in scope as your power to visualize, and this makes you emotionally rather stable yet able to understand the fears and prejudices of others. Your conversation is always worth listening to, possibly because you've got some way-out ideas that make sense when considered in the light of some of today's pressing problems.

You are agreeable, courteous and make a super collaborator. You are more comfortable working with groups than with individuals. Personal attachments make you feel hemmed in after a while. Your instincts are to serve humanity as a whole rather than to devote yourself to marriage or parenthood. This is not to say you can't enjoy a normal family life, but having to contend with a demanding and unimaginative partner or child can be awfully frustrating for you. Sooner or later you'll explode and do something quite unpredictable. Predictably, you could turn your back and walk out on any binding situation.

You are keenly interested in unusual subjects, especially those with a touch of mystery where you can employ your remarkable intuition. If you are a person living an ordinary kind of life without any great occupational opportunities for broad and original thinking, you have probably long ago dismissed the embryo signs described here as some sort of aberration peculiar to you. You could be hiding your creative potential under a bushel—and it's time the world had a look at it! It is the Aquarian Age that has given us marvelous electronic and mechanical aids. As a Lunar Aquarian, you share this inventive potential. It might be in scientific work, though you also have an aptitude for social work, politics and education. Moon in Aquarius usually gives a strong interest in occult matters and it is not unusual for the individual to possess some kind of ESP. Many of you have a very quick acceptance and understanding of Astrology, and sometimes a degree of clairvoyance. You seek knowledge, not for novelty or to impress, but to widen your understanding of universal principles.

With this combination, you are inclined to join clubs and associations having humanitarian or lofty aims. You possess a strong reforming instinct that desires to improve the lot of all human beings. When involved in a crusading venture, you do not go in for half-measures; you go all out to obtain public support. And you are not averse to making sensational announcements through the media aimed at surprising or shocking others into supporting your cause.

Friends and lovers are responsible for most of your sorrow and unhappiness.

The Other Side of the Story

You are likely to be a wanderer, moving from job to job and place to place, espousing ideas that never catch on. Your friends are probably dropouts and fruitless social rebels. Your anarchic views and erratic public behavior have probably led to a clash with the law or the Establishment. Notoriety and scandal may already have undercut any chance you had of success. Your attempts to show independence may cause unnecessary pain to others. Unexpected difficulties and sorrows are apt to make you bitter and quick to hurt others with thoughtless actions and a biting tongue.

MOON IN PISCES

You are an amazing, baffling, surprising, intriguing and beguiling personality, difficult to live with, in fact, a headache at times for those who feel responsible for you. But as a person to be with occasionally, as a companion, a buddy, a confidant, you are superb. You are either good news or bad news, depending largely on how emotionally attached the other party is to you.

You live in a world of fantasy where there is no pressure and you are the hero or heroine. Money problems and dealing with disharmonious situations leave you exhausted and feeling unstable and insecure. In these times—especially if you are a woman—you rush to the dependable person you usually have tucked away someplace and make a soul-elevating confession of your failures and inability to cope. Then, nestled in the warmth of your confidant's comforting and loving presence, you talk your head off until the harsh reality (as far as you are concerned) is dissolved. When you return to earth (you've probably been relating a dream or a childhood happening), you will start afresh until the pressures mount again.

That person you have around, especially if you are a woman, is the most important in your life. If it's a man, he certainly loves you in an abounding way, for in these dark, terrifying moments of self-doubt, you can be comforted only by undemanding and unselfish love. It is not difficult, mind you, for a man or an older woman to love a Moon-in-Pisces girl, for you epitomize sweet, cuddly, dependent, innocent helplessness. When you're feeling low, that is.

At other times, when the world's not treating you so badly, you want lots of company and plenty of change and stimulation. No one guy or gal for you now—it's life and excitement you require and anyone who tries to leash you (yes, even that old anchor guy) will feel your teeth sink deep into his cautionary or restraining hand.

When emotionally high, you are extremely optimistic, hopeful, gay and apparently outgoing. When the wind changes (as is likely in a few hours), you don't just go down, you plummet—into depression, fear and phobias, and if you're really a tough case, into various stages of paranoia. But no matter how far you fall, you rise again. Like the tides the Moon controls, you're either running in or running out. You're never one thing for very long.

It's this ambivalence that makes you such a fascinating and maddening character. But, of course, there is a grave danger in such behavioral extremes, and even at the best of times, you refuse to see the world as it really is. You are an incurable romantic. You weave your own dreams and expect reality to conform. Not surprisingly, you suffer from numerous disappointments and a great deal of misfortune. In adversity you retreat further into the world of your imagination. Consequently, under stress and without a strong and benevolent hand, you are in danger of losing touch completely.

You are self-sacrificing, generous and fundamentally placid. Being impressionable and compliant in worldly affairs, you are at the mercy of the unscrupulous and are often misused. Because of the Moon's position, you have a great emotional attachment to sensation, which sometimes leads to sexual promiscuity. In afflicted cases, there may be a recourse to drugs and alco-

hol to fortify the imaginative powers and make withdrawal from the world more complete. Most people with this combination have a compulsive need to be alone, usually after a period of excitation and fraternizing.

You love beauty and harmonious people. Art in all its forms appeals to you. Usually you have a particular creative talent for literature, poetry, dancing or acting. This may lie dormant unless you make a special effort to overcome the innate inertia, sometimes mistaken for laziness, that typifies this combination. Your unconscious tendency to reflect complementary emotions for the benefit of the people you are with makes you quite an unpredictable package. But it does ensure harmony in your casual relationships, which is terribly important to you. It is also your way of guaranteeing that people will like you—in you, often a desperate longing. You are highly psychic and sometimes have bad trips in dreams.

The Other Side of the Story

You may be a self-indulgent escapist, addicted to narcotics, drink and the search for sexual gratification. Chances are you will be a follower of some extremist sect or personality. Distorted emotionalism may render you vulnerable to dangerous practices such as trying to commune with disincarnate energies and even devil worship. You may be lazy, slovenly, indiscriminate and incapable of earning your own living in a conventional way. Prison, hospitals and mental institutions may figure prominently in your life. Your body may run to fat.

MERCURY

The Planet

Mercury is the smallest planet in the solar system and the nearest to the Sun. Its diameter is 3000 miles against the Earth's 8000. It is 36 million miles from the Sun, whereas the Earth is 96 million miles.

At times, Mercury can be seen just before sunrise, in the east, if you know where to look, and in the west, just after sunset. The planet revolves around the Sun just as the Moon revolves around the Earth. Its orbit is so close to the Sun that when it can be seen, it disappears from gaze beneath the horizon shortly after the Sun. The main problem spotting it with the naked eye (apart from glare) is its size. Mercury, relatively, is the size of a pea compared to the Sun's huge 54-inch-diameter sphere, and appears as a tiny black disc on the corona or halo of the solar giant.

Mercury has no atmosphere. If it had, the Sun's rays would be refracted and we would see a ring of light around the planet.

It is a planet of tremendous heat and cold. Because it takes the same time to rotate once on its axis as it does to complete a revolution of the Sun, one side is always exposed to the solar heat and light while the other remains in perpetual night and intense cold (as the Moon does in relation to the Earth).

Mercury's year—the time it takes to orbit the Sun—is only 88 Earth days. In keeping with its other "Mercurial" qualities, the planet's speed is a dashing 95,000 miles per hour compared with the Earth's ambling 25,000 mph.

Symbolism

Mercury, or Hermes as it was known to the ancients, was the herald of Zeus, the ruler of heaven and the supreme god. Since this planet is the closest to the solar lord by observation from the Earth, and since it appears to precede or follow the Sun (they are never more than 28 degrees apart), Mercury is said to represent the wisdom of the creator and the vital intelligence in man.

If thought is a linking process based on the mind's reflection on memory and experience, then Mercury is the flash of inspirational brilliance that gives thought new and meaningful connections with man's practical needs and developing consciousness.

The progress and evolution of the species depend on Mercury's analytical genius and its power to discriminate. It is pure intelligence that transcends time and place and appears in the consciousness from nowhere.

Symbolically, the planet's dual aspect—one side in perpetual sunlight and the other in perpetual shadow—denotes the constant and necessary distinction between the conscious and unconscious in man.

Mercury can explain the most complex ideas, formulate dazzling concepts. As the bridge between spirit, mind and matter, he has no preference of his own but provides the channel of immediacy. He will serve the basest desire and the most sublime aspiration.

He is the inventor of the lyre (having fashioned it by stringing a tortoise shell with cow gut). All music, art and science are of his devising. Magicians owe their skills to him. Those who would commune with the supreme intelligence in silence and solitude are dependent on his mediation. Mercury represents the power of man to study his inner world of thought and feeling without losing sight of external nature. Through his patronage, man discovered the correspondence between macrocosm and microcosm. "As above, so below," was the voice of Mercury.

To the ancients, he was the god of prudence and cunning as well as theft. To him is attributed the invention of astronomy, weights and measures, the musical scale and the arts of boxing and gymnastics. He was said to preside over games of dice. He was also regarded as the god of eloquence: in the Acts of the Apostles, the crowds of Lystra mistook St. Paul for Mercury "because he was the chief speaker." And because heralds promote peace and therefore trade, he was regarded as the god of peaceful commerce.

Mercury is usually depicted as a youth wearing a petasos (a traveling hat with wings)—or winged sandals, and carrying a caduceus or herald's staff made of olive wood, the ribbons of which were later changed to serpents, a tradiational symbol of wisdom.

Astrology

As a boy, Mercury is mischievous, a puckish prankster. He has little sense of responsibility or concentration. He is a cheery, cheeky messenger boy whose capers make even the sternest of the gods smile.

Mercury's cleverness requires positive direction, for he can just as easily turn into a confidence trickster and cheat as into a brilliant scientific investigator. Pure Mercurial intellect needs to be humanized, to connect with something worthwhile and significant, to discover lofty purpose; otherwise it may lose itself in the enjoyment of its own unemotional efficiency.

Mercury loves to pause briefly, and pass on. It is difficult for him to see things through, to build to last, because he is ever curious, always in motion. His task is to communicate his knowledge to others, and if he can't find one fulfilling way of doing this or a fertile field in which to work, he will either fritter away his fantastic intellectual energy in superficial activities or use his considerable persuasive powers to cast needless doubt, build up false hopes or undermine. His urge is to instruct in mental processes—and to hell with content!

Mercury has a high-strung, volatile and restless disposition. Like his metallic namesake, his moods rise and fall with the temperature of his surroundings, which includes the company he is in. He needs a fraternal hand on his shoulder, not so much to restrict as to guide him—a warm sagelike hand like that of the judicious and moral Jupiter, who has the good of all humanity in mind and is not beyond rebuking or chastising the errant boy when he needs it; or the steadying influence of Saturn, who can introduce Mercury to wisdom and curb his frivolity and vanity. The pleasure-loving Venus may overwhelm and distract Mercury further with her plethora of attractions. Mercury will never be short of good companions, but he needs to be careful of the impulsive element of Mars, the inconstancy and changeability of the Moon, and the excessive stimulation of the Sun.

Mercury, as the emissary of the Sun, allows us to discriminate beyond the confines of instinct. He is himself amoral, a connecting force between the essential being and our own individual propensities. He is the lightning in the pitch black sky of discursive thought that reveals the living earth to us in the reflection of our senses.

Without the flash of Mercurial intellect, the center of light and life—the Sun—would remain an incomprehensible mass. For this reason, Mercury, physiologically, is associated with the central nervous system, the brain and all sense perception and the sensory organs. It relates the exterior world to our own unique nature. It is the link between inner and outer, the interaction between objective and subjective realities.

MERCURY IN ARIES

You are a prolific and enthusiastic producer of new ideas, some of them quite brilliant. You are quick-witted, the dismay of slow thinkers, the pride of the office think tank. You are not afraid to suggest way-out ideas and have no trouble justifying them at a moment's notice with a superb display of mental gymnastics. Whether some of your ideas are practicable is doubtful, but few will be intrepid enough to challenge you to a public debate on that score. Repartee is like a rapier in your hand with which you thrust and parry with consummate skill. If your rivals or opponents suggest that you put your own plans to work, you may run for cover behind a convincing smokescreen of excuses.

You would normally make a first-class administrator, magistrate or governor because you are able to analyze and sum up situations swiftly. Your ability to think on your feet and to give orders off the top of your head makes you good at directing others; your precise instructions in an emergency are most impressive.

Although you are very original, you are incapable of sustained interest in one idea without the continual stimulus of twist, change and novelty. Your concentration is erratic and dissolves easily under the strain of repetition and forced effort. You can tell others, brilliantly, how something should be done, but you are incapable of following your own instructions to the end.

You are a lover of literature; you like to read, write and discuss subjects for hours on end when you meet a knowledgeable person. Writers and other literary people appreciate your ability to see the same situation from different angles. You can offer good common-sense advice, even though you may be unable to follow it yourself. You rely on your mind to control your supporters; if you want to be, you are the supreme demagogue.

You are not a stereotyped conversationalist. You like to put forward new opinions, some of which you have not considered until you utter them with all the panache of a deeply ruminative thinker. You are the loquacious life of the party socially, and can usually manage to keep even the dullest company amused provided you feel you are receiving sufficient attention. You may exaggerate and enjoy the sound of your own voice. As a raconteur who can switch topics to suit the audience you have few equals. People come to you because you will listen keenly to their problems without attempting to moralize or to judge them. Your intellectual energy is quite amazing. You are a fast communicator. Words can flow from you mouth or pen with riveting impact or persuasive charm.

If your Sun is in Pisces, you have a gift for describing human emotions with subtlety and deep understanding; if in Aries, you are passionately identified with your ideas, sometimes to the point of recklessness; if in Taurus, you possess an unerring instinct for business and financial manipulation.

With Mercury in Aries, the pioneering instinct of the Sign gives your intellectual activities an adventurous touch. You are prepared to experiment intellectually when most others would be daunted by fear of ridicule or failure. You are the propounder of the new theory, the first to express or approve a new style whether it is in writing, composing, thinking or inventing. Your mind, because it is so active and responsive, can be a wonderful servant or an oppressive master.

The Other Side of the Story

You are apt to want your own way immediately and be very impatient of opposition. As an employer, you may insist that your orders and instructions be carried out with an alacrity that borders on dictatorship. You are likely to lack method, order and perseverance, and skip from one thing to another. Some of you may suffer from fits of passion and anger that leave you physically exhausted; persistent and acute headaches may follow these temperamental outbursts. You may be perverse and willful, which could spoil your innate ability to lead.

You may lay down the law when compromise is essential, or be cruelly direct when tact is called for. You may be oblivious of your own power to hurt. In debate, you may see only your side of the argument, mistake cleverness for profundity, play to the gallery instead of playing the game. If others do not follow your rules, you may become peevish, critical, sardonic and quarrelsome. You may be quick to give an opinion on any subject but loath to listen to others. If you regard speech as your lifebuoy in any emergency, you may find that others are not as gullible as you

thought. Those whom you think you have converted to your ideas are likely to turn against you in the end.

MERCURY IN TAURUS

The plodding and methodical influence of Taurus brings your Mercurial qualities down to earth. You use your mind and considerable intellect to amass a greater share of material things. You are practical, you look before you leap and your ideas are not insubstantial. You are a deep thinker, or a true conservative or both. If you work in a scientific field, you are in your element, cautiously applying your well thought out theories, diligently observing and recording the results. You don't jump to conclusions. You are patient, solid, constructive. Your goal is to hold onto what you have, and if possible without running any extra risks, garner a great deal more. You are often obstinate and resist change. You like the old and proven ideas. In a position of power, you will see to it that progress is by cautious evolution, not revolution.

Historically, people born with Mercury in Taurus have made a great impact on their times, but their contribution usually came out of an unyielding self-repression that prepared the way for new eras of luminous advance. This position often confers political acumen, but not the spectacular kind. Politicians with this combination tend to come to power in times of chaos, when a return to solid and traditional methods is necessary to restore confidence and order. They lead their followers *back*—to fundamentals such as responsibility, perseverance, patience and economy. (Some might say now is a time for a Mercury-in-Taurus statesman or stateswoman to appear on the world scene.) It's not the creative achievement of these people that is impressive, but rather their ability to establish a firm basis others can use to go on to glorious accomplishment and discovery.

You stick to your opinions with great stubbornness. It may take you some time to decide what you want out of life, but when you make up your mind, you are usually unshakable. You will pursue your objectives with almost slavish application. Once an idea becomes fixed in your mind, you usually set about gathering large amounts of information to augment it.

With this planetary lineup, you have a fine chance of making money, as Mercury's usually capricious and flighty tendencies here are given direction. The acquisitiveness of Taurus and the mental wizardry of Mercury, together often produce wealth. You have the intellect to read and absorb facts, but you are a pragmatist who prefers to learn your lessons from life rather than from teachers, schools and books. As much as you respect theory, you realize it must be backed up by experience. You will never undertake a venture until you have carefully studied the ground and accumulated the necessary knowledge. You don't favor leaving success to chance, and you do believe in taking precautions. You like to build a solid framework and then patiently and doggedly fill in the panels. You are not easily distracted from your purpose. Slowly but surely, you wear down the opposition just as the sea erodes the coastline. You are the personification of the war of attrition.

You would make a sound banker because of your grasp of financial matters and your adherence to orthodox procedures and conservative policies. You are a good manager of both your own and other people's money. You are sociable, friendly and affectionate. Music, poetry and art often have more than the usual appeal. You have an innate appreciation of beautiful things and are often very knowledgeable about collecting objects of art. You enjoy the company of the opposite sex. You have enough intellectual pursuits to make you an interesting person to meet, and you are well aware of your ability to charm your way out of situations.

It is not unusual for people with this combination to acquire wealth, possessions or status through marriage. They tend to gravitate to more elevated social circles than their own. A pleasant, happy and relaxed disposition helps them gain acceptance where others would be considered rank interlopers.

Many famous popular singers have Mercury in Taurus. Music and dancing are also activities in which you may excel.

The Other Side of the Story

You may sink into a mental rut out of your dislike of change. If your ambitions are too earthy, you may not be able to make the best use of the abstractions and subtleties that Mercury has to offer. You may have the strength and massive solidarity of the Bull, but without the refining influence of the airy and volatile planet, your views will be fixed and repetitious. You may be excessively habitual, a bit of a bore. You can have lapses of uncontrollable rage and intense irritation. You may live for money or

position. Your mind may rule your heart. Cash, possessions and the social life could be your ultimate objectives.

MERCURY IN GEMINI

Life is not the puzzle to you that it is to others. You see things in a superrational way and are convinced that to you most problems can be sorted out intellectually. Because you believe logic is the simple answer to everything, you don't rely very much on feeling, even though you are naturally sympathetic. You think life should be lived intelligently, with reason as the guiding principle.

You are apt to generalize and skip over important considerations. At times your mind reaches great heights of lucidity. You are then fluent, clever, inquisitive and become irritated with others who do not see the facts as clearly as you do, although your "facts" are probably mere abstractions to them. You may win an argument by the sheer power of your logic, but leave the practical problem that provoked it just as far from solution. You are a master of superficial thought. You can dart here and there with a rapidity that leaves your weightier opponents continually on the wrong foot. You often make a fine public speaker who gains support by confining yourself popular ideas. You are on a wavelength with the common type of curiosity that requires interesting information but not necessarily the truth. You sometimes appear foolish, but never stupid or dull. Because you live in a mental world, your behavior at times may seem silly to more down-to-earth associates. You are ideally suited to journalism because you can report or interpret quickly without concerning yourself with practical consequences, and have the knack of clarifying issues and stringing ideas together in natural sequences. You are not actually as intuitive or instinctive as you may appear. Your real intellectual strength is in constant awareness, the ability to look two ways at once, both inwardly and outwardly. For you, everything must have a causal explanation and your mind works like a scanner, noting sequences and looking for flaws and gaps in the logical order.

You don't like mysteries; they exist for you to solve. You are contemptuous of people who believe blindly and impatient with those who allow sentiment and emotion to distort their thinking. You do not try much to communicate with those who live conventional and sluggish lives. You are polite, but . . . you need compatible company, people who grasp concepts quickly without the need for punctuation. You need to circulate, to travel, to exchange ideas. A change of environment can set you off in a totally new direction. You are easily influenced and distracted and won't concentrate on one idea for long. You are more versatile than profound. You long to be free and unbound by concepts or surroundings. You can make an excellent linguist. Your superb sense of humor helps you to communicate ideas in pleasing form. Your mind is machinelike in its precision. You are well informed, ingenious and resourceful. You are very seldom prejudiced and have a great many interests.

In manual occupations, you should shine where dexterity is required. You would make an able carpenter, painter, stenographer, dressmaker or magician. You are fond of specualtion, novelty, literature and science. You may be attracted to the study of occult subjects with considerable success. You enjoy acquiring obscure knowledge.

Your personality may be distinguished by a cold intellectual quality. This can be quite impressive in business or a position of authority, but in other circumstances, it may intimidate or repel others. You have a particular talent for seeing things as they are without allowing emotional considerations to distort your judgment. You may make unpopular decisions that are disputed, not because of their faulty logic, but because they disregard ordinary human feelings.

You're not a sentimentalist. But your Mercurial wit and humor communicate a warmth that others can't help but respond to. Many actors and comedians are born with Mercury in Gemini.

The Other Side of the Story

You may live too much on the mental plane and consequently lack human warmth. It may be hard for you to communicate at a serious level with ordinary people; gossip may be your main pastime. Nervous breakdowns are likely because of anxiety and overwork. Restlessness may make it impossible for you to settle down. Enduring accomplishment may always elude you. You are apt to imitate rather than originate. Nervous excitement may cause sleeplessness.

MERCURY IN CANCER

Your mind is passive and receptive. You have an uncommon capacity for absorbing facts, particularly about the past. You are often a student of history, a collector of antiquities, an antique dealer, a scholar. You are discreet, tactful and bend over backward to please people . You would make a first-class diplomat. In your eagerness to create a favorable impression, you are apt to ignore your own convictions and say what you think others want to hear. You are likely to lose yourself in whatever happens to take your attention. You are often a bookworm, a dedicated librarian. Any literary efforts will tend toward histories about races and families and sensitive biographies of famous figures of the past.

You are not particularly original, in fact, you depend a lot on precedent for your opinions and judgments. You would rather obey a rule than struggle with alternatives. You often find your self-expression in the backwaters of human activity where there is not a great deal of competition or stress. You are extremely sensitive. Your intuition amazes others, while to you it is an essential faculty. Labored explanations are not necessary for you; you get the point very quickly by intuitive transference, and frequently grasp a whole argument before the speaker has finished the preamble. You may know things without being told them; but not know how you know.

You can't stand being in the company of people who are out of harmony with you. You will withdraw quietly from discordant situations without offering an explanation, and preferably without making a scene. You can resent people who argue with you, but you are wonderfully sympathetic and understanding and your compassion is easily aroused. Pain and suffering in any living thing disturb you. You are quite intense in your likes and dislikes, but you are extremely tolerant of the opinions and beliefs of others. You like to live and let live.

You are a natural psychologist. You can stare deeply into the past (or into another person's mind) without a ruffle and without taking sides. Your appreciation of symbolism and fantasy exceeds the understanding that is normally ascribed to your type. You apprehend subtleties that at times are beyond the rational. For this reason, you sometimes find yourself accused of being illogical.

You have a way of winning the confidence and trust of others so that they often confide in you. You won't betray another's confidence and frequently offer advice that helps those in distress to carry on.

Your memory is often extraordinary but may deteriorate in old age. You are impressionable, sometimes too easily persuaded. You are creative and artistic. Your sense of rhythm can make you a competent dancer, gymnast or athlete, or a poet, musician or graceful writer. You are often successful in the entertainment field. You are inclined to have a close link with your mother or her side of the family. You are excited by travel, particularly when it means crossing water. You are a quietly social person, a good and generous friend to those whom you select. You are discreet and faithful. You like to be appreciated by your friends and are easily influenced by kindness. An appeal to the senses will have much more effect on you than an appeal to logic. Praise will make you try harder.

Your outlook on affairs is broad and comprehensive. Your intellect may not be as outstanding as that of those born with other Mercury combinations, but your humanity and respect for people's feelings, particularly their anxieties, make you a very special kind of person. Your imagination is extremely vivid and can cause you actual pain. You are inclined to become despondent through excess of sympathetic feeling. When you hear of a disaster, you visualize the scene with great and moving compassion for those affected. You are very aware of the needs of your family and will go to great lengths to protect and provide for them. Your children can be an especially tender spot. You look to your family for admiration. A greater faith in your own reasoning power is often needed. You have a genuine desire to help others.

The Other Side of the Story

You are likely to drift like a rudderless ship. You may live in a world of fantasy or bore everyone stiff with tales about the past, particularly your childhood. You may lack discrimination. You may resort to telling lies to secure approval and recognition. You are likely to become a creature of habit in an attempt to avoid asserting yourself. You may run from one worthy cause to another without achieving anything of permanent value. Your unusually impressionable nature makes you an easy victim of circumstance. You are too easily swayed by the opinions of others. You are likely to embrace an erroneous view briefly, turn away and immediately become attached to another false idea. Your mind may become inactive. You may be dishonest with yourself in trying to please others. Your need of approbation may turn you into a bit of a trickster. You could be narrow-minded.

MERCURY IN LEO

You believe in your ideas with all your heart and soul. You feel you have something to say and you want the world to know it—and usually, you are well worth listening to. This is one of the best positions for the Mercury influence; here it responds well to the steadying dignity of the Sun, which rules Leo. You have a warm personality and usually considerable presence. Your words convey a personal conviction that seldom fails to excite interest. Your audience may not agree with what you say, but it will be quick to respect the articulate and impressive manner in which you present your case.

You don't take kindly to disagreement, which you regard as a personal slight. This is a terrible reflection on your power to discriminate between fact and fiction, the pertinent and impertinent. You are a direct and positive thinker. There is seldom any malice in your reactions— when faced with a Doubting Thomas, you are likely to be astonished that he could possibly question your judgment or suggest there may be another way of looking at things. Believing yours is the only admissible point of view, you may surround yourself with yes-men.

You are ambitious and will probably get to the top in your field. You have a flair for management and organization and should make a top-flight company director. The communications industry could be especially favorable for you. You can issue orders quickly and cogently. You are progressive, persistent, determined. Your personality emanates vitality and assurance. You have the human touch, derived from the blending of a fine intellect (Mercury) with the sympathetic warmth of the Sun. You are intuitive. You like people. You like to help them with advice and give them the benefit of your experience. You are not the intellectual type who sits in an ivory tower devising fanciful schemes and handing them down for execution. You are a doer. If you can't do something yourself, you won't ask another to do it. You demand loyalty from both subordinates and those who love you. You have a lot of heart and a lot of brain: you combine the perceptive and emotional qualities in a rare balance of harmonious action and response. You are fond of children and pets, music, fine arts and the opposite sex. You are pleasure-loving and inclined to self-indulgence.

Usually you occupy a position of authority. You want your own way, mostly because you sincerely believe that your ideas are best for the common good. For yourself, you want recognition, admiration, respect. If these are forthcoming, your other needs are not great. You can be extraordinarily magnanimous, and selfless. As a born leader, you react very sharply to any form of disobedience. Your anger is explosive but it doesn't last long. You don't hold grudges. You seldom stoop to low actions. You are often flamboyant and ostentatious. You love to impress others with your accomplishments. You enjoy glamorous situations and the company of glamorous people. You think on a grand scale.

This combination often allows the exemplar of genius close contact with the masses. Not everyone with Mercury in Leo is a genius, but with this combination, even the most ordinary person projects ideas and influence beyond his or her immediate circle. Some of the greatest (and most infamous) empire builders of history were born with Mercury in this position. So were numerous thinkers whose bold ideas have helped to enlighten society on religion, Astrology, literature and other means of mass communication. There is frequently a strong element of physical courage in these people; they are not afraid to risk their reputations or even their lives for their beliefs. They are often distinguished by personal charisma.

You are likely to possess a good singing voice or some other quality that entertains and draws people to you. In proper circumstances, your speeches may seize the public imagination and carry you forward to a position of power. You may be popular in the acting or writing professions. You can sell your ideas as long as you believe in them. You aren't the best of demagogues or charlatans. In whatever you do, you are looking over your shoulder at a potential audience. Above all, you thrive on applause, which is why you will never seek obscurity. You will always do a good job, not only because of the nobility in your makeup, but also because the fire in you is fed by the adulation and love of others.

The Other Side of the Story
You may be conceited and overbearing. You are likely to be on a continuous ego trip that demands rather than deserves. You may be a snob. Your opinions could be too fixed. Your great sense of pride and authority may degenerate into tiresome boasting. You may be a showoff who upsets others with your patronizing attitude,

your pomposity. You may proffer advice where it is not wanted and display an intolerance and critical enthusiasm that alienate the very people who could be the most help to you. You may be an intellectual bully. Your urge for power may drive you to destruction; what you love most you may destroy out of misplaced sense of justice, zeal or a feeling of omnipotence. You may use alcohol and drugs to excess. Overindulgence is a danger for you in all pleasures.

MERCURY IN VIRGO
This is a very strong intellectual position for Mercury. The planet both rules and is exalted in Virgo, which means its powers are greatly enhanced here. You have a finely discriminating mind. You can dissect issues with great detail and precision. Your approach is by pure reason; you don't, as a rule, allow emotional considerations to override the mental. You are inclined to overlook or be intolerant of human failure—in fact, nothing annoys you more than the blind stupidity of others. Some of your associates may regard you as altogether too exacting and computerlike in your thinking.

You are skeptical, critical and analytical. Your greatest satisfaction is to set everything neatly in its place, and you try to accomplish this in every department of your life. Mercury here confers the Virgo quality that tries unconsciously to tidy up the household of the world. Considering the vast amount of disorder in this world, you are incessantly busy making mental assessments, endeavoring to compensate, rearrange and correct. In anyone less fitted for unrewarding effort, it would be an exhausting business, but you can cope, though the effort keeps you in a high-strung state and your intentions are sometimes misinterpreted. You find it hard to understand why everyone is not as aware as you are of the desirability of method and order. Frequently you are disappointed and frustrated by people's lackadaisical responses to your urgings. You are seldom contented. Unless you can direct your discriminative faculties into a worthwhile occupation you are apt to focus them on your associates and gain a reputation for being overly critical, interfering and fussy.

You are a down-to-earth person, devoid of the diffusiveness that characterizes Mercury in Gemini, the planet's other Sign. Your character is the polar—strictly practical, no-nonsense. You give the brilliant but unpredictable Mercury force stability. You apply your mental powers to practical affairs rather than abstract ends. You are ideally suited to scholarly research, because you are a master of detailed evaluation. You like to grind the particles down, sift, assimilate and digest the essential facts. Laboratory work, scientific inquiry, mathematics, accounting—any pursuit that requires a disciplined and controlled mind is one you will shine in. You enjoy activities that require involved planning and ingenuity. Crossword puzzles are child's play—or did you get stuck on a clue this morning? You are happier dealing with a multitude of details than with having to wrestle with the broader picture. You can be a great contributor to human knowledge through your ability to make painstaking studies and investigations. You are more adaptive than you are innovative. Exceedingly quick to learn, you are so quick that you may not concentrate enough to remember for long, though your power to memorize is unsurpassed if you wish to use it.

You aren't an easy person to convince; you insist on understanding a subject thoroughly before committing yourself. The way to appeal to you is through reason. With such concentrated intellectual power at your disposal, there is a danger you will overlook the human element in your calculations. You are apt to forget that though people often pay lip service to the power of reason, they more often run their lives according to a mixture of self-interest, prejudice and emotion.

You are naturally quiet and rather serious. You suffer from a painful lack of confidence, though you usually manage to disguise it. You try to avoid showdowns and taking strong stands on basic issues because you are so self-critical that you can't maintain a position of self-assertion for long.

You are interested in all intellectual pursuits, but you aren't showy or egotistical about these accomplishments. You would make an able linguist. Your powers of persuasion through the written and spoken word are considerable, though you have a tendency to go into too much detail and become tedious. You may also lack the warmth and fire of physical presence and thus fail to incite emotional fervor in others. You can make out an unarguable case why everyone should drink nothing but water, and the whole world will agree with you—and then go on drinking what they fancy.

Your love of solving mysteries sometimes inclines you to occult studies. You can write profusely on just about any subject that excites your interest and curiosity. You usually insist on having first-hand experience of things, and this enables you to give finely etched descriptions. Many writers with remarkable powers of observation have this combination. You usually endeavor to give others the benefit of your knowledge, although you are far from pushy (unless your Sun is in Leo).

You have a particular talent for devising special techniques for handling work. If there is a solution to a problem, you can be counted on to find it. Your discerning intellect will swiftly whittle away a mountain of conjecture into a molehill of fact and statistics.

Physical fitness especially interests you. Just as you strive to put details into place, so you endeavor to help people fit neatly and comfortably into their environment by staying healthy. You are a keen advocate of cleanliness and hygiene. You are strongly convinced of the healthiness of fresh and wholesome food, and try to set an example for others by keeping to a balanced and nutritious diet.

The Other Side of the Story

You are likely to ride roughshod over any opponent. Cold reason may be your god. The letter of the word may be so important to your judgments that any glow of human kindness is eclipsed. You may be too brittle, rigid and detached to deal effectively with practical affairs. You may be a harping critic, believing that only you know how things should be done. You are more likely to find fault than to praise, to quibble over unimportant details. You are probably selfish and sarcastic. You may be fanatical about health habits and inflict an unnecessary regimen on those you live with. Your penchant for neatness may become uncontrolled. You may be mean with money, and your reluctance to show love and feeling may eventually turn you into a dry, emotionless, unyielding individual. In a position of authority, you may be a trifling despot.

MERCURY IN LIBRA

This placing of Mercury makes you extremely broad-minded and intellectually capable. Your considered judgments are often impeccable for their justice and sheer logic, but in the rough and tumble of everyday living, you may be hesitant and indecisive. This can make life a bit difficult. An intuitive flash about how to go about something may be dissipated by an organized attempt to weigh all the pros and cons before proceeding. Thus are good opportunities lost. First thoughts are often best for you. It does not pay always to play safe. Remember, you can't hope to please everyone.

You are rather changeful. You sum up a situation admirably, decide on a course of action—and at the last second do something else. As refreshing as your openmindedness is, it does have certain drawbacks. For one, you are likely to be attracted to frivolous pursuits. Curiosity may lure you from one subject to another, preventing you from accomplishing any one thing that is really worthwhile.

You are ambitious for intellectual attainment. You will go to a lot of trouble to set up projects, discussing them with various people and assembling a large stack of reference material. But when the time comes for action, for disciplined effort, you may have flitted off (most gracefully) to some new interest. Therefore, you are apt to acquire voluminous knowledge about numerous topics but have little practical experience of anything in particular. You are not attracted to physical labor, though enjoy using your hands and can be quite deft and artistic with handicrafts and the like.

You have a charming way of saying the right thing. Quick to respond to the different factions in an audience, you have the knack of bringing them together or at least of convincing them all simultaneously that you understand their particular problem. You have a great eye for artistic detail and can fill a valuable role by putting the final touches to literary or artistic productions. You dot the i's as an artist, not as a pedant.

You have an air of authority, a suggestion of wisdom about you. You can combine the best of head and heart in your evaluations. If your Sun is also in Libra, you have an intellect of considerable polish and refinement. You are capable of expressing abstract ideas in a most interesting way. You are usually drawn to music, literature and public speaking.

With the Sun in Virgo, your outlook is more practical; you can be involved with the harsher side of life without bruising your finer sensibilities. With the Sun in Scorpio, you possess a flair for psychology that can be put to good use in business ventures.

Mercury in Libra should make you a well-balanced character, but equilibrium here, at the central Sign of the Zodiac, is so delicately poised that it can easily be upset by other aspects in the horoscope. No conclusions should be drawn until the other effects (indicated in the Yellow and Blue Tables) are studied and weighed—an exercise that will appeal tremendously to the typical Mercury-Libra person.

Your choice of career will depend largely on the people most influential in your life at the time. As you change your companions, you are also likely to alter your views and this will usually be reflected in the quality or style of the work you do. It is important for young people with this combination to choose associates who will stimulate their flexible and facile minds in positive directions so that they are always moving forward in their field—and not sliding sideways.

You love friends and a good social life. You are extremely well suited to work with partners. In marriage, you require intellectual companionship more than physical presence. Sometimes this combination leads to an inferior marriage—socially or financially. It can also mean marriage to a distant relative. Your refined taste, smooth social manner and gift for sophisticated conversation make you an ideal host or hostess and a popular guest.

The Other Side of the Story

You may be weak-willed and too easily influenced. Your tactlessness and manner of expression may make you unpopular. You may be insincere and easy to see through, eventually even a social outcast. You are apt to be devious and depend on the clever use of words to paper over situations rather than genuinely try to heal them. You may be a glaring opportunist. You are likely to agree with everyone to save yourself from contention, and may give in to an argument even though you know you are right. You may be an escapist who lies your way out of situations rather than face the truth. You may prefer to live in a world of daydreams or spend your time gossiping and maligning others.

MERCURY IN SCORPIO

Because the range of possibilities for good and evil is so extensive in this position and subject to modifications elsewhere in the horoscope, you must decide which traits apply to you personally in the following description. It is, by necessity, an analysis of extremes.

The typical person born with Mercury in Scorpio has a mind of almost unsurpassed clarity and intensity. You combine the heights of intellectual acuity with passionate fierceness of feelings. You can be most of what is best in man, and most of what is worst. Your reach is from heaven to hell. You are a visionary, able to see beyond the normal confines of the mind. Your perception is so shrewdly effective that it is almost impossible to deceive you. You can spot a phony a mile off.

You are hypercritical, highly suspicious and mistrustful. You have already observed in yourself all the inequities of which man is capable, so you recognize them instantly (though mostly subconsciously) in others. You are wary, cautious and possessed of a bitter intolerance that expresses itself eagerly in vitriolic condemnation. You are pitiless when opposed and will resort to any action or subterfuge likely to give you victory or revenge. Your capacity to hate and to wait patiently for vengeance can be diabolical. You are a vicious, ruthless and terrible enemy.

You are bold, reckless, ingenious and keen to demonstrate the penetrating swiftness of your mind. You enjoy the cat-and-mouse game, carefully baiting your unsuspecting opponent, skillfully maneuvering him or her into a vulnerable position. You strike to wound, not to kill; to ruin, not to destroy. You undermine by innuendo. Your insinuations are devilishly contrived. A sixth sense tells you exactly when and where to strike, when the psychological organism is at its weakest point.

You are secretive and cunningly protective of your personal interests. You hate committing yourself and refuse to take anyone into your confidence. But you like to listen to others' secrets, to hear their foolish, trusting statements. You are contemptuous of those who would oppose you and haughtily dismissive of the views of people you regard as your inferiors. You suffer many disappointments and have more trouble than most with relatives, neighbors and partners.

You would make a good undercover agent because you can keep up deception for an inordinate time. You are an inspired investigator of insurance frauds, conspiracies and complex financial swindles. You have great physical and nervous endurance. Your courage in the face of danger can be sublime. You enjoy pitting your wits against another, especially an adversary with a reputation. You are proud of your sharp mind and resourcefulness. You have a strong sexual drive and enjoy erotic reading and talk.

You are fascinated by mysteries and particularly enjoy solving those that have defied the ingenuity of others. You can be especially attracted to occult and metaphysical investigations. Your penetrative, subtle and intuitive mind allows you to be numbered among some of the most profound and inspirational mystics to have elevated the mind of man. Your bulldog tenacity and intellectual breadth fit you for a role in politics. You excel in a power struggle, especially if the in-fighting is rough and vicious. In a workshop, office or boardroom encounter, you don't expect sympathy or mercy and you certainly won't extend them. You have all the courage necessary to back up your convictions. Calmness under pressure is one of your most demoralizing weapons and you never fail to exhibit it.

The often pernicious effect of Mercury in Scorpio is softened if the Sun is in Libra. This personality is likely to be more yielding, less vitriolic, more given to satire than to straightout ridicule or vindictive criticism. But still, there is a strong inclination to argue and oppose.

The Sun conjoined with Mercury in Scorpio confers a greater capacity for noble endurance and fortitude and heightens the perceptive and intuitive faculties. The Sun-in-Sagittarius combination gives the mind a broader and less introspective vision and heightens the interest in philosophic studies.

The Other Side of the Story
This is largely told above. It is possible for poorly evolved persons with this combination to engage in sadism. They can be deeply brooding and find partial relief for their resentments in starting scandalous and despicable rumors about rivals and opponents. Their jealousy can reach peaks of destructive fury that would not shrink from even self-immolation to even a score.

MERCURY IN SAGITTARIUS
You are an extremely changeable person. Your mind is an open hotline that never ceases to receive and convey ideas. As one thought comes in, it quickly moves on and another takes its place. You are quite brilliant at times and can utter ideas and observations with the rapidity of a machine gun, hitting the target repeatedly with astounding accuracy. But your quick-fire thoughts lack depth and follow-through. You disappoint because your remarkable intuitions are never bolstered by digested knowledge and firsthand experience.

You enjoy being superactive physically as well as mentally and are apt to have one or two part-time jobs in addition to your main occupation. You are fond of doing several things at once. You love to talk to and meet people. You can scramble for hours, jumping from one topic to another, asking and answering questions, but remembering very little of consequence. Despite your brilliance, you talk off the top of your head and you often put your foot in things because you have neither the time nor the capacity to weigh a situation properly. Because your concentration is weak, you are bright but unwise and fail to consider the effect of your remarks.

Still, you are a sincere type of person, simple and honest. There is nothing underhanded about you. Unlike those with Mercury in Scorpio, you find it impossible to engage in deliberate cruelty. Such perversity would not even occur to you. If you tell a lie, it is on the spur of the moment. Since you lack malice, you are temperamentally unsuited to long drawn out feuds.

You love independence and are a strong and vociferous defender of free expression. You are impulsive and often rebellious, don't take kindly to authority and resent any overt display of its power. Because you can't stand injustice, you will often fight on the side of the underdog. You are ambitious and capable of surprising breadth of vision, but you seem unable to stick to one goal for any length of time and usually get diverted without noticing it.

Success often eludes you until late in life because you are inclined to move around too often to be there when the promotions are handed out. You live to live, not to work. You are interested in education, although you personally won't take it too seriously if it means being tied down in your early years. You enjoy traveling and probably wish to visit other countries, although you are very happy making numerous short trips, dropping in on people and cultivating contacts.

You often have a strong desire to understand life and its mysteries. You have great faith in the redemptive power of the moral law. You also respect science and religion and enjoy philosophic discussions. You imagine yourself, rightly or wrongly, to be well informed on these subjects.

A talent for writing and lecturing, which may lead to long-distance travel and unusual experiences, is indicated if your Sun is in also Sagittarius. Sun in Capricorn indicates a much more solid citizen, imbued with the ability to lay down the law and see that it is carried out. (The "law" in this case is usually a socio-moral concept the person enforces on his or her family or community.) Sun in Scorpio often turns the Mercury-Sag-ittarian vision inward, yielding great self-knowledge and a talent for sociology and psychology.

The Other Side of the Story

You may be incapable of reconciling your ideas with the facts of life, lacking in mature judgment and unable to weigh one idea against another—an absurd nonrealist. You may make an impressive show of urging others toward a greater life goal, while you yourself run around in foolish circles, patently achieving nothing. You may be tactless and carelessly hurtful, quick to make promises and slow to keep them. Your impatience and restlessness may prevent you from finishing anything worthwhile.

MERCURY IN CAPRICORN

This is a desirable position for Mercury. The brilliant and erratic planet has no chance of going off the rails here. It blends easily and advantageously with the Sign Capricorn, which epitomizes the cool, calculating and severe mentality, the mind that is rationalizing, disciplined and exacting. The result is a person of dignity, good sense, practicality, earnestness and prudence.

You seldom engage in frivolous or silly talk. You have an air of purposefulness. When you open your mouth, you are worth listening to. You can be counted on to have put your ideas through the strict acid-test of reason. And if they are wrong or unacceptable, it will be because of an error in judgment, not because of any neglect of detail or thorough investigation.

You have an excellent memory, which you don't bother to clutter with gossip and superficial information. The only details you decide to memorize are those you know will be useful. Your powers of concentration are likewise extraordinary. You have the knack of focusing your perceptive powers with unwavering intensity on the problem of the moment. Because your mind is usually engaged in some weighty consideration (the world is filled with problems for those who look for them), you may be intolerant of people who are interested in the lighter side of life. You may lack a sense of humor and find it hard to adapt to a purely social atmosphere.

You possess a great determination to succeed; Mercury ensures that you have the necessary wit and intelligence. You are very steady and sincere and tactfully curious about anything affecting your own ambitious interests. Your mind can attend to the smallest detail without losing sight for a second of the overall plan. You accept responsibility. You command respect even when you are wrong. Your deliberative seriousness gives you an air of wisdom.

You are reserved, cautious and suspicious. You have a moralistic outlook that may be too rigid to win many friends. Unless this Capricorn-Mercury combination is softened by other influences, you may tend to cut yourself off from people and make a cold and narrow intellectual world only you can live in

You are often consulted by others for your wise advice. You enjoy the role of confidant and counselor, but it is one in which you take yourself too seriously.

You are always trying to develop your mind. You are keenly interested in science, chemistry, philosophy and business management. You may be discontented with the way things are run in this world, but your natural diplomacy and correctness of manner usually prevent others from taking offense. You are intensely conscious of your own dignity and will seldom forgive anyone who undercuts it.

You need to guard against depression. Although your mind is steady, your moods can be quite changeable. You may swing violently from one extreme to another, and this innate ability to adapt quickly at the emotional level may leave you temporarily insecure and tormented by vague and unreasonable fears. Your mature and painstaking examination of the human condition can produce a pessimistic outlook. This may be countered by cultivating a more cheerful and elastic attitude.

If your Sun is in Sagittarius, you have a warm and expansive mind and your attention is less minutely concentrated. Your curiosity goes beyond the immediate task and your own self-centered interests. You may then see hope in religion and feel the glow of optimism. You may also use your wisdom to instruct others in practical, day-to-day matters.

If your Sun is in Aquarius, you are likely to fling yourself into organized research projects aimed at solving recognized scientific or social problems on a global scale. You are then more original and less restrictive in your perceptions. If both your Sun and Mercury are in Capricorn, you are a grave person who has great faith in his or her own opinions. If your ideas are correct, you may make a great contribution to human knowledge after struggling valiantly to overcome opposition. But if they are wrong, you may live a life of rigid isolation trapped in your own narrow thought-world.

The Other Side of the Story

You may be a religious bigot. Your close-mindedness may make you cruel and tyrannical, a wet blanket who spoils everyone else's fun and spreads gloom and depression. Your judgments may be unnecessarily harsh. You may also be stingy and selfish, and an unyieldingly severe boss who becomes increasingly tyrannical as your authority grows. You may be sullen and sulk at imagined insults.

MERCURY IN AQUARIUS

You have a gift for understanding both sides of an argument and resist siding with either. This equanimity may cause misunderstandings among associates and family members, who in emotionally charged moments usually demand a show of partiality. But you are too independent-minded to fall for this unless the subject happens to be one of your pet concerns. Then you can be as one-eyed as anyone, going so far as to verge on the fanatical.

You have a fine, versatile and broad mind. The petty issues of life and its superficial curiosities don't appeal to you much. You acquire knowledge to put it to work where it will do the most good for the greatest number. Scientific inquiry has a special attraction for you. Your mind can range over complex issues and with remarkable intuition light on the weakest point. You are capable of offering solutions that may be quite breathtaking in their originality and scope.

You are often drawn to the communications industries, using them to disseminate your ideas and to draw attention to necessary reforms. Broadcasting, television, magazine, book or newspaper publishing usually figure prominently in this combination.

You are an excellent judge of human nature but very tolerant of what you find. As a rule, you are not the type who goes in for deep emotional attachments—Aquarians embody the inventive and humanitarian impulses and thus need to be objective to function at their best. Emotionalism with its accompanying biases is something you try to exclude from your private life, too, so when it comes to love affairs, you're a bit too offhand and casual for the usual partner. You need a special kind of person who won't pester you with demands for devotion you are incapable of fulfilling. The exception to this may occur if your Sun happens to be in Pisces.

You are happier with groups where you can be friendly to everyone and get on with the business in hand. This "business" usually has some worthwhile objective, which may range from a plan for feeding the starving millions to a program for getting public support for a charity endeavor. You often join clubs, associations and movements connected with welfare.

You are a great mixer and enjoy conversing with people who have new and stimulating ideas like your own. Being intellectually bright, you enjoy the challenge and excitement of a controversial discussion. Sometimes you may go so far as to propound a proposition that you don't really believe in—purely for the satisfaction of sharpening your wits on an opponent.

Your social conscience is probably far more developed than that of your family and their friends. Your efforts to awaken in others an interest in the larger issues of life may earn you a reputation for heterodoxy or eccentricity.

If your Sun is also in Aquarius, the characteristics described above are more pronounced and you desire more effective expression. With this combination, you better appreciate the ramifications of what you are attempting and can see even greater possibilities in your mind. For the scientific thinker, deep theoretical speculation and inspired insights lead to inventions and innovations beyond those originally visualized. The artistic temperament is stronger.

With the Sun in Capricorn and Mercury in Aquarius, the emphasis is on action. Ideas are looked at more closely for their immediate practical application. There is a tendency to reject the more speculative and experimental propositions. Artistry is not so important. Words are used with clarity but in a down-to-earth style.

With the Sun in Pisces and Mercury in Aquarius, the person is supersensitive and capable of communicating his or her feelings and ideas in artistic ways. The humanitarian instincts are heightened and the desire to help others is much more personalized and emotional.

The Other Side of the Story

Your thought processes are erratic and confusing. Just when you have captured your audience, you dart off at a tangent, make some silly inappropriate observation or lose your train of thought. You probably find it hard to string three ideas together without being distracted. Your mind is curiously alert, flitting from one incidental happening to another, but incapable of sustaining one-track momentum. You choose friends who are your intellectual inferiors. When criticized or opposed in argument, you probably stutter or become spitefully indignant.

MERCURY IN PISCES

You're no great scientific mind. Your powers of reasoning are not conspicuous. But by golly, you've got tremendous understanding of people; and you know many things beyond the ken of others. It's not that you aren't intelligent. Far from it. It's just that the Piscean influence compels you to dispense largely with logical processes and rely mainly on instinct and intuition for your guidance.

You have a wonderful memory, especially for your childhood days. You spend much of your time wandering through these cerebral labyrinths, reflecting on this and that, and catching glimpses of astounding truths associated with past events. Whereas others grow brainier by absorbing great masses of useless information (much of which is only handy for watching television quiz shows), you educate yourself through the medium of inner feelings and emotions—that is, through self-knowledge. This is pretty powerful medicine. And that's why, on many occasions, you mentally poleax those who worship the god of reason by making uncanny prophecies that come true. You're a deep one, all right. And although you're pretty moody and exasperatingly vague at times, you prove consistently that there's something more profound in this wonderful life than a reasonable and clever mind!

You've got a lot of common sense, too. And when it comes to getting your own way by pretending, you'll win an Oscar every time. You absorb quickly and respond spontaneously. A tremendous capacity for showing sympathy to others and for understanding their intimate problems ensures a continual procession of friends. These people may not stay very long in your life, but they will certainly never forget you.

It is not unusual for Mercury-in-Pisces individuals to be employed in hospitals and other institutions where they can express their compassion in practical caring. Mind you, unless you are satisfying your urge for self-sacrifice, you will be easily upset by uncongenial environments. To everyone else, a place might seem cheery and harmonious, but you will pick up the discordant psychic impressions of previous occupants and events. Emotional turmoil and even physical illness can follow. Buying a house with a Mercury-in-Pisces person can be a long process of elimination by intangibles.

You are fond of pleasure and variety and enjoy exciting company until the urge for seclusion inevitably returns.

You tend to avoid responsibility and to

project your troubles onto the one who's nearest and dearest. You are assailed by feelings of unworthiness and may long to extirpate a vague guilt. You are not built to cope with sustained mental pressure, and if forced to, may suffer a nervous breakdown. You are capable of describing occult and mystical matters with great insight and fluidity.

If your Sun is also in Pisces, you may have impaired concentration and substitute an imaginative world for harsh reality. You are easily offended, supra-impressionable and so frequently misunderstood that you make as few social contacts as possible. Your inspiration is heightened by the Sun in this position, and you probably write poetry only a very few people will ever be allowed to read.

With the Sun in Aquarius, the urge to participate in large-scale humanitarian ventures may be irresistible, even to the point of interrupting an established career. You will probably travel to unusual places and absorb yourself at some time in trying to solve a mystery.

With the Sun in Aries, you are more positive and much less likely to be imposed upon or to delude yourself with fantasies. In this position, inspiration has a good chance of being translated into action. Revealing psychic insights may be written down and given to the world.

The Other Side of the Story

Your idealistic and wordy notions of how humanity can be saved are nothing more than gas-bagging. You'll talk about the past for hours, but when the time for action arrives, you'll disappear or blame someone or something for your slackness. You meet opposition with abject surrender and are incapable of facing up to your obligations. You are likely to live off others by stirring their sympathies with lying stories about your misfortunes. Doubts about your own mental health may exacerbate a fairly miserable and pathetic existence.

VENUS

The Planet

Venus is the brightest of all the planets. It orbits the Sun between Mercury and the Earth. It is the nearest planet to us and approaches to within 25 million miles.

Venus' size is roughly the same as the Earth's—7600 miles in diameter. The Venusian year is 225 Earth days, The planet's orbit is almost circular, so there is little variation in its 67-million-mile distance from the Sun.

In common with the other planets, Venus moves around the Sun in the same direction as the Earth. But it is the only one that rotates on its axis in the opposite direction.

Venus is often called the morning or evening star, depending on when it is visible, which varies with the time of the year. Observed from the Earth, the planet is never more than 48 degrees away from the Sun. When it is the evening star, we can see it for 3 hours and 12 minutes after sunset. At its brightest, Venus is 6 times as bright as Jupiter and 15 times as bright as Sirius, the brightest star in the sky.

In 1962, U.S. Mariner 2 recorded the surface temperature of Venus as 800° F. In 1967, the Russians soft-landed an instrumented canister on the planet from their Venus 4 research spacecraft. The data showed a very hostile environment of high atmospheric pressure and an atmosphere of almost pure carbon dioxide. Twin landings by Venus 5 and Venus 6 in 1969 provided information about the planet's mysterious veil of white clouds which account for its relatively high reflecting power.

The density of the planet is closest to the Earth's, being 5.23 times greater than water compared with the Earth's 5.52 times.

Symbolism

Venus or Aphrodite is the goddess of attraction, desire and eternal love. She was associated by the ancients with the spring, femininity and all things beautiful. She is said to have sprung from the seed of Uranus and to have risen naked from the sea, as in Botticelli's well-known painting, "The Birth of Venus."

According to Homer, Venus was unfaithful to her husband Vulcan and in love with Aries, or Mars, the god of war. Venus had many other lovers and several children. Her love for the mortal Adonis is the theme of Shakespeare's *Venus and Adonis.* Homer tells of her passion for Anchises, to whom she bore Aeneas, the hero of Virgil's epic poem. Venus is quite a girl.

She possesses a magic girdle that confers irresistible loveliness upon its wearer. Doves and sparrows are sacred to her.

Astrology

Venus in the horoscope indicates a person's love life, the pleasures and luxuries he or she enjoys, social adjustment and the refinements that lead to gracious behavior and artistic expression.

It also represents ease, beauty, indolence and pleasure seeking. If Venus is in a strong position in your birth chart, you can be rather superficial and a light thinker. You enjoy the perfumed distractions of life and ignore the essences, make charming but inconsequential conversation, are nice to everyone and extremely popular in the best of social circles. You can be the host or hostess with the mostest, possessing all the delightful attributes that make relationships amiable and satisfying as long as the harsher and sterner realities of existence can be held at bay.

Venus is essentially fruitful and feminine like the Moon. Both rule the gentler and finer emotions of men and women. On their own, they are inclined to be vacillating and lacking in direction and discipline. But given the support of more positive and purposeful influences in the horoscope, the Venus accomplishments are often splendid and always artistically pleasing or uplifting. Much depends on the Sign in which the planet is placed and the aspects it receives from the other planets in the horoscope. A description of Venus in the various Signs follows and the aspects for good and bad are given in the Yellow Tables, the Planetary Aspects.

Venus is known as the "lesser benefic" after Jupiter, the dignified, moralistic planet. Venus is more material, more physical. It gives earthly happiness to man and woman through mating. It is the finer part of lovemaking. It rules the clothes, the plumage, the colors, the dance, the song and the alluring gestures that are inseparable from the mating game. It keeps the lovers tantalizingly but exquisitely apart, insisting on the proprieties and gentle play before the consummating act of union. Venus is desire, never gross, salacious appetite. Any coarseness or "venal" influence comes from another source.

Venus rules the magnetic quality of beauty, which includes symmetry and proportion. It is the genius of the arts and the inspiration of the artistic. Venus personifies partnership, generosity, mutual giving, agreeableness, good humor —and most of all, harmony.

Venus rules two zodiacal Signs—Taurus and Libra. Taurus is an earth Sign and represents possessions, money, security, the sense of values— all that symbolizes unity by gathering in and attaching to oneself. Libra is an air Sign and represents the desire to bring together, to unify by an outward-going effort, to bring relationships into harmony, to balance circumstances, to equate so that all is at rest as one.

A Venus that is not unfavorably aspected invariably bestows remarkable quality of beauty. This may not be "handsomeness" or "prettiness" in the usual sense, but an etheric fineness of form, a feature, a curve—that certain something in a person that arrests the inner eye. Venus also endows a man or woman with good taste, an appreciation of clothes and grooming and a refinement of manner that is reflected in the way the home is furnished and decorated.

Venus people are usually very popular, especially with the opposite sex. As their role is to smooth out the rough and discordant by harmonizing relationships, they are extremely polite and charming people as a general rule and very agreeable company. They are sympathetic, pleasing, lovable and affectionate. Consequently, they are usually in demand as companions and receive many gifts, invitations and compliments. Sometimes they are showered with luxuries. All this ill-equips them to deal with physical adversity —poverty, squalor and deprivation usually leave them wilting on the vine.

Venus often shows a very determined and percussive streak. If you hit the detonator in the right place, it will explode in your face. The Taurus person will absorb a tremendous amount of provocation before putting his head down and charging with all the fury of an enraged Bull. The Libra person will bend over backward to placate and conciliate, but if he feels an injustice is being done, his eyes will flash and he'll hit out with an impulsive and aggressive indignation that springs from Venus' zodiacal lover and opposite number—none other than the fiery and impetuous Mars!

Your Venus is somewhere in your horoscope. With good aspects, its positive values are pronounced in accordance with the Sign where it appears. In Taurus and Libra, it is at "home," but if the aspects are bad, it won't be so comfortable. We are all Venus people to a larger or lesser extent.

Venus people have a fondness for poetry, music, good food, soft lights and genteel conversation. They often paint, sculpt or sing. They have a flair for interior design, architecture and sometimes flower arranging. They are often connected with the professional side of providing high-class furnishings for homes and offices.

Physiologically, Venus (not surprisingly) rules the venous circulation, the afferent nerves and the return phase of the bodily cycles to their respective centers. Eating, the assimilation of food, the feeling of satisfaction that this produces, and all the other gratifying processes, are the domain of Venus. So also are the throat and kidneys (throat, Taurus; kidneys, Libra).

VENUS IN ARIES

You are a passionate, restless and sexually attractive person. You have a roving eye that is quick to spot a possible conquest; and you act with alacrity and a great deal of impetuous charm. You are forever chasing the beautiful in life, whether it is a woman, a man, an experience or a possession—but it always seems to elude you. Although you are never satisfied, you will never give up the search.

You are exciting and brilliant. You flash from one activity to another. You are usually artistic and gifted, though you seldom manage to realize your full potential of creative expression because you have neither the time nor the patience. You direct your artistic drive into a bewildering variety of forms, some of them extremely energetic. You enjoy displaying your physical artistry and are often a stylish dancer, figure skater, gymnast or the like. Your prowess can also extend to the basketball court or the baseball field, but here you are not so much a combative type as a pure artist who keeps the crowd on its feet with your superb displays of skill.

You are an intense person but your emotions run along the surface. You are capable of great ardor but it quickly evaporates. You are an idealist and your conceptions of love and life very seldom match reality. You are searching for a perfection that can never be possessed. To your companions you seem fickle. No affair lasts for very long because your partners have very little hope of conforming to your abstract standards. To you, love is a mental thing that hides behind, but not in, the feelings. It waves enticingly—and off you dash, plunging impulsively into the stormy sea of emotion. You are single-minded in your pursuit because you are ruled by the head and not the heart. You fluctuate between ardent fire and cool detachment so that your loved ones are never quite sure of where they will stand from one hour to the next. If you do choose to settle down, you will aggressively fight off all rivals and contenders. You won't play second fiddle.

You are likely to marry early in life when your idealized conceptions lack the tempering of experience. Thus you may wed more than once. You may be woefully disappointed, but the scars won't last. Like that ancient Scottish King and the spider, you will try, try and try again. You need to love and to be loved, but you are not very good at going about it. You can be in love with the *idea* of love—and miss out on the real thing. Without love, you feel lost and sink into a brooding depression. You are a contradiction—an incurable romanticist and a sensationalist. You lose yourself in the glamor of the chase.

Venus in Aries is not a very good combination for a woman. The soft, feminine Venus is burned up in the aggressive masculinity of Aries, which, of course, is ruled by Mars. The Venus side of the nature gets no scope to charm, to gracefully arrange things into attractive patterns, to luxuriate. The love nature becomes demanding, impetuous, even ruthless—although always giving. Dashing Aries is more the knight in shining armor who races in quickly and rides off *alone* into the sunset as soon as it's over. For the feminine side of a person, which craves the stability of home and children, this is a disadvantage. Sometimes these people see themselves as their own persecutors. They have a need to be dominated, a factor which can resolve their basic problem.

You long for the security of love, but when you find it you tend to resent and rebel against the restrictions it imposes upon your freedom.

You are not a domesticated person. But you are far from hardhearted. You respond quickly to any appeal for help. Open-handed generosity can be almost a fault. You will give time and money to a person in need or to a worthy cause. Your sympathies lie very close to the surface and are easily touched. Quite often you accept people and situations as they appear, and are deceived.

The Other Side of the Story

You may be all head and no finer feelings, a heartless, roaming seducer. You are likely to be a promiscuous hedonist always on the lookout for sensation and gratification. You may use your artistic inclinations as a screen for your shallow intentions and excesses. You are likely to be ruthless and cruel. Your impulsive, thoughtless and inconsiderate actions may make life a torture for those who love you or live with you. You are apt to react violently when others fail to meet your impossible emotional demands. You may try to buy people and believe that money and gifts are a fair exchange for love and devotion. You may be discontented, frustrated and self-torturing. Bitterness and inner emptiness are likely to make growing old a travail.

VENUS IN TAURUS

You have a very simple and direct approach to love. To you, to love another person is to love them physically and with your heart. And if you can do this, and at the same time make your life more comfortable—for instance, by marrying into money—you will probably live happily ever after. Incidentally, this may be a universal dream of mortals, though with most others it usually remains just a dream. However, realization of this dream is almost a characteristic of the Venus-Taurus combination, all other things being equal.

Here, the planet that symbolizes romance, beauty and love of comfort is in her own Sign. Like the charming, affectionate and gracious woman she represents, she is at home. Taurus is the Sign of money and possessions. Between them, they usually have a ball.

You are practical and uncomplicated in your love life. You don't like making the best of things. You realize you have an innate longing for comfort and security and that it is much easier for you to be affectionate and loving in a pleasing environment. You are prepared to wait for these things—and (as often happens) for the right person to come along and provide them. This is one reason why people born with Venus in

Taurus are usually late developers sexually. They seem to know subconsciously they may have a long wait for the right marriage partner so they reject the risks and possible complications of premature sex. Other aspects in the birth chart must, of course, be considered.

Meanwhile, you work diligently toward providing yourself with all the comforts you long for. Seldom prepared to sit back and be idle, you know what you want and will work with great patience and determination to get it. You like to surround yourself with possessions because they ensure that you won't be victimized by harsh necessity, the thought of which appalls you. You also want what you own to be elegant and beautiful as possible. You regard your body as your first possession—and you make a point of keeping it attractively healthy and well groomed. You have a flair for tasteful and appropriate dressing.

You furnish your home with the same artistic discrimination—and your office, as well, if your position allows it. You enjoy good companionship and mixing at the highest social level you can command. You pursue pleasure in a leisurely but determined way. You are an amiable and friendly person; people warm to you quickly and are pleased to be in your company. You are fond of giving gifts—you relish the feeling of pleasure that others receive from them. One reason you desire wealth is that it will permit you to entertain and share the luxury of your home. You need to possess psychologically so that you can unite the act of giving and receiving into one delicious feeling of having harmonized two opposites.

You have a penchant for creating pleasing effects. You are an admirer of natural beauty. In sex, you are modest and decorous but quite straightforward and unashamed of nakedness and your body. Sex is the most natural thing in the world to you—once you have decided to yield to it. You are an emotional and feeling creature. Idealistic and platonic love mean very little to you. You are either attuned to someone or you aren't, but you are always aware of your personal magnetism and the subtle power of your physical presence and body movements. You give the impression of great passion and the capacity to love and be loved. And it is so . . . but not until it suits you. Then, and only then, are you capable of all that Venus promises.

You are likely to inherit money. You can be successful in business partnerships. Artistic pursuits offer you the chance of greatest satisfaction, but unless there are other favorable influences in the horoscope, you are probably not strikingly original. You are basically conservative and would rather put your trust in tried and proven methods than take risks experimenting.

Men with this combination have an intuitive understanding of women and are very attractive to them. They enjoy the domestic life and are good providers. Venus-Taurus women similarly appreciate masculine qualities and needs. They seldom remain single.

The Other Side of the Story

You may be a "sucker"—too quickly convinced, too easily taken in. You are likely to be ruled by your emotions and be incapable of mature, rational judgment. You can be horribly artificial, pretentious, affected in speech and mannerisms—an empty-headed social climber who is satisfied with basking in the reflected glory of the rich and famous. You may be mixed up, confused and unable to approach life's problems and joys simply and directly. The prospect of growing old is likely to horrify you. You can be inordinately susceptible to physical attractions and have little control over your sexual urges.

VENUS IN GEMINI

You are not a passionate person in the normal sense. Your sexual contacts are made with enthusiasm but not much fire. You are a bright spark but no glowing ember. The earthy, emotional Venus is at a disadvantage in the airy, heady, intellectual atmosphere of Gemini. Here she loses much of her physical warmth and devotional power. Instead of judging and valuing experience through the feelings, she rationalizes. This is the Sign of intellect, the world of thought, reason and cold logic. The loving Venus lives here in the mind and very little in the body.

You are a mental lover. You engage in affairs for the idea of love and are frequently disappointed. You dream up images and situations that people can't measure up to and circumstances won't allow. You idealize your attractions. You work yourself into a mental state of desire that is electrifying but short-lived. You can't maintain a passionate relationship for long—your love affairs have to be continually revitalized by the power of your imagination, for your energy is of restless, nervous origin and lives off the conflict and contrast of ideas.

You understand love—you can write about it, talk about it with extraordinary insight—but you don't feel love to the depths of its wonderful profundity as ordinary long-suffering and tormented lovers do. You experience a fleeting, superficial sensation. At times, you are even intensely jealous. But always it is an attachment of the mind, and it wanes as soon as you know the person sufficiently or a substitute new source of knowledge is available.

You enjoy having admirers and you usually manage to attract quite a few at a time. You are extremely interesting and amusing company. You can debate just about any subject. Venus gives you the artistic verve and panache to impress the most sophisticated audiences.

She refines your mind, makes it lyrical, poetical, imaginative. You can detach yourself from the human scene in a way others can't. As a writer, actor or entertainer reporting or miming the weaknesses and absurdities of the passing parade, you are peerless.

You enjoy attention and diversity. You love to flirt. Because your emotional anchors are short-tied and seldom get hooked on the bottom, you are capable of keeping several love affairs going at once. Though these dalliances often cause you a fair amount of trouble, you revel in the fun, excitement and danger of multiple affairs and slip in and out of romantic snares with a will o' the wisp dexterity. You don't really fancy the obligations of married life. If you do marry, you often marry twice. Rarely do you find the man or woman you are looking for, but by one of the foibles of human nature that you can lampoon so amusingly, you insist on fidelity in your romantic "entourage." Venus-in-Gemini people love to have a "harem" of vivacious and intelligent men or women whom they can visit or call up at any hour of the day or night.

You entice the opposite sex in an indefinably subtle way with a suggestion of promise, a floating seductiveness, an aura of refined and mysterious intimacy that when reached for, just isn't there. You delight. You disappoint. You delight again.

You are fond of traveling. You don't like hard physical work or the seamy side of life. You are attracted to quasi-artistic occupations where you can demonstrate your talents for original ideas and invention. Music, drama, teaching and writing also appeal, but sometimes you are hampered by a lack of formal education due to restlessness in your youth.

The Venus-in-Gemini woman has a rather material outlook where love is concerned. She is likely to use her wits and sex appeal to extract money and gifts from her beguiled admirers.

This combination gives a flair for trickery in both the male and the female, and an adroitness at providing remarkably plausible cover stories.

The Other Side of the Story

You may be a loquacious freeloader, eating and drinking off your friends, battening on any new acquaintances who happen to come along. You are likely to be immature and completely lacking in ambition. You may lie and cheat rather than go to work. You will probably get mixed up in some sort of fraud, possibly associated with fine arts, antiques, paintings or the like. You may be a bigamist. You are likely to use your charm and gift of gab to extort money and possessions from others, especially if they show a liking for you. You may indifferently betray those who have put their faith in you and blithely leave your responsibilities for others to cope with. You may be a barfly. Loneliness among the crowd may be your cross.

VENUS IN CANCER

Though you have a great need to love and be loved, you are not the type to go chasing after love or the companions whose company you enjoy. You prefer to sit and wait—knowing love will come. You will never say it hasn't come because tomorrow is another day. You have an abiding faith—a little too much at times—in the eternal life process that is said to provide everything with what it needs eventually. This probably explains why you find it so hard to resist the sensuous advances of another person. You need love, it is offered, you accept. Your propensity to take love as though it were the open-handed gift of destiny lands you in considerable trouble sometimes.

Venus is the planet of attraction and Cancer is the Sign of growth; together they make seductive melodies. But the love songs are not just those of physical attraction. You are deeply loving and sentimental about your family. Venus takes on a very maternal quality here, even in men. You are mothering and protective toward your near ones. You work to make the nest as comfortable, as soft and warm as humanly possible. You nourish, pet and cherish. You also want to be appreciated and fussed over yourself. To you, the home is the reassuring emotional center where you like to rest contented and undisturbed with all you love safe around you—and loving and admiring you in return for your good qualities. Given this, you are a loyal and domesticated partner.

But you are a bit too soft. Venus here makes you vulnerable to the machinations of loved ones who want to take advantage of you. You can be easily imposed upon—aggressive personalities can tear you to emotional shreds, even though you may not show your hurt. You may brood, become unhappy, sink into despondency. You may have a mother complex. There are likely to be obstacles to marriage. Your love life seldom runs smooth.

You need a positive outlet for your emotions. To bottle them up inside is like taking a dose of poison—it affects you physically. You are likely to suffer from digestive troubles and stomach complaints that are difficult to diagnose. To have something to love and serve is a kind of panacea—it keeps you fit psychologically, emotionally and physically.

If you can't lavish your affections on your family or another person, you are apt to turn your attention to the needs of humanity and serve some cause with slavish devotion. Sometimes you may devote your life to God. Martyrdom is not beyond you.

Secret love affairs are very likely with this combination. Your receptive, sympathetic and loving nature is extremely attractive to married people disillusioned by their partners. More than one marriage is likely. Someone much older or younger than yourself is apt to figure prominently in your love life. As well as a strong sharing of passion, there may be a deep mutual attachment to metaphysical or occult matters. You have a profound appreciation of spiritual and mystical things that goes far deeper than orthodox religious beliefs. You enjoy the mysterious side of life. You are "psychic," even though you may not publicize the fact.

You are charitable, sincere and kind-hearted. You enjoy talking and listening to people and would make an excellent teacher or nurse; others sense your understanding and are encouraged by it. Your love of the home makes you a competent cook and able housekeeper. You may sometimes choose an occupation that others regard as inferior to your talents or station. Your associates can be of a lower social status, and you are not averse to now and again befriending people down on their luck and taking them in.

Although naturally reserved, you may become a popular public figure. You can usually make money dealing in liquids. Land and houses can also be profitable.

You love beauty and are attracted to music, literature and art. You have a secret longing for the splendor and elegant living (and loving) of the past.

The Other Side of the Story

You may be exceedingly sensual, unable to say "no." You are apt to attract notoriety through your permissive behavior. You may be an emotional wreck, torn between simultaneous different passions and loves. You are likely to be ridiculously shy and self-conscious. Your hysterically emotional scenes may be the dread of your family and all who associate with you. You can be so unstable that you feel you have no permanent identity. On the other hand, you may be a social stick-in-the-mud. Your narrow possessiveness may make loved ones unhappy. You are likely to be absurdly responsive to flattery.

VENUS IN LEO

You can't help but attract the attention of the opposite sex. You love to be admired, and you're very good at dramatizing your entrances and timing your moves. You are always aware of who's looking and who's not but who ought to be. You are positive in speech and fluidly graceful in movement—the epitomy of an actor or actress who knows how to please an audience. You're Daniel or Danielle in the Lions' Den, and they're waiting to eat out of your hand.

You enjoy entertaining, particularly in luxurious surroundings. The most influential and glamorous people in town attend your parties. You are never awed or outshone. Your innate gift of showmanship ensures that you receive the Lion's share of attention, even in the most celebrated of company—and usually, not without merit. Your talent for self-expression is quite splendid to behold. The more personally demanding a social situation, the better you perform. Your art is the art of attraction; the result, understandably, is popularity.

You are often a pacesetter in fashions and fads. Venus gives you the capacity to combine color and form into universally pleasing patterns, and Leo provides the magic touch for projecting them as styles worth emulating. The thin line between a trend setter and an eccentric is often no more than the expressive flair this combination is able to bestow.

You are immensely warmhearted and kind, though on the proud side about receiving due respect. Although your gestures may be extravagant and at times ostentatious, your sincerity is unquestionable. You are out to impress, to be admired, there's no doubt about that, but you are conscious of people's deeper feelings. You have a loathing for all that is petty, spiteful, mean and unfair. You enjoy sharing your good fortune with others, an opportunity to do someone an unexpected good turn delights you.

You love excitement in all its sensual forms. Romance is something you can't live without, though it is often a source of disillusionment and sorrow. You love with your heart—each affair is the love of your life. You are generous to a fault with your emotions and possessions and tireless in your attempts to please the one you love. In return, you expect similar treatment and devotion. Not surprisingly, you are frequently disappointed and suffer bottomless despair. Nothing makes you more miserable than to discover your mate was only human after all and subject to the same frailties you sometimes turn a blind eye to in yourself. Until you learn that your great capacity to love has an altruistic function beyond individual desire, you go on loving, serving and being hurt, time after time.

You usually earn a living through a creative activity, especially writing and entertainment. In rarer instances, this combination can produce, through love, a saintliness that seeks to serve mankind without any attempt at personal aggrandizement.

If your social life becomes too absorbing, there is the danger your personality will become lost in superficialities. The need to be admired and talked about may induce an inordinate preoccupation with clothes, hairdressers, frivolous relationships, gossip and the like. The need to impress may lead to extreme forms of affectation, including speech. Overindulgence in food, drink and the party life may affect your health.

You have a knack of knowing a good investment when you see one and are quite likely to be a successful gambler or speculator as long as you refrain from acting until you know you are onto a good thing. Young people are good for you and often bring you luck. Most of your buddies are probably junior to you in age. You stand to gain from an inheritance, sooner or later.

The Other Side of the Story

You frequently fall in love with people who don't reciprocate your affections or who betray you. You have experienced some fearful heartbreaks in your love life. You are bombastic, conceited and a showoff. Although you crave love, your manner attracts those who are incapable of giving it. You may mistake lust for love. After you gain another's affection, you ruin things by being domineering and possessive. If you don't receive sufficient attention (one might almost say worship), you sulk, find fault and try to pick arguments. Your taste in clothes is garish and gaudy. If a woman, you overdo the perfume, jewelry and makeup. Your taste in artistic things is showy and vulgar; everything essentially fine in its appeal is overstressed.

VENUS IN VIRGO

Let's face it, you are *not* a spontaneous lover. In fact, you distribute your affections with deliberative care. You never really fall hopelessly in love, throwing discretion to the winds and passionately sharing your body and your being. No sir. You love in a very different way. You love—with service and with your mind. You seldom manage to express exactly what you feel. The world owes a lot to your type, although you are frequently misunderstood. You epitomize the goodness of supreme usefulness. You do not, as a rule, waste your energies in erotic or sentimental flights—or falls. You can be distraught, but rarely hysterical.

With this combination, the influences in the rest of the horoscope are exceedingly important. This description applies only to your Venus being placed in Virgo. On its own, it is a suppressed and intellectual position for the planet of love and beauty. Warmth elsewhere in the chart will soften the effects defined. The Sun in Libra or Leo, for instance, will help.

Above everything else, you are practical. You know you have to live in this world and make a go of it. You select your lovers to the best of your ability, always bearing in mind the possibility of marriage or a permanent association. You find it difficult to understand people who contract marriages based on passionate impulse when there are so many other things to be considered. You like to feel that you can help your mate by giving him or her the benefit of your experience—you want to improve your lover. Once you've found a reasonable partner to settle down with, you make the most of it. Even where there is contention and discord, you'll plug along rather than break up.

You are very sensitive and extremely aware of imperfections. Your impulse is to help, to serve, to improve, to reform, so when you spot weaknesses in people, you speak out. Though your intentions are the best, you often earn yourself a reputation for being hypercritical and outspokenly rude. The fact that what you say is usually true doesn't help you to hold friends. But that's you. And perhaps its one reason why you encourage acquaintances but are very wary of allowing close relationships. This reserve can attract people who admire cool indifference and self-possession.

Actually, you possess an acute desire to be appreciated and respected. You are not egotistical, but you want desperately to be needed. Once you are, the way is clear for you to serve diligently and without question—and you are at your happiest.

If you are incapable of strongly expressing the emotion of love, you are certainly more capable than most of the labors of love. There is no end to your dutiful devotion as an employee, husband, wife or parent.

You will make a comfortable home for your mate or family. Or you will serve a cause in the most menial way with selfless dedication. Quite often your inability to find personal love means that the world as a whole benefits. As a physician or nurse, you are capable of showing the utmost tenderness and care, tempered with an intelligent regard for the patient's good. Where others may indulge and harm someone out of pity, you have the strength and wit to withhold out of kindness.

If other influences are favorable, you can often gain materially through your partner. But this combination is not notable for happiness through the opposite sex. You are inclined to get involved with lovers who turn out to be materialistic, cold or callous. Secret romances that can never be revealed, delays in marriage and love affairs with people who are chronically ill or socially "inferior" are not uncommon.

The Other Side of the Story

Every attempt to express your emotions is probably misinterpreted and leads to sorrow. While you long to be loved, your fastidiousness and fault-finding rebuff and repel. You are apt to be all head and no heart, capable of deliberate mental cruelty. The absence of any real sympathy in yourself may make you ride roughshod over the feelings of others. In extreme cases, money may be made from drug pushing or other activities that show a pitiless disregard for human misery and suffering. Scandal is likely through associating with petty criminals and other similarly undesirable characters.

VENUS IN LIBRA

Beauty and harmony are essential for your enjoyment of life. This applies not only to your surroundings but also to your associates, right down to their attitudes, mannerisms and speech. Anything clumsy, jarring, coarse, blatant, uncouth or basically inelegant is distasteful to you. With this wondrously idealistic discriminating faculty functioning for you in a world more noted for its gaucheries than its graces, one would expect you to have a fairly rough ride, your sensibilities continually bruised. But not so. You're a subtle one. You weave, not a web like the spider, but in and out of the spider's web. You are adroit and entirely successful at building your own little private world of relative peace and harmony.

You have your bad moments and disappointments, of course, but they don't last long. If you can't harmonize a situation with your ineffable charm, you'll just take off.

You are a social creature above everything else. You adore dressing up in fine clothes, going to parties, entertaining, welcoming, greeting, conversing—all on a high-tone level. When the going gets too boisterous, you prefer to retreat to a comfortable armchair and discuss the weather or the latest in-topic with a like-minded companion while amusedly viewing the action. You love cultured pastimes and dignified novelty. Nothing pleases you more than to be with people in the higher strata of society—the wealthy and the influential (which often includes yourself). Your associates and friends are usually artistic and philosophical types and one or two of them are apt to be famous in their fields. You have a great fondness for painting, poetry, music and singing and could distinguish yourself in one of these areas. Your innate love of beauty and harmony is reflected in your extremely fine taste. You are probably capable of earning your living through one of the "beautifying" professions or industries, such as interior decorating, cosmetics, hair styling and architecture.

You possess strong magnetism, both physical and emotional. You unconsciously attract the people who appeal to you. In the old days, people would have said you were something of a sorcerer or sorceress. You beguile, emitting a promise so subtle that it exists only in the other party's awakened curiosity. You are sympathetic, kind and conciliatory, always ready with the oil at the first sign of troubled waters. You thrive on attention. You delight in the game of being nice, courteous, obliging, diplomatic—and tantalizingly unknowable. No one realizes better than you that familiarity breeds contempt. And as long as you can conceal your real self, you know that the magic is intact.

But love changes all this. In love, you give yourself totally with mind and spirit. Sometimes you are more in love with love than with the individual. You are blinded by the emotion. You tend to put your lovers on a level impossible of attainment by human nature. This is because you are more idealistic than physical in your rich love nature. Few people can live up to the consuming perfection demanded by this combination. So Venus-in-Libra folk sometimes garner a reputation for changing partners more frequently than others.

You love all the refinements of courtship, the flowers, phone calls, pretty words, chocolates, expensive note paper—and the full formal preliminaries. Sir Walter Raleigh, who threw his cloak on the muddy ground for Elizabeth to walk across, personifies the gracious sophistication that you adore as a woman and applaud as a man.

The ritual of love often means more to you than its consummation. Partnerships usually bring luck and money.

The Other Side of the Story

You are perversely cruel to those who love you, always changing your mind, flighty as a woman, inconstant as a man, flitting off and coming back with brand new promises you won't keep. You are lazy and play on the emotions of others to get what you want. You put on airs and graces about your artistic talents and tastes, which are quite mediocre. You have a deep longing for a refinement you can't find in yourself. Your social-climbing antics are a joke. You may be immoral and in constant danger of exposure. Partners defraud, disappoint and steal from you. You are extravagant and seldom out of debt. Witchcraft and secret cults where sex rites are practiced may attract you. Your domestic life is probably very unhappy.

VENUS IN SCORPIO

This is not a good position for Venus, the impulse of love and beauty. She becomes sluttish, waspish and heavy-handed. Love turns to lust and possessiveness. Violence, hatred and the desire for revenge creep in. Passion becomes a dreadful force that must be gratified . . . . or else. The feelings, instead of being rounded and subtly persuasive, work with the efficiency of a stone ax. Not much that is worthwhile will endure in a romance or marriage with a person having this combination.

But wait! That's the worst of it. It may not be a description of you or your life. There are numerous modifications in the horoscope that must be considered. Important though it is, this is but one isolated factor in your birth chart. For instance, if your Sun and Mercury are in Libra or Sagittarius, this will mollify the pure effects of Venus in Scorpio. You should also remember that the circumstances of your upbringing and education will also have an effect. If you are an evolved type who has learned the lessons of self-control—and Scorpio gives tremendous potential for this—these disturbing characteristics may never surface. You will feel their pressure, no doubt, but it can be directed into meaningful and productive activity. Otherwise, what follows will be evident in your life.

The opposite sex usually means trouble for you. Although you are a passionate and exciting lover, you overdo things. Only surfeit seems to suffice. You demand more and more. You want to possess body and soul. You are self-willed and absolutely determined to have your way. Your raging and tyrannical jealousy is likely to make married life a wretched misery. Your partner may be a nervous wreck imprisoned by your suspicion, distrust and cruelty. Violence, bitter quarreling, vindictiveness are all part of this depressing scene. You may marry for money and scheme in diabolical ways to benefit from inheritances. There is not much concerning the opposite sex that some people with this combination won't exploit for their own selfish enjoyment or profit.

From the social viewpoint, there is a tendency to gravitate to a low life, where sexual perversity can be indulged without question or risk of detection. The criminal class, with its passion for secrecy and attraction for violence, may have an irresistible appeal. Scandal and mayhem follow you like a long shadow.

You love pleasure, luxury and sensation. You are quite solicitous of the welfare of the person you love most and quick to demonstrate your affection. You share what you own with your mate. You are generous with friends and a lavish spender. Although you stand to inherit money or property sometime in your life, there will probably be a long delay before they are handed over. Partnerships are apt to be lucky only amid very great upheavals. Material gains are most likely to come to fruition when sorrow and pain are at their peak.

You are continually suppressing intense emotions, which makes you frustrated, irritable, restless and dissatisfied. Your energy buildup is often at the boiling point, and you may either explode into self-destructive actions or contain them. You can literally go to heaven or to hell. The peak of mystical and religious experience is within the scope of this combination, if you can harness your incredible passion and intense purposefulness.

You are not particularly artistic but you are efficient and practical. Your mind is sharp and penetrative, so you are very good at getting to the bottom of mysteries. Occult and mystical matters may fascinate you. At some time in your life you may be moved to sublimate your emotions with an extraordinary display of willpower and devote yourself entirely to some regenerative purpose. Then you will probably attract a powerful, disruptive but helpful personality.

The Other Side of the Story

Individuals with this combination can reach unnatural depths of depravity. They are also liable to commit despicably cruel acts. To satisfy their voracious emotional appetites, they may participate in all kinds of weird experiments, some of which may involve blood spilling and sexual excitation through involuntary physical pain. Dissipation may be so complete that the individual finds it impossible to pursue an ordinary livelihood. Death of the husband or wife is likely. Drunkenness and venereal disease are not uncommon. Tragedy and betrayal may lead to violent changes in life-style.

VENUS IN SAGITTARIUS

You are an idealistic lover and a bit of a disappointment when it comes to sensual delight. Oh, you emit an aura of promise, all right. You shine like a star in any company; as a woman, you are vivacious and seductive, as a man, masculine and sexy. But between the sheets, your light may be like a neon sign—less than lukewarm to the touch.

Your affections and passions are really too broad-based to be requited by any individual. You can't bring your mind to concentrate for long on one body and one other person's desires. Carnal passions are for release, you believe, not to be lingered over. Your gaze is forever returning to the horizon. You aspire toward the unknown. You wish, through your mind, to transcend the limitations of your body. And that means you need to keep moving, meeting new people and discovering fresh interests.

A single relationship very rarely transports you to fulfillment. If it does, you are very lucky indeed. Your basic need is for a partner who will help you to develop personally, share your love of refined pleasures—and give you plenty of free rein in the bargain!

You make a far better friend than lover. You are built for camaraderie, for the brief good-natured encounter, for fun and games—and the next happy meeting. With the opposite sex, you're a bit of a tease. You love change. You adore travel. You find it very difficult to settle down to domestic routine. Although you love your children, your mind is usually concerned with the possibility of getting away from them for a while, of being freed from your responsibilities just long enough to see what is over the horizon—and then to return. You are a less reliable wife or husband. Although your intentions are loyal, you find it very difficult to go through the rigmarole of establishing and running a home.

You feel you have something special to give to the world—but you're not sure what it is. It could be a kind of universal concern that you express in philosophic or religious ideals, or perhaps by dedicating yourself to some socially desirable project. Or maybe for you the secret lies in the simple act of giving your friendship to as many people among as many races and cultures as possible. Fundamentally, you would rather serve a cause than an individual.

You love the outdoors and have a refined sense of beauty. Nature delights you. Partnership is lucky for you and usually leads to material gain. It is not at all uncommon for people having this combination to marry for money or advancement.

Romantic partners seldom live up to your high expectations. One disappointment is enough to put you off. Habitual coarseness or indelicacy will kill the affair stone dead.

You are emotionally impulsive, fickle in your affections and likely to wed two or three times. You would rather flirt than have a deep affair. Frequently the love affairs of people with Venus in Sagittarius become so complicated that the only alternative they can see is to walk out.

Once they do, they only set about entangling themselves in a similar situation all over again. Because there is such a wide gap between the inner profundity of these people and their superficial behavior, they seem to take a long time to learn from their mistakes.

With Venus in Sagittarius, there is an odd attraction to foreigners. The emotions are intensified and passionate affairs are likely while traveling in other countries. The sense of freedom that goes with being in unusual and unfamiliar environments seems to intoxicate these people.

The Other Side of the Story

Your emotional irresponsibility has probably ruined your chances of happiness. You go on making the same errors over and over again, to your own and others' despair. Your friends are frequently people of ill repute whom you can't seem to shake off. You are apt to have an unhappy affair with a neighbor or a relative. You are cold to those who love you and all over those you think can help. As a parent, you will prefer to put your children into boarding school rather than make a home for them, making some excuse about its being good for them. You are wrapped up in your own selfish enjoyments. You are quite capable of two or three simultaneous affairs, while convincing each individual he or she is your only lover.

VENUS IN CAPRICORN

In love, caution is your catchword. You do not rush into permanent liaisons, and you certainly do not risk rebuff or reprimand by making premature advances. Love is generally a separate compartment in your life that you attend to when other more important matters such as work, income and position have been satisfactorily organized. But life seldom allows such tidy scheduling—as you've no doubt discovered!

This combination produces a higher and lower type of individual. The lower type is very earthy and saturnine in the dictionary sense of the word—heavy, gloomy and dull. The constrictive planet Saturn is the ruler of Capricorn, and in immature people, it literally squeezes the life out of Venus, the planet of love and beauty. These individuals make love by numbers, being incapable of spontaneous response and expression. Every action is thought out, calculated against their own self-interest. The temptation to play on the sentiments of others where there is a possibility of material gain is usually irresistible.

These people are mostly hurt through their wallets. They frequently marry for money or to improve their career chances.

But the goodies with this combination are far different. Although extremely ambitious and fascinated by power and position, you don't need to tread on heads to get to the top. You attract attention through your serious and responsible attitude to life. You work extremely hard and have a rare gift for organization. You epitomize willpower, concentration and enterprise in your chosen field. People in authority trust you instinctively and usually are quick to elevate you to an executive position.

You have an inordinate desire to be respected and esteemed. You will do nothing to risk your social status or business reputation. You are diplomatic, prudent, reserved and get along well with co-workers, associates and superiors. Elders can usually be depended on to help you.

Venus in Capricorn is often a slow developer sexually. The later you marry, the better your chances of making a go of it. In the beginning, you may find it difficult to settle down in double harness. Your mate will have to get used to your reluctance to demonstrate your affections, particularly in company. You may be jealous and rather demanding in love. Jealousy in you is a compensation for feelings of insecurity, which overwhelm your normally steady mind at times. Usually there is no real justification for these fears. When you do finally settle down with a person or into any situation, you identify with it completely. Your marriage will be for keeps, as far as you are concerned. You won't be interested in cheating on your mate.

You are apt to marry someone much older or younger than yourself. Domestic happiness can't be taken for granted; with this combination, you'll have to work hard at it. Sorrow and love are never far apart. The warm and fertile Venus can't really blossom in the cold and rocky domain of the Capricorn Mountain Goat. The danger is that either you or your partner will settle into a routine dedicated to outside interests that results in mutual alienation, indifference, coldness and finally rejection.

Your relentless drives are apt to make you wealthy and influential in later years. You may possess a fine house but not a home. You may tend to starve the emotions of your nearest ones, including your children. Too many practical considerations are liable to remove any chance of a normal, happy family life. You are not the type to gad about socially. When you can take a bit of time off from work, you're more likely to sit down by the fire with an informative book or watch an instructive program on TV.

You don't possess a great eye for beauty and seldom have any special aptitude for art. But you do respect proper conduct. Steadfastness, loyalty and all the qualities that contribute to moral rectitude are deemed by you the highest good.

You are easily slighted, and like the elephant, will never forget.

The Other Side of the Story

The human side of your development may be woefully lacking, leaving you a calculating, grasping and rather pathetically isolated creature. You probably have no friends to speak of. Your marriage was probably called off, or you are unhappily tied to a partner who is cold, exacting and indifferent. You live only to possess what you desire. Any finer emotions you once had have been blunted by selfishness and acquisitiveness. Your business chances are likely to be ruined by treacherous associates. You are apt to indulge a power complex by lording it over people in inferior positions or fraternizing with socially undesirable characters.

VENUS IN AQUARIUS

You love everyone, just about. Not sexually, of course. Sexually, you are fairly choosy, with a penchant for exciting, provocative and rather unconventional playmates. For most people, love usually ends in marriage or cohabitation, but Venus makes you crave much more than that. Love to you is more an idea than an emotion. You visualize it as a broad, sweeping, exciting, reforming, universal force—which it seldom is in ordinary relationships. You want a perpetuation of the romance, the novelty, the excitement —and sooner or later, you realize this is possible only by loving humanity as a whole.

You're a strange one in many ways, nowhere near as open and shut as you seem. You are one of fate's chosen victims. Odd things happen to you, out of the blue. As much as you try to be open and sincere, you are usually forced into secret love affairs at some time or other. You are no stranger to astounding and even bizarre happenings in connection with love affairs. These experiences can change your life-style virtually overnight, and even put you on the other side of the globe.

You have an extraordinary capability for discerning character. Your intuition cuts through the poses of personality right into the heart of the individual. As an artist—say, a painter or a writer—you can present vivid impressions of people that are unmistakable in character, though indefinably abstract. Attempts are often made to impose on you but this remarkable instinctive faculty usually provides an insight into the other's motives. However, you will go along with a mild deception without protest, as though unconsciously aware you must not misuse your gift. Music enjoyed with others probably provides your greatest relaxation. Apart from your acute appreciation of sound, you also have a strong sense of rhythm.

You delight in meeting people and make friends very easily. You probably have a wider circle of acquaintances than anyone else in your family, apart from those with the Sun in Aquarius. You enjoy chatting to strangers, too, and will arrive home occasionally with some poor guy or gal who needs a bed for the night. This open-house attitude may disturb other members of the household. You often attract bohemian and arty types of friends whose ideas may not jell with society's. Your own views are somewhat unconventional and ahead of the times, and you delight in discussing them with similar minded individuals. You are admirably tolerant of all beliefs. Even if these conflict with your own, you are genuinely interested in understanding the attitudes of their adherents and can listen without interrupting. You really prefer to have a lot of friends than one deep personal attachment.

At heart, you are a rambler and a traveler. Your independence and freedom mean more to you than you realize—until you lose either. Then you are constantly looking over your shoulder for a means of escape. In an effort to retain your sense of liberty, you may not marry until the second half of your life (if this is a second marriage, you felt fettered by the first, which was a youthful impulse).

You enjoy platonic relationships and have a cultured and intellectual approach that appeals to deep thinkers. You are almost fanatically sincere in some of your convictions and are not afraid to stick your neck out for your friends. Before you retire from active work, you will probably realize most of your earlier hopes and wishes.

Financially, you do best working with partners, societies, associations, cooperative concerns and public enterprises.

The Other Side of the Story

You're a drifter, an advocate of hopeless causes and a friend of the lunatic fringe. Women have been responsible for much of your unhappiness. You have no respect for marriage and other cohesive social conventions. You sleep with anyone, any time, not because you are highly sexed, but because you wish to dramatize your own cravings for freedom and expression. You are likely to support anarchy and lawlessness as a means of destroying detested authority, but have no clear idea of what should be substituted.

VENUS IN PISCES

You spend much of your life looking for love—real love. You may find it, you may not. If you don't, you will never feel you have fulfilled your earthly purpose. If you do, you will experience an ecstatic devotional completeness. But can it last? Is it forever? Chances are, you'll discover it is not. But you will have the satisfaction of knowing you have loved more profoundly and consumingly than most others even dream of.

Venus in Pisces is at her most idealistic, emotional and loving best. Here the goddess of love and beauty is searching for something that may not be attainable in this world. But that won't stop her from trying.

You are kind, generous, sensitive and extremely compassionate. Self-sacrifice in love is natural to you—in fact, you are inclined to be too willing to surrender yourself to another, too eager to worship your beloved. Wherever your tender feelings are aroused, you can't resist the role of selfless comforter or bemused, adoring lover. Of course, other strengthening influences in the horoscope can make you more practical and self-preserving, assuming that these qualities are to be preferred. Sun in Aries or Capricorn, for instance, will bestow a more urgent sense of self.

On its own, Venus in Pisces is a cherishing and self-abnegating impulse. At the same time, it helps to make you fickle. In the search for love, you are likely to spread your net of gentle affections over a very wide area. Quite unconsciously, you drag in a lot of odd fish, as well as the occasional real prospect. If it is not the real thing, you tire very quickly and move on. The idol you are seeking is the person who conforms to your peculiar ideals, some of which have no relation to human nature. But you are willing to plug the holes in the characters you find with your incredible plastic imagination. Consequently, you are frequently disillusioned or heartbroken.

Personal love is not the only string on your emotional violin. You are also passionately responsive to any form of human sorrow or suffering. You will pick up any tragic stray who catches your attention and minister to him or her with melting concern. As some of these people are not always victims of circumstances but suffering rather than from an overdose of self-inflicted maladjustment, you often emerge badly mauled here, too. You have an unfortunate habit of attracting individuals who play on your placid, yielding sympathy. Venus in Pisces can be very badly misused by rogues and opportunists. However, if you manage to fall in love with a genuinely helpless or underprivileged, dependent person, you can really have a ball. But the pressure of worldly responsibility, finding the money and paying the bills, has to be be left to someone else. You are a poor battler when it comes to coping with cruel reality. Loving—even dying—is easy for you; but living is hard. Venus in Pisces is fulfilled by the exquisite sensation of yielding all to another.

Trust is intrinsic to your nature. You don't hold grudges and are far too forgiving and understanding to make enemies.

Although sociable, cheerful, hospitable and fond of mixing with the opposite sex, you are more romantic than voluptuous. However, you may marry more than once. You enjoy ease and comfort and sincerely wish that the whole world could be at peace. As much as you love your family, you will not necessarily give them priority over a stranger you believe requires your help. People with this combination often take up voluntary work or are employed in hospitals and similar institutions.

The business of earning a living, which others take in their stride, may distress you. Unless your sympathies are aroused, you don't have much staying power. The need to be needed is paramount, and then your energies are formidable. Unneeded, you lose interest and retreat into a world of romantic daydreams.

You possess a deep appreciation of all that is beautiful in art and nature and are particularly fond of music. As a composer, dancer, writer, artist or poet, you have great inspiration.

The Other Side of the Story

You are devious, secretive and unable to face facts. You retreat from the slightest challenge. You are devoid of ambition and purpose and are prepared to drift along in a dream world, depending on your friends and family for subsistence. You are hysterically impressionable and emotional, putty in the hands of anyone who is prepared to tell you what to do. You may be so afraid of failure and criticism that you attempt very little outside of menial tasks. You are apt to lose money through deception and fraud or your own muddleheaded thinking. Your love life may contain numerous illicit affairs, as well as weird and shattering experiences.

The Planet

Mars is the first and nearest of the outer planets to the Earth. On the Sun side of us is Venus, on the other side is Mars. The mean distance between the Sun and the Earth is 93 million miles; between the Sun and Mars, it is 141 million miles.

The Martian year—the time it takes the planet to circle the Sun—is 687 days, just under two Earth years. Being an outer planet, Mars can never appear between the Earth and the Sun, as the Moon, Mercury and Venus do. Mars is smaller than the Earth. Its diameter is 4200 miles—just double that of the Moon. The planet rotates about itself in 24 hours 37 minutes 23 seconds. Its mass is one-tenth that of the Earth.

Mars is reddish in color and can be seen at night as a brilliant ruddy dot. Every 15 years it is at its closest distance to us—36 million miles, when it shines with the brilliance of Sirius, the brightest star. This proximity will be reached again in 1984.

The U. S. Mariner 9 space probe carried out an extensive study of Mars in 1971–1972, covering 85 percent of the surface in great detail. Earlier probes by Mariner 6 and Mariner 7 had indicated that Mars was a dead and featureless planet, but Mariner 9 showed it had extremely interesting and distinct characteristics, some of which raised new questions. Important new findings were that water played an active role in Mars's evolution. Photographs revealed four major geological regions: a polar region with terrace-like formations and deep grooves; an equatorial plateau scarred by deep canyons, with evidence of water erosion; a volcanic region; and a large cratered terrain like the Moon's. The Russians have also sent spaceships to Mars.

Mars has two small moons—Phobos and Deimos, each about 10 miles in diameter. Phobos revolves so incredibly fast that it rises and sets three times a day.

Symbolism

Aries or Mars, as he was known to the Romans, was the god of war and one of the 12 great Olympian deities. He was the son of Zeus (Jupiter), the supreme god, and Hera (Juno), the Great Goddess of the pre-Hellenic matriarchal society. He was a divinity of Thracian origin, representing dispute, destruction and war. Mars was said to delight in battle for its own sake. He was not popular with the Greeks, who disliked purposeless war and despised those (like the Thracians) who enjoyed it. The Greek myths about Mars reflect this hostile attitude.

According to legend, he was hated by all the other deities except three. One of these was Aphrodite or Venus. Mars was her lover and they were caught together by her husband in an invisible net and exposed to ridicule among the gods.

Mars was not invincible in war. The other gods wounded and conquered him many times. Once he was imprisoned for 13 months until Mercury freed him.

It is not surprising that the god of war was held in high esteem and honored in the Roman Empire. Mars ruled the first month of the Roman year (March—Aries) and was associated with the eighth month of the Roman year (October—Libra, which is ruled by Venus). Certain days in those months were given over to Martian ceremonies. Mars had two temples in Rome. One was an altar, the other a gate through which the army marched.

Astrology

Mars is dry, fiery and masculine. In the horoscope, it represents the outgoing physical force. It is significant of energy, both constructive and destructive, depending on its position and aspects in the horoscope. Mars is closely associated with ambition and desire. It symbolizes the senses and rules over the animal instinct in man. It is said to be a malefic planet, but if it is well aspected and allowed to express itself positively, it represents courage, endurance, strength, self-confidence and the driving impulse that all ventures, including deeds of heroism, require. Other Martian attributes are initiative, combativeness, sharp wit, the ability to argue, independence, imposing determination, the ambition to be successful in material matters against all odds, force of character—and above all, leadership.

Mars also endows a person with extraordinary muscular strength, the power of practical execution and great organizing ability in an active rather than armchair way. Without Mars, it would be impossible to make use of what the other planets offer. Mars is resourceful and ingenious and provides the wherewithal to reach just about any material goal desired. Like a good soldier, Mars knows when to strike and when to withdraw. He is not a person to tackle lightly.

The developed Mars person combines physical delight with spiritual well-being. But the negative side of Mars is dreadful. When the planet is at a bad angle to the Earth, violence erupts. Murders, accidents, fires, rapes and mayhem break loose. When it is afflicted in a horoscope, the person is rash, violent, contentious, quick-tempered and foolhardy. He wants to quarrel and can't resist a fight. According to the influence, he may be weak and cowardly, himself a victim of aggression. (Not enough Mars is as bad as an exaggerated amount of him.) Or he may be a ruthless bully, always spoiling for a fight but frequently losing it because he brings out the worst sort of animal fury in others. He may submit to drink. Where there is a difference of opinion, he will rely on brute force instead of reasoned argument. He will act first, think later, lash out, collide, stumble, trip over. He is accident-prone, careless, takes unnecessary chances, reacts pugnaciously and aggressively. In one way or another, he releases his excessive energy so as to bring disaster or some kind of trouble down on himself.

A well-aspected Mars produces a vigorous, forceful and well-knit character. These people usually succeed in what they undertake. They don't give in to superior forces but they don't take a blind smack at them either; they have a "feel" for combat and they understand the necessity for timing. They are busy clearing away obstacles that lie in the way of practical accomplishment. The role of these people is to win, to conquer. And all things being considered, they can do this in a strong and enterprising way that is socially acceptable. During times of war, these are the men who win the battles, brush aside the mediocrity of inherited command, claw and fight their way up from the ranks to leadership, victory and glory.

In love, Mars is responsible for the best and the worst. As the Earth stands between the orbits of Venus and Mars, so man is the collision point between love and force. Neither is complete without the other: they come together as a passionate, potent power. The worst type of sexuality is governed by Mars. These people will satisfy their sexual hunger without any thought for the pain they cause their partners or others. On the other hand, Mars and Venus together provide the sort of love that will sacrifice anything, even life, to save another. There is no one truer in a practical way than a Mars friend.

As a lover, Mars is filled with exuberance and creative energy. He is impulsive, simple and direct. He has a red-blooded need of sex. Until he has free and regular expression of this compulsive basic drive, he can't devote himself fully to his practical activities because thoughts about sex will distract him. These gnawing thoughts can only be disintegrated in one great percussive act of union with Venus.

Mars rules Aries and is the co-ruler of Scorpio. Aries is the positive first Sign of the Zodiac and typifies the initial thrust of energy into the world, the beginning, the pulsing seed, the body, the power, and the impulse; it also signifies initiative, enterprise, leadership, courage, independence and the pioneering, indomitable and adventurous spirit.

Scorpio is the negative, watery, mysterious eighth Sign, the powerhouse of repressed energy, intense emotion that unconsciously seeks to reunite itself with the source through the sexual function. It is subtle, secretive, purposeful, penetrating—the focal point of death and regeneration. It is the phoenix of immortality that waits in everyone to rise from the burned-out ashes of the self.

Physiologically, Mars is the body's resistance and attacking factor against invading disease and foreign bodies. Fevers and inflammations are the signs of this power at work. Mars also controls the elimination of waste products. As Venus governs the in-gathering forces of the body, so Mars rules the outgoing: the eliminating of waste as urine, the discharge of the male sperm from the testes, the shedding of eggs from the female ovaries and the release of sweat.

Mars is associated with the muscular system, the sympathetic nervous system and the red corpuscles of the blood. Where Mars is strongly emphasized, the person is prone to burns, fevers, cuts, accidents, scalds and inflammations. Mars is the physical side of sex—passion, lust. Venus provides the attraction, Mars supplies the phallic apparatus and the sensual stimulus.

MARS IN ARIES

You are iron-willed. You don't bend from your purpose. You may switch to something else before you finish a job—but only because it suits you to do so. You won't be dictated to. You are independent. You'll fight any opposition to the death if necessary, or you'll labor without help or encouragement until you drop to carry out your plans. Mars has always been associated with iron—it is the plowshare and the sword. In your hands, both get results.

In this position, the mighty Mars is in its own Sign so it is doubly strong and fiery. Whether what you undertake is for good or bad—and this will depend on the other influences in your horoscope—you will perform with great vigor and urgency. Aries and Mars represent the body, the dynamic principle of action. Here, the prime consideration is "me first." You are not so much naturally individualistic as a go-getter, an adventurer who is in it for him- or herself.

But you are not mean or selfish with money and worldly goods. You give freely, generously, often without thought. You crave excitement and freedom, not the deadening weight of accumulation. You'll leave everything behind on an impulse if you envision a new world to conquer. You'll upend your whole bag of goods for all to see and take what they want, so long as you can get where the action is. And you won't care if the prize is withheld—so long as you win.

You are open, frank and direct. There are no back doors to your nature. You march boldly through the main gate for all to see, with the sure-footed confidence of a soldier. You have nothing to hide. You are what you are. The fact that you might accidentally knock down a brick or two as you make your bustling entrance does not concern you.

Mars in this position gives brilliance and leadership. It is excellent for a man or woman of action. It provides determination and the practical ability to succeed in life, whether it be in the tug o' war of business or the rough and tumble of politics. You are a good propagandist—you know how to make an idea popular. Your work as a writer, musician or artist can gain wide acceptance. You are original and ingenious, a real pioneer in whatever field you choose. But when it comes to conspiracies or scheming, you are likely to be the odd one out. You are too impulsive and impatient to be successful in endeavors demanding diplomacy and tact. You would rather throw down the gauntlet and let whoever dares pick it

up. However, if the enemy fails to come forward, you are stymied.

You are quick-tempered and easily irritated. Unless you cultivate self-control, your rages are likely to be quite violent. You like to clear the air quickly and you don't hold grudges. You are prone to accidental injury. People with this combination usually have a scar on their head or face from some old wound. You may also need to wear spectacles earlier than usual or sunglasses as a therapeutic aid.

Your manner is sometimes blunt and aggressive. You sincerely believe you are the master of your own destiny and you don't intend to be caught napping. You aim at continual accomplishment, but sometimes you get so caught up in the action that you lose sight of the desired end. You need to use your willpower to see things through, to resist turning your attention to some fresh challenge before the old one has been satisfactorily concluded. You don't like detail. When the time for cleaning up arrives, you will probably vanish. People who object to noise and bustle do not like having you around. Steady plodding and patient cooperation are not your metier, and routine work nearly drives you mad. Even if you don't have to hurry a job, you'll put a time limit on yourself . . . and needle everyone else along at the same gallop.

You have a strong sexual urge and a tremendous amount of energy to get rid of. It is important to your health that you release your feelings and desires because you require free expression as well as self-control. You need a partner who is physically compatible and who understands the simplicity of your mental processes. You are an idealist. When you identify with a person, cause or principle, you go all the way.

You love active sports. You are physically tough. You do all in your power to keep your body healthy and fit.

The Other Side of the Story

You are likely to be oversexed and preoccupied with satisfying that basic urge. An extremely violent and uncontrollable temper may make you dangerous to life and limb. Recklessness and impatience can make it difficult for you to hold down a job. You may be brusque and bullying. Your language and manner of speaking may be vulgar and provoking. You are apt to be insensitive to other people's feelings as well as tactless and argumentative. An overly optimistic outlook may distort your judgment. Your hatred of detail may make you a slapdash planner.

MARS IN TAURUS

Mars here is in a bit of a quandary. He can't be outgoing, as in Aries, scattering his fiery brilliance and originality with scant regard for economy. Here he must hold onto what he owns and continually gather what he wants. He must be more material, more set on acquiring, on possessing—altogether more set—than his forceful, action-loving nature is comfortable with. Here in Taurus, the Sign of money and worldly goods, Mars is in his detriment. His driving energy turns to obstinacy. But despite his discomfort, this can be a good combination. Mars in Taurus means toil—but usually a substantial share of the world's comforts as well.

You want to make money. You are down to earth about it. You know the peace of mind that security confers, and you aim to get it. You are not interested in moralizing stories or philosophic theorizing about what methods should or should not be employed for success. When you see the chance for action, you move. And you keep moving with a dogged determination that won't admit defeat until the end is reached.

Though you are usually successful over the long haul, the climb may be painful and slowed by obstacles. (Sometimes—halfway up the summit—you may look back and wonder if it has been worthwhile.) You are likely to create difficulties by rushing ahead and grappling with problems before they emerge. You are a practical person. You know that, above all, you have to hang onto what you win.

But, paradoxically, after all your efforts to secure the prize, you are likely to let it slip away at the last minute. It is almost as though you are willing to surrender to the object desired, but never to the obstacles that would keep you from it. You stop. You change. You take a rest. And then you resume your efforts with the same tenacity. You tend sometimes to swing from one extreme to another—peacefully compliant, then obstinately aggressive; self-indulgent, then ascetic; open-handed, then grasping. In many ways, you are a living contradiction, ill-harmonized within yourself.

You are strongly sexual. The physical side of love is likely to dominate your thoughts and affections. The normal refinements of this Venus Sign are apt to be consumed in sensual desire.

Obstacles to your gratification may send you into a mood of fury or smoldering resentment, depending on the other influences in the chart. Your compulsion to retain possessions can extend to the people you love; you may be cruelly jealous—a suspicious, snarling guard dog. A well-aspected Mars in Taurus makes you a competent and satisfying lover who is usually very popular with the opposite sex. But there is a danger that the stability of your character may be undermined if you route too much of your energy into these relationships. Marriage may be a stormy and troublesome passage.

You are a conservative person who can be depended on to follow instructions and do a job well. You prefer, though, to be in a position where you can make decisions for yourself within an overall plan. With Mars in Taurus, the Sign of nature, the man is likely to be a capable engineer, bridge builder or construction worker, using his talents to change the look of the landscape. Formerly, a woman with this combination was usually employed or engaged in some sort of activity that called for stamina and perseverance—even if only in coping with an unruly family. Today, women are trained in these occupations and are equally capable of handling the same job.

You make a good executive with a talent for organizing and directing. You can visualize a goal with uncanny accuracy and make it materialize. You are most successful where there is a high element of self-interest.

You can be a successful writer or artist with a pronounced flair for expression that is sensual, rounded, voluptuous; the style is more earthy and classic than brilliantly stimulating, like that of Mars in Aries.

A vivid awareness of physical power, graceful movement and muscular coordination can produce fine ballet dancers, gymnasts, figure skaters and the like.

Although you are intent on acquiring money and assets, you can be a lavish spender when it comes to pleasure and the things you enjoy.

The Other Side of the Story
You may be stubborn and unable to see another person's point of view. Worries may come through property and sudden money crises. You are likely to steamroller your opposition, and with a little bit of authority, punish the innocent with the guilty just because they were on the wrong side. You may have a power complex that leads you to insist that antagonists be punished as

well as vanquished. You can be fiercely jealous and unreasonably possessive. Your appreciation of beauty and refinement may be confined to the things you own or can control. You may have legal difficulties and lose a legacy. Your arrogance may make you an overweening boss and an insensitive parent. You may be vicious in sex and a callous materialist in your aims. Any cruel means may justify the end.

MARS IN GEMINI

You get some really great ideas—at times you are even inspired—and you have no difficulty spurring others into action. You make an excellent politician, a convincing salesperson, a provocative writer and lecturer, a clever personal assistant or top secretary and an aggressive or rapier-tongued debater or lawyer. You not only are brilliant at putting an argument across, but you also arouse vital enthusiasm in an audience. You are forceful and blunt when you want to be; dancingly light and lacerating with your wit and sarcasm when it suits you. You are a rabble rouser, a morale booster, an ideologist who can tell people how to do the impossible.

But you are lacking in full-blooded physical energy. You do your best to avoid heavy work. Yours is a nervous energy that activates the mind. Here, in Gemini—the Sign of intellect—Mars' potent power expresses itself in an effusion of ideas and concepts. You are an energetic thinker. Your mind is always busy, restless. You want to change things—mostly to suit yourself—and you use other people to do it. You are the brains of the outfit, the master mind. You want action. You build verbal bridges for others to cross between the conceptual plane and the concrete world. Your ideas can literally set the world on fire. You are the type of person who proposes an ideology that the next generation might fight or die for.

If you are a Mars-in-Gemini thinker in a small world, you are just as effective; your friends, co-workers and acquaintances are equally impressed. You are talkative, an impulsive debater and disputant, but you seldom talk nonsense, unless there are upsetting influences in the horoscope. You are practical and speak in order to produce effective action. The fact that you might never *take* action is incidental. Your role is to show the way. You make an idealistic plan sound feasible and desirable.

You have mechanical aptitude. Although you may not be moved to dismantle a machine, you understand what needs to be done. You are deft with your hands. You are inventive, sometime marvelously ingenious. There are very few situations you can't deal with. You like to look through handbooks, to glance at plans to see whether you can improve on them.

You have many interests. You are continually running around, meeting people, making contacts, living largely off your nerves. You are high-strung and very excitable. You are also easily irritated. You sometimes show a remarkable inconsistency in your beliefs; you can take an opposite stand to one you've already advocated with magnificent aplomb.

You may have a love affair with a relative. Two marriages are common. You frequently have two affairs current.

You are not averse to exaggerating and telling untruths if it helps your cause—or the impact of your story. Physical violence is something you prefer to avoid. Your weapons are words and the influence they have on people and events. You can quickly cut an opponent down to size with the edge of your tongue. You verbally fence with the enemy to find his weak spot so you can puncture him, swiftly and neatly.

You enjoy reading and are drawn to educational activities. You would like to teach, to lecture. You are fond of travel, science and chemistry. You have great deductive ability and your conclusions usually make good sense and are extremely workable.

Your main fault is that you lack follow-through. Though your ideas are sound and wonderful, they must be carried forward by others. What you do seems to depend on the energy at your disposal, which is erratic and siphoned off by a variety of pursuits rather than one dearly held objective. You participate for the sake of the action, the excitement, the mental stimulus, more than for the result. Although your insight and perception are needle-sharp, you are easily distracted and need to cultivate concentration.

You are physically agile but don't possess the stamina to shine in strenuous competitive sports. You are sometimes accident-prone and are liable to injure your shoulder, arms or hands. There is also a possibility you will suffer from nervous prostration.

The Other Side of the Story

You are likely to be disagreeable in your speech and tiresomely fault-finding. You may use your quick wit to embarrass and discomfort others unnecessarily, particularly in company. Neighbors, relatives and those who work for you may cause you trouble. Brothers and sisters are likely to create special problems; or there could be painful separations or estrangements. Your education may have been neglected, making it hard for you to get ahead. You are likely to become an excessivily heavy smoker or drug user in an attempt to calm your nerves. Your lungs may give you pain. You are apt to be indecisive and possess a stutter or some other irritating speech impediment.

MARS IN CANCER

This is the combination that signifies the true artist, whether he or she be a painter, writer, sculptor, philosopher, musician—or gentle humanitarian. The fiery and energetic Mars, when immersed in Cancer, the deep receptive water Sign of the Moon, seems to bring out an unsuspected magical quality. Here are the men and women who serve the idea of art and not the fashion, the people who reveal its universal oneness and timelessness, those egos whose perish but whose essences linger on: Shakespeare, Michelangelo, Dante, Petrarch, Byron, Balzac, Kant, Copernicus. You, too, have some of this magic.

You are ambitious and industrious; you are also changeable and lacking in continuity. But you can wait for the things you really want. A master of the war of attrition, you can wear away the opposition as the sea erodes the hardest rocks. Mars stirs you at your deepest levels; you churn to the surface; you have sudden outbursts of temper and irritation. You are rebellious and refuse to be hemmed in and ordered about. Authority and its poses annoy you.

You want security, the security of the law as well as of the home. But you don't particularly like other people's ideas of security; you want things your way. The law in many ways fails the public, sets up power centers that restrict rather than resolve, pamper rather than protect, punish rather than prevent—and this is the source of your revolt and protest. You are often misunderstood and thought to be a sniping dissenter rather than a person with positive ideals. You would like to see the world run on home and family lines—with love—but you are enough of a realist (and sufficiently seasoned in domestic experience) to understand the odds against this becoming reality.

You are original, independent and enterprising. You love your home, and especially the family ideal, but your home life is often disturbed from inside as well as outside. You constantly have to deal with interference and never seem to be able to settle down for long.

You have an emotional approach to action rather than a reasoning one. Your instinctive knowledge is quite amazing and you have learned to rely on it. Because of this, the usual Mars impulsiveness is less rash and reckless in this position, drawing as it does on the deep subconscious knowledge of human experience stored in the profound reservoir of Cancer.

You are often in a ferment inside and this disturbs your stomach and digestive processes. Unless frustration and irritation are brought under control and a calmer temperament cultivated, you are apt to suffer from stomach ulcers and other intestinal disorders. A sense of humor can provide some release. If these self-destructive forces are channeled into a single effort, astonishing progress can be made; if not used constructively, these energies are pernicious.

You are easily offended and hold grudges. You resent, repress and smoulder. You are inclined to depend on alcohol, tobacco or drugs. Probably you clashed with your mother in younger years, and this may have left an unconscious traumatic scar. There is a possibility that death or separation occurred during childhood. Mars gives you a capacity for objective, no-nonsense self-analysis, which, if utilized, can release the emotional pressures you have allowed to build up through ignoring or rejecting issues.

You are likely to be involved in work requiring enterprise and initiative. A job that takes you abroad frequently or on long cross-country journeys can be profitable. Professions associated with children, houses, food and the sea may also lead to success. Some strenuous physical work is indicated, and here the rigorous demands of looking after a home and family can't be excluded.

You are likely to have to move home abruptly—several times. Unforeseen circumstances may involve you in sudden changes in numerous departments of your life.

The Other Side of the Story

Unhappy childhood experiences may still discolor your outlook on life. You are likely to be depressed by sad and sorrowful memories; when you try to snap out of it (as you continually do), you are irritable and psychologically ill at ease. You may have little in common with your marriage partner or the person you live with. Your home may be an arena of worries, difficulties and troubles. You are likely to be unfortunate where property and legacies are concerned. Accidents, thefts, fires, storms and danger through water are all possible causes of loss and injury. You may have eye trouble.

MARS IN LEO

You're a powerhouse of energy and vitality and know exactly where you're going—to the top, of course! It's not the pot of gold at the end of the rainbow that interests you, but the power and the glory—especially the glory. You're a showman, and you know it. You dramatize every emotion and action whenever someone is around to see. You never cease playing to the gallery. You are entertaining, enterprising and exciting. Your detractors might say you're proud and egotistical, but it must be admitted that you seldom fail to give the audience their money's worth.

You are a warmhearted, generous and passionate character. In love, you take over completely and in return give everything you've got. You are wildly emotional, recklessly romantic and inclined to make promises in the ardor of the moment that would be more wisely left unmade. Acutely conscientious—and as your critics say, proud—you endeavor never to go back on your word. Naturally, when your passion has cooled, you find yourself burdened with some tricky and/or irritating obligations.

Still, you're a man or woman of action. You get more done in a day than many others accomplish in a week. You work largely from intuition and are guided by your heart. When a challenge looms, you seem to know without deliberation what has to be done and fearlessly go on the attack. You have an extraordinary faith in life—not just in survival—that seldom measures the risk to yourself. If you bother to attempt something, you feel, it has to be worthwhile. So why hang about? You have no time for timidity or hesitation. It's in or out. Opportunities are seldom wasted on you Martian Leos.

But it's not all plain sailing, as you've probably noticed. You're a demon for going that little bit too far—which, to others, is overboard. Extremes have a fatal attraction for you. In love, as has been mentioned, you are frequently overhasty and impulsive, contemptuous of indecision and disdainful of consequences. Your love of pleasure and the party life costs you a packet. You're a bit ingenuous and foolishly trusting. Sometimes cunning types penetrate your guard (you're surprisingly easy to deceive with flattery and praise, and a personal compliment, no matter how outrageously extravagant, seldom seems inappropriate to you).

You are a born leader who invariably enjoys the trust and confidence of those in authority. Power and command pass to you with a natural affinity. You have a passion for justice and fair play and will defend the case of the underdog or any minority as though it were your own. Sometimes you are overassertive to the point of dogmatism. The result is you stir up unnecessary opposition and enmity. For instance, you may go too far when presenting arguments to superiors; although they are usually on your side, you are not averse to pushing them to the extremity of their tolerance. It is easy for you to earn a reputation for defiance and aggression. Rashness and recklessness can lead to your downfall.

Although rather fixed in your opinions, you are willing to listen to what others have to say. This willingness never prevents you from arguing your own ideas readily and forcefully. You are a resourceful debater and inclined to present fiction as fact if you think you can get away with it. Whatever your field, you will rise to an executive position. It is in your own interests to curb excessive zeal and to resist becoming exclusively identified with a particular idea or belief. Fanaticism lurks in this particular combination, especially where political and social crusades are concerned.

You are apt to be most successful in occupations connected with the government, stock exchange and entertainment industry. A musical ability is often latent with Mars in Leo.

You are fond of exercise and competitive sports. Although sometimes accident-prone, you enjoy speed and taking risks.

The Other Side of the Story

You are power mad but lack the positive qualities of leadership. Your dictatorial and belligerent manner makes you more enemies than friends—you even antagonize those you believe you are helping. Your love life has probably been marred by tragedy, most of your romantic affairs ending in disappointment or sorrow. Gambling and reckless extravagance keep you poor and worried. People in authority trust you to begin with, but soon lose confidence. You are brash and a braggard, clumsy, irritable and prone to blame others for your misfortunes. When opposed, you are bullheaded, threatening and violent.

MARS IN VIRGO

It may not be easy, but you'll probably attain your goals in the end. Mars makes you a little impatient, too eager to move on to something else when you should be persevering in what you have already begun. The fiery, energetic planet produces peculiar setbacks and reversals, but once you have settled on a particular aim—really settled on it—not much can thwart you. The secret is to know what you want.

In your job, you are a born specialist. You have a particular talent for organizing work into formularized systems. Your ideas are original and extremely practical, and you are sure to stand out in any profession or trade you follow. Science often provides a fertile field for your inventive and analytical mind. You are keenly interested in medicine, hygiene, foodstuffs and diet—in any of these fields, you could succeed. Your ability to handle vast amounts of detail without losing concentration or interest fits you admirably for research projects. You should also be able to make your mark as a medical technician, a mechanic or engineer.

You are not a passionate person. All your feelings are well and truly under control. To some of your acquantances, you may appear a bit cold-blooded. Emotional and excitable types find you difficult to understand and may not be prepared to try very hard. You're a handy person to have around in emergencies because your detachment allows you to take an impersonal view. Sometimes, though, you act out emotions you don't feel—this happens particularly when loved ones are upset or being demanding. It is this facility for acting that often leads Mars-in-Virgo people to a successful stage or film career.

You possess a lot more energy than you display. Because you are inclined to be conservative, you go about your work in a quiet and methodical manner. Even when pressures reach the screaming point, you manage to keep your cool and carry on efficiently as though nothing unusual were happening. You are strong-willed, shrewd and ambitious in a subdued way. Setbacks don't affect your work; you are quite prepared to start all over again. In many ways, Mars in Virgo produces the "perfect" employee.

Being inclined to worry and determined not to show it, you suffer from nerves that may affect your digestion. Otherwise, through close attention to hygiene and diet, you manage to keep fairly fit and healthy.

You don't go out of your way to look for love affairs. You enjoy the company of the opposite sex, like to talk about romantic matters and sometimes flirt a little, but when it comes down to the nitty-gritty, you'd rather avoid the emotional turmoil love invariably means. You are more intellectual than sensual. You enjoy talking and love to gossip.

You are rather puritanical in your beliefs, favoring the old-fashioned values that have stood the test of time. If you become fixed on a moral idea or ethic, you can espouse it with a degree of conviction that may verge on sermonizing.

You believe in a fair day's work for a fair day's pay, and that much current talk about individual freedom is merely an excuse to avoid responsibility. You are acquisitive but not money-hungry. Economy is natural to you.

You enjoy the social life and are a pleasant and efficient host or hostess. You don't believe in being lavish nor are you particularly attracted by luxuries. Comfort, a clean house and everything in good working order are your most important domestic priorities. You are not the type to intrude on others and will wait for an invitation rather than "drop in." You are tactful, modest and a lot less self-assured than your detached and "professional" manner would suggest.

You are a careful planner and seldom initiate an action without having calculated that the odds are in your favor. Although bold and enterprising in your approach to working problems, you have very little stomach for risks or venturesome activitity in your personal life.

The Other Side of the Story

You are a cold fish with haughty contempt for the emotions of ordinary people. You are proud, obstinate, irritable and terribly lonely in your aloofness. Unless constantly encouraged in your work, you lose heart. You make many starts and few finishes. Your nerves are continually on edge, even though you may present a controlled facade. You remember slights and will take revenge at the first opportunity. Loss comes through friends, co-workers, subordinates, strikes and labor troubles. You are sarcastic and argumentative, capable of thinking one way, then doing the other.

MARS IN LIBRA

You possess a strong social conscience. You

are very much aware of the inequalities and in-justices imposed on your fellow man—sometimes you seethe with resentment on their behalf. Though you truly don't enjoy violence, you can understand why many of the champions of humanity in the past have had to resort to force to rid the world of an evil. You might be tempted to do the same yourself, given the right circumstances. War to stop war! Can it ever really work! This is the conflict that you must learn to live with—or resolve—in yourself.

Mars, the god of war, is not too comfortable here. Libra is ruled by Venus, the goddess of love and harmony. Love and war are an uneasy mixture, but that's your chemistry. In sex, the soldier Mars and the beautiful goddess Venus fall together in a wild embrace of passion and ecstacy. But when it comes to cohabitation, they fight with the fury of cat and dog.

You usually marry early in life and probably more than once. Disappointment invariably follows each attempt to establish a permanent love relationship. Quarrels, accusations and unhappiness are the rule, not the exception. The opposite sex has a great influence on your life. Even the direction of your work or career seems to be affected by these relationships.

You are a rash and impulsive lover. As a man, you dazzle your women with suavity and charm and then sweep them up with thrilling red-blooded ardor. As a woman, you satisfy with a mind-blowing carburetion of feminity and pure animalism. Inevitably, it ends in love and war—or at its worst, a snarling truce.

The person with Mars in Libra needs a goal in life, not just for his or her own sake, but because the individual has something tangible to contribute to society. This position endows you with keen judgment and a discerning eye, backed by a determination to see your decisions through to the bitter end. You can view a situation from both sides without becoming emotionally committed. Others listen to your advice. You are realistic and refined, and given the opportunity, may become a popular public figure or prominent in your particular set.

Your gift for presenting the sword edge with a firm and gentle gesture makes you an impressive diplomatist and a formidable opponent in the political arena. You would make a wily statesman, a top-ranking military man or a reforming lawyer. A steady mind as well as a steady hand when there is a delicate job to do also fits you for the role of surgeon. You are an idealist who ob-serves life closely and, too often for your own good, becomes upset by the injustice of what you see. Despite the controlling power of your reason, you occasionally flare up in anger and righteous indignation and involve yourself in conflicts and discord that have an amazing habit of spreading. One inflammatory word or action by you seems enough to start a chain reaction among innumerable people. Frequently you have to overcome your own ground swell before getting started. You are no stranger to obstacles, enmity and determined opposition.

You have strong artistic leanings, especially toward poetry, painting and music. Whatever you produce of a creative nature has an urgency and unmistakable vitality to it. You have many friends, most of whom are in the professions. You enjoy getting together with them over drinks and dinner and having a free-ranging discussion that may go on until the early hours. You are a night owl and come to life with great vigor when the dancing starts. You enjoy animated speculation about philosophic and religious matters. Your views on politics are interesting and usually sound.

Your main problem is trying to balance the disharmonious and irritating elements you feel. If you attempt to correct the wrongs outside without resolving the belligerence in your own peace-aspiring nature, you will have trouble finding happiness. The key is to realize the means does *not* justify the end; the means *is* the end.

The Other Side of the Story

You have to battle for everything you get. Nothing comes easy. If it does, it soon disappears or is destroyed. You are unfortunate in love. Vindictive women have cost you much. You quarrel easily with friends and partners and are often unreasonable. Bad luck and open hostility have prevented you from achieving your most treasured ambitions. You often feel cheated by a cruel fate. You rise to an occasion with a tremendous show of energy and enthusiasm, but soon lose heart or burn yourself out. You are a flash in the pan. Jealous associates make a habit of undercutting you. Your own faulty judgment can be seen as the cause of most of your troubles.

MARS IN SCORPIO

Good or evil? Call it what you like, the choice is yours. Nowhere else in the Zodiac does such a tremendous reservoir of energy await direction than when Mars, the planet of energy and force, pulsates in Scorpio, the Sign of repressed or hidden power. Energy and repressed or hidden power? There's a three-letter word for it: *sex*. The sex drive starts here.

This should not be interpreted as meaning that everyone with Mars in Scorpio is a sexual maniac. Far from it. These people have access to a mighty energy at its very source, deep in the nonphysical unconscious. True, it takes some handling as it surfaces through the senses into the mind. True, the propensity of such a fundamental, assertive force is toward some kind of violent, willful and piercing expression. That could be sexual gratification, cruelty for its own sake or a ruthless quest for power. Or, this force could just as easily be used to root out iniquity from the world in one dedicated through rigid self-discipline to altruistic aims.

Not surprisingly, this combination gives a steel-nerved capacity for self-control and unswerving determination—once the individual has decided which course he or she is to take. All people with Mars in Scorpio discover early in life that they live on an emotional volcano. They develop a repressive temperament that appears to others as a cool, calculating shrewdness and total self-sufficiency.

You are practical, hard headed and one of the most hard-working types in the Zodiac. To attain your goals, you are capable of toiling under the most punishing conditions with almost superhuman endurance. Once committed, you never give up. But the aim must be personally desirable. No one on earth can make you perform against your will, although you'll go through the actions out of economic necessity, if it pleases you. Sometimes you are thought to be lazy, by those who don't understand that you are one of nature's self-starters. It is not unusual for you to have to sacrifice physical comfort and happiness to achieve your ambitions.

You are a hard-driving, relentless individual who cannot be placated with half-measures and good intentions. Give you an inch and you'll take a foot—and immediately make a stand for more from there. You are unstoppable. At the same time, you are diplomatic, urbane if it suits you. You realize the importance of social formalities in achieving cooperation, though when off your guard, you can be rather blunt.

Your mind is quick and penetrating. You have a knack of getting to the bottom of things. You can probe another person's mind with the same impersonal precision that a Mars-in-

Scorpio brain surgeon uses to excise a tumor. This combination is found in people who earn their living through various forms of analysis in mining, psychotherapy and science. They also enjoy solving mysteries and may be attracted to occult and psychic investigations. Sometimes a profound flash of mystical insight changes their entire life-style. Frequently, people with Mars in Scorpio possess an innate mechanical ability. Being quite physically strong themselves, they enjoy the feel of using powerful machines.

You are not an adaptable person. Your opinions are fixed. You prefer to have one clear aim and stick to it through thick and thin. This way, you are never confused. In fluid situations where you are denied predetermined references, you suffer considerable inner strain, though you may never show it. Uncertainty you regard as your worst enemy. Fortunately, you rarely feel it.

You find danger attractive and are prone to taking physical risks. With this combination, there is always the chance of a violent and unexpected death. Without softening influences elsewhere in the horoscope, you will be selfish and think nothing of riding roughshod over others.

Secretiveness, a liking for revenge and a mute awareness of their own erotic thought patterns characterize Mars-in-Scorpio people.

The Other Side of the Story

You have no respect for the rights of others. You take as much as you can of what you want whenever you see it. You are contemptuous of ordinary people and use them outrageously to indulge your sensual and other selfish desires. You are despotic and tyrannical, quarrelsome, sarcastic, vitriolic and revengeful. You are oversexed, obsessed with luridly erotic thoughts, cruel, unscrupulous, violent and probably sexually deviate. Or you may be the victim of others with the same traits. Troubles come through those who work for you; a secret affair with one of these individuals is likely to end tragically. Major operations and serious accidents are likely.

MARS IN SAGITTARIUS

Given the chance, you'd love to be a rolling stone. You're fond of travel, adore adventure, make friends instantly and have a pounding lust for life. But above all, you're independent. You are in love with liberty—the freedom to go where you like, when you like, as you like, and to say what you like. Obviously, you're not a very safe bet as a marriage partner. But despite your transitory habits and inclinations, you often manage to acquire a substantial place in the community.

You're a good sport, popular and have immense vitality. Not many people can keep up as you whisk from one situation to another, intrigued by novelty, fascinated by experiment and exploration, and dauntless when it comes to physical danger. In a risky situation, you're down right foolhardy.

Yet you're not a stayer, a sticker. When it comes to perseverance and tenacity, you don't want even to be consulted. You're a sportsman in heart and soul, a kind of light-footed pugilist, one might say. Your style is to prance into the fray, knock 'em down, drag 'em out, bleed like fury if you have to, and then move on smartly to the next contest or tournament. Although Mars is a warrior, he has no stamina for the war of attrition or lackluster siege.

Your mind is sharp, active and original, your thinking supremely optimistic and futuristic. You're constantly questioning and seeking, but seldom stay around long enough to make enough use of the answers. Tomorrow and not today seems to be your main interest. Over the horizon is the promise this moment lacks. When you can manage to apply yourself, you are often brilliant, but your concentration soon ebbs, leaving you chasing that end of the rainbow where you know it's all happening.

You do well in any occupation where your natural urges can be expressed. Any other kind of job will seem drudgery. You would make a fine traveling sales representative, itinerant lecturer or teacher, crusading politician, adventure writer, military commander or space explorer. If you can set your mind on a single objective and marshal all your energetic and intellectual resources, there's no limit to how far you can go. The vital point is to know what you want and to deal with the problems as they occur instead of rushing out to meet them.

You have a keen interest in social, philosophic and religious matters. Although you hesitate to reject outright the orthodox dogmas, you are impatient with the restrictions they impose on the individual's thinking. Frequently you are drawn into good-humored arguments and express your views in an articulate and forceful manner. Your opinions are often at variance with those of the Establishment. Your style of speaking is open and candid, and combined with your strong views on morality and justice, usually guarantees you a hearing in any company. Some-

times you upset others with personal observations that are remarkable for their accuracy, if not for their tact.

You love company and have many boon companions. Most exciting outdoor sports and games appeal to you. You're a lucky and impulsive gambler and seem to have a sixth sense. If you lose, you have a happy knack of being able to forget it and plunge into the next adventure with the same optimism and high spirits.

Simplicity in all its forms appeals to you. You dislike insincerity and affectation and can be depended on to give an honest opinion at all times. You are particularly critical of people in high places who put on airs and graces, and are not afraid to publicly say so. You will never allow the fear of what others may think to inhibit your free speech.

You stand to gain financially through marriage and may wed more than once. Money may also come through legacies and social position.

The Other Side of the Story

Court actions are likely to go against you with ruinous results. You lack a sense of proportion and create unnecessary difficulties and hardship for yourself through rash and careless actions. You exaggerate to impress others and make impossible promises. Neighbors, brothers, sisters and other relatives are unlucky. The death of one of these people may have a profound effect on your life. Your religious beliefs, unorthodox ideas and skepticism are likely to wreck your career or social status. You might foolishly risk all on what amounts to the throw of the (probably loaded) dice.

MARS IN CAPRICORN

This is the best position in the horoscope for the fiery energy of Mars. Here the planet's wonderful driving force links up with the astute organizing ability of Capricorn and produces you—a person who commands respect in whatever field you choose and who is certain (other influences in the chart being equal) to rise to the position of executive or chief.

Your work or career is the most important thing in your life. You are aggressively ambitious and determined to make a name for yourself. No amount of responsibility deters you—on the contrary, you thrive on it. You are even prepared to shoulder the responsibilities of others if you feel it's necessary. You possess remarkable persistence and (as a tactic), patience. You will work day and night to achieve your goals and are not afraid to get out the sledgehammer and deliver a few well-aimed blows when the obstacles or opposition gets too tough. It's an exceptional man or woman who can stand against you. Fortunately, few wish to try.

Your progress is generally smooth because you have a talent for marshaling all available forces into one mighty continuing effort, with you very active as the guiding and cohesive spirit. This stratagem eliminates much of the need for struggle, which so often wears out the subject before the object. Like an old sailing master, you use the crosswinds to drive you forward. This strategy may cost a few miles, but the going is easier for all, and the end result more productive.

Your personality is magnetic and commanding. You are able to inspire others from the workshop floor to top management. People enjoy working with you and for you; above all they respect you. And nothing makes you feel happier or nobler than being esteemed for your practical qualities and wisdom.

You are severe and stern when necessary. You insist on obedience from subordinates and have the happy knack of getting it without confrontations. You are precise, know exactly what you want and can usually do any job you ask of another. Austerity is no hardship for you. You have supreme confidence in your own ability, but your impressive acumen and expertise may inhibit initiative in your associates.

Financially powerful people can usually be counted on to give you assistance. You're what's regarded in business circles as a good bet. You're also prepared to take a chance, to grab an opportunity boldly when others might hesitate. It is your style to know exactly what is going on in all departments of your organization and to keep informed of market developments and trends. So although you delight in a bit of venturous plunging, it's rarely that much of a gamble!

This astuteness and assiduous concern for responsibility may not be so evident in the youth of a person born with Mars in Capricorn. Sometimes these young people may seem to have an intractable love of pleasure and appear quite undisciplined. This, however, is a development phase. Capricorn usually affects the circumstances so that the youth enjoys himself but only by surmounting constant difficulties and setbacks. The underlying seriousness and gravity in the character can usually be discerned, even though the glimpse may be fleeting.

Now, what of love for the mature person born with this combination? Here is a guy or gal who responds to only real affection. It pierces the tough layer of inhibitions that protects their love nature from hurt, and stirs the intense sensual longings throbbing there. But love has got to be for real. Let someone love them truly and they'll be loyal forevermore. Lovers with this combination are easily offended, and if rejected, suffer excruciatingly.

There's always a chance you will blow your top. Although you can take a tremendous amount of sustained mental and physical effort, it must be justified by progress. Prolonged delays and irritations cause a buildup of frustration that's finally released in a violent way.

The Other Side of the Story

You have an atrocious temper, which is a danger to life and limb. None of your affairs ever seems to advance smoothly; you are usually the victim of delays, mistakes, inefficiency and other people's nastiness. Even at this moment, a project important to you is probably held up for unaccountable reasons. You may have the best of plans but be incapable of stirring the interest of those whose cooperation is necessary. You have a habit of wasting time on detail and ill-conceived projects. A love affair early in life with a person much older or in an inferior position probably proved disastrous in more ways than one.

MARS IN AQUARIUS

You probably want to change the world with your ideas and make it a better place to live in. The trouble is, you're in a terrible hurry and in your rush you'll probably succeed only in turning everything upside down—and making us all unhappy and very uncomfortable.

Slow down, be patient and keep up the good work. You have flair and imagination. You're the type of person who gives the world some of its best reforming ideas. You are a genuine intellectual with the good of humanity at heart. You discern the hairline cracks in society long before they open into fissures of political clamor and discontent. You are visionary. You demand action. Your mind is sharp, incisive and dynamic. Your unique and original thinking puts you out in front—sometimes so far out that you are a voice crying in the wilderness.

You are very convincing in your arguments.

Your reasoning power is impeccable. You are fearless in debate and will say exactly what you think. But you do occasionally get overexcited. At these times, you are impulsive, self-willed and rash in speech. Overall, with Mars in Aquarius, you are susceptible to acting in spurts and spasms. Your opinions are fairly fixed and you don't like to water them down.

You are more a thinker than a doer, equipped to whip others into action with your galvanizing presence and slogans. You enjoy a free and easy life. Restrictions imposed by job or family irritate you. You are much happier with groups of people than in an emotional entanglement with one or two others. Bohemian types attract you most; you enjoy their informality and uninhibited ways, which are very similar to your own. These characters are inclined to be enthusiastic about your more revolutionary views and make you feel less eccentric than misunderstood.

Mars in Aquarius usually confers an ability to write as well as a wide-ranging interest in literature. You are apt to use your pen (more likely an electric typewriter) to propagate your advanced ideas or to secure public support for a pet project. You are never content with results. You must move forward. When one project ends, you immediately pick up another with the same enthusiasm and idealistic fervor. Whatever your circumstances, you manage in some way or other to stand out from the crowd—even if through a simple gesture such as affecting an unusual style in clothes.

It is not uncommon for people with this combination to win public acclaim. They are often connected with international welfare organizations such as the United Nations, the Red Cross and other groups dedicated to the eradication of disease, hunger and poverty, as well as the protection of human rights.

Mars in Aquarius is a catalyst that produces unusual events and lightning changes around the people born with this combination. Even in quiet and private conversations, their unusual ideas may set others in motion with far-reaching and even violent repercussions. They typify the revolutionary spirit and the release of idealogical forces that ignite mass emotions long suppressed by injustice and inequality.

You are well suited for a career in medicine, welfare, social work, politics, psychiatry or science. Electronics and the solving of problems of stellar-space travel should appeal to your enterprising and inventive mind. You may also make a competent lecturer in psi (parapsychic sensitivity) subjects and have a talent for experimental work in these fields.

In all your activities, you will be more effective if you exert a constant pressure on yourself rather than work by fits and starts.

The Other Side of the Story

You are too independent to be taken seriously. Your blunt and insensitive manner turns off people who might otherwise support you and your views. You're all talk and hopelessly ineffective when dealing with practical problems. Inwardly, you are a mass of nervous tension and project an image of instability and restrained hysteria. If you lose your temper, you are apt to go berserk. You are unreliable, reckless and fanatical. You may be betrayed by friends and separated quite early in life from a parent.

MARS IN PISCES

You are frequently tortured by your own thoughts and frustrated by your inability to put your plans across. *You* know precisely what you mean—in your imagination you can visualize every detail—but when it comes to tangible expression, you often flop. There are exceptions to this, powerful ones, because Mars is the planet of force and energy. If well aspected (which can be ascertained from the Yellow Tables) Mars confers the necessary strength to overcome Pisces' debilitating effect. Even so, you will always have difficulties to surmount in practical endeavors. Pisces is self-sacrificing, sensitive and psychic, the very antithesis of Mars' warriorlike aggression and rambunctiousness. This is probably the most difficult position in the whole Zodiac for fiery Mars.

You are most likely to be successful in occupations that depend on tuning in to other people's emotions, or in those in which you can express yourself in abstract and subtle ways so as to arouse the finer feelings of others. As an actor or actress, you can communicate to your audience on a very satisfying but indefinable wavelength. Mars provides the vigor for physical action, Pisces restrains it. The result may be an intriguingly languid movement, exciting in its suggestion, even sexy, but exasperatingly ellusive. This combination could produce a first-class dancer.

You could also be successful as a writer or an artist, again arousing emotions and even passions with an insinuative style, rather than an explicit one. The power to switch emotions quickly is extremely evident in people with this combination. But as beneficent as this trait may be in creative expression, it can cause great internal confusion. These people's constant ambivalences make them wary of their own moods. They are subject to depression because of the hopeless feeling that they'll never be as normal as they imagine those around them to be. What they fail to realize is that the "normalcy" they covet so much in despairing moments would destroy their wonderful artistic potential.

You have a great desire to be liked, to be popular, but circumstances usually work against this, particularly where the larger public is concerned. In any case, no matter how highly regarded you are—by the world or only by your own friends—you'll never feel satisfied. It is not that you want more acclaim. It's that in your dreams where you act out much of your life before it happens, the feeling of success and acceptance is . . . well, different.

You are courageous in the face of misfortune, and this often comes through love affairs. You adore excitement and mystery and can fall head-over-heels in love with those you feel project these qualities. But unless it's the real thing—which is very rare with Mars in Pisces—your affections quickly fade. Ordinary person-alities, no matter how attractive, don't possess the depth of character to stand up to your intuitive scrutiny, which is actually searching for Love Everlasting! You revel in other people and read them like books—and the "paperback" types take no time at all to get through.

You are extremely impressionable and sometimes easily led. You'd rather comply than resist if there is no great issue at stake. You can't be bothered raising objections just to have your own voice heard. Your egotism is far deeper than that—you like to manipulate people and situations quietly and unobtrusively, and a compliant and receptive nature (as you know only too well) is ideal for this.

The Other Side of the Story

You suffer deeply from your own indecision and vacillating moods. Your friends learn to be cautious of you, knowing you are likely to be pleasant and obliging one moment and bitterly resentful the next. Marriage is likely to be delayed. You may be deserted by lovers or plunged into scandal through an illicit affair. Because of your inability to cope with normal life, you are apt to seek escape in drink or drugs. You are probably promiscuous and permissive but unable to satisfy your sexual cravings. You are lazy, easily depressed and cannot seem to remain in one job for very long.

JUPITER

The Planet

Jupiter is the largest planet in the solar system. After Venus, it is the brightest. Its diameter is 88,000 miles compared with the Earth's 8000 miles. Jupiter is nearly 500 million miles out from the Sun, and is never closer than 367 million miles to the Earth.

The huge "empty" space between Mars and Jupiter—an inconceivable 342 million miles—is littered with cosmic rubble. This is called the asteroid belt.

Jupiter takes 12 Earth years to circle the Zodiac. Despite its tremendous size, the planet rotates in less than 10 hours, against the Earth's 24. The sections near the poles are not completely solidified, so the period of rotation for all parts of Jupiter is not uniform. Because of the planet's lack of density and its speed of rotation, its poles have a pronounced "flattened" appearance.

The striking features of the planet's atmosphere are light- and dark-colored belts paralleling the equator, which slowly change, and the Great Red Spot. This "spot" is 20,000 miles long, and although fading, appears to be more permanent than the belts.

In January 1610, Galileo made history by discovering Jupiter's satellites. He named them the Medician planets after his patron Cosimo Medici. These can easily be seen through good binoculars. They have diameters of 2300 to 3200 miles and revolve around Jupiter in 2 to 17 days. There are eight other Jovian moons, all of which are less than 100 miles in diameter. One, very close to the planet, revolves at a speed of over 1000 miles a minute.

Jupiter is largely or entirely composed of gases. Hydrogen, methane and ammonia have been detected in its atmosphere. Pioneer 10 passed within 81,000 miles of the planet in December 1973 and sent back color pictures and information as it flew out of the solar system.

Symbolism

Zeus or Jupiter, as he was called by the Romans, was the greatest of the Olympian divinities. He was the omnipotent ruler of the ancient Greek gods who lived on the summit of Mount Olympus. He was regarded as the father of men and thought possibly to be even the master of fate. The Romans considered him the guardian of the law, protector of justice and virtue, and defender of the truth.

Jupiter was the son of Cronus who, fearing he would be deposed by his sons, swallowed them one by one at birth. But his wife, Rhea, gave Cronus a stone to swallow when Jupiter was born, and the young god was brought up in a cave in Crete. In 1900, archeologists explored this reputed "birth cave" and found votive offerings to Jupiter believed to have been there since the year 2000 B.C. It was said that Rhea's priests clashed their weapons in the cave to drown the infant Jupiter's cries and that a goat acted as his nurse. The goat was rewarded by being placed among the stars as Capricorn. (The Goat is, of course, the symbol of the Sign Capricorn.)

Jupiter fathered four Olympian deities by mortal women: Mercury, Artemis or Diana (the Moon), Apollo (god of prophesy) and Dionysus (god of wine).

Jupiter was called the Thunderer and his chief weapon was the thunderbolt. Sacred to him were the oak, the eagle and mountain summits. His sacrifices were usually goats, cows and bulls. He sometimes wore a wreath of oak or olive leaves. The rustling of oak leaves was said to be his voice.

Jupiter's attributes were the scepter, a thunderbolt, an eagle and a figure of victory held in the hand.

Astrology

Jupiter is fiery, noble, benevolent, fruitful and masculine. It typifies all that is jovial, optimistic, expansive, buoyant, positive and dignified in man. It is the good provider, the respecter and upholder of the law, the generous and genial helper.

Jupiter in Astrology is called the "greater fortune." It not only brings abundance of material benefits, but is also the source of philosophical wisdom. It teaches frequently by coming to the rescue at the last minute, when all hope seems lost. Saturn is also a great teacher, but teaches by restriction, denial and adversity without any (immediately apparent) saving grace. Jupiter's nature is to fulfill; it delivers the goods at the end of the lesson. Jupiter is the strength that allows us to endure trials with philosophic steadiness in the knowledge that we are growing in wisdom and experience. It is the happy ending, the great protector. The only danger from a well-placed Jupiter is that you may fail to see or take full advantage of the opportunities it offers.

People with Jupiter prominent in their horoscope are generous and candid. They have a good intellect and astute judgment. Their observations are often uncannily on the mark. They aspire a greater understanding of morality and religious ideals and have a deep respect for law and order. Their conscience continually reminds them that in the final analysis, justice and decency depend on the individual. These men and women are broad-minded, logical, determined and extremely self-confident.

The Jupiterian is usually a happy, outgoing, sociable and likable person. He or she enjoys a good time, is hospitable and has many friends. These people often display an interest in the law and enjoy philosophic and religious studies. They have a penchant for foreign travel, and until they can make such a journey, will read and talk avidly about the places they want to visit.

The influence of Jupiter is expanisve, creative and prosperous. Unless the planet is ill placed, it invariably bestows a great amount of what appears to be good luck. The person is either born with money, is provided with an income or becomes well off later in life. These men and women usually display great faith in their good fortune by being lavishly generous when economy is indicated, or exceedingly easygoing about their possessions. Easy come, easy go is often their attitude.

Jupiter people love sports and physical exercise. They usually develop a strong, muscular frame and in later years become stout or fat. Since this is the planet of expansion, they are readily susceptible to middle-age spread. They like to move about freely. Jupiter rules Sagittarius, the ninth Sign of the Zodiac, which is associated with long journeys and higher studies. It also has co-rulership, with Uranus, of Pisces, the watery twelfth Sign of the Zodiac, which is disposed to long journeys, life in a foreign place and acute religions insight.

The Jupiterian is very interested in educational matters. He or she makes a competent judge, lawyer, banker, broker or physician. These people are usually fitted for positions of dignity, trust or power in business or social circles. Large charities, religious foundations and philanthropic organizations often provide them with the scope they need for the exercise of their particular talents.

A badly placed Jupiter causes restlessness and uncertainty. The person may be an extremist in his or her views and become a religious or political fanatic. Excessive optimism and carelessness may mar judgment. Losses are likely through bad investments, gambling and extravagance. These people may run up debts, borrow money indiscriminately, fail to honor their obligations and generally lead a lazy, luxury-loving, shallow life devoid of any uplifting philosophic or religious thoughts.

Jupiter represents the power of uniform growth throughout the organism. The urge is to mature, to expand the consciousness through understanding what has been experienced rather than merely to accumulate knowledge. Jupiter strives to counterbalance our inadequacies and failures by developing compensation features elsewhere. The subconscious awareness of these weaknesses form the conscience. The conscience is the motivating factor in the Jupiterian. Hence he is continually reminded of the need for justice, morality, mercy and the law—both manmade and religious.

Physiologically, Jupiter rules the expansion of the body and is associated with the disposition of fats, the liver (the largest gland) and the pituitary gland, which regulates hormone production.

JUPITER IN ARIES

You are a person with great and grand ambitions. You aim to get to the top in whatever field you choose. You are not content to follow in the footsteps of others. You consent to knuckle down to an apprenticeship for as short a time as possible out of sheer necessity, but as soon as *you* think you are qualified, you will be off into the wide blue yonder where you can display your originality, initiative and leadership—and do as you like.

You won't settle for second place in anything. This combination gives an aggressive determination to succeed for the good of all concerned and not just the self. You genuinely feel you have a mission in life. You don't have faith in the orthodox sense—in fact, you are a bit of a skeptic where religious doctrines are concerned

—but you believe wholeheartedly that forces deep within you are pushing you toward a pre-destined point.

You are intent on broadening your mind. You love to travel, to do big things on the spur of the moment. You detest detail, and routine jobs you avoid like the plague. You have a flair for organization, for handling numbers of people and big concerns. You are a born leader. Men make excellent military chiefs. Women are just as gifted in other fields. Both sexes have an impelling desire to establish a reputation. If this can be done with dash and a flourish of heroics, you will be delighted. You can burst into politics—enrich and enliven the scene with outrageous policies that catch the popular imagination and leave the die-hards standing flatfooted. Your ideas are likely to be so original that at first they may seem impractical. But you have the ability to put your point of view across forcefully and intelligently. You are at your best when defending an idea that is under attack from reactionary and conservative forces.

You don't like working under others and you usually succeed finally to a position of independence and authority. People respect you because you always seem to know where you are heading. You have tremendous enthusiasm and energy—sometimes you get carried away by your own optimism and self-confidence and make promises you can't keep. Your generosity and desire to be helpful also get the better of you. You say you will do things and then find you can't.

You have a natural aptitude for literature, science and the law. You are generally lucky with speculative investments, though this depends specifically on other influences in your chart. Gambling can be your making or ruin. Young people usually play a prominent and fortunate role in your affairs. You often make a successful marriage that brings you money or raises your social standing. Otherwise, you make your mark in the world through your own qualifications and unremitting effort.

You are likely to change your career at some time in your life. Your business interests may be widely diversified so that you have to be on the move to keep a check on what's going on because you are known for your open-handed habits; you have plenty of company when ever you want it. You prefer the congenial, intellectual type of friend with whom you can discuss a wide range of topics. You enjoy nothing better than new places and new faces. You are keenly interested in expanding your experience of life; you want to feel that you have tried everything at least once. You develop a definite philosophy that is pragmatic rather than idealistic, but once your views are formed, they may become fixed and dogmatic. You may enjoy laying down the law and arguing with people. You love sports and displaying your excellent physical coordination, but you are not much of a spectator.

The Other Side of the Story

You may expect too much from life and be constantly disappointed. Gambling is likely to be a compulsive and ruinous disease. You may be a big talker, promising anything to anybody to get attention, and avoiding people you have let down. You are likely to be unrealistic and count on luck when common sense warns otherwise. Your desire for experience may degenerate into a bustling search for sensual gratification.

JUPITER IN TAURUS

You have a great love of pleasure and home comforts. Money seems to come easily (you are lucky that way) but you are also prepared to work hard for what you want. The combination of the abundant Jupiter in Taurus, the Sign of material acquisition and income, makes you a naturally favored individual.

You are warmhearted, generous, reserved and affectionate. You love beauty in all its forms. You may not be an artist yourself, but you could easily be a connoisseur or collector. You like to fill your home with elegant and beautiful things that others will admire. Apart from aesthetics, you also enjoy the feeling of security derived from owning valuable objects. You usually possess a fine collection of books, many of them to do with religion, metaphysics and philosophy.

You go all out to make money and to build up your estate. You have a flair for making money earn money. Whether you work for yourself or an employer, you can usually be counted on to turn a profit. You are especially able in fields connected with building, banking, the land and mining. With this combination, you are a potential tycoon. A wizard at building up businesses, you tend to rely on solid and proven methods and are reluctant to take unnecessary chances. But you spread your investments widely and wisely. You are determined; you work toward your planned objectives with untiring persistence. Your Midas touch often extends into the oil business, ranching, massive construction projects, agriculture and industry. Although your ideas are often advanced, even radical, you like to apply them in a systematical manner. The quicker you can reduce your procedures to a routine, the happier you are. At heart, you are cautious and conservative.

Your love of the good life is likely to make you extravagant. You enjoy reveling in luxury. You may run into debt supplying yourself with the best in food, drink, entertainment and accommodations. You can very easily go to extremes where sensual pleasures are concerned. You are strongly attracted to the opposite sex.

Although you enjoy reading and talking about other countries, you aren't a great one for traveling unless it is connected with business or education. If you do have to visit a foreign city, you enjoy it (provided you're traveling first class), but in your heart of hearts, you prefer the psychological comfort of familiar surroundings, particularly your own home. You are devoted to your family and like to feel you are a good provider. Sometimes you may have an exaggerated idea of what you are doing for loved ones; other times, you make lavish promises you have no hope of fulfilling. You take to domestic life like a duck to water: you enjoy sitting in your favorite chair, feeling the fine wood of your furniture, walking on quality carpets. You are fond of entertaining and showing off your possessions. You have a penchant for jewelry, paintings, miniatures, porcelain and fine hand-crafted objects.

You believe in helping people who help themselves, that is, you prefer to create opportunities for others to take advantage of rather than give them a straight handout. You are a fair and a generous employer but you won't tolerate goldbricking. You want to see justice done on both sides. You can be very firm when the occasion demands it.

You have strong religious leanings but you don't allow them to interfere with your day-to-day activities. Your ethics are practical and straightforward: you believe that if you treat others fairly and justly in your worldly affairs, you are largely obeying all the religious tenets.

With Jupiter in Taurus, you may possess a good singing or speaking voice. Many talented actors and singers have the Jupiter-in-Taurus combination.

You are likely to gain financially through marriage, partnerships and legacies. Your children may give you reason to be proud of them.

The Other Side of the Story

Your love of luxury may wreck your health.

You are likely to overeat and have a weight problem, overspend and always be in debt. Gambling may ruin your chances. Your children may fail to come up to your expectations. Your taste is such that you are likely to clutter your home with cheap and junky ornaments, believing them to be artistic and desirable. You may be an out-and-out materialist who lives only for the pleasure your possessions (including the people you love) give you. Your own ability to love may be as shallow as the platitudes you constantly spout. You are likely to be a hypocritical religionist. Your marriage or business partners may take you down. You may lose a legacy or an inheritance. You are likely to be easily fooled with promises. You may be lackadaisical and quick to give up.

JUPITER IN GEMINI

Your ideas are grandiose. Your mind can stretch beyond the normal horizons—out of this world, in fact. You are a master at seizing hold of abstract ideas and propounding them in ingenious ways. You are voluble, eloquent, amusing, intelligent, articulate, likable, knowledgeable and persuasive. But one question usually remains unanswered when you have finished holding forth: Will your scheme actually work? Frequently the answer is no.

In this position, the expansive, jovial and optimistic Jupiter combines with the nervous, restless intellectual and airy Sign of Gemini. The result is often insubstantial. Jupiter here is at its detriment. It is not that the planet is incompatible with Gemini; it is just that it can't manage to contribute its heavyweight qualities to this often scatterbrained Sign.

You are a person who has great faith in the mind's ability to solve all the world's problems. Your aim is to gather knowledge. You believe in higher education and would like to have at least one academic degree yourself. You want to travel as far afield as possible, to see things first hand, to meet people, talk, exchange ideas, correspond, to become a well-informed person.

You are not only a quiz kid but a whiz kid. You are constantly on the move. You love to make friends—to pop in on them, call them up. You scatter your views and opinions around with the abandon of someone throwing wheat to chickens. You are seldom around long enough to collect any eggs. You know a little about a great many subjects, but you lack the power to concentrate long and deeply on any single study. Actually, you are seldom at a disadvantage because your fine intellect and retentive memory allows you to ad-lib in most situations with an amazing show of erudition.

You aim to earn a living through mental pursuits. You are not a very practical person. Physical routine and manual labor are anathema to you. You are a theorist, a visionary. You have the brilliant answer in your mind; it is for others with an aptitude for detailed procedures to apply your solutions. You make an excellent diplomat, writer, teacher, lawyer, actor, linguist, banker, stockbroker, underwriter. You can be successful in air transport, broadcasting or television. With maturity, those of you who are writers may gravitate to the publishing field and enjoy considerable success. You probably play a musical instrument. If you try, you should be able to compose music and may even be able to earn a living from it.

You are an idealist who limits your chances of lasting accomplishment by jumping from one new activity to another. You scatter your energies, both mental and physical. You live for the satisfaction of the moment; the promises of tomorrow are just promises. Still, you build in a practical fashion despite yourself and are often fortunate and successful. Your instincts are strongly humanitarian. Although your approach to other people's problems is usually a reasoning one, you are kind and sympathetic.

You make friends very quickly and sometimes attract the wrong type—the go-getters and the schemers. You are so trusting and overconfident at times that you can be taken in by these people, especially in business matters. New ventures and propositions, especially the way-out kind, need to be vetted thoroughly.

You will probably marry twice. You are not the domestic type but will do your best to make your mate happy. You need a partner who is intellectual rather than emotional, one who understands your need to come and go much as you please. You are a rather disorganized person and your home sometimes reflects this. Travel, relatives and correspondence are likely to cause marital problems. You may even marry a relative or a close associate.

You show a pronounced flair for philosophic reasoning. Your ideas in this field are sometimes provocative and original. You are worth listening to, but your appeal is principally to the intellect and fails to satisfy deeper human longings that depend on faith rather than reason.

The Other Side of the Story

Your writings and beliefs may stir others up against you. Sudden difficulties can make it impossible for you to continue in your profession or job. You may be forced by circumstances to keep traveling and be unable to settle down when you wish to. Your marriage is likely to break up and divorce or separation may involve you in considerable expense. You may have to work to support another person and have very little money for yourself. Differences and separations from relatives are likely to occur in distressing circumstances. A publishing venture may flop. Your best ideas or plans may be stolen. You are likely to talk your way into jobs and then out of them. You may be a compulsive gossip.

JUPITER IN CANCER

This is a most auspicious placing for Jupiter. It generally means roses all the way. The person is charitable, popular, enterprising and good-humored. Circumstances are usually fortunate and fulfilling. Jupiter, the influence of good fortune and growth, is at its strongest in Cancer.

You are a person whose sympathies are easily aroused. You will put yourself out to help another in a practical way and genuinely endeavor to understand people's problems. You combine thought and feeling in a rare balance, which makes you a kind, benevolent and well-integrated human being.

You have a great attachment to your home and family. You are fiercely protective of your loved ones and will do all in your power to help them get on in the world, even if they don't deserve your aid. You try very successfully to live up to the traditions of elegance and good living you have assimilated. You don't deny yourself any comforts. You aim at being surrounded in your home with all the things you admire. These include not only objects that are pleasing to the eye but also those redolent of the past. You have a penchant for antiques, relics and memorabilia. You are likely to keep a family bible, handed down from generation to generation, in a special place. Your furnishings or decor will reflect your admiration of classical lines and historical form. There will be no shortage of sentimental bric-a-brac. Old photographs, letters, a family coat of arms and well-worn leather-bound books, if not displayed, will be tucked away with loving care.

You enjoy traveling, especially over the sea or to places by the water. You may travel for education or business purposes but are not averse to making a trip just for pleasure. While you are away, you think about your home, and vice versa. You often manage to get away once or twice a year, and this helps you appreciate both your home and your love of travel.

Your financial judgment is extremely good. More often than not, you are helped by good luck. You enjoy making money, but no more than you delight in spending it. You are a very self-possessed person; you have it all together in a natural and unaffected way. The influence of a stable and happy childhood usually creates a deep inner sense of security in people born with Jupiter in Cancer. An understanding and provident mother is also characteristic of this group, other things being equal. The image you present to the world is one of restrained optimism and confidence. This suggests—quite rightly—that you are able to handle your affairs more than capably. Women with this combination can take good care of themselves if anything happens to their male providers. All of you tend to share in inheritances or legacies at some time in your life and to receive money without having to work for it. The men frequently benefit materially from the women in their lives.

You are a gracious host or hostess. You enjoy the domestic life. You love to serve the best of food and drink. Your fondness for food and good living can create a weight problem, which will have to be dealt with eventually to safeguard your health. You enjoy a good time. By pouring too much energy into pleasurable activities, you risk stultifying your deeper development.

You are patriotic and very interested in public and national affairs. You like to keep yourself well informed of what is happening in the world. You are intuitive about the needs of people and your political views are well worth heeding.

You are suited for a wide variety of occupations. Usually you are most successful in fields requiring an assessment of the public mood and tastes, or in providing the masses with life's necessities. These include politics, the manufacturing industries, wholesale distribution, shipping and large-scale ventures connected with liquids and refreshments. Women with Jupiter in Cancer frequently marry prominent public figures. They also make exceptional nurses.

Your religious views are usually carried forward from your childhood. You are apt to be a staunch supporter of the church or to espouse a homespun philosophy that stresses the basic interdependence of social groups and the moral law expressed through the family unit.

The Other Side of the Story

Blind extravagance is likely to lead to all kinds of complications and unhappiness if this combination is badly influenced by other factors. Excesses such as overindulgence in sex, food and drink are likely trouble starters. Your health may suffer through gluttonous habits and obesity. Inner misery brought about by an inability to cope with the conflict between intellect and emotions may make you seek relief in drugs or liquor.

JUPITER IN LEO

Everything about you is expansive—and probably expensive, if you reflect the full potential of this very fortunate zodiacal placing. In some cases, it is a little too good and the person concerned becomes a slave of his own grandiose ambitions to be the wealthiest, best-dressed, most popular or influential guy or gal in town. Thus he or she misses out on the enjoyment money and position can give in moderation. Jupiter unrestrained tends toward excess; Leo often means a double-dose.

Still, the fact remains that with Jupiter in lordly Leo you have the capacity and the luck to raise yourself to a position of prominence in your particular community. Whether you spoil it by going to extremes is your decision.

As a mature person with this combination, you are generous, warmhearted and very keen on seeing justice done for your fellow man. You intend to make an impact for good on the world and to be remembered with genuine affection. Your ambitions are unlimited (everything you attempt is on a grand scale), but your lofty aspirations are supported by a magnanimous, dignified and noble temperament.

Although you enjoy comfort and luxury and are basically extravagant, you tend to accept these boons as your "right" while they are available. A sincere and honest type, you possess an innate sense of purpose, a feeling of being directed by powers greater than yourself—why should you dispute with a benevolent fate? Others may think you're a little too grand at times.

You inevitably rise to a position of authority and revel in all the honors and privileges it confers. You possess excellent executive ability and are particularly well suited for high government office and work in large well-established public companies. You have dash, loads of self-confidence, good humor and a splendid sense of the dramatic. Employees respect and admire you. You inspire loyalty and even hero-worship, which may arouse the jealousy of superiors.

You are ideally suited for heading a public

relations or advertising firm. You would make an excellent figurehead, ready to step in and do the lesser tasks if necessary, but prepared to enjoy the lavish living and entertainment if not. The film-making industry may also be a suitable medium for your talents; as may be the promotion and organizing of tours by international celebrities. You are quite likely to rise to fame yourself.

You are a proud and passionate lover—as a man, masterful, as a woman, utterly yielding to the guy who can demonstrate (to your satisfaction) that he is worthy of you. You love being pursued. The center of attention in any company you feel is reserved for you. Social popularity means so much that you spend much of your income (or expense account) on entertaining to keep up your position. You make a wonderful host or hostess.

You possess a flair for art as well as a genuine love of it. Your artistic preferences, whether they take the form of color, sound or shape, reflect either the flamboyant and spectacular or the richly conservative—nothing in between. You know precisely what you like and don't like. You are seldom confused or undecided. You lean toward philosophic subjects and literature and may try your hand at writing a book sometime.

You have exceptional judgment in business and financial matters, and usually acquire a reputation for wisdom and foresight in regard to everyday affairs. You are unusually lucky with speculative investments.

The Other Side of the Story

You may hog all the glory and conveniently forget to give credit where credit is due. You are puffed up with your own importance, boastful, domineering and an incorrigible spendthrift. Your health is poorer than you think because you won't exercise, you overeat and you drink too much. You are always in debt and constantly borrow from friends. You are a social climber and a poseur, blinded by appearances and affectation. You choose the wrong friends nearly every time. Your love of glamor and all that is gawdy, ostentatious and phony makes you easy to deceive. Your love life is a procession of disappointments and arguments over money and possessions.

JUPITER IN VIRGO

Yours is a mind ideally suited for coping with the frenzied activity and pace of modern business. You are not the tycoon type who sits in his or her ivory tower controlling or figureheading a vast organization. Your aim is to be down where the day-to-day and job-to-job action is, where you can have a hand in the actual production, distribution and on-the-spot management. You're not an empire builder; you are, rather, the type who keeps commercial enterprises growing at the grassroots level.

Expansion, based on impeccably sound, prudent and practical reasoning, is your theme. You never overlook the little things. You have an instinct for turning the simplest ideas into paying propositions. Any hobby of yours can usually earn money. Detail intrigues you—your acute discriminative powers help you to isolate the smallest essentials so they can be applied in proper sequence. You know that with a mind as analytical as yours, attention to detail leads to practical solutions—minute atoms strung together make up the world of matter, after all!

You are an intricate planner, and if allowed too much latitude, are likely to get bogged down in materialistic considerations. Under your capable direction, all systems providing for efficiency, order and creature comforts are likely to be "go"—but where does this lead ultimately? To you, the question may have no relevance; but to others, who know that human happiness is not based on a well-paid 35-hour week, a smooth production line or a domestic deep-freeze unit, it's not that simple. To put it bluntly, you're excessively intellectual and, unless there are other mitigating influences in the chart, emotionally undeveloped. The quality of life does not depend on what can be weighed or measured.

Personally, you are inclined to be unbending and stereotyped, not lacking in imagination by any means, but short on spontaneity and the ability to relax in company. Your reserve and formal manner put a damper on your social life. You don't make friends easily and are inclined to choose those who share your intellectual interests rather than look for empathetic connections.

Scientific subjects have a fascination for you. You love probing possibilities such as whether there is life on the other planets. Philosophic speculation also appeals to you. You possess an innate talent for technological research. People with Jupiter in Virgo are frequently found working with computers and other highly advanced electronic devices used in modern industry and experimental laboratories. You have a very special interest in diet and hygiene and busy yourself in one way or another with propagating your discoveries and views on these subjects.

You are likely to make business trips to foreign countries and possibly marry someone you meet there. Chances are your wife or husband will not be as well off or as intellectually advanced as you. The circumstances in which you marry could be peculiar. In middle life, you will probably enjoy a more comfortable and sophisticated existence than people would have predicted in your earlier years.

You have a gift for writing and speaking clearly and are equipped to produce books about your travels as well as manuals and textbooks dealing with your particular line of work. You would also make a capable lecturer or teacher.

You get along well with co-workers and employees. Your honesty and openness is attractive. Superiors trust you. Sometimes you are overly critical and this upsets others. You are also rather skeptical about religious matters, and if outspoken in this regard, can sound intolerant. You believe that if people were to do the right thing in their daily lives, there would be no call for dogmatic reminders.

The Other Side of the Story

Your ideas lack depth and betray an inability to see life as it really is. Your proposals usually paper over problems rather than provide solutions. You lack concentration and rely on quick-witted cunning to get you through. You write and speak for effect. You exaggerate the simplest situations and have a reputation for wasting your own and other people's time with trivia. Your ambitions far exceed your capabilities. You are unlucky in love. Marriage is likely to lead to irritating restrictions and lost chances. You read avidly but learn very little of consequence.

JUPITER IN LIBRA

Once upon a time there was a kind, obliging and gentle person who saw more good than evil in everyone, who sincerely tried to promote peace wherever he went and who consistently denied his own self-interest to see justice done to others. Recognize him or her? It's you—provided there are no spoilers among the rest of the influences in your horoscope.

This combination confers a breadth of vision that exceeds the limited ego and embraces the aspirations of humanity as a whole. As a pure reflection of Jupiter in Libra, you would rather serve than be served—not in menial ways, mind you, for it is not in physical effort that your gifts and abilities lie. You are an intellectual and aesthetic being. You possess a rare balance of most

that is refined or admirable in man. You embody the spirit of fair play. Being just, you can judge.

Now, everyone with Jupiter in Libra can't be a saint or sit on the Supreme Court. But the basic principle holds true and expresses itself through the individual irrespective of how ordinary or seemingly undistinguished his or her life may be.

You need an occupation that allows you to express these basic urges. Being a sensitive soul, you are not going to be happy in disharmonious and squalid surroundings or where the people coarse and aggressive. (If these are your present working conditions, then Jupiter is probably badly aspected.) You will be most contented in work that has a light artistic element or a profound humanistic value. You shine where you can employ your superlative judgment, which is not restricted to a judiciary role. You may just as easily receive satisfaction from employment in the chemical industry, weighing one ingredient against another to produce a better cosmetic, synthetic material or pleasing dye color, or as a jeweler or fine-metal worker. An appreciation or talent for writing, poetry and singing is natural to this pleasant combination. But it is in expressing your social conscience as a lawyer and judge, or in your devotional insight as a prophet, mystic or religious leader, that you seem to fulfill your highest potential. You may also be successful as a banker, broker, engineer, electrician, architect or designer. You do not adapt well to the harsh competition and methods of the business world.

Although you can often manage to sort out other people's affairs, you are not so good at managing your own. You are inclined to let financial matters slide and to get yourself into a muddle. You are very fond of entertaining and mixing in higher social circles. This and a predilection for beautiful and expensive things, including fashionable clothes, makes you an extravagant spender—when you have the money.

You are tormented by what could be described as a pernicious desire to be liked and accepted by your associates. As long as any doubt on this score remains in your mind, you will suffer painfully and go to extraordinary lengths to win people over with courtesy and hospitality. You are so addicted to the need to make a good impression that you will sometimes even neglect old friends for a casual acquaintance.

Friends are usually luck for you, both financially and socially.

You are often on close terms with influential people in the community. Money and social position often come through partners. You are lucky in love and generally enjoy a happy marriage. Children of people with Jupiter in Libra are usually very bright.

The Other Side of the Story

The women in your life are vindictive, extravagant and two-faced. You are frequently disappointed and let down by friends and associates. As much as you try, you can't seem to break into the right social circles. People are put off by your unctious manner and obvious insincerity. You have a weight problem, or you dress in an ostentatious and gawdy style. You are affected, boastful and can't adjust to your position in life. You are always trying to go one better than the other person. Lawsuits and lawyers are unlucky for you. You are often confronted with hostile people who refuse to see your point of view.

JUPITER IN SCORPIO

Mysteries, secrets and other people's confidences are usually prominent in the lives of people born with Jupiter in Scorpio.

You have a strange attraction for those who are looking for someone to confide in, and often the information imparted is serious enough to give you a "hold" of sorts over the other party. In normal circumstances (depending on other influences in the chart), you would never betray another. But that doesn't alter the fact that you have a knack of conveying you know more than you are telling so that you can "induce" others to make "confessions." Not surprisingly, this combination is often found in the horoscopes of spies, detectives, private investigators, psychiatrists—and religious extremists!

You are an emotionally charged person, but very capable of concealing your feelings. You can go to extremes, dangerous extremes, but seldom do you allow others to detect any sign of weakness that may impair their faith in you as a person who knows exactly what he or she is doing at all times. It is this tremendous capacity for self-control that makes you such an asset in an emergency. You don't crack under pressure, or doubt your own ability to eventually get the upper hand. You are basically the steel-nerved type who would make a competent surgeon, dentist or military commander.

One of your problems is you tend to make the same serious mistakes more than once. It's as though you are attracted to the same situations and mesmerized, by your sheer faith in yourself, into believing that this time you can overcome.

Unfortunately, you seldom do. Few people are better able to endure difficulties and physical discomfort than you. You possess an iron will; once you've fixed your goal, you won't be deflected from it under any circumstances.

You are enthusiastic and shrewd, absorbingly ambitious and have a great yearning for power. Once this is achieved, you usually attempt to change conditions so fundamentally that they can never be reversed; thus do you irrevocably destroy the old order. "Destroy" is a word most appropriate to this combination: these people can be powerful agents for destruction (or construction). They enjoy handling and manipulating masses of people, equipment or construction materials. The religiously inclined can become fanatical and, given the opportunity, cause drastic upheavals in the immediate community.

Jupiter-in-Scorpio people are often engineers engaged in large-scale building projects, especially dams, as well as huge drainage and sewerage schemes. High government jobs also attract them. But, as usual, wherever Scorpio is involved, the danger exists that the person may misuse power for his or her own selfish ends. In public life, this combination permits unlimited lawlessness and tyrannical behavior.

You are proud—sometimes haughty—but not egotistical. Your mind is extremely subtle and capable of the most abstruse analytical reasoning. If there are two ways of approaching a problem, you can be counted on to try the most indirect first. You believe in gentle persuasion and deft tactics, but if these fail, you do not hesitate to crack the whip or, given the right circumstances, use force.

You usually manage to move in circles where power and authority are exercised. Your ability to sense money-making opportunities is quite phenomenal. You have a way of quietly noting significant but small signs or changes and waiting with astounding patience for the right time to make your move. Timing is your specialty in most things. You have an intuitive capability for spotting investments that will pay off later on.

There is a danger that younger people with this combination will be tempted to experiment with drugs out of a desire to penetrate deeper into experience. The addictive perils involved are completely overlooked.

The Other Side of the Story

Your judgment has proved to be unsound, but still you persist with speculative investments and go on losing. Your love life is unhappy and has probably landed you in more than one legal tangle. Arguments, hostility and jealousy are apt to mar your professional progress. Your "friends" are unreliable and more than once have sold you out. Your bitter envy of someone in a more powerful position is likely to provoke his or her enmity and spoil your own chances. Any money gained from legacies will probably be lost or absorbed in legal costs. Sex may well be a major problem area.

JUPITER IN SAGITTARIUS

This is a "lucky" combination. Genial Jupiter, said to be the planet of greater fortune and success, is in its own Sign and therefore strong. Sagittarius itself stands for activities not normally associated with the hard grind of earning a living—travel, philosophy, religion and outdoor sports. The result is an active, independent and good-humored person—you.

You've probably noticed that you attract money or the things you need in life. Not that you necessarily have an overabundance, but sufficient amounts of what you require to proceed with the job at hand seem to be provided (as long as you don't wory excessively). That's the first phenomenon that often accompanies this combination. The second is a caveat: you're only lucky so long as you don't lose faith in your luck! In other words, if you have money, you've got to spend it, not try to hold onto it. As a general rule, as long as you spend, it keeps coming. When you stop, the fountain shuts off.

Not surprisingly, you are incurably optimistic. And your optimism—along with your free and easy manner—makes you popular with your associates and a welcome visitor. You enjoy conversation and mixing with as many different types of people as you can. You're a very acute observer of others and this emerges as an interest in their problems and a desire to help as much as possible. You have a broad-minded interest in most topics, especially science, serious literature, law and animals. You are remarkably candid and at times your comments to people about themselves are so accurate that they offend. But your open and patently sincere manner usually guarantees that any ill feeling will evaporate immediately. You also possess a lively sense of humor and a love of fun, which enables you to win friends quickly.

Your mind is sharp and clear and particularly adroit at producing ideas for making money. You rely a great deal on your intuition and be-

cause of it are quite successful at gambling and speculation. A sixth sense warns you when others are lying or situations are dangerous. You are the type who can walk out of a crowded public building seconds before the roof collapses just because you "felt it was the best thing to do."

You love to entertain and visit others at their homes, and are generous both as a guest and as a host or hostess. Whatever you do in the way of entertainment, you do lavishly with a touch of panache. Your parties are probably very popular events. You also enjoy night life.

You possess a great sense of humor and try to be kind and considerate. You won't knowingly hurt or deceive another person. Your conscience, literally, is your guide, and if ever you should feel remorseful, you will go well out of your way to make amends with a generous gesture and heartfelt apologies. You are tolerant of other people's weaknesses and it is natural for you to sympathize and offer help. You are generally high-minded, just and farseeing.

Although contemptuous of bureaucractic restrictions and many outdated traditions, you can be quite orthodox in your approach to religious matters. You usually feel that it is the moral code espoused by the great religions that prevents society from collapsing under undue contemporary stresses and strains. You tend to favor reforms that are acceptable to a majority of thinking people like yourself rather than subscribe to revolutionary ideas and tactics.

You are keenly interested in education but have doubts about the usefulness of some of the knowledge taught in classrooms. You are more likely to support an education system that puts the emphasis on practical experience and participation. You also believe that travel is one of the finest teachers.

It should be remembered that this combination can produce a person whose views on life are serious and profound, as befitting a basically metaphysical Sign. This outlook may curb much of the outward-going joviality. The personality may be kind and pleasant, but reserved and ponderous.

The Other Side of the Story

Parties, entertainment and other social affairs have a habit of ending unfortunately. Quarrels and misunderstandings are frequent. Your efforts to please others seldom work out. Love partners complicate your life and saddle you with many unnecessary expenses. Although you probably enjoy sports, you may have had some trouble or bad luck through them. You are sometimes a lucky gambler, but in the long run, you are a loser and this might be an incurably compulsive habit. Travel abroad usually leads to loss or aggravation of some kind.

JUPITER IN CAPRICORN ✓

There is not much doubt that you will work your way steadily to the top in the occupation of your choice. You have an abiding sense of responsibility, a flair for financial manipulation, good business sense and a powerful urge to succeed. You may take longer than is actually necessary to attain your goals, for you are very thorough and don't enjoy taking risks.

Jupiter-in-Capricorn people often feel pulled in two directions at once. Jupiter is the planet of optimism and expansion; Capricorn is the Sign of caution, restraint and deliberation. The combination creates some stresses and strains in the personality, which are often alleviated by understanding the basic causes.

For instance, you are inclined to be conservative and thrifty when dealing in small amounts of money—but where large sums are concerned, and especially if your reputation or business image is involved, you will spend as though the sky's the limit. This is not a bad trait. It permits you to build up your savings and make a good start at something, and it prevents you from squandering your money to make an impression. Clear and astute thinking always lies behind your financial actions. You may lay out four dollars to earn one, but it's a safe bet you are not taking that much of a gamble. However, you can be rather glib at justifying your mistakes and occasional excesses.

You are also a mixture of enthusiasm and caution. When you have a bright idea—which is quite often—you are likely to get carried away with the possibilities for success, only to be assailed at the last moment (or when the first obstacle is encountered) by sudden doubts and indecision. This also is not a bad trait. Your natural restraint will force you to thoroughly examine facts that you might have skated over in the first wave of optimism. Of course, hesitation means you will sometimes miss out on good opportunities, but once you learn to handle this paradoxical part of your nature, you will generally make solid progress.

People with Jupiter in Capricorn are natural leaders, usually on the business scene where weighty and sound achievement counts most. They are extremely well suited to executive positions where practical experience has to be augmented with the power to command and organize. The larger the business and the responsibility, the more likely these people will distinguish themselves. They possess a serious approach that impresses their superiors and engenders the respect and obedience (or cooperation) of employees. A high government post or a career culminating in heading a large public foundation or financial institution is likely to eventuate for those who have the opportunities. These people are also capable of running international conglomerates where the interests are widely diversified and complex.

You are inventive and occasionally unorthodox, especially when it comes to self-education in mature years. You enjoy reading and study, and probably have some practical connection with politics, science and even a religious organization. Your personal philosophy is well worth listening to if you can be persuaded to disclose it.

You have far less self-confidence than your manner suggests. In truth, you suffer severely from insecurity, even though it may be unjustified. To compensate, you do all in your power to preserve your reputation and good name. The respect and esteem of others, particularly those in authority, are enormously important to you. You are deeply pained by criticism, especially if it is delivered in public. Your fear of what others might think can be quite self-torturing. To be made a fool of in company is excruciating—and you will never really forgive the person responsible for your mortification.

You have a great capacity for handling detail and for devising economical and efficient measures. Occupations connected with the land, such as farming, mining and real estate, are likely to attract you. You should also be successful in the manufacturing industries or as a wholesaler or merchandiser. Wherever there is a need for perseverance, planning and prudence, with a dash of style, you should do well.

The Other Side of the Story

You plunge into projects with great enthusiasm, then back out for no apparent reason. Inside, you may be nearly a nervous wreck, afraid to attempt anything really constructive for fear of failing. Your fears of what others think of you may be almost phobic. Excessive worry could lead to stomach disorders. You may be mean and miserly. You are unnecessarily critical and severe with those who work for you and kow-tow to those in authority. Sexual perversity and a coarse sense of humor are sometimes associated with the negative side of this combination. Friends are likely to be a source of trouble. You may be forced to pay for others' mistakes.

JUPITER IN AQUARIUS

Your capacity for doing good in the world is considerable. Others may be more practical and possess greater stamina to serve in a physical sense, but you are, literally, the "brains of the outfit." You are supremely idealistic, a visionary in your way, a person who can see beyond obvious effects to the causes that need eliminating or remedying. You are sometimes called unrealistic by the more down-to-earth characters, who would prefer to give a starving man another bowl of soup than try to eradicate the conditions responsible for his poverty.

Aquarius is the Sign associated with the latest electronic inventions that have taken much of the drudgery out of our lives, especially in the modern home. Jupiter is the planet of material fortune and wisdom. Sign and planet blend naturally together here to produce a person who not only wishes to help his fellow man in practical and lasting ways, but frequently does so through new and novel means.

You are ideally suited for social, scientific and charitable work. You would make an excellent sociologist or union leader. You have a breadth of vision that allows you to visualize and plan large-scale humanitarian projects like those associated with the Red Cross, the Salvation Army and global campaigns against hunger. You have a flair for administration, for handling group funds and for distributing resources in complex conditions, particularly at the international level. You usually excel working abroad.

In ordinary business, you may be casual about your own best interests and inclined to put the welfare of employees and others before profitability—with predictable results. Your type of person is not particularly materialistic in his or her ambitions. You are usually better off working for an organization where your energies are not drained by accounting problems. In a nutshell, you are not so much an acquisitive type as a dedicated one.

In the professions, the independence and originality conferred by Jupiter placed in Aquarius makes you particularly creative in a social sense, so that through architecture, medicine, banking, politics, education, town planning and the like, you can implement reforms and lay down sweeping new lines, styles and patterns for the next generation to follow.

You enjoy unusual work of the kind that constantly tests your ingenuity, imagination and inventiveness. An ordinary nine-to-five routine job would drive you mad. Commercial businesses do not have any great appeal, unless they offer opportunities to satisfy and exhibit your innate unconventionality.

You make friends very easily and can harmonize with just about any type. You're not a sentimental person and are sometimes perceived as detached and cool in your affections. This is largely true—but not because you don't care. You see beyond the confines of limited personal attachments and realize that these can obstruct the grand principle of brotherhood and the breaking down of social barriers— principles you feel are so worthwhile.

You stand to gain in various ways through your friends and acquaintances. You do well in just about any group situation. You don't want power for its own sake, but you do respect it as a means for achieving reform. Friends often involve you in peculiar situations. Your life is subject to sudden and dramatic changes. You have a fondness for reading about ESP and other psychic experiences. Your intuition is first-rate.

The Other Side of the Story

You are alarmingly unpredictable and erratic. You can't be depended on from one moment to the next. You possess extraordinary ideas about politics and social reform, some of which are so far-fetched that no one will listen to them. Though you constantly advocate changes or some kind of revolution, you never seem to do anything concrete yourself. Oddballs, misfits and others belonging to the lunatic fringe of society are numbered among your friends. You don't remain long enough in one job to get anywhere. You have very little chance of making a success of marriage. Love affairs invariably end in separation. You are far too easily influenced by the opinions and ideals of others.

JUPITER IN PISCES

People can't help but like you. You go straight to their hearts. Others can probably tell better stories, make more scintillating conversation and appear more clever and intellectual. Yours is a more simple appeal, a soul appeal. You care about people, all people, and frequently suffer personally when you see them sorrowful or in pain. With Jupiter in Pisces, you can often touch and stir in others emotions they didn't realize lay within them.

You need work that is not intellectual. There's not much doubt you will find what you are looking for—in the end—but for some time you are likely to go from job to job. You will never stay where you are unhappy. You cannot endure work that involves pressure and concentrated thought. Your ability to charm and get along with employers and co-workers does not satisfy you—you must have a function you consider worthwhile. You want to be of use to humanity in some way. If you understand this peculiar need, you should be able to save yourself a lot of time and aggravation the next time you have to change positions or go looking for satisfaction elsewhere.

Many of you can find sufficient contentment in an artistic occupation, especially acting or dancing. This type of activity allows you to communicate directly to an audience and to feel their emotional response. Without the stimulus of emotional exchange, your life is very empty. The intellectual type of person has very little appeal for you. Unless you can reach empathetic union with your companion, you become bored, restless and unhappy.

You are kind, sympathetic and unbelievably idealistic. Your love of humanity and sympathy for the downtrodden, poor, and sick is very moving in a world that doesn't exactly overflow with compassion. You will work with selfless devotion to help people in prison, sanitariums, hospitals and the like, provided they possess that tiny spark you know lingers in nearly every human breast but is sometimes obscured by worldliness and sophistication. When you don't find this in an individual, you quietly move on. Often, people with Jupiter in Pisces receive public honors and recognition for their humanitarian work. Unfortunately, not all are able to find the correct means to serve, and suffer considerable frustration and despair.

You are acutely sensitive, psychic and spiritual. Hardly a night passes that you don't have some kind of prophetic dream or peculiar experience. You are often clairvoyant and probably have had some visions. Sometimes it is difficult for people with this combination to distinguish between reality and their daydreams, mainly because so many of these seem to come true.

It is important for you to have a friend or lover who understands your feelings of other-worldliness and to whom you can confide your dreams and secret wishes. Before you allow intimate relationships of this nature, the person must demonstrate deep love, loyalty and understanding. You are more discriminating, as a rule, in your choice of confidants than you are in ordinary love affairs. Because you don't possess the keen body consciousness of most people, you tend to ignore physical pain and even ill treatment. In illness, you often feel you can heal yourself—but only after you've suffered a sufficient amount of discomfort. You don't complain.

As much as you enjoy lively company, you need regular periods of seclusion. Without these, you become irritable, depressed and fiercely self-critical. Communion with nature restores your spirits. Music soothes or stimulates you, according to your mood. The sea and the forest can provide idyllic delight.

You have to be careful not to lose interest in worldly affairs and retreat into a personal dream world. This is most likely if you can't find a means of expressing your altruistic urges, or if you are forced to work or live in a highly competitive or disharmonious environment.

The Other Side of the Story

Members of the opposite sex may take advantage of your cooperative, kind and placid nature. You are likely to be easily deceived and imposed upon. You may prefer to drift aimlessly without ambition rather than to make a place for yourself in the world. You probably never feel settled or contented. Although anxious to succeed and be respected, you are not prepared to make the necessary effort. You may be lazy, indecisive, moody—and self-hating. Some people with this combination are inveterate liars who can't help exaggerating even the simplest statement. They may resort to fraud to live in comfort and peace.

SATURN

The Planet

Saturn is said to be the most visually beautiful planet in the solar system. It appears as a bright "star" to the unaided eye, but the unique system of rings that surround the planet and its lustrous, contrasting colors can be clearly seen through a telescope. It appears as a blue ball with three yellow rings against the velvet black of deep outer space.

Saturn is the sixth planet out from the Sun and the second largest (after Jupiter). Its diameter is 75,000 miles, more than nine times that of the Earth. It spins once every 10¼ hours, an enormous rate for such an immense sphere. Its volume is 736 times that of the Earth, but its mass or weight is only 95 times greater.

Saturn is 886 million miles from the Sun. The closest it gets to the Earth is 745 million miles. Its orbit takes nearly 29½ years, which means it spends a leisurely 2½ years in each Sign of the Zodiac.

Like Jupiter, the planet is covered with banded clouds. The bands are not as clear as Jupiter's, but seem more nearly permanent. Bright spots occasionally appear in them.

The Saturnian rings were discovered in 1655 by telescope. They are composed of myriads of tiny satellites or cosmic dust particles. The first is a dull outer ring, next to a dark area, and the second is the widest, brightest ring. Inside this is a thin dark space and then the third ring, which is described as the "crepe" ring because it resembles the texture of the dress material.

The total width across the three rings is 41,000 miles. The outer ring is 10,000 miles wide, the second about 16,000 miles and the crepe ring about 11,000 miles. The crepe ring begins about 7000 miles above the surface of the planet.

Outside the rings, Saturn has at least ten moons. One of these, Titan, with a diameter of around 4000 miles, is one of the largest satellites in the solar system.

Symbolism

Saturnus, or Cronus as the Greeks called him, was the god of agriculture and the founder of civilization and social order. He was the rebellious son of Uranus, the first supreme god. Armed with a flint and a sickle, Saturn overthrew his father, who cursed him predicting that Saturn himself would in turn be deposed by his own son. To forestall this, Saturn swallowed each of his children at birth. But when Zeus (Jupiter), the youngest was born, his mother deceived Saturn by giving him a stone to swallow instead. The young god was brought up secretly in a cave. In a war that lasted ten years, Jupiter overthrew Saturn. The old man, still with his sickle or scythe became Father Time, a bitter, decrepit figure whose eyes looked meaningfully from the hourglass in his hand to all that was new and young in the world.

Astrology

Saturn's influence is heavy, restrictive and long-lasting. It is melancholy, cold, dry, barren, constant, defensive, hard, secretive, nervous, binding and masculine. It is ponderous, slow-moving, serious and has an extremely powerful and important effect on the horoscope.

Saturn is called "the law-giver." It is the last of the personal planets. Beyond its orbit, the three remaining known planets—Uranus, Neptune and Pluto—take so long to go around the Sun (84, 165 and 248 years, respectively) that their effects are more generalized and register as gradual changes and developments in the characteristics of groups and generations of people rather than individuals.

As Saturn stands in space, so it stands in relation to individual man. It is the periphery. It represents the time man has on earth—and the end of it. It is the boundary no one can cross over in physical form. Saturn keeps man and life within specific bounds. As such, it represents the law that governs human behavior; the self-discipline that allows man to govern himself; the sense of duty that permits responsible action; the patience and perseverance that make accomplishment possible; and the practical reflection that gives rise to self-consciousness, including the inevitable realization of separateness from other beings, of isolation and aloneness.

Saturn is the ruler of Capricorn, the tenth

Sign of the Zodiac. Capricorn represents the individual's social status, accruing from responsibility and self-discipline. Saturn is the co-ruler (with Uranus) of the eleventh Sign, Aquarius.

Saturn stands for the skin and the skeleton. As the skin, it restricts and yet protects—from without. As the skeleton, it gives form and hardness and protects—from within. Between the two lie the vital functions and organs.

From the above it is not difficult to conclude that Saturn is the planet of restriction, hardship and delay. Its influence gives a hard time. By imposing inherited burdens, uncontrollable events and the consequences of errors arising from the past. Saturn represents the distance between man and his goals. Saturnian law is supremely just. Every man gets exactly what he deserves, whether he thinks so or not. Saturn's law gives at the same time it exacts—by ensuring that an individual faces in circumstantial form the weaknesses flawing his or her character. These must be overcome before the person can finally enjoy that which lies beyond skin, skeleton and all limitation: the freedom to be him- or herself.

Saturn squanders the individual's time, halts his progress despite redoubled efforts, wastes his resources, uses others to impede, disappoint and frustrate. However, once Saturn's discipline is accepted and the lessons are learned, "the lawgiver" reveals its true nature and rewards in full.

Saturn will sometimes delay things that are promised by the other planets in the horoscope. As master of time, it can do this. Its function is to see that no one receives anything of lasting value that is not deserved. At other times, Saturn will not deny—and the individual will suffer as a result of boons and abundance because he was not ready to cope with them.

A well-aspected Saturn has an ennobling and dignifying effect. The person is conscientious and industrious. He or she may choose the hard way to go about things, but this is often out of thoroughness and a tendency to equate patience and painstaking care with responsibility. This person can always be depended on to do a job to the best of his or her ability. These men and women also have a sense of moral rectitude that compels them to do the right thing. They are discreet and can be relied on to keep a secret. They can get to the bottom of a problem, put it in its correct perspective and suggest practical solutions. Their advice is objective, realistic, always down to earth. They are conservative, tread warily in new territory. Under attack, they are nervously aware but show restraint and self-control. Under pressure, they are superbly in command. Their approach to life is serious and cautious. They do not waste money and can account at any time for all their resources. They are thrifty but not mean.

A badly aspected Saturn produces a person who is inclined to complain and moan a lot. He or she has bad luck, misses opportunities, is slow off the mark. The tendency is to be selfish, gloomy, given to self-pity and censurous of those who enjoy themselves. This person is mean, stingy, unpopular. Either he has a hard time earning money or is too miserly to spend it on normal comforts and pleasures. He is fearful and usually suffers from prolonged obscure and often depressing illnesses.

Physiologically, Saturn controls the bone and skin systems, the crystallization and constriction of the body's growth. As time, it gives shape to form, imposing the necessary limitations on growth; and then the drying and ossifying constrictions of age. Saturn is also associated with the spleen, gallbladder, knees, teeth, inner ear and anterior lobe of the pituitary gland, which promotes masculinity as well as regulating the sex glands.

Toothache and colds are among the most common Saturnian ailments.

SATURN IN ARIES

Although you are ambitious, the way up is extremely hard. You have to work for everything you get. This is a hard-slog combination. Saturn here sits on the strong and impulsive shoulder of Aries like a ton of bricks. It is difficult to move. To move with speed and flourish, as you so often try to do, is impossible.

Despite these severe limitations, you are determined to succeed. The first half of your life is usually the worst, but this is the time when you are likely to develop the strength of character that will eventually bring success. Saturn will see you are tested by plenty of obstacles and adversity.

Your best chance of making a name for yourself—which is what you most long to do—is through ventures that appeal to the public imagination. You are probably more capable of building a reputation than of becoming a millionaire. As you have a great desire for respect and esteem, this order of things will probably appeal to you. Your capacity to persevere in the face of seemingly overwhelming odds makes you an excellent pioneer type. You are the sort who could disappear into the hostile wilderness for years, undergo dreadful privations, and finally emerge with the holy grail to immense public acclaim.

You are not a person who gets along very well with others. You are more a loner, a toiler; some might say (in the beginning) a loser. You continually feel frustrated. The pace of your life never seems to synchronize with your lofty ambitions. You miss out on the big chance—arrive too early, too late or just don't hear about it. You are sometimes envious of others who seem to get all the breaks. You are easily irritated. You build up heat inside slowly, like a pile of lawn clippings, and suddenly flare into an angry outburst. Then the iron hand of self-discipline comes down and you quickly get a grip on your emotions. And the cycle of spontaneous combustion starts again.

You make a good military type because you are a disciplinarian. Seldom do you show your feelings except in a corrective, critical way. You know the value to authority of clipped aloofness. If you do not try to relax your self-imposed constrictions, you will become overbearing. As a parent, you can be too strict; as a human being, too intent on maintaining your position against whatever the odds.

A happy marriage is seldom your luck. Your mate may be jealous or project his or her feelings of insecurity onto you. Your reluctance to join in the usual social activities does not help. You may be grumpy in lighthearted company, quick to find fault and plunge into an argument. At heart, you prefer to be alone or with a crony who shares your rather jaded views on life. Underneath, you are somewhat distrustful of people and inclined to be selfish.

You have good reasoning ability, though your mind may not possess the depth your manner and mien suggest. However, when left alone, you can be quietly contemplative and this helps to stabilize your emotions. You are quite sure of yourself when dealing with practical matters. It is the inner stresses and strains that you have the most difficulty coping with.

You are diplomatic when you want to be and quite impressive. Your reserved and austere manner suggests hidden strength, capability and wisdom. You would like to occupy a position of power in a large organization. You want to be admired for your accomplishments, particularly for your sense of responsibility. You yearn to transform your outer show of these qualities into an inner reality.

You may suffer from chronic health problems that make it difficult to compete with others on even terms. But you have the fortitude to bear up and not allow physical impediments to get the better of you. In moments of despondency or depression, it may help you to remember that Saturn, the law-giver whose influence is afflicting you, pays off in full measure at the end.

The Other Side of the Story

You may be a puritanical despot, the terror of your home, office or community. You are likely to be lonely and friendless. Your depression and whining complaints may get on everybody's nerves. The only lesson you may have learned from a domineering father is how to be even more oppressive and severe as a parent or boss. You may try to reform others for their own good and make their lives a misery. You could be a typical zealous missionary who sets out to "save" an uncivilized people but succeeds only in destroying their culture and self-respect. You may be tortured by feelings of personal inadequacy. You are likely to suffer from severe headaches, toothache, deafness or eye trouble.

SATURN IN TAURUS

You are too intent on holding onto your worldly goods to really enjoy them. Possessions and money come to you so slowly and laboriously that you are in constant dread of losing them to some capricious act of fate. But you won't give up what you own without a grim struggle—any more than you will surrender your impelling ambition to acquire more and more. You know that with wealth comes status, prestige, respect—and these mean just about as much to you as the security you crave.

You are thoughtful and kind. You are not given to rash actions, although you will lose your temper suddenly if badgered enough. As much as you are able to, you lead a steady sort of existence. You prefer to think long about things before making any moves because you like to know in advance exactly where you are going. You fix your goals well ahead, and because all the pros and cons have been considered (you hope!), you seldom see any need to change your plans or to listen to others' advice. You plow on, regardless. The unexpected unnerves you. You find it hard to make sudden adjustments. You are not adaptive. You really prefer to work for someone else or under the auspices of a large organization where you can express your authority without having to worry about security.

Your greatest strength is the ability to persevere and overcome obstacles. Your determination is prodigious. The things you strive for in life do not come easily. You are not a lucky individual. But your dogged persistence often gets you there in the end. You are frugal with money, and can go without luxuries, although you enjoy life's comforts once you feel you can afford them. You try hard to save but it is a slow and daunting process: something usually drains off your accumulated funds. Many of your problems come through relatives, especially elders. You may have to support or care for a parent over a long period. Other unfortunate domestic experiences may bring loss and sorrow. There may be ill feeling between you and your neighbors.

Most of your anxieties stem from money and love. You are indecisive and seldom able to strike when the iron is hot. You lack confidence in your own timing: you hesitate. In love, when you evenually do act, it is often at the wrong moment, or with the wrong person. You may become quite depressed at the topsy-turvy way your personal relations seem to operate compared with the experiences of others. You keep your emotions too much to yourself. You need to give your feelings and deeper thoughts an airing, to open up to another person. Your continual reserve and restraint lead to brooding, a kind of emotional in-breeding that gives rise to fear, imagined slights and seething resentment. You don't forgive or forget easily.

You acquire money through judicious investments. You play it safe. You know all about the hazards of get-rich-quick schemes, the nail-biting and sleepless nights when things go wrong. They are not for you. You are an excellent person to have on the payroll to keep costs down because you know how to economize and can explain economical moves to others diplomatically. In your personal affairs, you are prudent and thrifty. You can be trusted implicitly with other people's money. You will do nothing that might undercut your reputation or cause others to be disrespectful. You have a high sense of moral duty. Despite your nervous disposition, you are dependable under pressure and can help others overcome their panic and hysteria.

You possess a love of natural beauty. The order and precision of nature fascinate you. You are often drawn to scientific studies or occupa-

tions associated with horticulture, stock breeding and botany.

The Other Side of the Story

You may be pitifully self-conscious and incapable of mixing socially. Your fear of insecurity may make you miserly and avaricious. You are likely to worry yourself into a nervous breakdown. Your home may be an unhappy place. You are likely to begrudge showing others simple kindnesses. You can be unresponsive in love and have no feeling for beauty. All your thoughts may be calculated to bring about materialistic ends.

SATURN IN GEMINI

You are a person with great intellectual capacities. You can write and think with depth and inspiration. You would make an excellent mathematician, theoretical or practical scientist, penetrating lecturer, wise teacher or impressive lawyer. You would also do well in commerce as a merchant, a publisher, printer or broker. In even the most humble walks of life, you will be noted for the astuteness of your views and the nimbleness of your mind.

In this position, the effervescent intellectual Sign of Gemini receives the steadying influence of the wise and experienced Saturn. It is a sound and fruitful alliance.

You are intensely aware of all that is going on around you. You are continually picking up information but holding only onto that which will be of some practical use later on. You have the ability to forget the inconsequential and remember the profound. Still, you can tell a droll story with an admirable turn of wit.

You are inclined to study a number of subjects at one time. Although you move quickly from one topic to another, it is not in a superficial way. You absorb in depth; you understand; you don't just study to accumulate a lot of useless information. You are an intellectual being. It is essential to your health and well-being that you keep your mind engaged. Other more earthly temperaments would wilt and verge on a nervous breakdown under the constant cerebral activity, but you are in your element.

You are urbane and sophisticated. Given the proper circumstances, you would make a fine diplomat, elder statesman, head of state, titular president. You are deeply serious and yet retain a refreshing, youthful sense of humor, a naiveté that makes you rather lovable, especially in later years. You are capable of great literary effort. You possess extraordinary powers of observation and have the mental equipment to describe what you see in graphic and moving language. Your comprehension is quite remarkable.

You are usually plagued with difficulties, trials and sorrows brought about by relatives, especially brothers and sisters. Responsibilities impinging on you from this direction may restrict your freedom and independence. False accusations are likely to be made against you. Court proceedings you institute may fail or succeed only after long drawn out delays. In the end, charges against you may be dismissed, but the damage to your reputation will never quite be repaired. There is also the possibility that some period of your life may have to be spent in another country in a form of exile. Travel is likely to be unfortunate for you. Words written or spoken in haste or anger may result in libel or slander actions. Neighbors may also be a cause of aggravation.

The above experiences, plus the strong intellectual nature of Saturn in Gemini, can make you rather bitter and cynical. Without other good aspects, there may be an absence of warmth in your personality. You could be a bit too hard and exacting. A deviousness and lack of candor may also creep in.

As a general rule, the Saturn-Gemini position produces a person with lofty ideals. You have a fine sense of the correct way to do things and practice what you preach. You are responsible and serious-minded, but sometimes trust the wrong people and are therefore let down. Disillusionment usually leads to depression. The imagination sometimes colors the judgment and you see situations, especially adverse ones, as you would like them to be. Disappointment is then inevitable. A philosophic approach helps to allay your natural nervousness and apprehension.

This combination frequently means that early education is interrupted or delayed. It is then difficult to get a start in a chosen field. Or you may lack direction, certainty about what you want to do for a living. Early hardships are more than likely. You may have trouble with your chest and lungs.

The Other Side of the Story

Depression may lead to suicidal thoughts. You are likely to yearn for love, but do nothing about attracting it. You may be an incorrigible pessimist living under the delusion that you are a realist. You are likely to be offensively critical of others. Opportunities may be missed through fear of failure; nothing is ventured, nothing is gained. Your thinking is likely to be dull and ponderous, your manner of speaking irritatingly halting and slow. An obstinate and pigheaded attitude may make you a monologuist. You are likely to be illogical and a bit scatterbrained.

SATURN IN CANCER

You are an inveterate worrier. You worry about your mother, your family, your home, your future, your childhood, your children, your past. You seldom throw off the feeling of insecurity and personal inadequacy—except when you plunge into the delights of sensual gratification through sex, food, liquor and the like. Afterward you go back to worrying again.

Saturn in Cancer is like dipping bread in water. The bread loses its consistency, falls to pieces. Saturn is in its detriment here, almost at its weakest. Its discipline, morality and persistence are largely dissolved.

But there remains a possibility of outstanding accomplishment. When Saturn-in-Cancer people apply themselves to a job—whether it be a profession, an artistic venture or a business pursuit—they rally the best of both the Saturn and Cancer qualities, with extraordinary results. But when the work is over, they sink back into inertia, laziness or dissipation.

You are supersensitive. Your emotions, which were tuned so finely by your surroundings when you were a child, still dictate your responses. You either had too much love or not enough of it. If you had an excess, you miss it now, long for it, feel deprived, insecure. If you were starved for love, you still miss it, long for it, feel deprived, insecure. You are a prisoner of the past who is too plastic, fearful and lacking in self-confidence to break away.

You don't like making new moves. The pioneering and competitive urges disturb you. You think about being original and stepping out on your own, but you quickly dismiss the idea. You prefer to stick to what you know you can do, what's been proved, what's been accepted by your associates and especially those you love. You are confined by the limitations imposed by your childhood. Usually your background includes sorrow or suffering connected with your mother or home. You may have seen your mother coping in difficult circumstances and had to share her troubles or shoulder her burdens. Sometimes there is a history of harsh maternal discipline, which conditions adult responses. Sometimes the mother died at an early age. Any of these produce a complex, a vacuum of uncertainty and insecurity. Your usual defense is to take no risks, do nothing—which makes you appear lax or lazy. You fall back on the things you know you can trust and enjoy—your own senses, sensual pleasure—or you throw yourself into work you love, if you have been fortunate enough to find it.

Saturn, unless very favorably aspected, deprives the child of many comforts and normal enjoyments. Or it denies the person in later years, ruining his or her career or inflicting an impoverished or lonely old age—or both. This combination also causes distressing illnesses usually associated with the stomach and women's breasts. Wasting diseases or obstructions such as ulcers and tumors — and obesity—are common.

People born with Saturn in Cancer desperately need to justify their existence. This is their main problem. In the attempt to justify themselves, they constantly look for admiration from their loved ones, and sulk when they don't get it. They may pose as martyrs to the rest of the family, overstressing their slavish and thankless devotion as housewife or breadwinner. They may strive desperately to win the approval and the nod of approbation from their boss, the police chief, the society leader—any figure of authority. They even enjoy passing a policeman in the street to feel the satisfaction of being law-abiding, on the law's side. They want to be told over and over: "You are doing well. Your existence is justified." Then they are happy—for a while.

People born with this combination can couple the protective urge of Cancer with Saturn's discipline, and at the same time satisfy their inner longings, by fighting at the authority level for the rights of the sick, the distressed, the needy and the underprivileged.

The Other Side of the Story

You may be insufferably moody, changeful and unreliable. The more promiscuous you are sexually, the more depressed and dissatisfied you will become. Overeating may make you fat, sloppy and miserable. A dependence on drugs could be disastrous. People may laugh behind your back at the excuses you make to justify your excesses; or you may be an object of pity. You are likely to have a punishing mother or father complex. Your unhappiness may be largely due to the lies you tell yourself.

SATURN IN LEO

Situations involving leadership or love are likely to make great personal demands on you and culminate in disappointment or heartache. You are a born leader, but in many ways a severe one. You're not the congenial Leonine type who steps down off his thrown to mix freely with his subjects. You're a Saturnian Leo—although suited to rule, you are too aware of the dignity and distinction of your position. These, you believe implicitly, can only be maintained if you yourself remain aloof and isolated.

Leo is a warm, human and generous Sign; Saturn is the planet of weighty responsibility and cold constriction. It is an odd combination and often leads to power and enviable success in worldly affairs, but rarely results in personal satisfaction or real happiness.

You are a stickler for hard work and doing your duty. Although you may be drawn to the entertainment industry or be occupied in a profession that gives pleasure to others, you seldom let your hair down and actually join in the fun. This sort of behavior, you feel, would demean you. You may be extremely good at your job and gifted at pleasing the masses, but it's always only a job, never an expression of your true feelings.

What your true feelings are is a bit of a mystery even to yourself. Like everyone, you want love. And deep down inside, you have a vast quantity of it that groans and strains to be released and shared. But, generally speaking, with Saturn in Leo, this is not to be. You have great difficulty expressing your emotions. Often when you try, the result is awkward, inappropriate, inadequate. People with this combination frequently resolve early in life not to bother trying to demonstrate their affections anymore. As a protection, they adopt an aloof and self-contained attitude that discourages others from reaching out to them emotionally. They settle comfortably into this armor-plated style and very rarely manage to break out of it again.

Sometimes Saturnian Leos find a release for their emotions by engaging in love affairs with socially inferior people. In these situations, they feel their actually being with the person is sufficient expression of their affection or regard and that no further demonstrations are necessary. It doesn't always work out so smoothly, however;

bitterness and scandal are too often the outcome.

You an excellent organizer, cool in an emergency and able to handle large groups of people with an authority that others seldom think to question. You are constructive, practical, impressive and, given the opportunity, should have no difficulty rising to a powerful position in government or politics. Your talent for diplomacy is quite remarkable.

In business and employment, you are the ideal "company man" or woman. You put the organization first, your personal concerns second. Obviously, you are soon singled out for promotion by discerning and progressive management.

In your personal life, your mode of living usually reflects extremes of austerity and splendor. If wealthy, you may surround yourself with all the creature comforts and yet have no one to share them with. In ordinary circumstances, you may treat yourself now and again to the best meal in town—and eat alone. "Splendid isolation" may be your way.

You are bold in action when committed, but cautious in reaching your conclusions. It is not easy to deflect you from a course; you can be counted on to have weighed all the pros and cons well in advance. You are seldom persuaded by appeals to sentiment. Justice and logic carry much more power of conviction.

The Other Side of the Story

You are a rigid disciplinarian and fixed in your views, which are largely out of date. You desire to move with the times but an inner mistrust and reserve hold you back. With children, you are apt to be far too strict and unbending. Some unhappiness has probably come to you through youngsters. You believe your way is the only way. Subordinates and members of the opposite sex enjoying less social status than you are likely to cause serious trouble. Secret enemies may work against you. You sometimes suffer from mental depression and vague aches and pains. Your love life has always been a source of problems, misunderstandings and sorrow. You endanger your health by working far too hard.

SATURN IN VIRGO

You are capable of considerable accomplishment. Your mind is sharp, original, practical and disciplined. You can be depended on to do a job properly and to work without slacking for as long as necessary. You are a person of your word, an excellent employee and ideally suited for a position of authority in one of the professions, especially where there is a tutorial element.

But you are a worrier. Hardly a day goes by that you don't feel a vague uneasiness. Gloom and depression descend on you without warning. Your mind remains clear and able during these times as far as work is concerned, but your personal relationships suffer. Others may find your moods melancholy and difficult to put up with. The fact that often there is no real justification for them makes your associates even less tolerant.

You enjoy work for work's sake. Nothing pleases you more than to be tucked away in an office grappling with a difficult problem that requires prolonged concentration. You are especially interested in scientific inquiry. Your analytical mind can sift detail with amazing precision. All types of research and laboratory work are apt to appeal to you. You should excel as a university professor.

People with Saturn in Virgo often distinguish themselves in work connected with diet, health and hygiene. They pay strict attention to these disciplines in their personal life and sometimes become food faddists and hypochondriacs. They are often competent speakers and writers and may turn to lecturing or writing books or articles about their "pet" subjects. Efficiency and order have tremendous appeal for them. Their studies are usually aimed at improving something or someone (very seldom themselves). Because of this, they seem to be uncommonly critical and fussy individuals and tend to alienate the more lighthearted and less discriminating types who are content to live and let live.

You are a little suspicious of your fellow man and very distrustful of new situations. You are extremely observant and rather prudish about the relaxation of moral restraints in modern society. Your views are traditional and orthodox and you seldom find any reason for changing them. You don't make friends easily, although you do enjoy conversing with people who share your intellectual interests. Your manner is quiet, serious, reserved. You prefer to remain in the background and to observe life from there. You are courteous, diplomatic and discreet.

With money, you are conservative and sometimes a bit stingy. You feel less vulnerable when there is cash in the bank. You tend to live a frugal life. It would never occur to you to throw your money around on lavish entertainment. Other people's extravagance irritates you.

You derive most of your relaxation and pleasure from simple pursuits that are usually not far removed from your working habits. Many people born with this combination spend considerable time with hobbies. Sometimes these are developed to such a high standard that they become commercially viable.

Your ability to work for long periods without distraction usually enables you to forge to the forefront of your field eventually. The middle years are generally the most successful and productive. Your early life is apt to have been difficult at home and in school. You will probably end up in a comfortable financial position as a result of steady effort and careful investment.

The somber, dour and somewhat pessimistic outlook of people born with Saturn in Virgo does not help them to be happy in marriage. They may also have difficulty with teenage children, who are likely to resent minor tyrannies.

The Other Side of the Story

Marital and business partnerships are likely to be most unfortunate. Your constant criticism of others makes you irritating company. You are also too quick to condemn your own shortcomings without making positive endeavors to correct them. Negative thinking can be a form of illness with this combination. You are unnecessarily mean with money and have probably lost the art of spontaneous giving. Your early years may have been marked by ill health and sorrow. Memories you can't erase may still prey on your mind. Unless you adopt a more optimistic frame of mind and stop worrying about trivial matters, you may be heading for a nervous breakdown.

SATURN IN LIBRA

Here is the artist who triumphs after years of obscure and dedicated effort. Here is the wisest judge. Here, also, is the honest, clever but frustrated politician who must watch the corrupt and inefficient rule of others while awaiting the call that may never come.

Saturn is the eternal taskmaster—he makes things hard wherever he appears. And yet, if the job has been well done with discipline and selflessness, he usually distributes the rewards with impeccable fairness. Our own opinion of how we've worked pulls no weight with Saturn; he considers himself the only judge. In Libra, Saturn is in the Sign of balance. If you've balanced your accounts, you're okay. If you haven't . . . watch out!

You are an artistic and high-minded person who gets most of his or her pleasure through relating to others. You have many friends and social acquaintances. Because art and entertainment are good means of reaching others, these activities appeal to you. In the back of your mind, you always aim to bring people closer together, to eliminate their differences and harmonize their positive qualities, with you at the center.

You believe in moderation in everything—in reserved and refined behavior, manners, tastes, and most of all, in goodwill and peace. But as much as you strive to stay on this middle path, you are constantly swept from one side to the other like an emotional pendulum. Where you work for order, you usually get turmoil. Yet your extraordinary tact and good judgment frequently save the day.

In marriage, much depends on whether Saturn is badly aspected. (This can be ascertained from the Yellow Tables.)

Generally speaking, people born with Saturn in Libra benefit from the stabilizing influence of a partner. Libra is the Sign of partnership but Saturn makes severe demands, which, if not met in the right spirit, create obstacles and difficult circumstances. Partnerships often contain deep flaws (undiscernible in the beginning) that cause sorrow and unhappiness.

Both business and marital relationships may continue in harassing conditions for several years, or be quickly terminated and new ones begun with exactly the same results. People with Saturn in Libra frequently marry more than once. They seldom achieve their romantic ideals, although these persist right to the end. They never allow what *is* make them lose sight of what *might be*.

Women are generally unfortunate for people with this combination. If you are a woman, the women in your life are likely to stir up trouble behind your back, to undermine your position or reputation in some way. Lifelong feuds are a distinct possibility. If you are a man, you have probably suffered considerable loss or psychological pain through the open enmity or indifference of a woman. Early heartbreak that will never really be repaired is likely. Separations in the midst of happiness and the reemergence of old love problems long forgotten are to be expected. Women are also apt to cause you employment difficulties.

You are intelligent, eminently suited for scientific work or for distinguishing yourself in medicine or law. In art, your success depends largely on your mastery of fundamental techniques. If you attempt to short-cut experience or training, you will probably fail at a distant future point when success seems crucial to your career.

Although you naturally shrink from contentious situations, you frequently become in-'ved in arguments and sharp exchanges. You find it necessary to correct wrong assumptions, especially when another person is being unfairly criticized. The underdog has a particular place in your heart and you will risk a great deal on his or her behalf.

The Other Side of the Story

Loss is likely through broken contracts, lawsuits and the dishonesty of partners. Your love life is probably remarkable for the number of affairs that end unhappily. Marriage will probably be delayed. Sometimes with this combination, the person achieves wide success and influence and suddenly is discredited or falls from favor. The faults and weaknesses most prominent in your own nature will probably be encountered in your closest associates. Until you learn to live with these and assimilate the right lessons, you have little chance of overcoming your frustrations.

SATURN IN SCORPIO

You are a very forceful character, though you mightn't show it, for you are shrewd and know precisely when an agreeable and pleasant facade will create the desired effect. In most of the relationships you encourage, you usually have an ulterior motive. Basically, you are a loner, so when you reach out to others, they can be fairly sure you have more in mind than friendship or interest.

You are serious, painstaking and secretive. Much goes on inside of you that no one on earth ever hears about. You suppress your emotions deliberately, control yourself with rigorous persistence, so that most of your true self is concealed and you appear something of an enigma to others. Your basic drive is for power, and you are more dangerous than the average power seeker because you have learned the crucial secret of achieving power, which is to first gain power over oneself.

In people with this combination, emotion burns with a suppressed fury. Scorpio is the Sign of sexual energy, which must be released in one way or another. And Saturn, the cold, heavy, restrictive planet, sits on it here like a giant stopper. As the pressure builds up, the need to express the creative Scorpion force becomes intense and the person is propelled toward art, domination, mystical achievement, lawlessness or sexual gratification. Fortunately, Saturn dampens the destructive potential of this energy and generally allows it to be harnessed in dynamic but socially acceptable ways.

You favor working behind the scenes. Your subtle and penetrative mind is ideally suited for manipulating others and for solving all kinds of mysteries. In the sciences, you can apply this faculty as a geologist or archeologist, probing the secrets of the past; or as an astronomer, probing time and space. You may also excel in microscopic research or psychiatry. Mysticism and the occult also intrigue you because you like to penetrate the depths of the mind and emotions. Training is essential so you can marshal your innate capacities into an effective method.

In love, you are extremely passionate and liable to suffer excruciating jealousy. You are true to your loved ones and expect their fidelity in return. When betrayed in love, you hit out cruelly, wait patiently to take revenge, or withdraw into yourself and suffer in searing but dignified silence. You are proud but not arrogant, haughty but not vain, fiercely determined once decided, and fixed in your attitudes.

People with this combination make first-class spies, undercover agents and insurance investigators. They have a knack of getting results by indirect or "backdoor" methods. Being naturally suspicious and distrustful, they are seldom surprised by any human foible or weakness. They are capable of enduring incredible deprivation, physical hardship and mental harassment to achieve their ends. They can also be supremely selfish and despotic.

You have a violent temper but usually manage to keep it under control (provided Saturn is not badly aspected—see Yellow Tables). You regard your independence as inviolable and can react viciously if someone attempts to curtail it.

You are seldom as cool, calm and collected as you appear. Sometimes, in fact, you are swamped by feelings of failure and insecurity, though you usually manage to conquer these by the sheer power of your will.

The Other Side of the Story

Health may be indifferent in the early years, but once maturity is reached, physical stamina may be exceptional. However, unless the energies at your disposal are directed toward higher aims, sex may be a problem and lead to health difficulties. Someone's sudden death is likely to bring about major changes in your life-style. You have probably made the same serious mistakes in your life more than once. Complexes about wealth, sex and power are apt to create serious personality difficulties.

SATURN IN SAGITTARIUS

This is a favorable position for several reasons. It means you have high ideals, a strong desire to help humanity, and that you are prepared to do something practical about your beliefs rather than just engage in enthusiastic discussions. You are, in your way, a driving force for good. However, since Saturn, the planet of restriction and delay, is posited in Sagittarius, the Sign of bounding optimism, you can expect some hard going, including tedious and infuriating detours. But there's not much doubt that by persisting you will finally win through.

You have a strong social conscience. You would make a first-rate politician, writer, lecturer or minister who uses his or her knowledge and position to draw attention to the ills of the community. You possess the energy, vision and administrative ability to organize crusades at the grass-roots level, where continual contact with the public gives you the opportunity to mold opinion.

Not everyone, of course, can be a shining light in this world, but this combination gives you the capacity to display these talents to some degree in whatever walk of life you choose. Half the battle is to realize that your inner urges to be committed to a worthwhile cause are not aberrations. They are real, valuable, and you are capable of taking the initiative.

You are a wise and philosophic person, particularly after you have reached your middle years. You learn from adversity and setbacks. The more you are required to struggle while maintaining a confident and good-natured outlook, the wiser you will become. Your opinion is highly regarded by your friends and associates. You don't act or speak lightly, although you always manage to convey a cheerful and independent attitude. You believe in looking behind the obvious—in meditating on your problems but not worrying about them. You depend a lot on your intuition, which throws up solutions without a great amount of deliberation.

In business, you are down to earth and

straightforward, unafraid to call a spade a spade. You are open and fair in your dealings and don't like fools or crooks. You have a flair for seeing possibilities a long way off and are almost certain to make money out of projects anticipating future trends. You can afford to play your hunches because you know from experience that they are reliable. You can't explain this because it is derived from the prophetic nature of the metaphysical Sign Sagittarius. The presence of Saturn, the planet of business and administration, introduces the commercial angle.

Your feelings are easily hurt. They are also easily touched by the sorrow and unhappiness of another. You are kind, obliging and compassionate. But criticism cuts you to the bone. You feel you don't really deserve this kind of treatment; you don't dish it out nor do you try to hurt others unnecessarily. In fact, you are very wary about doing anything that may cause people to lose their respect for you.

You want to be liked, and sometimes this desire conflicts with your innate urge to be frank and honest, causing uncertainty and pangs of conscience. One of the drawbacks of this combination is that despite your high regard for ethical and moral rectitude, your own methods or motives may be publicly questioned sometime during your life. Considerable anguish may result. You may be perfectly innocent but be forced to carry the blame for someone else. In one way or another, your honor and reputation are likely to suffer.

You are also a bit like the elephant and slow to forget a slight. When censured by superiors, you are apt to overreact and be too outspoken for your own good. Promotion and advancement may be delayed as a consequence. If you can learn to curb and control this rather irrational resentment, your positive qualities such as persistence, responsibility and creative thinking should bring you quickly to the notice of those who count.

The Other Side of the Story

You may think that sermonizing is a practical way of helping others. Your outdated ideas may have little application to today's conditions. You probably have very little grasp of modern economic trends; your investments may be safe but yield very little profit. Your judgment is poor, basically because you're not prepared to take any risks—except with your reputation, which you endanger through odd personal alliances and indiscreet moves. Scandal is likely to hurt your family and associates. Slander and libel suits are possible. If you have known success, you will probably be deprived of it. Health and nervous strains in the latter part of your life may lead to progressive depression.

SATURN IN CAPRICORN

Saturn in Capricorn produces a very worldly and materialistic outlook. It is an exceedingly good placing for the achievement of ambitions and for the rise to power, but without softening influences elsewhere in the horoscope; this personality may be too harsh, disciplined, self-centered and grasping to achieve the happiness that normally comes from a relaxed state of mind. Here, life is a very serious business and work with its concrete rewards may represent the beginning and end of all aspirations.

You are fiercely determined to succeed. You wish to build a reputation so that others will respect and esteem you. You are very reliable and hardworking. You will never let a superior down—or anyone else, for that matter, who may be able to help you in attaining your goals. You make a point of quietly cultivating people in authority, believing you can't have too many contacts for future success. You are suavely tactful, persuasively diplomatic and incurably conservative—and you persevere.

When it comes to making friends and selecting lovers, you are very choosy. The thought of deep emotional involvement makes you uneasy. You are not nearly as composed and in command of your feelings as you like to make out. You are actually terrified of being hurt, or ridiculed. You would rather venture nothing in the way of love or friendship than risk a rebuff.

Yet you often seem to draw unhappy experiences to you. Friends frequently fail you in one way or another. In love, you are also apt to be unlucky. Perhaps it is your unnatural wariness. You try so hard to play it safe all the time that you end up making impossible compromises in your personal relationships. Unless your Venus, Sun or Jupiter are in Virgo or Taurus, or—to a lesser degree—in Pisces or Scorpio, your marital affairs will probably be wearyingly depressing. Whether married or living with your parents, you have little chance of avoiding unhappiness and worry. People with this combination frequently end up living alone—or living only for their work. Their chronic anxieties may cause illness and sometimes mental problems.

Not without justification, you have great faith in your own abilities. Your intellect is sharp and your reasoning powers well above average. You can strip a business proposition down to the rawest details and expose its flaws with consummate brevity. At the same time, you can plan the largest venture without overlooking a single important detail—and then set up the organization to handle it. Given the circumstances, you can pull yourself up to just about any commercial height. Fundamentally, you are tycoon material, but you may have to pay a price in isolation from human sentiment (which some others regard as a reason for living).

You have a flair for writing, even though this may not yet have occurred to you. You can express abstract ideas clearly and put the most complex data into simple, cogent English. You are also suited for scientific work where the object is to crystallize facts and formulate workable theories. As a teacher, you should shine. But it is probably in running your own business (if you get the chance) that you will be able to make the best use of your talents and at the same time satisfy your strong desire for independence.

Despite your immense persistence, you are likely to become depressed and melancholy. The progress you make is seldom sufficient to satisfy your ambition. You also seem to run into more than your share of obstacles and hindrances. Opposition sometimes infuriates you, breaks down your reserve—and you lose your temper. In a position of authority, you are quite capable of throwing your weight about and insisting that others fulfill their obligations to the letter of the law. When treasured goals are threatened, you may become ruthless.

With this combination, you should try to remember that success is likely to come only after perseverance in the face of prolonged difficulty and aggravation.

The Other Side of the Story

You may marry to escape an unhappy family life only to experience even greater sorrow. Your love partners are apt to be unfaithful, your friends unreliable. You are suspicious and distrustful of others, and this makes them avoid your company. You are probably lonely and unhappy, weighed down by worries emanating from your own selfishness. In the home, you may be a tyrant and unnecessarily severe on children. You will probably become attached to someone intellectually inferior. You usually choose the hard way to do things rather than take normal risks. You are obstinate and refuse to listen to good advice.

SATURN IN AQUARIUS

This is a fine position for Saturn, possibly the best in the horoscope. It makes you an outgoing and very responsible person. You sincerely care about your fellow man. You are keenly aware of the limitations imposed on him, but are convinced half are unnecessary and can be gradually thrown off by more liberal and enlightened thinking. You realize that political and social ills can't be remedied overnight—in this, you are not a radical like some solar Aquarians. You believe in evolution rather than revolution. But you are willing to take an active part in giving things a kick in the right direction.

You have a great deal of common sense, the product of an observant mind that learns from every experience. Your policies are down to earth. You are at your best working in a job where the team spirit is essential. You understand the value of cooperation and have a talent for bringing together in working harmony totally different personalities. You don't play one person against the other. Although you may show some autocratic tendencies at times, you respect the individual's longing for freedom and independence. Your style is to inspire unity of effort that allows everyone to do his or her own thing, preferably under your direction. Authority comes easily to you and others don't seem to question it. This makes you an ideal group leader. Many people with Saturn in Aquarius are occupied in research laboratories where numbers of scientists combine to find a single solution.

You are likely to enjoy an unusual, but lasting, marriage or love attachment. You may be parted from this person on numerous occasions, but separation never severs the deep link that binds you together. You are not the type to form frivolous liaisons. You won't play around with another's affections. You are true and faithful. Whatever you undertake, you approach with a serious and responsible attitude. You have many social acquaintances and a very wide range of contacts in your field.

You are probably an authority on your work, or will be in later life. In your early years, the particular direction of your career may be uncertain. Seemingly insuperable difficulties may discourage you from pursuing the occupation of your choice. But eventually, people with Saturn in Aquarius usually win through on the merit of their fine intellects, perseverance (when they are interested in a project) and ability to get along with others.

You are friendly and considerate, courteous and well meaning. If something needs to be done, you take direct action. You enjoy study, especially in maturity, and regard it as a means of keeping your mind fresh and vital. You are a deep thinker, drawn to subjects that others consider profound and abstract. You are often accomplished in refined artistic expressions that verge on the mathematical, such as musical composition and modernistic stage routines and body rhythmics. Games and gadgets employing odd magnetic and electronic phenomena are apt to originate in the mind of someone with Saturn in Aquarius. These people are also responsible for bringing into the home exciting technical advances and inventions which they use to decorate or entertain. They originated psychedelic colors and effects.

You are extremely able at putting your ideas into words. As a lecturer, you can make the dullest subject vibrate. You have a knack of pleasing an audience. Any work that brings you into contact with the public or depends on public support is likely to project you into prominence.

Quite often you are prepared to play a ''back room'' role and allow others to receive the acknowledgment that is rightly due you. This is because you are not egotistical; you value the work more than the recognition. The esteem of your colleagues generally means more to you than public plaudits.

This combination often produces great interest in occult subjects, especially in the practical study of Astrology.

The Other Side of the Story

Your high-handed attitude makes you an unpopular teammate. You always seem to want to go in the opposite direction to everyone else. You are a troublemaker; you talk too much about topics you don't understand and provoke others to complain. You can't stand being told what to do without retaliating in some way. You are apt to hold extreme political views that may be offensively autocratic or communistic. But you don't have the courage of your convictions; excuses are your subtitute for action. Your radical opinions may arouse public hostility and lead to your being ostracized. Or, on the other hand, you may be regarded as a crank and have no impact whatever. Trouble with the law is indicated.

SATURN IN PISCES

You are a person with unique qualities, some of which may not have surfaced yet. You are basically creative, artistic and refined. What you have to give to the world comes through your ability to tap the nature of things—the universal spirit, if you like, or the plane of psychic causes. This is a bit confusing—especially for you who has to live the strange in-between existence that epitomizes Pisces, the watery final Sign of the Zodiac. The presence of Saturn, the earthy and practical planet, makes it a little easier for you to express in concrete terms the extraordinary things that go on in your mind.

Many inventors, philosophers, poets and sensitive writers have this combination. At its best, it enables them to pluck inspiration out of the nebulous mass of impressions they feel, project it through the Saturnian menstruum in their mind and . . . *eureka*, the world-shaking discovery or classical masterpiece materializes!

Saturn brings Pisces, the Sign of mysticism and self-sacrifice, down to earth, in more ways than one. It usually exposes these supersensitive people to the full rigors of worldly struggle. Frequently, especially if the planet is badly aspected (see Yellow Tables), they undergo considerable physical hardship and for a long time may be denied the material success and recognition they deserve. Their friends and acquaintances are often their worst enemies, or so it seems.

The big problem people with this combination have is to remain hopeful and resolute in the face of obstacles. Their tendency is to give up at the first sign of opposition—to throw in the towel before any blows are even struck. However, these individuals are acutely sympathetic, and if their emotions can be sufficiently aroused, they are capable of great achievement. The humanitarian fields attract them particularly, and they are often found working in hospitals, prisons and other institutions for the destitute, underprivileged and crippled. Sometimes they are widely acclaimed for their devotion and dedication. These people really understand that there are others worse off than themselves, so they suffer their own disabilities and misfortunes with saintly silence.

You are not so materialistic as many others. Still, you would like to get ahead and be popular and respected. Your difficulty is in summoning up the willpower to stick to something long enough to achieve results. You can't help wondering if worldly ambition is worth such a struggle, especially since the fruits of your efforts will all disappear one day. You understand serving others, you enjoy comfort and ease, but you don't comprehend the need for acquisitiveness and the sacrifice of peace of mind required to succeed in the material sense.

When you do reach a position of honor and prestige, it is very difficult for you to hang onto it. You can't perform as others expect you to; you don't have the same solid and convenient values as the masses. When the chips are down, money doesn't matter that much to you beyond its power to provide the necessities of life. Sometimes people with Saturn in Pisces can even get satisfaction out of the martyrdom of destitution.

However, you are well equipped mentally to deal with worldly affairs because you are ingenious, can spot opportunities instantly and have a rare gift for assessing character at first meetings. Many people with this combination are intensely interested in mysticism, the occult and parapsychology. Their emotional receptivity confers first-hand knowledge and experience of these matters. If they are unable to make a career in connection with their psi gifts, they are apt to use them in seclusion, often with results that may be unstabilizing.

The Other Side of the Story

You are badgered by hard luck and misfortune. Your love life is filled with sorrow and disappointment. You tend to link up with people who are so dominant that they take over your entire life and give you very little freedom. Or you choose weak but unscrupulous partners who exploit you, ill treat you, defraud you or misuse you. You have probably suffered more than your share of sadness, even tragedy. Much of your unhappiness and frustration is probably owing to your own pessimistic outlook, dependence and lackadaisical habits.

URANUS

The Planet

Uranus is the seventh planet out from the Sun, after Saturn. Its diameter is 32,000 miles, four times that of the Earth. It is 1782 million miles from the Sun, takes 84 years to complete one orbit and rotates on its axis in 10 hours 48 minutes.

Uranus is an "eccentric" planet—it has eccentric bands around it and its axis is tilted a unique 98 degrees (compared with the Earth's 23.5 degrees). This means that the planet lies virtually on its side, and that at opposite ends of its orbit, the Sun seems to stand directly over one of its poles. When this is the North Pole, the Southern Hemisphere lies in total darkness—for 20 years at a time. At the other end of the planet's orbit, the Northern Hemisphere has its 20-year "night."

Uranus was officially discovered in 1781. The discovery is attributed to William Herschel (1738—1822), a professional musician whose hobby was astronomy. But actually it had been seen and recorded on several occasions almost a century before by John Flamsteed, the first English Astronomer Royal. Flamsteed (1646—1719) was the astrologer for whom Charles II built the Observatory at Greenwich. He timed the laying of the foundation stone from astrological data, and the horoscope he cast for the Observatory is still on view today.

Uranus is the last of the planets that can be seen with the naked eye. But an observer on Uranus would not be able to see the Earth—the planet is so far out in space that the Earth would appear to be about 3 degrees away from the Sun, making observation from Uranus impossible.

Uranus has five satellites, all named after characters created by William Shakespeare and Alexander Pope.

For more than 100 years, the planet was called "Herschel" after its discoverer, although a famous contemporary astronomer, Johann Bode (1747—1826), had suggested the name "Uranus."

(Bode was the man who discovered the intriguing proportions in the distances of the planets from the Sun—Bode's Law.) It is little wonder that the name "Herschel" did not stick when the symbolic and astrological significance of the planet is taken into account.

Symbolism

Mythologically, Uranus was the first of the gods. He was the son of Earth, or Ge, who sprang from the original empty space, known as Chaos. He was the father of Saturn, the grandfather of Jupiter and the great-grandfather of Mars and Mercury. Urania is the muse of astronomy.

Astrology

In accord with the extraordinary consistency of the evolution of astrological knowledge, Uranus was not discovered until the human mind was ready to cope with its influences in a constructive way. Prior to that, its strange and eccentric potencies affected only the unconscious; Uranus was part of the sum of life's forces, one of the vagaries of existence that just had to be borne, as contrasted with a positive power that could be harnessed for the betterment of man and the deepening of human knowledge.

The discovery of Uranus coincided with the scientific epoch (Age of Reason) and ushered in the sudden and shattering events and upheavals of the Age of Revolution. The Uranian epoch encompassed the French Revolution and the Napoleonic Wars, the first experiments with electricity, the abolition of the slave trade, antiseptic surgery, the invention of the locomotive, the airplane, television and so on.

Uranus is the first of the three Extra-Saturnian planets, which are considered to be more general than personal in their effects. Since the planet spends seven years in each Sign, it affects large groups of people in the same basic way. Uranus is said to produce the differences in outlook, attitude and tastes that so clearly distinguish one generation from another. It is the generation gap.

Uranus is the planet of genius that goes beyond the intellect. It includes the power of intuition, ESP, Astrology, warning dreams, clairvoyance, clairaudience, visions, electricity, magnetism, inventions.

It is regarded as a strange and malefic planet. It acts without premeditation. It is the force nature employs to disrupt established patterns, societies and civilizations so that entirely new orders and cycles can begin. It is the power behind new political certainties that sweep away the old, often with devastating destruction and misery. It was the power behind the Bolshevik Revolution, the American Revolution and all the other social and political revolutions of the last two centuries; and it will be the power that overthrows these when they become effete, stagnant or sterile.

Uranus is disruption, originality, inventiveness, rebellion, freedom, fanaticism, shock, separation. It is independent, electrifying, unconventional, unexpected, virulent, drastic, radioactive, modern. It represents divorce, bombing, explosives, adventure, gas, astrologers, automobiles, microscopes, electrical goods, alloys, electrons, astronomy, spaceships.

It is reform, creative inspiration, anarchy—and free and illicit sexual behavior.

Uranus is the main ruler (with Saturn) of Aquarius, the eleventh Sign of the Zodiac.

The Uranian influence makes a person prophetic and able to predict the outcome of business and scientific matters with great accuracy. These people have a "feel" for knowing, outside the normal reasoning process. They are quick to act on their insights. Because they can see far ahead of their times, they are frequently branded eccentric, by conventional minds. Their imagination is extremely constructive and strong; they can find a way to improve on just about anything. And they are always convinced they are right.

The Uranian person loves electronic gadgets, especially radios, tape recorders and all electrically operated musical instruments and appliances. He or she delights in the cyclic rhythms of music and usually likes loud sounds.

These men and women have a great number of friends and acquaintances and mix with ease. But they are not emotional, and feel more affinity with groups than with individuals. They cultivate companions who appreciate their way-out ideas and who are intellectually supple enough to discuss them. They enjoy listening to the unorthodox views and opinions of others and are remarkably free of prejudice. They attract odd kinds of people who (like themselves) are sometimes regarded as the lunatic fringe of society. In reality, these people are the vanguard of new social customs and political ideas. The flower children, hippies, and dropouts of the 1960s were eruptions of the Uranian soul-wave. Not all succeeded in revolutionizing society or becoming permanent fixtures, but they left their mark in one way or another.

The Uranian is a great humanitarian. He fervently believes in freedom for all. And he understands that the individual must suffer, even perish, to bring about the new order. His realistic approach to change makes him appear dispassionate and detached by sentimental standards. Sometimes he gets carried away with his progressive aims and becomes autocratic, even despotic, a megalomaniac. The imagined good of the whole prevents any consideration for the part. The individual is expendable. This person, out of obsession for a cause, can deviate from his own lofty ideals and become a cheating, lying propagandist.

The Uranus influence prompts people to act erratically. Unexpected things happen to them and around them. Sudden changes, new situations, fateful meetings, unexpected partings—all are the work of Uranus. It is hopeless to cling to the past or the old. To be free of Uranus, or united with its power, requires a willingness to move on without looking back.

Physiologically, Uranus is associated with the pathetic nervous system. It is said to cause sudden nervous breakdowns, spasms, fits and paralysis, all kinds of convulsive and violent mental disorders, hysteria and freak growth.

Sexual perversion and homosexuality are also attributed to Uranus, through its control of the sex glands of the endocrine system.

URANUS IN ARIES

You are exceedingly impatient to tell and show the world what you can do. Your ideas are often brilliant and your flair for originality well known among your associates. But you are frequently in too much of a hurry. You go off half-cocked without thinking your moves through. You start off wonderfully, then lose direction. You make superb suggestions, propose instantaneous solutions—and drop some terrible clangers. You are unpredictable and impetuous, but you are never a bore.

You have an almost obsessional love of freedom and independence. You won't accept any situation that ties you down. A nine-to-five existence drives you mad. Unless a job or profession allows you to show your initiative and originality, you will quit. You are resourceful and inventive, extremely well suited to work connected with scientific discovery and development. You are the ideal space-age technician. You have a special affinity for electronics, and on the human side, social reforms. You have the kind of mind that in a flash can solve problems that may have been delaying progress in a whole technology. You are inspirational and intuitive. You enjoy improving on things, employing new and advanced ideas. You have a lively interest in education and a firm belief that children should be taught in liberal and up-to-date ways.

You possess a flair for attracting attention to yourself. If you move in public circles, your name is often in the newspapers. The publicity you receive is not always favorable. You are too much of a free thinker to conform to a comfortable public image. Your fiery and headstrong temperament often rubs people the wrong way. Uranus in Aries can mean notoriety. You are sometimes brusque and tactless. You always want to get things moving and sometimes streamroller over those patient, plodding people who like to think first. You have great intellectual vigor and insight; you are often intolerant of slower minds, particularly when they fail to grasp your radical ideas. You frequently despair that the Establishment will ever understand what you are trying to do. You may be just too advanced for the times.

Your enthusiasm is formidable. You are a live wire—continually turned on. You spend most of your leisure time contacting a wide circle of acquaintances. You frequently fall out with your associates but quickly find new companions. You are argumentative and erratic. You lose interest suddenly in people and ventures. You have the irritating habit of changing horses in midstream, switching from one contradictory course to another with the dexterous unconcern of a pony express rider. You are "for this" today and "for that" tomorrow. And you seldom appreciate your own inconsistencies.

You have trouble with your love life. Partners find it difficult to put up with your way of living. After you have your cake, you want to eat it too. You desire a mate, but you want to be able to come and go as you please. Because of your unusual vitality and personal magnetism you have no difficulty attracting the opposite sex. Your ideas about liberty and equality are terribly appealing. Your way of life is exciting; you seem to promise so much. But when it's time for sharing, you lack heart. Generosity isn't enough.

Disputes, separations and divorce are not uncommon for this combination. Being self-willed and headstrong, you are often careless and lacking in self-control. You do silly, upsetting things, speak out of turn and unintentionally offend others with your bluntness. You also tend to be reckless and somewhat accident-prone.

You are a compulsive traveler. You like to roam unimpeded, meeting different groups, sampling other cultures, spreading your ideas, living as much as possible from day to day. You tire quickly of the same suburban environment and move quite often.

The Other Side of the Story

You may have a reckless disregard for safety and often endanger your own life and that of others. You should be extremely careful when handling explosives, firearms and electricity. As a driver, you can be a menace. You are likely to be a mental bully, making life miserable for subordinates and those not as bright as yourself. You may reject good advice and fail or suffer as a result. Any form of restraint can make you uncontrollably violent. You may be a misfit who has no respect for authority. If your revolutionary urges get out of hand, there may be trouble with the law. Justice to you may be anything you manage to get away with. You are too easily bored to build consistently.

URANUS IN TAURUS

You are the type who can build an empire—and lose it overnight. You have probably noticed long before this that your financial and business fortunes are subject to extraordinary ups and downs when compared with other people's. You are always running into unexpected reverses; yet, on the other hand, you gain or things fall happily into place with the same abrupt tempo. This is the result of the rather incongruous alliance between Uranus and Taurus.

Taurus is the Sign of income, possessions and landed property—the solid, earthy comforts. Uranus is the force of startling and electrifying change bringing a new order. Together they make some strange music.

You are best fitted to acquire money and possessions in unorthodox ways. Although yours may be a traditional job or profession, you can spot new and novel possibilities. You see opportunities long before others. And when you act on your intuitions, you are usually successful. You are especially good with financial and property investments; here you are usually the first one in. You are the type who may start a new fashion or cycle in commercial enterprise. You are ingenious, inventive.

You are at your best when working as a member of a group or in a loose kind of partnership. You are too independent to be tied down by hard and fast rules and binding agreements with others. But if you strike the happy balance in your cooperative efforts, you can be a catalyst, producing the ideas and energy for all concerned to benefit from. The biggest threat to your material security and advancement is your inability to accept advice. You either think you know it all or pigheadedly stick to your plans because you don't like the idea of changing them. In this way, you court loss and disaster. Some would say Napoleon, who was born with Uranus in Taurus, was defeated because he ignored the advice of his friends.

You attract numerous people to you in both business and personal life. But when successful, you are inclined to gather an entourage of hangers-on who aim to separate you from your money or to use your influence. You need to be cautious about whom you trust and to make sure that the schemes and people you support are sound. Your money-making ideas are also likely to be stolen by these types.

You have remarkable willpower and determination to succeed. You can push ahead against great odds as long as you have confidence in what you are doing. But you tend to have several goals at once. Since you can't give each the attention it needs, you work in fits and starts, pushing this activity and then that activity. Although you seem to pour yourself out in a continual stream of energy, you get a bit bored doing one thing at a time. You have a one-pointed aim to succeed, but you choose a dispersive way of going about it.

You possess considerable artistic ability. This may be expressed through music or literature. Being born with Uranus in Taurus also gives an impressive quality to the voice; many prominent singers and actors have this combination in their horoscopes. If Uranus is poorly aspected, you may have trouble with your throat or generative organs.

Your love life is not likely to run smoothly, although you can gain financially through your mate. Your free-wheeling ways and popularity are likely to antagonize your lovers. Your partner's jealousy, suspicion and attempts to make you conform to accepted patterns of married life may make it impossible for you to settle down. These negative effects can be largely offset by good aspects in the horoscope; a congenial and prosperous marriage is then possible. The influence of the Moon, Jupiter and Venus, as given in the Pink Tables, must be considered.

The Other Side of the Story

You may have poor taste in colors or dress badly or in an old-fashioned way. You are likely to be absurdly obstinate, refusing to listen to the good advice of others and pushing ahead with unpopular and unfortunate plans. Your artistic efforts may lack the necessary refinement and show a garish style. In financial matters, you are likely to take foolish risks; a lack of discretion and judgment may make you a poor money manager. Conflicting desires for security and freedom may cause nervousness and uncertainty. You are likely to have cruel and vindictive ways toward those who oppose you. In group activities, you may be a destructive element, proposing radical ideas that undermine harmony and cohesion.

URANUS IN GEMINI

You are a superactive and inspired thinker. Your mind is especially suited for advanced scientific studies. You can understand the most abstract ideas, from atomic fission to the intricacies of the computer. But that is not all. You have the potential to expand these fields of knowledge by contributing new and original notions. You would make an excellent logician, a first-class theorist in any branch of science or a facile and interesting writer.

But you are not the kind of person who can get much done physically. You prefer to work in your mind, at lightning speed. Ideas flash into your consciousness like X-rays, giving you insights and solutions to all sorts of problems, some of which don't even concern you at the time. You have an extraordinarily penetrative vision that keeps producing advanced and novel thoughts.

Unless you can find a suitable profession or occupation to hitch your ideas to, you may get a reputation for being a bit odd. Your views may be too radical, revolutionary, ultramodern for normal minds to accept. Your written or spoken opinions on sex education in schools, abortion and other contentious subjects may shock and cause resentment. Success and association with publicly recognized endeavors give your wilder or more advanced ideas greater credence and acceptance. It is not unusual for people born with Uranus in Gemini to be considered eccentric. They also have unusual ways of expressing themselves. They are sharp, often too frank without meaning to cause offense. They can appreciate several points of view simultaneously, and in disputes, quickly perceive an acceptable compromise. Writing offers an excellent field of expression. It enables them to get their ideas across in logical form and to anticipate and answer conservative opinion, which usually opposes them.

With Uranus in Gemini, you have an undoubted capacity for psi and ESP and, given the chance, can write on these subjects. Whether you know it or not, you are an expert in one way or another at the art of communication. You merely have to find the role that suits you. Your versatile and clever mind can convey ideas in ingenious and interesting ways. You would make a fine teacher, musician, secretary, lawyer, public speaker, lecturer or popular commentator on scientific subjects. You have a flair for languages and would be a capable interpreter. The probability of travel, which this field offers, would make it doubly attractive.

You enjoy travel and meeting people. You usually gravitate toward the intelligentsia and number among your associates those with radical and extreme views. Literary and scientific people are among your closest friends. You have a sympathetic understanding of reformers. Most out-of-the-ordinary subjects attract your attention sooner or later.

You have probably had to adapt to a number of abrupt changes in your life. Many moves of residence disrupted your formal education, or circumstances may have prevented you from making a normal start in a profession or occupation. Your strong desire to study and learn may only be fulfilled in adults years. You may find that although you are intellectually superior to your rivals, you can't secure the recognition you deserve because of educational drawbacks. Your professional advancement will probably be jeopardized by this deficiency.

Some of the above problems may have been caused by relatives. Uranus in Gemini signifies problems with and estrangements from relatives, especially brothers and sisters. Neighbors can also be a source of trouble and unhappiness. Letters, telephone calls and gossip may produce unfortunate effects.

The Other Side of the Story

You may be so lacking in vital force and energy that you seldom manage to get your own way. You are likely to be the victim of scurrilous talk and be unable to vindicate yourself. Friendship with dubious people may damage your reputation. Unexpected difficulties, including loss of baggage, may beset you whenever you travel. Happiness at home may always elude you. You may be forced to change your profession or bring yourself up to date in your field in later years. You are likely to be disorganized in your thoughts and unable to sustain a logical argument for long.

URANUS IN CANCER

You can catch the imagination of the public if you care to develop your talents and act positively. You have great sensitivity. You are reserved and most times prefer to retire rather than advance. You are ambitious and would like to make a name for yourself, but when the time comes for action, you feel it is too much effort. Uranus in Cancer gives you the chance to make your mark, not in a rip-roaring way (which would only unsettle you), but pervasively (which better suits your placid disposition).

You can be successful in the arts. You possess a keen sense of beauty and a deep inner longing for completeness that enable you to contribute a unique flavor to any creative line you develop. You can be a superior artist, writer, sculptor—or humanitarian—bringing to these activites Uranian verve and originality without its usual jarring effects. You bring evolution, not revolution. But first of all, you have to overcome your passivity.

You may also be successful in an unaggressive way in politics, advertising, literature or publishing. You are a gentle persuader. In business, your innate ability to sense what the public does and does not want gives you an advantage to be exploited. You have a fine magnetic quality that attracts groups of people. They will listen to what you have to say, read your works or patronize your enterprises. You can do well as a quality restaurateur, a gourmet, a connoisseur or a supplier of food and drinks. Your penchant for custom and things of the past makes you a natural collector of antiques. This combination produces the popular radio and TV personality who, with Old-World charm and urbanity, gives his or her views on the important social and community issues of the moment.

You are more likely to obey your feelings and intuitions than your reason. You are acutely sensitive to your environment, especially to the deeper emotions of the people around you. You are strongly motivated by your subconscious and often do things without quite knowing why. The sorrow of other human beings and the sufferings of animals can distress you profoundly. Injustice—either against yourself or others—arouses your anger and indignation.

You are intensely psychic. If you wish, you can use this faculty to help others who are troubled. Because you are so high-strung and your emotions so easily moved, you are susceptible to sudden nervous disorders; hysteria and palpitations may be problems. You are also prone to stomach disorders, ulcers and cramps.

Your domestic life may be very unsettled. As much as you may love your home and family, it may be impossible to keep familial relations on an even keel. Upheavals and sudden departures may result in long absences from the people you love most. You may no sooner be reunited than another separation is forced on you. In love, you may be unpredictable and too fond of other company and parties to forge a strong marriage tie. You may find temporary escape from your sorrows and disappointments by having love affairs with whoever happens to come along at the time. Legal proceedings concerning your home or property are likely to cause loss, worry and illness. The childhood influence of an eccentric parent may still inhibit you and color your views on life.

You are ardently patriotic and may take an active part in a political organization, especially in a national crisis. Your views may not be consistent enough for political loyalty, but you like to feel that this is because you keep an open mind. Your heart is with your country. Your main political concern is to maintain national unity so that the traditions and values of the past are not lost.

The Other Side of the Story

You may be restless, changeable, unreliable and a stranger to your own mind. Your behavior may seem odd to friends and co-workers. Your radical and peculiar views may be publicly criticized. You are likely to be oversensitive to what other people say and quick to take offense. Being alone may hold a special horror for you. You are likely to be irritable, cranky, sulky and impatient when you fail to get your own way or sufficient attention. If a man, your reputation may be destroyed by a woman. If a woman, you may have been severely and erratically disciplined by an eccentric mother. You may suffer from obsessional fears. Nervous indigestion and ulcers of the stomach are possible.

URANUS IN LEO

You have a great desire for freedom and independence, and yet are likely to deny them to others. You believe in yourself. You feel—with some justification—that you are the leader of any group you happen to be in. You think you know what is best for others, and when you appear bossy or domineering, it is usually because you genuinely feel you have the other party's interests at heart.

That's all very well. You do have a lot of positive qualities. But you're a trifle too erratic and excitable to instill great confidence in those you want to follow you.

Leo is the royal Sign of kingship and rulers; Uranus is the planet of the unusual and unexpected, the abrupt and jarring change. These two hardly go hand in hand, but the combination often produces brilliant ideas (sometimes approaching genius), original schemes and thrilling scientific discoveries.

You are a person whose life is punctuated by remarkable changes. You don't seem to be able to keep on one course for very long not because your mind is changeable or because you are unable to concentrate (far from it), but rather because circumstances seem to seize you and fling you in the opposite direction. Hence, you don't get much chance to follow through on things. Making plans for the future can be a nightmare.

Still, you have an exciting life. You won't settle for a humdrum existence. You insist on being that little bit different.

You are apt to be attracted to the entertainment and leisure industries. Film-making could easily be the field in which you will shine. You enjoy glamorous situations and everything that contributes to spectacle. As a stuntman (or woman), an originator of special effects or a public relations or advertising executive specializing in gimmickry, the Uranus-in-Leo type is without a peer. You enjoy being in the limelight, adore a personal audience and can be counted on to take just about any kind of risk for the sake of applause or hero-worship.

You are attracted to odd types of people and frequently clash with those who support the Establishment.

Your love life is turbulent, often tempestuous. You reach the peaks of happiness and the depths of despair. It is difficult for you to stay on one emotional level for long. You have frequent love affairs—or none at all for long stretches. If married, it is not easy to avoid separations and estrangements. Strange and sudden eventualities are just as likely to part you from a loved one as to bring you together. Not a great deal that is "normal" or pedestrian happens where your affections are involved.

Your views often verge on the eccentric. You frequently upset co-workers, associates and even superiors with your unconventional actions and unorthodox methods. You will deliberately try a different way of doing something rather than use a tried and trusted procedure. Anything can be improved on, is your motto. You will only be happy in a job where you may experiment and test your ideas in practical and dynamic ways.

It's not surprising that such an independent and often rebellious character has difficulty taking orders. Unless you are handled carefully, or respect the person in charge, you will walk out at the first sign of high-handedness. You won't tolerate being told what to do. But if you are in a position of authority yourself, you won't brook contradiction.

You are beaverishly industrious and will give a project all you've got. You wish to change the world with your ideas and you make no secret of the fact that you want to be noticed while you're doing it. People with this combination are inclined to draw attention to themselves by dressing in unusualy ways, affecting way-out hairstyles or driving exotic cars.

The Other Side of the Story

Your father may have been an eccentric and caused family hardship through his unreliable habits. The sudden death of a dear one may have left you deeply grieved. You are probably a troublemaker, a bit of a showoff and a braggard. People resent your dogmatic attitude. You have inordinately strong likes and dislikes that border

on the irrational. You are dangerously headstrong and impulsive. Your recklessness and disregard for convention make you a poor example for younger people. Loss and sadness are likely through children. You have violent outbursts of temper, which, although not long-lasting, may distress those near to you. If you are a woman, the men in your life are probably erratic and very difficult to live with.

URANUS IN VIRGO

You can turn your hand and your mind to a great many occupations, with a good chance of success in all of them. You are not particularly ambitious for yourself but are intent on producing a good article or performing a worthwhile job. You prefer to be engaged in work where you can employ your flair for devising novel methods and inventing helpful gadgets. If there's a bottleneck anywhere in the production line, you can be depended on to come up with a simple solution. Whether in the professions or at the workbench, you are solidly effective.

You have to avoid working in spurts to be at your happiest. Your need is for a job you can get your teeth into, such as solving mechanical problems, teaching groups of people practical subjects or generally overseeing continuous work.

Your specialty is scientific research, if you can manage to get started in it. Your mind is brilliantly analytical and ideally suited for sifting large amounts of detail without losing concentration or interest.

People with this combination are often in the forefront of laboratory work connected with the chemical industries. They are intensely interested in the latest attempts to control air, water and soil pollution. They are intrigued by all aspects of diet and are often able to devise new formulas for slimming as well as for improving the vitamin effectiveness of staple foods in developing countries. Their contribution to the fields of hygiene, biology and particularly sophisticated electronics have won many of them world renown.

You are generally quiet and reserved in manner but fearfully obstinate when you believe you are right. You tend to affect an unruffled exterior even when your emotions are undergoing intense turmoil. This happens quite frequently. Unless people with this combination learn to relax, to laugh, not to take themselves too seriously and to confide more in others, they are apt to become introverted and eccentric in their behavior.

Uranus in Virgo epitomizes the absentminded professor who is so identified with his overriding interest that he merely goes through the motions in his other relationships. This can be undesirable here. Pent-up pressure should be released in adequate social activity and not in odd habit patterns. The longer the electric energy of Uranus is suppressed in Virgo, the greater is the chance of mental instability.

You have an inquisitive mind. You are continually questioning the environment and trying to put the pieces together in a new and original way. You want your achievements to be of practical benefit to as many people as possible.

You would do well working in a government or municipal department where your advanced ideas would be of direct assistance to the public. Another good area for you is the manufacturing industries, where mass production techniques help to make life easier for everyone. You should be able to write books about your work or make a living from lecturing. You can be an entertaining speaker, explaining your pet subjects, and are seldom stuck for a clever or humorous phrase.

The Other Side of the Story

Your manner is abrupt and unsettling. You seldom get along well with co-workers or subordinates. Your management or executive skills seem to consist chiefly of carping and bullying. Trenchant criticism is your long suit. As a boss, your success is marred by labor troubles, noncooperation, excessive rule enforcement and ill will. You lack concentration; your brain works in spurts and spasms. You are fanatical in your ideas about food and hygiene, though inconsistent in practicing them. You are unreliable and prone to forget where you are at times. Nerves and mental aberrations are common among immature people born with Uranus in Virgo.

URANUS IN LIBRA

Your personal and social life undergoes numerous jarring fluctuations. For a while, you get along swimmingly with people. Then suddenly a violent change occurs, either in the other person, yourself or circumstances. And nothing is ever quite the same again. It's annoying, exciting, exasperating, amusing. But one thing is certain: it's not as boring.

This on-off electric impulse is due to Uranus, the planet that activates everything it touches—briefly. Libra is the Sign of balance, a state achieved by putting a little more or less on either side of the scales. When Uranus steps in

(or on), balance fluctuates wildly. You, therefore, are kept very busy trying to maintain the harmony you crave in your relationships.

Friends are a great help. They have been responsible for much of your success in life as well as for providing the pleasure and intellectual stimulus your expansive mentality requires. Work and social acquaintances usually become your buddies, and many of them are influential. You have a way of attracting the people who appeal to you, and are usually surrounded by more companions than the average person. But . . . it is a constantly changing scene. As new friends arrive, others move on—and not always in peace! Uranus turns friends into enemies. Sharp and heated exchanges frequently shatter your dreams of idyllic friendship.

The same problems afflict your love life. And yet, you enjoy intense moments of happiness—sometimes even physical ecstacy—as the scale rises to heights others may never experience. The lows, of course, can be shatteringly disruptive. But as people with this combination mature and learn to live with their fluctuating emotions, they find sufficient compensations to make it all very much worthwhile. With Uranus badly aspected, though (see Yellow Tables), there is likely to be a considerable disproportion of discord and unhappiness.

You are an artistic type of person with a special interest in music, painting or literature. People with a knowledge of these subjects are among your closest confidants. You are fascinated by the latest scientific discoveries and enjoy discussing developments in electronics and space research, as well as trendy pseudosciences such as the Geller effect. The possibilities of Astrology excite you, and although you may not have time for practical study, you are likely to be an avid reader of the latest books. Your own ideas on the topics that interest you are often original and advanced. Given the opportunity through an appropriate career, you have the capacity for making a unique contribution in your field.

Your ideas are often considered ahead of the times, perhaps even a little eccentric. Because of this, you tend to choose unconventional companions who are prepared to listen to you. Aside from being a good audience, these people appeal to you because they are intellectually flexible and creative and therefore better company. Your living habits are somewhat bohemian. You like to dress in noticeably different styles or furnish your home modernistically. You are restless and enjoy change. Your temper is volatile but brief.

People with Uranus in Libra often marry suddenly, sometimes very young or in astonishing circumstances. Eventualities in their love life often shock their families and conventional-minded associates. Partnerships, both marital and business, have a way of turning upside down—not necessarily for either bad or good —but usually to the amazement or consternation of others.

The Other Side of the Story

The sudden death of a loved one or friend may leave a vacuum in your life. You have many enemies and rivals. Friendship can seldom stand the strain of your violent temper and abrupt changes of mood. You lose your best friends and keep those who indulge your liking for luxury and pleasure. Marriage is apt to end in divorce or death. The unpredictable conduct of a partner may result in scandal and ridicule. You arouse people's hostility and antagonism, and never seem to attract understanding or sympathy even when these are well deserved.

URANUS IN SCORPIO

This is an extremely powerful position—the possibilities for material success and making an impact on society are tremendous. But . . . so are the chances of failure. Much depends on the aspects to Uranus (see Yellow Tables). Theoretically, there are three paths for those with this combination to choose from: first, a career in science, medicine or another constructive occupation where their penetrative intellect and love of investigation can be used for the benefit of all; second, treachery, cunning and lawlessness, at which the Uranus-in-Scorpio person unfortunately can excel; third, uncontrolled passion and sensuality, which can enslave the underdeveloped person with this combination. In any of these three paths, the person will show relentless dedication.

You are determined to succeed. You like to fix a goal well in advance and work persistently toward it. Circumstances often change suddenly and force you to make detours, but your faith in yourself and your ultimate victory never falters. You are one of the most self-willed types of the Zodiac. You never give in either to opposition or obstacles.

Your methods are novel and unconventional and frequently arouse the admiration of associates. You have a knack of visualizing future eventualities, and with your shrewd mind and diplomatic artfulness can manipulate people into making the moves your strategy requires. However, your tactfulness is usually limited to situations where you feel some advantage can be gained. Otherwise, your manner is rather blunt and aggressive. You have a stinging tongue when you want to use it and are likely to withdraw your cooperation abruptly at any time.

In many ways, you are erratic and unpredictable—one moment bold and adventurous, the next conservative and cautious. As a rule, you are secretive and for no apparent reason may withold even unimportant information from your associates. You prefer to work alone, within a group. You understand the value of cooperation, but will not involve yourself in any scheme that does not have a solid and practical objective. Light chat is not your scene. Hen parties don't interest you.

When working, you believe in using the most modern equipment available. You are quite mechanically minded yourself and often enjoy tinkering with machines and electronic gadgets or reading articles about inventions in these fields.

You have an explosive temper. Your family, co-workers and (especially) subordinates have probably learned never to push you too far. You tend to rub others the wrong way, to be haughtily dogmatic and dictatorial. But at the same time, you have a magnetic appeal so that people tend to see your strong and positive qualites rather than your flaws. Weaker types, although apprehensive in your company, draw strength from you. Few who know you would ever try to provoke your animosity or endeavor to outfox you.

You deride many of society's most respected values and would like to see them replaced with your own. The fact that you are in a minority does not deter your enthusiasm or forcefulness.

You are a sensual and passionate lover, though your relations with the opposite sex seldom run smooth. Marriage is usually marked by violent arguments, tempestuous emotional scenes and lusty reconciliations.

If your energies are properly directed, you possess great artistic and creative powers. These are sometimes manifested in exceptional mystical insight. Uranus in Scorpio has produced some of the finest musicians, painters and writers—artists who reveal rather than merely relate. It also endows exceptional potential for surgical medicine, psychiatry, invention, philosophy—and just plain moneymaking.

The Other Side of the Story

You are likely to be crude, coarse, bad-tempered, violent, brooding, cruel, vindictive and revengeful. Your love life is apt to be devoid of romance. Your relations with the opposite sex may end in tragedy or scandal. Lower types with this combination are bewilderingly erratic and unreliable. They may be preoccupied with the search for sexual gratification. Their perverse ways usually bring them into contact with shady and underworld types.

URANUS IN SAGITTARIUS

People with this combination are often instrumental in reforming and refining public opinion. They have a sense of identity with the common man that explodes limited material desires and opens up brave new worlds of thought and accomplishment for him.

You believe in freedom and independence for everyone. You realize that man often imprisons himself in worn-out dogmas and automatic support of discredited authority. You want to do away with these fetters—not by rebellion and physical violence, but by reeducation and enlightened thinking.

So, out of Uranus in Sagittarius comes a new message, giving a more realistic meaning to religion, philosophy, morals, ethics, education and the law. And at the more mundane level, people with this combination are likely to be the initiators and innovators of new methods of long-distance travel, technical advances that speed up communications between nations, and scientific discoveries that help eliminate poverty and suffering. The end of their activities is to bring humanity as a whole closer to the concept of universal dignity.

You are an adventurer at heart. If you can't get away to visit other countries or participate in daring exploits, you manage to travel in your mind. You are an avid reader and listener. Progressive and helpful ideas crackle through your brain day and night. Whatever your line of work, you have something valuable to contribute. "Broad-minded visionary" is an appropriate description of this combination at its best. If you get the chance, you will be daring, courageous and quite contemptuous of physical danger. You would have made a wonderful old-time explorer—and how you would have enjoyed rapping with the natives!

You change your views often and abruptly, but generally in a progressive direction. You are continually replacing old ideas with new ones. To you, to live means to experience, so one should keep one's mind moving with the times. Since (deep inside) you are mainly interested in the truth about man and universal principles, you are not weighed down by many opinions. You know personal opinions are notoriously unreliable and depend largely on individual conditioning and circumstances. You'd much prefer to stick to facts. That's probably why you would favor any system of education based on actual experiencing. You are suspicious of classroom learning and academic certainties. Life itself and an observant and responsive mind, you believe, are the ideal teachers. But then, most of your beliefs are ahead of the times. Occasionally they land you in hot water with those who esteem conservative and traditional values.

You are not a character who can be browbeaten into silence. You believe vehemently in free speech. Frequently you offend others with your candid remarks, though your spontaneous and sincere nature usually soften the blow of these telling barbs.

Generosity is your second nature. You give without a thought to anyone in need. (Few even have to ask.) You place great value on comradeship. You are not so keen on emotional attachments because you see them as restrictions on your freedom.

You are acutely intuitive and have powerful hunches. Your dreams can be prophetic. People with this combination sometimes have visions.

The Other Side of the Story

You are constantly on the move but never succeed in doing anything worthwhile. Your reckless nature and inability to concentrate make you unreliable and forgetful—though you always come up with a good excuse for your chronic unpunctuality. You like to imagine yourself a sage or leader, but run at the first sign of responsibility. You are a big and impulsive spender, especially of money that dosen't belong to you. You can't resist a bet and will gamble wildly against hopeless odds. You depend on a glib tongue to get you out of most of your troubles. Long journeys are unlucky. Difficulties come through partners and their relatives.

URANUS IN CAPRICORN

You are intensely ambitious and very capable—a force to be reckoned with. Not much can stand against your indomitable will. It is important with this combination to know where you are going, what you want out of life, for there is very little doubt—given favorable aspects to Uranus (see Yellow Tables)—that you will reach your goal eventually. It would be a pity to waste power and ability on inconsequential activities.

Despite the seriousness and discipline of this combination, it *is* possible for you to dart off in a totally different direction without apparent rhyme or reason. This is because of the dual effect of Uranus on Capricorn. Capricorn is the Sign that literally means business. It stands for responsibility, restraint, prudence and perseverance. Uranus, on the other hand, is the planet of abrupt changes, the unexpected, which strikes like an electric shock. Uranus takes a lot of the heaviness and dullness out of Capricorn and reinforces its resourcefulness.

But Uranus is upset at times by the movements of other planets in the heavens, and on these occasions those inexplicable inconsistencies that you must have noticed in your temperament come to the fore. And you, along with your colleagues, are often amazed at the change. You become suddenly restless and even a bit eccentric. In yourself, you feel uneasy and not so sure of the direction you are heading in. At these times, you are likely to espouse quite radical views and want to see the established order changed abruptly. You may act impulsively—and unwisely—and obstinately refuse to consider other people's viewpoints.

However, Uranus in Capricorn generally makes you a first-class business person and executive. Your mind is quick and penetrating, and yet profound in its ability to reason in practical terms. Your business methods are novel and progressive. You are determined to get to the top, and as you climb higher, you update the system and organization under your control. You admire broad-minded and creative people and gather this type around you. You have no time for fogies and old-fashioned ideas.

You work very hard and have a special talent for getting the best out of your employees. They and your colleagues are pleased to cooperate because they know you are capable and usually successful in whatever you undertake. You are particularly adapted to take charge of a large organization, especially municipal and public works. You gravitate to positions of trust and those that require exceptional responsibleness.

You respect the independence of the individual and will always listen to the protests, objections and arguments of others—even though you may not agree with them. You have an acute sense of fair play. You won't ask someone to go against his or her principles, if you believe in this person. Although somewhat conservative, you do believe in taking the initiative. The bold enterprise that offers a challenge but not a gamble will attract you every time.

You have a flair for making accurate long-range assessments. Your logic, vision and developed social conscience all fit you for a role in politics and government.

You are also capable of writing and speaking in a revealing way, particularly when drawing attention to social ills. You seldom speak unless you have something to say. Satire is a field in which you may excel.

The Other Side of the Story
Your early home life may have been unhappy, possibly because of the death of or separation from your father or another patriarchal figure. People in authority may tend to treat you unjustly and be responsible for financial loss and anxiety. You have probably had to start a new career or been forced by circumstances beyond your control to change jobs frequently. Promotion may depend on one person who hinders or dislikes you. This combination often involves public criticism or false accusations by superiors, when the person is of the negative type. It also makes the individual weak-willed, changeable and erratic.

URANUS IN AQUARIUS
You probably run into difficulty at work and around the home through your inability to appreciate the points of view of others. Some people might call you perverse—you invariably want to go the other way to accepted opinion. This is most admirable when you take up a worthy cause and try to institute reform in the face of unyielding authority, but at the personal level it can be quite annoying.

Still, the irritation that Uranus in Aquarius may cause other individuals is often downtrodden society's gain. For people with this combination, even in ordinary life, have a deep concern for their fellow man. They genuinely desire to see him emancipated, and they will do all they can at their own level to help, whether it is by spreading propaganda in conversation and in letters to newspapers, or by organizing their own little quasi-political groups of agitators, activists and protesters.

It's the Aquarian Age, remember, and since it dawned about the turn of the century, never in history have so many kings, rulers, despots and tin-god authorities been deposed and discarded.

You are a high-minded, well-intentioned freedom lover. You love peace, but not at the price of surrender. Although your views may be unconventional or a bit ahead of the times, people respect your ebullience and sincerity. You are popular among a very wide circle of casual acquaintances. Whatever line of work you follow, you soon build up a long list of helpful contacts. Your informal, friendly and easygoing manner, together with your bright and interesting conversation, combine to make you very pleasant and entertaining company.

You are exceptionally loyal to your friends. You don't form deep emotional attachments but find your link at the intellectual level—and through brotherhood, which is a rapport you feel with most people. You like to move around a lot, circulating among club or society friends. You are interested in odd and unusual subjects, and this brings you into contact with similarly minded companions. Quite often Uranian Aquarians and their friends are bohemian types who dress differently and have little in common with established society.

In your love life, you are faithful to the partner of the moment. You won't double-cross that guy or gal as long as it's understood that you're a twosome. But you must have a constant change of scene, not for sensual reasons, but because you're basically a mental creature and depend on different viewpoints to spark your ideas. The partner who does not understand this and tries to restrain you will lose you.

You are ideally suited for working with teams and groups or in large organizations whose aims are humanistic. Science has a special attraction. You prefer to be associated with some kind of advanced technology such as that encountered in space programs, electronics, radiation research and the like.

Uranus in Aquarius produces a person whose mind is particularly quick and ingenious. A highly developed intuition gives you flashing brilliance. Your capacity for original thinking and invention can approach the genius level. Sometimes your mind and imagination expand so fast that an "otherworldliness" creeps in and you appear odd.

When politically inclined, an individual with this combination is likely to get carried away with his or her own enthusiasm and slogans to the point of losing sight of the original aim. In these cases, excessive zeal may become fanaticism.

Taken to an extreme, a worthy humanitarian effort may degenerate into a dictatorial rampage.

The Other Side of the Story

You may be violently antisocial, believing that all that is customary is wrong. Friends and partners may desert or betray you. Those in authority may loose a vendetta against you. You are apt to suffer from sudden falls and injuries and may be physically assaulted by a mob. You could be rude, tactless and lacking in principles. Friends may be used for your own power-grasping ends. You are probably erratic, unruly and fanatical.

URANUS IN PISCES

This is not a particularly strong position from the materialistic point of view. It's something like immersing a red-hot poker in a dish of water. Clouds of obscuring steam are the result rather than dynamic power.

The power you possess is an inner one. It is expressed in a refinement, a sensitivity, a gravitation to art and a deep appreciation and understanding of the pain and suffering that exist throughout the world.

You are also profoundly psychic. You are likely to hear voices, see visions and sense atmospheres that others in the same room are oblivious of. You also have weird and peculiar dreams, some of which are amazingly prophetic. You sometimes wake up startled in the middle of the night for no apparent reason. You are apt to take a pessimistic view of your psychic experiences. Sometimes they depress you for days.

Uranus in Pisces is the conjunction of two exceptionally intuitive forces. Uranus is flashing and positive; Pisces is subdued and negative. If the rest of the horoscope is favorable, the person will have the strength to utilize his or her extreme sensitivity in probing and understanding the unseen forces that regulate much of our lives. In this way, he or she can fulfill the basic urge to be of service and to help mankind by describing in rational terms what is experienced.

This combination with its affinity for art and creative expression often produces singularly talented writers whose work is notable for its subtlety and finesse. Their own love of the unusual ensures that the topic will not be trite or dull.

Uranian Pisceans are also likely to be proficient students of Astrology and active in other occult investigations. They can be a great personal comfort to others who may have lost loved ones.

If positive use is not made of their psychic gifts, these people are likely to become overly introspective and slip into a world of daydreams and delusion.

A career associated with hospitals, orphanages and similar public institutions often appeals to people with this combination. In the medical and welfare fields, especially, they are able to put their splendid inventive minds to work and make life easier for the sick and the handicapped. Their innovations and success in these fields may not always be featured in the newspapers, for public recognition does not come easily with the Uranus-in-Pisces lineup, and if achieved, may be transient. But these people will receive delicious personal satisfaction from the knowledge that they are serving those less privileged than themselves.

Pisces is a self-sacrificing Sign and, despite its spasmodic ambitious urges, is more attracted by the achievement of good than the prospect of fame. These people radiate a sympathetic aura that communicates at the unconscious level. Others recognize their innate kindness and concern and are inclined to go out of their way to help them without being aware of it. It's as though the forces of good in these individuals attract a similar response from the people around them. A sick person served by a Uranian Piscean may be moved to extreme expressions of gratitude and deep-felt love.

The Other Side of the Story

You are constantly disillusioned by life, mainly because it seldom measures up to your self-deluding dreams. Although you possess the highest ideals, you lack the willpower and resolution to act on them. You are depressed by your own failures and yearn constantly for a chance to start anew, which seldom materializes. You change accommodations frequently. Unexpected reversals and difficulties often make you despair. Progress in your job or career is slow. Friends are unreliable, superiors hostile and lovers unsympathetic. You are usually separated from the people you enjoy being with most. Scandal and notoriety may be hard to avoid.

NEPTUNE

The Planet

Mysterious Neptune is the eighth and second most distant planet in the solar system. It was discovered less than 180 years ago. It is so far out from the Sun (2793 million miles) that it appears as no more than a disc through the most powerful Earthbound telescopes. No markings are visible.

Neptune is another giant planet. With a diameter of 27,700 miles, it is about four times the size of Earth. Although very slightly oblate, it is the most perfectly spherical of all the planets. Neptune, like the other outer giants, spins quite rapidly, having a day of 15 hours 48 minutes.

Neptune takes 165 years to orbit the Sun. It has not completed one round since its discovery, and won't have done so until the year 2011. This means the planet spends nearly 14 years in each Sign of the Zodiac.

Interesting circumstances surrounded the discovery of Neptune on September 23, 1846. For years, astronomers had been speculating and calculating, trying to account for the increasing deviation of Uranus from its regular path. It was suspected that another large cosmic body was in the vicinity, exerting a pull on Uranus—but where was it? The French astronomer Urbain Jean Joseph Leverrier postulated the position of the hypothetical planet by mathematical reckoning. A few months later, Johann Gottfried Galle, a German astronomer, spotted Neptune through a telescope—within 1 degree of the position Leverrier had calculated!

Neptune has two moons, Triton and Nereids. Triton, discovered in 1846, is the largest known satellite in the solar system. With a diameter of nearly 5000 miles, it is larger than the planets Mars and Venus. Triton orbits Neptune at 219,000 miles, which is closer than our Moon is to the Earth. Nereids, discovered in 1949, has an orbit that takes it 3 to 5 million miles away from Neptune.

Symbolism

Neptune, called Poseidon by the Greeks, was the eldest son of Saturn. After Saturn was deposed, Neptune and his brothers, Jupiter and Hades, cast lots for sovereignty and Neptune won the sea. He lived in an underwater palace. Neptune's symbol of power was the trident, thought to have originally been a lightning bolt, with which he could shake the Earth or subdue the waves.

Astrology

Neptune is associated with formlessness and refinement through dissolution, immateriality and subtlety. It is the force behind the appearance of things, the deceiver and the revealer. It is the psychic as opposed to the physical, the spirit as opposed to the flesh. It represents escape from the mundane world through the awakening of supersensitive perceptive faculties. It is the mystical link between the planes of inspiration and genius and the artists and visionaries who give the world the finest music, poetry, literature, form, uplifting spiritual truths and melting compassion. It is the medium for good or evil between man and his highest aspirations, whatever they may be.

Neptune is a higher octave of Venus, the planet of love and beauty. Neptune idealizes these emotions into one potent and discerning force, scalding but intangible and nebulous, which pervades rather than persists, flounders rather than floats, redeems rather than reforms. It is the mysterious and unknowable force that releases man from matter and reveals to him what does and does not signify. It is terribly personal. It is the path through the body and the ego mechanism to high consciousness. It is matter attuned to its own finest vibrations.

Neptune links man with the deceptive forces of his subconscious. With Neptune, things are seldom what they seem. It produces queer and indefinable feelings, sensations and emotions. It is the psychic power behind spirtual mediums, the hypnotist and the hypnotized. It creates impressionability, mystical experience, daydreaming and all that is associated with the "supernatural." It raises the sensitivity to such a pitch that the feelings of others—even the feelings others impress by their presence on inanimate objects—are discerned and emotionally identified without making use of the reasoning process. This psychometric faculty is a refined extension of the Venus-ruled sense of touch.

If you are strongly influenced by Neptune in your horoscope, the total number of good and adverse aspects between Neptune and the other planets will exceed neutral aspects. (This can be easily determined from the Yellow Tables.) It is up to you to draw conclusions from the descriptions that follow.

Neptune well aspected means you are a gentle and unassuming person. You are receptive, subtle and visionary. Since you are ultrasensitive and impressionable, your emotions are very close to the surface and easily disturbed. You have a great need of silence and solitude at times to restore your psychic balance. Unless your companions understand this, they will not understand you. You appear extremely charming and gracious, but this is largely a persona or mask, and although you are compelled by your nature to don it, you are aware it is illusory. You have strong and vivid spiritual insights, which can produce vague yearnings to burst through to understanding through renunciation. You find it very difficult to stand up to pressure for long; you sag, and without respite are likely to suffer a nervous breakdown.

A badly aspected Neptune can produce an escapist who retreats into his or her own dream world rather than try to improve or change the environment. This type is irresponsible and will turn to drugs and liquor to sustain a hallucinatory existence. Psychosomatic illnesses are very common among these people; they have an extraordinary capacity for producing symptoms of particular illnesses with a thought. Given the environmental stimulus they want (or their own way), they can snap back into glowing health in a moment. Negative Neptunians use their considerable charm to deceive others in business and personal life. They make the most plausible villains and confidence tricksters. They are also capable of being promiscuously permissive with their bodies.

Neptune rules Pisces, the twelfth and last zodiacal Sign, and is at its strongest in Cancer. Both are water Signs. The planet controls the sea, oil, chemicals and other liquids. Its discovery coincided with distinct new human trends that correlate with its nature: mesmerism (later to lead to hypnotism) swept Europe; the famous "Rochester Rappings" in the United States gave birth to modern spiritualism in America and England; anesthetics began to be used in surgery; and so on. Because the planet spends nearly 14 years in a Sign, its effects are less specific on the individual than those of the personal planets and even Uranus (7 years). However, these effects will be expressed through the characteristics of the Sign Neptune occupied at birth. Neptune is not the precise "generation gap" typified by Uranus; it represents the hidden undercurrents in the collective psyche that work partially in the minds of men and women and guide each generation haltingly to a point from which the next can step up in consciousness. To Neptune, war and peace, famine and plenty, are virtually irrelevant externals, the province of other planetary forces. Neptune is concerned with the *inner* changes these events work. The Neptune influence, like the lightning bolt the old god used to shake the earth and quell the sea, shatters the inner temples of materialistic values that individuals and generations would put their faith in.

The planet's energy is a transmuting force that, for the want of a better or more scientific word, is called "spiritual." The spirit, like Neptune, can never really be defined but its effects are unmistakable. Whereas the revolutions of Uranus occur outside of man, Neptune revolutionizes from within. Neptune's mists seem to drift in confusion, but the nebulousness is part of the transmutation process.

The materialist who is ready for the next evolutionary step up in his consciousness will be pitilessly driven by Neptune until confusion dissolves his certainty. The person already moving toward spiritual awareness and truer values will be inwardly elevated and exalted in his feelings by the same force.

Neptune, compared with the planets out to Saturn, is an otherworld force. Its power relates to a period longer than a lifetime and to a life purpose that is intangible. It gives no real inklings, no promises—just more stirrings to go on. The Neptune impulse is to share, so the Neptunian (or true Piscean) is passionately, impassionately and compassionately involved in humanity's progress. This personal commitment to the elevation of a species can be deluding, enlightening, confusing, inspiring, misguiding, sublime, divine or chaotic—depending on the individual.

Physiologically, Neptune is associated with the optic and hearing nerves, the spinal canal and the nervous and mental processes generally. When afflicted, it causes deep-seated neuroses, several emotional and mental disturbances and incurable insanity.

NEPTUNE IN CANCER (1902—1916)

You are a person who has experienced some very unusual happenings connected with your family or home. Your childhood was not what it appears to others to have been. You may have had reason to keep secret some of the circumstances of your earlier years, or perhaps you were deceived by a family member and the memory and its associations are still clear in your mind.

You were born at a time when the world was making traumatic adjustments. Your generation was raised by people who experienced the rigors of war on a world scale for the first time. Yours was the task of trying to build a viable modern society on the shaky ground of inherited mistakes and uncertainty. You are a generation of transitions, and you are never too sure that what you have accomplished is essentially better than what went before.

You are inclined to be too passive and allow things to slide. You are not disposed to determined and positive actions. With Neptune in Cancer, you feel your way ahead very carefully; the grand and sweeping gesture is not in your repertoire. You are somewhat negative in your approach to problems. People, especially your family or children, may tend to take you for granted, to walk over you in a sense. You are too sympathetic and affectionate. You have known many disappointments in the past.

You love to travel and have probably made at least one ocean cruise. You would prefer to travel by ship than by air, but have to do the modern thing to save time and expense. You don't like being away from home for long. You are a person who was probably overindulgent as a parent. Discipline was never your strong point; you preferred to bring up your children in a relaxed and homely atmosphere. Some of your ideas about domestic affairs may have been regarded as a bit odd. But you probably found that no matter how much you tried to guide your children with love and affection, they seldom responded as you would have expected. You may feel at times that you were not (and still are not) really appreciated by your dear ones. But this does not prevent you from continuing to care and concern yourself deeply with family affairs.

You have always possessed a psychic faculty, which probably first revealed itself in childhood. You are extremely sensitive to other people's moods, and without their saying a word, you know exactly what they are feeling. You also have deep spiritual insights. Although you may not speak about these very often, they help you to cope with daily affairs and to understand life better. Sometimes you have premonitions that are amazingly accurate.

You are idealistic, refined and love nature. You are exceedingly sentimental and enjoy all contact with the past. You remember the good old days with a great deal of nostalgia. You surround yourself with antiques and other relics of the periods you admire most, especially objects and souvenirs handed down by older family members. Your love for your mother was or is quite profound. She had a great influence on you as a child, and may have helped to develop your psychic powers or encouraged you spiritually.

You really love your country. Although normally reserved, you can display fervent patriotism in a national crisis or political emergency. Other times, you take an active interest in what is going on by keeping yourself informed through newspapers and magazines. You are a loyal supporter of whichever political party you feel stands for the preservation of standards.

The Other Side of the Story

You are restless, discontented and rarely able to settle in one place for long. Your impressionability makes you neurotic and a difficult person to live with. Peculiar and even weird experiences in your childhood have probably left deep scars on your mind, which have never really healed. Your domestic life may be complicated and unhappy. You may suffer from nervousness and anxiety. A pessimistic and gloomy frame of mind may repel others and reduce you to loneliness. You are likely to suffer from chronic indigestion or stomach ulcers. You may have to engage in some sort of deception in connection with your home or family. Your political views may be extreme and you may be thought a little eccentric.

NEPTUNE IN LEO (1917—1929)

This is an excellent position for Neptune. It

gives an innate desire and ability to serve the world and your fellow man in practical ways. You want to throw over the old and help bring on the new. But whether your objectives are worthwhile or worthless depends largely on how Neptune is aspected in your horoscope. You may be a source of hope or a source of trouble. In between, stands misguided optimism.

Many of the world's most effective revolutionaries were born when Neptune was in Leo. The leading lights of the American Revolution and many of the fighting men had this combination. So did numerous figures in the French Revolution, including Robespierre, Danton—and Marie Antoinette. Although on the other side, she believed (misguided optimism?) in what she stood for and did try to negotiate with the revolutionaries before losing her head. Another example of opposing forces, both fighting for their idea of freedom, were President Kennedy and the Communist revolutionary Fidel Castro, who brought the world to the brink of nuclear war when Russia moved atomic missiles into Cuba. Both were born with Neptune in Leo. So was Oliver Cromwell (nearly four hundred years earlier) who led the Puritan Rebellion against the English monarchy; and Christopher Columbus, who proved revolutionary theory—the Earth was not flat.

You are ambitious, conscientious and considerate. You are spiritually inclined and are moved to improve conditions rather than allow them to continue as they are. You have a keen intellect and sensitive emotions. You can interpret the feelings of the masses and express yourself in artistic and entertaining ways, which are received with acclaim. You are the product of the generation that gave the world the motion picture industry. Through this make-believe medium, glamor, romance and movie-star adoration were introduced into the otherwise prosaic lives of vast numbers of people. Neptune in Leo often bestows the charisma of irresistible charm and popularity that reaches the level of hero-worship. Many of the modern superstars of politics, screen, medicine and philosophy and psychology have this combination.

Neptune in Leo makes you social-minded and a lover of pleasure and the outdoors. You have a special way with children; you can guide them toward a less materialistic outlook without destroying their natural ambitions. You encourage the artistic and creative urge in others because you sincerely want them to develop to their highest potential. Your own interests include poetry, music, painting and drama. You can be a capable author, playwright, actor, actress or entertainer.

At times, you have peculiar feelings and intuitions, some of which are indescribable. Usually you know what you must do without any great thought about it. You trust your emotions and sympathies a little more than you do your reason. But you insist on being rational in your relationships and channel your energies into practical and purposeful endeavors. Art, spirituality and reform, to you, are not just topics to be talked about; they require action, determination and dedication—qualities you inspire in others by your own example.

Your love life is unsettled. Over the years you have had quite a few crushing disappointments. Love as a personal expression or selfish need does not have much chance of success where you are concerned. You may be deceived or suffer heartbreak through separation from the great love of your life. You are never short of individuals to love or to love you, but circumstances usually intervene after a while and force you apart, either physically or psychologically. The inner drive of Neptune is toward a more detached and pervasive love, which sacrifices egotistical satisfaction for the universal good. You need to find a humanitarian cause big enough and worthy enough to absorb the love and devotion you have to give.

The Other Side of the Story

You may live for pleasure and thus undermine your health and chances. You may go from one love affair to another, never finding satisfaction. Your search for physical gratification may lead to gluttony and drunkenness. Your father may have taught you low principles. You may attract degenerate company. You are likely to be a slave to your feelings and emotions and lack reasonable restraint. You can spend money as quickly as you get it on lavish living and entertainment. You may make a show of generosity in an attempt to win attention and applause. You are likely to be self-centered, boastful and loud. You may have been poorly educated and forced to fabricate qualifications. You are likely to be weak, cowardly, lazy or bullying. Your closest companions may be yes-men.

NEPTUNE IN VIRGO (1930—1942)

You are a gentle and patient individual, particularly when dealing with what are often thought to be the less important things in life. You give the smallest detail its correct place in the scheme of things, and this attention extends to animal and plant life. You are compassionate for the little creatures—the grasshoppers, fish, worms, birds, wild flowers, small animals, shrubs—and assume the bigger things are capable of looking after themselves.

You are also drawn to help people who can't help themselves—the sick, the aged and children who are poor or underprivileged. You don't have such sympathy for others; ordinary people you find necessary, but not easy to love. In fact, you are quite reserved and even shy in a social sense. You enjoy company and conversation, but your emotions are not easily aroused; you give the impression of being animated but lukewarm. You would make an excellent nurse or horticulturalist, zoologist or agriculturalist. Scientific matters relating to health intrigue you. You would find it easy and satisfying to make a living from medicine, chemistry, pharmacy. You have some unusual views about diet, which you put into practice with lively enthusiasm until you discard them for even better (or more peculiar) nutritional ideas. You enjoy writing about health and food and are not averse to sending off letters to friends or a newspaper detailing your latest theories and discoveries. You are a quite competent cook. You are acutely conscious of the necessity for hygiene and may go to extremes with perpetual handwashing and the like.

You have definite views about labor conditions and the plight of the workers. You want to improve the lot of those who are exploited, but you are inclined to overlook the shortcomings of some of the individuals in these conditions. If Neptune is badly aspected, you may be confused in your judgments and mistake laziness for lack of opportunity. You are keenly interested in education generally; you want to see everyone educated to the hilt, zealously ignoring the fact that those who find it hard to learn would be very unhappy under your prescription.

You possess exceptional psychic powers, which allow you to predict situations with amazing accuracy. You can visualize a set of circumstances and immediately see the flaws and advantages that events will present. Napoleon had this occult insight. He knew men. He could gauge what they would do. In matters of state, he could look years ahead and erect a detailed conceptual structure of what the future would require. Parts of his Code Napoleon, which reformed the French legal system, are still in use. Posterity is continually reminded of him by the ideas he projected. (Even the incidentals of his thought system seem to endure: the Italian flag was Napoleon's design.) But the general tendency with Neptune in Virgo is to allow psychic vision to take the place of spiritual insight, to be caught up in the desire to leave things in good order without harmonizing inner conditions. Material considerations, including man-made laws and wisdom, become paramount values (this, no doubt, is what finally led to the Emperor's downfall).

Your psychic perception makes you an especially capable researcher into occult fields. You also possess the literary ability to describe your findings in clear and logical language. Many astrologers are born with this combination.

You have an affinity for city and suburban life. Even if you live in the country, you will work in a more populated area and visit the city regularly. You have a talent for architectural work and draftmanship. You can conceive schemes for vast building projects—industrial complexes, shopping centers, new towns—and either construct them or design them down to the last quantitative detail.

The Other Side of the Story

You may be a cold fish who doesn't care for anyone. You may live a life of fastidious and efficient selfishness and not be averse to keeping up a long deception to get your own way. You are likely to be a hypochondriac with a special weakness for drugs and liquor. You may feel the world owes you a living and exist on the dole, handouts and your own cunning. You may be perverse in your sexual appetites. In employment, you may seldom contribute a fair day's work if it can be avoided by cheating or falsifying. You may use your talents for writing and public speaking to extract or extort money from others. You have a sharp, destructively critical tongue that causes much pain to others.

NEPTUNE IN LIBRA (1943—1956)

You people of the 1940s and 1950s have been called the "love generation" because you tried to introduce this concept to the world. You did it quietly and passively with love and sit-ins. But if you were successful, it is a reforming impulse that has now sunk deep into the human psyche. The effects are superficially obscured by the fundamental drives of the generation that followed yours—those born with Neptune in Scorpio. As an individual, you still believe in love, peace and equality. But your generation, which produced the extraordinary era of the flower and love cults, petered out as a reigning world force in 1957 when Neptune left Libra for another 154 years.

You are an idealist and a humanitarian. Your mind is continually considering how man's lot can be improved. Libra is the Sign of art, love, beauty and justice; Neptune is the planet of pervasive, reforming spiritual power. So your higher aspirations are even more refined than is normally the case in the creative and humanistic worlds. This makes you an individual who is filled with idealism but lacking in force. Although your convictions about the rights of man are firmly entrenched, you don't have much power to change the order of things. Because the reforms you want to make are dependent on inner workings, you won't see any great evidence of the lasting effects of your efforts.

You are refined in your tastes and behavior. You are more intellectual than physical. You have an extremely active imagination that likes to soar beyond mundane problems to the realm of lofty ideals and magnificent aspirations. When it comes down to everyday lick-and-polish activity, you are easily discouraged. You don't wish to be involved in the drab tasks of life and you make no secret of your distaste. You desire elegant living, gracious forms, gentle manners and peaceful and pleasant surroundings, as well as the company of artistic and sophisticated people. You are drawn to art, music, philosophy, literature and social reform.

You love love, you tend to idealize it, and in the hands of harsh reality, your illusions are often destroyed. But you invariably manage to create another ethereal vision. This is because you believe in love, not as it is practiced by a cynical society through hypocritical conventions, but as you know it can be. Your dream of love allows you to hang on to the ultrareality, to believe that it will one day be realized on Earth.

You are popular and much in demand socially. You have a tender spot for the underdog and will go out of your way to befriend neighbors and others who are unhappy or worse off economically than yourself. Your compassion, understanding, charm and love of harmony make you a desirable and pleasing companion. As a lover you are tender and affectionate. But if Neptune is badly aspected, you are likely to be overly emotional, changeable and sexually promiscuous. Your love affairs often lead to peculiar situations and frequently result in mutually unwanted separations.

You are very firm in your views about the need for justice in the world. You can be quite forceful and aggressive when debating this subject. But Neptune is inclined to cloud your judgment when you identify with a cause, and you need to listen to advice or you may ruin the very thing you are trying to promote.

Mystical, mysterious and magical subjects hold a fascination for you. You are extremely interested in the occult. But you need the encouragement or inspiration of another person or a group to become active in this field. You have a special liking for good films and television. You love dancing and music. Scientific discoveries, especially space explorations, excite you.

The Other Side of the Story

If a woman, you may be a crybaby, a hysterical person who is likely to break into tears at any moment for no apparent reason. If a man, you may be emotionally unstable and unable to discuss a contentious subject without feeling under personal attack. Your love life may be a succession of disasters that lead to broken homes. You may be oversexed and unable to resist any opportunity to gratify your appetite. You may aim at promoting harmony between people and succeed only in stirring enmity, misunderstanding and anger. You are likely to be an interfering do-gooder who collapses at the first sign of hard work, opposition or pressure. You may run from responsibility. Your idea of social reform may extend no further than having your name published in the society columns.

NEPTUNE IN SCORPIO (1957–1969)

Neptune is in each Sign of the Zodiac for about 14 years. Its effects are more visible in generations than in individuals. It has much to do with influencing the unconscious actions and modes of thought that, although expressed through individuals, become what might be called collective characteristics of that time.

Neptune was in Scorpio from approximately 1957 to 1970. This was the time when those in a position to mold public opinion decided to bring sex out from under wraps and place it squarely in the public eye. There was fierce and outraged opposition to plays like *Oh, Calcutta!* and *Hair*, and the increasing permissiveness of the screen, but gradually the protests became a drone that few really heard.

Neptune is the planet of subtle revelation and Scorpio is the Sign of sex, secrets and the investigation of mysteries. Scorpio also is a harsh and perverse Sign, and anyone looking back on those times cannot help but notice the rash of entertaining but murderously slick spy stories and films, the ferocity and torment of the war in Vietnam, the assassinations of the Kennedy brothers and others, and the prominence of the drug scene with its Neptunian delusions and Scorpionic wretchedness.

But out of the agony and anguish came much that was regenerative in human thought. And those of you who were born with this influence will have the opportunity of showing exactly what that means when you begin sitting on the benches of power and authority starting about the year 2000.

You can't stand hypocrisy and affectation. You want to see the world stripped of pretentiousness and insincerity. You believe in being honest—even if it hurts—though your methods sometimes make others suspect you believe the means justifies the end. But most of all, you believe in being honest with yourself. This can be a traumatic discipline not only for you, but also for those who have to live and work with you. You don't always measure up to your rigorous ideal, but you keep trying. You are intractably self-willed and have unshakable faith in your ultimate victory over all resistance.

You have a fierce temper, which you usually manage to keep under control; in fact, you don't like showing any of your feelings. Although your emotions are intense and quite often in a repressed state of turmoil, no one can tell this from your appearance. You are reserved and secretive, slow to make friends and rather doubting and suspicious. You have learned not to accept things at their face value.

You are fascinated by stories about the occult and have had numerous psychic experiences of your own, especially when you were young. Your dreams are often extremely vivid and sometimes symbolize events yet to come. People with this combination have visions at times of immense stress or just after a crisis.

You would do well in any occupation that requires a penetrative or inventive mind. Psychiatry, engineering, mechanics, investigation, chemistry, surgery or an army career could provide a field for your considerable talents.

One of the dangers of Neptune in Scorpio may be a tendency to drink excessively or to experiment with drugs. You have a deep attach-ment to all forms of sensation and a desire to expand your experience.

The Other Side of the Story

You are probably obsessed with some weird ideas that make life very difficult for those you live with. If this combination is afflicted by bad aspects, your nature is likely to be twisted with brutal urges to satisfy an insatiable lust for power over others and sexual gratification. In some cases, you are yourself the helpless victim of malicious and degenerate types. Bad luck may dog you at every step and cease only when there is nothing left to you in the material world. Some form of spiritual regeneration is possible in the midst of final despair.

NEPTUNE IN SAGITTARIUS
(1970–1983)

This generation will be incurable idealists and incredibly optimistic about the future of mankind—if only other people will see things as they do. While they will recognize that there are many ills in the world, they will be inclined to fight them with words and ideas, by stirring up public opinion rather than by taking direct action to eliminate the causes. They will look to the future rather than to the present.

Their vision will be broad, sweeping and original. Demanding details of their expansive schemes would be like asking a millionaire exactly how much he's worth—it's irrelevant: he's a millionaire! Using a few broad brush strokes to show what they mean, they will leave the filling in to those of lesser inspiration and intellect.

This will work very well both in business and in humanitarian schemes, for they will undoubtedly manage to surround themselves with willing helpers before racing off to launch another idea somewhere else.

Their intuition will sometimes be astonishing. They will seem to be able to look down the line of time and conceive exactly what will be required to make the most of events yet to happen. They will go out on a limb to carry out their hunches and will even back them with money and reputation.

Their public-spiritedness will extend to a keen interest in education, especially the kind that makes minds receptive to loftier principles and ideas. In the realm of religion and metaphysics, they will probably have some very original notions. Neptune in Sagittarius tends to link mystical experience with some of the less explicable phenomena in today's psi experiments and occultism. They will be inclined to pull down the barriers and demonstrate how the golden rules of the old-time religions still hold true: they will require wider application, not necessarily wider interpretation. They may believe that ideas have the power to change human minds, and they will demonstrate that power in measurable ways. They will be against hidebound reasoning, but will believe in truth—and that every thought should begin afresh from there.

Just as they will like to let their minds run free, so will they love to keep their bodies on the move. They will crave the outdoor life and all sports and games. They will demand travel, as far and as often as possible, both through the spaces of their minds as well as to other countries.

The ability to express themselves will fit them for a career in journalism or as authors of travel books and articles. The more they are able to move around and explore, the happier and more productive they will be. They will be also competent or itinerant artists who refuse to be tied down by their many possessions. A career in science, which would allow them to explore exotic places or to live with other races and study comparative cultures, will also be enticing to these idealists.

Deep-seated emotions will sometimes reach fever pitch and make them exceedingly restless in both mind and body. On these occasions, they may well act without thinking and then live to regret it.

Their dreams may sometimes be weirdly prophetic. A sense of humor will often be crucial in preventing lapses into vague depressions.

The Other Side of the Story

Long journeys and visits to other countries will probably end in odd experiences for these people. Foreigners may try to deceive them, especially those who pretend to be friendly. The political and religious views they hold will undoubtedly be criticized by those in important positions and public ridicule may result. Psychic experiences and terrifying dreams may make sleep itself a nightmare. Their concentration may be weak, their religious ideas misleading; these factors could result in torment and unhappiness for others.

NEPTUNE IN CAPRICORN (1984 -- 1997)

These persons, still unborn, will want to see greater order established on Earth. They will show that the resources of the world can be better organized. They will feel strongly that efficient—and possibly global—political and bureaucratic control can be the only answer to man's age-old struggles for supremacy. They will prove that, if given the chance, they can make life much easier for everyone—if they are free to put their ideas into play. The biggest problem will be their inclination to concentrate on man's material needs, ignoring the intense human longing for aesthetic fulfillment.

Neptune spends an average of 14 years in each Sign, so its influence (largely of an unconscious nature) works through all the individuals born during that time as an expression of their generation. The planet's effect is more pervasive than direct, more motivating than activating. It is a powerful force moving behind the scenes. What is described will generally be manifested as "mood" and attitude.

These people will be brilliantly practical and painstakingly thorough. They will seldom make a move without considering every possibility. Their minds will seem almost inspired in their ability to gauge, weigh and measure. They will have the makings of gifted physicists, chemists, engineers; as top executives, they will run the largest organizations and can be counted on to increase profits and reduce costs.

As politicians, they may not be so popular, but will have the compensating virtue of delivering promised results. They may live by the letter of the law rather than its spirit. Those who support this group may hope, in a way, that they will fail. Their methods, although effective, may become quite wearying for all concerned after a time. While likely to awaken man's desire for a change—any sort of change—they will free him from the imposed sterility and regimen of security. In the face of opposition, they will show great courage and determination. Although naturally careful and cautious, they will be quite versatile and resilient when it comes to defending their position.

Their personal lives may very likely be rather unhappy, beginning with problems in the home during childhood. Married life is apt to be spoiled by the absence of warmth and spontaneity in either partner. What begins with high promise may well degenerate into impersonal compromises or total disregard.

This group will probably be connected with

the entertainment industry through dancing, music or acting, but they will be more than likely to take an organizational or servicing role rather than an artistic one. Any artistic flair in this combination will undoubtedly be limited to qualitative excellence in the things produced, manufactured or supplied. For instance, a person with Neptune in Capricorn may be a printer of attractive packaging, reading matter, cards, sheet music and other high-class color work.

They will have a strong tendency to suffer from painful and vivid dreams in which they find themselves being publicly rebuked by someone in authority. In these dreams, they may be horrified by their own irresponsible actions or may have to face the reality of poverty in old age.

Insecurity, failure and the feeling that they are not respected may frequently depress them, even though these have no foundation in fact.

The Other Side of the Story

This group will be uncertain and vague and will tend to rely on others to make decisions for them. They will wait too long and will miss opportunities. They will be fearful worriers and their digestion will suffer as a result. They may resolve to be decisive and definite, but will fail as soon as any pressure is brought to bear. Family affairs will contain some peculiar situations; there will probably be a skeleton in the closet that will depress them; or a business scandal may leave their reputations in tatters and thus ruin their hopes. Family members will complicate their lives in unusual ways.

PLUTO

The Planet

Pluto was discovered less than 50 years ago. It is the last-known planet out from the Sun. Like Neptune, the planet's presence was suspected before it was located. Around the turn of the century, astronomers noted that Neptune's orbit was being increasingly disturbed by a body that seemed to be farther out in space. In an attempt to find the new planet, Dr. Percival Lowell built an observatory at Flagstaff, Arizona. He installed a 13-inch telescope—quite a sizable apparatus for those days—but was unsuccessful in his search. Then, in 1930, at the same Lowell Observatory, a student astronomer, C. W. Tombaugh, spotted the planet and photographed it.

This was quite a feat. Pluto is only about half the size of the Earth—3650 miles in diameter—and it is an inconceivable 3600 million miles out in space—about 39 times the distance of the Earth from the Sun.

Pluto takes the longest time of all the planets to complete its orbit round the Sun—248 years—and its movement is highly irregular. While all the other planets move within degrees of the Sun's path (called the ecliptic), Pluto moves within 17 degrees. It spends an average of 24 years in each zodiacal Sign, but because of its irregular movements, this period can vary from 13 to 32 years.

Symbolism

Pluto, or Hades as he was known to the Greeks, was the ruler of the dead and the underworld. He was the son of Saturn and brother of Jupiter and Neptune. When Saturn was deposed by his sons, the three divided the government of the world by lot. Pluto won the underworld. The ancients associated Pluto with wealth because gold and precious stones in their raw form and buried treasure were said to be in his custody. Hence the word "plutocracy": government by the wealthy.

Pluto's most treasured possessions were the helmet of darkness, a two-forked scepter and the staff with which he drove the ghosts or shades of men. He ruled with his queen, Persephone, whom he had forcibly abducted from the upper world. She was forced to spend half the year with Pluto and the other half on the surface of the Earth. Pluto was usually accompanied by Cerberus, the dog-monster of Hades that had three heads, a serpent's tail and a mane of snakes. Pluto was not depicted as a tempter of men, like the Christian devil. He was certainly a physical seducer of women, but not a psychological one. Mostly he was the custodian of the dead, the ruler of the house of the dead, who had to be stern and pitiless, but only in those roles.

Astrology

When a planet is discovered, its basic characteristics coincide with the trends and events then beginning to show in human affairs. Invariably, it seems, the broad mythological connotations apply. Pluto's discovery in 1930 coincided with the rise of gangsterism, the rule by those of the underworld who enslave, rob and kill for money and power. It marked the rise to power of Hitler and his attempt to produce a super-race through exterminating those he deemed "subhuman"— Jews, Poles, Slavs. It was the era of racketeers, the mob and machine-gun justice; the Mister Bigs with massive psychoses and paranoic drives, who liked to remain mysteriously respectable while pulling villainous strings behind the scenes. It was the buildup period to the most devastating war in history, beginning with the worst financial depression ever known.

The task for astrologers was to decide which Sign of the Zodiac was Pluto's. All the planets rule a Sign—that is, there is one Sign (sometimes two) that has a characteristic affinity with the life principle or force each planet represents. In the case of Pluto, the Sign was never really in doubt, although the surmise had to be verified by events. This has taken nearly 50 years, but there are few serious astrologers today who dispute that Pluto rules Scorpio.* Scorpio is the Sign of death, and such other things as redemption, secrecy, elimination, repression, suspicion, legacies, inheri-

*Until the discovery of Pluto, the rulership of Scorpio was attributed to Mars, which is still regarded as co-ruler. Over the centuries to come, Mars' influence will gradually give way to Pluto's in Scorpio. Mars is, of course, the sole ruler of Aries.

tances, penetration, intensity, investigation, sewage disposal—and sex.

Other Signs and planets affect a person's love life, but Scorpio and Pluto relate to the sex act devoid of the desire for progeny, love or the finer emotions. It is the act of sex as the power to penetrate into the very origins of being, beyond conscious motive; the urge to concentrate the libidinal force into a point so intense ethat it sears through the obstruction of desire to reach release, self-forgetfulness and unity with one's source.

Pluto represents the power of money and sex, but not as universal currencies that confer some sort of preference or privilege when exchanged. In Pluto, money and sex represent the two root drives that every human being sooner or later must learn to control in himself, and in so doing convert force—the personal need of preference or privilege—into the wealth and power of individual self-sufficiency.

Pluto, because it spends an average of 24 years in each Sign, controls the mass movements of change in each generation. It is constructive and destructive. It is the principle that gave us the blessings of nuclear power and the horror of the atom bomb. It is soothing psychology, healing psychiatry, the bludgeoning of brainwashing and the debasement of propaganda. It is the benefits of mass communication through newspapers and broadcasting, and the mass hysteria generated by the same media. It is a contradiction: a transformer and an annihilator.

Wherever Pluto appears in your horoscope, you will find contradictions in yourself. You can be forceful and strong, but suffer from nerves. You can know intense dislike and consuming love. You may be acquisitive, and yet be indifferent to possessions once they are yours.

Pluto is the last of the three known "spiritual" planets. All its effects on the individual are designed to change the physical habits that have straitjacketed the psychological being. It upsets established patterns and order. It destroys suddenly, then teaches the individual to build again, not as things were before, but with the exhilarating and creative freedom to make a fresh start while remembering the mistakes of the past.

Pluto splits opinion, usually on issues that involve masses of people. It divides tidy, close-knit groups, setting one fraction against the other, so that hard-won reform must itself yield to progressive thought and perhaps revolution. Pluto stands for automation. It makes human labor obsolete compared to machines so that man must create new thresholds of activity that machines cannot duplicate—for a while. Pluto represents endless repetition and reproduction. It is the spirit of mass production. It has set the marveldogs of modern science howling after man's necessity so that he must work ceaselessly at learning and developing new skills to stay out in front.

Pluto gives a person a dual view so that his or her personality ranges from one extreme to the other. When well aspected, the person is able to contain these opposites within himself and pour out the resultant energy in progressive, positive ways. Pluto provides a talent for medicine and science, particularly for theoretical work that grapples with the problems standing in the way of progress. Radical political action is Plutonian. Pluto endows great spiritual insight leading to popular new philosophies like those expounded by the Beatles and subsequent pop heroes, gradually idealizing the crass and hysterical emotions of each generation.

Badly aspected, Pluto makes a person a victim of his or her own extremes. Thus the individual can be an evil genius, a magnificent scoundrel, a cruel dictator, a vicious gangster—or suffer under these types.

Physiologically, Pluto is associated with the sex glands and their influence on the mind and will. It is the force of renewal through elimination, and this applies to the psychological as well as the physical. Pluto forces to the surface the unconscious blockages in the psyche; neurotic causes must be eliminated by being faced or lived through. If the planet is afflicted, this process may be difficult and lead to nervous and mental disorders. In extremes, violence, viciousness and self-destruction are likely.

PLUTO IN GEMINI (1882—1914)

You are a person who always likes to speak your mind. You have firm views on many subjects and you are not constrained by other people's feelings from expressing them. You say what you think is true or needs to be said. You don't have much time for people with narrow and closed minds, nor do you like conversing with those who cling to obsolete ideas. Although you are of mature age and have many memories to reflect on, you do not stick to old-fashioned ideas for sentiment's sake. The values you prize today are those you consider have stood the test of time. You are unsure of some contemporary standards and are especially doubtful of the values espoused by current world political leaders.

You take an active interest in all that is going on around you. You enjoy reading the newspapers, watching the news on television and keeping abreast of the times. In your way, you have achieved recognition of your talents. Even if you have never been a public figure, you have made sufficient impact in your field to give you a fair amount of personal satisfaction.

You are an individual used to many changes in your personal life. Nothing shocks you much now; you are prepared for just about anything. You have followed several vocations, probably changed your career entirely at least once and/or have had a great variety of jobs. You have a good mind for figures and have probably managed to earn quite a lot of money in your time, even though you may not have held on to much of it.

You are a bit of an extremist and inclined to be self-contradictory at times. You suffer from sharp changes of mood and sometimes feel dejected or negative about life. You can be inspiringly positive and depressingly gloomy. But you soon swing back onto a progressive course. You can usually hold your own in any sort of debate and are pretty clever when it comes to covering up your mistakes or concealing your weaknesses. You sum up situations quickly and are an excellent judge of character. No one fools you for very long.

You have an inventive turn of mind. You are always looking for ways of improving on things. You never feel that the ultimate has been reached. It is second nature for you to believe in life after death. You know there is always something else to be discovered.

You have always shown a talent for handling or dealing with groups of people, for being able to sway and convince them with the force of your logic. You would make a capable teacher, textbook writer, designer, theoretician. You enjoy sweeping the board clean of old ideas and laying down new easy-reference criteria that help people to do and produce things quickly and efficiently.

You are highly sensitive and nervously alert. You have always enjoyed a psychic ability, which gives you an acute understanding of occult matters. You also have spiritual depths, which can help you to appreciate the reasons for any personal failure.

The Other Side of the Story
You may never have really made a success of anything. Your inability to concentrate on one activity and to control your sudden mood changes have probably left you little to show for your working life. If a woman, you are likely to have married several times and still not found what you are searching for. You may have a perverse sense of humor that gets satisfaction out of teasing and lampooning others. Or you may be cruelly critical, tormenting or a vicious scandalmonger. You may judge others by harsh standards that you fail dismally to live up to yourself. You may be a cheat, capable of defrauding your friends in games or business with the same detachment with which you would embezzle from a corporation.

PLUTO IN CANCER (1915–1938)
Your nature reflects a generation that threw off many of the traditional yokes, especially in relation to the home and family. You were not prepared to be a slave to outmoded ideas. You were the first of the modern moderns, particularly where the emancipation of women was concerned. For a start, your generation started the kitchen revolution. Out went the dark old drudgery equipment and in came the bright new stoves, refrigerators, washing machines, sinks and so many other time-saving gadgets that women were able to start functioning outside the home. They kicked up their skirts and raised their hemlines to unheard of levels. They discovered that there is comfort, style and femininity in simple, lightweight gear.

But you didn't discard all of the past. That is not your nature. In fact, you have found that the greatest satisfaction comes from improving on what went before. And this is what you aim to do in most departments of your life. You like to develop new standards based on what has already been proved by experience. You have endeavored to bring up your family along these lines. You probably would not have gone as far as today's permissive society. But you try to keep an open mind because you appreciate the necessity for trial and error.

You have profound inner feelings. You draw most of your strength and understanding from your emotions—reasoning and intellectual considerations seem to come second. You have a highly developed sense of knowing what is right for you without having to think about it a great deal. Your convictions seem to rise up from your subconscious mind. You enjoy spreading new ideas. You are determined to give others the benefit of your experience. You have a talent for getting the things you recommend accepted by the majority. Once an idea has your imprimatur, it seems to become acceptable and popular.

Your memory is phenomenal. You can recall the most obscure details about your personal life with amazing clarity. You can tell anecdotes galore. You have a keen interest in archeology; historical topics never bore you. You especially enjoy reading biographies of people who were responsible for significant social changes.

You are often able to tune into what others are thinking or feeling. This gives you an uncanny ability to anticipate what people will do, especially in an emergency or crisis. You also have an affinity with the earth that often creates an interest in geological studies. Sometimes people born with Pluto in Cancer have a sixth-sense knowledge of where certain minerals can be found. This makes them particularly suited for mining careers.

As Pluto is often responsible for reversing situations, it is not uncommon for mothers or wives to go out to work and for husbands to take over some or all of the usual housekeeping duties.

Many of you have found careers in the entertainment world. You are also likely to be successful in advertising. Careers where there is intense competition are most likely to attract you. Television and radio can have special appeal. The manufacture of frozen and prepared foods, as well as packaging and the production of lines of products, are also areas in which people with this combination can shine.

The Other Side of the Story

You may cut yourself off from others and live a lonely, introverted and reclusive existence. Or, you may be insufferably domineering, especially toward relatives and friends. You are likely to be an ambitious egotist who never really achieves anything because you are so busy telling others what they should do or trying to deprecate their efforts. If a woman, you may neglect your children or family to further a career. You may be bored by the trivialities of home life and spend your time and money looking for diversions.

PLUTO IN LEO (1940–1957)

Everything you do or want to do is on a grand scale. You are artistic and creative. You want to give all and sundry the benefit of your talents. There are no half-measures about you. You possess tremendous energy and drive, which you apply to whatever you undertake. You

would be an excellent actor, entertainer or creative artist: you are keen on making a public impression. You are also likely to be drawn to one of the sciences, where you may make some timely discoveries. Whatever line you are in, you will tend to attract public attention and generate an aura of glamor and showmanship.

You and your generation think you can do better—and you have, in many ways. Yours was the age that swept away a record number of the world's kings and started the syndrome of 30-day governments. You insisted that the old regime must go. But no one—including yourselves—seems quite sure of what to erect in its place. But you did get rid of many of the old heavy hands. This is your nature—to try to improve conditions, often by taking the opposite course.

Yours was the era that turned the spotlight on the young people of the world. Teenagers discovered their massive vocal strength; and what a noise they made! They also realized they had formidable economic power; from then on manufacturers who wanted their support had to do things their way. Television came and boomed. Everyone had more money. Entertainment was paramount. Sex lost a couple more of its seven veils.

You and your generation are about to take control of the world. Over the next few years, in every country and society, you will be in the driving seat in politics, science, medicine, law and the rest. You can be counted on to make many changes. And you will have your chance to deal with the problems that were born with your own generation and that will, by then, have matured along with you. The elder statesmen and the custodians of the obsolescent will have to give way to sit on the sidelines and watch you battle with the dragon of your own times. You like an audience. Well, here's your chance.

You are a leader. You have never liked the idea of making the best of things. You want to make things better. You have new ideas for art, entertainment and the theater. You intend to overhaul education, and some of your proposals will be unconventional and highly contentious. But you will introduce them, nevertheless. Every Lion must have his day.

You are adventurous and the thought of taking responsibility for the future doesn't daunt you. You prefer that affairs be in your hands rather than anyone else's. You know that at least you have the good of the majority at heart. You won't flinch in the face of difficulties or danger; you have a natural daring and a deep faith in your own mission in life. Your generation will do more with space than travel to the Moon. You will explore new places. This will include expeditions into the field of parapsychology. The world of unseen forces—clairvoyance, clairaudience and the etheric double—waits to be mapped, a challenge beyond the capabilities of yesterday's materialists.

The Other Side of the Story

You may be a racist who tries to spread his or her ideas with hatred and violence. Bloodshed, force and revolution may be your chosen methods of bringing about change. You are likely to be a troublemaker, a glory seeker who leaps on any popular bandwagon. Your only aim may be to build a reputation for yourself, good or bad. You are likely to be a dictator at heart who rules his or her family and subordinates with fear and threats of reprisals. You may be sexually promiscuous and perverse.

PLUTO IN VIRGO (1958—1971)

Yours is the age that brought great changes in the practice of medicine and in the use of chemicals. Attempts were made to clean up the earth and improve on the chemistry of the human body. Virgo is the Sign that rules health; Pluto is the force of rejuvenation, death and rebirth, often through reversed procedures. So it was your era that pioneered the heart transplant and went on to develop even more refined techniques of spare-parts surgery. The use of drugs to induce mind-blowing experiences became widespread. The psychedelic age dawned and human beings, under the influence of LSD, tried to take off like birds—from buildings.

Virgo also is concerned with food, and this was the age of awareness of contamination. For the first time, the public became conscious that the excessive use of insecticides, preservatives and hormones was slowly poisoning them, and that the industrial wastes being discharged into the water and atmosphere were killing us just as effectively. *Ecology* became the new word. Pollution of the environment had to be stopped. Governments passed all sorts of laws. And the oceans, the rivers, the lakes and the air accumulated poisons.

When you and your generation sit in the plastic seats of power and influence about the end of this century, there will be a revival of these anxieties in much more virulent form. Then you will have your chance on behalf of mankind to find a final solution to the ills that accompanied you into the world.

Virgo also stands for work and workers. Pluto's passage through the Sign saw the beginning of the end of exploitation: employees began to feel their power, flex their industrial muscles, demand, picket, strike. Servants disappeared. And the Third World nations forced their way onto the international scene, determined to secure recognition and equal opportunity, even if it took force and disruption.

In accord with Pluto's extreme nature, lawlessness in pernicious ways such as skyjacking, international kidnapping, parapolitical violence and murder, drug pushing, built-in obsolescence, campus revolutions, all made a bewildered world wonder—what comes next?

PLUTO IN LIBRA (1972—1983)

This generation is being born at a time when the world's haves and have-nots are confronting each other in surprisingly reversed situations—a typical Plutonian effect. The most globally significant and eruptive of these (as the planet became established in Libra) was the oil embargo.

In late 1973 and early 1974, the Arab oil-producing states raised the price of oil 400 percent, claiming they could not otherwise afford inflated Western prices for essential goods. Among the Western nations, crisis followed crisis year after year as governments battled to right the disastrous imbalances in their finances that this sudden action had caused.

Libra is the Sign of balance; its symbol is the Scales; it stands for justice through equality. It is the Sign of peace, but also the Sign of war and aggression, which are often thought necessary to correct injustice and restore a workable harmony.

Pluto is the planet of violent extremes marking the end of one phase and the beginning of another. It rules the underworld, the depths of the earth, the source of gold (finance) and oil. Through Libra, without taking sides, Pluto naturally strives to correct the balance by using the wealth tokens under its control.

The generation of children born with Pluto in Libra will embody the characteristic urge to restore equality wherever they may find it lacking. This will have a profound impact at the national and international levels when their generation assumes positions of power and influence in the world around the year 2016.

This generation will face tremendous problems (laws to enforce a world economy?), which may seem impossible of solution to the generations of today. But tomorrow's Pluto-in-Libra rulers will possess the consciousness to deal effectively with the consequences of these crises that began appearing in their world.

PLUTO IN SCORPIO (1984—1995)

During these eleven years when Pluto is in Scorpio, man will probably decide whether or not to wipe most of his kind off the face of the Earth.

Scorpio is the most destructive and cruelly unsentimental Sign of the Zodiac. Power and power alone counts here. Ultimate victory against any odds and at any price is the parapathetic drive. With Pluto, the planet of extremes and brand-new beginnings after sudden endin.s, the result seems almost a foregone conclusion.

Almost . . .

Scorpio is also the Sign that stands for man's ability, through courageous self-discipline, to gain power over himself. It is the Sign of the loftiest aspirations, as well as the lowest. Here alone can the soul soar through self-mastery to fantastic levels of consciousness, which may bring man to the start of the long-awaited Golden Age.

Pluto has the right transforming energy for this process. It is the planet of regeneration. Its extremes include death and rebirth. It also represents money and all the untapped resources lying deep in the earth, such as (perhaps) a new source of energy from the Earth's molten core.

With maturity of consciousness, Pluto in Scorpio can provide man with all the material means to bring about undreamed of social and economic reforms on a global scale. Then, perhaps, peace and goodwill on Earth may be more than a beautiful concept.

Children born with Pluto in Scorpio have the potential to reach such heights (or depths) of consciousness. They will begin taking their places in the seats of power around the year 2029. Their generation will be equipped in one way or another to deal with the aftermath of the crises born into the world with them.

PLANETARY

ASPECTS

Reading the Planetary Aspects (Yellow Tables) is the next step in constructing your AstroAnalysis.

You've already looked up the positions of all your planets on your birthday (Pink Tables) and have found the meanings of all those planetary positions. Now you can go deeper by discovering the all-important Planetary Aspects in your horoscope.

As the planets move around the Sun, they form different angles with the Sun and with each other. Planetary Aspects are the relationships and angles made by all the planets, with respect to the Earth. Each angle relationship has a meaning all its own. You will be able to tell at a glance whether the aspects between your planets are "good," "adverse," or "neutral."

A Note on Good *and* Bad

No characteristic in Astrology can be considered in isolation. We are not one-celled creatures reacting to one event. We are *individuals* because we are constantly responding to numerous events, and each response will condition every other response. No doubt about it, we are complex beings with intriguing personalities and fascinating dimensions to our behavior.

In Astrology, some planetary relationships cause stress, tension and unease. Others are smoother, easier vibrations, more harmoniously integrated energies. "Bad" aspects are the stress aspects, the struggle to grow and integrate conflicting forces and seemingly opposing facets of character. "Good" aspects are the stable planetary relationships, the clear-flowing, easy-to-combine energies.

All the energies flow and work together to produce one whole human being. Some lives are filled with struggle, turmoil and conflict. Others are joyous, easy and beneficent. Good aspects and adverse aspects *together* are the creative raw material of human personality and spiritual growth.

Too many good aspects can produce the sort of person who misses out on life; everything comes too easily. Inner development is lacking because there seems to be no impetus, no need to try—nothing to strive for, nothing to overcome. Adverse aspects provide the catalyst for the strengthening of fiber. The most successful people, people who transform their lives, are rarely those whose charts are too "easy." So be thankful if you find a few adverse aspects.

Whatever your Sun Sign is, look up the Table for that particular Sign. All the other planets are listed in the first column, beginning with the Moon. Across the top of the table you'll find all 12 Signs of the Zodiac. To find the aspect of any planet to your Sun, look under the position of the planet and read "G" for *Good*, "A" for *Adverse* and "N" for *Neutral*.

Then turn to the following pages headed *Sun and Moon, Sun and Venus, Sun and Mars,* etc., and read the meanings of all the aspects. Go back to the Tables and do exactly the same for all the other planets in their Signs—Moon, Mercury, Venus, Mars, etc.

SUN IN ARIES

	ARIES	TAURUS	GEMINI	CANCER	LEO	VIRGO	LIBRA	SCORPIO	SAGITT.	CAPRICORN	AQUARIUS	PISCES
MOON	G	N	G	A	G	N	A	N	G	A	G	N
MERCURY	G	N	G	A	G	N	A	N	G	A	G	N
VENUS	G	N	G	A	G	N	A	N	G	A	G	N
MARS	A⁻	N	G	A	G	N	A	N	G	A	G	N
JUPITER	G	N	G	A	G	N	A	N	G	A	G	N
SATURN	A	N	G	A	G	N	A	N	G	A	G	N
URANUS	A	N	G	A	G	N	A	N	G	A	G	N
NEPTUNE	A	N	G	A	G	N	A	N	G	A	G	N
PLUTO	A	N	G	A	G	N	A	N	G	A	G	N

G = GOOD   N = NEUTRAL   A = ADVERSE

SUN IN TAURUS

	ARIES	TAURUS	GEMINI	CANCER	LEO	VIRGO	LIBRA	SCORPIO	SAGITT.	CAPRICORN	AQUARIUS	PISCES
MOON	N	G	N	G	A	G	N	A	N	G	A	G
MERCURY	N	G	N	G	A	G	N	A	N	G	A	G
VENUS	N	G	N	G	A	G	N	A	N	G	A	G
MARS	N	A	N	G	A	G	N	A	N	G	A	G
JUPITER	N	G	N	G	A	G	N	A	N	G	A	G
SATURN	N	A	N	G	A	G	N	A	N	G	A	G
URANUS	N	A	N	G	A	G	N	A	N	G	A	G
NEPTUNE	N	A	N	G	A	G	N	A	N	G	A	G
PLUTO	N	A	N	G	A	G	N	A	N	G	A	G

G = GOOD   N = NEUTRAL   A = ADVERSE

SUN IN GEMINI

	ARIES	TAURUS	GEMINI	CANCER	LEO	VIRGO	LIBRA	SCORPIO	SAGITT.	CAPRICORN	AQUARIUS	PISCES
MOON	G	N	G	N	G	A	G	N	A	N	G	A
MERCURY	N	N	N	N	N	N	N	N	N	N	N	N
VENUS	G	N	G	N	G	A	G	N	A	N	G	A
MARS	G	N	A	N	G	A	G	N	A	N	G	A
JUPITER	G	N	G	N	G	A	G	N	A	N	G	A
SATURN	G	N	A	N	G	A	G	N	A	N	G	A
URANUS	G	N	A	N	G	A	G	N	A	N	G	A
NEPTUNE	G	N	A	N	G	A	G	N	A	N	G	A
PLUTO	G	N	A	N	G	A	G	N	A	N	G	A

G = GOOD   N = NEUTRAL   A = ADVERSE

SUN IN CANCER

♋	ARIES	TAURUS	GEMINI	CANCER	LEO	VIRGO	LIBRA	SCORPIO	SAGITT.	CAPRICORN	AQUARIUS	PISCES
MOON	A	G	N	G	N	G	A	G	N	A	N	G
MERCURY	N	N	N	N	N	N	N	N	N	N	N	N
VENUS	A	G	G	N	G	G	A	G	N	A	N	G
MARS	A	G	N	A	N	G	A	G	N	A	N	G
JUPITER	A	G	N	G	N	G	A	G	N	A	N	G
SATURN	A	G	N	A	N	G	A	G	N	A	N	G
URANUS	A	G	N	A	N	G	A	G	N	A	N	G
NEPTUNE	A	G	N	A	N	G	A	G	N	A	N	G
PLUTO	A	G	N	A	N	G	A	G	N	A	N	G

G = GOOD   N = NEUTRAL   A = ADVERSE

SUN IN LEO

♌	ARIES	TAURUS	GEMINI	CANCER	LEO	VIRGO	LIBRA	SCORPIO	SAGITT.	CAPRICORN	AQUARIUS	PISCES
MOON	G	A	G	N	G	N	G	A	G	N	A	N
MERCURY	N	N	N	N	N	N	N	N	N	N	N	N
VENUS	G	A	G	N	G	N	G	A	G	N	A	N
MARS	G	A	G	N	A	N	G	A	G	N	A	N
JUPITER	G	A	G	N	G	N	G	A	G	N	A	N
SATURN	G	A	G	N	A	N	G	A	G	N	A	N
URANUS	G	A	G	N	A	N	G	A	G	N	A	N
NEPTUNE	G	A	G	N	A	N	G	A	G	N	A	N
PLUTO	G	A	G	N	A	N	G	A	G	N	A	N

G = GOOD   N = NEUTRAL   A = ADVERSE

SUN IN VIRGO

♍	ARIES	TAURUS	GEMINI	CANCER	LEO	VIRGO	LIBRA	SCORPIO	SAGITT.	CAPRICORN	AQUARIUS	PISCES
MOON	N	G	A	G	N	G	N	G	A	G	N	A
MERCURY	N	N	N	N	N	N	N	N	N	N	N	N
VENUS	N	G	A	G	N	G	N	G	A	G	N	A
MARS	N	G	A	G	N	A	N	G	A	G	N	A
JUPITER	N	G	A	G	N	G	N	G	A	G	N	A
SATURN	N	G	A	G	N	A	N	G	A	G	N	A
URANUS	N	G	A	G	N	A	N	G	A	G	N	A
NEPTUNE	N	G	A	G	N	A	N	G	A	G	N	A
PLUTO	N	G	A	G	N	A	N	G	A	G	N	A

G = GOOD   N = NEUTRAL   A = ADVERSE

SUN IN LIBRA

	ARIES	TAURUS	GEMINI	CANCER	LEO	VIRGO	LIBRA	SCORPIO	SAGITT.	CAPRICORN	AQUARIUS	PISCES
MOON	A	N	G	A	G	N	G	N	G	A	G	N
MERCURY	N	N	N	N	N	N	N	N	N	N	N	N
VENUS	A	N	G	A	G	N	G	N	G	A	G	N
MARS	A	N	G	A	G	N	A	N	G	A	G	N
JUPITER	A	N	G	A	G	N	G	N	G	A	G	N
SATURN	A	N	G	A	G	N	A	N	G	A	G	N
URANUS	A	N	G	A	G	N	A	N	G	A	G	N
NEPTUNE	A	N	G	A	G	N	A	N	G	A	G	N
PLUTO	A	N	G	A	G	N	A	N	G	A	G	N

G = GOOD   N = NEUTRAL   A = ADVERSE

SUN IN SCORPIO

	ARIES	TAURUS	GEMINI	CANCER	LEO	VIRGO	LIBRA	SCORPIO	SAGITT.	CAPRICORN	AQUARIUS	PISCES
MOON	N	A	N	G	A	G	N	G	N	G	A	G
MERCURY	N	N	N	N	N	N	N	N	N	N	N	N
VENUS	N	A	N	G	A	G	N	G	N	G	A	G
MARS	N	A	N	G	A	G	N	A	N	G	A	G
JUPITER	N	A	N	G	A	G	N	G	N	G	A	G
SATURN	N	A	N	G	A	G	N	A	N	G	A	G
URANUS	N	A	N	G	A	G	N	A	N	G	A	G
NEPTUNE	N	A	N	G	A	G	N	A	N	G	A	G
PLUTO	N	A	N	G	A	G	N	A	N	G	A	G

G = GOOD   N = NEUTRAL   A = ADVERSE

SUN IN SAGITTARIUS

	ARIES	TAURUS	GEMINI	CANCER	LEO	VIRGO	LIBRA	SCORPIO	SAGITT.	CAPRICORN	AQUARIUS	PISCES
MOON	G	N	A	N	G	A	G	N	G	N	G	A
MERCURY	N	N	N	N	N	N	N	N	N	N	N	N
VENUS	G	N	A	N	G	A	G	N	G	N	G	A
MARS	G	N	A	N	G	A	G	N	A	N	G	A
JUPITER	G	N	A	N	G	A	G	N	G	N	G	A
SATURN	G	N	A	N	G	A	G	N	A	N	G	A
URANUS	G	N	A	N	G	A	G	N	A	N	G	A
NEPTUNE	G	N	A	N	G	A	G	N	A	N	G	A
PLUTO	G	N	A	N	G	A	G	N	A	N	G	A

G = GOOD   N = NEUTRAL   A = ADVERSE

SUN IN CAPRICORN

	ARIES	TAURUS	GEMINI	CANCER	LEO	VIRGO	LIBRA	SCORPIO	SAGITT.	CAPRICORN	AQUARIUS	PISCES
MOON	A	G	N	A	N	G	A	G	N	G	N	G
MERCURY	N	N	N	N	N	N	N	N	N	N	N	N
VENUS	A	G	N	A	N	G	A	G	N	G	N	G
MARS	A	G	N	A	N	G	A	G	N	A	N	G
JUPITER	A	G	N	A	N	G	A	G	N	G	N	G
SATURN	A	G	N	A	N	G	A	G	N	A	N	G
URANUS	A	G	N	A	N	G	A	G	N	A	N	G
NEPTUNE	A	G	N	A	N	G	A	G	N	A	N	G
PLUTO	A	G	N	A	N	G	A	G	N	A	N	G

G = GOOD   N = NEUTRAL   A = ADVERSE

SUN IN AQUARIUS

	ARIES	TAURUS	GEMINI	CANCER	LEO	VIRGO	LIBRA	SCORPIO	SAGITT.	CAPRICORN	AQUARIUS	PISCES
MOON	G	A	G	N	A	N	G	A	G	N	G	N
MERCURY	N	N	N	N	N	N	N	N	N	N	N	N
VENUS	G	A	G	N	A	N	G	A	G	N	G	N
MARS	G	A	G	N	A	N	G	A	G	N	A	N
JUPITER	G	A	G	N	A	N	G	A	G	N	G	N
SATURN	G	A	G	N	A	N	G	A	G	N	A	N
URANUS	G	A	G	N	A	N	G	A	G	N	A	N
NEPTUNE	G	A	G	N	A	N	G	A	G	N	A	N
PLUTO	G	A	G	N	A	N	G	A	G	N	A	N

G = GOOD   N = NEUTRAL   A = ADVERSE

SUN IN PISCES

	ARIES	TAURUS	GEMINI	CANCER	LEO	VIRGO	LIBRA	SCORPIO	SAGITT.	CAPRICORN	AQUARIUS	PISCES
MOON	N	G	A	G	N	A	N	G	A	G	N	G
MERCURY	N	N	N	N	N	N	N	N	N	N	N	N
VENUS	N	G	A	G	N	A	N	G	A	G	N	G
MARS	N	G	A	G	N	A	N	G	A	G	N	A
JUPITER	N	G	A	G	N	A	N	G	A	G	N	G
SATURN	N	G	A	G	N	A	N	G	A	G	N	A
URANUS	N	G	A	G	N	A	N	G	A	G	N	A
NEPTUNE	N	G	A	G	N	A	N	G	A	G	N	A
PLUTO	N	G	A	G	N	A	N	G	A	G	N	A

G = GOOD   N = NEUTRAL   A = ADVERSE

MOON IN ARIES

☽ ♈	ARIES	TAURUS	GEMINI	CANCER	LEO	VIRGO	LIBRA	SCORPIO	SAGITT.	CAPRICORN	AQUARIUS	PISCES
SUN	G	N	G	A	G	N	A	N	G	A	G	N
MERCURY	G	N	G	A	G	N	A	N	G	A	G	N
VENUS	G	N	G	A	G	N	A	N	G	A	G	N
MARS	A	N	G	A	G	N	A	N	G	A	G	N
JUPITER	G	N	G	A	G	N	A	N	G	A	G	N
SATURN	A	N	G	A	G	N	A	N	G	A	G	N
URANUS	A	N	G	A	G	N	A	N	G	A	G	N
NEPTUNE	A	N	G	A	G	N	A	N	G	A	G	N
PLUTO	A	N	G	A	G	N	A	N	G	A	G	N

G = GOOD   N = NEUTRAL   A = ADVERSE

MOON IN TAURUS

☽ ♉	ARIES	TAURUS	GEMINI	CANCER	LEO	VIRGO	LIBRA	SCORPIO	SAGITT.	CAPRICORN	AQUARIUS	PISCES
SUN	N	G	N	G	A	G	N	A	N	G	A	G
MERCURY	N	G	N	G	A	G	N	A	N	G	A	G
VENUS	N	G	N	G	A	G	N	A	N	G	A	G
MARS	N	A	N	G	A	G	N	A	N	G	A	G
JUPITER	N	G	N	G	A	G	N	A	N	G	A	G
SATURN	N	A	N	G	A	G	N	A	N	G	A	G
URANUS	N	A	N	G	A	G	N	A	N	G	A	G
NEPTUNE	N	A	N	G	A	G	N	A	N	G	A	G
PLUTO	N	A	N	G	A	G	N	A	N	G	A	G

G = GOOD   N = NEUTRAL   A = ADVERSE

MOON IN GEMINI

☽ ♊	ARIES	TAURUS	GEMINI	CANCER	LEO	VIRGO	LIBRA	SCORPIO	SAGITT.	CAPRICORN	AQUARIUS	PISCES
SUN	G	N	G	N	G	A	G	N	A	N	G	A
MERCURY	G	N	G	N	G	A	G	N	A	N	G	A
VENUS	G	N	G	N	G	A	G	N	A	N	G	A
MARS	G	N	A	N	G	A	G	N	A	N	G	A
JUPITER	G	N	G	N	G	A	G	N	A	N	G	A
SATURN	G	N	A	N	G	A	G	N	A	N	G	A
URANUS	G	N	A	N	G	A	G	N	A	N	G	A
NEPTUNE	G	N	A	N	G	A	G	N	A	N	G	A
PLUTO	G	N	A	N	G	A	G	N	A	N	G	A

G = GOOD   N = NEUTRAL   A = ADVERSE

MOON IN CANCER

	ARIES	TAURUS	GEMINI	CANCER	LEO	VIRGO	LIBRA	SCORPIO	SAGITT.	CAPRICORN	AQUARIUS	PISCES
SUN	A	G	N	G	N	G	A	G	N	A	N	G
MERCURY	A	G	N	G	N	G	A	G	N	A	N	G
VENUS	A	G	N	G	N	G	A	G	N	A	N	G
MARS	A	G	N	A	N	G	A	G	N	A	N	G
JUPITER	A	G	N	G	N	G	A	G	N	A	N	G
SATURN	A	G	N	A	N	G	A	G	N	A	N	G
URANUS	A	G	N	A	N	G	A	G	N	A	N	G
NEPTUNE	A	G	N	A	N	G	A	G	N	A	N	G
PLUTO	A	G	N	A	N	G	A	G	N	A	N	G

G = GOOD   N = NEUTRAL   A = ADVERSE

MOON IN LEO

	ARIES	TAURUS	GEMINI	CANCER	LEO	VIRGO	LIBRA	SCORPIO	SAGITT.	CAPRICORN	AQUARIUS	PISCES
SUN	G	A	G	N	G	N	G	A	G	N	A	N
MERCURY	G	A	G	N	G	N	G	A	G	N	A	N
VENUS	G	A	G	N	G	N	G	A	G	N	A	N
MARS	G	A	G	N	A	N	G	A	G	N	A	N
JUPITER	G	A	G	N	G	N	G	A	G	N	A	N
SATURN	G	A	G	N	A	N	G	A	G	N	A	N
URANUS	G	A	G	N	A	N	G	A	G	N	A	N
NEPTUNE	G	A	G	N	A	N	G	A	G	N	A	N
PLUTO	G	A	G	N	A	N	G	A	G	N	A	N

G = GOOD   N = NEUTRAL   A = ADVERSE

MOON IN VIRGO

	ARIES	TAURUS	GEMINI	CANCER	LEO	VIRGO	LIBRA	SCORPIO	SAGITT.	CAPRICORN	AQUARIUS	PISCES
SUN	N	G	A	G	N	G	N	G	A	G	N	A
MERCURY	N	G	A	G	N	G	N	G	A	G	N	A
VENUS	N	G	A	G	N	G	N	G	A	G	N	A
MARS	N	G	A	G	N	A	N	G	A	G	N	A
JUPITER	N	G	A	N	N	G	N	G	A	G	N	A
SATURN	N	G	A	G	N	A	N	G	A	G	N	A
URANUS	N	G	A	G	N	A	N	G	A	G	N	A
NEPTUNE	N	G	A	G	N	A	N	G	A	G	N	A
PLUTO	N	G	A	G	N	A	N	G	A	G	N	A

G = GOOD   N = NEUTRAL   A = ADVERSE

MOON IN LIBRA

☽ ♎	ARIES	TAURUS	GEMINI	CANCER	LEO	VIRGO	LIBRA	SCORPIO	SAGITT.	CAPRICORN	AQUARIUS	PISCES
SUN	A	N	G	A	G	N	G	N	G	A	G	N
MERCURY	A	N	G	A	G	N	G	N	G	A	G	N
VENUS	A	N	G	A	G	N	G	N	G	A	G	N
MARS	A	N	G	A	G	N	A	N	G	A	G	N
JUPITER	A	N	G	A	G	N	A	N	G	A	G	N
SATURN	A	N	G	A	G	N	A	N	G	A	G	N
URANUS	A	N	G	A	G	N	A	N	G	A	G	N
NEPTUNE	A	N	G	A	G	N	A	N	G	A	G	N
PLUTO	A	N	G	A	G	N	A	N	G	A	G	N

G = GOOD   N = NEUTRAL   A = ADVERSE

MOON IN SCORPIO

☽ ♏	ARIES	TAURUS	GEMINI	CANCER	LEO	VIRGO	LIBRA	SCORPIO	SAGITT.	CAPRICORN	AQUARIUS	PISCES
SUN	N	A	N	G	A	G	N	G	N	G	A	G
MERCURY	N	A	N	G	A	G	N	G	N	G	A	G
VENUS	N	A	N	G	A	G	N	G	N	G	A	G
MARS	N	A	N	G	A	G	N	A	N	G	A	G
JUPITER	N	A	N	G	A	G	N	G	N	G	A	G
SATURN	N	A	N	G	A	G	N	A	N	G	A	G
URANUS	N	A	N	G	A	G	N	A	N	G	A	G
NEPTUNE	N	A	N	G	A	G	N	A	N	G	A	G
PLUTO	N	A	N	G	A	G	N	A	N	G	A	G

G = GOOD   N = NEUTRAL   A = ADVERSE

MOON IN SAGITTARIUS

☽ ♐	ARIES	TAURUS	GEMINI	CANCER	LEO	VIRGO	LIBRA	SCORPIO	SAGITT.	CAPRICORN	AQUARIUS	PISCES
SUN	G	N	A	N	G	A	G	N	G	N	G	A
MERCURY	G	N	A	N	G	A	G	N	G	N	G	A
VENUS	G	N	A	N	G	A	G	N	G	N	G	A
MARS	G	N	A	N	G	A	G	N	A	N	G	A
JUPITER	G	N	A	N	G	A	G	N	G	N	G	A
SATURN	G	N	A	N	G	A	G	N	A	N	G	A
URANUS	G	N	A	N	G	A	G	N	A	N	G	A
NEPTUNE	G	N	A	N	G	A	G	N	A	N	G	A
PLUTO	G	N	A	N	G	A	G	N	A	N	G	A

G = GOOD   N = NEUTRAL   A = ADVERSE

MOON IN CAPRICORN

	ARIES	TAURUS	GEMINI	CANCER	LEO	VIRGO	LIBRA	SCORPIO	SAGITT.	CAPRICORN	AQUARIUS	PISCES
SUN	A	G	N	A	N	G	A	G	N	G	N	G
MERCURY	A	G	N	A	N	G	A	G	N	G	N	G
VENUS	A	G	N	A	N	G	A	G	N	G	N	G
MARS	A	G	N	A	N	G	A	G	N	A	N	G
JUPITER	A	G	N	A	N	G	A	G	N	G	N	G
SATURN	A	G	N	A	N	G	A	G	N	A	N	G
URANUS	A	G	N	A	N	G	A	G	N	G	N	G
NEPTUNE	A	G	N	A	N	G	A	G	N	A	N	G
PLUTO	A	G	N	A	N	G	A	G	N	A	N	G

G = GOOD   N = NEUTRAL   A = ADVERSE

MOON IN AQUARIUS

	ARIES	TAURUS	GEMINI	CANCER	LEO	VIRGO	LIBRA	SCORPIO	SAGITT.	CAPRICORN	AQUARIUS	PISCES
SUN	G	A	G	N	A	N	G	A	G	N	G	N
MERCURY	G	A	G	N	A	N	G	A	G	N	G	N
VENUS	G	A	G	N	A	N	G	A	G	N	G	N
MARS	G	A	G	N	A	N	G	A	G	N	A	N
JUPITER	G	A	G	N	A	N	G	A	G	N	G	N
SATURN	G	A	G	N	A	N	G	A	G	N	A	N
URANUS	G	A	G	N	A	N	G	A	G	N	A	N
NEPTUNE	G	A	G	N	A	N	G	A	G	N	A	N
PLUTO	G	A	G	N	A	N	G	A	G	N	A	N

G = GOOD   N = NEUTRAL   A = ADVERSE

MOON IN PISCES

	ARIES	TAURUS	GEMINI	CANCER	LEO	VIRGO	LIBRA	SCORPIO	SAGITT.	CAPRICORN	AQUARIUS	PISCES
SUN	N	G	A	G	N	A	N	G	A	G	N	G
MERCURY	N	G	A	G	N	A	N	G	A	G	N	G
VENUS	N	G	A	G	N	A	N	G	A	G	N	G
MARS	N	G	A	G	N	A	N	G	A	G	N	A
UPITER	N	G	A	G	N	A	N	G	A	G	N	G
SATURN	N	G	A	G	N	A	N	G	A	G	N	A
URANUS	N	G	A	G	N	A	N	G	A	G	N	A
NEPTUNE	N	G	A	G	N	A	N	G	A	G	N	A
PLUTO	N	G	A	G	N	A	N	G	A	G	N	A

G = GOOD   N = NEUTRAL   A = ADVERSE

MERCURY IN ARIES

☿ ♈	ARIES	TAURUS	GEMINI	CANCER	LEO	VIRGO	LIBRA	SCORPIO	SAGITT.	CAPRICORN	AQUARIUS	PISCES
SUN	N	N	N	N	N	N	N	N	N	N	N	N
MOON	G	N	G	A	G	N	A	N	G	A	G	N
VENUS	G	N	G	A	G	N	A	N	G	A	G	N
MARS	A	N	G	A	G	N	A	N	G	A	G	N
JUPITER	G	N	G	A	G	N	A	N	G	A	G	N
SATURN	A	N	G	A	G	N	A	N	G	A	G	N
URANUS	A	N	G	A	G	N	A	N	G	A	G	N
NEPTUNE	A	N	G	A	G	N	A	N	G	A	G	N
PLUTO	A	N	G	A	G	N	A	N	G	A	G	N

G = GOOD   N = NEUTRAL   A = ADVERSE

MERCURY IN TAURUS

☿ ♉	ARIES	TAURUS	GEMINI	CANCER	LEO	VIRGO	LIBRA	SCORPIO	SAGITT.	CAPRICORN	AQUARIUS	PISCES
SUN	N	N	N	N	N	N	N	N	N	N	N	N
MOON	N	G	A	G	A	G	N	A	N	G	A	G
VENUS	N	G	N	G	A	G	N	A	N	G	A	G
MARS	N	A	N	G	A	G	N	A	N	G	A	G
JUPITER	N	G	N	G	A	G	N	A	N	G	A	G
SATURN	N	A	N	G	A	G	N	A	N	G	A	G
URANUS	N	A	N	G	A	G	N	A	N	G	A	G
NEPTUNE	N	A	N	G	A	G	N	A	N	G	A	G
PLUTO	N	A	N	G	A	G	N	A	N	G	A	G

G = GOOD   N = NEUTRAL   A = ADVERSE

MERCURY IN GEMINI

☿ ♊	ARIES	TAURUS	GEMINI	CANCER	LEO	VIRGO	LIBRA	SCORPIO	SAGITT.	CAPRICORN	AQUARIUS	PISCES
SUN	N	N	N	N	N	N	N	N	N	N	N	N
MOON	G	N	G	N	G	A	G	N	A	N	G	A
VENUS	G	N	G	N	G	A	G	N	A	N	G	A
MARS	G	N	A	N	G	A	G	N	A	N	G	A
JUPITER	G	N	G	N	G	A	G	N	A	N	G	A
SATURN	G	N	A	N	G	A	G	N	A	N	G	A
URANUS	G	N	A	N	G	A	G	N	A	N	G	A
NEPTUNE	G	N	A	N	G	A	G	N	A	N	G	A
PLUTO	G	N	A	N	G	A	G	N	A	N	G	A

G = GOOD   N = NEUTRAL   A = ADVERSE

MERCURY IN CANCER

☿♋	ARIES	TAURUS	GEMINI	CANCER	LEO	VIRGO	LIBRA	SCORPIO	SAGITT.	CAPRICORN	AQUARIUS	PISCES
SUN	N	N	N	N	N	N	N	N	N	N	N	N
MOON	A	G	N	G	N	G	A	G	N	A	N	G
VENUS	A	G	N	G	N	G	A	G	N	A	N	G
MARS	A	G	N	A	N	G	A	G	N	A	N	G
JUPITER	A	G	N	G	N	G	A	G	N	A	N	G
SATURN	A	G	N	A	N	G	A	G	N	A	N	G
URANUS	A	G	N	A	N	G	A	G	N	A	N	G
NEPTUNE	A	G	N	A	N	G	A	G	N	A	N	G
PLUTO	A	G	N	A	N	G	A	G	N	A	N	G

G = GOOD   N = NEUTRAL   A = ADVERSE

MERCURY IN LEO

☿♌	ARIES	TAURUS	GEMINI	CANCER	LEO	VIRGO	LIBRA	SCORPIO	SAGITT.	CAPRICORN	AQUARIUS	PISCES
SUN	N	N	N	N	N	N	N	N	N	N	N	N
MOON	G	A	G	N	G	N	G	A	G	N	A	N
VENUS	G	A	G	N	G	N	G	A	G	N	A	N
MARS	G	A	G	N	A	N	G	A	G	N	A	N
JUPITER	G	A	G	N	G	N	G	A	G	N	A	N
SATURN	G	A	G	N	A	N	G	A	G	N	A	N
URANUS	G	A	G	N	A	N	G	A	G	N	A	N
NEPTUNE	G	A	G	N	A	N	G	A	G	N	A	N
PLUTO	G	A	G	N	A	N	G	A	G	N	A	N

G = GOOD   N = NEUTRAL   A = ADVERSE

MERCURY IN VIRGO

☿♍	ARIES	TAURUS	GEMINI	CANCER	LEO	VIRGO	LIBRA	SCORPIO	SAGITT.	CAPRICORN	AQUARIUS	PISCES
SUN	N	N	N	N	N	N	N	N	N	N	N	N
MOON	N	G	A	G	N	G	N	G	A	G	N	A
VENUS	N	G	A	G	N	G	N	G	A	G	N	A
MARS	N	G	A	G	N	A	N	G	A	G	N	A
JUPITER	N	G	A	G	N	G	N	G	A	G	N	A
SATURN	N	G	A	G	N	A	N	G	A	G	N	A
URANUS	N	G	A	G	N	A	N	G	A	G	N	A
NEPTUNE	N	G	A	G	N	A	N	G	A	G	N	A
PLUTO	N	G	A	G	N	A	N	G	A	G	N	A

G = GOOD   N = NEUTRAL   A = ADVERSE

MERCURY IN LIBRA

☿ ♄	ARIES	TAURUS	GEMINI	CANCER	LEO	VIRGO	LIBRA	SCORPIO	SAGITT.	CAPRICORN	AQUARIUS	PISCES
SUN	N	N	N	N	N	N	N	N	N	N	N	N
MOON	A	N	G	A	G	N	G	N	G	A	G	N
VENUS	A	N	G	A	G	N	G	N	G	A	G	N
MARS	A	N	G	A	G	N	A	N	G	A	G	N
JUPITER	A	N	G	A	G	N	G	N	G	A	G	N
SATURN	A	N	G	A	G	N	A	N	G	A	G	N
URANUS	A	N	G	A	G	N	A	N	G	A	G	N
NEPTUNE	A	N	G	A	G	N	A	N	G	A	G	N
PLUTO	A	N	G	A	G	N	A	N	G	A	G	N

G = GOOD   N = NEUTRAL   A = ADVERSE

MERCURY IN SCORPIO

☿ ♏	ARIES	TAURUS	GEMINI	CANCER	LEO	VIRGO	LIBRA	SCORPIO	SAGITT.	CAPRICORN	AQUARIUS	PISCES
SUN	N	N	N	N	N	N	N	N	N	N	N	N
MOON	N	A	N	G	A	G	N	G	N	G	A	G
VENUS	N	A	N	G	A	G	N	G	N	G	A	G
MARS	N	A	N	G	A	G	N	A	N	G	A	G
JUPITER	N	A	N	G	A	G	N	G	N	G	A	G
SATURN	N	A	N	G	A	G	N	A	N	G	A	G
URANUS	N	A	N	G	A	G	N	A	N	G	A	G
NEPTUNE	N	A	N	G	A	G	N	A	N	G	A	G
PLUTO	N	A	N	G	A	G	N	A	N	G	A	G

G = GOOD   N = NEUTRAL   A = ADVERSE

MERCURY IN SAGITTARIUS

☿ ♐	ARIES	TAURUS	GEMINI	CANCER	LEO	VIRGO	LIBRA	SCORPIO	SAGITT.	CAPRICORN	AQUARIUS	PISCES
SUN	N	N	N	N	N	N	N	N	N	N	N	N
MOON	G	N	A	N	G	A	G	N	G	N	G	A
VENUS	G	N	A	N	G	A	G	N	G	N	G	A
MARS	G	N	A	N	G	A	G	N	A	N	G	A
JUPITER	G	N	A	N	G	A	G	N	G	N	G	A
SATURN	G	N	A	N	G	A	G	N	A	N	G	A
URANUS	G	N	A	N	G	A	G	N	A	N	G	A
NEPTUNE	G	N	A	N	G	A	G	N	A	N	G	A
PLUTO	G	N	A	N	G	A	G	N	A	N	G	A

G = GOOD   N = NEUTRAL   A = ADVERSE

MERCURY IN CAPRICORN

♍♑	ARIES	TAURUS	GEMINI	CANCER	LEO	VIRGO	LIBRA	SCORPIO	SAGITT.	CAPRICORN	AQUARIUS	PISCES
SUN	N	N	N	N	N	N	N	N	N	N	N	N
MOON	A	G	N	A	N	G	A	G	N	G	N	G
VENUS	A	G	N	A	N	G	A	G	N	G	N	G
MARS	A	G	N	A	N	G	A	G	N	A	N	G
JUPITER	A	G	N	A	N	G	A	G	N	G	N	G
SATURN	A	G	N	A	N	G	A	G	N	A	N	G
URANUS	A	G	N	A	N	G	A	G	N	A	N	G
NEPTUNE	A	G	N	A	N	G	A	G	N	A	N	G
PLUTO	A	G	N	A	N	G	A	G	N	A	N	G

G = GOOD   N = NEUTRAL   A = ADVERSE

MERCURY IN AQUARIUS

☿♒	ARIES	TAURUS	GEMINI	CANCER	LEO	VIRGO	LIBRA	SCORPIO	SAGITT.	CAPRICORN	AQUARIUS	PISCES
SUN	N	N	N	N	N	N	N	N	N	N	N	N
MOON	G	A	G	N	A	N	G	A	G	N	G	N
VENUS	G	A	G	N	A	N	G	A	G	N	G	N
MARS	G	A	G	N	A	N	G	A	G	N	A	N
JUPITER	G	A	G	N	A	N	G	A	G	N	G	N
SATURN	G	A	G	N	A	N	G	A	G	N	A	N
URANUS	G	A	G	N	A	N	G	A	G	N	A	N
NEPTUNE	G	A	G	N	A	N	G	A	G	N	A	N
PLUTO	G	A	G	N	A	N	G	A	G	N	A	N

G = GOOD   N = NEUTRAL   A = ADVERSE

MERCURY IN PISCES

☿♓	ARIES	TAURUS	GEMINI	CANCER	LEO	VIRGO	LIBRA	SCORPIO	SAGITT.	CAPRICORN	AQUARIUS	PISCES
SUN	N	N	N	N	N	N	N	N	N	N	N	N
MOON	N	G	A	G	N	A	N	G	A	G	N	G
VENUS	N	G	A	G	N	A	N	G	A	G	N	G
MARS	N	G	A	G	N	A	N	G	A	G	N	A
JUPITER	N	G	A	G	N	A	N	G	A	G	N	G
SATURN	N	G	A	G	N	A	N	G	A	G	N	A
URANUS	N	G	A	G	N	A	N	G	A	G	N	A
NEPTUNE	N	G	A	G	N	A	N	G	A	G	N	A
PLUTO	N	G	A	G	N	A	N	G	A	G	N	A

G = GOOD   N = NEUTRAL   A = ADVERSE

VENUS IN ARIES

♀ ♈	ARIES	TAURUS	GEMINI	CANCER	LEO	VIRGO	LIBRA	SCORPIO	SAGITT.	CAPRICORN	AQUARIUS	PISCES
SUN	G	N	G	A	G	N	A	N	G	A	G	N
MOON	G	N	G	A	G	N	A	N	G	A	G	N
MERCURY	G	N	G	A	G	N	A	N	G	A	G	N
MARS	A	N	G	A	G	N	A	N	G	A	G	N
JUPITER	G	N	G	A	G	N	A	N	G	A	G	N
SATURN	A	N	G	A	G	N	A	N	G	A	G	N
URANUS	A	N	G	A	G	N	A	N	G	A	G	N
NEPTUNE	A	N	G	A	G	N	A	N	G	A	G	N
PLUTO	A	N	G	A	G	N	A	N	G	A	G	N

G = GOOD   N = NEUTRAL   A = ADVERSE

VENUS IN TAURUS

♀ ♉	ARIES	TAURUS	GEMINI	CANCER	LEO	VIRGO	LIBRA	SCORPIO	SAGITT.	CAPRICORN	AQUARIUS	PISCES
SUN	N	G	N	G	A	G	N	A	N	G	A	G
MOON	N	G	N	G	A	G	N	A	N	G	A	G
MERCURY	N	G	N	G	A	G	N	A	N	G	A	G
MARS	N	A	N	G	A	G	N	A	N	G	A	G
JUPITER	N	G	N	G	A	G	N	A	N	G	A	G
SATURN	N	A	N	G	A	G	N	A	N	G	A	G
URANUS	N	A	N	G	A	G	N	A	N	G	A	G
NEPTUNE	N	A	N	G	A	G	N	A	N	G	A	G
PLUTO	N	A	N	G	A	G	N	A	N	G	A	G

G = GOOD   N = NEUTRAL   A = ADVERSE

VENUS IN GEMINI

♀ ♊	ARIES	TAURUS	GEMINI	CANCER	LEO	VIRGO	LIBRA	SCORPIO	SAGITT.	CAPRICORN	AQUARIUS	PISCES
SUN	G	N	G	N	G	A	G	N	A	N	G	A
MOON	G	N	G	N	G	A	G	N	A	N	G	A
MERCURY	G	N	G	N	G	A	G	N	A	N	G	A
MARS	G	N	A	N	G	A	G	N	A	N	G	A
JUPITER	G	N	G	N	G	A	G	N	A	N	G	A
SATURN	G	N	A	N	G	A	G	N	A	N	G	A
URANUS	G	N	A	N	G	A	G	N	A	N	G	A
NEPTUNE	G	N	A	N	G	A	G	N	A	N	G	A
PLUTO	G	N	A	N	G	A	G	N	A	N	G	A

G = GOOD   N = NEUTRAL   A = ADVERSE

VENUS IN CANCER

♀♋	ARIES	TAURUS	GEMINI	CANCER	LEO	VIRGO	LIBRA	SCORPIO	SAGITT.	CAPRICORN	AQUARIUS	PISCES
SUN	A	G	N	G	N	G	A	G	N	A	N	G
MOON	A	G	N	G	N	G	A	G	N	A	N	G
MERCURY	A	G	N	G	N	G	A	G	N	A	N	G
MARS	A	G	N	A	N	G	A	G	N	A	N	G
JUPITER	A	G	N	G	A	G	A	G	N	A	N	G
SATURN	A	G	N	A	N	G	A	G	N	A	N	G
URANUS	A	G	N	A	N	G	A	G	N	A	N	G
NEPTUNE	A	G	N	A	N	G	A	G	N	A	N	G
PLUTO	A	G	N	A	N	G	A	G	N	A	N	G

G = GOOD   N = NEUTRAL   A = ADVERSE

VENUS IN LEO

♀♌	ARIES	TAURUS	GEMINI	CANCER	LEO	VIRGO	LIBRA	SCORPIO	SAGITT.	CAPRICORN	AQUARIUS	PISCES
SUN	G	A	G	N	G	N	G	A	G	N	A	N
MOON	G	A	G	N	G	N	G	A	G	N	A	N
MERCURY	G	A	G	N	G	N	G	A	G	N	A	N
MARS	G	A	G	N	A	N	G	A	G	N	A	N
JUPITER	G	A	G	N	G	N	G	A	G	N	A	N
SATURN	G	A	G	N	A	N	G	A	G	N	A	N
URANUS	G	A	G	N	A	N	G	A	G	N	A	N
NEPTUNE	G	A	G	N	A	N	G	A	G	N	A	N
PLUTO	G	A	G	N	A	N	G	A	G	N	A	N

G = GOOD   N = NEUTRAL   A = ADVERSE

VENUS IN VIRGO

♀♍	ARIES	TAURUS	GEMINI	CANCER	LEO	VIRGO	LIBRA	SCORPIO	SAGITT.	CAPRICORN	AQUARIUS	PISCES
SUN	N	G	A	G	N	G	N	G	A	G	N	A
MOON	N	G	A	G	N	G	N	G	A	G	N	A
MERCURY	N	G	A	G	N	G	N	G	A	G	N	N
MARS	N	G	A	G	N	A	N	G	A	G	N	A
JUPITER	N	G	A	G	N	G	N	G	A	G	N	A
SATURN	N	G	A	G	N	A	N	G	A	G	N	A
URANUS	N	G	A	G	N	A	N	G	A	G	N	A
NEPTUNE	N	G	A	G	N	A	N	G	A	G	N	A
PLUTO	N	G	A	G	N	A	N	G	A	G	N	A

G = GOOD   N = NEUTRAL   A = ADVERSE

VENUS IN LIBRA

♀ ♎	ARIES	TAURUS	GEMINI	CANCER	LEO	VIRGO	LIBRA	SCORPIO	SAGITT.	CAPRICORN	AQUARIUS	PISCES
SUN	A	N	G	A	G	N	G	N	G	A	G	N
MOON	A	N	G	A	G	N	G	N	G	A	G	N
MERCURY	A	N	G	A	G	N	G	N	G	A	G	N
MARS	A	N	G	A	G	N	A	N	G	A	G	N
JUPITER	A	N	G	A	G	N	G	N	G	A	G	N
SATURN	A	N	G	A	G	N	A	N	G	A	G	N
URANUS	A	N	G	A	G	N	A	N	G	A	G	N
NEPTUNE	A	N	G	A	G	N	A	N	G	A	G	N
PLUTO	A	N	G	A	G	N	A	N	G	A	G	N

G = GOOD   N = NEUTRAL   A = ADVERSE

VENUS IN SCORPIO

♀ ♏	ARIES	TAURUS	GEMINI	CANCER	LEO	VIRGO	LIBRA	SCORPIO	SAGITT.	CAPRICORN	AQUARIUS	PISCES
SUN	N	A	N	G	A	G	N	G	N	G	A	G
MOON	N	A	N	G	A	G	N	G	N	G	A	G
MERCURY	N	A	N	G	A	G	N	G	N	G	A	G
MARS	N	A	N	G	A	G	N	A	N	G	A	G
JUPITER	N	A	N	G	A	G	N	G	N	G	A	G
SATURN	N	A	N	G	A	G	N	A	N	G	A	G
URANUS	N	A	N	G	A	G	N	A	N	G	A	G
NEPTUNE	N	A	N	G	A	G	N	A	N	G	A	G
PLUTO	N	A	N	G	A	G	N	A	N	G	A	G

G = GOOD   N = NEUTRAL   A = ADVERSE

VENUS IN SAGITTARIUS

♀ ♐	ARIES	TAURUS	GEMINI	CANCER	LEO	VIRGO	LIBRA	SCORPIO	SAGITT.	CAPRICORN	AQUARIUS	PISCES
SUN	G	N	A	N	G	A	G	N	G	N	G	A
MOON	G	N	A	N	G	A	G	N	G	N	G	A
MERCURY	G	N	A	N	G	A	G	N	G	N	G	A
MARS	G	N	A	N	G	A	G	N	A	N	G	A
JUPITER	G	N	A	N	G	A	G	N	G	N	G	A
SATURN	G	N	A	N	G	A	G	N	A	N	G	A
URANUS	G	N	A	N	G	A	G	N	A	N	G	A
NEPTUNE	G	N	A	N	G	A	G	N	A	N	G	A
PLUTO	G	N	A	N	G	A	G	N	A	N	G	A

G = GOOD   N = NEUTRAL   A = ADVERSE

VENUS IN CAPRICORN

	ARIES	TAURUS	GEMINI	CANCER	LEO	VIRGO	LIBRA	SCORPIO	SAGITT.	CAPRICORN	AQUARIUS	PISCES
SUN	A	G	N	A	N	G	A	G	N	G	N	G
MOON	A	G	N	A	N	G	A	G	N	G	N	G
MERCURY	A	G	N	A	N	G	A	G	N	G	N	G
MARS	A	G	N	A	N	G	A	G	N	A	N	G
JUPITER	A	G	N	A	N	G	A	G	N	G	N	G
SATURN	A	G	N	A	N	G	A	G	N	A	N	G
URANUS	A	G	N	A	N	G	A	G	N	A	N	G
NEPTUNE	A	G	N	A	N	G	A	G	N	A	N	G
PLUTO	A	G	N	A	N	G	A	G	N	A	N	G

G = GOOD   N = NEUTRAL   A = ADVERSE

VENUS IN AQUARIUS

	ARIES	TAURUS	GEMINI	CANCER	LEO	VIRGO	LIBRA	SCORPIO	SAGITT.	CAPRICORN	AQUARIUS	PISCES
SUN	G	A	G	N	A	N	G	A	G	N	G	N
MOON	G	A	G	N	A	N	G	A	G	N	G	N
MERCURY	G	A	G	N	A	N	G	A	G	N	G	N
MARS	G	A	G	N	A	N	G	A	G	N	A	N
JUPITER	G	A	G	N	A	N	G	A	G	N	G	N
SATURN	G	A	G	N	A	N	G	A	G	N	A	N
URANUS	G	A	G	N	A	N	G	A	G	N	A	N
NEPTUNE	G	A	G	N	A	N	G	A	G	N	A	N
PLUTO	G	A	G	N	A	N	G	A	G	N	A	N

G = GOOD   N = NEUTRAL   A = ADVERSE

VENUS IN PISCES

	ARIES	TAURUS	GEMINI	CANCER	LEO	VIRGO	LIBRA	SCORPIO	SAGITT.	CAPRICORN	AQUARIUS	PISCES
SUN	N	G	A	G	N	A	N	G	A	G	N	G
MOON	N	G	A	G	N	A	N	G	A	G	N	G
MERCURY	N	G	A	G	N	A	N	G	A	G	N	G
MARS	N	G	A	G	N	A	N	G	A	G	N	A
JUPITER	N	G	A	G	N	A	N	G	A	G	N	G
SATURN	N	G	A	G	N	A	N	G	A	G	N	A
URANUS	N	G	A	G	N	A	N	G	A	G	N	A
NEPTUNE	N	G	A	G	N	A	N	G	A	G	N	A
PLUTO	N	G	A	G	N	A	N	G	A	G	N	A

G = GOOD   N = NEUTRAL   A = ADVERSE

MARS IN ARIES

♂♈	ARIES	TAURUS	GEMINI	CANCER	LEO	VIRGO	LIBRA	SCORPIO	SAGITT.	CAPRICORN	AQUARIUS	PISCES
SUN	A	N	G	A	G	N	A	N	G	A	G	N
MOON	A	N	G	A	G	N	A	N	G	A	G	N
MERCURY	A	N	G	A	G	N	A	N	G	A	G	N
VENUS	A	N	G	A	G	N	A	N	G	A	G	N
JUPITER	A	N	G	A	G	N	A	N	G	A	G	N
SATURN	A	N	G	A	G	N	A	N	G	A	G	N
URANUS	A	N	G	A	G	N	A	N	G	A	G	N
NEPTUNE	A	N	G	A	G	N	A	N	G	A	G	N
PLUTO	A	N	G	A	G	N	A	N	G	A	G	N

G = GOOD   N = NEUTRAL   A = ADVERSE

MARS IN TAURUS

♂♉	ARIES	TAURUS	GEMINI	CANCER	LEO	VIRGO	LIBRA	SCORPIO	SAGITT.	CAPRICORN	AQUARIUS	PISCES
SUN	N	A	N	G	A	G	N	A	N	G	A	G
MOON	N	A	N	G	A	G	N	A	N	G	A	G
MERCURY	N	A	N	G	A	G	N	A	N	G	A	G
VENUS	N	A	N	G	A	G	N	A	N	G	A	G
JUPITER	N	A	N	G	A	G	N	A	N	G	A	G
SATURN	N	A	N	G	A	G	N	A	N	G	A	G
URANUS	N	A	N	G	A	G	N	A	N	G	A	G
NEPTUNE	N	A	N	G	A	G	N	A	N	G	A	G
PLUTO	N	A	N	G	A	G	N	A	N	G	A	G

G = GOOD   N = NEUTRAL   A = ADVERSE

MARS IN GEMINI

♂♊	ARIES	TAURUS	GEMINI	CANCER	LEO	VIRGO	LIBRA	SCORPIO	SAGITT.	CAPRICORN	AQUARIUS	PISCES
SUN	G	N	A	N	G	A	G	N	A	N	G	A
MOON	G	N	A	N	G	A	G	N	A	N	G	A
MERCURY	G	N	A	N	G	A	G	N	A	N	G	A
VENUS	G	N	A	N	G	A	G	N	A	N	G	A
JUPITER	G	N	A	N	G	A	G	N	A	N	G	A
SATURN	G	N	A	N	G	A	G	N	A	N	G	A
URANUS	G	N	A	N	G	A	G	N	A	N	G	A
NEPTUNE	G	N	A	N	G	A	G	N	A	N	G	A
PLUTO	G	N	A	N	G	A	G	N	A	N	G	A

G = GOOD   N = NEUTRAL   A = ADVERSE

MARS IN CANCER

♂ ⊙	ARIES	TAURUS	GEMINI	CANCER	LEO	VIRGO	LIBRA	SCORPIO	SAGITT.	CAPRICORN	AQUARIUS	PISCES
SUN	A	G	N	A	N	G	A	G	N	A	N	G
MOON	A	G	N	A	N	G	A	G	N	A	N	G
MERCURY	A	G	N	A	N	G	A	G	N	A	N	G
VENUS	A	G	N	A	N	G	A	G	N	A	N	G
JUPITER	A	G	N	A	N	G	A	G	N	A	N	G
SATURN	A	G	N	A	N	G	A	G	N	A	N	G
URANUS	A	G	N	A	N	G	A	G	N	A	N	G
NEPTUNE	A	G	N	A	N	G	A	G	N	A	N	G
PLUTO	A	G	N	A	N	G	A	G	N	A	N	G

G = GOOD   N = NEUTRAL   A = ADVERSE

MARS IN LEO

♂ ♌	ARIES	TAURUS	GEMINI	CANCER	LEO	VIRGO	LIBRA	SCORPIO	SAGITT.	CAPRICORN	AQUARIUS	PISCES
SUN	G	A	G	N	A	N	G	A	G	N	A	N
MOON	G	A	G	N	A	N	G	A	G	N	A	N
MERCURY	G	A	G	N	A	N	G	A	G	N	A	N
VENUS	G	A	G	N	A	N	G	A	G	N	A	N
JUPITER	G	A	G	N	A	N	G	A	G	N	A	N
SATURN	G	A	G	N	A	N	G	A	G	N	A	N
URANUS	G	A	G	N	A	N	G	A	G	N	A	N
NEPTUNE	G	A	G	N	A	N	G	A	G	N	A	N
PLUTO	G	A	G	N	A	N	G	A	G	N	A	N

G = GOOD   N = NEUTRAL   A = ADVERSE

MARS IN VIRGO

♂ ♍	ARIES	TAURUS	GEMINI	CANCER	LEO	VIRGO	LIBRA	SCORPIO	SAGITT.	CAPRICORN	AQUARIUS	PISCES
SUN	N	G	A	G	N	A	N	G	A	G	N	A
MOON	N	G	A	G	N	A	N	G	A	G	N	A
MERCURY	N	G	A	G	N	A	N	G	A	G	N	A
VENUS	N	G	A	G	N	A	N	G	A	G	N	A
JUPITER	N	G	A	G	N	A	N	G	A	G	N	A
SATURN	N	G	A	G	N	A	N	G	A	G	N	A
URANUS	N	G	A	G	N	A	N	G	A	G	N	A
NEPTUNE	N	G	A	G	N	A	N	G	A	G	N	A
PLUTO	N	G	A	G	N	A	N	G	A	G	N	A

G = GOOD   N = NEUTRAL   A = ADVERSE

MARS IN LIBRA

♂ ♎	ARIES	TAURUS	GEMINI	CANCER	LEO	VIRGO	LIBRA	SCORPIO	SAGITT.	CAPRICORN	AQUARIUS	PISCES
SUN	A	N	G	A	G	N	A	N	G	A	G	N
MOON	A	N	G	A	G	N	A	N	G	A	G	N
MERCURY	A	N	G	A	G	N	A	N	G	A	G	N
VENUS	A	N	G	A	G	N	A	N	G	A	G	N
JUPITER	A	N	G	A	G	N	A	N	G	A	G	N
SATURN	A	N	G	A	G	N	A	N	G	A	G	N
URANUS	A	N	G	A	G	N	A	N	G	A	G	N
NEPTUNE	A	N	G	A	G	N	A	N	G	A	G	N
PLUTO	A	N	G	A	G	N	A	N	G	A	G	N

G = GOOD   N = NEUTRAL   A = ADVERSE

MARS IN SCORPIO

♂ ♏	ARIES	TAURUS	GEMINI	CANCER	LEO	VIRGO	LIBRA	SCORPIO	SAGITT.	CAPRICORN	AQUARIUS	PISCES
SUN	N	A	N	G	A	G	N	A	N	G	A	G
MOON	N	A	N	G	A	G	N	A	N	G	A	G
MERCURY	N	A	N	G	A	G	N	A	N	G	A	G
VENUS	N	A	N	G	A	G	N	A	N	G	A	G
JUPITER	N	A	N	G	A	G	N	A	N	G	A	G
SATURN	N	A	N	G	A	G	N	A	N	G	A	G
URANUS	N	A	N	G	A	G	N	A	N	G	A	G
NEPTUNE	N	A	N	G	A	G	N	A	N	G	A	G
PLUTO	N	A	N	G	A	G	N	A	N	G	A	G

G = GOOD   N = NEUTRAL   A = ADVERSE

MARS IN SAGITTARIUS

♂ ♐	ARIES	TAURUS	GEMINI	CANCER	LEO	VIRGO	LIBRA	SCORPIO	SAGITT.	CAPRICORN	AQUARIUS	PISCES
SUN	G	N	A	N	G	A	G	N	A	N	G	A
MOON	G	N	A	N	G	A	G	N	A	N	G	A
MERCURY	G	N	A	N	G	A	G	N	A	N	G	A
VENUS	G	N	A	N	G	A	G	N	A	N	G	A
JUPITER	G	N	A	N	G	A	G	N	A	N	G	A
SATURN	G	N	A	N	G	A	G	N	A	N	G	A
URANUS	G	N	A	N	G	A	G	N	A	N	G	A
NEPTUNE	G	N	A	N	G	A	G	N	A	N	G	A
PLUTO	G	N	A	N	G	A	G	N	A	N	G	A

G = GOOD   N = NEUTRAL   A = ADVERSE

MARS IN CAPRICORN

♂ ♑	ARIES	TAURUS	GEMINI	CANCER	LEO	VIRGO	LIBRA	SCORPIO	SAGITT.	CAPRICORN	AQUARIUS	PISCES
SUN	A	G	N	A	N	G	A	G	N	A	N	G
MOON	A	G	N	A	N	G	A	G	N	A	N	G
MERCURY	A	G	N	A	N	G	A	G	N	A	N	G
VENUS	A	G	N	A	N	G	A	G	N	A	N	G
JUPITER	A	G	N	A	N	G	A	G	N	A	N	G
SATURN	A	G	N	A	N	G	A	G	N	A	N	G
URANUS	A	G	N	A	N	G	A	G	N	A	N	G
NEPTUNE	A	G	N	A	N	G	A	G	N	A	N	G
PLUTO	A	G	N	A	N	G	A	G	N	A	N	G

G = GOOD   N = NEUTRAL   A = ADVERSE

MARS IN AQUARIUS

♂ ♒	ARIES	TAURUS	GEMINI	CANCER	LEO	VIRGO	LIBRA	SCORPIO	SAGITT.	CAPRICORN	AQUARIUS	PISCES
SUN	G	A	G	N	A	N	G	A	G	N	A	N
MOON	G	A	G	N	A	N	G	A	G	N	A	N
MERCURY	G	A	G	N	A	N	G	A	G	N	A	N
VENUS	G	A	G	N	A	N	G	A	G	N	A	N
JUPITER	G	A	G	N	A	N	G	A	G	N	A	N
SATURN	G	A	G	N	A	N	G	A	G	N	A	N
URANUS	G	A	G	N	A	N	G	A	G	N	A	N
NEPTUNE	G	A	G	N	A	N	G	A	G	N	A	N
PLUTO	G	A	G	N	A	N	G	A	G	N	A	N

G = GOOD   N = NEUTRAL   A = ADVERSE

MARS IN PISCES

♂ ♓	ARIES	TAURUS	GEMINI	CANCER	LEO	VIRGO	LIBRA	SCORPIO	SAGITT.	CAPRICORN	AQUARIUS	PISCES
SUN	N	G	A	G	N	A	N	G	A	G	N	A
MOON	N	G	A	G	N	A	N	G	A	G	N	A
MERCURY	N	G	A	G	N	A	N	G	A	G	N	A
VENUS	N	G	A	G	N	A	N	G	A	G	N	A
JUPITER	N	G	A	G	N	A	N	G	A	G	N	A
SATURN	N	G	A	G	N	A	N	G	A	G	N	A
URANUS	N	G	A	G	N	A	N	G	A	G	N	A
NEPTUNE	N	G	A	G	N	A	N	G	A	G	N	A
PLUTO	N	G	A	G	N	A	N	G	A	G	N	A

G = GOOD   N = NEUTRAL   A = ADVERSE

JUPITER IN ARIES

♃♈	ARIES	TAURUS	GEMINI	CANCER	LEO	VIRGO	LIBRA	SCORPIO	SAGITT.	CAPRICORN	AQUARIUS	PISCES
SUN	G	N	G	A	G	N	A	N	G	A	G	N
MOON	G	N	G	A	G	N	A	N	G	A	G	N
MERCURY	G	N	G	A	G	N	A	N	G	A	G	N
VENUS	G	N	G	A	G	N	A	N	G	A	G	N
MARS	A	N	G	A	G	N	A	N	G	A	G	N
SATURN	A	N	G	A	G	N	A	N	G	A	G	N
URANUS	A	N	G	A	G	N	A	N	G	A	G	N
NEPTUNE	A	N	G	A	G	N	A	N	G	A	G	N
PLUTO	A	N	G	A	G	N	A	N	G	A	G	N

G = GOOD   N = NEUTRAL   A = ADVERSE

JUPITER IN TAURUS

♃♉	ARIES	TAURUS	GEMINI	CANCER	LEO	VIRGO	LIBRA	SCORPIO	SAGITT.	CAPRICORN	AQUARIUS	PISCES
SUN	N	G	N	G	A	G	N	A	N	G	A	G
MOON	N	G	N	G	A	G	N	A	N	G	A	G
MERCURY	N	G	N	G	A	G	N	A	N	G	A	G
VENUS	N	G	N	G	A	G	N	A	N	G	A	G
MARS	N	A	N	G	A	G	N	A	N	G	A	G
SATURN	N	A	N	G	A	G	N	A	N	G	A	G
URANUS	N	A	N	G	A	G	N	A	N	G	A	G
NEPTUNE	N	A	N	G	A	G	N	A	N	G	A	G
PLUTO	N	A	N	G	A	G	N	A	N	G	A	G

G = GOOD   N = NEUTRAL   A = ADVERSE

JUPITER IN GEMINI

♃♊	ARIES	TAURUS	GEMINI	CANCER	LEO	VIRGO	LIBRA	SCORPIO	SAGITT.	CAPRICORN	AQUARIUS	PISCES
SUN	G	N	G	N	G	A	G	N	A	N	G	A
MOON	G	N	G	N	G	A	G	N	A	N	G	A
MERCURY	G	N	G	N	G	A	G	N	A	N	G	A
VENUS	G	N	G	N	G	A	G	N	A	N	G	A
MARS	G	N	A	N	G	A	G	N	A	N	G	A
SATURN	G	N	A	N	G	A	G	N	A	N	G	A
URANUS	G	N	A	N	G	A	G	N	A	N	G	A
NEPTUNE	G	N	A	N	G	A	G	N	A	N	G	A
PLUTO	G	N	A	N	G	A	G	N	A	N	G	A

G = GOOD   N = NEUTRAL   A = ADVERSE

JUPITER IN CANCER

♃☋☊	ARIES	TAURUS	GEMINI	CANCER	LEO	VIRGO	LIBRA	SCORPIO	SAGITT.	CAPRICORN	AQUARIUS	PISCES
SUN	A	G	N	G	N	G	A	G	N	A	N	G
MOON	A	G	N	G	N	G	A	G	N	A	N	G
MERCURY	A	G	N	G	N	G	A	G	N	A	N	G
VENUS	A	G	N	G	N	G	A	G	N	A	N	G
MARS	A	G	N	A	N	G	A	G	N	A	N	G
SATURN	A	G	N	A	N	G	A	G	N	A	N	G
URANUS	A	G	N	A	N	G	A	G	N	A	N	G
NEPTUNE	A	G	N	A	N	G	A	G	N	A	N	G
PLUTO	A	G	N	A	N	G	A	G	N	A	N	G

G = GOOD   N = NEUTRAL   A = ADVERSE

JUPITER IN LEO

♃☌☊	ARIES	TAURUS	GEMINI	CANCER	LEO	VIRGO	LIBRA	SCORPIO	SAGITT.	CAPRICORN	AQUARIUS	PISCES
SUN	G	A	G	N	G	N	G	A	G	N	A	N
MOON	G	A	G	N	G	N	G	A	G	N	A	N
MERCURY	G	A	G	N	G	N	G	A	G	N	A	N
VENUS	G	A	G	N	G	N	G	A	G	N	A	N
MARS	G	A	G	N	A	N	G	A	G	N	A	N
SATURN	G	A	G	N	A	N	G	A	G	N	A	N
URANUS	G	A	G	N	A	N	G	A	G	N	A	N
NEPTUNE	G	A	G	N	A	N	G	A	G	N	A	N
PLUTO	G	A	G	N	A	N	G	A	G	N	A	N

G = GOOD   N = NEUTRAL   A = ADVERSE

JUPITER IN VIRGO

♃♍	ARIES	TAURUS	GEMINI	CANCER	LEO	VIRGO	LIBRA	SCORPIO	SAGITT.	CAPRICORN	AQUARIUS	PISCES
SUN	N	G	A	G	N	G	N	G	A	G	N	A
MOON	N	G	A	G	N	G	N	G	A	G	N	A
MERCURY	N	G	A	G	N	G	N	G	A	G	N	A
VENUS	N	G	A	G	N	G	N	G	A	G	N	A
MARS	N	G	A	G	N	A	N	G	A	G	N	A
SATURN	N	G	A	G	N	A	N	G	A	G	N	A
URANUS	N	G	A	G	N	A	N	G	A	G	N	A
NEPTUNE	N	G	A	G	N	A	N	G	A	G	N	A
PLUTO	N	G	A	G	N	A	N	G	A	G	N	A

G = GOOD   N = NEUTRAL   A = ADVERSE

JUPITER IN LIBRA

♃ ♎	ARIES	TAURUS	GEMINI	CANCER	LEO	VIRGO	LIBRA	SCORPIO	SAGITT.	CAPRICORN	AQUARIUS	PISCES
SUN	A	N	G	A	G	N	G	N	G	A	G	N
MOON	A	N	G	A	G	N	G	N	G	A	G	N
MERCURY	A	N	G	A	G	N	G	N	G	A	G	N
VENUS	A	N	G	A	G	N	G	N	G	A	G	N
MARS	A	N	G	A	G	N	A	N	G	A	G	N
SATURN	A	N	G	A	G	N	A	N	G	A	G	N
URANUS	A	N	G	A	G	N	A	N	G	A	G	N
NEPTUNE	A	N	G	A	G	N	A	N	G	A	G	N
PLUTO	A	N	G	A	G	N	A	N	G	A	G	N

G = GOOD   N = NEUTRAL   A = ADVERSE

JUPITER IN SCORPIO

♃ ♏	ARIES	TAURUS	GEMINI	CANCER	LEO	VIRGO	LIBRA	SCORPIO	SAGITT.	CAPRICORN	AQUARIUS	PISCES
SUN	N	A	N	G	A	G	N	G	N	G	A	G
MOON	N	A	N	G	A	G	N	G	N	G	A	G
MERCURY	N	A	N	G	A	G	N	G	N	G	A	G
VENUS	N	A	N	G	A	G	N	G	N	G	A	G
MARS	N	A	N	G	A	G	N	A	N	G	A	G
SATURN	N	A	N	G	A	G	N	A	N	G	A	G
URANUS	N	A	N	G	A	G	N	A	N	G	A	G
NEPTUNE	N	A	N	G	A	G	N	A	N	G	A	G
PLUTO	N	A	N	G	A	G	N	A	N	G	A	G

G = GOOD   N = NEUTRAL   A = ADVERSE

JUPITER IN SAGITTARIUS

♃ ♐	ARIES	TAURUS	GEMINI	CANCER	LEO	VIRGO	LIBRA	SCORPIO	SAGITT.	CAPRICORN	AQUARIUS	PISCES
SUN	G	N	A	N	G	A	G	N	G	N	G	A
MOON	G	N	A	N	G	A	G	N	G	N	G	A
MERCURY	G	N	A	N	G	A	G	N	G	N	G	A
VENUS	G	N	A	N	G	A	G	N	G	N	G	A
MARS	G	N	A	N	G	A	G	N	A	N	G	A
SATURN	G	N	A	N	G	A	G	N	A	N	G	A
URANUS	G	N	A	N	G	A	G	N	A	N	G	A
NEPTUNE	G	N	A	N	G	A	G	N	A	N	G	A
PLUTO	G	N	A	N	G	A	G	N	A	N	G	A

G = GOOD   N = NEUTRAL   A = ADVERSE

JUPITER IN CAPRICORN

♃ ♑	ARIES	TAURUS	GEMINI	CANCER	LEO	VIRGO	LIBRA	SCORPIO	SAGITT.	CAPRICORN	AQUARIUS	PISCES
SUN	A	G	N	A	N	G	A	G	N	G	N	G
MOON	A	G	N	A	N	G	A	G	N	G	N	G
MERCURY	A	G	N	A	N	G	A	G	N	G	N	G
VENUS	A	G	N	A	N	G	A	G	N	G	N	G
MARS	A	G	N	A	N	G	A	G	N	A	N	G
SATURN	A	G	N	A	N	G	A	G	N	A	N	G
URANUS	A	G	N	A	N	G	A	G	N	A	N	G
NEPTUNE	A	G	N	A	N	G	A	G	N	A	N	G
PLUTO	A	G	N	A	N	G	A	G	N	A	N	G

G = GOOD   N = NEUTRAL   A = ADVERSE

JUPITER IN AQUARIUS

♃ ≈	ARIES	TAURUS	GEMINI	CANCER	LEO	VIRGO	LIBRA	SCORPIO	SAGITT.	CAPRICORN	AQUARIUS	PISCES
SUN	G	A	G	N	A	N	G	A	G	N	G	N
MOON	G	A	G	N	A	N	G	A	G	N	G	N
MERCURY	G	A	G	N	A	N	G	A	G	N	G	N
VENUS	G	A	G	N	A	N	G	A	G	N	G	N
MARS	G	A	G	N	A	N	G	A	G	N	A	N
SATURN	G	A	G	N	A	N	G	A	G	N	A	N
URANUS	G	A	G	N	A	N	G	A	G	N	A	N
NEPTUNE	G	A	G	N	A	N	G	A	G	N	A	N
PLUTO	G	A	G	N	A	N	G	A	G	N	A	N

G = GOOD   N = NEUTRAL   A = ADVERSE

JUPITER IN PISCES

♃ ♓	ARIES	TAURUS	GEMINI	CANCER	LEO	VIRGO	LIBRA	SCORPIO	SAGITT.	CAPRICORN	AQUARIUS	PISCES
SUN	N	G	A	G	N	A	N	G	A	G	N	G
MOON	N	G	A	G	N	A	N	G	A	G	N	G
MERCURY	N	G	A	G	N	A	N	G	A	G	N	G
VENUS	N	G	A	G	N	A	N	G	A	G	N	G
MARS	N	G	A	G	N	A	N	G	A	G	N	A
SATURN	N	G	A	G	N	A	N	G	A	G	N	A
URANUS	N	G	A	G	N	A	N	G	A	G	N	A
NEPTUNE	N	G	A	G	N	A	N	G	A	G	N	A
PLUTO	N	G	A	G	N	A	N	G	A	G	N	A

G = GOOD   N = NEUTRAL   A = ADVERSE

SATURN IN ARIES

♄♈	ARIES	TAURUS	GEMINI	CANCER	LEO	VIRGO	LIBRA	SCORPIO	SAGITT.	CAPRICORN	AQUARIUS	PISCES
SUN	A	N	G	A	G	N	A	N	G	A	G	N
MOON	A	N	G	A	G	N	A	N	G	A	G	N
MERCURY	A	N	G	A	G	N	A	N	G	A	G	N
VENUS	A	N	G	A	G	N	A	N	G	A	G	N
MARS	A	N	G	A	G	N	A	N	G	A	G	N
JUPITER	A	N	G	A	G	N	A	N	G	A	G	N
URANUS	A	N	G	A	G	N	A	N	G	A	G	N
NEPTUNE	A	N	G	A	G	N	A	N	G	A	G	N
PLUTO	A	N	G	A	G	N	A	N	G	A	G	N

G = GOOD   N = NEUTRAL   A = ADVERSE

SATURN IN TAURUS

♄♉	ARIES	TAURUS	GEMINI	CANCER	LEO	VIRGO	LIBRA	SCORPIO	SAGITT.	CAPRICORN	AQUARIUS	PISCES
SUN	N	A	N	G	A	G	N	A	N	G	A	G
MOON	N	A	N	G	A	G	N	A	N	G	A	G
MERCURY	N	A	N	G	A	G	N	A	N	G	A	G
VENUS	N	A	N	G	A	G	N	A	N	G	A	G
MARS	N	A	N	G	A	G	N	A	N	G	A	G
JUPITER	N	A	N	G	A	G	N	A	N	G	A	G
URANUS	N	A	N	G	A	G	N	A	N	G	A	G
NEPTUNE	N	A	N	G	A	G	N	A	N	G	A	G
PLUTO	N	A	N	G	A	G	N	A	N	G	A	G

G = GOOD   N = NEUTRAL   A = ADVERSE

SATURN IN GEMINI

♄♊	ARIES	TAURUS	GEMINI	CANCER	LEO	VIRGO	LIBRA	SCORPIO	SAGITT.	CAPRICORN	AQUARIUS	PISCES
SUN	G	N	A	N	G	A	G	N	A	N	G	A
MOON	G	N	A	N	G	A	G	N	A	N	G	A
MERCURY	G	N	A	N	G	A	G	N	A	N	G	A
VENUS	G	N	A	N	G	A	G	N	A	N	G	A
MARS	G	N	A	N	G	A	G	N	A	N	G	A
JUPITER	G	N	A	N	G	A	G	N	A	N	G	A
URANUS	G	N	A	N	G	A	G	N	A	N	G	A
NEPTUNE	G	N	A	N	G	A	G	N	A	N	G	A
PLUTO	G	N	A	N	G	A	G	N	A	N	G	A

G = GOOD   N = NEUTRAL   A = ADVERSE

SATURN IN CANCER

♄♋	ARIES	TAURUS	GEMINI	CANCER	LEO	VIRGO	LIBRA	SCORPIO	SAGITT.	CAPRICORN	AQUARIUS	PISCES
SUN	A	G	N	A	N	G	A	G	N	A	N	G
MOON	A	G	N	A	N	G	A	G	N	A	N	G
MERCURY	A	G	N	A	N	G	A	G	N	A	N	G
VENUS	A	G	N	A	N	G	A	G	N	A	N	G
MARS	A	G	N	A	N	G	A	G	N	A	N	G
JUPITER	A	G	N	A	N	G	A	G	N	A	N	G
URANUS	A	G	N	A	N	G	A	G	N	A	N	G
NEPTUNE	A	G	N	A	N	G	A	G	N	A	N	G
PLUTO	A	G	N	A	N	G	A	G	N	A	N	G

G = GOOD   N = NEUTRAL   A = ADVERSE

SATURN IN LEO

♄♌	ARIES	TAURUS	GEMINI	CANCER	LEO	VIRGO	LIBRA	SCORPIO	SAGITT.	CAPRICORN	AQUARIUS	PISCES
SUN	G	A	G	N	A	N	G	A	G	N	A	N
MOON	G	A	G	N	A	N	G	A	G	N	A	N
MERCURY	G	A	G	N	A	N	G	A	G	N	A	N
VENUS	G	A	G	N	A	N	G	A	G	N	A	N
MARS	G	A	G	N	A	N	G	A	G	N	A	N
JUPITER	G	A	G	N	A	N	G	A	G	N	A	N
URANUS	G	A	G	N	A	N	G	A	G	N	A	N
NEPTUNE	G	A	G	N	A	N	G	A	G	N	A	N
PLUTO	G	A	G	N	A	N	G	A	G	N	A	N

G = GOOD   N = NEUTRAL   A = ADVERSE

SATURN IN VIRGO

♄♍	ARIES	TAURUS	GEMINI	CANCER	LEO	VIRGO	LIBRA	SCORPIO	SAGITT.	CAPRICORN	AQUARIUS	PISCES
SUN	N	G	A	G	N	A	N	G	A	G	N	A
MOON	N	G	A	G	N	A	N	G	A	G	N	A
MERCURY	N	G	A	G	N	A	N	G	A	G	N	A
VENUS	N	G	A	G	N	A	N	G	A	G	N	A
MARS	N	G	A	G	N	A	N	G	A	G	N	A
JUPITER	N	G	A	G	N	A	N	G	A	G	N	A
URANUS	N	G	A	G	N	A	N	G	A	G	N	A
NEPTUNE	N	G	A	G	N	A	N	G	A	G	N	A
PLUTO	N	G	A	G	N	A	N	G	A	G	N	A

G = GOOD   N = NEUTRAL   A = ADVERSE

305

SATURN IN LIBRA

♄ ♎	ARIES	TAURUS	GEMINI	CANCER	LEO	VIRGO	LIBRA	SCORPIO	SAGITT.	CAPRICORN	AQUARIUS	PISCES
SUN	A	N	G	A	G	N	A	N	G	A	G	N
MOON	A	N	G	A	G	N	A	N	G	A	G	N
MERCURY	A	N	G	A	G	N	A	N	G	A	G	N
VENUS	A	N	G	A	G	N	A	N	G	A	G	N
MARS	A	N	G	A	G	N	A	N	G	A	G	N
JUPITER	A	N	G	A	G	N	A	N	G	A	G	N
URANUS	A	N	G	A	G	N	A	N	G	A	G	N
NEPTUNE	A	N	G	A	G	N	A	N	G	A	G	N
PLUTO	A	N	G	A	G	N	A	N	G	A	G	N

G = GOOD   N = NEUTRAL   A = ADVERSE

SATURN IN SCORPIO

♄ ♏	ARIES	TAURUS	GEMINI	CANCER	LEO	VIRGO	LIBRA	SCORPIO	SAGITT.	CAPRICORN	AQUARIUS	PISCES
SUN	N	A	N	G	A	G	N	A	N	G	A	G
MOON	N	A	N	G	A	G	N	A	N	G	A	G
MERCURY	N	A	N	G	A	G	N	A	N	G	A	G
VENUS	N	A	N	G	A	G	N	A	N	G	A	G
MARS	N	A	N	G	A	G	N	A	N	G	A	G
JUPITER	N	A	N	G	A	G	N	A	N	G	A	G
URANUS	N	A	N	G	A	G	N	A	N	G	A	G
NEPTUNE	N	A	N	G	A	G	N	A	N	G	A	G
PLUTO	N	A	N	G	A	G	N	A	N	G	A	G

G = GOOD   N = NEUTRAL   A = ADVERSE

SATURN IN SAGITTARIUS

♄ ♐	ARIES	TAURUS	GEMINI	CANCER	LEO	VIRGO	LIBRA	SCORPIO	SAGITT.	CAPRICORN	AQUARIUS	PISCES
SUN	G	N	A	N	G	A	G	N	A	N	G	A
MOON	G	N	A	N	G	A	G	N	A	N	G	A
MERCURY	G	N	A	N	G	A	G	N	A	N	G	A
VENUS	G	N	A	N	G	A	G	N	A	N	G	A
MARS	G	N	A	N	G	A	G	N	A	N	G	A
JUPITER	G	N	A	N	G	A	G	N	A	N	G	A
URANUS	G	N	A	N	G	A	G	N	A	N	G	A
NEPTUNE	G	N	A	N	G	A	G	N	A	N	G	A
PLUTO	G	N	A	N	G	A	G	N	A	N	G	A

G = GOOD   N = NEUTRAL   A = ADVERSE

SATURN IN CAPRICORN

♄♑	ARIES	TAURUS	GEMINI	CANCER	LEO	VIRGO	LIBRA	SCORPIO	SAGITT.	CAPRICORN	AQUARIUS	PISCES
SUN	A	G	N	A	N	G	A	G	A	G	N	A
MOON	A	G	N	A	N	G	A	G	A	G	N	A
MERCURY	A	G	N	A	N	G	A	G	A	G	N	A
VENUS	A	G	N	A	N	G	A	G	A	G	N	A
MARS	A	G	N	A	N	G	A	G	A	G	N	A
JUPITER	A	G	N	A	N	G	A	G	A	G	N	A
URANUS	A	G	N	A	N	G	A	G	A	G	N	A
NEPTUNE	A	G	N	A	N	G	A	G	A	G	N	A
PLUTO	A	G	N	A	N	G	A	G	A	G	N	A

G = GOOD   N = NEUTRAL   A = ADVERSE

SATURN IN AQUARIUS

♄♒	ARIES	TAURUS	GEMINI	CANCER	LEO	VIRGO	LIBRA	SCORPIO	SAGITT.	CAPRICORN	AQUARIUS	PISCES
SUN	G	A	G	N	A	N	G	A	G	N	A	N
MOON	G	A	G	N	A	N	G	A	G	N	A	N
MERCURY	G	A	G	N	A	N	G	A	G	N	A	N
VENUS	G	A	G	N	A	N	G	A	G	N	A	N
MARS	G	A	G	N	A	N	G	A	G	N	A	N
JUPITER	G	A	G	N	A	N	G	A	G	N	A	N
URANUS	G	A	G	N	A	N	G	A	G	N	A	N
NEPTUNE	G	A	G	N	A	N	G	A	G	N	A	N
PLUTO	G	A	G	N	A	N	G	A	G	N	A	N

G = GOOD   N = NEUTRAL   A = ADVERSE

SATURN IN PISCES

♄♓	ARIES	TAURUS	GEMINI	CANCER	LEO	VIRGO	LIBRA	SCORPIO	SAGITT.	CAPRICORN	AQUARIUS	PISCES
SUN	N	G	A	G	N	A	N	G	A	G	N	A
MOON	N	G	A	G	N	A	N	G	A	G	N	A
MERCURY	N	G	A	G	N	A	N	G	A	G	N	A
VENUS	N	G	A	G	N	A	N	G	A	G	N	A
MARS	N	G	A	G	N	A	N	G	A	G	N	A
JUPITER	N	G	A	G	N	A	N	G	A	G	N	A
URANUS	N	G	A	G	N	A	N	G	A	G	N	A
NEPTUNE	N	G	A	G	N	A	N	G	A	G	N	A
PLUTO	N	G	A	G	N	A	N	G	A	G	N	A

G = GOOD   N = NEUTRAL   A = ADVERSE

URANUS IN ARIES

♅ ♈	ARIES	TAURUS	GEMINI	CANCER	LEO	VIRGO	LIBRA	SCORPIO	SAGITT.	CAPRICORN	AQUARIUS	PISCES
SUN	A	N	G	A	G	N	A	N	G	A	G	N
MOON	A	N	G	A	G	N	A	N	G	A	G	N
MERCURY	A	N	G	A	G	N	A	N	G	A	G	N
VENUS	A	N	G	A	G	N	A	N	G	A	G	N
MARS	A	N	G	A	G	N	A	N	G	A	G	N
JUPITER	A	N	G	A	G	N	A	N	G	A	G	N
SATURN	A	N	G	A	G	N	A	N	G	A	G	N
NEPTUNE	A	N	G	A	G	N	A	N	G	A	G	N
PLUTO	A	N	G	A	G	N	A	N	G	A	G	N

G = GOOD   N = NEUTRAL   A = ADVERSE

URANUS IN TAURUS

♅ ♉	ARIES	TAURUS	GEMINI	CANCER	LEO	VIRGO	LIBRA	SCORPIO	SAGITT.	CAPRICORN	AQUARIUS	PISCES
SUN	N	A	N	G	A	G	N	A	N	G	A	G
MOON	N	A	N	G	A	G	N	A	N	G	A	G
MERCURY	N	A	N	G	A	G	N	A	N	G	A	G
VENUS	N	A	N	G	A	G	N	A	N	G	A	G
MARS	N	A	N	G	A	G	N	A	N	G	A	G
JUPITER	N	A	N	G	A	G	N	A	N	G	A	G
SATURN	N	A	N	G	A	G	N	A	N	G	A	G
NEPTUNE	N	A	N	G	A	G	N	A	N	G	A	G
PLUTO	N	A	N	G	A	G	N	A	N	G	A	G

G = GOOD   N = NEUTRAL   A = ADVERSE

URANUS IN GEMINI

♅ ♊	ARIES	TAURUS	GEMINI	CANCER	LEO	VIRGO	LIBRA	SCORPIO	SAGITT.	CAPRICORN	AQUARIUS	PISCES
SUN	G	N	A	N	G	A	G	N	A	N	G	A
MOON	G	N	A	N	G	A	G	N	A	N	G	A
MERCURY	G	N	A	N	G	A	G	N	A	N	G	A
VENUS	G	N	A	N	G	A	G	N	A	N	G	A
MARS	G	N	A	N	G	A	G	N	A	N	G	A
JUPITER	G	N	A	N	G	A	G	N	A	N	G	A
SATURN	G	N	A	N	G	A	G	N	A	N	G	A
NEPTUNE	G	N	A	N	G	A	G	N	A	N	G	A
PLUTO	G	N	A	N	G	A	G	N	A	N	G	A

G = GOOD   N = NEUTRAL   A = ADVERSE

URANUS IN CANCER

♅ ♋	ARIES	TAURUS	GEMINI	CANCER	LEO	VIRGO	LIBRA	SCORPIO	SAGITT.	CAPRICORN	AQUARIUS	PISCES
SUN	A	G	N	A	N	G	A	G	N	A	N	G
MOON	A	G	N	A	N	G	A	G	N	A	N	G
MERCURY	A	G	N	A	N	G	A	G	N	A	N	G
VENUS	A	G	N	A	N	G	A	G	N	A	N	G
MARS	A	G	N	A	N	G	A	G	N	A	N	G
JUPITER	A	G	N	A	N	G	A	G	N	A	N	G
SATURN	A	G	N	A	N	G	A	G	N	A	N	G
NEPTUNE	A	G	N	A	N	G	A	G	N	A	N	G
PLUTO	A	G	N	A	N	G	A	G	N	A	N	G

G = GOOD   N = NEUTRAL   A = ADVERSE

URANUS IN LEO

♅ ♌	ARIES	TAURUS	GEMINI	CANCER	LEO	VIRGO	LIBRA	SCORPIO	SAGITT.	CAPRICORN	AQUARIUS	PISCES
SUN	G	A	G	N	A	N	G	A	G	N	A	N
MOON	G	A	G	N	A	N	G	A	G	N	A	N
MERCURY	G	A	G	N	A	N	G	A	G	N	A	N
VENUS	G	A	G	N	A	N	G	A	G	N	A	N
MARS	G	A	G	N	A	N	G	A	G	N	A	N
JUPITER	G	A	G	N	A	N	G	A	G	N	A	N
SATURN	G	A	G	N	A	N	G	A	G	N	A	N
NEPTUNE	G	A	G	N	A	N	G	A	G	N	A	N
PLUTO	G	A	G	N	A	N	G	A	G	N	A	N

G = GOOD   N = NEUTRAL   A = ADVERSE

URANUS IN VIRGO

♅ ♍	ARIES	TAURUS	GEMINI	CANCER	LEO	VIRGO	LIBRA	SCORPIO	SAGITT.	CAPRICORN	AQUARIUS	PISCES
SUN	N	G	A	G	N	A	N	G	A	G	N	A
MOON	N	G	A	G	N	A	N	G	A	G	N	A
MERCURY	N	G	A	G	N	A	N	G	A	G	N	A
VENUS	N	G	A	G	N	A	N	G	A	G	N	A
MARS	N	G	A	G	N	A	N	G	A	G	N	A
JUPITER	N	G	A	G	N	A	N	G	A	G	N	A
SATURN	N	G	A	G	N	A	N	G	A	G	N	A
NEPTUNE	N	G	A	G	N	A	N	G	A	G	N	A
PLUTO	N	G	A	G	N	A	N	G	A	G	N	A

G = GOOD   N = NEUTRAL   A = ADVERSE

URANUS IN LIBRA

♅ ☌ ♎	ARIES	TAURUS	GEMINI	CANCER	LEO	VIRGO	LIBRA	SCORPIO	SAGITT.	CAPRICORN	AQUARIUS	PISCES
SUN	A	N	G	A	G	N	A	N	G	A	G	N
MOON	A	N	G	A	G	N	A	N	G	A	G	N
MERCURY	A	N	G	A	G	N	A	N	G	A	G	N
VENUS	A	N	G	A	G	N	A	N	G	A	G	N
MARS	A	N	G	A	G	N	A	N	G	A	G	N
JUPITER	A	N	G	A	G	N	A	N	G	A	G	N
SATURN	A	N	G	A	G	N	A	N	G	A	G	N
NEPTUNE	A	N	G	A	G	N	A	N	G	A	G	N
PLUTO	A	N	G	A	G	N	A	N	G	A	G	N

G = GOOD   N = NEUTRAL   A = ADVERSE

URANUS IN SCORPIO

♅ ☌ ♏	ARIES	TAURUS	GEMINI	CANCER	LEO	VIRGO	LIBRA	SCORPIO	SAGITT.	CAPRICORN	AQUARIUS	PISCES
SUN	N	A	N	G	A	G	N	A	N	G	A	G
MOON	N	A	N	G	A	G	N	A	N	G	A	G
MERCURY	N	A	N	G	A	G	N	A	N	G	A	G
VENUS	N	A	N	G	A	G	N	A	N	G	A	G
MARS	N	A	N	G	A	G	N	A	N	G	A	G
JUPITER	N	A	N	G	A	G	N	A	N	G	A	G
SATURN	N	A	N	G	A	G	N	A	N	G	A	G
NEPTUNE	N	A	N	G	A	G	N	A	N	G	A	G
PLUTO	N	A	N	G	A	G	N	A	N	G	A	G

G = GOOD   N = NEUTRAL   A = ADVERSE

URANUS IN SAGITTARIUS

♅ ☌ ♐	ARIES	TAURUS	GEMINI	CANCER	LEO	VIRGO	LIBRA	SCORPIO	SAGITT.	CAPRICORN	AQUARIUS	PISCES
SUN	G	N	A	N	G	A	G	N	A	N	G	A
MOON	G	N	A	N	G	A	G	N	A	N	G	A
MERCURY	G	N	A	N	G	A	G	N	A	N	G	A
VENUS	G	N	A	N	G	A	G	N	A	N	G	A
MARS	G	N	A	N	G	A	G	N	A	N	G	A
JUPITER	G	N	A	N	G	A	G	N	A	N	G	A
SATURN	G	N	A	N	G	A	G	N	A	N	G	A
NEPTUNE	G	N	A	N	G	A	G	N	A	N	G	A
PLUTO	G	N	A	N	G	A	G	N	A	N	G	A

G = GOOD   N = NEUTRAL   A = ADVERSE

URANUS IN CAPRICORN

♅ ⚹ ♑	ARIES	TAURUS	GEMINI	CANCER	LEO	VIRGO	LIBRA	SCORPIO	SAGITT.	CAPRICORN	AQUARIUS	PISCES
SUN	A	G	N	A	N	G	A	G	N	A	N	G
MOON	A	G	N	A	N	G	A	G	N	A	N	G
MERCURY	A	G	N	A	N	G	A	G	N	A	N	G
VENUS	A	G	N	A	N	G	A	G	N	A	N	G
MARS	A	G	N	A	N	G	A	G	N	A	N	G
JUPITER	A	G	N	A	N	G	A	G	N	A	N	G
SATURN	A	G	N	A	N	G	A	G	N	A	N	G
NEPTUNE	A	G	N	A	N	G	A	G	N	A	N	G
PLUTO	A	G	N	A	N	G	A	G	N	A	N	G

G = GOOD   N = NEUTRAL   A = ADVERSE

NEPTUNE IN CANCER

♆ ♋	ARIES	TAURUS	GEMINI	CANCER	LEO	VIRGO	LIBRA	SCORPIO	SAGITT.	CAPRICORN	AQUARIUS	PISCES
SUN	A	G	N	A	N	G	A	G	N	A	N	G
MOON	A	G	N	A	N	G	A	G	N	A	N	G
MERCURY	A	G	N	A	N	G	A	G	N	A	N	G
VENUS	A	G	N	A	N	G	A	G	N	A	N	G
MARS	A	G	N	A	N	G	A	G	N	A	N	G
JUPITER	A	G	N	A	N	G	A	G	N	A	N	G
SATURN	A	G	N	A	N	G	A	G	N	A	N	G
URANUS	A	G	N	A	N	G	A	G	N	A	N	G
PLUTO	A	G	N	A	N	G	A	G	N	A	N	G

G = GOOD   N = NEUTRAL   A = ADVERSE

NEPTUNE IN LEO

♆ ♌	ARIES	TAURUS	GEMINI	CANCER	LEO	VIRGO	LIBRA	SCORPIO	SAGITT.	CAPRICORN	AQUARIUS	PISCES
SUN	G	A	G	N	A	N	G	A	G	N	A	N
MOON	G	A	G	N	A	N	G	A	G	N	A	N
MERCURY	G	A	G	N	A	N	G	A	G	N	A	N
VENUS	G	A	G	N	A	N	G	A	G	N	A	N
MARS	G	A	G	N	A	N	G	A	G	N	A	N
JUPITER	G	A	G	N	A	N	G	A	G	N	A	N
SATURN	G	A	G	N	A	N	G	A	G	N	A	N
URANUS	G	A	G	N	A	N	G	A	G	N	A	N
PLUTO	G	A	G	N	A	N	G	A	G	N	A	N

G = GOOD   N = NEUTRAL   A =ADVERSE

NEPTUNE IN VIRGO

♆ ♍	ARIES	TAURUS	GEMINI	CANCER	LEO	VIRGO	LIBRA	SCORPIO	SAGITT.	CAPRICORN	AQUARIUS	PISCES
SUN	N	G	A	G	N	A	N	G	A	G	N	A
MOON	N	G	A	G	N	A	N	G	A	G	N	A
MERCURY	N	G	A	G	N	A	N	G	A	G	N	A
VENUS	N	G	A	G	N	A	N	G	A	G	N	A
MARS	N	G	A	G	N	A	N	G	A	G	N	A
JUPITER	N	G	A	G	N	A	N	G	A	G	N	A
SATURN	N	G	A	G	N	A	N	G	A	G	N	A
URANUS	N	G	A	G	N	A	N	G	A	G	N	A
PLUTO	N	G	A	G	N	A	N	G	A	G	N	A

G = GOOD   N = NEUTRAL   A = ADVERSE

NEPTUNE IN LIBRA

♆ ♎	ARIES	TAURUS	GEMINI	CANCER	LEO	VIRGO	LIBRA	SCORPIO	SAGITT.	CAPRICORN	AQUARIUS	PISCES
SUN	A	N	G	A	G	N	A	N	G	A	G	N
MOON	A	N	G	A	G	N	A	N	G	A	G	N
MERCURY	A	N	G	A	G	N	A	N	G	A	G	N
VENUS	A	N	G	A	G	N	A	N	G	A	G	N
MARS	A	N	G	A	G	N	A	N	G	A	G	N
JUPITER	A	N	G	A	G	N	A	N	G	A	G	N
SATURN	A	N	G	A	G	N	A	N	G	A	G	N
URANUS	A	N	G	A	G	N	A	N	G	A	G	N
PLUTO	A	N	G	A	G	N	A	N	G	A	G	N

G = GOOD   N = NEUTRAL   A = ADVERSE

NEPTUNE IN SCORPIO

♆ ♏	ARIES	TAURUS	GEMINI	CANCER	LEO	VIRGO	LIBRA	SCORPIO	SAGITT.	CAPRICORN	AQUARIUS	PISCES
SUN	N	A	N	G	A	G	N	A	N	G	A	G
MOON	N	A	N	G	A	G	N	A	N	G	A	G
MERCURY	N	A	N	G	A	G	N	A	N	G	A	G
VENUS	N	A	N	G	A	G	N	A	N	G	A	G
MARS	N	A	N	G	A	G	N	A	N	G	A	G
JUPITER	N	A	N	G	A	G	N	A	N	G	A	G
SAUTRN	N	A	N	G	A	G	N	A	N	G	A	G
URANUS	N	A	N	G	A	G	N	A	N	G	A	G
PLUTO	N	A	N	G	A	G	N	A	N	G	A	G

G = GOOD   N = NEUTRAL   A = ADVERSE

NEPTUNE IN SAGITTARIUS

♆ ♐	ARIES	TAURUS	GEMINI	CANCER	LEO	VIRGO	LIBRA	SCORPIO	SAGITT.	CAPRICORN	AQUARIUS	PISCES
SUN	G	N	A	N	G	A	G	N	A	N	G	A
MOON	G	N	A	N	G	A	G	N	A	N	G	A
MERCURY	G	N	A	N	G	A	G	N	A	N	G	A
VENUS	G	N	A	N	G	A	G	N	A	N	G	A
MARS	G	N	A	N	G	A	G	N	A	N	G	A
JUPITER	G	N	A	N	G	A	G	N	A	N	G	A
SATURN	G	N	A	N	G	A	G	N	A	N	G	A
URANUS	G	N	A	N	G	A	G	N	A	N	G	A
PLUTO	G	N	A	N	G	A	G	N	A	N	G	A

G = GOOD   N = NEUTRAL   A = ADVERSE

NEPTUNE IN CAPRICORN

♆ ♑	ARIES	TAURUS	GEMINI	CANCER	LEO	VIRGO	LIBRA	SCORPIO	SAGITT.	CAPRICORN	AQUARIUS	PISCES
SUN	A	G	N	A	N	G	A	G	N	A	N	G
MOON	A	G	N	A	N	G	A	G	N	A	N	G
MERCURY	A	G	N	A	N	G	A	G	N	A	N	G
VENUS	A	G	N	A	N	G	A	G	N	A	N	G
MARS	A	G	N	A	N	G	A	G	N	A	N	G
JUPITER	A	G	N	A	N	G	A	G	N	A	N	G
SATURN	A	G	N	A	N	G	A	G	N	A	N	G
URANUS	A	G	N	A	N	G	A	G	N	A	N	G
PLUTO	A	G	N	A	N	G	A	G	N	A	N	G

G = GOOD   N = NEUTRAL   A = ADVERSE

NEPTUNE IN AQUARIUS

♆ ♒	ARIES	TAURUS	GEMINI	CANCER	LEO	VIRGO	LIBRA	SCORPIO	SAGITT.	CAPRICORN	AQUARIUS	PISCES
SUN	G	A	G	N	A	N	G	A	G	N	A	N
MOON	G	A	G	N	A	N	G	A	G	N	A	N
MERCURY	G	A	G	N	A	N	G	A	G	N	A	N
VENUS	G	A	G	N	A	N	G	A	G	N	A	N
MARS	G	A	G	N	A	N	G	A	G	N	A	N
JUPITER	G	A	G	N	A	N	G	A	G	N	A	N
SATURN	G	A	G	N	A	N	G	A	G	N	A	N
URANUS	G	A	G	N	A	N	G	A	G	N	A	N
PLUTO	G	A	G	N	A	N	G	A	G	N	A	N

G = GOOD   N = NEUTRAL   A = ADVERSE

PLUTO IN GEMINI

♇♊	ARIES	TAURUS	GEMINI	CANCER	LEO	VIRGO	LIBRA	SCORPIO	SAGITT.	CAPRICORN	AQUARIUS	PISCES
SUN	G	N	A	N	G	A	G	N	A	N	G	A
MOON	G	N	A	N	G	A	G	N	A	N	G	A
MERCURY	G	N	A	N	G	A	G	N	A	N	G	A
VENUS	G	N	A	N	G	A	G	N	A	N	G	A
MARS	G	N	A	N	G	A	G	N	A	N	G	A
JUPITER	G	N	A	N	G	A	G	N	A	N	G	A
SATURN	G	N	A	N	G	A	G	N	A	N	G	A
URANUS	G	N	A	N	G	A	G	N	A	N	G	A
NEPTUNE	G	N	A	N	G	A	G	N	A	N	G	A

G = GOOD   N = NEUTRAL   A = ADVERSE

PLUTO IN CANCER

♇♋	ARIES	TAURUS	GEMINI	CANCER	LEO	VIRGO	LIBRA	SCORPIO	SAGITT.	CAPRICORN	AQUARIUS	PISCES
SUN	A	G	N	A	N	G	A	G	N	A	N	G
MOON	A	G	N	A	N	G	A	G	N	A	N	G
MERCURY	A	G	N	A	N	G	A	G	N	A	N	G
VENUS	A	G	N	A	N	G	A	G	N	A	N	G
MARS	A	G	N	A	N	G	A	G	N	A	N	G
JUPITER	A	G	N	A	N	G	A	G	N	A	N	G
SATURN	A	G	N	A	N	G	A	G	N	A	N	G
URANUS	A	G	N	A	N	G	A	G	N	A	N	G
NEPTUNE	A	G	N	A	N	G	A	G	N	A	N	G

G = GOOD   N = NEUTRAL   A = ADVERSE

PLUTO IN LEO

♇♌	ARIES	TAURUS	GEMINI	CANCER	LEO	VIRGO	LIBRA	SCORPIO	SAGITT.	CAPRICORN	AQUARIUS	PISCES
SUN	G	A	G	N	A	N	G	A	G	N	A	N
MOON	G	A	G	N	A	N	G	A	G	N	A	N
MERCURY	G	A	G	N	A	N	G	A	G	N	A	N
VENUS	G	A	G	N	A	N	G	A	G	N	A	N
MARS	G	A	G	N	A	N	G	A	G	N	A	N
JUPITER	G	A	G	N	A	N	G	A	G	N	A	N
SATURN	G	A	G	N	A	N	G	A	G	N	A	N
URANUS	G	A	G	N	A	N	G	A	G	N	A	N
NEPTUNE	G	A	G	N	A	N	G	A	G	N	A	N

G = GOOD   N = NEUTRAL   A = ADVERSE

PLUTO IN VIRGO

♇ ♍	ARIES	TAURUS	GEMINI	CANCER	LEO	VIRGO	LIBRA	SCORPIO	SAGITT.	CAPRICORN	AQUARIUS	PISCES
SUN	N	G	A	G	N	A	N	G	A	G	N	A
MOON	N	G	A	G	N	A	N	G	A	G	N	A
MERCURY	N	G	A	G	N	A	N	G	A	G	N	A
VENUS	N	G	A	G	N	A	N	G	A	G	N	A
MARS	N	G	A	G	N	A	N	G	A	G	N	A
JUPITER	N	G	A	G	N	A	N	G	A	G	N	A
SATURN	N	G	A	G	N	A	N	G	A	G	N	A
URANUS	N	G	A	G	N	A	N	G	A	G	N	A
NEPTUNE	N	G	A	G	N	A	N	G	A	G	N	A

G = GOOD   N = NEUTRAL   A = ADVERSE

PLUTO IN LIBRA

♇ ♎	ARIES	TAURUS	GEMINI	CANCER	LEO	VIRGO	LIBRA	SCORPIO	SAGITT.	CAPRICORN	AQUARIUS	PISCES
SUN	A	N	G	A	G	N	A	N	G	A	G	N
MOON	A	N	G	A	G	N	A	N	G	A	G	N
MERCURY	A	N	G	A	G	N	A	N	G	A	G	N
VENUS	A	N	G	A	G	N	A	N	G	A	G	N
MARS	A	N	G	A	G	N	A	N	G	A	G	N
JUPITER	A	N	G	A	G	N	A	N	G	A	G	N
SATURN	A	N	G	A	G	N	A	N	G	A	G	N
URANUS	A	N	G	A	G	N	A	N	G	A	G	N
NEPTUNE	A	N	G	A	G	N	A	N	G	A	G	N

G = GOOD   N = NEUTRAL   A = ADVERSE

PLUTO IN SCORPIO

♇ ♏	ARIES	TAURUS	GEMINI	CANCER	LEO	VIRGO	LIBRA	SCORPIO	SAGITT.	CAPRICORN	AQUARIUS	PISCES
SUN	N	A	N	G	A	G	N	A	N	G	A	G
MOON	N	A	N	G	A	G	N	A	N	G	A	G
MERCURY	N	A	N	G	A	G	N	A	N	G	A	G
VENUS	N	A	N	G	A	G	N	A	N	G	A	G
MARS	N	A	N	G	A	G	N	A	N	G	A	G
JUPITER	N	A	N	G	A	G	N	A	N	G	A	G
SATURN	N	A	N	G	A	G	N	A	N	G	A	G
URANUS	N	A	N	G	A	G	N	A	N	G	A	G
NEPTUNE	N	A	N	G	A	G	N	A	N	G	A	G

G = GOOD   N = NEUTRAL   A = ADVERSE

ASPECTS

SUN AND MOON

Good

You are a well-integrated person, sincere, loyal and adaptable. You are ambitious and have the will and capacity to go to the top. Success frequently crowns your efforts, especially in business activities. Influential people tend to be helpful. Obtaining a suitable job with satisfactory pay is never much of a problem. Promotion generally comes pretty quickly. Your home life is usually harmonious and you strive to keep it that way. You are inclined to be lucky and to gain through investment, speculation and enterprise. A position of responsibility suits you. With Jupiter favorable, you are even more successful and are likely eventually to accumulate wealth.

Adverse

Although ambitious, you are apt to take foolish risks. Your actions are contradictory in many ways. You seldom seem to get very far ahead. You have difficulty accumulating money, and if ever you do, it soon slips through your fingers. Inwardly, you are very unsure of yourself. Restlessness is a problem. You are constantly frustrated because you are unable to express your deeper creative urges. Striving can bring about the odd achievement. You are emotionally sensitive and troubled by vague inner conflicts. Bursts of willpower quickly burn out. Overconfidence leads to loss and disappointment. Superiors are often unsympathetic. Childhood traumas linger. If Saturn is unfavorable, difficulties may come through women and illness.

SUN AND MERCURY

The Sun and Mercury are always so close together that good and bad aspects can't occur.

SUN AND VENUS

Good

You love the good life and are usually fortunate enough to be able to afford it. Ease and luxury suit your style. You are sociable and hospitable and enjoy entertaining in pleasant and comfortable surroundings. You are lucky in business and frequently successful where there is a bit of a gamble. You are popular with co-workers and superiors. In your affections, you are sympathetic, loving and kind. Your cheerful and agreeable manner attracts many friends. Courtesy is a strong characteristic. You usually enjoy a full and exciting love life, though you change partners quite often. Art, elegance and harmonious relationships bring out the best in you.

Adverse

Venus, like Mercury, is so close to the Sun that there is no really unfortunate aspect. But the mild adversity that is possible may produce a person who is fickle, extravagant, overfond of luxury and pleasure, and somewhat lazy.

SUN AND MARS

Good

You are a vital, courageous and enterprising person. You have an enviable frankness and an urgent, assertive temperament. Although aggressively ambitious, you do your best to stick to your principles and will avoid underhanded tactics as much as possible. You are progressive, generous and a natural leader. You take command quickly and have great faith in your ability to overcome obstacles. Your enthusiasm, determination and purposefulness attract others, especially in times of crisis or uncertainty. You have unusual stamina and vigor. You should shine in sports or athletics. Key people generally cooperate with you. A top executive post would suit you well. Your perception is quick. You'll take a chance. You are practical.

Adverse

You are your own worst enemy. You lack application, staying power. You try to do much, make a lot of dust and noise, but do not accomplish a great deal. You are forever looking around when you should be looking where you are going. You meet many obstacles head-on. You are impulsive, aggressive, combative and headstrong. You impress superiors at first meetings, but they tend to lose faith in you. You are impatient, bossy, obstructive and too easily hurt when your pride is touched. Your anger can be destructive. You are argumentative and likely to get into fist fights. You rub people the wrong way. Hasty actions often ruin your best chances. You have strong sensual desires. You tend to wear yourself out. Life has many ups and downs.

SUN AND JUPITER

Good

This is a very fortunate aspect. It will help to counter any adverse factors elsewhere in the horoscope. You are a broad-minded, farseeing person with a benevolent attitude toward others. People can't help liking you. You are honorable, generous, kind, a sympathetic listener, a wise counselor and a loyal friend. You are popular with influential people, who will usually go out of their way to help you. You are sincere, optimistic, honest and magnanimous. Chances are you are either wealthy or will be—or your mature optimism will keep you comfortable and contented as you are. You are inclined toward philosophic and religious thought. Good fortune seems to smile on you in most respects.

Adverse

You make frequent miscalculations. Financial problems often come through extravagance and social affairs. You are careless with your possessions and often have to borrow money. Gambling, poor judgment in making investments and silly ostentatious gestures designed to impress or infiltrate are likely to land you in constant difficulties. You are a sucker for taking the wrong tip and poor advice. Court actions can be costly. Your love of pleasure may cause ill health. You are indiscriminate in your choice of friends and are apt to become tight with any bar-fly who throws you a wave, a laugh and a few compliments. At times, you are bombastic, boastful and conceited. You live an indolent life and trust too much to luck—which often lets you down.

SUN AND SATURN

Good

You succeed mostly through your own ef-

forts. You are the typical self-made man or woman. You have the ability to persevere and concentrate on what you want out of life. You climb slowly but very surely. You have a talent for assessing situations down to the last detail, and for organizing the means to deal with them. You never take anything for granted. You are extremely ambitious and can take the most depressing setbacks in your stride. Your readiness to accept limitations and to make the best of what's offered will help you to become successful in later life. You are sincere, conservative and methodical. You are not inhibited by other people's opinions or fears. Responsibility is second nature to you. Practical, authoritative and patient, you are often admired for your practical wisdom.

Adverse

You are no stranger to disappointment and sorrow. Obstacles continually hinder your progress. When you do succeed, there is usually a condition attached to your rewards, or they are snatched from you at the last moment and you have to start all over. You run into more than your share of enemies, opposition and competitors. Business affairs are unlucky, especially those connected with government or large companies. It is unlikely you enjoy the sympathy of the public, superiors or those in important positions. There may be difficulties connected with your father. Self-pity is a danger, pessimism a chronic complaint. For a woman, marriage will have its trials.

SUN AND URANUS

Good

There's a touch of genius about your thinking. Whatever line you follow, you can be depended on to produce some sensational ideas. You should be in an occupation where your inventive mind and its flashes of inspiration can be practically utilized. You have a good chance of success in public or government projects. Big-time promotion and entertainment may appeal to you. Although fiercely independent, you do best working with a group toward some noble or humanitarian objective. You would make an admirable leader in the scientific or medical research industry; electronics could be your specialty. You are a rebel and a reformer in many ways, with a talent for originality and enterprise. You are magnetic and have many friends and acquaintances.

Adverse

You are rash, erratic and unconventional. There is not much hope of a happy marriage. Your friends and many acquaintances are unreliable, like yourself. You are impulsive and willing to take risks that aren't worth the odds. You endure many sudden and shattering changes in your life. Love affairs often end unfortunately, sometimes disastrously. Your involvement with groups and organizations is usually disruptive. When you think you are helping most, you are dividing. You are insistent on the rightness of your ideas and on getting your own way. You have an awkward manner with ordinary people and often upset them. It is hard for you to remain very long in one job or one place.

SUN AND NEPTUNE

Good

You have refined feelings and emotions and possess a powerful and vivid imagination. Your keen appreciation of the intangibles of beauty and art sometimes puts you in a world apart. You tend to express yourself through music, poetry, literature or dancing. You are intensely idealistic. Although you feel propelled toward higher aims you may have difficulty in defining them. You are capable of psychic experiences, including visions, and are drawn to religion, mysticism and the occult. You enjoy the sun and the sea. Often you are inspired when speaking, thinking or writing. You strive for fineness and elegance.

Adverse

You are inspired in your head but can't find a suitable means of self-expression. You are vague, ambivalent and in many ways a muddler. If you are not deceitful, you are apt to be a victim of treachery, fraud or scandal. A desire to escape from the world may lead to excessive use of drugs and alcohol. Sexual permissiveness is also a possibility. Resistance to suggestion is low. Weird dreams are likely to disturb your sleep. Peculiar feelings and desires may cause restlessness. Loss is probably through children, love affairs and speculation. Illnesses may be hard to diagnose.

SUN AND PLUTO

Good

You will always be prepared to cut old ties to begin anew if necessary. You are the type who would make a strong politician or law enforcement officer, capable of cleaning up rackets and corruption in high places. Your investigative na-

ture gives you a fresh approach to old problems, although other factors in the horoscope will determine how long you may postpone action. It delights you to start building after the old has been discarded. You are daring, self-confident and self-contained. You endeavor to eliminate all unwanted bonds. You strive to free yourself of habitual and rigid situations. Pluto's influences tend to be more general than individual. With this aspect, it offers the possibility of self-renewal.

Adverse

There is a strong potential in you for callous and ruthless action. Although other zodiacal factors will probably mitigate the full effects of this unfavorable aspect, even so, it tends to be antisocial and relentless in its selfish drives. The tendency for self-destruction is evident through overestimating personal capacity, taking unnecessary risks and ignoring consequences. You are apt to use other people with devilish disregard for their feelings and physical welfare. The egotistical urge for power is your dominating drive. The megalomaniac dictator could very well have this aspect in his chart. So could the all-powerful "respectable" gangland boss.

MOON AND MERCURY

Good

You are a fluent, entertaining and interesting person to talk to. If you haven't tried your hand at writing or public speaking, you should. If other aspects are favorable, your mind and senses should be beautifully coordinated and your communications unmistakably true to life. You are quick-witted, ingenious and could make a capable linguist. You enjoy change, revel in new ideas and are always on the lookout for novel experiences. You are sympathetic and possess sound common sense. You are a great comfort to those who bring their troubles to you, being able to feel and describe their emotions with rare sensitivity. You enjoy pleasure and possess a fine appreciation of art in most of its forms. Your intuition is remarkable.

Adverse

You are a chatterbox and forever complaining or blaming others for your misfortunes. You are ruled by a frenetic and superficial imagination. Vague and uncomprehended fears torment you. You look everywhere for reassurance. You are uncertain, anxious, aimlessly speculative about the future. You have a sharp and stinging tongue. But there is no deep-seated desire to hurt in you: just a need to reduce others to your own self-doubting level. You are ingenious, clever and devious. You lack stability and concentration and are not much good at business. Your painfully tense nervous system may cause chronic stomach upsets. Although at times entertaining, you seldom win wide popularity.

MOON AND VENUS

Good

You are a nice person to know, good natured, kind and agreeable. You enjoy the company of the opposite sex and are usually very much at ease in social situations. Something about you is distinctly attractive to others, even though you may not be what is called baautiful or handsome. You dress tastefully, have a flair for fashion. You are affectionate, loving and gentle. Your manner is mild and refined. You have a penchant for pleasure, and although not terribly intellectual, enjoy light literature. You love artistic and beautiful things. You like meeting people and usually possess sufficient money and a comfortable home in which to entertain.

Adverse

You may be sloppy and careless around the house. Domestic relations are not likely to be too happy. You may be the innocent victim of another family member's cruelty or tyranny; or you could bring unhappiness on yourself through a stubborn disregard for the feelings of others. Chances are you're a rather cold and unsympathetic person who uses people. But when it comes to sensual pleasures, you may be extremely self-indulgent. Sexual promiscuity is a danger with this aspect. You are not lucky with money and seldom are able to accumulate property or attractive possessions. You may be slovenly in your habits and appearance.

MOON AND MARS

Good

You are a vibrant and stimulating person with loads of energy and acute senses. You enjoy working and being out of doors. Even though you may be employed in an office, you probably like nothing better on weekends than digging vigorously in the garden or going for stiff hikes through the forest or along the shore. You feel a lot of life pounding in your body. You are very quick-acting—perhaps a little too quick at times (no sooner said than done is your style). You inspire the confidence of others with your live-wire

common-sense approach. When you make a decision, you stick to it. You are ambitious, resourceful and very hard working. You are well fitted for responsibility and should succeed in any activity that caters to public taste.

Adverse

You are always putting your foot in it, upsetting others by your actions or your words. Your moods are notoriously changeable—effusive one minute, withdrawn and sullen the next. You don't seem to enjoy peace, although you may spend most of your time looking for it. If you're not picking an argument or quarreling, you're blaming someone else for your problems. You're also impulsive. You'll take risks, lash out unthinkingly, incite gossip and scandal through your indiscretions and make enemies unnecessarily. You often compete to combat. You are irritable, bad-tempered and careless of consequences. You're brave enough, but you leave trails of sorrow. Unhappiness through your mother, family or marriage partner is most likely.

MOON AND JUPITER

Good

You should have a fortunate and fairly easy ride through life, other influences being equal. Good health and an optimistic and hopeful outlook make you a desirable partner and companion. You won't surrender to depression; you look on the brighter side, usually with justification. You are compassionate, honest, friendly and have a fine sense of justice and fair play. You should make a happy marriage. You probably come from a home where love and understanding were practiced and taught by your mother or some maternal figure. A literary career would suit you, as would publishing or education. You are intuitive, imaginative and admire beauty. Generosity and a genuine respect for the rights of others no matter what their station of life ensure your popularity.

Adverse

You are always making changes in your life but few of them turn out the way you desire. You are apt to be involved in scandal at some time or other. You are likely to lose out through overconfidence and ill health. Long journeys may bring misfortune. Foreigners may be unlucky for you. Friendly people with ulterior motives will dupe you. If you gamble, you are sure to lose in the long run. Any dishonesty will eventually catch up with you. Money gains may come to you easier than to others, but they will be intercepted in some way or quickly dissipated. Your extrvagance will provide little satisfaction. You are likely to be alienated or separated in unhappy circumstances from your mother or home.

MOON AND SATURN

Good

You are tactful and diplomatic, preferring to accomplish your ends without force. Although ambitious, you take your time, always assessing the obstacles and the resources of the opposition before making a start. Your conservative and thoughtful manner engenders respect and trust of superiors and those with whom you work. You are likely to make your mark in any enterprise dependent on public support, or where there is an appreciation of methodical and persistent effort. You can borrow money easily and stand to gain through employers, parents, friends and older people. You wish to be esteemed, and for this alone, you will toil without respite. You are orderly and systematic and much more timid than you appear.

Adverse

You don't have much luck. Though hardworking and industrious, you seldom realize your ambitions. If you have money, you'll probably lose it. Even in good times, you find it hard to make ends meet. The burdens of elders may make it impossible for you to get ahead. Three steps forward, two back, is the general rule for this aspect. Opportunities just don't seem to be there; or if they are, unexpected obstacles prevent you from seizing them. Marriage is likely to be unhappy or unfulfilling, at least the first time. Too much concentration on practical needs may dull your natural sympathies. Chances of happiness may be missed through shyness and feelings of inadequacy.

MOON AND URANUS

Good

Changes are good for you. Even in steady employment you should find you progress faster by doing different kinds of work rather than one repetitive job. This sort of variety makes you highly productive. You have a strong intuition and an excellent grasp of what the public wants. Commercially, this can be very profitable. But you usually aim to do some kind of good through your work. You are humane and acutely aware of mankind's sufferings and difficulties. You have

an eye for the unusual; you can obliterate the past and see new ways of attacking problems and overcoming obstacles. You enjoy the friendship of the opposite sex. You are independent, progressive, inventive and curious.

Adverse

You are temperamental, cantankerous and quick to take offense. Your friendships break up easily under the strain of your emotional instability. You are frequently beset with love troubles. The women in your life are very changeful. If you are a woman, your own fickleness will cause you constant problems. You are high-strung and intellectually receptive, but easily irritated. People always seem to be letting you down. Your likes and dislikes are pronounced and everchanging. You can't stand the confinement of one job or one place for long. You swing from one extreme to another. Others may think you're a bit peculiar.

MOON AND NEPTUNE

Good

You may daydream yourself out of existence unless this aspect is countered by a more compelling one. The tendency to sit back and let everything happen while you retreat into your own mental world is dangerously attractive here. The pipeline to the unconscious is a wide one and this access to your own depths is almost certain to result in an unusual but aesthetic form of self-expression. Apart from music, art, dancing and acting, you have an aptitude for ESP and other types of psychism. If developed, this could have considerable public impact. All careers associated with satisfying the public taste should provide opportunities for success. Your imagination is incredibly real to you.

Adverse

There is a grave danger here of self-delusion. You may convince yourself that your dream world is truer than reality, and be setting yourself up for a percussive and painful awakening. The opposite sex causes difficulties. Marriage for men will be delayed and encounter obstacles. You may be fascinated by peculiar people and weird ideas. Your great sensitivity makes you susceptible to all influences, especially the sensuous. Eagerness for sense experience may overcome your judgment and lead to indiscretion, and in some cases, disgrace. You pick up on good and bad environments instantly—some can actually make you physically sick.

MOON AND PLUTO

Good

Remember that Pluto's influence tends to show in generations of people more than individuals because the planet spends an average of 24 years in each Sign. But with this aspect, you have the capacity to make and accept changes in your way of life with smooth and harmonious adjustment. Changes are probably quite common. Your moods also fluctuate quite widely, but without disturbing or alienating others. You are variable without caprice, and are often secretly admired or envied for this trait. Sometimes your fortunes twist violently, but you have a way of turning whatever eventuates to good account.

Adverse

A thread of sudden, mind-shaking upsets runs through your life. People and situations you become accustomed to tend to be whipped away, leaving you nonplussed and insecure. The more stabilizing the other factors in the horoscope, the less likely this will be noticed overtly. But there is an ever-present danger of neurosis. Your emotions and moods are subject to jolting extremes that bewilder both you and your associates. You are a person who frequently has to begin all over again. Secretive, sullen brooding makes you a pain in the neck to be with at times. Acrimonious outbursts are not unusual.

MERCURY AND VENUS

Good

You are amiable, cheerful and witty. Your manner is pleasing, your speech articulate and charming. There is a sophisticated, cultured air about you. You enjoy the artistic side of life. You are fond of pleasure and ease and seek the company of refined and thoughtful people. You are popular with the opposite sex and have a penchant for entertaining and fraternizing at a high social level. You have many friends and are likely to marry at least once. You should make a comfortable living, possibly from writing, speaking or art. Other influences being equal, you epitomize the polished diplomat. You are expressive with your hands.

Adverse

As Venus is always so close to Mercury, they are never really in bad aspect. In fact, the little pressure that an adverse aspect might produce is likely to be productive. Instead of sitting back and enjoying the genteel life (as is the likelihood

with a good aspect), you are apt to strive to communicate your artistic leanings in some definite form, such as designing, painting or handicrafting. You want to use your mind and bounce creative ideas off it rather than absorb them into an amorphous harmony. You may be hindered by a speech defect and find making decisions is difficult for you.

MERCURY AND MARS

Good

Your mind is splendidly active and intensely practical. No airy-fairy discourses for you; you want progress—activity plus enterprise. You like to put your concepts down on paper, to make workmanlike plans, to give ideas concrete form. You have a natural talent for designing, music, engineering and science. In your work, you endeavor to devise new and practical methods. Your mind is constantly examining and investigating. You are a rapid and enthusiastic talker, witty, entertaining and ingenious. Few can equal you in debate. You enjoy speed and being on the move. Fast cars and sexy, intelligent playmates delight you and vice versa.

Adverse

You are easily irritated, sarcastic, impatient and very shrewd. You feel strongly about what you want out of life, but lack the persistence necessary to achieve it. You fall short, make do with compromise, and then resentfully reject the result. You don't know much peace. You are excitable, quick-tempered, argumentative and very bright intellectually. Your stinging criticisms and thoughtless actions create enemies and opposition. Frustration and anger can inflame your highly charged nervous system to the point of breakdown. Loss is likely through recklessness, carelessness and hasty conclusions.

MERCURY AND JUPITER

Good

Your judgment is A1. You take the broadest view of things. There is nothing small or petty about your mental attitudes. You are a type capable of great accomplishment in literature, science, business or the professions. Your power to earn money with your mind is greater than most. Although you can grasp the most complex arguments, you are not a great one for detail. You prefer to formulate sweeping concepts and leave the punctuation marks to others. You are extremely versatile and creative.

You have a high regard for honesty and truth. As a companion, you are generous, jovial and humorous. There's something of the sage in your utterances. You enjoy change and traveling; both are usually fortunate for you.

Adverse

You are indiscreet and often lose sight of the conventional curbs society has found necessary to impose to protect itself from temperaments like yours. What you regard as funny or amusing often strikes others as offensive or bad form. Though your judgment is poor, you persist in airing your views. You can be a crushing bore. You tend to ramble on, exaggerating childishly and making statements likely to make you the object of a slander action. You are impressionable, verbose, and too often loud and conceited. You're a bit devious but lack the concentration for any prolonged deception. Misfortune comes to you through backing and filling.

MERCURY AND SATURN

Good

You are methodical, painstaking and a stalwart. You are inclined to get hold of an idea and stick to it through thick and thin until it is realized. Your mind is extremely practical. You possess an extraordinary talent for organizing work into manageable departments, which you then proceed to control with great executive ability. There is always sound common sense behind your thinking. With people, you are tactful and diplomatic, though not overfriendly at first. You like to proceed cautiously in all your relationships. Much of your time is spent summing up others. You have an excellent memory and make shrewd assessments. Your judgment is tops.

Adverse

Your education was probably neglected or disorganized. You lack self-confidence and therefore miss chances through timidity and indecision. Most of your efforts are marred by complications and delays, not necessarily of your own making. Your thinking tends to be narrow and rigid. You are a carping critic of those who enjoy fun and light conversation. In business, you are constructive, if you can get beyond planning, detail and finding fault. Your mind is too cut off from others to maintian much humor or elasticity. Decisions are weighed against practical results rather than for their effect on people's feelings. Ill will and pique often result.

MERCURY AND URANUS

Good

This is a brilliant aspect that usually produces an original mind with a scientific bent. You are unconventional. You refuse to approach life or the practical problems of your career from the same old standpoint. In the social sense, this may make some of your responses seem a bit peculiar, but from the inventive angle, they could be regarded as strokes of genius responsible for a revolutionary new theory, product or method. Independence is very important to you. You won't conform just because others do. In fact, you are just as likely to deliberately go the other way. You are drawn to investigate the curious and unusual. Your speech is quick and dramatic, your actions sudden and unexpected.

Adverse

You are mentally acute, but a little too much the old-fashioned revolutionary to gain wide acceptance for your views. You are a bit of a knockdown, drag-out slogan man or woman. You are clumsy at communicating and abrupt, tending to separate rather than bridge. You may be a fanatic, a victim of your own war cries; or you may be dismissed as an eccentric. Equipped with the best idea in the world, you would convey it in such a way that it would be ignored or laughed at. Although you have the spirit of a reformer, you lack the panache to be effective. You are a restless and discontented person who has to cope with numerous reversals.

MERCURY AND NEPTUNE

Good

You will have noticed that you are somewhat psychic, having deep inspirational insights into people and yourself. Your sensitivity is extremely refined and you receive impressions that most others miss. Your imagination is fertile, an ideal source of ideas if you are an author, poet or artistic innovator. You use words with mellifluous ease. You are quick and practical, versatile and resourceful. You reach deep into your emotions and observe your own thought processes making you mystically perceptive or aware. Your dreams are frequently prophetic. You would make a sensitive dancer, mimic or artist. Clairvoyance and other psi abilities are well within your range.

Adverse

Your mind is disorganized, vacillating, vague. A soaring and ceaseless imagination makes it difficult for you to relate for long to practical realities. Your judgment and concentration are impared by flights of fantasy. You are often confused and frequently duped by the clever and unscrupulous. You are touchy. At the first sign of discomfort or opposition, you retreat into your mind. There you repair any damage to your own satisfaction but leave gaping holes in your worldly relationships. You are absentminded and irresolute. You have a strong intuition, which you substitute for reason. You may be a heartless rogue, tricking others with your plausible stories and sham innocence.

MERCURY AND PLUTO

Good

Your mind is incisive and penetrating. You have a natural talent for psychoanalysis. You can temporarily rid your mind of its inhibitions and conditioning and perceive the emotions working in another. You can throw off worry and thus ease your own nervous tensions, which could otherwise be a problem. You are able to reason from new angles and get refreshing results. Since Pluto spends an average of 24 years in each Sign, its effects are mainly on generations of people rather than on individuals. But the characteristics mentioned are intrinsic to your nature and therefore capable of development if not already active.

Adverse

You may use your keen mind to harass or tyrannize others and take advantage of their weaknesses. You are sarcastic, vitriolic and explosive. Your nerves are continually on edge and you choose the most perverse ways to ease the strain. You are secretive, scheming and capable (if there is no restraining influence in the rest of the horoscope) of using the written or spoken word, innuendo or rumor, in the most despicable ways. The poison pen writer who destroys another's reputation or life could have this aspect.

VENUS AND MARS

Good

You are ardent and enthusiastic in your relationships. You make a passionate and pleasing lover. You are affectionate and concerned for the younger ones in your family. You don't just talk about pleasant plans—you try to put them into action. You appreciate art in most forms, especially when it has practical application. You

would make a good architect, sculptor, fine engraver or civil engineer concerned with balance and shapes. You are romantic and chivalrous and possess great sex appeal. You have a head for business and can earn money better than you can hold on to it. You are a cheerful free spender. You are likely to marry very young or suddenly.

Adverse

Your love life is intense, compulsive and eruptive. Love seldom runs smooth for you. You may mean well in your affections, but usually you manage to hurt or cut with an impulsive word or action. You are quarrelsome and crude. Your sexual appetite may lead to you excesses that result in scandal or unhappiness. Misfortune comes through partnerships; loss through recklessness, carelessness and extravagance. Friends may turn against you in jealousy and desert you. Gambling and speculative pursuits rarely prove profitable. You'll take a swipe at anyone who gets in the way when you're after what you want.

VENUS AND JUPITER

Good

This is an excellent aspect. It creates harmonious and profitable relationships both in business and marriage. You possess an innate charm that attracts others and usually projects you into the highest echelons of society. You have numerous happy love affairs, and seem to attract money, position and comfort. Your tastes are refined and you enjoy all that is elegant, luxurious and expensive. You are keenly interested in artistic pursuits and usually earn your living from these. You are well-informed on foreign affairs and political matters. Your opinion is sought and respected by those in authority.

Adverse

All the qualities mentioned above become exaggerated and turn sour. Too much charm translates into affectation and insincerity. Overindulgence in pleasure causes ill health and dissolute habits. Your companions often detract from your reputation or damage your chances. Notoriety is likely. Despite your yearning for the good things in life, you are forced to settle for second best. Love affairs are unhappy, partners resentful, demanding. Excessive eating and drinking leads to a weight problem. Business partnerships are both unsuccessful and costly. You lose through offhandedness, fraud, deception and desertion.

VENUS AND SATURN

Good

Love to you is a very serious matter. You believe in being faithful to one person. Sometimes you have to serve the person you love in a menial or dedicated way and make considerable sacrifices on his or her behalf. You are resolute, though, and you enjoy doing your duty as you see it, as though it were a compensation for the affection you are often denied. Good, in the form of material benefit, usually comes to you in the end. Your social life is not particularly active, but this does not trouble you. Business partnerships work well, especially when elders are involved. You are thrifty, trustworthy and held in high esteem by those in authority.

Adverse

Marriage may be delayed or result in onerous responsibilities for many years. Early divorces or separations from those you like best are probable. Parents, relatives and elders may cause reversals and problems. The promiscuous behavior of a partner may result in disappointment, humiliation and prolonged distress. A solitary life may deaden your emotional responses and make you depressing and unpopular company. Your sensuality may be a coarse and repulsive, your sense of humor crude and obscene. Any show of affection on your part is likely to lead to sorrow or be misinterpreted. Although diplomatic, your cold, self-centered nature may repel all but those who are like you.

VENUS AND URANUS

Good

You intrigue people with your unusual ideas about sex, love and marriage. Because you stimulate the interest of the opposite sex, you are seldom without an attractive partner, but these associations do have a habit of breaking up after a time, although usually for good reason and without rancor. Your ideas on art are radical and impressive, but once you've made your point, you like to move ahead and experiment with more progressive departures. You are fortunate in business and usually gain through partnership. Strangers, chance meetings and unexpected happenings seem to work in your favor.

Adverse

Partnerships have very little chance of permanent success and usually end in violent ructions. You arouse others with your uncon-

ventional and provocative views, but are a bit of a straw man or woman and usually prove a disappointment on closer acquaintance. Your ideas of independence and freedom may be intolerable because they amount to license. You are erratic in your affections and infuriatingly unpredictable. You link up with all kinds of odd people, including strangers who are usually as eccentric as yourself. You need a sounding board for your ideas, and any old head with an ear will do. You may wish to revolutionize the art world, but succeed only in getting a reputation as a nut.

VENUS AND NEPTUNE

Good

This aspect produces heightened creativity. The temperament can be almost ideal in its power to create pleasing, rhythmic and profoundly satisfying art forms. Dancing, music, poetry, painting and vividly descriptive literature that excites rather than soothes the emotions are among your latent abilities. Even if you don't express your artistry in a tangible way, you need a refined enviornment to be happy. You are sensitive and consummately understanding. You possess a wonderful ability to calm the anxieties of people who are compatible with you. But exacting types distress you. Your intuition regarding others is incredibly accurate.

Adverse

Your head may be too far above the clouds for you to come down to earth and realize your potentialities; or you may delude yourself, pouring constructive effort into ideas that have no chance of succeeding. You are prone to disappointment, especially in love and marriage. Your disillusionment may be monumental. In sex, you may be used abominably. Partnerships usually turn out disastrously—always when it's too late for you to back out. You have strong and compulsive feelings, but difficulty in finding a harmonious outlet for them. The idea of voluptuous escape appeals to you, but your attempts in this direction usually end in nagging discontent or are confined to erotic daydreams.

VENUS AND PLUTO

Good

Since Pluto averages 24 years in each Sign, its influence is more general than individual. Still, it always has a background effect, discernible through the play of the more personalized planets. Your love life is often marked by violent changes that, oddly, produce favorable results in the end. Partnership matters seldom run as planned. Disclosures and exposures may force you to make new starts. You become attached to people and situations and often have to give them up. Once you make a change, something inside you prevents you from going back. You are sexually attractive and a bit of a fatalist. Your thoughts range from the lustily erotic to the spiritually profound.

Adverse

Shattering reversals are not uncommon in your love affairs. Many of your associations end unpleasantly. Try as you may, you rarely succeed in putting the pieces back together. Attachments invariably result in wrenching unhappiness; or you have a habit of mistaking infatuation for love and being disenchanted. Once entrenched, your desires are obsessive. Money may mean more to you than people. Sex can be a major problem. Divisive and unhappy experiences are repeated until the lessons are learned.

MARS AND JUPITER

Good

You exhibit the best qualities of leadership; a combination of courage, determination and intelligence. You inspire confidence in others and can exhort them to action. Money never seems to be a great problem for long. You have a rollicking sense of humor and enjoy gaiety and fun. You are firm and commanding when necessary, but fair. Your views are broad and you are concerned about the root problems of the world. You are prepared to do something concrete about the things you believe in. You would make a competent business executive, capable of controlling large industrial and commercial enterprises. You enjoy helping people who help themselves. In debate, you are a lively and resourceful opponent. You are active in mind and body. You have a knack for getting the best out of people.

Adverse

You are wildly impulsive and suffer through your own extreme actions. You seem incapable of maintaining a steady or moderate course. Other factors in the horoscope may modify this aspect, but if not, you are in constant danger of damaging your health through working or playing too hard. You may be absurdly and recklessly generous. Compulsive gambling may keep you in debt, leading to evasion of creditors and brazen lying. Aggravation and difficulty may come

through long journeys and contact with distant people or places. In business, broken contracts and deception may add to your troubles.

MARS AND SATURN

Good

You are an indomitable sort of individual, able to combine energetic action with dogged perseverance. There is not much you put your mind to that you can't accomplish in time. You make an excellent top executive. You have great endurance and remarkable initiative, though you may be a bit too dogmatic and overbearing at times. You are well suited for pioneering conditions—when the going is tough and others are losing heart. Danger and the possibility of defeat seldom deter you. You are skillful, ambitious and usually rise to a position of prominence or power. You manage to cope with emotional strain by releasing it through work.

Adverse

Injury through accidents is likely. Falls, burns and scalds will leave their mark. You are not a well-integrated person; you suffer from a chronic inner conflict, the tugging and pulling of two inimical forces. You are hasty and impulsive, though also grindingly patient when it suits you. Your temper is atrocious, and if ever it gets out of control, you can be dangerous. You resent opposition in any form and are revengeful. With rivals, you are likely to be cruel and deceptive. You are cynical and selfish and have to battle for most of what comes your way. Without failing disastrously in any one thing, you're something of an all-around loser—and too stern or harsh to engender much affection or sympathy.

MARS AND URANUS

Good

You are capable of great achievements, given the challenge. Space travel and research could easily be your field, or some advanced engineering or scientific project may benefit from your inventive and productive mind. Your unusual talents, which may border on genius in your particular line, often put you at the head of things. If you aren't recognized as a leader, you are apt to break away from the group and set up in opposition, with disruptive results for all concerned. You are ambitious and practical, though very intellectual. You possess flair and style. You love the independent kind of life and usually manage to get your own way.

Adverse

You are restless, unsettled and unsettling. Although a magnetic and galvanizing leader, you are apt to be reckless and overstretch yourself or your resources. You suffer from nervous strain, which drives you to thoughtless actions. You are headstrong and impatient, a terror when you get the bit in your mouth, for you don't know when or where to stop. Your partnerships—either business or marital—usually burst apart. You are tactless and antagonistic, eccentric and erratic. You want to throw off all limitations, but lack the judgment to set correct priorities. You are often forced to change your objectives.

MARS AND NEPTUNE

Good

You are an activist, an idealist, a crusader. You want to see the world put right, especially for the poor and suffering. You are likely to pour your considerable energies into any cause that seeks to end pain and suffering in some form or other. You are often successful, but seldom in a way that provides a great deal of personal satisfaction. You can't rest on your laurels. You are psychically sensitive. You have the temperament to explore the unknown, the unusual. You enjoy experimenting and acting out dramatic roles. You are drawn to the arts, especially those expressed through body movements and rhythms. Some of your cherished goals are unattainable. You are intrigued by the call and the sound of the sea.

Adverse

Your energies may be wasted in hopeless causes. You are likely to be attracted to glamorous people and situations that lead to scandal or disrepute. Weird and peculiar experiences are common in your life. Strange, inexplicable fears may make it difficult for you to live normally. Chaotic conditions can result from forays into the world of imagination and emotive daydreams. Your appetite for sensual gratification may be insatiable. Dependence on alcohol or narcotics may lead to involuntary confinement. Sadistic tendencies may have to be resisted. The pursuit of glory as a reason for being may lead to your downfall.

MARS AND PLUTO

Good

Since Pluto spends an average of 24 years in each Sign, its influence is more general than individual, but it always has a background effect that is discernible through the play of the more personalized planets. Your life is notable for disintegrating upheavals that tend to turn out for the best in the end. Painful new beginnings are forced on you. You have splendid recuperative powers and bounce back into action after a setback with a great energy. You enjoy power, especially stepping in to take command in nearly hopeless situations. You are aggressive, bold and combative. You don't dwell on the past.

Adverse

Explosive changes force you to face new conditions. No sooner do you throw yourself into a challenge than it takes an abrupt or violent new turn. Though you endeavor to cling to situations, you are compelled to let go. You possess a deep, aggressive self-tormenting drive that impels you to speak cruelly and vindictively. Happiness and fulfillment always seem to beckon on the other side of a fight. Your combative nature continually gets the better of you no matter how often you may resolve to cool it.

JUPITER AND SATURN

Good

This aspect produces sound financial prospects. Although you have a temperament that could easily go to extremes, you manage to control it and therefore get the best of two worlds. General good fortune seems to be your lot. You make the most of opportunities. Your business judgment is good, and you are likely to inherit wealth, especially in later years. You are optimistic and always thinking about expansion in common-sense terms. You are a serious and profound thinker, well suited for science, politics or a judicial position. Your mind is acute and absorbs knowledge easily. In your expansive moods, you learn to work productively; when your mind becomes withdrawn and introspective, you reflect, meditate and grow wiser.

Adverse

Success comes only after much hard work. You often feel you are getting nowhere and, understandably, find it difficult to remain enthusiastic. When pessimism intervenes, hope recedes, opportunities are missed. Your timing in financial matters never seems quite right; investments seldom yield the optimum. If money comes your way, you try to cling to it to the point of denying yourself the ordinary pleasures of life, or you indulge in bouts of self-gratification and afterward suffer excruciating remorse. You decide on one thing one moment and do the other the next. Despair can have tragic consequences.

JUPITER AND URANUS

Good

You possess a remarkably different—almost unique—reasoning power. Your logical processes are highly refined, but you require scope to use them. You really should be involved in some advanced scientific research or profound philosophic study. Certainly you won't be content making light conversation or gossiping. You stand to gain from travel, foreign investment, currency speculation, publishing, inventions and group research. Higher education and the law are also likely to interest you. You are generally lucky and may benefit through a legacy. You are a riveting original thinker with a broad progressive outlook.

Adverse

Your radical views are likely to land you in trouble with the Establishment. Although you're probably worth listening to, you have the unfortunate habit of choosing the wrong moment to make your point or your move. Too much militancy will lead to a clash with the law. You are impetuous and ever ready to assert your "rights," which the majority may regard as license. You are apt to lose through court actions and unexpected eventualities. Property is unlucky for you. Inheritances may be delayed or suddenly disputed by determined and powerful groups. Friends may be a source of trouble and annoyance.

JUPITER AND NEPTUNE

Good

Good things tend to flow to you, usually in intangible but personally satisfying ways. You have an inspirational temperament that, with steadying, may be a help to the world. Your ultra-refined imagination and emotions can be expressed in religion, work or art. You have a heart-rending sympathy for those in distress and may devote yourself to nursing and caring for them. If drawn to artistic effort, you will try to express intangibles, possibly in the rhythms of music or dancing, light patterns or diffusive colors. If wealthy, you have a tendency to philanthropy. The mystical and devotional side of religion has great appeal for you. You are likely to benefit from hidden sources. You have some remarkable dreams and psychic experiences.

Adverse

All that is favorable above may cause trouble and hardship. The danger of fantasy taking over from reason is great. Excuses may be found for practically any kind of behavior, including treachery, moral degradation, drug addiction, alcoholism and just plain dropoutism. You may be fanatical in your beliefs and suffer from severe emotional disturbances. Your health may be indifferent and your whole mental outlook distorted by secret sorrows and irrational self-condemnation.

JUPITER AND PLUTO

Good

You will probably become suddenly famous or prominent in the community at some time during your life. Whenever you discard old ways or methods or break with contacts of the past, there is apt to be rapid progress. You are a particularly resourceful person and are never really stuck for a way in or out. You have deep insights into people's character and can be relied on to evoke courage and enthusiasm from others in the face of danger and adversity.

Adverse

You are likely to be a rabble-rousing revolutionary who destroys his or her chances through impatience. Your desire for violent change and overthrow may be more important than any transforming principles involved. This is the aspect of a person who out of compulsion to escape blows up the wall of his cell and spends the rest of his life limping around with one leg. The "freedoms" gained through violent action are often more binding than the old order. The capacity for fiendish cruelty toward others in the name of a cause or ideal typifies this aspect. The Papal Inquisition, in which the Church condoned the torture and burning of people, is an example.

SATURN AND URANUS

Good

You have exceptional ability for galvanizing action in unusual ways and for maintaining control of it so that unusual results are achieved. This aspect brings into harmony two ordinarily inimical qualities—freedom and limitation. You, being the point where they meet, are apt to suffer from a degree of nervous tension—but this mild stress keeps you on the ball, alert to new opportunities. You are inventive and efficient, systematic and resourceful. You won't acknowledge any limitations to your thinking when facing a problem, yet, once the decisions are made, you have a fixity of purpose that will see a thing through right to the finish.

Adverse

You have an aggressive and lawless streak. Violent and insurgent acts appeal to you. Your attitudes to society are quite peculiar at times—you have an urge to institute reforms no one else may want. You are impulsive, imaginative and eccentric. If other aspects are unfavorable, this combination can produce a treacherous and thoroughly dispicable character who will stop at nothing to impose his or her radical ideas. The destructive tendency may be reflected in bad health, possibly a long drawn out or incurable illness. Riotous behavior and an inclination to serious injury from blows, falls and collisions are typical.

SATURN AND NEPTUNE

Good

Neptune's brilliant intuitions and impressionability are given form and practical significance by this favorable Saturn aspect. You have remarkable depth and clarity of thought. Insights into the psychic world, often vaguely and unsatisfactorily described by others, you can define in precise and meaningful terms. You would make a fine ESP and psi investigator. Weird and mystical subjects attract you. You are deeply sympathetic, good-hearted and not beyond making sacrifices on behalf of others who are in need. You are studiously reserved and thoughtful.

Adverse

Your ideas are impractical and lack cohesion. You start projects and find it impossible to follow through. Misunderstandings, confusion and criticism are common in your life. You suffer from weird feelings and distressing psychic conditions. Your financial affairs, usually in a mess, are a constant worry to you. You suffer from the frustration of wanting to organize your affairs on a proper footing but somehow never being able to do so. Your diet often causes health problems. It is easy for you to be discredited or to become involved in scandal.

SATURN AND PLUTO

Pluto spends and average of 24 years in each Sign, Saturn an average of 2½ years. The good and bad aspects between them occur so rarely and last so long that they are regarded as being more applicable to generations than to individuals.

URANUS AND NEPTUNE

Good

Here gifted scientific inquiry is combined with inspirational ideas. The usual vague idealism of Neptune is given direction (in unusual ways) by the galvanizing force of Uranus. You may have your daydreams, but always you are intent on applying them for the practical benefit of all. You are the inspirational mystical leader who never loses sight of the fact that man has to live in the material world; or the scientific researcher who knows that the physical law is only the rational and visible part of the universal law.

Adverse

Nervous hypertension makes the practical application of the Uranus and Neptune principles virtually impossible. Their combined effect is to make you appear out-of-this-world—eccentric, nebulous, self-deluding, erratic and uselessly self-sacrificing.

NEPTUNE AND PLUTO

Pluto spends an average of 24 years in each Sign and Neptune 14 years. The good and bad aspects occur so rarely and last so long that they are regarded as applicable to generations rather than to individuals.

ASCENDANT

SIGNS

How to Use the Blue Ascendant Tables

Your Ascendant—the Sign rising on the eastern horizon at the time of your birth—is a major influence in the formation of your personality. It shows, among other things, how you appear to other people.

Your Ascendant has been clearly worked out in the Blue Ascendant Tables. By referring to the hour of your birth under the day of the month you were born, you will see which Sign was rising or ascending at the time. (The year of birth is not important.) You can then turn to the relevant description in the following pages and see what may well be an explanation of the hidden or unsuspected in your makeup.

If you don't know your birth time, try to think of someone you can contact who might be able to help, as the Ascendant is a very valuable guide. If that fails, there is a good chance you can pinpoint your Ascendant by reading through all the 12 descriptions and finding the one most applicable to you.

It is quite possible to have the same Ascendant and Sun Sign. For instance, a person with a Leo Sun Sign and Leo Ascendant would be a "double" Leo, in whom the warm, dramatic, and attention-getting characteristics of that Sign are powerfully reemphasized. But a Leo with Sagittarius Ascending would be more restless; with Taurus Ascending, a more practical and security-oriented personality all-round.

That is why you might come across people who don't seem to conform to the characteristics of their Sun Sign. Their Ascendant, combined with the placings of the planets in their horoscope, may be the stronger influence, and consequently modify or distort the basic character. But this is rare. The Sun Sign invariably shines

through, even though, because of adverse aspects, it may take a negative form. You have to observe the person concerned more closely, or if it is yourself, more honestly than previously.

All this is the fascination and fun of AstroAnalysis. It is a test of your skill to synthesize, to blend the various dominant and subtle influences described in this book so that you perceive the person concerned as he or she actually is and not just the public persona. In a way, it's like looking through three or four different-colored eyeglasses simultaneously; as you become more adept, the final image appears in its true color.

It is interesting to touch on Astrology's rationale for the existence of the Ascendant. To begin with, what exactly is it?

The Ascendant Sign is your Earth point. Here at the moment of your birth you inherit your fate—your genetic future, your hereditary limitations, and the circumstances of your home and family. Your fate is what you can't avoid—for now. At the same moment, the Sign in line with the Earth—as demarcated by the eastern horizon at that geographical location—becomes operative as an information reciprocal in the personal organism.* This regulates the personality, the person or mask that you present to the world. To fashion this mask, you draw, consciously or unconsciously, on the character type of the rising Sign, adapted, of course, to your particular circumstances.

As the Earth is rotating at a constant speed and the 12 zodiacal space/types are "fixed" in a circular electromagnetic field against the heavens, one of the Signs is always ascending on the eastern horizon at any time, at any place on Earth, just as the Sun at every moment is appearing to rise somewhere.

Each Sign measures 30 degrees across and takes approximately two hours to clear the horizon so that every 24 hours, in rotation, each Sign rises again.

---

*See Cybernetics, "Introduction," pages 16-17

The Ascendant Sign, deriving as it does from the person's birthplace, as marked by the horizon, represents your adjustment and immediate response to the world outside yourself. It is your business face, your social face, the various conscious and unconscious poses that you adopt in cultivating the sophistication that acts to hide your true (Sun Sign) self from others, but not necessarily from yourself. It is how you appear to your associates. But not necessarily how you *are*, deep down.

The Ascendant is a most significant part of the horoscope. It ties together on Earth the outward-going characteristics of the Sun and the unconscious emotional responses of the Moon. The Sun is heavenly, the Moon is sentimental, the Ascendant is worldly. The Sun reminds you of the present and allows you to identify yourself immediately as a conscious being. The Moon reminds you of the past, shows you habit patterns, memories and subjective feelings. The Ascendant reveals the means you will use to arrive at the future.

Ascendant Conversion for the Southern Hemisphere:

Here is a simple way to find your Rising Sign if you live south of the Equator. It is really quite simple. Just add twelve hours to your birth time, then follow the steps outlined above for finding the Rising Sign. When you locate the appropriate Sign, refer to the list below to determine your Rising Sign south of the Equator.

If you are located in,	your Rising Sign is
Aries	Libra
Taurus	Scorpio
Gemini	Sagittarius
Cancer	Capricorn
Leo	Aquarius
Virgo	Pisces
Libra	Aries
Scorpio	Taurus
Sagittarius	Gemini
Capricorn	Cancer
Aquarius	Leo
Pisces	Virgo

LEO
YOUR ASCENDANT

	JULY 23	JULY 24	JULY 25	JULY 26	JULY 27
MIDNIGHT	TAURUS	TAURUS	TAURUS	TAURUS	TAURUS
1 AM	GEMINI	GEMINI	GEMINI	GEMINI	GEMINI
2 AM	GEMINI	GEMINI	GEMINI	GEMINI	GEMINI
3 AM	CANCER	CANCER	CANCER	CANCER	CANCER
4 AM	CANCER	CANCER	CANCER	CANCER	CANCER
5 AM	LEO	LEO	LEO	LEO	LEO
6 AM	LEO	LEO	LEO	LEO	LEO
7 AM	LEO	LEO	LEO	LEO	LEO
8 AM	VIRGO	VIRGO	VIRGO	VIRGO	VIRGO
9 AM	VIRGO	VIRGO	VIRGO	VIRGO	VIRGO
10 AM	LIBRA	LIBRA	LIBRA	LIBRA	LIBRA
11 AM	LIBRA	LIBRA	LIBRA	LIBRA	LIBRA
NOON	LIBRA	LIBRA	LIBRA	LIBRA	LIBRA
1 PM	SCORPIO	SCORPIO	SCORPIO	SCORPIO	SCORPIO
2 PM	SCORPIO	SCORPIO	SCORPIO	SCORPIO	SCORPIO
3 PM	SAGITTARIUS	SAGITTARIUS	SAGITTARIUS	SAGITTARIUS	SAGITTARIUS
4 PM	SAGITTARIUS	SAGITTARIUS	SAGITTARIUS	SAGITTARIUS	SAGITTARIUS
5 PM	SAGITTARIUS	SAGITTARIUS	SAGITTARIUS	SAGITTARIUS	SAGITTARIUS
6 PM	CAPRICORN	CAPRICORN	CAPRICORN	CAPRICORN	CAPRICORN
7 PM	CAPRICORN	CAPRICORN	CAPRICORN	AQUARIUS	AQUARIUS
8 PM	AQUARIUS	AQUARIUS	AQUARIUS	AQUARIUS	AQUARIUS
9 PM	PISCES	PISCES	PISCES	PISCES	PISCES
10 PM	ARIES	ARIES	ARIES	ARIES	ARIES
11 PM	ARIES	ARIES	ARIES	TAURUS	TAURUS

	JULY 28	JULY 29	JULY 30	JULY 31	AUGUST 1
MIDNIGHT	TAURUS	TAURUS	TAURUS	TAURUS	TAURUS
1 AM	GEMINI	GEMINI	GEMINI	GEMINI	GEMINI
2 AM	GEMINI	GEMINI	GEMINI	GEMINI	GEMINI
3 AM	CANCER	CANCER	CANCER	CANCER	CANCER
4 AM	CANCER	CANCER	CANCER	CANCER	CANCER
5 AM	LEO	LEO	LEO	LEO	LEO
6 AM	LEO	LEO	LEO	LEO	LEO
7 AM	LEO	LEO	LEO	LEO	VIRGO
8 AM	VIRGO	VIRGO	VIRGO	VIRGO	VIRGO
9 AM	VIRGO	VIRGO	VIRGO	VIRGO	VIRGO
10 AM	LIBRA	LIBRA	LIBRA	LIBRA	LIBRA
11 AM	LIBRA	LIBRA	LIBRA	LIBRA	LIBRA
NOON	LIBRA	LIBRA	SCORPIO	SCORPIO	SCORPIO
1 PM	SCORPIO	SCORPIO	SCORPIO	SCORPIO	SCORPIO
2 PM	SCORPIO	SCORPIO	SCORPIO	SCORPIO	SCORPIO
3 PM	SAGITTARIUS	SAGITTARIUS	SAGITTARIUS	SAGITTARIUS	SAGITTARIUS
4 PM	SAGITTARIUS	SAGITTARIUS	SAGITTARIUS	SAGITTARIUS	SAGITTARIUS
5 PM	CAPRICORN	CAPRICORN	CAPRICORN	CAPRICORN	CAPRICORN
6 PM	CAPRICORN	CAPRICORN	CAPRICORN	CAPRICORN	CAPRICORN
7 PM	AQUARIUS	AQUARIUS	AQUARIUS	AQUARIUS	AQUARIUS
8 PM	AQUARIUS	AQUARIUS	AQUARIUS	AQUARIUS	AQUARIUS
9 PM	PISCES	PISCES	PISCES	PISCES	PISCES
10 PM	ARIES	ARIES	ARIES	ARIES	ARIES
11 PM	TAURUS	TAURUS	TAURUS	TAURUS	TAURUS

LEO
YOUR ASCENDANT

	AUGUST 2	AUGUST 3	AUGUST 4	AUGUST 5	AUGUST 6
MIDNIGHT	GEMINI	GEMINI	GEMINI	GEMINI	GEMINI
1 AM	GEMINI	GEMINI	GEMINI	GEMINI	GEMINI
2 AM	CANCER	CANCER	CANCER	CANCER	CANCER
3 AM	CANCER	CANCER	CANCER	CANCER	CANCER
4 AM	CANCER	CANCER	CANCER	CANCER	CANCER
5 AM	LEO	LEO	LEO	LEO	LEO
6 AM	LEO	LEO	LEO	LEO	LEO
7 AM	VIRGO	VIRGO	VIRGO	VIRGO	VIRGO
8 AM	VIRGO	VIRGO	VIRGO	VIRGO	VIRGO
9 AM	VIRGO	VIRGO	VIRGO	VIRGO	VIRGO
10 AM	LIBRA	LIBRA	LIBRA	LIBRA	LIBRA
11 AM	LIBRA	LIBRA	LIBRA	LIBRA	LIBRA
NOON	SCORPIO	SCORPIO	SCORPIO	SCORPIO	SCORPIO
1 PM	SCORPIO	SCORPIO	SCORPIO	SCORPIO	SCORPIO
2 PM	SCORPIO	SCORPIO	SCORPIO	SCORPIO	SCORPIO
3 PM	SAGITTARIUS	SAGITTARIUS	SAGITTARIUS	SAGITTARIUS	SAGITTARIUS
4 PM	SAGITTARIUS	SAGITTARIUS	SAGITTARIUS	SAGITTARIUS	SAGITTARIUS
5 PM	CAPRICORN	CAPRICORN	CAPRICORN	CAPRICORN	CAPRICORN
6 PM	CAPRICORN	CAPRICORN	CAPRICORN	CAPRICORN	CAPRICORN
7 PM	AQUARIUS	AQUARIUS	AQUARIUS	AQUARIUS	AQUARIUS
8 PM	AQUARIUS	PISCES	PISCES	PISCES	PISCES
9 PM	PISCES	PISCES	PISCES	PISCES	PISCES
10 PM	ARIES	ARIES	ARIES	ARIES	ARIES
11 PM	TAURUS	TAURUS	TAURUS	TAURUS	TAURUS

	AUGUST 7	AUGUST 8	AUGUST 9	AUGUST 10	AUGUST 11
MIDNIGHT	GEMINI	GEMINI	GEMINI	GEMINI	GEMINI
1 AM	GEMINI	GEMINI	GEMINI	GEMINI	GEMINI
2 AM	CANCER	CANCER	CANCER	CANCER	CANCER
3 AM	CANCER	CANCER	CANCER	CANCER	CANCER
4 AM	LEO	LEO	LEO	LEO	LEO
5 AM	LEO	LEO	LEO	LEO	LEO
6 AM	LEO	LEO	LEO	LEO	LEO
7 AM	VIRGO	VIRGO	VIRGO	VIRGO	VIRGO
8 AM	VIRGO	VIRGO	VIRGO	VIRGO	VIRGO
9 AM	LIBRA	LIBRA	LIBRA	LIBRA	LIBRA
10 AM	LIBRA	LIBRA	LIBRA	LIBRA	LIBRA
11 AM	LIBRA	LIBRA	LIBRA	LIBRA	LIBRA
NOON	SCORPIO	SCORPIO	SCORPIO	SCORPIO	SCORPIO
1 PM	SCORPIO	SCORPIO	SCORPIO	SCORPIO	SCORPIO
2 PM	SAGITTARIUS	SAGITTARIUS	SAGITTARIUS	SAGITTARIUS	SAGITTARIUS
3 PM	SAGITTARIUS	SAGITTARIUS	SAGITTARIUS	SAGITTARIUS	SAGITTARIUS
4 PM	SAGITTARIUS	SAGITTARIUS	SAGITTARIUS	SAGITTARIUS	SAGITTARIUS
5 PM	CAPRICORN	CAPRICORN	CAPRICORN	CAPRICORN	CAPRICORN
6 PM	CAPRICORN	CAPRICORN	CAPRICORN	CAPRICORN	AQUARIUS
7 PM	AQUARIUS	AQUARIUS	AQUARIUS	AQUARIUS	AQUARIUS
8 PM	PISCES	PISCES	PISCES	PISCES	PISCES
9 PM	PISCES	ARIES	ARIES	ARIES	ARIES
10 PM	ARIES	ARIES	ARIES	ARIES	TAURUS
11 PM	TAURUS	TAURUS	TAURUS	TAURUS	TAURUS

LEO
YOUR ASCENDANT

	AUGUST 12	AUGUST 13	AUGUST 14	AUGUST 15	AUGUST 16	AUGUST 17
MIDNIGHT	GEMINI	GEMINI	GEMINI	GEMINI	GEMINI	GEMINI
1 AM	GEMINI	GEMINI	GEMINI	GEMINI	GEMINI	GEMINI
2 AM	CANCER	CANCER	CANCER	CANCER	CANCER	CANCER
3 AM	CANCER	CANCER	CANCER	CANCER	CANCER	CANCER
4 AM	LEO	LEO	LEO	LEO	LEO	LEO
5 AM	LEO	LEO	LEO	LEO	LEO	LEO
6 AM	LEO	LEO	LEO	LEO	VIRGO	VIRGO
7 AM	VIRGO	VIRGO	VIRGO	VIRGO	VIRGO	VIRGO
8 AM	VIRGO	VIRGO	VIRGO	VIRGO	VIRGO	VIRGO
9 AM	LIBRA	LIBRA	LIBRA	LIBRA	LIBRA	LIBRA
10 AM	LIBRA	LIBRA	LIBRA	LIBRA	LIBRA	LIBRA
11 AM	LIBRA	LIBRA	SCORPIO	SCORPIO	SCORPIO	SCORPIO
NOON	SCORPIO	SCORPIO	SCORPIO	SCORPIO	SCORPIO	SCORPIO
1 PM	SCORPIO	SCORPIO	SCORPIO	SCORPIO	SCORPIO	SCORPIO
2 PM	SAGITTARIUS	SAGITTARIUS	SAGITTARIUS	SAGITTARIUS	SAGITTARIUS	SAGITTARIUS
3 PM	SAGITTARIUS	SAGITTARIUS	SAGITTARIUS	SAGITTARIUS	SAGITTARIUS	SAGITTARIUS
4 PM	CAPRICORN	CAPRICORN	CAPRICORN	CAPRICORN	CAPRICORN	CAPRICORN
5 PM	CAPRICORN	CAPRICORN	CAPRICORN	CAPRICORN	CAPRICORN	CAPRICORN
6 PM	AQUARIUS	AQUARIUS	AQUARIUS	AQUARIUS	AQUARIUS	AQUARIUS
7 PM	AQUARIUS	AQUARIUS	AQUARIUS	AQUARIUS	AQUARIUS	AQUARIUS
8 PM	PISCES	PISCES	PISCES	PISCES	PISCES	PISCES
9 PM	ARIES	ARIES	ARIES	ARIES	ARIES	ARIES
10 PM	TAURUS	TAURUS	TAURUS	TAURUS	TAURUS	TAURUS
11 PM	TAURUS	TAURUS	TAURUS	TAURUS	TAURUS	TAURUS

	AUGUST 18	AUGUST 19	AUGUST 20	AUGUST 21	AUGUST 22	AUGUST 23
MIDNIGHT	GEMINI	GEMINI	GEMINI	GEMINI	GEMINI	GEMINI
1 AM	CANCER	CANCER	CANCER	CANCER	CANCER	CANCER
2 AM	CANCER	CANCER	CANCER	CANCER	CANCER	CANCER
3 AM	CANCER	CANCER	CANCER	CANCER	LEO	LEO
4 AM	LEO	LEO	LEO	LEO	LEO	LEO
5 AM	LEO	LEO	LEO	LEO	LEO	LEO
6 AM	VIRGO	VIRGO	VIRGO	VIRGO	VIRGO	VIRGO
7 AM	VIRGO	VIRGO	VIRGO	VIRGO	VIRGO	VIRGO
8 AM	VIRGO	VIRGO	VIRGO	LIBRA	LIBRA	LIBRA
9 AM	LIBRA	LIBRA	LIBRA	LIBRA	LIBRA	LIBRA
10 AM	LIBRA	LIBRA	LIBRA	LIBRA	LIBRA	LIBRA
11 AM	SCORPIO	SCORPIO	SCORPIO	SCORPIO	SCORPIO	SCORPIO
NOON	SCORPIO	SCORPIO	SCORPIO	SCORPIO	SCORPIO	SCORPIO
1 PM	SCORPIO	SCORPIO	SCORPIO	SCORPIO	SAGITTARIUS	SAGITTARIUS
2 PM	SAGITTARIUS	SAGITTARIUS	SAGITTARIUS	SAGITTARIUS	SAGITTARIUS	SAGITTARIUS
3 PM	SAGITTARIUS	SAGITTARIUS	SAGITTARIUS	SAGITTARIUS	SAGITTARIUS	SAGITTARIUS
4 PM	CAPRICORN	CAPRICORN	CAPRICORN	CAPRICORN	CAPRICORN	CAPRICORN
5 PM	CAPRICORN	CAPRICORN	CAPRICORN	CAPRICORN	CAPRICORN	CAPRICORN
6 PM	AQUARIUS	AQUARIUS	AQUARIUS	AQUARIUS	AQUARIUS	AQUARIUS
7 PM	PISCES	PISCES	PISCES	PISCES	PISCES	PISCES
8 PM	PISCES	PISCES	PISCES	ARIES	ARIES	ARIES
9 PM	ARIES	ARIES	ARIES	ARIES	ARIES	ARIES
10 PM	TAURUS	TAURUS	TAURUS	TAURUS	TAURUS	TAURUS
11 PM	GEMINI	GEMINI	GEMINI	GEMINI	GEMINI	GEMINI

ASCENDANT

PERSONALITIES

THE ARIES—ASCENDANT PERSONALITY

You who were born with Aries ascending are lovers of action. You want to be out in front. You are the pioneering impulse of mankind. As soon as you get a good idea, you immediately try to put it into action. Since you are so impulsive, you will spend some time licking your wounds because you failed to make a thorough evaluation of the opposition or obstacles. But you are not easily discouraged from beginning again. You are at your best when you can lay down a plan of action for yourself and others to follow. Your mode of operation is to move on to greener pastures before the task is finished, leaving others to press on or clean up.

You enjoy a position of command. You have the ability to guide, control and govern yourself as well as others. You are an admirer of scientific thought and have some distinct philosophical leanings. You are a lover of independence who doesn't like sharing your secrets or revealing your plans. You prefer to demonstrate your tactical inspiration in activity rather than talk about what you intend to do. Like a good general (Mars is the ruler of Aries ascending), you don't like to risk having your plans fall into enemy hands.

You possess strong and penetrating willpower. You are quite versatile, able to change from one action to another without losing a beat as long as your interest is sustained. You sometimes miss out on the rewards of your considerable efforts because you moved before they were handed out. You are enterprising and ambitious and usually headstrong. You reach out eagerly for what you want, but are easily put off by complicated situations that might slow your progress. You react indignantly if imposed upon or abused, and are apt to speak out and let others know quickly that they have offended you. Your temper can be quite fiery, but you don't hold grudges for long. You prefer to settle differences quickly and get your battles over in a hurry, whichever way the result may go. You are brimful of initiative and make an able executive, though you may lack persistence. Quite often you are interested in physical sports and your physique reflects this. You will do best in a vocation that requires instant decisions and action.

Possessions and Personal Security

You are likely to be very good at acquiring property, especially land and buildings. You don't allow cash to lie idle in the bank; you would rather invest it in bricks and mortar. Tangible assets that give you a solid hold on the earth are what you like most. In business, where you are also prone to be impulsive you are likely to drive a hard bargain. You are more conservative in financial matters than in most others. You spend money to increase the value of your property. You don't allow anything you own to fall into disrepair, and that includes your body. You are health conscious and very aware of the need to keep your body fit.

Communication with the Environment

You are apt to scramble your words at times because your tongue can't keep up with the speed of your thought. Your expressive Aries speech may develop a stammer when you are excited or intense. You may be accused of opportunism because you can genuinely see the validity of several people's points of view at once. You tend to be hasty or explosive in speech when defending yourself. The unguarded word may give you cause for regret. You are restless and impatient, eager for new meetings. Your ingenious ideas impress those you work for. You are on the move a lot and may be inclined to stumble or knock things over.

Home, Family, Tradition

You are very sentimental about your family. Your mother or another close elder has a special place in your heart. Your home means a great deal to you. If you have not yet settled down, you long to do so and often think about it. You think a lot about the past. You are an admirer of tradition and the good old days. You are fond of reading about history and archeological subjects; you may also display this interest in a physical way by visiting museums and even taking part in digs at old ruins. You may make numerous changes of residence before finding the home you are looking for. You work hard at making your home a comfortable place to live in.

Self-Expression, Love Life, Entertainment

You have a longing to be noticed and applauded. Your Aries aggressiveness may cause others to accuse you of being bossy or dictatorial. You take satisfaction in dramatizing your efforts, in producing spectacular effects. Your accomplishments are impressive. Your head can be turned by flattery and glamor. An impatience to fulfill your ambitions may drive you into taking risks, although you usually hedge your bets so as to preserve your basic security. You enjoy a good time. Your love affairs are largely ego trips. You need to be proud of your children and revel in situations where you can show them (at least the successful ones) off.

Work and Health

You are a steady worker, though no one would describe you as a plodder. You toil with deft dedication. You can separate the chaff from the wheat with great ease whether you are dealing with people or detail. You are efficient and disciplined in your personal life. You are keenly conscious of hygiene and sometimes can be finicky. You enjoy delicacies but seldom eat or drink to excess. You take more than average care of your body because good health means you can continue to be active. Sickness irritates you, makes you nervous and snappish. At times you are too quick to find fault with co-workers; but however annoying, your criticisms are very often right on the mark.

Partnerships and Marriage

In this department, the Aries is not an independent loner. You need to share your life with others, especially a love partner. You expect the admiration of your mate, and at times, adoring attention. You try to get along with your partners. Harmony is intensely important to you, but you don't always find it. Your directness and sometimes rugged manner may offend even your own

finer sensibilities. You feel the pull of inner extremes and are constantly striving to rest or your inner balance. You usually marry early after a romantic adolescence. Marriage to a compatible and charming person is important to you. You can be adamant, but at heart you are a peacemaker.

Shared Resources, Legacies, Sex

Secretive about your deeper feelings, you seldom engage in intimate discussions with outsiders. In your love life, you are sensual rather than sentimental. You have numerous secrets. You feel a need to rise above the temptations of your lower nature, although this may be neither easy nor personally desirable. You are a powerhouse of emotional energy that needs to be properly harnessed. Sometimes strenuous physical activity will work off your excess energy. By sublimating your deeper drives, you can reach towering heights of attainment. You are a realist. You understand human failings. You don't like pretense. You can be torn by jealousy.

Higher Development and Long-Distance Travel

You have an interesting religious or philosophic outlook, although not really unconventional. You seek new vistas of the mind. You are highly intelligent and sometimes astound your acquaintances with your penetrative powers of perception. You are an expansive personality, forever trying to widen your horizons. You like to travel afar to absorb new cultures, meet different types of people and encounter fresh situations. You often do things on the spur of the moment through sheer inspiration. Your optimistic, frank and generous nature helps you to attract companions who have something out of the ordinary to offer.

Public Standing, Career, Prestige

Your Aries talent as an organizer in this position fits you for big business. You are sure to rise in your field, especially in later life. You are responsible and ambitious, though your methods may be conservative. You want to be recognized as an authority because you don't like to take orders. You are capable of great and enduring effort; persistence here is your long suit. You like to assume responsibility for others. You appear somewhat aloof and unfriendly, but this is just your customary manner when important matters have to be attended to. You are happier in charge of the big scene than coping with details, which you prefer to leave to others.

Friends, Group Activities, Hopes, Wishes

Your Aries love of independence may be overemphasized here. You may kick up your heels, break with some traditions and choose friends who do the same. But your business companions will be more conventional; you have the knack of coping well with the two extremes. You are a bit of a revolutionary, more intellectual than sentimental. Your advanced ideas may attract some odd-bods. You need to be able to express your broader views freely, and the bohemian types of this world are the most receptive listeners. You are tolerant of others' eccentricities. Your flair for originality is exceptional; you shine in group activities.

Hidden Motives, Selfless Service,
Psychic Feelings

You are instinctively able to decide the right thing to do. Although you may be impulsive, your actions will probably turn out for the best. You have a very tender side to your nature, which you may unconsciously repress. Any excessively sympathetic responses you manage to control in one way will erupt into compulsive action in another. You may have difficulty understanding some of your own emotional reactions. The plight of your suffering fellow man is apt to move you to actions of self-denial. You may feel a need for solitude and introspection, but seldom be able to find the time for either. Your intuition is acute.

THE TAURUS—ASCENDANT PERSONALITY

You who were born with Taurus ascending are self-reliant people capable of working hard for long periods to accomplish the goals you set for yourself. You are also extremely good at working for others. You are an ideal person to have on the payroll; you have a flair for earning money for whoever employs you.

You usually possess a pleasing or attractively distinctive voice. You give an impression of grace and compact movement, even though some of you may be on the chubby side. You like gold—literally. You strive to amass money so you can convert it into solid assets. Nothing would please you more than to own a gold mine, for the sheer, deliciously secure feeling of it. You don't like taking risks with what you own. You would rather depend on your practical capacity for dogged effort than take a big win-or-lose chance.

You are a gentle person at heart and don't go looking for trouble. You are not easy to provoke to anger, but once stirred, your rage can be formidable. When opposed, you can display an extraordinary stubbornness. It is this unyielding quality that allows you to hang on like a bulldog to tasks and causes that would daunt any other type in the Zodiac. Once you make up your mind, that is the end of it; you stick to your decision through thick and thin. There is a great deal of latent energy behind your powers of endurance. But if it is misplaced, you can be overly sensual, too dependent on comfort and indolent. You are sincere, reliable and trustworthy. You have a good deal of common sense. You make a very loyal friend. You have a flair for financial manipulation and considerable organizing ability, which will be helpful in your career.

You need time to think things over, to weigh all the pros and cons before reaching a decision, and for this reason, others sometimes regard you as ponderous and slow. You have a compelling need to get everything on a firm basis before proceeding. You are rather secretive and reserved concerning your personal affairs. Although usually of a quiet disposition, you can be surprisingly dogmatic. You are deeply influenced by sympathy. You love beauty in nature, music, literature or art. You are also fond of pleasure and the comforts of this world. You are keen to surround yourself with beautiful things. Good food and the refinements of entertaining that go with it are important to you. You are a most relaxed person and can have a calming and beneficial effect on those who are nervous or irritable. Although affectionate and loving, you can be exasperatingly unreasonable and prejudiced.

Possessions and Personal Security

You set your mind to making money. You think about different schemes, testing them with your considerable powers of imagination to make sure they work before putting them into action. You are very likely to take on an extra job to augment your income. You use wit and intelligence to diversify your financial interests so that your security is never really vulnerable. Money usually comes to you through various channels. You like to cultivate the friendship of people with wealth and material possessions. Since you also like to give the impression that you are doing well yourself, you don't mind spending money on gifts, traveling and other communications.

Communication with the Environment

You are in regular touch with your closest relatives. You have an urgent need to know that all is well with those who love you and with those to whom you feel related. You are sensitive to your surroundings, particularly to the neighborhood in which you live. If your home is not in a desirable area, you are unhappy. Although you are unsettled by the thought of a major change, you will probably move house more than once to find the right surroundings. Uninterfering neighbors can be a big consideration. Just as Taurean children learn much faster if the subject is given emotional meaning, you absorb knowledge slowly but surely, once the "feeling" is right.

Home, Family, Tradition

Your home is your castle, and you leave no doubt in anyone's mind that you want to be the lord or lady of it. Domestic life probably revolves around your preferences, even though there may be others to consider. You like to dispense hospitality from a well-stocked larder and an impressive wine cellar (or rack). You are an entertaining and gracious host with a flair for providing lavish and glamorous flourishes. If you can manage it, you'll buy yourself a mansion, fill it with luxurious things and arrange an endless parade of admiring guests. If "home" is only a cave, you can be depended upon to make it comfortable, impressive and homelike.

Self-Expression, Love Life, Entertainment

You enjoy love affairs but they don't obsess your thinking. You aren't partial to romantic daydreaming or to coloring your relationships with imagination. You believe in having everything in its right place, and that includes your emotions. You may be a bit prudish and critical of contemporary permissiveness. You select a love mate with great caution, but once having made your commitment, you like to get on with what happens next—so that you'll always *know* what's happening next. You are a bit too methodical for spontaneous gamesmanship. A stimulating discussion or an activity highlighting food is often your idea of entertainment. Strenuous games or sports don't appeal to you.

Work and Health

You need to work in harmonious conditions. Any degree of discord will throw you off balance and send you running for the exit or the escapist's bottle. Your health depends very much on your being able to maintian an amicable and agreeable atmosphere around you. You work very well with others. You are cooperative, good-natured and cheerful. Tact and diplomacy are your special qualities. You are prepared to work as one of a team and can frequently manage to bring together warring factions. Peace at almost any price is your slogan. But sometimes your exactitude irritates co-workers. Your work is often in fields that require the artistic touch.

Partnerships and Marriage

You are probably a quite demanding marriage partner, because you pour the considerable intensity of your emotions into your closest relationships. Jealousy and possessiveness can make life miserable at times for you both. You are much happier if you enjoy a satisfactory sexual relationship with your marriage partner. Disloyalty by the other person may have deep psychological repercussions. Partnerships for you are a serious business and you don't shirk from sharing your material wealth and means with those you live with. Your intuition acts like a sixth sense where partners are concerned. Although you are strongly physical, you need someone with intellectual qualities as well.

Shared Resources, Legacies, Sex

You are apt to benefit from an inheritance of money, property or title. The ending of a partnership could be particularly rewarding in material terms. Big business settlements may suddenly affect you and coincide with an abrupt change in your way of life. You have a strong social conscience about the way people handle the reproductive instinct and the effect of this on the community. You believe in the moral law, and this is reflected in your lofty ethics regarding sex. Whatever freedoms you may seem to take in sexual activity, you still observe strict principles of your own. You have faith in a life hereafter.

Higher Development and Long-Distance Travel

Although your religious beliefs tend to be conventional, you have the intensity to inspire others to an enlightenment possibly greater than your own. You are conservative and rather orthodox in your opinions about the deeper questions of life. You are prepared to accept or live with doctrines handed down from the past until some authority proves they are wrong or lays down an alternative. You don't enjoy speculating about philosophic possibilities and you are a bit suspicious of those who do. Like the lawyer (a profession in which you should shine), you want concrete evidence before committing yourself. Travel doesn't usually hold special appeal unless it is connected with commerce.

Public Standing, Career, Prestige

You feel more secure and happy in a profession where you work with a group. You have much to contribute, being both a cohesive and persistent influence as well as an original thinker. You like to feel you are doing a good job and are pulling your weight. Emotionally, you are more involved with the cause than with the people concerned. Your ideas are often ingenious. You could be an able inventor. Science may provide a field where you can work with satisfaction and renown toward solving mankind's graver problems. You are prepared to sacrifice much for the greater cause. You are a tireless worker for the species rather than for the individual.

Friends, Group Activities, Hopes, Wishes

You have true friends, the kind who don't forget you even though you may seldom meet. You sincerely want to understand all your friends, but you are particular about who gets really close to you. You get along well with people. You are prepared to listen to their problems without trying to introduce your own. You have a deep reservoir of sympathy for your fellow man, especially for the underdog, the underprivileged and the sick. You depend on your companions a great deal to fill your need for emotional sharing. You are more easily hurt than most if you feel your friends are neglecting you. You identify with suffering people and are not beyond a grand but unostentatious gesture of self-denial on their behalf.

Hidden Motives, Selfless Service, Psychic Feelings

You initiate as many moves as you can behind the scenes. You don't announce what you are up to until you have to. The facade you present to the public sometimes bears little resemblance to the person inside. A sympathetic, vigorous and often secret imagination plots the course for your compelling actions. You feel sometimes that your decisions are made for you. This is the dynamic point in the Zodiac from where all your Taurean activity stems. The position gives you the power to repress impatience and to be rather long-suffering. Once your anger flares, it can become a self-paralyzing fury that explodes within you, causing debilitating results more harmful than suppressing your anger.

THE GEMINI–ASCENDANT PERSONALITY

With Gemini ascending, you must be constantly busy to be happy. You crave change and diversity; deprive you of these, and life loses its meaning. You live a mental existence. Your world is the world of ideas. You unrealistically expect your physical environment to move at the same pace as your mind; hence, you are frequently bored and restless

You are ambitious and curious. You aim to develop an inquiring mind and a quick wit: these are the implements you use to get ahead and to defend yourself the moment trouble looms. You are not a very physical entity. You use your body as you use your mind, sometimes driving it to a state of near exhaustion. "Jack be nimble, Jack be quick, Jack jump over the candlestick"—is you! A usually slender and agile frame allows you to move with speed and flowing precision.

You are sympathetic and sensitive, very quick to pick up the thoughts and attitudes of others. Your lucid perception is often mistaken for intuition, but you are essentially an intellectual creature. Being naturally idealistic, you often feel you can solve the problems of the world—in your head. You are not beyond helping a good cause in a practical way, especially if you can take on the job of whipping up enthusiasm and support with letters, telephone calls and the personal power of your rhetoric.

You like pleasure and adventure. Your fertile imagination is always at work, trying to introduce novelty into your activities. You enjoy all kinds of mental recreation, including brain-teaser games. You are interested in experimentation and investigation. Education in its wider sense attracts you, and you will often take up a study to amuse yourself or just to stay well informed. You are attracted by scientific subjects because they are concerned with facts and these are more important to you, basically, than opinions. You are extremely adaptable and can tailor your conversation and language to suit any company you happen to be in. You like to chat. To others, you seem to have an extraordinary zest for living and your acquaintances are often amazed at how you retain your youthful looks and outlook. Like Peter Pan, you don't seem to grow old as ordinary mortals do. As long as you are fired by enthusiasm's vital spark, you seem to be able to go on forever, dancing from project to project, never appearing to weary of incessant diversity.

At times, you become anxious, restless and indecisive. You can also be mentally timid. When inactive, you become impatient and irritable. Your high-strung nature makes you extremely excitable. You possess inherent literary ability and are fond of reading and writing. You are quick to learn and either admire or enjoy music, painting, drawing, languages, travel and most forms of innovation and invention. You are capable of doing several things at once and are very good at carrying on an intelligent conversation and deftly using your hands at the same time.

Possessions and Personal Security

You are best at increasing your income and building up assets in situations where you can appeal to people's emotions, particularly in their homes. You can be successful in this way through television, magazines, newspapers, books and radio. You could also be a con artist. You have a keen sense of values. You can prosper in trade and commerce, especially in the role of agent or middleman. You try to conserve your resources and don't throw your money around, except sometimes when you are chasing pleasure. You like to make your home comfortable and to provide well for your family. In doing this, you sometimes appear to be extravagant.

Communication with the Environment

You have a great talent for expressing yourself, for commanding the attention of others with a dash of showmanship. You are not just a fluent talker and writer; you have a style and presence that come through however you choose to communicate. Writing and speaking, to you, are arts that exist not only for persuading others but also for gaining their admiration and respect. You are the journalist who not only gets the scoop but who also feelingly conveys the atmosphere; the amusing storyteller, the entertaining public speaker, the absorbing lecturer. Sometimes you get carried away and in your enthusiasm, exaggerate, present fiction as fact, and also say the wrong thing.

Home, Family, Tradition

You are a tidy person and your home reflects this. You like orderliness and cleanliness. You would prefer to earn your living by working at home, and this thought is often in your head as you methodically strive to better yourself. You feel it is important to your health to live in peaceful surroundings where you can recuperate quickly and quietly from the rigors of your constant communication with the outside world. The country will often suit you as long as you have easy access to the brighter lights. You are a much deeper person than your flippant conversation sometimes suggests. You can be quite sharp for their own good with family members who step out of line.

Self-Expression, Love Life, Entertainment

You like a good balance to your activities and manage to mix sociability, creativity and working with considerable dexterity. It's not beyond you to go to work, give a party and produce something of artistic merit in the same day. You intend to behave in socially acceptable ways but it is not unknown for you to occasionally go off the wall when your spontaneity and enthusiasm get the better of you. You enjoy the company of artistic people and possess a flair for dressing well or stylishly either in traditional or modern mode. You are popular with children and have a gift for talking *with* them rather than *at* them. In your love life, you are basically a roamer and may have two or three affairs going at once.

Work and Health

You have a fine talent for ferreting out facts and you do well in any profession or field that demands this ability. You are well suited for laboratory work, scientific research programs, psychiatry, psychology and investigative journalism. You are able to cut through trivia with razor-sharp keenness and expose the reality that lies behind. In your work, you are able to overcome your natural Gemini flippancy and become deeply involved. Dedicated effort is not beyond you. You are often revitalized by unremitting endeavor. Co-workers who provoke you may feel the sting of your tongue.

Partnerships and Marriage

You marry more for mental than physical reasons. You are happiest with a companion who is intellectually bright and able to share your ideas. Sex is secondary to your need to be understood by your partner, to feel that your mental boundaries are being continually pushed back by the close contact between two intelligent people. You won't be nagged and you won't be imprisoned; you would rather be single. You want a mate who can handle your affairs and provide the sense of purpose you require, without limiting your freedom and scope for self-expression. It's a tall order. In turn, you offer a very adaptable, witty, communicative and hopeful personality.

Shared Resources, Legacies, Sex

Your sex life is fairly clear cut and you are able to keep it proportional to your other interests. You seldom have any serious hangups about sex; you are not a sentimental type and your approach is somewhat matter-of-fact. You usually have to wait until rather late in life to benefit from legacies. Settlements are often delayed. Your views on an afterlife are conservative and you have no great desire to speculate about death. Your interest in occult subjects, however, can be quite intense and you have a flair for digging out the truth. You enjoy exposing trickery.

Higher Development and Long-Distance Travel

You are seldom a conformist in your religious beliefs. You think that the truths contained in traditional religions can be expressed in rational terms and require no mumbo-jumbo. You feel that the established churches should keep up with the times. You have a great urge to share your ideas with as many people as possible and to travel long distances. You like to disseminate information. You aim to understand other races, to visit and stay among them if you get the chance, to learn about other cultures firsthand. You are tolerant of other people's beliefs and don't set out to convert them to your own.

Public Standing, Career, Prestige

Your main problem in life is trying to make up your mind about what you want to do with it. The trouble is you can be successful in just about any career that appeals to you, which gives you little incentive to stick to one occupation. You never seem to find the occupation that can satisfy you for long. Once you know you can handle a job, you tend to move on. Often you use your versatility to follow more than one vocation simultaneously. You may switch from one job to another, looking for the golden one that will fulfill you. Some of you would rather be drifters than settle for a humdrum or mundane position. Your search for a dream may serve to reduce your immediate chances of recognition and renown.

Friends, Group Activities, Hopes, Wishes

Friendship is one of the most important spheres of your life. You have many friends and keep in regular touch. Friendship means variety, change, conversation, animation, movement, discussion—all the things you love most. As this department is the zodiacal point that gives rise to Gemini activity through enterprise, you are exceptionally good at making acquaintances. You get to know the right people, have a flair for enlisting cooperation and are particularly successful at initiating group activities. You join things to meet others, and once this is accomplished, often withdraw. You are apt to squander your energies marshaling support for too many projects at once and run out of steam before any are completed.

Hidden Motives, Selfless Service, Psychic Feelings

Although you may not show it, you are frequently shaken by feelings of material insecurity. You may try to affect a certain detachment from the things of this world, but underneath you worry about your bank account and try to put pennies aside for a rainy day. You are often a silent saver—busily, between other activities, stamping down the earth around your money chest. It is this vague anxiety about financial matters that accounts for much of your Mercurial versatility. You reason unconsciously that the more talents you can develop and have at your disposal, the less chance there is of falling on hard times. Your methods are sometimes devious.

THE CANCER—ASCENDANT PERSONALITY

If the Sign of Cancer was ascending at the hour of your birth, you are a person of changing moods and emotions. You are extremely sensitive and of retiring disposition. You know what it's like to be hurt and you do your best to shield those you love, especially your family, from painful experiences. You are particularly solicitous of your mother or the matriarchal figures in your family. Although circumstances may force you to lose touch with these people, you are never really free of concern for them. You have strong memories of your childhood. Whether your recollections are happy or unhappy, you can't help reminiscing about the past.

You are sentimental, sympathetic and rather talkative. Your imagination is fertile and inventive. You feel first and think after; thought, to you, is almost unnecessary. Your ideas emerge as vivid "feeling" pictures, with which you can identify with great pain or pleasure. Although you are fond of your home, you are inclined to wander and may never really manage to settle down in one place. If you do set up a permanent residence, you are apt to pack up and move off again after two or three years.

You have a fine retentive memory, especially for family and historical events. You file away feelings rather than concepts. As you have a strong emotional attachment to the past, this probably accounts for your often phenomenal power of recall. You are fond of possessions and will work industriously to acquire them. Your personal needs are not great and you can be very economical, even frugal, with money. You like to travel and enjoy visiting people in their homes. You are especially liable to drop in on relatives. Novelty and change appeal to you in almost any form. Although you are careful with money, you are often imposed upon. Your sympathetic nature makes it difficult for you to refuse another person who appeals for help or appears to be in need. But you have an extremely tenacious streak, which manifests itself in a variety of ways but is particularly vehement when you adopt a protective role.

You shy away from pressure. You can give the impression of hardy self-assurance and toughness and can cope with the best of them for a limited period. But then you must scuttle off to some warm and secure retreat where you can quietly restore your self-confidence. You fear criticism and ridicule and will go to great lengths to avoid either. This makes you rather conventional and very discreet. You are inclined to follow an occupation that will bring you in touch with the public. You enjoy praise and approbation; this, again, makes you exceedingly diplomatic. You are a lover of beauty and usually possess a psychic and mediumistic faculty.

Possessions and Personal Security

You like to do well so you can provide for your children with style. You are one of the real collectors of the Zodiac. You love to assemble objects of art, sets of beautiful things and relics of antiquity. You enjoy displaying these in your home for others to see. Your collections are often valuable, but this is not a prerequisite; you are just as capable of saving worthless objects with the same affection and pleasure because they give you a reassuring feeling of material security. You are painfully affected when anything you own is broken or destroyed. But no emotional scar hurts you for too long.

Communication with the Environment

You are rather apprehensive about the future so you tend to take refuge in the past. You think and talk a lot about the good old days. You feel that traditional attitudes are more desirable than contemporary ones. You like to quote precedents. You take pride in your patriotism. You are often critical of the ideas of others and try to put them on the right track. You like to feel that you and your associates are eating health-giving foods. You collect dietary books and articles to help all concerned. Your eye for descriptive detail is remarkable. You often exaggerate your problems to yourself and worry unnecessarily.

Home, Family, Tradition

You regard your home as the pivot of your life. As sentimental as you are about your family, you would rather have an empty house than disturb it with discord and disagreement. You aim to maintain harmony in your surroundings, and to achieve this, show tact and diplomacy to those with whom you live. If you fail to secure the balance you crave, you will leave the house temporarily or retire to the seclusion of your room. You spend much of your leisure time making your home a more attractive and congenial place to live. You like to feel that your family thinks and speaks well of you in your absence.

Self-Expression, Love Life, Entertainment

You are capable of producing work of superior artistic merit, but to do this, you have to overcome a curious self-repressive tendency, which is to be overly possessive of your loved ones, especially your children. You are inclined to play a watchdog role, continually "guarding" or brooding over them, and this introverted centering of your emotional forces reduces your creative fire and inspiration. In romance, you veer toward secret love affairs, finding excitement in the thought of tasting forbidden fruit and calculatedly ignoring the painful consequences that might be involved. You can suffer deeply through jealousy, which is often matched by an intensity of physical passion.

Work and Health

Your work as an employee is marked by an optimistic outlook that allows you to cope cheerfully with considerable detail. As long as you believe that what you are doing is useful and a step to bigger things in the future, you will apply yourself with diligence. You are an industrious worker. In organizing and planning, you use the lessons of the past with considerable discernment to get around the problems that lie ahead. As much as you dislike emotional scenes, you seem impelled to get involved in squabbles and arguments among co-workers. It is important to your health that you avoid eating while you are emotionally upset.

Partnerships and Marriage

You take marriage very seriously and often choose a partner who is helpless, lazy or unable to cope. Your inherent desire to nourish and protect induces you to accept responsibilities that others would find impossible. You are frequently the long-suffering husbands and wives of the Zodiac, although it is not in your character to complain. You are also ambitious for your mate to get on in the world and you do all in your power to encourage and to help it. The Cancer woman makes an excellent partner for men struggling to get to the top—particularly in occupations that depend on public support. The career woman could not have a more solid supporter than a Cancer husband.

Shared Resources, Legacies, Sex

You have advanced and original ideas about sex and the community. You are the type of person who is a leading advocate of enlightened approaches to abortion, homosexuality, the Pill for teenagers and similar subjects once not discussed in polite gatherings. You may also hold forth with some independent thoughts about death and survival and participate in group inquiries into occult and metaphysical experiences. You have strong feelings about sharing with others and might visualize some sort of communal existence as a means of human regeneration.

Higher Development and Long-Distance Travel

Experience of the higher consciousness is not uncommon among some of the more advanced Cancer types. You begin with as much zest, if not more, than the next person to fulfill your worldly ambitions, but eventually you discover that (as you've often suspected) your personal fulfillment lies in service and the surrender of egocentric desires. You have little time for orthodox religions and avoid discoursing with people who espouse dogma. You are a true meditator and spiritual pragmatist. Less evolved Cancer types are apt to lose themselves in dreaming, wishful thinking and regret.

Public Standing, Career, Prestige

You are a person who has to live with rhythm, the ebb and flow of a highly sensitive and in-drawn nature with an instinctive, outgoing urge. You are ambitious and more eager than some apparently less retiring types to get ahead. You are determined from the start to make a name for yourself, and the fact that you don't always succeed is no reflection on your efforts or tenacity. Your frequently aggressive drive helps to compensate for your lack of self-assurance and natural reserve. You often succeed in maritime occupations and those that offer the opportunity to travel, especially overseas.

Friends, Group Activities, Hopes, Wishes

Friendship is one of the mainstays of your life. Your friends are a buffer between you and the realities of the outside world. As you walk out of your home, you like to feel there are numerous other welcoming and comfortable places for you to go. You may stride into the thick of combative reality with an admirable display of aggression, but when the day is over, you heal your psychological wounds by contact with your friends. You enjoy helping your comrades and are the first to lend cash if you have it. You also like to spend money on friends. You tie yourself to your companions with deep bonds of affection and often form lifetime friendships. You are particularly loyal and caring. You enjoy the physical warmth of groups and the opportunity they provide to extend your sphere of influence by discussion.

Hidden Motives, Selfless Service, Psychic Feelings

Despite their overt need of friends, Cancer-Ascendant people can be among the recluses of this life. The strength of your feelings, acting on a richly imaginative disposition, provides you with an inner life that often approaches self-sufficiency. You learn more from observing people and situations than from formal tuition. You have periods of soul-searching introspection. Your more abstract ideas clash with your sentimental nature, and while you are sorting out the contradictions, you can give the impression of moodiness. You have strong psychic powers and mediumistic ability. Intuition is more natural to you than thinking.

THE LEO—ASCENDANT PERSONALITY

You love power and distinction. You succeed

most where you have authority. You usually occupy some high or responsible position in managing or executive work. You have the gift of inspiring others to great accomplishments—unless you become power-happy, in which case you can lead them to their ruin. You are ambitious, self-confident and fearless. Although high-strung and quick to anger, you are very forgiving and don't hold grudges for long.

You have great energy and are apt to pour it, without restraint, into any activity that arouses your sympathy or interest. Therefore you are always in danger of overdoing things (it is not unknown for a Leo-born person to work himself to death). Although you are usually strong, there is a distinct limit to how far you can push yourself before undermining your health. You have great hope and faith in the future. You are outgoing and magnanimous and scatter your goodwill in all directions while everything is going well. In adversity, you are easily troubled and may seem to withdraw from all other pursuits to attend to one problem. You are not, in fact, neglecting any responsibility; your aim is to gather the sum of your forces to attack the problem that occupies you. You are impatient to come to grips with problems and to eliminate them. You have the fortitude to endure considerable discomfort and pain if it will lead to a peaceful life. Like the Lion, who is the symbol of this Sign, you are a great fighter, but you must also have your quiet hours lazing in the sun.

And again, like the King of Beasts, you are of noble disposition. You have dignity and integrity. You are philanthropic, charitable and loyal. You often receive favors as though they were your due and dispense them with much the same flourish. You are imperious and fond of command. You tend to dominate the social sphere in which you move. You are a physically attractive and vital person and gravitate to a position of leadership as though it were the most natural thing in the world. You are good-natured, generous and kind-hearted. You are also independent, outspoken and at times brutally frank. Your aim, to grant freedom through your own ability to lead, sometimes degenerates into a power complex resulting in arrogant dictatorship. You enjoy nothing quite as much as an admiring audience.

Possessions and Personal Security

You are a bit of a paradox where money is concerned. You have quite extravagant tastes and yet your spending habits are conservative. You can put your pennies away with punctilious care and then blow the lot (well, almost the lot) on a night out or on some expensive luxury item. You enjoy manipulating money and balancing your accounts. You can teeter on the razor's edge between good living and bankruptcy with an adroitness that would make less confident types shudder. Usually, though, you know what you are doing and have calculated the extent of your resources and reserves down to the last coin. If you get into financial difficulty, you worry incessantly and this affects your health.

Communication with the Environment

Since you like people to agree with your ideas, it is fortunate that you are usually very good at the art of persuasion. You make, in fact, a fine salesperson. Articulate and polished in speech, you have the knack of communicating your enthusiasm through the vitality of your presentation. You are pleasing and tactful. Because you usually believe in whatever you recommend, you exude an air of sincerity. You are even prepared to risk an argument to make your point. On the other hand, if you don't have faith in what you are saying, the solar charisma tends to evaporate, making you fairly easy to see through. You strive to create harmony in your immediate environment, even to the extent of bringing like-minded or romantically inclined people together.

Home, Family, Tradition

You insist on being the master or mistress of your home. This is probably the reason why many Leonine types do not enjoy a great amount of domestic happiness. You are imperious and extremely conscious of the dignity of a healthy family tree and the advantages of good breeding. If your ancestors are unknown quantities, you will set about establishing your own dynasty, however modest your circumstances may be. You are a proud descendant of admirable forebears, you prefer to ignore family skeletons and hope they'll go away. You run a tight (family) ship and expect the unquestioning loyalty and support of your dependents.

Self-Expression, Love Life, Entertainment

Your natural desire and flair for being noticed makes it possible for you to reach considerable heights of accomplishment. Although your compulsion to be recognized degenerates at times into sheer showmanship or showoffmanship, you are driven by the same forces to exploit your artistic and finer creative abilities. You will never rest content with what you attain; you will always have the conviction that far greater possibilities lie within you—and, for that matter, within others. You are especially capable of instilling exalted ideas in children and of awakening them to their potentialities. For this reason, you make an inspiring parent or teacher. You love to gamble—with money, love, your skills . . . even your own destiny.

Work and Health

Your profound sense of responsibility for whatever job you take on makes you a most diligent and industrious employee. Your ability to work hard with creative inspiration, together with your innate leadership powers, usually ensures that you get to the top. Although ambitious, you are impelled mostly by the desire to do a job well for its own sake. The fact that you can then bask in the sunlight of other people's admiration is a hidden motivation. Your health can be affected by overwork, the most vulnerable areas being the heart and back. Self-confidence sometimes causes you to overestimate your powers of physical and mental endurance.

Partnerships and Marriage

You are not an easy person to be married to, although you can be devoted and disarmingly generous. You often choose the wrong type of partner. You have a strong streak of independence and a love of freedom, and if you choose a mate with similar characteristics—as you usually do—the result is fireworks. Your imperious nature makes it difficult for you to share authority in the home. You want a royal subject as well as a mate. You are often attracted to an artistic type, and this temperament is known more for rebellion than servitude. You need an intelligent partner who is keen and earnest enough to pay the relatively harmless doses of homage you require in exchange for royal munificence.

Shared Resources, Legacies, Sex

A degree of sacrifice and pain usually accompanies the Leo experience of sharing. To share with mankind is your greater purpose, befitting the son of the Sun's own Sign. You must learn to resist the natural urge to use up your energies and passion in satisfying personal desires and concupiscence. You are required, often after long suffering, to rise to compassionate heights where you can renew yourself in concern for your fellow man rather than for your own superficial self. You can do this by intense dedication to an artistic pursuit. Legacies are often surrounded by confused and disordered circumstances. There can be a long battle to win what you believe to be your rightful inheritance, whether it be property, title or the vindication of your family name. The Leo person usually succeeds in whatever he or she undertakes.

Higher Development and Long-Distance Travel

Your deep-rooted optimism is based mainly on faith in yourself. And this, in turn, is frequently supported by the conviction that you are filling a destined role and being guided by inner forces you do not need to explain or understand. It is this faith, either consciously or unconsciously held, that enables you to assume a position of authority or rulership in practically any situation. The so-called divine right of kings is a postulate not hard for you to understand. You like to travel far afield, but you are not a rubberneck tourist type; you need to know that your journey has greater purpose than mere sightseeing to make it worth your while.

Public Standing, Career, Prestige

You are a lover of the vestments and tokens of office. If you become lord mayor or police chief, you want the 24-carat-gold chain around your neck, the big badge or the ivory-handled pistols. As soon as you can afford it, you surround yourself with status symbols. Apart from artistic considerations, all the objects you choose are usually workable, for you appreciate practicality as long as it doesn't cramp your style. Once in a position of power, you are often reluctant to step aside and may ferociously resist any order to step down. As a superior, you can be one of the boys as long as the boys remember you are the one. By learning to delegate, you can help protect your health.

Friends, Group Activities, Hopes, Wishes

You need a mixed group of people around you to stimulate your mind and to prevent you from becoming too fixed in your attitudes. You usually attract friends who, although they may be overindulgent as an audience, are intelligent and vivacious. Many of your companions are young, clever and admiring, and in this company you allow others to shine beside you with an amused, paternal or maternal beneficence. You are generous to your friends and select the closest of them with care. Sometimes you ally yourself with humanitarian group efforts, usually on the organizational side. Philosophic movements and seminars also appeal to you, but only until you can formulate your own abstract ideas. Then you may well set up a "school" of your own.

Hidden Motives, Selfless Service, Psychic Feelings

You sometimes feel neglected and unappreciated and this causes you to retreat sulkily into yourself. Your towering pride won't allow you to disclose the reasons (such pettiness is rather unkingly, or is it?), so everyone in your vicinity feels a little bit uncomfortable without quite understanding why. Unless you have identified with a purpose in life, you are apt to drift off into glorious daydreams. You have considerable capacity for serving others selflessly, but sometimes spoil it by looking for applause and commendation. You will give up money and time, but rarely the right to recognition or attention. You suffer most when these plaudits are not immediately forthcoming.

THE VIRGO—ASCENDANT PERSONALITY

If Virgo is your Ascendant, you are a person who has an unusual amount of common sense. Basically, you are a very active thinker and you strive to implement your ideas rather than allow them to lie around in your head. You aim to "tidy up" your environment, to set things and people straight; therefore, you are sometimes perceived as fastidious or hypercritical. You possess a great aptitude for handling details, regarding them as the first essentials for establishing the order you love so much.

You are extremely good at work that requires precision and special skills. You can be counted on to have done your homework well and to possess a keen idea of sequences and procedures before you start. You learn readily and quickly and have impressive powers of endurance. You make a competent accountant, clerk, secretary and personal assistant. Your very practical way of looking at things also makes you an able worker in more menial occupations such as foreman, housekeeper, institution orderly or aide and the like.

You are not easily contented. Although conservative in outlook, you have a speculative turn of mind and often become anxious about your affairs. You desire wealth and expend considerable effort building up your savings. You are economical and prudent. You don't enjoy making a scene about money, but you indicate clearly to others that you know what's going on. You are cautiously protective of your own interests and are not likely to plunge into financial ventures without thorough reflection. You can also be counted on to look after the interests of others, which makes you a trusted and valuable employee, guardian or companion.

You seek perfection, not so much in yourself, but in the outer world. You aim to put everything in its place and are extremely methodical and neat to this end. Your interest in order extends to your associates and you often endeavor to correct them by pointing out their faults. Despite your good intentions, this may be resented. If not controlled, your impulse to criticize can descend into trifling fault-finding. Otherwise, you prefer to remain in the background. You are a modest and rather nervous type, somewhat lacking in self-confidence. You like to dress neatly or well but not conspicuously. You are diplomatic, shrewd—and tactful when you want to be. A thoughtful person, you are much attracted to the study of diet and hygiene. You are frequently an enthusiastic cook, with a special bias toward foods and dishes that are regarded as contributing to good health.

Possessions and Personal Security

You prefer to earn your money through partnerships, through working with or for people. You dislike working alone. You are happiest making your living in a job or profession where you can follow a clear-cut course, using your great flair for selecting and filling in details as you go. You are very good at carrying out instructions. You would make an excellent number two to a top executive. You enjoy owning quality objects and would prefer to miss a bargain than to gamble on poor workmanship or inferior quality. You know you can be depended on to do a first-class job yourself, and you see no reason to settle for anything less from others. You are good at balancing budgets and take great care to try to save something out of everything you earn. The extravagance of others distresses you deeply if it upsets your own financial affairs.

Communication with the Environment

You are often cutting in your observations. You have a capacity for puncturing human vanity, but this ability to discern sham and self-delusion in others is not always appreciated. You would make an excellent media critic who could be counted on to start public controversy and debate. You are not particularly voluble and may refuse to explain or elaborate on your criticisms. You may be a little too fixed in your opinions.

You possess a penetrating business mind and are capable of shrewd and subtle assessments. You can swiftly sort out confused situations and get down to the nitty-gritty.

Home, Family, Tradition

You are efficient at staying within a budget, paying bills on time and keeping the home spick and span. You enjoy supervising domestic and family affairs. You are deeply conscious of the importance of the family unit in maintaining a healthy, cohesive and well-ordered society. You have a keen sense of morality and would never aim to do anything that would harm or endanger the traditional family concept. You don't as a rule enjoy being away from your family for any extended period. And you are not so keen to travel long distances, except in connection with buying or moving into a grander or more spacious home.

Self-Expression, Love Life, Entertainment

Your approach to pleasurable activities is rather restrained, although you are not beyond breaking out on occasions. You tend to choose the safest or more socially acceptable course, and this can be inhibiting when it comes to romance and other exciting diversions. This reserve is not so pronounced in Virgo men as in women. The Virgo woman may appear frigid and politely unresponsive as a lover because she is never quite sure (nor anxious to find out) where her emotions will lead her. The man is more naturally responsive to his passionate desires. When face-to-face with his own spontaneous urges, the Virgo person usually manages to do the conventionally correct thing.

Work and Health

You are an able and persistent worker who will do his or her best to cooperate with fellow employees. You like being a member of a team. You share your ideas—often original and ingenious—without looking for special approbation. You excel in laboratory work. But whatever your occupation, you like to surround yourself with the very latest scientific equipment or tools designed for the job. You are acutely health conscious and have advanced views on food and diet. You are prone to overlook the fact that the strain of too much work can affect your highly sensitive nervous system.

Partnerships and Marriage

You need a mate who truly appreciates your unflagging efforts and endeavors to carry out your share of the bargain. You don't look so much for praise and admiration as for sympathetic understanding of your problems. Given the right treatment, you are easily soothed and prepared to go on serving and working with very little complaint. If your partner is not the placid and gentle type, you are apt to accept your lot with somewhat philosophic resignation. A Virgo person is often prepared to surrender his or her own personal desires to ensure an agreeable and workable union. Perhaps because of this, Virgo is not one of the Zodiac's most marrying types and sometimes makes an early and inflexible resolve to remain single.

Shared Resources, Legacies, Sex

Sharing is the department of your life that gives rise to activity through enterprise, so you yourself are continually involved with possessions, property and responsibilities belonging to other people. You are one of the great managers and caretakers of the Zodiac, as distinct from a principal or owner. In relation to sex, the Virgo person often regards his or her thoughts and longings as undesirable character elements and seeks to sublimate them in practical though sometimes obscure or complex ways. Virgo people are usually more concerned with sex than the chaste Virgo of tradition implies. Behind their controlled outward appearance may be a deep, though self-conscious, passion.

Higher Development and Long-Distance Travel

You are inclined to be orthodox in your attitudes toward religion and metaphysical matters. You may also desire to teach in these fields. Although your vision of a particular religion may be wide and comprehensive, you will probably apply its tenets in recognized ways. Hence the Virgo person is often to be found conducting a bible study class, organizing a church bazaar or giving instruction at a Sunday school. You are keen to judge the merits of any philosophy or doctrinaire way of life on its practical results. Generalities irritate you because you think they are a way of ducking issues. Travel generally holds no great attraction except as a means of increasing material holdings or income.

Public Standing, Career, Prestige

It is said the Virgo people often become prominent because they are so inoffensive that no one opposes them. This is especially so in politics, which is frequently a game of nominating the compromise candidate to avoid a stalemate. But someone has to perform the myriad nonspectacular but necessary tasks of the world such as assembly-line work, clerking and machine operating, and no one is more efficient or better suited temperamentally to these occupations than Virgos. As computer and electronic technicians working on small and complex circuits, you are without a peer. You often acquire renown through an aptitude for words and therefore make able editors, journalists, broadcasters, commentators and the like. You also make good librarians, secretaries, record keepers and assistants in publishing firms.

Friends, Group Activities, Hopes, Wishes

You like to entertain your friends in an informal atmosphere—preferably at home—and you enjoy cooking for them. You are keenly solicitous of their welfare and health and spend a fair amount of time doing the rounds on the telephone and a little less in visiting them at their homes. You enjoy the company of homey people. You have an avid interest in the latest developments in domestic aids and appliances. You like to talk about decorating schemes, furniture and furnishings. You are not a great one for joining groups, but once you give your word, you are a dependable social worker, especially for deprived people, children and animals. You usually own one or two domestic pets, to which you are deeply attached. You are also likely to support societies whose aim is to preserve old homes, antiquities and community landmarks.

Hidden Motives, Selfless Service, Psychic Feelings

You people with Virgo ascending frequently rise to become a power behind the throne. Although outspoken and open, you are adept at organizing activity behind the scenes, at erecting and running little systems within the main power structure. You often fail to receive the recognition that your accomplishments entitle you to. It is this capacity of yours to perform thankless service for exceptionally long periods that fits you for many of the ennobling tasks of the world, such as caring for the sick, insane and underprivileged in conditions of obscurity and even penury. This characteristic self-sacrifice can produce a deeply religious state of mind that works for heavenly rewards and no others.

THE LIBRA—ASCENDANT PERSONALITY

You love balance and harmony. You are said to be the judges of the Zodiac, because of your constant attempts to restore equilibrium in a world where injustice is the norm. You admire neatness and order. Peace is not just a desire to you, but a deep-seated need. You can be quick to anger but are easily appeased. You love companionship and are usually pleasant, very courteous and agreeable.

You are extremely diplomatic and generally try to please everyone at the same time. This calculated balancing of the Scales (the symbol of Libra) sometimes inclines you to vacillate. Not quite knowing what course to take next, you often sit on the fence, try to sense which way the wind is blowing, and then jump onto the nearest bandwagon. You are a person who relates to rather than initiates. You feel there are enough causes in the world without your starting up any new ones. You are fundamentally against aggravation and are aware of any aggressive move by you that will upset someone somewhere. This acute awareness often makes you mentally indecisive. You are better adapted to waiting placidly and agreeably for events to occur than to strike out assertively for yourself.

You admire beauty in most forms, especially nature, art, music and literature. You enjoy cultured and refined pleasures and amusements. You are a bright and congenial companion in social situations. You are usually endowed with remarkable grace and charm, which complements a well-formed body and symmetrical features. Your favorite companions are happy and cheerful types who frequently possess some artistic appreciation or talent. You are an admirer of courage and positive action in others. You are idealistic, adaptable, intuitive and constructive. A keen perception makes you very good at drawing comparisons. You are highly impressionable, and if your imagination is not curbed, it can soar to dizzy heights of daydreaming, wishful thinking, and impractical projects.

You are humane, sympathetic, modest and usually amorous. Although a very loving person, you are inclined to be changeable. You are ambitious, but dislike all discordant and unclean types of work. You enjoy getting out and about and have a feel for the social swing. You have good taste in clothes and furnishings and enjoy wearing expensive jewelry. Your love of fine things can lead to extravagance.

Possessions and Personal Security

You keep the details of your financial and property affairs fairly hidden. Although you may appear to be quite open and offhand about these matters, you seldom reveal the true situation. You can be secretly concerned about losing your possessions even though this fear has no actual foundation. You enjoy dealing in land if you get the chance and are very quick to see a potential bargain or to spot flaws in the sales talk. Most Libra-born people spend money freely and frequently live beyond their means. Financial strain can create an intensity in them that may erupt in greater extravagance! You enjoy the comfort of fine possessions and like to share this feeling by giving handsome gifts.

Communication with the Environment

Libra people often keep a diary about their travels or write long detailed letters to their family and friends. You also enjoy taking photographs of where you have been and distributing them to anyone who might be interested. You like to put your intinerary and plans neatly down on paper and have as many things as possible organized so there are no slipups. In conversation, you favor broader issues, but there is a danger here that you will focus on affairs that don't really concern you and neglect matters closer to home. Sometimes you waste your time and energy gathering and filing away useless details.

Home, Family, Tradition

You are admirably efficient and organized in the home. You enjoy having things arranged down to the last detail so there is a place for everything and a minimum of clutter. If things are disordered through no fault of your own, you will work hard and systematically to restore them to their original state, doing this over and over again if necessary. Your patience where your home and family are concerned can be quite remarkable. And you extend this quality by being a conscientious and law-abiding citizen. It is important to your sense of security to have a home of which you are proud; you seldom really settle down until this is achieved. You are usually interested in ancestral history, and if building or renovating a home, will often copy a tasteful feature from the past.

Self-Expression, Love Life, Entertainment

You are keen to express yourself through group efforts. You favor aims that are socially admired and, if possible, of notable and noticeable benefit to the community. Most Librans are deeply sympathetic to the needs of children—not necessarily just to their own offspring. They are frequently to be found taking an active part in parents' and teachers' associations as well as the Boy Scouts and Girl Scouts. In romance, they are usually guided by their head rather than their heart. They prefer to stay aloof from the untidy involvement that falling in love can mean. They don't have great trust in the strength of their emotional detachment, though they like to pretend to the world that they do. Sometimes, though, Librans lose their cool in unusual love affairs that produce drastic changes.

Work and Health

Physical labor doesn't have much appeal for you. You also find it hard to apply yourself for any length of time to mundane or repetitive work. You try but . . . it just doesn't seem to come off. Anyway, you feel you are fitted for better things than being a cog in a series of wheels, though often you aren't sure just what these might be. You prefer to work in the background where you can do a little secret string pulling, manipulating those who perform the more menial tasks. If you have to, you can somehow muddle through in routine jobs, using your charm and affable disposition to conceal from others your painful feeling of failure. You often suffer physical disorders induced by an active imagination.

Partnerships and Marriage

You are usually better at introducing harmony into other people's relationships than into your own marital affairs. You have a flair for bringing similar-thinking individuals together, for combining the different idiosyncrasies of character into an agreeable unity. You are a tactful matchmaker and a dependable mediator. But your own marital relations can be tempestuous. By attempting to maintain a balanced atmosphere for yourself, you frequently manage to stir up aggression in your mate. You are a natural fighter for the rights of others, and if these can be identified with your own rights, you are indeed a formidable antagonist. You genuinely love peace, but not always at the price of surrender.

Shared Resources, Legacies, Sex

The Libra personality often attracts wealth and affluence without any great striving. In fact, the more these people struggle to acquire the possessions of this world, the less success they are apt to enjoy. Acting along preconceived lines of endeavor seems to push the object of their desire further away. Librans sometimes marry for money and almost inevitably regret it. Or they may resolve "never again," and then repeat the experience with the same result. Despite your pleasant, easygoing manner, you have a good business mind. You can make money on the stock market and in corporate ventures. You also stand to gain through legacies. You usually reach mature age owning fairly substantial assets.

Higher Development and Long-Distance Travel

You often develop a very, workable philosophy as you approach middle age. Although you have the ability to absorb abstract ideas, your style is to formulate them in concrete terms so they can be passed on to others. The more evolved Libran is often a respected and erudite pundit who may be found lecturing on philosophy or metaphysics at a university or for a quasi-religious organization. You are happy to study in other countries or to travel to spread your views; you may be just as happy at home, in the comfort of an armchair with a good book.

Public Standing, Career, Prestige

You Libra people feel a deep connection between your career and your home. You often show a preference for the professions that improve or beautify the residence, such as interior design, needlepoint, architecture and decorating. You like to work at or from your home. Your city office is frequently a streamlined version of it in decor, tasteful finishing touches. Your professional life is usually marked by a procession of ups and downs. You often make your reputation through activities involving the public. You make keen real estate and rental agents.

Friends, Group Activities, Hopes, Wishes

You are a lavish and extremely considerate host or hostess. Your friends are always given the royal treatment, irrespective of expense. You are basically "high society" in your social aspirations. If you can't afford to move in "the best" circles, you keep yourself informed through chic magazines and acquaintances of what the rich and famous are doing. You desire to mix and be seen in the company of socially important and influential people. You are usually renowned for superb taste in clothes. In group activities, you lean to enterprises where your flair for promotion, entertainment and decoration can be exploited. The grander events such as large charity balls and political convention benefits are your ideal scene. Your flair and enthusiasm usually guarantee you a leadership position in club affairs.

Hidden Motives, Selfless Service, Psychic Feelings

Libras often appear to lose interest and seem drained of energy. Some have to retire to the bedroom or another place of isolation to restore the psychological face they would present to the world, for they are periodically assailed by indefinable anxieties that sap their psychic forces. It is also not unusual for Libra women, despite naturally endowed beauty, to feel compelled to remake their faces frequently with new cosmetics and hairstyles. This is because of a largely hidden contradiction in the Libran personality: these people are continually suppressing a surprisingly virulent critical attitude toward all their relationships, which conflicts terribly with their deep-rooted longing for harmony.

THE SCORPIO-ASCENDANT PERSONALITY

If Scorpio was ascending at the hour of your birth, you are one of the Zodiac's most steadfast and determined types. You possess true grit. You are an unflappable tower of strength in emergencies. You can be depended on to remain cool and practical while others are emotional and on the verge of panic. You can work under strain and pressure for remarkably sustained periods. You have unusual strength of will and will use subtlety and even force to achieve your purposes.

You are proud and reserved. You never allow others to get close enough to really know you. You seldom show your deeper feelings and you strive continually to repress your basic impulses. You are secretive and suspicious. Your habitual restraint can give you an air of inscrutability and poised intensity. You are the type of person one unconsciously likes to have on one's side.

You are quick in speech and action, often brusque, blunt and provoking. Your tongue can be venomous with a power to sting like the tail of the Scorpion, who symbolizes this Sign. Sudden and violent outbursts of rage mark the point where your self-enforced restraint ends. This, combined with a talent for quick-witted scalding retorts and sarcasm, makes you an enemy or opponent to be approached very warily. But as a friend, there are few more staunch or loyal.

You are enterprising, keen, shrewd and of acute judgment. You are fond of investigating mysteries and usually have a particular penchant for occult subjects. You are not easily influenced or imposed upon. You have a suspicious nature that on social occasions may manifest itself as good-humored mocking. Your views are bold and fixed, although your mind is exceedingly subtle. You are courageous and energetic and often possess a magnetic quality that suggests tremendous passion and power of conviction. You are fond of travel. Men make good naval officers. Both men and women are attracted by scientific subjects, especially research. You have an innate mechanical skill, along with constructive, as well as pronounced destructive, capabilities. You are very practical and realistic and make a fine executive, businessman or woman, contractor or the like.

You have been described as the workhorses of the Zodiac, usually possessing a strong, stocky body, a robust constitution and an amazing capacity for seeing something through to the end. A quirk in your character is that you remain active as long as you are interested in what you are doing; at other times, you can be indolent and pleased to let the rest of the world go by.

Possessions and Personal Security

You are a person who fixes his or her financial goals clearly and well ahead, and then works with great energy toward them. You have a flair for discerning future trends; you can often put your finger on an area of profitable investment years in advance. You take the wider view. You have the patience and endurance to wait and work for long-term profits. You like to have money for the power and prestige it imparts, but you are not a greedy person. You enjoy having possessions around you, but prefer to put your spare cash into land and property. Your income is usually derived from business. (Sometimes you are drawn to mining investments. It is not unusual for you to earn money through travel.)

Communication with the Environment

You are one of the less communicative types of the Zodiac. You talk in facts or about things that are important to you personally, but you seldom engage in idle chat. Your lighter conversation usually has an ulterior motive; otherwise, you are inclined to be silent. You enjoy analyzing people as they talk, particularly the more intelligent ones. Your own speech is cautious and controlled. You aim to give little away. The early education of Scorpio people is sometimes disjointed and they may evince little interest in formal instruction. As they mature, however, they are often drawn to study and extensive reading as necessary aids to their ambitious drives.

Home, Family, Tradition

The home and family is an area where your views and attitudes are likely to be quite advanced and even unconventional. Usually inclined to be cautious and conservative, you like to equip your home with the very latest gadgets, especially electrical gear. You are original in your ideas about structural and decorative changes. You have a broad-minded approach to family matters, which may seem natural and modern to you, but which could strike others as radical or even odd. Although you are firm in your opinions while you hold them, you are willing to convert to more progressive ideas as often as your inner growth and development demand.

Self-Expression, Love Life, Entertainment

You love to imbue your activities with an aura of secrecy and your love life is usually indicative of this. This Sign has a reputation for sexual excess that is not always deserved because the Scorpio person has strong self-repressive powers. However, there are often emotional perturbations that lead to secret love affairs, sometimes of great emotional intensity, and often with tragic or unhappy results. Your ability to sacrifice yourself to overcome the demands of your lower nature often produces a sublimation of energy that leads to soaring heights of creative attainment. You are often successful in the arts, especially in the entertainment professions.

Work and Health

You are the single-handed worker who could literally shift a mountian with a shovel, if you had the mind to. But fortunately for the rest of us, you like to throw your tremendous energies into projects that will make the world a better place to live in. You are accomplished in things requiring muscular skill and aggressive enterprise. You would make a fine industrial chemist. Because a job is rough or dirty doesn't put you off. You are excellent at solving pollution problems. You are often a specialist in drainage, sanitation and waste disposal. Medicine and scientific pursuits attract you. Because your nature is to take the initiative, you are better adapted to an executive position than an ordinary one.

Partnerships and Marriage

You are extremely cautious when it comes to choosing a marriage partner. You have very fixed ideas about what you want in a mate, and your expectations are frequently too exacting. Or, you may hesitate to take the plunge because of past hurts and experiences. You are "old-fashioned" in your ideas about marriage and are usually very possessive. Jealousy and suspicion can burn in you with volcanic fury. You are usually a loyal partner and will be inclined to see a marriage through even though it is unhappy. You often increase in wealth and influence through marriage.

Shared Resources, Legacies, Sex

The Scorpio person's supposed preoccupation with sex stems from a primitive urge to penetrate to the roots of life and uncover its mysteries. You are often just as curious about death and the afterlife or rebirth. Psychologically, you associate all three issues with your search for truth. You are intense about your sexual relationships but your approach is largely intellectual. You like variety and tend to flit from one sensual experience to another. You enjoy experimentation, so homosexuality is not uncommon among your type. As seething as your passions may be, they remain a vehicle for your incisive mind to probe deeper into your, and life's inexplicable motivations. Often you are a shrewd investigator of psychic phenomena and mediumistic contact with the so-called dead. You may write or lecture on your findings.

Higher Development and Long-Distance Travel

The evolution of the Scorpio-type person depends largely upon extremes of experience. Just as you plunge into the depths of carnal enjoyment and gratification, so you are impelled to soar to the mental heights sometimes associated with mysticism. This is your essential ying and yang. The Scorpio person is a natural traveler who feels at home in any country. You often enjoy the feeling of seclusion and perverse distinction that you receive from living among foreigners. You take pleasure in voyages and like to settle near water. During your travels, you sometimes suffer from hurt and frustration in connection with your emotional needs.

Public Standing, Career, Prestige

You are intensely ambitious and usually achieve your objectives through sheer tenacity and an inordinate desire for personal power and prestige. You work according to a long-range plan whenever you can. You fix your sights on an influential position, and then toil toward it with single-minded determination. You use your amazing reserves of physical and mental energy to outflank the strongest opposition, sometimes endangering your health and even risking your

life in the process. Your desire to make good is obsessive throughout your working life. You are not a notable egotistical type, but you expect due recognition for your accomplishments. You gravitate toward self-employment or a position where you can make the decisions without reference to others.

Friends, Group Activities, Hopes, Wishes

You must trust a person first to make him or her your friend; then he or she can join the chosen few you allow to gather around you. You have a magnetic quality that attracts a certain type of companion who will have respect as well as affection for you. It is your nature to keep one last barrier between you and all others, and this may be manifested as aloofness. You are staunch in friendship and will work unstintingly on behalf of your comrades if necessary. Being a loner, you are not at your best in groups and don't extend yourself with any great enthusiasm. However, you appreciate the common-sense advantages of the democratic vote and are prepared to go along with majority decisions.

Hidden Motives, Selfless Service, Psychic Feelings

Partnerships are not very fortunate for you (outside of material gains) and often result in deception and bitter disappointment. You seem to sense this intuitively; hence your cautious approach to partnership and your basic motivation to go-it-alone. The law courts can be particularly unlucky for you. You are likely to find that in disputed wills and the like you will fare better by settling out of court, even though it may mean accepting a smaller sum than you feel you deserve. The Scorpio person often fails to profit from the lessons of the past and may repeat the same painful error several times.

THE SAGITTARIUS—ASCENDANT PERSONALITY

You are a lover of personal liberty and freedom. Although it is your nature to be jovial and good-humored, you don't take kindly to being ordered about. You like to be able to come and go as you please and will eventually gravitate to an occupation that provides this opportunity. You try to choose a love partner who respects your need for independence; if he or she doesn't, you are likely to rebel and go your own way.

You are bright, optimistic, generous and charitable. You are a consistent good friend, neighbor and relative. You have a strong sense of honor and fair play, which you do your best to live up to. Your manner is open, frank and helpful. Combining these qualities with a cheery and easygoing breeziness, you are never short of companions or a cordial welcome.

You are an expansive thinker. You like the big scene and the horizons that extend beyond. You enjoy visiting foreign countries and meeting people of differing backgrounds and cultures. You are drawn to big business and large financial deals. There is very little that is restrictive or narrow in your makeup.

You are the sportsmen of the Zodiac. There is hardly a sporting activity in which Sagittarians don't shine or lead the field. Movement, freedom, opportunity to display your energy and physical prowess and the possbility of travel—all these make sports a compelling attraction.

You have a strong feeling for religion, law, medicine—and sometimes philosophy. You make a capable teacher where moral guidance is required, but have to guard against a tendency to sermonize or lay down the law.

You are intuitive and prophetic and quick to arrive at conclusions. Though you sometimes appear blunt and abrupt, your observations are often uncannily on the mark. You are fearless, demonstrative and outspoken—and often restless. You are also impulsive and frequently too anxious to be on the move again to develop the concentration of which you are capable.

You are ambitious and quick to take advantage of opportunities. You make a good promoter or public relations expert. But, easily carried away by your own exuberance, you incline toward making superoptimistic predictions that have very little hope of fulfillment. Your interest and enthusiasm are quickly aroused by innovation, novelty and all that is ingenious. In commercial life, you have to restrain yourself from jumping from one promising new activity to another. You are a sympathetic and humane type of person who sincerely does what he can to help others. You have a soft spot for animals.

Possessions and Personal Security

You have a deep-seated interest in security that belies your offhand manner. You aim from the start to acquire wealth and possessions. And you usually succeed, provided you overcome the speculative and less dependable side of your nature. This is attracted to gambling and dabbling in get-rich-quick schemes. You are fortunate in business—big business and big connections. You

prefer to invest your funds in gilt-edged securities and government-guaranteed bonds. You like to feel that you can spend your income freely while keeping the principal intact. You take pride in owning luxuries that imply status and have a special liking for expensive cars, yachts and other prestigious conveyances.

Communication and the Environment

You are extremely good at carrying on a knowledgeable conversation without knowing too much about the topic. You have a rare flair for putting snippets of information together so that they make sense and carry conviction. You are ingenious, inventive and original when you talk and write. Your ideas are often visionary, even though you may not have given the subject any great thought. You will go to some trouble to encourage others to learn and to pass on information that will be helpful to them. You have a great respect for education in its broadest sense and belive that its value lies in enabling all men to develop a workable moral ethic for themselves.

Home, Family, Tradition

You are deeply sentimental about your home and family. You need to feel that wherever you may roam, you have a secluded place with people who care to return to. You are prepared to make sacrifices for the happiness and welfare of your loved ones, though you sometimes doubt that your self-denying actions are sufficient. You seldom communicate your personal doubts and fears to anyone. You can be rather fixed and assertive in your opinions around the house, although you do your best to create an atmosphere of freedom and liberal thinking. As much as you love your family, you don't let them tie you down. Your idealism can go to extremes.

Self-Expression, Love Life, Entertainment

You are a lover of all pleasures and entertainments that keep you on the move. You aren't the kind of person who enjoys staying in one place for long unless there is plenty of action. Activity is your standard for amusement. You are positive and forceful in your love affairs; the waiting game is not for you. Competitive sports and physical exercise are your particular strong points. Here you can show your personal skill and fine coordination, inspiring others, especially children to emulate you. You combine physical prowess with a noble sense of sportsmanship that often makes you the captain of a team, a star player with a big following or a respected coach.

In later years, you may channel your energy into the study of philosophic subjects, and again show a flair for teaching.

Work and Health

You are a very conscientious person once you take on a job. You like to have a sure and steady income so you can indulge your many interests without having to worry about basic expenses. This is why many Sagittarians are found in solid jobs like the teaching profession. You may appear offhand in your attitude to work, but this is purely a reflection of your unfailing confidence in life. You are intent on establishing yourself. Once the vision of what you want to do becomes fixed in your mind, you can produce the energy and staying power to make it materialize. You are vividly aware of your dependence on good health for worldly accomplishment. You are usually diet-conscious and not only an advocate of physical fitness, you practice it.

Partnerships and Marriage

The Sagittarius-Ascendant person can be rather casual about marriage and more permanent emotional relationships. Basically you have a great need for mental stimulation, and only meetings with numerous people of different types can satisfy it. Although these contacts may be quite innocent, they can monopolize your time and make life miserable for a devoted partner who doesn't understand your motivations. Sagittarians frequently marry more than once. You look for someone to share your diverse interests with rather than a partner with whom you can plunge into exclusive intimacy. You are a pretty basic physical lover. Sometimes you find it easier to stay wedded to your work and mental pursuits.

Shared Resources, Legacies, Sex

The person influenced by this Sign can be highly sensuous in his or her sexual relationships. Your deeper feelings may occasionally be excited to the degree of licentiousness. Sexual relations provide an opportunity to probe deeper into your nature than you are normally prepared to go. On these occasions, you may discover you are two people—breezy and amicable on the surface, brooding and unsure inside. Death and the afterlife concern you more than you are prepared to admit. You often have vague intuitive feelings that you are not prepared to conceptualize except in uncomplicated conventional terms. Sagittarians frequently share in legacies.

Higher Development, Long-Distance Travel

To you, life is a university and the obvious way to prepare for graduation is to travel. Visits to other countries you find particularly informative and interesting. You are absorbed not only by what new acquaintances have to say, but also in airing your own ideas. You take considerable pleasure and pride in these. Religion and topics with moral overtones are often your favorites. Although you are an abstract thinker, you tend to identify your conclusions with one of the traditional faiths. You are more an idealist than a realist. And your zeal at times suggests dogmatism.

Public Standing, Career, Prestige

Your professional aspirations are conventional in a way. You like to be close to big business or linked with a large "umbrella" organization where you feel fairly safe and secure. Given this protection, you then feel free to spread your wings and show your intellectual inventiveness and capacity. You would do well in a public relations or advertising firm handling several large company accounts. You like to occupy a position where you can guide or enlighten others—the church or an educational situation would be ideal for this. You possess a keen critical faculty and writing ability. You excel in implementing detailed programs and grand strategies.

Friends, Group Activities, Hopes, Wishes

Your special ability is bringing people of different points of view together. In group activities, and especially in business, this can be of inestimable value. You often find yourself playing the role of arbitrator, negotiator, chairman and common friend. You are, in fact, never short of friends, probably because you go out of your way to be diplomatic and seldom lose your affability. Group discussions in which you usually shine give you great pleasure. In club activities, you sometimes get carried away with enthusiasm and advocate an exciting but impractical idea. You are a stickler for a fair deal for all, even though your own interests may be affected.

Hidden Motives, Selfless Service, Psychic Feelings

You are often not altogether honest with yourself when it comes to your deeper feelings. You are inclined to run away from mystical insights because you find them fundamentally upsetting and in severe contrast to your innately expansive and outward-going nature. All that is formless and vague you tend to reject; or you convert it to ideologies and beliefs that are socially tenable. You are suspicious of the occult; the closer it gets to the truth, the more uncomfortable you become. You prefer to take refuge in safe concepts. And yet, you possess the intellectual and emotional equipment to make an outstanding occultist.

THE CAPRICORN—ASCENDANT PERSONALITY

You are basically a serious and thoughtful person with an unusually high regard for dignity. You have a tendency to look out for yourself most times, but your self-esteem usually ensures that your actions are not easily reproachable. You are cautious and practical and seldom act without due consideration. You are prudent and economical and capable of depriving yourself of life's comforts in order to realize your goals.

Often you are more ambitious for prestige and position than for actual wealth and possessions. You are capable of hard and enduring effort wherever there is the slightest opportunity of making good, especially in business. Your powers of concentration seem indefatigable, and you can exhaust the strongest opposition with your persistence. You possess great organizing ability, along with a cautious, calculating and (when appropriate) conniving mind. Thus you are extremely well fitted for planning and carring out the schemes of large corporations and conglomerates. Your aim is to become a recognized authority in your chosen field. You want to be looked up to and sought out for the stream of wisdom that you feel you have to impart to the world. Even when you become rich and famous, you are apt to live frugally, in modest style.

You are not a demonstrative type of person. You don't show sympathy readily. You prefer to be judged on your actions (if anyone dare judge you) and to evaluate others' effectiveness in the same way. Words and promises don't have much significance for you. Your disposition is somewhat cold. You suffer from bouts of despordency. You are secretive, reserved, self-willed —and very responsible.

You have a scientific turn of mind that is drawn to investigate, dig out facts, make notes, file away, arrange in logical order. You succeed by determined and steady action rather than by bursts of effort.

In youth, you often look older than your years, and in maturity, you look younger. The Capricornian often has a difficult childhood;

your education may be interrupted and your health indifferent. This is usually more pronounced if in youth you tried to subordinate your innately serious nature. In adulthood, you generally grow steadily tougher and wirier and seldom run to fat.

Possessions and Personal Security

The best outlet for your talents and the most lucrative is usually one connected with the sciences. Your unusual type of mind makes it possible for you to make money through commercializing the discoveries of science, particularly on a national or international scale. Your thinking is advanced and original. You are the distributor or wholesaler of the life-saving drug or the new smelting process. You are the industrial chemist who revolutionizes a technology through an inspired discovery. You are also a key member of any team that is engaged in global projects and research of too vast a magnitude for individual effort. You shine where you can establish authority, in drawing up systems and in working for the benefit of the community.

Communication with the Environment

You don't use words lightly. You like to say what you mean or remain silent, mostly out of a desire to avoid being misunderstood. You are not quick to communicate with all and sundry. People have to prove serious and trustworthy before you confide in them. Then you can be quite vocal. You perceive more in others' conversation than the words they use; you are aware of hidden connections, and whenever others speak, you are looking for subtle implications (what is not said also comes into your calculations). You can have a profound appreciation of music since it does not depend on words to convey meaning. To you, music is the embodiment of an otherworldliness you can readily understand.

Home, Family, Tradition

You take a keen interest in the day-to-day running of your home. You feel you know what is best for all concerned and you insist on having your ideas adhered to. Anyone who does not conform is likely to be urgently rebuked. Domestic rebellions are not rare these days in the Capricorn-dominated household. But you will rarely go to any extreme that might threaten family solidarity. Many of you with this Sign ascending have had to overcome a lack of self-confidence in childhood, frequently with the assistance of an ambitious maternal influence. You feel that a solidly secure home life is a desirable base from which to confront life's ambitious struggle.

Self-Expression, Love Life, Entertainment

You find your amusements in rather conservative ways. You are not a party lover or given to rash or reckless escapades, but you do enjoy entertaining in a quiet and dignified way, particularly if it allows you to display your affluence or influence. You are more likely to give a dinner party to create an impression than to enjoy social warmth and conviviality, although this could never be inferred from the quality of your hospitality. Despite their reserved manner, Capricorn men are reputed to be exceedingly sensual. Women are more inclined to express their creative drives in artistic endeavors. Both enjoy physical warmth and a comfortable home.

Work and Health

You can be depended on to do an excellent job at work because you are conscientious and persevering. You also have the gift of clear and straightforward written expression, and since you are often drawn to scientific occupations, you can produce a lucid and compact technical report from a bewildering collection of data. You aim at versatility in your job and often develop new methods and techniques that are very profitable for your employers. Your logical mind prefers to deal in facts. You don't waste time or effort on fantasy. You are admirably suited for work in financial institutions, businesses and all kinds of research establishments. Your nerves are sometimes affected by overwork, but generally you have the good sense to take care of your body, particularly through diet.

Partnerships and Marriage

Capricorn people are avidly sentimental about marriage. Men require a partner who will be almost motherly in her attentions. Capricorn women will put a protective ring of affection around their husbands and do all they can to make them comfortable and secure at home. Both sexes have a great desire to keep the family intact, for this is the taproot through which they cling to the earth and from which they reach up and out into the competitive world. Those of you influenced by Capricorn will repeatedly give way to your mate and even endure an unhappy marriage for the sake of your family. Your partnerships mature and become more binding with time.

Shared Resources, Legacies, Sex

To realize your full potential, you need to direct your creative energies along purposeful paths. If you squander your vital drive and look for self-renewal in sex, you are likely to miss the point as well as the boat and become lost in your own frustrated ambitions. If you are the advanced type of Capricorn, you have the ability to share in large-scale business and financial operations; through these you have a great chance of becoming a respected force in the power game, which so intrigues you. You can succeed with natural ease in mastering the intricacies and complex problems of giant conglomerates and combines; you and the computers will be among the few who grasp and understand the total picture. And the rewards can be enormous. The dedicated Capricorn person in later years usually obtains the recognition which he or she craves.

Higher Development and Long-Distance Travel

You are a stickler for the letter of the law, a sturdy pillar of society and a weighty influence on the side of rules and regulations. But in philosophic and higher-minded matters, you are not easily convinced. You don't have much time for abstractions and subtleties. Your approach is critical and analytical. You want proven systems and tidy thoughts that fit without any leftovers. If an idea can't be slotted into a definite place in your experience, then you will discount it. Your preoccupation with practical values can make you rigid and dogmatic, and if carried too far, depressingly closeminded.

Public Standing, Career, Prestige

You often make a name for yourself in businesses and professions that require a partner. Numerous Capricorns are respected and influential partners in law firms. You are also likely to make your mark in fields that necessitate working in close collaboration with others and where your unemotional qualities can be exercised and developed. The administrative side of large institutions, the civil service and the sciences frequently offer appropriate opportunities. You also gravitate to dignified positions where your flair for arbitration and conciliation can be utilized.

Friends, Group Activities, Hopes, Wishes

Above all, you look for loyalty and steadfastness in the select group you choose to call friends. In return, you offer them the same earnest and staunch support. You have very few intimate associates. You don't have much time to spare for friendly gatherings with others. You prefer to devote yourself to the serious issues of life (you are proud you are not an escapist) and choose companions who share your stolidly realistic views. You are fond of meetings in old haunts and seldom alter your routines. Your band of cronies does not welcome newcomers easily. You are a bit suspicious of people who want to get too close too soon. You have a fondness for societies and movements that foster esoteric knowledge and teachings.

Hidden Motives, Selfless Service, Psychic Feelings

You have a talent for outscheming the best of the zodiacal schemers. Often you sum up a situation and decide on a series of moves before others have any idea of what's going on. You have the advantage of being extremely practical. You don't allow your nebulous feelings the luxury of useless daydreaming; you try to pare down each emotion with your practical intellect and make it work or discard it. When one does get past, you become despondent. Less evolved Capricorns live for their work and responsibilities; they seldom dwell on "significance." They can, indeed, be pretty drab people. Advanced types, although reticent about their beliefs, may leave a life-trail blazed with words of wisdom.

THE AQUARIUS—ASCENDANT PERSONALITY

With Aquarius ascending at the hour of your birth, you are among the most humanitarian of mankind's zodiacal helpers. You are drawn to projects that will benefit the great majority rather than the individual. Your sentiment is to advance the race. You are usually a leader in the search for truth, not as a philosophical exercise, but with the firm intention of applying it in practical ways. You often become a physician or a socialistic reformer.

Although you are pleasant and friendly, you are a person of strong likes and dislikes. You usually have a very large circle of acquaintances and friends, but your attitude toward them is somewhat detached. You are determined, sincere and fond of honor and dignity. Although sympathetic, you develop a dispassionate and reasoning outlook that fits you to be one of the progressive thinkers of the community. You have strong ideals and are attracted by all humanizing activities that lead to reform.

You are clear-minded and very capable of dealing with facts, your memory is extremely reliable and everything of a mental nature appeals to you. But you are an exceedingly independent person. Although keenly cooperative in a general sense, you retain a deep need for personal freedom. Unless this is appreciated by others, you can be badly misunderstood. Even though you are usually law-abiding, your impulse is to try to change things for the better. Your idea of "better" doesn't always agree with ruling opinion. You may be unorthodox and even revolutionary in your ideas. You put intense energy into a cause. An overzealous Aquarian always runs the risk of becoming so identified with his slogans that he veers away from the truth he is trying to propagate.

You are imaginative and broad-minded. Your capacity for originality can be quite electrifying. Your fertile mind makes you an inspired scientific worker. Inventive genius often appears in people born with Aquarius rising.

You are unpredictable. You have a penchant for all that is unusual. You may on occasions be considered eccentric because of your freewheeling attitude. You can be a force in the artistic world. You enjoy literature, music, art and scenery.

Your disposition is unobtrusive, quiet and patient. You try to be faithful. It is necessary for you, both physically and mentally, to keep circulating so that you are well informed of what's going on and get sufficient exercise.

Possessions and Personal Security

You love possessions but can be quite impractical about them. Your ways of handling money may be hopelessly muddled. When you have money, you literally try to make your dreams come true—with some disillusioning results. You may receive income from unusual, and at times, quite unexpected, sources. You are a frequent recipient of gifts. Funds also are inclined to come from large institutions; sometimes in the form of grants and awards. Lack of money depresses you, makes you feel hamstrung. Sooner or later, most Aquarians have to go through the discomfort of loosening their attachment to material things. Or, they may be forced by circumstances to arrange their financial affairs with a more conscious sense of proportion.

Communication with the Environment

You are vigorous and precise in your contacts. You like to have plenty of channels of communication open. You are seldom stuck for ideas or words or unsure of the next step to take. You have a clear and incisive way of expressing yourself. Often you propose remarkably original ideas that leave others wondering why the heck they didn't think of them. Your quiet manner belies the great intellectual strength and energy that powers your reasoning. Aquarians are often pioneers in the communications industry, particularly in electronics, radio and television. You don't hesitate to make public statements if you think you've got something important to say.

Home, Family, Tradition

You have a greater need for security than your unpredictable nature would suggest. You love your home for the reassuring substantiality it provides. You like it to be paid for, to hold the deed of ownership in your hands. You enjoy filling it with attractive furniture and furnishings as well as modern labor-saving devices. You dislike buying goods on credit but are sometimes forced to because there seems no other way to get what you want. You aren't fond of moving; once you're settled, you can be a bit of a stick-in-the-mud, so long as your mental activities are not restricted. You enjoy living in places where you can feel close to nature.

Self-Expression, Love Life, Entertainment

You enjoy variety in your love life. You are not a sentimentalist and are more inclined to have numerous casual romances than to fall deeply in love too quickly or too easily. Your approach to love is more intellectual than emotional; you personify the cool, calm and collected lover. As a parent, you foster intelligence in your children rather than sentiment. You find your entertainment mostly in mental ways: you enjoy conversing with different people in different places as often as possible. You can be a great traveler, preferring to move on when everyone else is just getting settled. You are deft and clever with your hands and often sew or make things in your spare time. You also write competently.

Work and Health

You usually choose a job where your efforts will directly or indirectly benefit others. You have an avid interest in the welfare and health of all humanity. This will often lead you into the laboratory or onto committees concerned with eliminating hunger in the world and alleviating other human suffering. When you find a satisfying job, you immerse yourself in it completely; you are the type who may even forget to go home! It is therefore not surprising that you try

to make your office as homely as possible. You are a good employer, with an eye to efficiency, who likes his or her workers to feel they are one big happy family. You are aware of the need to keep fit, but may be too busy intellectually to get enough exercise. Many Aquarians manage to combine this critical intellectual faculty with talent for research and become renowned in professions requiring detailed discrimination. Some of the world's best detectives have been Aquarians. You also make able astrologers, psychologists and chemists. You possess a pronounced ability to keep professional secrets and to remain cooly detached in emotional situations.

Partnerships and Marriage

You usually take your time selecting a marriage partner. You marry for love but you also need someone whose accomplishments you can take pride in. You can be an easy person to live with and have a happy marriage provided you choose the right partner. Those Aquarians who select a bossy mate have little chance of domestic harmony; a clash of wills is almost certain. You have no great desire to seek glory for yourself; in fact, you are inclined to allow others to take credit that belongs to you. But you will not be dominated or dictated to. You must retain your independence in any partnership for it to work. Your ideal mate will be on the same mental wavelength, allowing an easy exchange of creative ideas.

Shared Resources, Legacies, Sex

You have a quite critical tendency, which can be off-putting. When this is restrained, you give out a coolness that can be inhibiting in your sex life. You are a mental creature and unless your intellectual interest is first stirred and then confirmed, you make no effort to encourage intimate relationships. Any legacies you receive are more likely to be in the form of numerous objects, possessions and small pieces of property and real estate rather than large, lump sums and extensive holdings. Positions or jobs that are inherited—even when lucrative—may involve a fair amount of work and personal attention.

Higher Development and Long-Distance Travel

Your admirable humanitarian instinct springs from a desire for universal justice and equality. To you, the individual is deserving of sympathy and consideration, but the urgently greater task is to eliminate the basic causes that afflict and degrade the human condition. You choose the broader outlook. Your impartiality allows you to listen to others and to make fair and practical assessments. You present your findings either as a scientist or humanitarian with honesty and forthrightness. You are a keen traveler, and if you get the chance, will often visit many countries in a short time.

Public Standing, Career, Prestige

You enjoy nothing quite as much as meeting a challenge. You make your way in the world, when you can, by embracing king-size tasks that for time and dedication would daunt most other types. You will toil for years to unlock nature's secrets as a medical researcher, engineer, physicist. Once committed, you will never quit halfway through a job. You have tremendous powers of concentration. Although your prefer mental activity, you are capable of considerable physical exertion if it is necesssry for the success of a project or the attainment of your goals. Prestige does not mean as much to you as accomplishment; fortunately, both go together for you.

Friends, Group Activities, Hopes, Wishes

You have more acquaintances than friends. You are the type of person people find easy to talk to, a very intelligent and interesting conversationalist. You enjoy listening as much as talking. Since you need to range freely, exchanging views among a wide variety of people, you have neither the time nor the inclination to form deep friendships. You are more at home with groups of people, especially those who are not bound by conventional thinking. Your own views are advanced and frequently radical enough to split and disrupt groups and organizations if you press them hard enough. The strength of your ideas is a force to be reckoned with.

Hidden Motives, Selfless Service, Psychic Feelings

In this department of life, the typical Aquarian can be negatively disposed in one of two ways. He may make a lot of speeches about the need for progress and liberated thought, but when the time for action comes, he may be busily engaged elsewhere in strictly conservative pursuits. Or, he may be a truly inspired visionary who is so far ahead of his time that no one will listen to him. To be an effective force worthy of his brilliant ideas, the Aquarian sometimes has to learn the discipline of frustrated desire. Most people influenced by this Sign manage to conceal the great amount of energy they put into their enterprises so that their accomplishments seem rather effortless and natural.

THE PISCES—ASCENDANT PERSONALITY

If Pisces was ascending at the hour of your birth, you are among the most affectionate, sympathetic and trusting people of the Zodiac. You are also among the most modest and timid. This is not surprising when you consider that Pisces is the summation of the other 11 types. As Pisces stands at the "end" of the zodiacal wheel, so man stands at the end of his life with only his essential qualities of feeling—and much uncertainty.

You are kind and loving, easygoing, good-natured and charitable. You are very quick to understand. You have a strong and profound psychic faculty that you rely on to an immense degree: you "know" things most of the time without having to say or know what you know (a true Piscean will understand exactly what this means). You are skilled in detail, especially in putting the finishing touches to things. And paradoxically, though very orderly in manner, you are changeful in disposition—so you live a rather disjointed existence, leaving many things unfinished that were begun so well. You are quick to observe deficiencies in others; a lack of completeness in any thing or situation immediately catches your attention.

You are impressionable, emotional and imaginative. The intensity of your idealism can be quite painful to you at times, especially when you tune into others' sufferings and sorrows. You have a highly developed intuitive and inspirational faculty. You are often telepathetic and mediumistic.

You are courteous, confiding, affable and hospitable. You don't like to push yourself forward. You lack confidence and self-esteem. At times, you become overanxious, indecisive and disheartened, but in an emergency, your uncertainty seems to fall away, revealing a resolute, determined and very effective person.

You are extremely creative if you can discover the correct medium for your self-expression. You love music, good literature and all that is intrinsically beautiful. Your tastes are refined and at times impeccably subtle. You often write exquisite poetry. Your daydreams are very real to you and are an important part of your psychic processes. You are usually not very body conscious and can compensate for this by directing your vital energies into physical accomplishments—becoming an excellent dancer, gymnast or teacher of yogic and other disciplined postures and exercises.

You usually succeed in occupations where you are required to add the finer details to ensure completeness. Your hypersensitivity makes you a competent dramatic actor, an inspired painter or artist. You excel in situations where it is necessary to make the best of things and where discretion and understanding are required. You have a talent for publishing and social service. Many Pisceans find an outlet for their humanitarian instincts by working in hospitals and institutions.

Possessions and Personal Security

You usually manage to have a fairly good income. You put considerable effort into your money-making activities and do a fair amount of scheming and manipulating behind the scenes. You work on the basis that if you have several enterprises going at once, you can afford a couple of failures. This often occurs and you accept it philosophically. You are a free spender, although not a particularly wise one. Unless you invest your funds in property, you will have a job holding on to them. You look for a quick turnover. You are frequently a successful promoter of one-time publishing ideas and "pop" events that appeal to the masses. The lucrative film industry attracts Pisceans. Possessions, prestige and money help you maintain confidence in your own worth.

Communication with the Environment

Though you give the impression of flexibility, you can be surprisingly stubborn. You have a gift for dissolving your attitudes so that you remain receptive and open-minded most of the time, but once you get stuck on an idea, you will not relinquish it without a great deal of obstinate maneuvering. You are much more a feeling creature than a thinking one. You are continually picking up psychic sensations from your environment, which you act on with conceptualizing them. Because the Piscean child finds it hard to relate to a formal education with its intellectual emphasis, he is sometimes thoughtlessly branded as a slow learner. If the child is approached through his feelings, which are acutely sensitive to beauty and emotional stimulus, he can understand a subject quickly and profoundly.

Home, Family and Tradition

You want your home and family relationships to be ideal. You look for story-book perfection, and when you don't find it, you are hurt, disappointed or disillusioned. You never really comprehend why things aren't as you imagine them. You are a mental creature where your loved ones and domestic life are concerned. Because it is not easy for you to adapt to the earthy realities of these relationships, you sometimes get in a muddle, unable to cope with the exigencies of children, mate and household duties all at the same time. You like to move often because this gives you a chance to make new and exciting starts—not to mention the opportunity to try yet again to materialize your dreams.

Self-Expression, Love Life, Entertainment

You enjoy parties at home but are not greatly attracted by noisy or boisterous amusements in public places. The more intimate types of recreation and pleasure appeal to your nature. You are happy visiting others in their homes. Piscean women welcome the opportunity to dress up. Their personal appearance is very important to them, and they will walk out of any function (or hide for hours in the background) rather than see it through inappropriately dressed. You have a strong sense of personal pride, which is easily dented. You get touchy if there is any criticism of your children or if they fail to come up to your expectations. You need continual praise and encouragement for your creative efforts. You have a romantic chocolate-box approach to love affairs and want to cherish and pet as well as be petted and cherished.

Work and Health

You have a compelling need to be proud of the job you do, so it is essential that you choose work you can perform well. If you don't, you will be miserable and downhearted most of your working hours. You like to be your own boss but you don't mind following instructions if you enjoy the work. Your talents are better suited to artistic occupations and to those that give you the chance to display something. You need to feel that your job carries prestige, or at least that it is glamorous enough to attract the interest and approval of your friends. Despite your retiring nature, you like to show off about your accomplishments. If you can't find an esteemed position, you may make out that lesser tasks are obviously unworthy of your talents and do nothing, but make gracious excuses.

Partnerships and Marriage

You aren't such the easy person to live with that your pliant nature suggests. You are intensely critical—of your partners as well as yourself. You have a way of projecting your inadequacies onto your mate and then paradoxically looking to him or her to provide the reassurance and confidence you can't find in yourself. You need to live with a reliable, methodical and efficient person who will serve you conscientiously. Being a sentimentalist at heart, you will work hard in your way to make the marriage conform to your dreams, but unless you choose the right mate, the psychological pressures may be too great for the union to stand. As much as you love the idea of romance, you may marry for security or even because you think it is the right thing to do. Pisceans are sometimes happier and attain to greater self-sufficiency by remaining single.

Shared Resources, Legacies, Sex

Your fortunes largely depend on partners, but you can lose all through these people just as easily as gain. The balance of the scales of Piscean sharing are finely set. Partners can take you down to the depths or raise you to the heights. This applies in a sensual sense, as well as to spiritual and economic matters. You have a high expectation of others, which may be unjustified. You can seize greater control of your own destiny by becoming more balanced in yourself, by getting rid of ambivalence and psychological dependence on others, and by achieving a sense of purpose. Art and your love of beauty are the most powerful means of regeneration for you. You need to cultivate faith in yourself. When this is achieved, the Piscean Fishes swim purposefully in the same direction.

Higher Development and Long-Distance Travel

You have the power to reach extraordinary heights of spirituality. Unfortunately, your dreams and illusions stand in the way. You have a fundamental longing to tear aside the veil, but this can only be done by coming to terms with your own past. For this reason, you are intolerant of formal religious "paths" and logical "methods." You have faith only in direct experience—of yourself. It is not unusual for you to embrace the emotional side of orthodox religions, but the path always leads back to you. You are a spiritual pragmatist who relies on attunement with psychic and spiritual forces for eventual enlightenment. What others achieve by drugs, you achieve naturally. You are a spiritual "mainliner" who should understand that the induced experience, however vividly described, falls far short of your constant intuitions. You enjoy long voyages—both worldly and hallucinatory.

Public Standing, Career, Prestige

You are quite a lucky person. You often have only to think about something and hold the idea in your consciousness for it to happen. You aspire to greatness, or at least to a position of eminence or fame. You love to be popular. You choose to make your way in a profession that offers a wide scope; you like to be respected for your ethical rectitude. In business, your word is your bond. You are frequently required to travel in connection with your career. (Piscean women often marry men whose occupations take them on journeys to distant places.) You are basically a curious person who is well satisfied by the delights and novelty of travel. You aim high. You would rather lose than not try at all—for the biggest stakes.

Friends, Group Activities, Hopes, Wishes

Your friends are probably the most solid side of your life. You like to see in them the substance of your dreams. In fact, you are not beyond promoting someone to the highest pedestal of regard and then smashing his image to the ground with iconoclastic fervor. You would never hurt a friend, though you just grow out of them. You create and dissolve your friends with a rhythmic passion that leaves even you horrified at times. This makes you a bit hesitant to reach out, a bit of a loner. You are also cautious about joining in group activities. Quite often you may accept an invitation personally and then back out by letter or telegram. You relate to people through their emotions but tend to favor those who are tried and true. You admire people who are dashingly original, but finally settle for those who are reliable and dutiful.

Hidden Motives, Selfless Service, Psychic Feelings

Despite your sometimes vague otherworldliness, you have a practical and scientific approach to occult studies. It is as though this is *your* world, and in it you have all the confidence and authority you may lack in what others call "the world." You are often a leading light in research into spiritualism, parapsychology and extrasensory perception. But you seldom achieve public admiration or recognition for your efforts; more likely, you devote years to a study only to have your findings annexed by another person or distorted for popular consumption. Pisces is the Sign of spiritual transcendance, which begins with the study and understanding of universal law and the sacrifice of egotistical impatience.